CRUISING GUIDE TO
NEW YORK WATERWAYS
AND LAKE CHAMPLAIN

Homes on dots of land make for interesting scenery in the Thousand Islands.

CRUISING GUIDE TO
NEW YORK
WATERWAYS AND
LAKE CHAMPLAIN

By Chris W. Brown III
Edited by Claiborne S. Young

PELICAN PUBLISHING COMPANY
GRETNA 1998

All maps by the author
Photographs by the author and Linda Kempin

*The word "Pelican" and the depiction of a pelican are trademarks
of Pelican Publishing Company, Inc.,
and are registered in the U.S. Patent and Trademark Office.*

Library of Congress Cataloging-in-Publication Data

Brown, Chris W., III.
    Cruising guide to New York waterways and Lake Champlain / by Chris
W. Brown III ; edited by Claiborne S. Young.
        p.   cm.
    Includes bibliographical references (p.) and index.
    ISBN 1-56554-250-9 (pbk. : alk. paper)
    1. Boats and boating—New York (State)—Guidebooks. 2. Boats and
boating—Champlain, Lake—Guidebooks. 3. Waterways—New York
(State)—Guidebooks. 4. New York (State)—Guidebooks.
5. Champlain, Lake—Guidebooks. I. Young, Claiborne S. (Claiborne
Sellars), 1951- . II. Title.
GV776.N7B76 1998
917.4704'43-dc21

                                                       98-17842
                                                          CIP

Information in this guidebook is based on authoritative data available at the time of printing. Prices and hours of operation of businesses listed are subject to change without notice. Cruisers must
have and use current charts and exercise prudent judgment. Readers are asked to take this into account when consulting this guide.

Manufactured in the United States of America
Published by Pelican Publishing Company, Inc.
P.O. Box 3110, Gretna, Louisiana 70054-3110

To my children —

Jennifer and Chad Brown —

who bring so much joy to my life.

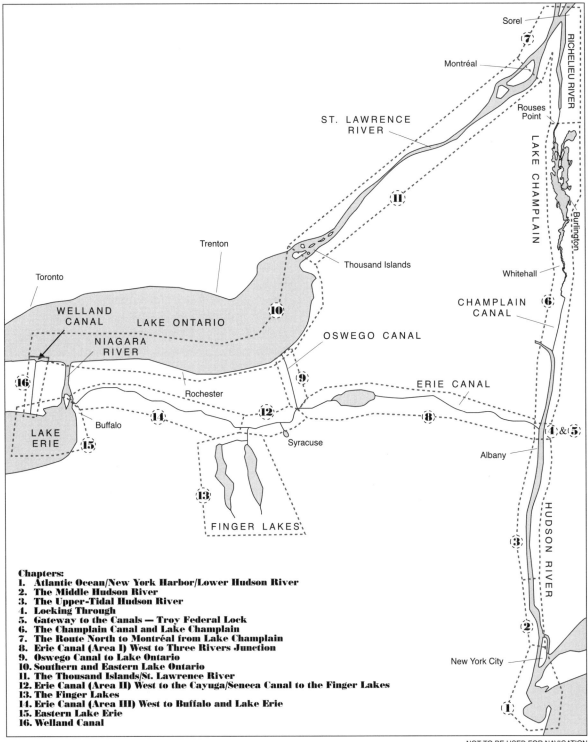

Sorel

Montréal

Rouses Point

ST. LAWRENCE RIVER

RICHELIEU RIVER

LAKE CHAMPLAIN

Burlington

Trenton

Thousand Islands

Whitehall

Toronto

WELLAND CANAL

LAKE ONTARIO

NIAGARA RIVER

OSWEGO CANAL

CHAMPLAIN CANAL

Rochester

ERIE CANAL

Buffalo

Syracuse

LAKE ERIE

Albany

FINGER LAKES

HUDSON RIVER

New York City

Chapters:
1. **Atlantic Ocean/New York Harbor/Lower Hudson River**
2. **The Middle Hudson River**
3. **The Upper-Tidal Hudson River**
4. **Locking Through**
5. **Gateway to the Canals — Troy Federal Lock**
6. **The Champlain Canal and Lake Champlain**
7. **The Route North to Montréal from Lake Champlain**
8. **Erie Canal (Area I) West to Three Rivers Junction**
9. **Oswego Canal to Lake Ontario**
10. **Southern and Eastern Lake Ontario**
11. **The Thousand Islands/St. Lawrence River**
12. **Erie Canal (Area II) West to the Cayuga/Seneca Canal to the Finger Lakes**
13. **The Finger Lakes**
14. **Erie Canal (Area III) West to Buffalo and Lake Erie**
15. **Eastern Lake Erie**
16. **Welland Canal**

NOT TO BE USED FOR NAVIGATION

Contents

One of over 85 tie-ups on the first 160 miles of the tidal Hudson River.

Acknowledgments

Cruising is fun, but it also provides challenges. Cruising while trying to write a book about an area adds several more complications to each day: visit one more marina, investigate both sides of the waterway, take one more photo.

I may be the skipper, but Linda Kempin was the admiral of this project. Her expertise gave me immeasurable guidance, and her tireless energy gave me incredible support during all the research, writing, and refinement of this book. She surprised us both by turning out to be almost as good on a boat as she is behind a camera lens. Since her grandfather was a career naval officer, I guess it's in her blood—but it turned out to be a surprise bonus for me!

Speaking of incredible support, I also want to thank my mother, Elizabeth Brown, who continues to give me all the love a son could ever need. I share both her thirst for adventure and her love of the water. She still lives within view of Barnegat Bay, on the Jersey shore, where my water experiences began.

A special thanks also goes to my sister, Judy Brown Basedow. More than anyone else, she probably best understood my need to do this book. Her perspective and wisdom are a constant source of encouragement.

Family thanks would be incomplete without an acknowledgment of my two uncles, Tom and Charlie Brown. I have so many wonderful memories from my early years with them, including the day when Uncle Tom said, "Paint it, caulk it, and you can use it." At the age of eight, I was suddenly captain of my own rowboat!

Nadine Conley also needs to be recognized for her unfailing assistance on this book. Not only did she create the electronic versions of all of my maps, but she was always available to keep the computer running. She's an unstumpable computer expert!

Thanks to Kim Smith, too, whose advertising agency in Albany turns out creativity on par with the best efforts that I've seen from the large Los Angeles agencies.

A special acknowledgment goes to the Maklers in southern California. More than just my scuba buddies, they have been there for me whenever I needed them. And thanks to Philippe Stoner, the best of best friends. He didn't just teach me how to handle a twin-screw vessel—he demonstrated to every one of us how to prioritize life's issues and value what's really important.

Canal cruising includes stretches of scenic man-made waterways.

Introduction

Landscapes are formed by landscape tastes. People see their surroundings through preferred and accustomed glasses and tend to make the world over as they see it. Such preferences long outlast geographical reality.
—David Lowenthal, *The American Scene*

Ahh . . . the boating life. It combines all of the elements that make America great: freedom, opportunity, determination, discovery. These inland waterways offer cruisers some of the best of each.

For boaters who are used to open waters, cruising on rivers and canals provides the freedom of traveling a weekend or a week—or longer—without ever having to plan on "sea only" days. While these waters provide their own challenges, they are generally more protected from disruptive weather and are more accessible to the usual amenities on land. They offer endless opportunities for fun and adventure, no matter how large or small your vessel, and a little determination goes a long way toward learning the skills that will successfully take you through the channels and locks that characterize these waterways.

Finally, these cruising grounds are also a revelation to anyone whose familiarity with New York State is limited to New York City. While that exciting metropolis is there to explore, here's a chance to encounter apple and peach orchards and a varied topography that includes not only rolling hills but also forests and mountains. The Hudson River Valley echoes with the legends of the Catskills, while the lakes and canals are flanked by the Adirondacks to the west and the Green Mountains to the east. There is always a bay to check out and another city or town to explore. Anchorages and marinas are plentiful, as are museums and historical sites. Going through the locks is an adventure in itself, with your boat rising or descending as much as 30 feet at a time to bypass rapids and falls. Visit these waterways and you will discover a way of cruising that offers something for everyone in your crew.

We spent four years cruising these waters during a variety of seasons. We also backtracked by car, visiting and revisiting to see the territory from different angles. We also researched the area, digging into maps, articles, and books, talking to people, hiking around, sampling menus . . . and sampling some more menus.

What we discovered is that these rivers, lakes, and canals are rich with beauty, diversity, and history. There are new experiences waiting around each bend—breathtaking vistas, landmarks of American history, and the challenges of locking through—yet you are rarely, if ever, out of sight of land!

We captured the essence of our discoveries in a bottle, shook it up, distilled it, and poured it out here for you. In this book, we will guide you through some of the most magnificent waterways on the eastern seaboard. We hope to inspire you before you go and point the way. Read about your cruise ahead of time, letting your mind soak up the spirit of the region. Then let this book help you prepare your gear, plan your stops, and anticipate each new experience. Finally, read it while you cruise for helpful hints about water depths and clearances, as well as where to refuel, grab a meal, buy hay bales, or find the best gunk hole for the night. If you take this book as you cruise these waterways—along with the necessary government charts and your boating knowledge—you just might make this your best cruise ever.

CRUISING GUIDE TO
NEW YORK WATERWAYS AND LAKE CHAMPLAIN

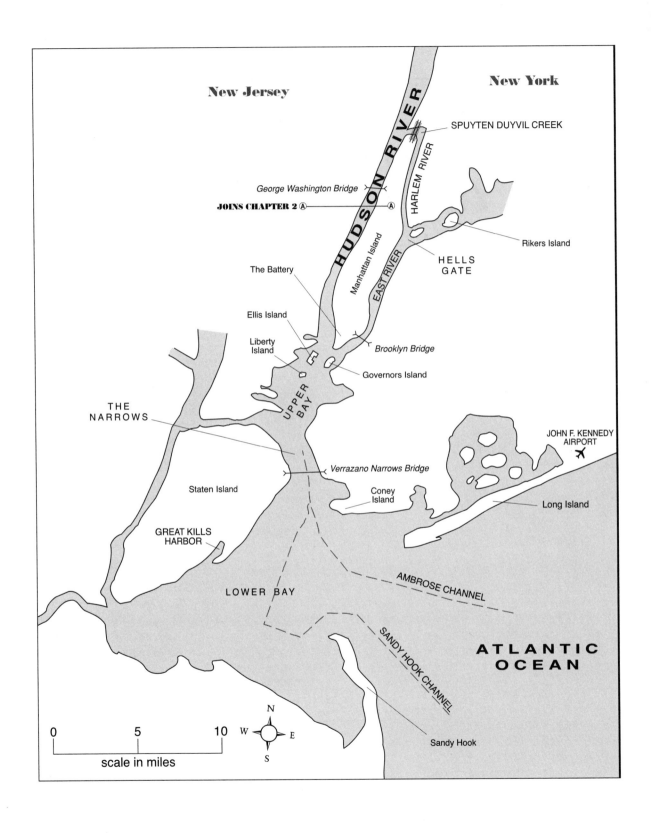

New Jersey

New York

HUDSON RIVER

SPUYTEN DUYVIL CREEK

HARLEM RIVER

George Washington Bridge

JOINS CHAPTER 2 Ⓐ ────────── Ⓐ

Rikers Island

Manhattan Island

EAST RIVER

HELLS
GATE

The Battery

Ellis Island

Liberty
Island

Brooklyn Bridge

Governors Island

UPPER
BAY

THE
NARROWS

JOHN F. KENNEDY
AIRPORT

Verrazano Narrows Bridge

Staten Island

Coney
Island

Long Island

GREAT KILLS
HARBOR

LOWER BAY

AMBROSE CHANNEL

SANDY HOOK CHANNEL

**ATLANTIC
OCEAN**

0   5   10

scale in miles

N
W   E
S

Sandy Hook

CHAPTER 1

The Atlantic Ocean, New York Harbor, and the Lower Hudson River

Beginning the Cruise

Hudson River Mileage (From Port Imperial/Lincoln Harbor Marinas)
(All distances are +/- 3 miles.)

Tarrytown/Nyack: 24 miles
Haverstraw: 33 miles
Peekskill: 40 miles
West Point: just short of 50 miles
Newburgh: 55 miles
Poughkeepsie: about 70 miles
Kingston: 85 miles (very popular stop)
Saugerties: 97 miles
Catskill: shy of 108 miles (popular stop)
New Baltimore: 125 miles (popular stop)

Coeymans: 125 + 2 miles (popular stop)
Albany Yacht Club: 140 miles (most masts unstepped by now)
First 25-foot vertical clearance bridge: 141 miles
Troy Town Docks: 147 miles (very popular stop)
Troy Federal Lock: 148 miles
First lock of Erie Canal: 150 miles
First lock of Champlain Canal: 156 miles

(Add 21 to 23 miles to all of the above when starting at the Atlantic Ocean/Sandy Hook.)

SKIPPER TIP: You will need NOAA charts 12327, 12341, 12343, 12347, and 12348 for the run to Albany.

Cruising from the Atlantic Ocean up the Hudson River is like traveling through a panorama of American life. From the bustling excitement of New York City to the inspiring beauty of the Palisades, and from the captivating tradition of Indian lore to the charm of old Dutch legend, the Hudson River Valley offers something for everyone in the family. It has often been called the "Rhine River of North America." The cruise itself is an opportunity not just to see something new around each bend but also to relax in the knowledge that a marina or anchorage is waiting just ahead. Never out of sight of land, yet meeting the challenge of navigating around points and bays and through swiftly changing scenery, boaters hone different skills from those required on the open sea. Whether your craft is a small runabout or a luxury sail craft, I urge you to embark on these waters, which have inspired artists, storytellers, and historians for three centuries.

Are you coming from the south from Manasquawn, Ocean City, Norfolk, Beaufort, Bermuda, or from the northern points of Long Island, the Cape Cod Canal, or Newport? All can lead to your river-, lake-, or canal-cruising adventure. It is just ahead.

Approaching the Statue of Liberty from the Upper Bay of New York Harbor.

Approach from the Southern Points

Coming in from the south (New Jersey), most boaters will pick up the Sandy Hook Channel at least one and a half miles off the bathing beach shore of Sandy Hook.

> **SKIPPER TIP:** Most harbor charts will shade in blue and outline in black all water less than 3 fathoms (18 feet) deep, draw a second black line at 12 feet (2 fathoms), and then again at 6 feet (the 1-fathom line).

Know the numbers of the buoys you need to locate before you start each section, and then check them off as you pass them.

This channel turns the corner (left) around Sandy Hook and comes quite close to shore at this point. Although there reportedly is a nude beach in this area, it is not at this point (sorry). Then you must pick up the Chapel Hill South Channel and the continuing North Channel by making a right turn. Here, make sure you locate the navigation light on a rock island, which is at an elevation of 69 feet, 3½ miles after the turn. It is just off the channel's west side, and mere water-depth changes (shallowing) alone may not warn you adequately. This channel then merges with the Ambrose Channel, and at that point one sees the Verrazano Narrows Bridge (217-foot clearance). Once under the bridge, try to locate the red buoy #20A that is 1 mile ahead. It is to starboard, a quarter-mile off the east shore. The pilot's base on the western shore is about an equal amount inward from the bridge also.

Approach from the Northern Points

The Ambrose Channel is used by boaters entering the Hudson River from the north. Pick it up east of buoys #3 and #4. Ambrose is a wider channel, with the aids to navigation often spaced 1 mile apart. It is used by all traffic from the continent, including Queen Mary-sized vessels. One does feel small within it. About 3 miles farther in, a shallow swing to the right (north) takes you into a merge with the Chapel Hill North Channel and onto cruising under the bridge. Know the numbers of the aids to navigation you intend to use to locate yourself through this section and check them off as they pass. Doing so should provide a sense of comfort in these oversized surroundings. The Verrazano Narrows Bridge is now in view, just ahead.

Lower New York Bay

Coming from the Atlantic Ocean into Lower New York Bay is an uplifting experience. After all, you are approaching the most diverse and exciting city in the world. This is the city of the Statue of Liberty, Times Square, and Broadway. The magnitude of the Big Apple is reflected in the waters approaching it. Because everything here is sized for large, oceangoing vessels, there is a feeling of wide-open space that might overwhelm some pleasure boaters. A prudent skipper will clearly identify beforehand which channel she wants to follow and know which buoy numbers mark that channel. The numbers are important: They help you be sure you are still in your selected channel. The channels are wide and deep, but there are a couple of spots where you can get caught in somewhat shallow water between channels. Some aids to navigation themselves might have rock outcroppings surrounding them for protection from ice and flotsam and jetsam. Locate them well before you enter the path you have selected.

If for some reason you need the services of a marina before proceeding into the Manhattan Island area 10 miles ahead, there are marina facilities on Staten Island inside Great Kills Harbor. At the inside end of the Sandy Hook Channel and the split between the Chapel Hill South Channel and the Raritan Bay East Reach, head about 318° magnetic (see appendix B to create a course to steer from this heading) to pick up Great Kills Light at a 35-foot height and the series of buoys that define the channel into this harbor. It is a 4¾-mile run to the harbor from the end of the Sandy Hook Channel.

Although Staten Island Boat Sales Marina is primarily an organization that sells new and used boats, they are well equipped and staffed to repair boats. However, transients are accommodated on an "as available" status only. Follow the marked channel into the harbor. Staten Island Boat Sales is in early off the channel.

Staten Island Boat Sales Marina (718) 984-7676

Storm protection: √√√
Scenic: * *
Marina-reported approach depths: 5-6 feet
Marina-reported dockside depths: 4-5 feet
Gas
Diesel
Waste pump-out
Rest rooms
Showers
Dockside water
Power connections: 30A/125V, 50A/125V, 50A/220V
Fiberglass repairs
Below-waterline repairs
Mechanical repairs
Gas-engine repairs
Diesel repairs
Stern-drive repair
Generator repairs
Travelift/hoist: two 30-ton hoists
Ship's store
Restaurant: off site
Grocery: off site
Convenience store: off site

Nichols Great Kills Marina is the largest marina facility in Great Kills Harbor. It serves seasonal tenants.

Nichols Great Kills Marina (718) 351-8476
Storm protection: √√√

Scenic: * * *
Marina-reported approach depths: 6-18 feet
Marina-reported dockside depths: 6-15 feet
Rest rooms
Showers
Dockside water
Picnic tables
Power connections: 30A/125V
Mechanical repairs
Travelift/hoist: 30 ton

The commercial traffic around New York can be intimidating. Fifty billion dollars in waterborne trade passes through here each year. If you are entering the Lower Bay from Sandy Hook, you must cross or share the channel that is used by container ships heading into Perth-Amboy and Newark, New Jersey. There is also traffic going into the Narrows, where you are going. It is that section of water that separates the Lower and Upper bays. As its name indicates, the water narrows down here, becoming a throat leading to New York Harbor, the East River, and the Hudson River.

The Narrows Bridge

The Verrazano Narrows Bridge is a fixed-suspension bridge that connects Staten Island and Brooklyn across the Narrows. The bridge is a modern wonder, with a vertical clearance of just over 200 feet—even with the maintenance basket in place—and a center span from the supporting pilasters of 4,260 feet. The towers above you are some 690 feet high. The foundations for these go underwater to a maximum of 170 feet. The bridge accommodates a six-lane highway, part of Interstate 278. It opened in 1964 and was expanded by the addition of a second tier in 1969.

The Hudson River was first explored by the Europeans in 1524, when Italian navigator

Giovanni da Verrazano, sailing under the French flag, anchored his ship, *La Dauphine*, outside of what we now call Staten Island. From there he took some of his crew and rowed his shore boat up to the mouth of the river, reportedly on the New Jersey side. It turned out to be an inauspicious event. Once off the ocean, they were spotted by the natives of the area, who crowded the wooded banks to greet them. These natives decided to launch their boats and row out to the explorers to welcome them. Then, before the two could meet, the foreigners noticed that the wind had shifted. Realizing they had to take advantage of the wind to sail, Verrazano and his crew suddenly turned their small craft around, went back to the main ship, weighed anchor, set sail, and took off out of view of the disappointed natives.

Main or Upper New York Bay

Many of us who skipper private vessels are used to cruising areas that are scaled for us. The impressively wide New York Harbor and the very first few miles of the Hudson River are on a scale more for commercial traffic. Remember, for several hundred years this was the No. 1 gateway to the New World, so channel depths, navigation aids, and bridge clearances are sized for them. The George Washington Bridge, for example, has a vertical clearance of more than 200 feet, so that oceangoing vessels with fixed masts and an array of antennas can pass underneath.

Once you pass under the Verrazano Narrows Bridge, you are out of the lower bay and into the upper bay of New York Harbor. Upper New York Bay contains shipping wharves and anchorages for every kind of vessel. On the east side of the channel, on Governors Island, there is the Coast Guard station that is closed. To your port are the Statue of Liberty and Ellis Island, the famous immigration stop for many of our ancestors. Each has its own side channel you can take to get closer, but watch your water depth outside any channel.

To Governors Island

While the entire width of the logical waterway has far deeper water depth than you need, I still recommend that, absent local knowledge, you follow a channel and check off buoys as you pass them. I run near the green buoys on the eastern side of the channel passing west of the Bay Ridge Flats. Then I stay a quarter-mile to half-mile west of the south end of Governors Island. At this point your decision is to make a run closer to Liberty Island and Miss Liberty, to Ellis Island, to continue on up the Hudson, or to choose a side trip to the East River.

Viewing New York's skyline from the water is an exhilarating experience.

SKIPPER TIP: Note that red buoys are now switching from starboard to port and then back again just north of here.

The Origins of the Hudson River

Long before man walked on the earth, the Hudson River made its way from a lake high in the Adirondack Mountains, first narrow and winding, then wider and deeper, until finally finding the Atlantic. During the last Ice Age, most of New York State was covered by a glacier. This glacier blocked the St. Lawrence River route to the Atlantic Ocean, forcing the Mohawk River and the Great Lakes to drain through the Hudson, thereby sending water rushing through, creating a level more than 100 feet higher than it is today. This massive flow of water deepened the river channel and forged a deep gorge through the rock. The length of the river also has changed. Today we know that the bed of the river continues far into the ocean, for a good 90 miles offshore. One theory holds that at various times the ocean was also 300 to 10,000 feet lower than it is today, and the river channel had to continue that much to reach the open water of the Atlantic Ocean.

There also is a second theory that in ancient times the Hudson River, rather than following the course that we are now riding up, had wandered off to the southwest and through parts of Pennsylvania and there joined the Susquehanna River, and together they emptied into the Chesapeake Bay. This theory further holds that when the glaciers came, they redirected the Hudson to its current path.

Statue of Liberty

The Statue of Liberty is not only a symbol of freedom, but it also is an outstanding piece of artwork. The statue stands 305 feet tall on tiny Liberty Island in the harbor. It faces southeast, welcoming travelers to America's shores. Created by French sculptor Frederic-Auguste Bartholdi, it is clad in copper over an iron skeleton, which was designed by Alexandre-Gustave Eiffel, the builder of the Eiffel Tower. The giant goddess was presented to the United States by the people of France to commemorate the 100th anniversary of the signing of the Declaration of Independence. Before that, the island was named Bedloe's Island after its owner, Isaac Bedloe, in 1689. Be aware that you can't circumnavigate the Statue of Liberty. I know of at least one vessel that hit bottom here, and private vessels are not permitted to land on Liberty Island. To really appreciate this national monument, go over to Liberty Harbor Marina, which is on the New Jersey shore side (to the west) in Jersey City, and from there take a private tour boat over to the island and visit the statue as a day trip off your vessel.

Ellis Island

In 1892 the country's biggest immigration station was established on what was renamed Ellis Island. It also had been previously known as Bucking, Gibbet, Oyster, and Gull Island. In use until 1954, the station was renovated in 1989 as a historical site. It handled a huge load of people from its opening in 1892 through 1924. Then a change in the law dramatically reduced the need for an immigration station. The new U.S. law required preapproval before you left your mother country. After securing visas, most immigrants were

From 1892 to 1954, Ellis Island was the clearinghouse for millions of immigrants to the United States. Today, this historic site has been renovated for thousands of tourists to enjoy.

processed upon arriving on board the ship and at a 15-minute customs inspection. With this law was in place, only a few thousand exceptions per year were required to visit Ellis Island. Even given that, about 90 percent (12 million to 14 million people) of all the immigrants coming to America passed through here—40 percent of the families in the United States have some relative who first touched U.S. soil on this island. Watch water depths if you come in fairly close.

Fishing

New York was blessed with three things that made it a notable fishing area: temperate waters that nourished many of the same species of fish and oysters as those near Boston and Chesapeake Bay; a publishing empire that perhaps let local techniques and catches be popularized quickly; and the Fulton Fish Market, the largest fish market in the United States.

There are fish. March brings shad, a popular specialty at old-time local restaurants (the Hudson River population of shad is the third largest in the United States), plus winter flounder. April and May are the season for sturgeon, whose roe is processed into caviar, and menhaden, a fish used from Indian times as a crop fertilizer. May through October is the time for bluefish. Weakfish season spans July through October. Eels can be caught April through November. Other fish include striped bass (particularly around Ellis and Liberty islands), kingfish, black fish, butterfish, flounder, sheeps-head, and porgy. Shellfish species here in some areas include oysters, clams, lobsters, and blue-claw crabs.

Well over a hundred years *before* the American Revolution, two men caught more than 1,000 codfish in a single day's fishing. Sharks were noted and caught in the harbor area from 1760 until after the Civil War. At the beginning of this century, three men in a locally built skiff caught 200 striped bass while night fishing. Of course, because today's large people population heavily affects the natural water supply, there have been better times to eat this harvest of fish. However, today some or all of these fish are around for the catching. When you buy a fishing license, check with the locals to see if there are limits on how much or what kinds of fish you are permitted by law to catch.

The first of seven marinas and one anchorage that offer ready access to Manhattan are just ahead. All provide a secure and friendly overnight stay. I will brief you on how to access New York City from each as well as describe the amenities available both on site and nearby. And, of course, I will give you my opinion of each. Note: There is no advertising in this book; any opinions are mine alone. Marinas are listed in order of appearance on the waterways. Please review the information for all of them in an area before picking one that suits you. Often an extra mile or an early stop will make a world of a difference in your cruise. Please review at least up to the George Washington Bridge section of this book before choosing a marina.

Liberty Harbor Marina (201-626-5550) requires a walk to a PATH (the New Jersey commuter train) station, and from there an underwater tunnel PATH train takes you into

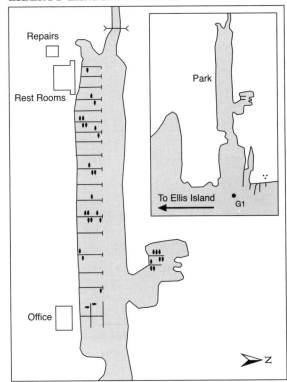

LIBERTY LANDING MARINA

NOT TO BE USED FOR NAVIGATION

Manhattan. It is set back off the main river channel on the New Jersey (port) side of the waterway. They have a limited number of transient berths. This facility, like many others on these waterways, is consistently evolving its offerings to boaters, so call to confirm that the new bathrooms and cafe are open. Also, they cater to commercial and tour vessels. In mid-June each year, pleasure-boat versions of off-shore-racing powerboats hold a rally/poker run from Liberty Harbor Marina. Up to 60 boats go buzzing around this section of the Hudson River and harbor, making several stops to pick up a playing card in order to complete a poker hand. Then everyone returns to the marina for a barbecue and dancing. It is quite lively. Also, inside this side channel called Clermont Cove is the Liberty Landing Marina.

Liberty Harbor Marina (201) 451-1000

Storm protection: √√√
Scenic: *
Marina-reported approach depths: 15 feet
Marina-reported dockside depths: 12 feet
Gas
Diesel
Waste pump-out
Rest rooms
Showers
Laundry
Dockside water
Power connections: 30A/125V, 50A/125V, 50A/220V
Below-waterline repairs
Mechanical repairs
Travelift/hoist
Ship's store
Restaurant: on site
VHF-monitored channel: 68

Liberty Landing Marina (201) 985-8000

Storm protection: √√√
Scenic: *
Marina-reported approach depths: 15 feet
Marina-reported dockside depths: 12 feet
Gas
Diesel
Waste pump-out
Rest rooms
Showers
Laundry
Dockside water
Power connections: 30A/125V, 50A/220V
Below-waterline repairs
Mechanical repairs
Travelift
Restaurant: on site

What's special: a shuttle connecting these two marinas
VHF-monitored channel: 09, 68

Newport Marina (201-626-5550) is on the same side of the Hudson about three-fourths of a mile north and also a walk to the PATH train to get into New York City. This is, as one of the marina's ads says, "an integral part of . . . a waterfront community." Adjacent are luxury apartments and a mall that includes shops, a supermarket, restaurants, and movie theaters. The marina has had up to 20 percent of its slips available for transients. Find it by looking for the large Colgate clock. Enter on the marina's south end near its sign with white and blue coloring. Go slowly. Take care to not

NEWPORT MARINA

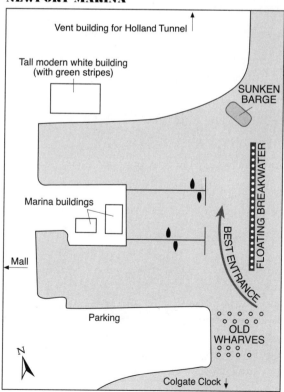

NOT TO BE USED FOR NAVIGATION

run over the floating breakwater to the north of the entrance channel that dampens harbor wakes for the marina.

Newport Marina (201) 626-5550

Storm protection: √√√
Scenic: * *
Marina-reported approach depths: 10 feet
Marina-reported dockside depths: 10 feet
Waste pump-out
Rest rooms
Showers
Laundry
Dockside water
Power connections: 30A/125V, 50A/125V, 50A/220V, 100A/125V
Restaurant: on site
Deli: on site
Convenience store: on site

What's special: part of a newer retail/apartment development
VHF-monitored channel: 16, 72

Scheduled Traffic

It's important to note that there are many ferryboats and other kinds of regularly scheduled traffic that cross here, including executive helicopters. The helicopters often sweep down fairly low (at least that's the feeling you get if you're traveling in a pleasure boat). To feel comfortable, stay well off any heliport landing routes. Also, watch out for regularly scheduled ferry traffic. To keep to their schedules, the ferries' speed and docking techniques tend to favor efficiency more than caution. They also throw a larger-than-expected wake, and some might be a bit rude as far as the rules of the waterway go.

Helicopter activity near the Staten Island Ferry landing on Manhattan Island.

They figure you're out there for a pleasure cruise and you can go around them, rather than they should avoid you and fall behind schedule.

The East River

There are various traffic patterns through the Upper Bay, and you're likely to find yourself in the midst of traffic going in several directions. Just know where you want to go, both by buoy and landmarks, and you'll do fine. My recommendation here is to take a little side trip up the East River to just under the Brooklyn Bridge and back. Pass Governors Island on your starboard side and make a turn east and up the East River, passing the bottom of Manhattan Island on your port side. This very bottom tip of Manhattan Island is the area known as the Battery. Soon you will see a ferry station and the helicopter landing pads for celebrities such as Geraldo Rivera and for

some of the Wall Street executives who come in and out of town on a regular basis. As you go farther up the East River, to your port is the South Street Seaport, with several large historical vessels on display. The seaport has been developed into a spiffy eating and shopping area and has the bonus of an active, wooden boat-building shop on site. They put out a great publication that is available as one of several benefits of an inexpensive membership program. A recent issue featured articles on the murals of the old-time U.S. Customs House in New York City (now the home of the Museum of the American Indian), a reflective discussion on the life of one of the owners of New York Harbor's biggest transport companies in the mid-nineteenth century, and photographs of the Fulton Fish Market just before World War II. It also pointed out that New York City had its own Manhattan Island-based postal

A few of the assets of New York City's maritime museum at the South Street Seaport—just a few steps away from the Fulton Fish Market.

system that was selling postage stamps years before the federal government began to in 1847. All in all, this stop is very interesting. Inquire by calling (212) 748-8735 or (212) 669-9400; the World Wide Web address is: www.southstseaport.org. Unfortunately, there is no docking here. The best access is by taxi across Manhattan after you have berthed at one of the marinas on the Hudson River listed in this guide.

East River History

During the late 1700s and early 1800s, the East River was considered the region's commercial waterway, whereas the Hudson was thought of as a recreational river. Both rivers had equal access to the Atlantic Ocean, but the East River alone had access to Long Island Sound and therefore to New England and Boston. Thus, early on the East River became the site of commercial business and trade activity. The Hudson, on the other hand, with a slower-growing population on its banks as it heads north, became a playground, first for the moneyed class of New York City and then for the laboring classes. This pattern changed completely, however, with the advent of the Erie Canal in 1825.

Brooklyn Bridge

Ahead is the Brooklyn Bridge, which was designed by John A. Roebling. He, his son Washington, and—to a large extent—his son's wife, Emily, supervised its construction. Their family business made most of the wire cable used in the bridge's construction. The bridge was completed in 1883 and connects Manhattan Island to Brooklyn with a complex and

A boater's view of the Brooklyn Bridge's elegant structure.

beautiful construction of wire cables. The bridge was considered to be a triumph of modern engineering, and with a span of 1,595 feet it remained the longest suspension bridge in the world for more than twenty years.

The East River eventually opens into Long Island Sound, but for this trip I suggest that once you have passed beneath the Brooklyn Bridge, make a 180-degree turn and cruise back down to the Battery. Then, make a turn around the tip of Manhattan and head once again into the main channel of the Hudson River.

Manhattan from the Hudson River

The Battery is the area at the bottom of Manhattan Island. Stay at least a quarter-mile off the bulkheaded land area to clear shallower water. Named after the ninety-plus cannons placed here by the British in 1693, the Battery was a military point in various configurations through the Revolutionary War. Later it was an area where Manhattanites strolled in their Sunday finest. Immigration was handled here from 1855 to 1892. Finally, an aquarium was established when the immigration station shifted to Ellis Island, which was in use through 1954 but used less after the post-World War I laws to restrict immigration were enacted. Almost all of the above uses have disappeared, although the area has a small re-creation of earlier times.

SKIPPER TIP: There can be flotsam in all of the waters detailed in this guide, although New York City has vessels constantly in circulation to pick up whatever is floating around in the immediate city waterways. Keeping a sharp watch is your best protection, especially after a hard rain, when the many small creeks and feeder waterways disgorge their flotsam in the runoff.

Many believe it is safer to cruise down the middle of a channel than near shore. I also believe that, but cruising is also soaking up life—and Manhattan is a destination not to be missed. Use your judgment and your charts, but the impact of a front-row center seat here requires you to cruise nearer the docks, skyscrapers, and people of this island. It is something to tell your grandchildren about.

Deep water is everywhere except directly in front of the Battery. For 300 years the water around New York City was used but not cared for. Now the river has been cleaned up over the last 10 years through millions of dollars from a state Superfund and other funding that continues. The river is open enough so that traffic competing with you for a piece of waterway can be spotted early on and easily accommodated. Do not let the absence of markers annoy you. This is the Big Apple, the most energetic city in the United States, all for you to enjoy.

SKIPPER TIP: As you navigate northward, be sensitive to current and tide levels. The Hudson River is a substantial body of water, and during tidal changes you can experience some current. The current also has been known to change directions from one shore to the other as one goes across it. Current at flow averages under about 1½ mph and a half-mile per hour higher at ebb on the Hudson. Look for this to be higher where the river is narrow or shallow and less in the wider sections. This is more noticeable in a human-powered craft than others. In fact, during the Depression years, people who kept their row boats in the 79th Street area would use the current to float 5 miles first upstream and then back down for a full day on the river with only a minimum of paddling. That knowledge was passed down from the local Indians. They always thought of the Hudson as "the river that flows both ways." Tides run all the way to Troy Lock with a rise and fall of about four feet. Although they are not that predictable because of spring runoffs, cities' water needs, and rainstorms. The Hudson River meets the definition of an estuary. One outstanding joy: Water depth in the channel here runs as much as 35 feet or more.

There are two marinas on Manhattan Island: North Cove Yacht Harbor (212-938-9000) was developed to provide upscale marina facilities for large megayachts. It bills itself as "Wall Street's International Yacht Harbor." Although North Cove can handle 150-footers like all the other facilities mentioned here (except for the 79th Street Boat Basin), it is a compact facility inside its own harbor in high-rent Manhattan. It was quite the site for this skipper to have dock attendants pull up in electric-powered carts to greet me. Fees are upscale, and there are minimum charges regardless of the size of your vessel. This marina

is near the World Trade Center (one block east); Wall Street is four short blocks east/five short blocks south, as is Trinity Church; City Hall is four blocks east and four blocks north.

On the same side of the river and close by (two miles north) is Chelsea Piers/Surfside 3 Marina (212-336-7873). This is a major rehab of former transatlantic-liner piers. It is designed to be a complete sports facility on a grand New York scale. The marina is home to the Sea Ray dealer, Surfside 3. They can provide support if you want to buy a new vessel or need to get something repaired, but no repairs or sales are offered on site. There are just a few transient slips here, however, and they are priced to reflect Manhattan rent levels. Note that its 23rd Street location (land-side entrance) puts

CHELSEA PIERS/SURFSIDE 3

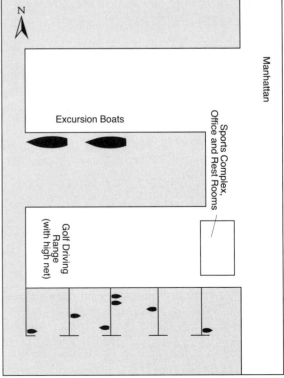

you close to Washington Square (5½ blocks east/17 blocks south), which is the center of Greenwich Village and is near the New York Nautical Instrument and Service Corporation at 140 W. Broadway (7 blocks east/22 blocks south). New York Nautical (212-962-4522) is a must-stop for pleasure boaters who have never visited a chart agency that serves commercial freighters or for those of us who are in awe of row upon row of drawers carrying charts for exotic ports and places. Plus, it has all the navigational equipment, ship clocks, nautical and local lore books, and some decor items—the most complete inventory I've seen.

Breakfast, lunch, and dinner should be available on site at the marina sports complex, and the marina staff will facilitate ordering and delivering meals from some nearby restaurants. A temporary membership at Surfside 3 not only makes all of the fabulous sports facilities accessible to transient pleasure boaters but also includes the benefit of transient dockage. If you need anything, just ask; they might be able to help. As an example, they try to have staff available for more extended hours in-season than the other marinas in this area. Therefore, it's your best choice for a late-night arrival. Also, the marina offers day slips or slips by the hour if you just want to quick-hit Manhattan and then continue on your cruise.

The marina is on the south side of the outdoor golf driving range. That driving range's multistory enclosure screen to catch the golf balls is a unique sight against the backdrop of the skyline.

North Cove Yacht Harbor (212) 938-9000

Storm protection: √√
Scenic: * * *
Marina-reported approach depths: 25-30 feet

Marina-reported dockside depths: 15 feet
Pump-out
Floating docks
Rest rooms
Laundry
Power connections: 50A/125V, 50A/220V, 100A/220V
What's special: a superyacht marina
VHF-monitored channel: 69

Chelsea Piers/Surfside 3 (212) 336-7873

Storm protection: √√
Scenic: * *
Marina-reported approach depths: 20 feet
Marina-reported dockside depths: 8-15 feet
Floating docks
Waste pump-out
Rest rooms
Showers
Dockside water
Power connections: 30A/125V, 50A/125V
Mechanical repairs
Ship's store
Restaurant: on site
Deli: off site
Grocery: off site
Convenience store: off site
What's special: a part of a major sports complex
VHF-monitored channel: 16, 68

Manhattan Access

Back on the Hudson and cruising north, you will see Battery Park on your starboard side and then the twin towers of the World Trade Center. They were the world's tallest buildings when they were constructed between 1966 and 1976. Standing 110 stories, they reach some 1,380 feet high and have an observation deck at the top open to the public. The famous Windows on the World restaurant and upscale bar is here, too, which was recently renovated. Another full selection of restaurants is inside its base. The multistory basement of the complex required so much excavation that the removed material created more than 20 acres of waterfront level when it was used as fill in nearby waters. Under the water and in the mud beneath you run the Holland and the Lincoln Tunnels, taking automobile traffic back and forth into the city. Stretching out before you is all of Manhattan Island, the heart of New York City.

Manhattan is about 13 miles long and roughly 2½ miles wide. This is the Big Apple, where you can see and do everything from Central Park to Greenwich Village, including restaurants serving every type of cuisine, museums that rival any in the world, architecture spanning three centuries, naval displays, Broadway shows, piano bars, high tea, and world-class shopping.

George Washington was inaugurated as president on Manhattan Island in 1789. You can retrace his footsteps and see the buildings he visited that historic day. It was the first capital of the young United States.

When traveling by boat, the most convenient way to visit Manhattan is to arrange for dockage at Port Imperial (201-902-8787), which is on the western shore of the Hudson River in Weehawken, New Jersey. The property next door on the northern edge of the marina functions as a ferry terminal for commuters going from New Jersey to New York. The sight of the ferry traffic is often the easiest way to locate the facility. The Port Imperial ferry runs from Weehawken to the landing at the Jacob Javits Convention Center, at 39th Street in Manhattan. The Javits Center is known to boaters as the site of the New York

Boat Show, which is held each year in early January.

If you take the ferry from Port Imperial, you will land within a few blocks of the aircraft carrier *Intrepid,* which is docked on the Hudson River at 42nd Street. The *Intrepid* houses a fascinating aerospace museum, and a submarine, a destroyer, and other craft also are on hand for you to explore.

On-site ferry service from Port Imperial runs year-round and is available almost to midnight. Included in the price is bus fare for up to five buses that will take you from the ferry terminal to just about any area in the city. All this also applies to the Lincoln Harbor Yacht Club, a marina, for the purposes of this guide, not a private-membership club, except that its on-site ferry only operates from there Monday through Friday until about 10 P.M. If you do not intend to use the ferry, by all means use Lincoln (201-319-5100) because it might provide a quieter slip. Any marina near a ferry landing or that has nighttime, commercial, or excursion traffic will be somewhat disrupted by the traffic. Plus, Lincoln offers the upscale Chart House and Ruth's Chris Steakhouse restaurants in its complex as well as a food court and other eating venues. Arthur's Landing restaurant at Port Imperial is top of the shelf, too. They serve outstanding shrimp and other innovative cuisine, and the bar staff has the flair for mixology that only the best of their profession exhibit and that is often found only in urban areas. I have had several memorable meals there. Port Imperial also offers the services of a concierge inside its ship's store. This is a great benefit for boaters, because the concierge will arrange for theater tickets—and you can't cruise through New York without taking a night to dine out and see a Broadway show, the height of live entertainment!

Naturally, these benefits and conveniences come at a cost. Port Imperial is around $2 plus extras per foot per night. Two other marinas—both on Manhattan Island itself, the newest being Surfside 3, at 23rd Street—charge more (in the area of $4 per foot, per night plus electricity), while the others on the New Jersey (west) shore are about the same.

Lest you reflect too hard on the economics of cruising, ponder instead this bit of history: A field on the western bluffs above you in Weehawken, New Jersey, was the location of the famous duel between Alexander Hamilton and Aaron Burr. Burr challenged Hamilton to the duel after Hamilton exerted his influence to prevent Burr from being elected governor of New York. On July 11, 1804, they squared off against one another and fired their pistols. Hamilton lost the duel and died from his wounds.

Lincoln Harbor Yacht Club (800) 205-6987; (201) 319-5100

Storm protection: √√
Scenic: * * *
Marina-reported approach depths: 20 feet
Marina-reported dockside depths: 4-7 feet
Gas
Diesel (limited)
Waste pump-out
Rest rooms
Showers
Dockside water
Power connections: 30A/125V, 50A/125V
Mechanical repairs
Restaurant: off site
Deli: off site
Convenience store: off site
What's special: second-best facility-and-access package to New York City
VHF-monitored channel: 74

LINCOLN HARBOR YACHT CLUB

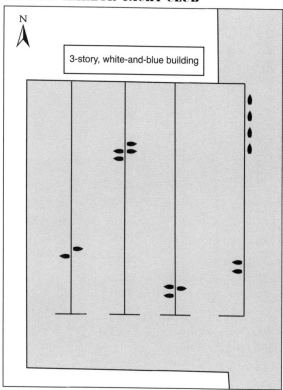

N

3-story, white-and-blue building

NOT TO BE USED FOR NAVIGATION

Port Imperial Marina (201) 902-8787

Storm protection: √√
Scenic: * * *
Marina-reported approach depths: 12 feet
Marina-reported dockside depths: 3-8 feet
Floating docks
Gas
Diesel
Waste pump-out
Rest rooms
Showers
Laundry
Dockside water
Power connections: 30A/125V, 50A/125V, 50A/220V
Mechanical repairs

PORT IMPERIAL MARINA

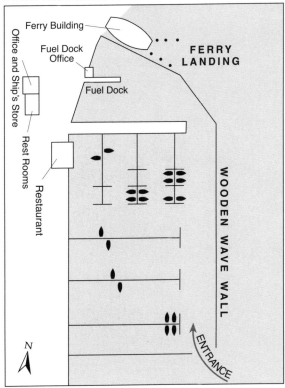

NOT TO BE USED FOR NAVIGATION

Ship's store
Gift shop
Restaurant: on site
What's special: top notch and best access to New York City
VHF-monitored channel: 09, 16

Now coming up, 79th Street Boat Basin is a different kind of New York City marina. Rescued from becoming a derelict property several years ago, its services and amenities continue to evolve. Although it mainly serves seasonal live-aboard tenants who want affordable boating, transient boaters are accommodated in rare cases, but detailed city-access instructions (it would be buses or a cab from here) could not be ascertained during my visit. Also, your craft should be well-fendered if you follow instructions and tie up to the bulkhead while awaiting a slip assignment. River traffic creates quite a wave action, which is why all the marinas around here put in the bulkhead in the first place.

79th Street Boat Basin (212) 495-2105

Storm protection: √√√ (inside-none outside the bulkhead)
Scenic: *
Marina-reported approach depths: 20 feet
Marina-reported dockside depths: 2-5 feet
Rest rooms
Picnic tables
Power connections: 30A/125V
VHF-monitored channel: 16

79th Street Anchorage Area (212) 495-2105

Storm protection: √
Scenic: * *
Please be sure to make arrangements to use the dingy dock at the 79th Street Boat Basin. This is a secure area; do not use the 79th Street facilities without checking in. It is a mud bottom here, with 25- to 35-foot water depth. Anchor either north or south of the marina. Pay attention to the current and tides because you will swing with them.

If it's more important to get something on your craft repaired than any amenity for yourself or your crew, you might be interested in the Von Dohln Bros. marina on the New Jersey (port) side, a mile south of the George Washington Bridge.

A visit at the Port Imperial Marina on the western shore of the Hudson River affords a spectacular view of the Manhattan skyline.

Von Dohln Bros. (201) 943-3424

Storm protection: √√
Scenic: *
Marina-reported approach depths: 10 feet
Marina-reported dockside depths: 6-8 feet
Rest rooms
Power connections: 30A/125V
Welding
Below-waterline repairs
Mechanical repairs
Gas-engine repairs
Diesel repairs
Generator repairs
Ship's store
What's special: more of a repair yard than
   an overnight stop; family-run
VHF-monitored channel: 16

SKIPPER TIP: New York City Weather
   Average daily high temperature runs in the low 80s in June, July, and August, just under that in September, and the high 60s in May.

Neighborhoods of Manhattan

   Manhattan is an island and one of the five boroughs of New York City. Although more than 1½ million people live on this island, they might identify themselves more with their neighborhood; that is, instead of calling themselves Manhattanites, they're more likely to say, "I live in the Village, Greenwich Village."

And sometimes they might talk in terms of a subset of that area, say the West Village, which means within Greenwich Village and west of Broadway. The East Village is on the opposite side of Broadway. The Village is known for its poets, artists, and cutting-edge political and cultural thinkers, and it has parks, shopping, and bars for all tastes, and a strong sense of community. In the West Village, past residents have included Edgar Allan Poe, Edith Wharton, Mark Twain, Dylan Thomas, and Eugene O'Neill. Its streets are not in a grid-pattern; it is an older area of Manhattan that predates the organization effort of the city. Greenwich Village has lots of alleyways and byways and is more like a plate of bent paper clips in terms of street layout.

There are jazz clubs here, gourmet food stores, coffee shops, and even some wholesale markets. Music goes to the latest fashion, much of it coming from clubs and restaurants that have intruded out onto the street. There are delis, Russian baths, and Irish pubs here.

SoHo—another Manhattan neighborhood—stands for **so**uth of **Ho**uston St. (pronounced How-ston). Much of SoHo's charm lies in its artists' colony, where artists have renovated loft spaces and built live-in studio apartments. The light and airy feeling inside the apartments seems to continue on as you walk down SoHo's streets, which exude a tremendous amount of art and creativity. There are probably 200 art galleries in this neighborhood. If you go into a restaurant in SoHo, you're likely to see a creative, eclectic menu. After spending some time in SoHo, you will have a sense of openness that you wouldn't get in most of the other neighborhoods of Manhattan.

Less well known is NoHo (**no**rth of **Ho**uston St.). It is a working-class neighborhood with artist-in-residence spaces above the retail street level. It is home to my newest favorite New York City restaurant—NoHo Star—at Bleeker and Lafayette Streets. Inquire by calling (212) 925-0070. There is even a subway stop here. The NoHo Star is open for breakfast, lunch, and dinner. Out of a sense of obligation to you, the reader, the author has sampled brunch, burgers, and crab cakes there and recommends them.

Now imagine an old New York City street scene out of a *Godfather* movie, and you might come up with Little Italy. Mulberry Street is probably the last best street in Little Italy. Eat the pasta, enjoy the Parmesan, see how many different red sauces you can sample, and enjoy some of the many flavors of the area.

Chinatown is really an area not only for Chinese but also for the broader group of immigrants and descendants of immigrants from Pacific Rim nations. Supposedly the 150,000 residents here make up the largest Chinese community outside Asia. The Chinese use a different approach to medicinal health, and here you can find an herbalist store, a source for many of the tools of alternative medicine. Chinese specialty items such as Chinese five spices can be found in the produce markets and little restaurants.

TriBeCa is perhaps the newest area amongst the neighborhoods of Manhattan to come into high-profile recognition. The name TriBeCa stands for the **Tri**angle **Be**low **Ca**nal St. There's jazz, theater, poetry, art studios, art galleries, and restaurants. Its retail area is Chambers Street. Of course, Robert DeNiro's restaurant, the TriBeCa Grill, is here, too.

Chelsea is located between 19th and 20th Streets in a north-to-south direction, and between 8th and 9th Avenues from east to west. It's an area mostly of townhouses. Chelsea was built after the 1830s, when one of the major landowners decided to divide up his family holdings into lots, thus providing the neighborhood's infrastructure. Again, you can enjoy many good neighborhood stores, restaurants, and taverns here. The Antiques Building in Chelsea is at 25th Street between 6th and 7th Avenues. Ninth Avenue also offers good antique shopping around 20th and 22nd Streets. Flower shops, food stalls, and flea markets abound. The Joyce Theater in Chelsea is a mecca for people who enjoy dancing. The list of recreational opportunities goes on and on.

Central Park splits the upper part of Manhattan into the Upper West Side and, logically, the Upper East Side. The West Side is known for the Lincoln Center for the Performing Arts. The 1884 Dakota building, where John Lennon was murdered, also is nearby. The terrific American Museum of Natural History and the famous Tavern on the Green, generally considered the highest-dollar-volume restaurant in the United States, are here too. There's a great Barnes and Noble bookstore on the Upper West Side. Do not miss it. Coffee is on the top floor. Buy a boating book and read it here alongside the locals. In this neighborhood, with people walking by the outdoor cafes with sidewalk seating, you can almost feel like you're in Europe. Ernie's, a great dinner house, is in the 70s on Broadway here.

The Upper East Side is home to the Whitney Museum of American Art at 75th Street and, of course, the fine, upscale shopping area for haute couture, with Ralph Lauren's Polo store, Armani, and Valentino all present. The Guggenheim Museum and the Metropolitan Museum of Art are up here too. Gracie Mansion, the mayor's official residence, is in this area as well.

North of both Upper West Side and East Side is Harlem, the area above Central Park. Harlem starts at about 110th Street and goes north from there. The world-famous Apollo Theater is on West 125th Street.

Midtown, roughly considered to be the area from 59th Street south to Times Square, is home to the Jacob Javits Center, where the New York Boat Show is held each January, and Madison Square Garden. The Theater District is in a subset of Midtown.

Exploration of the Hudson River

Eighty-five years after Giovanni da Verrazano, the Englishman Henry Hudson, working for the Dutch East India Company, explored New York's great river in 1609 as he was searching for a water route across the continent to China. While offshore at Sandy Hook, Hudson and his crew fished and caught 10 mullet and a ray so big it took four sailors to haul it in. Once on the river, the *Half Moon's* crew was visited by some of the local natives, riding in their dugouts and clad in tanned hides of deer with a few feather mantles around them. They brought with them as gifts some tobacco leaves, some yellow ears of maize (corn), and some loaves of cornbread.

The Indians called the river *Manna*hatta or *Shatemuc*, depending on tribe affiliation. Hudson called the river "the Great River of the Mountains," also from an Indian name, or the river of the Prince Mauritius, in honor of the Dutch soldier, Maurice of Orange. Later it was called the North River to distinguish it from the East River and the South (Delaware) River between Pennsylvania and New Jersey. It's now named the Hudson River.

TIME LINE FOR BOATERS VISITING NEW YORK STATE

1524—Giovanni da Verrazano sailed through New York City Harbor, just past the narrows now named for him.

1540—Fur traders from France established a trading post at present-day Albany (or so some historians believe).

1609—In the fall, the Englishman Henry Hudson, employed by the Dutch East India Company, sailed up the Hudson River as far north as today's Champlain Canal System's Lock 1. He was looking for a passage to China.

In the summer, while establishing additional fur-trading posts, French explorer Samuel de Champlain discovered the lake he named for himself.

1614—First trading post, Fort Nassau, was established in present-day location of Port of Albany.

1618—Adrien Block named Block Island in Long Island Sound before heading north to build a fort at Albany.

1624—The first 18 families settled in Fort Orange, known today as Albany.

1626—Manhattan was purchased for 60 guilders, about $24.

1629—Without ever leaving Holland, Kiliaen Van Rensselaer, a Dutch jeweler, established his ownership of the east side of the Hudson River across from Albany. Although at first this patron system of ownership hastened settlement of the area, by the 1800s settlement slowed down because the land was never sold, just rented.

1650—Peter Stuyvesant established the Connecticut-New York boundary.

1656—Jesuit missionaries worked among the Indians in the Finger Lakes region.

1664—King Charles II granted his brother, James, Duke of York and Albany, much of what is now New York. Within five months the Dutch surrendered the Manhattan area to the British without a shot being fired.

1665—New Amsterdam was renamed New York; Fort Orange is changed to Albany.

Fort Saint Louis de Chambly was built at Chambly, Canada.

1669—The explorer La Salle traveled through the Finger Lakes.

1678—Upstate versus downstate competition began when New York City is declared the sole port of entry.

1724—Cadwallader Colden, surveyor general of New York State, first talked publicly about the idea of a water connection between the Hudson River and the Great Lakes.

1727—Fort Ontario was built, later becoming the terminus of the Oswego Canal on Lake Ontario.

1754-63—The French and Indian War was fought in the New World.

1759—Fort Ticonderoga was built on Lake Champlain.

1761—Gen. Philip Schuyler of Albany visited England to examine its canals.

1774-83—The colonists sought freedom in the American Revolutionary War.

1783-84—Gen. George Washington toured New York State and suggested a link between the Great Lakes and the Hudson. He wanted to keep western New York part of the United States and not lose it to Canada.

1784—Chase Manhattan Bank was founded as the Bank of New York. It was the second bank in the United States.

1785—Christopher Colles from Ireland drafted a pamphlet proposing that private companies be formed to build a canal to open up the West.

1791—The first canal law was passed, authorizing the survey and estimates for a canal program.

1792—Two private corporations were created to try to build the early version of New York State Canal, including the Erie and Champlain routes.

1793—The Northern Canal Company began work on a canal between Fort Edward and the Hudson, the route of the Champlain Canal. The canal failed, and the company dissolved soon after.

1795—Union College was founded in Schenectady.

1797—The second canal company, the Western Canal Lock Company, created two miles of canal near the current Erie Canal path. It was 37 feet wide and 4 feet deep, with two locks at Rome, New York.

1798—Another 1¼ miles of canal and two additional locks, for a total of four, were completed.

1807—Thomas Jefferson recommended to Congress that surplus revenue of the federal government be used to finance canals and turnpikes.

Fulton's steamboat made a pioneering trip up the Hudson.

1808—James Geddes' survey of New York State indicated that building canals to Lake Erie would be feasible.

1812—One of the canal commissioners, De Witt Clinton, became the unsuccessful peace candidate for president of the United States in the 1812 election.

1812-14—Americans fought the British in the War of 1812.

1816—The canal bill became law on April 17.

1817—Canal commissioners presented a report to New York's legislature, complete with maps and profiles of the proposed canals. They recommended a canal 353 miles long, from Albany to Lake Erie, that would be 40 feet wide at its surface, 28 feet wide at the bottom, and 4 feet deep. The longest canal in America at this time was only 27 miles long. It was suggested that this canal would accommodate boats of 100 tons each. A canal connecting the Hudson River to Lake Champlain also was recommended.

Groundbreaking began the construction of the Erie Canal on July 4 near Rome, New York. A local, Judge John Richardson, did the honors.

Spending on the canal's construction topped $200,000 this year.

1818—Laborers on the canal made 50 cents a day to $1 and a half-pint of whiskey per day; assistant engineers, $4 per day; principal engineers, $1,500 to $2,000 per year; and canal commissioners, $2,500 per year. More than $466,000 was spent this year on canal construction. (Note: Back in 1812, nobody believed that current technology or surveying techniques could meet the needs of the canal. However, two surveys, started at opposite ends, 100 miles apart, showed a difference at the junction of less than 1½ inches.) The canal became a school of engineering for the state of New York, the United States, and the world. No formal training was then available in the United States to adequately prepare anyone for this monumental task.

Water was let into the first three-quarter mile of the canal.

1819—Washington Irving, a Hudson River Valley author, made the region famous with his story "Rip Van Winkle."

Using horses, three men could dig out a mile of canal section in a work season spanning spring, summer, and fall.

Though almost $600,000 was spent on canal construction, the Business Panic of 1819 ensued.

1820—Ninety-four miles of canal were now open to navigation.

The canal was dug through the Cayuga marshes west of Syracuse. With at least six inches to a foot of standing water in this section, all the construction crews fell ill.

1820-21—The Senate passed a bill appropriating $1 million annually for the next two years on top of the $600,000 regular appropriation for each year—all for canal construction.

1821—Nine thousand men were working on the canal construction.

1822—Foreign investors began to buy stock in the Erie Canal.

The Champlain Canal opened.

Water from the Genesee River filled the section of the Erie Canal at Rochester.

The newest canal section dried out at the end of summer due to lack of water.

One hundred-eighty miles of navigable canal opened from Rochester to Little Falls. However, the embankment was not trusted, and the commissioners ordered the Erie Canal to be drained nightly.

Businesses formed freight-line companies of canal barges to carry freight through the Erie Canal. One sold its stock at $100 per share in 1820, then paid a dividend of $86 in the fall of 1822.

1823—Joseph Smith found the golden plates of the Book of Mormon near Palmyra, New York, site of his family farm.

The 66-foot rise in the canal at Lockport—accomplished through a flight, or grouping, of five locks—was under construction according to plans drawn up by Nathan B. Roberts. He considered these plans the greatest achievement of his career.

The canal commissioners involved themselves in contracting to cut the canal channel through the rock. In the history of the young United States, this was the first public-works project in which the U.S. government took direct responsibility.

"Cash for Wheat" headlines in the newspaper indicated that good times for farmers were imminent. Wheat sold for $1 per bushel, up from 25 cents, because the freight rate had dropped so low that farmers could raise the price of the wheat and remain competitive.

After an expenditure of $83,000, the 802-foot aqueduct, one of the longest on the canal, was completed.

The eastern section of the canal was

ready to open. The run from Schenectady to Albany required 27 locks to cover just 30 miles—about one-third of the entire lock count on the whole canal, but less than 10 percent of the length.

1824—A bookstore built on a barge ran up and down the canal to supply canal builders with books.

1825—New York celebrated the opening of the completed Erie Canal with a bang on Wednesday morning, October 26. To celebrate the connection of Lake Erie to the Hudson River, and from there to the world, there was a sound-off of weaponry stretching 500 miles from Buffalo to New York City. The canal was 4 feet deep and 40 feet wide and could float a 30-ton cargo load.

Three days after the canal opened, 50 immigrants heading west arrived in Buffalo. One year later, 1,200 arrived *in one day,* all seeking to go west.

On Friday, November 11, at 7 A.M., the procession celebrating the opening of the canal arrived at New York Harbor.

The canal had 83 locks, with lifts ranging from 6 to 12 feet each. It also had 18 aqueducts to facilitate the canal path in and around the river system.

The middle section of the canal was calculated to have cost an average of $12,000 per mile, the eastern section $18,000 per mile, and the short section from Schenectady to Albany $30,000 per mile, for an overall average of $26,241 per mile.

Eight thousand men were employed in the transportation of goods on the Erie Canal, along with 9,000 horses, pulling 2,000 boats, in shifts of six hours on, six hours off, around the clock.

A museum was fitted into a line freighter, offering access to canalers by floating up and down the waterway.

1826—Tolls worth $762,000 were collected, about 10 percent of the total cost of the canal, in just one year.

Bushels of wheat numbering 14,000 were transported from Lake Erie on the canal. By 1840, the number was up to 8 million bushels.

Freighters, using mules, traveled from 2½ to 3 miles per hour.

Going from Albany to Schenectady via stagecoach became popular. The overland route was 15 miles versus a 30-mile (and 27-lock) route by canal. The stage took only three hours and shaved a full day from the canal trip.

1827—"Low bridge!" had become a popular refrain on the Erie Canal. Canal contractors built more than 100 bridges across the canal to let farmers access fields bisected by the canal. Most were built low.

1828—The Oswego Canal was completed, providing access to Lake Ontario.

1829—Passengers on a canal packet boat paid roughly four cents per mile, which included meals and a fold-down bunk bed to sleep on while passing through the canal. A freight canal barge, cramming in immigrants, charged about 15 cents per 10 miles.

The Cayuga and Seneca Canals—or C/S Canal, as we call it today—was completed.

The Well and Canal was completed in Canada, circumventing Niagara Falls and connecting Lake Ontario with Lake Erie.

This canal was enlarged in 1841 and is still used today.

The closing of the canal each winter because of ice affected the daily lives even of people not directly involved with the canal: Mail slowed, perishable goods could not come to market via the slower land-based freight system, and what was freighted cost a fortune.

1830—On Christmas day, the first American-made railroad ran in the United States on a railway in Charleston, South Carolina.

1831—A railroad was constructed from Albany to Schenectady to compete with the stagecoach.

Packet boats that had weighed as much as 20 tons when first used on the Erie Canal were now down to just over 10 tons, because they were being used only on protected waters.

1832—Cholera broke out. It came down from Canada, where it killed 3,000 people in 11 days, to Albany, and up from New York City to Albany. From Albany it went west, right along the route of the Erie Canal. Doctors didn't know the cause of cholera, and people took various defensive measures. Some wore wooden shoes so as not to absorb cholera through their feet. When a side of beef was hung outside and spoiled in the air, some towns started to believe the cholera was airborne. Large pieces of meat were hung out to soak up whatever vapor or mist the cholera epidemic was thought to produce. Similarly, people burned tar in barrels to burn off or absorb the cholera germs and put lime in vats on street corners to create fumes to dismiss the disease.

Boston and other port cities also suffered from cholera as infected people passed through. The disease spread rapidly through the eastern half of the United States. New Orleans alone lost 10,000 people to cholera that summer.

1833—A canal opened between Keuka Lake and Seneca Lake. It later closed when a railroad line replaced it. Today, a hiking trail follows the path of both, ending in the town of Penn Yan.

Businessmen cried "Eureka!" New York City processed just over a million barrels of flour, twice as much as was being shipped to Baltimore, the port with the next highest ranking in the New World, and four times the amount being shipped through New Orleans. Montréal, Canada, was not even in the ranking.

1835—The canal increased property values. Mr. Barton bought two North Tonawanda lots in 1815 for $250. In the fall of 1835, he accepted an offer of $20,000 for the same two lots.

Half the boats working the Erie Canal were owned or controlled by Rochester-based businesses. Rochester was a center for lumber, sending by canal about 753,000 feet of boards, 885,000 pounds of staves, and 2,000 pounds of furniture. Rochester also shipped beef, pork, potatoes, peas, beans, ashes, wool, dried fruit, whiskey, cheese, butter, lard, and other goods.

1836—Construction on the second-generation Erie Canal began. The new dimensions were to be 70 feet wide with a 7-foot-deep waterway and rectangular-sized double locks, one eastbound, and one westbound, of 110 feet by 18 feet. This enlargement was completed in 1862. It could transport barges carrying 240 tons of cargo instead of the 30 tons of the previous canal. The canal never closed during its operating season while the expansion was occurring.

Three thousand boats were now on the canal. Fifty or more boats often lined up at peak hours, waiting to lock through.

Bridges in populated areas were frequent, about every quarter-mile. Passengers had to lie prone or go inside their boats, missing the scenery while passing under these bridges.

Martin Van Buren was the first New Yorker to be elected president of the United States.

1837—Canal lock operators were very efficient at their job. They could move a canal boat through a lock in as little as three minutes—for a tip of two beers. At the height of the season, as many as 250 boats, going one at a time, passed through a canal lock in a given day.

1839—The canal still had political implications. The Whig party came into power in the state legislature and removed every canal-system superintendent, save one.

1840—The Erie Canal System's 363 miles of canal were now supplemented by some 4,000 miles throughout the eastern United States. Most were far less successful.

1842—The invention of Dart's grain elevator, used to load product into a barge, was a big advance for the canal's grain trade.

Buffalo's boat-building industry began to rival that of Rochester.

Six railroad lines linked together finally connected Albany with Lake Erie by rail.

At peak periods traffic congestion at locks delayed passage by as much as 36 hours.

1843—The Seventh-Day Adventist Church was established.

New oversized packet boats were built to fill the enlarged Erie Canal.

1845—The number of boats on the canal reached 4,000, compared with 3,000 in 1836. Twenty-five thousand men, women, and children worked on them.

The cost of the canal was finally paid off.

1846—Some canal packet boats started carrying bands to entertain passengers.

Rum, gin, brandy, wine, beer, cider, bread, milk, and groceries were offered at the locks every few miles.

1847—For the first time, more tonnage was shipped east than west. Typical cargoes were furs, lumber, staves, potash, wheat, flour, barley, beef, pork, butter, cheese, whiskies, furniture, and salt.

1848—Elizabeth Cady Stanton organized the first Women's Rights Convention just three blocks north of the Cayuga-Seneca Canal. She lived a half-block south of the canal.

1849—A train could travel from Albany to Buffalo in 15 hours. This achievement was the handwriting on the wall for the canal system's future.

The first woman, Elizabeth Blackwell, graduated from Geneva Medical College on Seneca Lake near the terminus of the Cayuga/Seneca Canal.

1850—A break in the canal near Rochester took 2,400 men working 24 hours a day for 10 days to repair. The resulting backup continued for weeks.

1852—New York City's ports processed 300,000 immigrants, compared to 192,000 in 1848, 63,000 in 1840, 30,000 in 1830, and 9,000 in 1825. Roughly 25 percent of these immigrants would remain in the greater New York City area. Many of the rest traveled up the Hudson and via the canal to Albany and to other points north and west along the canal.

Two local boys, Henry Wells from Port Byron, New York, and William G. Fargo of Auburn, New York, joined together to form the Wells-Fargo Express Company.

1853—The canal helped populate and develop such towns as Troy, Ilion, Utica, Rome, Syracuse, and Macedon, all of which carry names from Roman and Greek history. Indian names were also popular, including Schenectady, Canajoharie, and Canastota.

The New York Central Railroad was created out of 10 smaller railroads and establishes a viable railroad connection between New York City and Chicago. As a result, New York railroads carried three times the freight of Pennsylvania railroads and more than twice the freight all Ohio railroads. The Erie Canal still transported a greater tonnage of freight than all these railroads combined, but the canal was doomed due to the efficiency and power of the railroads.

1855—New Yorker Walt Whitman published his first edition of *Leaves of Grass*.

1857—William S. Burroughs, an accountant working in a bank alongside Cayuga Lake, off the Cayuga-Seneca Canal, left the bank because of the boring nature of the work. He learned how to operate machine tools and lathes and, motivated by his repugnance of current accounting methods, invented the adding machine. Burroughs, by the way, was born in Rochester, though he worked in the Finger Lakes region.

1859—A fellow named George M. Pullman from Auburn invented an oversized railroad car called the Pioneer. The invention didn't go anywhere because its size prohibited it from going around bridges, platforms, and curves. In 1865 it was used as a part of Lincoln's funeral train, forcing the railroad to modify that particular set of tracks to accommodate it. The invention was renamed the Pullman car and came into widespread use, changing forever the ride quality and comfort of railroad passage.

1861-65—The Civil War divided the nation. New York City voted on secession but remained in the Union.

Schenectady's Clute Machine Works built the turret mechanism for the Union's ironclad ship, the *Monitor*.

1863—The military draft started in New York City.

1865—Ezra Cornell, a millwright, constructed a line for Samuel Morse, of Morse-code fame, between the cities of Washington, D.C., and Baltimore, Maryland. Cornell University, in Ithaca on the south end of Cayuga Lake off the Cayuga-Seneca Canal, was named after him.

1867—Commodore Vanderbilt achieved effective control of the New York Central Railroad.

1872—Tonnage transported on the New York canal system reached an all-time peak.

1881—President William Garfield was assassinated, and Vice-President Chester

Arthur, a New Yorker, succeeded him. President Garfield had worked as a "hoagie" (canal barge boatman) as a youth.

1882—J. Pierpont Morgan bought his first boat—a used one, but still 185 feet long.

1883—All tolls on the Erie Canal were abolished, and revenues since inception totaled $121,461,871. The cost of the canal at that point totaled $80 million: $50 million for construction and $30 million for supervision and repairs since inception. The rest was profit. Still, the railroads shipped more freight than the canal.

The Brooklyn Bridge, a modern engineering wonder, was built to span the East River.

The Metropolitan Opera House opened in New York City.

1887—The Statue of Liberty was erected in New York City.

1890—The first electric chair was put to use at the state prison at Auburn, New York.

1891—Carnegie Hall opened.

1896—Motion pictures, invented by Thomas Edison, were first shown at Bial's Music Hall in New York City.

1897—New York's Steinway Piano Company ended its boat-building activity.

1902—Without a speed limit, the Hudson River became home to higher-performance motor boats such as the metal-framed, wood-planked *Arrow*, built in New York by Sam Ayers. Measuring 130 feet by 12 feet, 5 inches, the boat was clocked at 45 miles per hour in trials.

1903—Construction began on the third major generation of the canal.

1905—New York hosted its first boat show.

1910—The National Association for the Advancement of Colored People (NAACP) was founded.

1917-19—The United States fought in World War I.

1918—Barges as long as 300 feet moved through the newly opened third-generation Erie Canal, which was renamed the New York State Barge Canal System. This third incarnation of the canal did not really use very much of the initial or second versions and sometimes had shifted the canal routings a number of miles from the prior canal paths. The new Champlain Canal (opened in 1916), the Oswego, and the main Erie Canal were all widened, and larger locks with higher lifts were installed to reduce the number of locks. The Erie Canal then ran roughly 340 miles; the Champlain, 63; Oswego, 24; and the C/S Canal, 27 miles. Fleets of four or five barges, self-propelled or towed, could carry up to 2,300 tons combined in one raft-up. No towpaths for horses on this version.

1919-20—Prohibition started, and high-speed boats were developed for rumrunning.

1921—Boat designer and racer Gar Wood raced a train from Miami, Florida, to New York City. Over the 1,260 miles the boat beat the train by 21 minutes. Then 41 years old, he had "retired" to a second career of designing and building fast boats, including many Gold Cup winners and boats specializing in straightaway speeds. He originally made his fortune inventing the dump truck.

1924—Gar Wood designed and built a five-engine, 70-foot-by-11½-foot fast commuter for Gordon Hamersley to use going between Wall Street and his home in Long Island. She could break 50 miles per hour in trial conditions. (Everything was perfect: tuned engines, clean bottom, no accouterments on board.)
1925—Madison Square Garden opened; *Time* magazine started publication.

The commuter yacht *Teaser,* a George Crouch design, beat the scheduled time of the railroad traveling from Albany to New York City.
1926—The NBC coast-to-coast radio network was formed.
1927—Babe Ruth hit 60 home runs, a season record.
1928—Franklin Delano Roosevelt was elected governor of New York.
1929—The fastest commuter, *Rascal,* broke 55 miles per hour with a step athwart ships in her bottom. The step, however, caused vibration, so it was removed, and she slowed down 10 percent.

The stock market crashed on October 24, signaling the start of the Great Depression.
1932—Franklin Delano Roosevelt was elected president.
1933—Prohibition was repealed on December 5 at 5:32 A.M.
1935—New York implemented unemployment insurance at the state level.
1939—The World's Fair opened in New York.
1941-45—The United States fought Germany and Japan in World War II
1946—Leo Durocher left the New York Dodgers to manage the New York Giants.
1947—The *Pardon Me,* a 47-foot Hacker bright-finished mahogany boat nicknamed the "World's Largest Runabout," was launched.

At Oyster Bay, Long Island, Lawrence Rockefeller launched his first aluminum yacht, built by Jakobson Shipyard.

John D. Rockefeller's donation of 20 acres of land along the East River established the United Nations' home base in New York City.
1948—Alger Hiss was indicted by a New York grand jury for perjury in an investigation of his spying for the U.S.S.R.

Your author was born on November 8.
1950—The New York State Thruway Authority was established.
1952—Dr. Norman Vincent Peale's book *The Power of Positive Thinking* went on sale.
1957—The Billy Graham crusade filled Madison Square Garden.
1959—The St. Lawrence Seaway opened. Waterborne freight could be moved west more cheaply through this route than the canals.
1960—More than 70 percent of New York State's population lived within two miles of the New York State Barge Canal System.
1962—Johnny Carson took over the *Tonight* show from Jack Parr.
1964—The second New York World's Fair opened.
1971—Inmates rioted in western New York's Attica State Prison.
1975—The Antique & Classic Boat Society was established.

1980—The Winter Olympics were held in Lake Placid.

1985—The Dow Jones industrial average broke 1,400 for the first time.

1986—"Tall ships" joined in the celebration of the 100th birthday of the Statue of Liberty. They stole the show.

1987—The New York Boat Show opened at its new home in the new Jacob K. Javits Convention Center in Manhattan.

1994—Your author traveled from California to New York to begin researching this book.

1996—Albany-area car dealer Jim De Nooyer Sr. and his son Jim Jr. made a record run of three hours and 20 minutes from Albany to the Statue of Liberty in their 28-foot catamaran powerboat.

North Tarrytown, located on the Hudson River in Westchester County, renamed itself Sleepy Hollow to commemorate the town's connection to Washington Irving, who made the area famous in his story "The Legend of Sleepy Hollow."

1997—The U.S. Department of Housing and Urban Development announced $120 million in grants and loans for towns along the Erie Canal to encourage development, boating, and recreation.

The Dow Jones industrial average broke 8,000.

1998—The first million-dollar boating improvements under the U.S. government's new financing were in place at Seneca Falls in the Finger Lakes region off the Cayuga/Seneca Canal section of the Erie Canal System.

The Dow Jones industrial average broke 9,000.

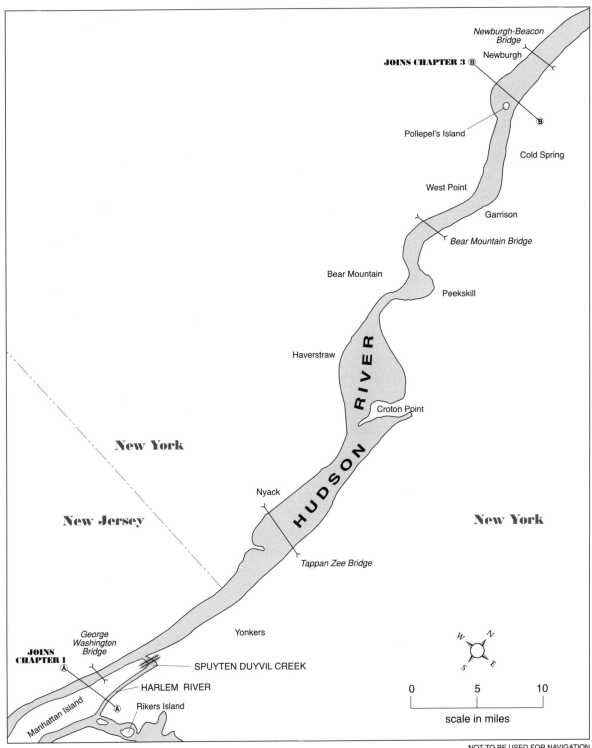

JOINS CHAPTER 3 Ⓑ

Newburgh-Beacon Bridge

Newburgh

Pollepel's Island

Cold Spring

West Point

Garrison

Bear Mountain Bridge

Bear Mountain

Peekskill

HUDSON RIVER

Haverstraw

Croton Point

New York

Nyack

New Jersey

New York

Tappan Zee Bridge

Yonkers

George Washington Bridge

JOINS CHAPTER 1
Ⓐ

SPUYTEN DUYVIL CREEK

HARLEM RIVER

Ⓐ

Rikers Island

Manhattan Island

N
W   E
S

0   5   10

scale in miles

NOT TO BE USED FOR NAVIGATION

CHAPTER 2

The Middle Hudson River

> **SKIPPER TIP:** While the Hudson River does not have a speed limit per se, everyone is expected to slow down near fuel docks, swimmers, and other situations that demand prudence and adherence to boating regulations. Marine police craft are on hand to help prevent accidents and enforce regulations. Watch your wake and you'll be fine. The Hudson is one of the greatest runs on the entire East Coast for a planing powerboat. Trip planners need to factor in tide (allow for swiftness wherever the river narrows on your chart). It averages about 1½ knots flood and about a half-knot more on ebb the length of the Hudson River south of Troy. Another factor for sailors is the effect of wind blockage when their boats are behind some of the bigger mountain peaks. The towering beauty has a price.

> **SKIPPER TIP:** Please use NOAA charts 12343 and 12347 for this section.

The George Washington Bridge

If you stayed at Port Imperial overnight or at nearby Lincoln Harbor Yacht Club, Surfside 3, or at an anchorage, and are now starting your run north up the Hudson, you will soon come to the George Washington Bridge. The bridge connects Manhattan Island, at 178th Street on the east shore, to Fort Lee, New Jersey, on the west. The road crossing via the George Washington Bridge is Interstate 95. A toll is charged for cars going from New Jersey to New York, but to keep traffic flowing, no toll is charged going from New York to New Jersey. The George Washington Bridge was built in 1931, and at that time it was the longest suspension bridge in the world, with a span of 3,500 feet. In 1960 the bridge was expanded to add a second deck. Now about 46 million cars cross it each year. There are now 14 lanes of traffic on these two decks, which a few locals euphemistically refer to as "George" and "Martha."

As you go under the George Washington, keep a sharp eye out on the east shore, right at the base of the bridge. There is an inactive lighthouse there named Jeffrey Point. H. Swift wrote about it in his children's book *The Little Red Lighthouse and the Great Gray Bridge*, and I think the attention the book created is what saved it from destruction after World War II. This Jeffrey Point lighthouse was a manned station built in 1920 to replace two fixed lights originally set up there in 1885. The lighthouse was open for only 12 years before being deactivated. The bridge's lights are now a more effective warning to boaters than the lighthouse was. Now it is listed in the National Register of Historical Places.

On Manhattan Island, a little over a mile north of the George Washington Bridge, is Dyckman Marina. Look for its rounded white building.

Dyckman Marina (212) 567-5120

Storm protection: ⩗
Scenic: *
Marina-reported approach depths: 10 feet
Marina-reported dockside depths: 2-5 feet
Rest rooms
Showers
Dockside water
Barbecues
Power connections: 15A/125V
Mechanical repairs
What's special: limited to smaller craft
VHF-monitored channel: 16

On the opposite shore is another marina facility, about 1½ miles north of the George Washington Bridge. You must use the privately maintained markers to properly approach this facility. Because it is located in a park, you must drive some distance from the marina for additional services. This also applies to the Alpine Boat Basin, about 5 miles north of here.

Englewood Boat Basin (201) 894-9510

Storm protection: ⩗
Scenic: * *
Marina-reported approach depths: 5 feet
Marina-reported dockside depths: 3-5 feet
Gas
Diesel
Rest rooms
Showers
Dockside water
Picnic tables
Power connections: 30A/125V
What's special: few transients
VHF-monitored channel: 16

Spuyten Duyvil Creek and The Harlem River

Looking at your chart, you will see that the next waterway is to the east: the Spuyten Duyvil Creek (Dutch for "spitting devil"). It was named in the seventeenth century, and the reference to it as a "creek" might seem deceptive today, because it's quite wide at this point.

By traveling through the Spuyten Duyvil, you will reach the Harlem River. This is the route to the East River, which lets you go on to Long Island Sound or back to New York Harbor.

Although boaters can use this route, it does have its limitations. First of all, Amtrak railroad service uses the swing bridge that crosses the entrance to the creek for trains to and from New York City. Second, depending on the tide, currents and eddies can affect your craft at the juncture of the Hudson River and Spuyten Duyvil Creek waterways. When the train bridge is closed, depending on the tide, clearance can be less than four feet. Because so much of the northeast rail traffic uses this bridge, it is often a limiting factor for boaters.

SKIPPER TIP: Hail the bridge tender on VHF channel 13 or sound one long followed by one short blast on your ship's horn. He will either open or answer with five blasts if he cannot open. You also must acknowledge his five blasts with an answering five blasts to show that you understand that he cannot open.

Another concern is that farther east of this first bridge just discussed here are other

These bridges mark the entrance to the Spuyten Duyvil Creek, which leads to the Harlem River. The bridge in the foreground—just a few feet above the water—carries Amtrak trains to and from New York City. Because of heavy train volume, this photo captures one of those rare times when the bridge has been swung open to accommodate boat traffic.

bridges, with height limitations of some 20 feet, and you have to be able to cruise beneath these heights. If you are in a sailboat, forget it—unless you're willing to take down your mast. Note: Like most of Manhattan's shoreline, these channel edges are mostly man-made. The natural creek course was so convoluted that on old maps it looks like a curved snake ready to strike. The switch-backed water path was strewn with rocks and boulders in such a way that the water seemed to spit as it flowed, particularly during tidal changes (hence the name). A bit of history: This general area of Manhattan Island was the scene of the first American victory of the Revolutionary War in the Hudson Valley.

Yonkers

Proceeding north up the Hudson River, you pass the city of Yonkers. You have probably heard of Yonkers in connection with Yonkers Raceway, a popular harness-racing horse track over the years. Yonkers started out as a land grant in 1646, becoming a village in 1855 and a city in 1870. Yonkers is both an industrial city and a bedroom community. There is not much docking, and most of what is available is limited either by shallow water or a lack of tie-up space. The largest city in Westchester County, Yonkers was the nickname of its first Dutch owner and means "young lord" in Dutch. The local Indians called it Kekeskick.

We will review some of the docking

choices in this general area, but most boaters will have stayed down in Weehawken and do not need to hear about any facilities in this area. Your first choice is Alpine Boat Basin, (201) 768-9798, which is across the river from here. You are going to have to watch your water depth during the tides, and once you have slipped you still are not near enough to ancillary facilities, such as restaurants, to reasonably walk to them.

An interesting side note: The idea of a suburb first started here. The cost of living in the city, Manhattan Island, actually forced people to start thinking about taking their living into homes located in the river country, a distance from their workplace in Manhattan, as reported in the *New York Times* in 1871.

The Palisades

The breathtaking rock cliffs and foliage you see on the west shore are the Palisades. They extend about 30 miles, from Hoboken, New Jersey, up to and through Haverstraw, New York, though the defining section is a 12-mile stretch that runs from Fort Lee northward to Sparkhill Creek, south of both the Piermont Pier and the Tappan Zee Bridge.

> **SKIPPER TIP:** Sailors, this was known as the Great Chip, and thus it was the "Great Chip Reach" in the days of sail.

The cliffs range in height from about 100 to 540 feet at their highest point. For years people have been trying to describe this crest line of old volcanic rock. The Palisades have been called "massive stone logs," "Titanic pickets," "a great wall of posts," "a sandwich of sandstone and molten rock," and other such expressive phrases. Centuries of weathering has caused much of the column effect: Water made its way into fissures, froze, and pried off pieces of rock, leaving scars in the cliff sides. A couple of million years passed before the rock that forms the Palisades accumulated in the lowlands, most of which were in what is now New Jersey. First sand and mud were washed down from the higher areas. These deposits solidified and, under great pressure, eventually formed the sandstone that lies beneath the Palisades and Hackensack Meadows. After the sandstone layers were formed, molten rock was forced up through gaps or rifts, creating immense dikes or sills some 700 to 1,000 feet thick. When that mass of hot molten rock cooled down, it broke the rock into sheets that resemble huge vertical columns, which are what you're now looking at to port. The Palisades' diabase is a heavy rock primarily made of feldspar and pyroxene. It shows a dirty gray color where it's been exposed for a long time. The more recently exposed rock surface weathers to a brown color. The red-colored rock is typically a layer of shale within the sandstone. It seems natural that stone quarrying was done in this area as early as 1736. By 1820, iron mining and manufacturing were also under way in these western-shore highlands.

In the post-Revolutionary War period, boat building and rock quarrying were ongoing at the base of the Palisades cliffs. In fact, various industries were so well established that housing for the stonecutters, masons, woodcutters, and even some fishermen were built along the water's edge. Evidence of this includes a map drawn in 1818 by John Eddy that shows large quarry holes on the shorelines of Bergen (New

Jersey) and Rockland (New York) counties. Also, the red sandstone underlying the Palisades was used prior to 1825 as a material for building blocks. Stonemasons farmed the stuff by carving building blocks out of the rock pits. By 1790 the Fort Lee ferry connected these areas to Manhattan. Records from 1830 indicate that 12 vessels were engaged in the hauling of stone from here. And so, the freighting and boat-building industry continued.

North New Jersey Early History

In the November 29, 1862, issue of *Harper's Weekly,* an illustration of a monitor-style gunship named the *Passaic* shelling the Palisades highlands appeared. People in this time lacked our present-day understanding of the need to preserve the natural landscape—the idea of protecting the environment would not have occurred to them. During the postbellum period, dynamite became popular and greatly accelerated the ability to quarry some of the native stone in this Hudson River area. By 1894, from Fort Lee, New Jersey, to the New York State border just north of Cloister, 15 quarries had been plotted on a local map. In addition, the need for housing and factories destroyed some of the highland scenery of the Hudson River Valley.

Because the quarrymen's activity was destroying the area, the Palisades Interstate Park was established, and all quarrying stopped on New Year's Eve 1900. This cessation was extended upriver from the New Jersey/New York border all the way up to Newburgh in the extension of 1906, when the federal government was authorized to buy up land. Entrepreneurial and philanthropic families had earlier donated some of this land.

The northeast New Jersey area was not very

populated during the 1660s and 1670s. Some Indians were still living there, and hostilities between them and the settlers were ongoing. There were just a few plantations, which started northward from Hackensack. In 1643 there were a few settlements in what is now known as Jersey City, then called Communieaw. The 1643 census confirmed that there were no people living in Bergen County (Weehawken, New Jersey, and inland from there). It was later, around 1709, that this western shore area finally had some 70 families. Historians theorize that the threat posed by the Indians, whose land was being encroached upon, prevented any earlier development

All this scenery and history are in these Palisades highlands high above your vessel's port side as you head north up the Hudson. Many people consider this historically rich scenery some of the best in the world—maybe some of the most romantic scenery, too. Enjoy it; don't hurry on past it.

Before the Revolutionary War this whole area of New Jersey was called the King's Woods. Because all timberland in England was the property of the king, the term King's Woods was used in the American colonies too. During the Revolutionary War these woods were suddenly no longer off-limits because of the war; therefore, a lot of the trees were harvested for firewood. In fact, there was a cold winter in 1779-80. The Hudson River froze hard enough that the British, who were occupying Manhattan Island, took their horses and sleds across it, stripped whatever wood there was in New Jersey, and came back across the frozen Hudson with it to Manhattan. These Fort Lee woods were also regularly clear-cut to provide wood for ships' use.

Some 30 years after the Revolutionary War,

the devastated King's Woods, which had been clear-cut at least once for firewood by each opposing army of the war, had regenerated itself. It was cut down again for use as firewood, but this time by the city dwellers of that town called New Amsterdam, which we now call New York City. In 1858 railroad-tie material was forested from the top of the Palisades. A sawmill was established to cut these ties in Englewood, New Jersey, which is inland from the cliffs.

After the Civil War, the deforested Palisades plain contained apple orchards, vineyards, and cabbage patches. These farming activities extended north as far as the Rockland Lake area. At this same time, any dairy farms along the Hudson were abandoning cheese making in favor of milk production for the growing population of Manhattan.

Besides producing food, this whole section tied in with the lower Hudson River to meet Manhattan's recreational needs. The Palisades, as you've probably heard before, is the former location of the Palisades Amusement Park, which began operating in 1890. Sadly, it has since been torn down.

Leisure Time

Manhattanites vacationed both in the Harlem area of Manhattan and on the New Jersey side of the Hudson River, where they took day trips via the ferry service. There also were some boating activities such as yacht and rowing clubs. These clubs held regattas and other yachting events. Bicycling, fishing, some camping, hiking, and bathing also were popular. This was another stage in the development of the Hudson River Valley. The area grew as people felt more comfortable about going on a pleasure day trip on Sunday rather

than observing the Sabbath—a hard step for earlier Americans who clung to the Puritan work ethic. They also had to be successful enough in their work to have this leisure time.

Then, as the Hudson River Valley mode of transportation moved from sailboats to steamboats to railroads, the speed of these vehicles allowed the successful New York residents to reach farther and higher up the valley. First they did so for short-term recreation and vacation purposes. However, as time went on, each of these areas would be sought after by the rich and famous as a place for a summer home (or year-round residence). Thus, most of these major palatial estates that you'll see resulted from inventions and improvements in the transportation system.

Rockefeller Family

Boaters have the ideal vantage point for appreciating the spectacular formations of the Palisades, so enjoy the beauty of this rock wall, rising from the water like a row of giant sentinels. At one time the Palisades were at risk of human encroachment because portions of the area were mined and quarries operated at the base of the cliffs. However, in 1910, the Rockefeller family bought up all the remaining land along the river not owned by the government and donated it for use as an interstate park area for New York and New Jersey. Now its beauty is preserved for the future.

A couple of reference points along the Palisades include the Alpine Boat Basin, which is an old landing terminal for the ferry system that used to land here. It is 7 miles north of the George Washington Bridge on the west shore of the Hudson River. Just north of the boat basin is an old Boy Scout camp called Camp Alpine, which is a very popular fishing spot. Locals call this area Boat Point. They like to catch crab with a trap or a line, using dead fish or chicken parts to bait the crabs.

Alpine Boat Basin (201) 768-9798

Storm protection: √√
Scenic: *
Marina-reported approach depths: 5 feet
Marina-reported dockside depths: 2-5 feet
Gas
Rest rooms
Showers
Dockside water
Picnic tables
Power connections: 30A/125V, 50A/125V
What's special: few transients

New York Boat Clubs

While traveling the New York waterways, I noticed that often a yacht club will call itself a boat club. Some members seem to think that when these clubs were being formed, primarily in the 1950s and 1960s, the term "yacht club" meant the New York Yacht Club, which was the defender of the America's Cup and the stomping grounds of the wealthy and famous. The members of boat clubs generally believe that boating is a less grandiose sport and a more family-oriented activity, and that these clubs are designed to make the average middle-class American feel comfortable and at home. After all, I think that a yacht is often perceived to be a vessel that is luxuriously outfitted, sharply styled, and too big to be carried as a tender to a larger vessel. Therefore, anything that doesn't meet that definition would just be called a boat, and the boat clubs were founded to serve and be a source of enjoyment to people who own boats as well as yachts. For those of you who continue your

pleasure cruise onto the Great Lakes area, you'll find that old-timers there call everything a boat, even the largest 600-foot freighter, rather than using the term "ship." People from the Great Lakes region also use "laker" or "Great Laker" today.

Hoboken

With the advent of the steamboat activity on the Hudson River, the idea of a destination resort was viable—and within reach of New York City residents. Of course, some New Yorkers were getting successful and had money to spend. People started to spend some of this money on the new transportation in their pursuit of out-of-town recreations and vacations.

The Catskill Mountain House, which opened in 1823, had a client base of New York City residents. The time was ripe for steamboats to expand their business. The Erie Canal was under construction. Elysian Fields, which was on the New Jersey side across from New York, was a conveniently located resort for New Yorkers. This resort area had been frequented as early as the Revolutionary War period, when the rich and famous were the only ones who could afford the private sailcraft to get over there. When the steamboats began offering regular ferry service, the Elysian Fields became a playground for the working man.

In 1837 G. T. Strong, who happened to be a very class-conscious individual, wrote in his diaries that loafers were socializing in Hoboken. Strong was very disappointed about the type of people who were there—including strumpets—and he observed a couple engaged in, according to his diary, "the commission of gross vulgarity."

Tower Ridge Yacht Club, another private club, is now visible. Readers should expect that any club or other facility listed as "private" in this guide will not welcome newcomers. At a minimum, call ahead of your visit to ask if a club accepts transients. Many of those that do need prior correspondence with your home club to establish proper billing. A few might be sufficiently dazzled by your craft or your predicament that someone will relax the procedures, but do not count on it.

A quick word about yacht clubs in general: Yacht clubs frequently "reciprocate" with other yacht clubs. Members of foreign yacht clubs are welcomed at other clubs as if they were members there too. The visiting boater can often stay the first night free, use all club facilities, and participate in any ongoing activities. Boaters who avail themselves of a foreign club's amenities are encouraged to either join the club (if they intend to make repeat visits in the future); make a donation to the foreign club's treasury; or offer their home club's burgee (flag) for the foreign club's display. Some clubs do limit visitors on a "space available" basis, but almost any reciprocating club will honor a visitor who has contacted the foreign marina well in advance through written correspondence. However, some clubs, especially those on heavily traveled routes, do not reciprocate because of past abuses of courtesies they extended. Any number of competing circumstances can affect a club's policy toward nonmembers, so you're better off calling ahead if you're planning to pass through an area and need a yacht club's services. Note: If a yacht club's phone number is not listed in this guide, chances are that that club has requested its number not be given in order to discourage requests for accommodations.

Tower Ridge Yacht Club (914) 478-9729

Storm protection: √√
Scenic: * *
Marina-reported approach depths: 15 feet
Marina-reported dockside depths: 2 feet
Rest rooms
Power connections: 15A/125V
What's special: private yacht club

While this yacht club is on the east shore at the town of Hastings-on-Hudson, the New York-New Jersey border is on the west shore.

SKIPPER TIP: Now there is a substantial stretch of shallower water to the west of the marked channel, and the channel slowly shifts to the right side of the natural river width.

Piermont

In 1854 the town of Piermont had twice the population of the town of Nyack. The boom was driven by the railroad-support facilities of a pier, a ferry stop, an engine house, repair shops, and maintenance buildings for the railroad trains. Piermont also had hotels, a depot, shops, stores, and a cemetery—all supported by these activities.

Piermont, called Tappan Slote prior to the opening of the Erie Canal in 1825, was the main loading point in this area for farm produce grown in inland hamlets and farms on both the New York and New Jersey sides of the Hudson. In about 1820 this area produced cash crops of apples, raspberries, and potatoes. Prior to the construction of the pier, which could handle larger boats, crops had to be transported across the Hudson from the

New York side via small boats. By 1841 the eastern end of the Erie Railroad was situated in Piermont.

On the western shore of the Hudson River, the Piermont Pier has served as a landing for Columbia University's geological and research vessels, but much of it is a park. Built in 1841 as a railroad and steamboat terminal, the pier extends about a mile into the river, hence its nickname of the "mile-long dock." If you want to go off the main channel and towards the Piermont Pier, make sure that you pick up the unmarked side channel correctly. If you look at your chart, you can see that much of the water immediately outside the channel is as shallow as 1 foot. North of the pier the water is somewhat deeper, and there are a few docks. Piermont Pier itself does not offer boater access.

You may see the boats (anchored and otherwise) and marinas from the channel over 1½ miles away. People visiting the businesses in Piermont enjoy the stores, restaurants, and even the grocery stores, but the water around these amenities is shallow enough that most need local knowledge. Contact the business you intend to visit by cellular phone (they do not seem to monitor VHF radio channels) and ask for their specific approach instructions, or follow in a local craft that requires more water depth than you do.

Tappan Zee Marina (914) 359-5522

Storm protection: √√
Scenic: *
Marina-reported approach depths: 4 feet
Marina-reported dockside depths: 2-3 feet
Floating docks
Gas
Rest rooms

Dockside water
Barbecues
Picnic tables
Mechanical repairs
Travelift/hoist
What's special: few transients

Cornetta's Marina (914) 354-0410

Storm protection: √√
Scenic: *
Marina-reported approach depths: 4 feet
Marina-reported dockside depths: 1-3 feet
Rest rooms
Showers
Power connections: 30A/125V
Mechanical repairs
Travelift/hoist
Restaurant: on site
What's special: few transients

Lyndhurst

Lyndhurst on the east shore is a mansion open to visitors. It is one of the premier properties on the Hudson. Built in 1838-39 on 67 acres, it is made of greystone in the Gothic Revival style. The house and grounds are worth seeing. The house's second owner, George Merritt, enlarged it in 1865. However, its third owner, Jay Gould, was the most famous. One of the "robber barons" of the nineteenth century, he was a prominent financier, railroad speculator, and owner of the Western Union telegraph company. One of Gould's daughters donated the property in 1964 to the National Trust for Historic Preservation, which operates it today. Inquire by calling (914) 631-4481. Boaters should dock in one of the Tarrytown facilities and taxi back.

The main house at Jay Gould's Lyndhurst estate in Tarrytown, New York. The estate has been designated a National Trust for Historic Preservation property, and tours are frequently conducted.

The Tappan Zee Bridge

North of the Piermont "mile-long dock" is the Tappan Zee Bridge. This bridge spans a wide part of the Hudson River within the Tappan Reach and connects Tarrytown on the east shore with South Nyack on the west shore. The route over the bridge is part of Interstate 87 and the New York State Thruway. The bridge is three miles long and has a vertical clearance of 129 feet. When the bridge opened in 1955, more than 2,200 cars crossed it during the first two hours, and the population of Rockland County on its western landing grew from 89,000 in 1950 to 230,000 in 1970. *Tappan* is an Indian word meaning "cold springs." The word *zee* means "sea" or "large body of water" in Dutch. Some support facilities for boaters are here on both sides of the river.

Tarrytown and North Tarrytown (Sleepy Hollow)

Located on the eastern shore, just above the Tappan Zee Bridge, is Tarrytown (population about 10,000), former home of a General Motors assembly plant, and North Tarrytown, which renamed itself Sleepy Hollow in 1996. Tarrytown means "wheat town" in Dutch. Tarrytown has two marinas, both of which require a 10- to 15-minute walk to get into town. There you'll find a large Grand Union supermarket, some good antique shopping, a donut shop, and a variety of restaurants, from fine dining to McDonald's. North of town you can spot the Tarrytown Lighthouse, which is neither active nor open to visitors.

After a visit to Lyndhurst, boaters should take a cab north to the Old Dutch Church, the Sleepy Hollow Cemetery (nearby is where Ichabod Crane met the headless horseman in the Washington Irving story!), and Philipsburg Manor, where hardtack (biscuits for boaters) was made as early as 1690. Washington Irving's home, Sunnyside, is south, however, on Route 9 (try the lemonade at the cafe there). Inquire by calling (914) 631-8200.

Tarrytown Lighthouse

Opened in 1883, the Tarrytown Lighthouse had a strong light that was said to be visible for 10 to 15 miles. It also had a foghorn and bell for use during times of reduced visibility. The lighthouse was operational until the Tappan Zee Bridge was lit up and made it obsolete. In 1979 it was listed in the National Register of Historic Places. This is the second of seven lighthouse structures that still exist on the Hudson. The construction of these lighthouses was driven mainly by the traffic on the Erie Canal, which opened in 1825 and whose traffic volume continued to grow for more than 50 years. The Tarrytown Lighthouse used to sit freestanding on a small rock promontory, and you either had to walk out to it over the frozen river in the winter or row to it in a small

A boater's view of the Tappan Zee Bridge.

boat during the summer. Now that it has been deactivated, a land bridge has been created with fill, allowing easy access on foot. The lighthouse stands at the base of the area that is now the closed General Motors assembly plant, north of the bridge.

Marinas

Local-marina approach instructions: Immediately north of the Tappan Zee Bridge is a secondary channel (one-third of a nautical mile long) that takes you into the east shore. Pick up green buoy #1 and red buoy #2 and follow the channel in. Keep between buoy #3 and #4 and finally #5 and #6. There is a range that you can also follow in. Following it will direct you in properly. As you approach the shore, look

for the sign reading Tarrytown Marina on the building; then turn right after red buoy #6. It is 2 to 5 feet deep outside the channel.

The restaurant at the marina has entertained boaters with live jazz on Thursday, Friday, and Saturday in past cruising seasons. It has an outside patio and a raw bar and is generally open for lunch and dinner.

Tarrytown Marina (914) 631-1300

Storm protection: √√√
Scenic: *
Marina-reported approach depths: 8 feet
Marina-reported dockside depths: 8 feet
Gas
Diesel
Waste pump-out
Rest rooms
Showers
Laundry
Dockside water
Power connections: 30A/125V, 50A/125V, 50A/220V
Below-waterline repairs
Mechanical repairs
Gas-engine repairs
Diesel repairs
Generator repairs
Travelift/hoist: 25 tons
Mast stepping
Ship's store
Restaurant: on site
What's special: great dockside dining, but some slips are narrow
VHF-monitored channel: 16

The Washington Irving Boat Club's restaurant next door—with lobster nights on Wednesdays as well as the regular Italian and seafood menus—is open for lunch and dinner. Both marinas are very near a train stop that has service from New York City to Albany and then all

TARRYTOWN MARINA

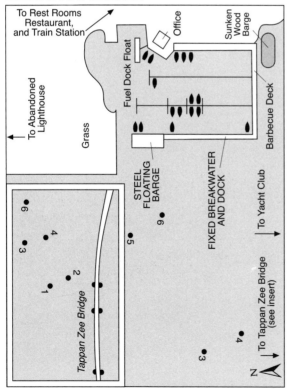

NOT TO BE USED FOR NAVIGATION

the way up to Montréal, so it's easy for friends from elsewhere to join your cruise via a train.

Washington Irving Boat Club (914) 332-0517

Storm protection: √√
Scenic: * *
Marina-reported approach depths: 4 feet
Marina-reported dockside depths: 2-3 feet
Gas
Rest rooms
Showers
Laundry
Dockside water
Power connections: 30A/125V
Restaurant: on site

Sail on the Hudson

The earliest Dutch colonists developed some sailing directions for their Hudson River sloops. As the boats were sailing upstream in the area of the Tappan Zee, where the bridge is now, sailors kept an eye on the top of Hook Mountain. In fact, because it was in view for so long during that particular tack, Hook Mountain got nicknamed "Tedious Hook." Without any engines, the Dutch often had to scull past Haverstraw Bay, which is ahead, or they would anchor when they had a tide or wind that was against them. It just was more effective to anchor than to let themselves lose ground against the unfavorable wind and tide.

Until river dredging began later, European ships coming to America across the Atlantic needed more water to navigate the river than was available. The Dutch early on built a specialized Hudson River sloop, which was about 70 feet long and sometimes as long as 100 feet. These sloops had a very large main sail—the mast was well forward—and the jib and the topsail were small. The Dutch also favored the balloon-style cut sail. Of course, we now know that this is inefficient, but at the time they thought this sail shape was best.

A summer afternoon of sailing on the Hudson River.

Gunboats on the Hudson

This section of the river was the site of an ill-fated Revolutionary War naval battle. British warships had been anchored above the Tappan Zee for more than two weeks when the Americans decided to send out five small boats to engage them in battle. The battle lasted an hour and a half before the Americans turned around and went home. They had failed to drive off the enemy craft. It was the Revolutionary War's first and last naval engagement fought on the Hudson River.

One of the aftereffects of the Revolutionary War was the problem of how to treat British loyalists still living in America. Americans were very hostile toward these people. The British government eventually arranged for some of them to be sent to England, the West Indies, or Nova Scotia. The American soldiers wanted the Tories to leave, hoping to get the land they would relinquish. However, the departing Tories sold most of the land to neighboring American landowners. General Washington himself didn't care if these people were hanged, so it was get-out-of-town-quick time for the Tories.

Nyack, Grandview, and Hook Mountain

Grandview was a source for trap rocks, now known as Belgian paving stones, which were used for roads. In the 1820s and '30s, this part of the Hudson River Valley competed for this business with nearby New Jersey to spur New York City's growth. This industry essentially died by the end of the Civil War because other materials were used for roads. Nyack then diversified its industries, manufacturing shoes, straw hats, matches, and—after 1900—carriages, pianos, ships, boilers, and smoke-stacks.

Starting around 1720, Nyack and the area northward through the Haverstraw lowlands were home to Dutch, German, Danish Huguenot, and some Flemish immigrants. In the 1730s, many New Englanders who had earlier settled along the New England seacoast, having exhausted the soil's fertility there, crossed the valleys and started to mix with this group of newer immigrants. By the 1750s the greater Haverstraw area was populated by a mixture of Long Islanders and Connecticut migrants who were both now second-generation Yankees.

Nestled in surrounding hills ranging from 400 feet to 700 feet high, Nyack, nicknamed "the Gem of the Hudson," is still a small town, rich in history. During the early 1800s, Nyack was very rural, with only seven homes in the village limits and a single trading post at the landing, operated by a fellow named Abram Tallman. In 1806 New York's legislature authorized the first road between Albany and New York City. After the Nyack Turnpike was completed in 1825, the town grew quickly and by 1830 had a population of 300. By the early 1870s and 1880s, Nyack had become a popular resort area, attracting upper-class vacationers from the city and doubling its population during the summer months.

In its early days, Nyack's sloops were generally thought to be the most colorful of all those on the Hudson River. They were decoratively painted with gold, red, green, and blue stripes. Some of the decrepit docking facilities along the tidal beaches of the river's edge below the landings date from the time when ice harvesting and rock quarrying were big activities on this part of the river. Northward and behind the Hook Mountain area are three lakes: Rockland, Congers, and

Swartwout. They used to be ice-harvesting sites. Just north of Hook Mountain you'll see a couple of "almost" fault coves—one natural, the other artificially cut. Over time both of them have had roads nestled in them.

In the 1830s Rockland Lake, fed by natural springs and brooks, was considered the most extensive ice station of many on the Hudson River. This industry began in 1826, when workers sawed some blocks of ice out of the lake, slid them down the cliff's side to a boat landing, and barged them down to storage cellars in the Greenwich Village area of Manhattan. By the 1830s the ice was run down the hill in a sluiceway, which was replaced by a gravity-incline railway in the 1850s. This Rockland Lake ice company was running a fleet of 13 steamboats and 80 barges and employed almost 3,000 workers during the winter. Remnants of this business can be found today. The old landing for the Knickerbocker Ice Company is best identified on your chart by the area marked as "cable area," approximately at 41 degrees and 8.75 seconds north. It's just north of Rockland Lake on the west shore of the Hudson River.

These ruins at the base of Rockland Lake just north of Hook Mountain were the Rockland Lake Landing, also nicknamed Slaughter's Landing. A popular version of how Slaughter's Landing got its name dates from Revolutionary War times, when the British used this landing to load their slaughtered cattle onto their ships. However, the landing was likely named for the Slaughter family, which had settled in this area as early as 1711. Nevertheless, the first story is the better one and, in fact, can be found in several books on Hudson River/New York State history.

Much of the wood from the oak and hickory trees that were plentiful on the slopes of Hook Mountain was used for the brick industry and also for some shipbuilding in Nyack and Haverstraw. As these woods were cut down for shipyards, brickyards, sawmills, and charcoal furnaces, other uses for the land were created. Cattle and sheep herds, for example, grazed here among the tree stumps.

From the Revolutionary War to the opening of the Erie Canal in 1825, this whole Hook Mountain region developed slowly. The poor soil conditions caused by glacier activity millions of years ago were blamed. In addition, the somewhat rugged terrain was not easily farmed, and the continual lack of roads was a problem. In 1820 development began inland from Rockland Lake, when an iron works was built and sandstone was quarried. Cottoncloth and twine mills followed. Finally, nail manufacturing began, and flour- and sawmills were opened.

Anchorage

Today Nyack has a population of about 10,000 people, and its sister town of Upper Nyack offers an attractive anchorage for boaters. Designated on your chart as a special anchorage, you can locate it at the north end of town. However, because this area has a very large permanent population of moored boats, perhaps the largest on the entire Hudson River, the situation is crowded. Here the Palisades sweep around Hook Mountain, creating what is known as the Tappan Zee. To find the anchorage, look for Hook Mountain, which at 700 feet tall is quite prominent from the river. The anchorage provides protection from northwest winds, which generally blow in if there is a cold front passing through. This pretty popular area also draws local people who drop anchor, have dinner on board, enjoy the evening, and then go back to their home slip.

Nyack Anchorage

Off the west shore 2 miles north of the Tappan Zee Bridge.

This area is designated for anchorage, but all landing areas for your dingy are private. Secure permission to land from the yacht club. Approach from the south in 10 to 15 feet deep water. Anchor in a mud bottom with 8 feet to 10 feet of water. You usually will swing with the tide changes. Many permanent moorings are already here; do not disturb their property

Note: Although it is not a designated anchorage, a few people choose to anchor close to shore at the base of the sheer rock face of Hook Mountain, about 1½ nautical miles north.

If you stop in the town of Nyack, be sure to visit the mansion of De Witt Clinton, which was George Washington's base of operations in the 1780s. It is open to the public, but you'll need to take a cab from the marinas.

There are two private yacht clubs, the Nyack Boat Club and the Hook Mountain Yacht Club, and two marinas 2 miles north of the Tappan Zee Bridge. Julius Peterson Boat Yard, (914) 358-2100, is a working (or repair) facility with a longstanding reputation for an ability to fix anything. They also operate the Julius Peterson South Marina. The marina offers easy access to Upper Nyack via local transportation (inexpensive trolley), but it accepts few transients overnight.

Julius Peterson Boatyard (914) 358-2100

Storm protection: √√
Scenic: *
Marina-reported approach depths: 12 feet
Marina-reported dockside depths: 3-10 feet
Floating docks
Rest rooms
Showers
Picnic tables
Power connections: 30A/125V, 50A/125V, 50A/220V
Woodworking repairs
Fiberglass repairs
Welding
Below-waterline repairs
Mechanical repairs
Gas-engine repairs
Diesel repairs
Generator repairs
Travelift/hoist
Crane
Mast stepping: to 100 feet
Ship's store
What's special: 60 ton travelift; a repair yard that is a Hudson River institution; and nice people
VHF-monitored channels: 16, 09

Julius Peterson South Marina (914) 358-2100

Storm protection: √√
Scenic: * *
Marina-reported approach depths: 12 feet
Marina-reported dockside depths: 3-8 feet
Floating docks
Power connections: 30A/125V
What's special: for seasonal tenants only (contact their main marina for repairs and transient stays)

Aid to Navigation

The channel defined now by both red and green buoys delineates water depths of more than 34 feet, while the white area of the chart indicates water more than 18 feet deep. As the river bends to the left, you will see an additional aid to navigation, but not to mark the channel location. The aid is near the west bank on a rock-pile island. These special aids to navigation pop up occasionally on the Hudson River. Commercial rafts—the ones composed of a series of barges tied together that use more swing room to turn but do not need the channel's 30-foot-plus water depths to operate—use these to assist themselves in navigating the river.

Ossining and Sing Sing Prison

Sing Sing Prison is on the south side of the town of Ossining on a low, flat shore. If you're a sailor, the Croton sailing school is located in Senasqua Park, which also is the site of a public boat-launch ramp. You'll see some small sailboats (they are on offshore moorings), and you have the option to tie up there. If you do tie up, you can visit a small shopping center in Croton-on-Hudson, which is a town of about 8,000 people. The shopping center has a deli, a pharmacy, a newsstand, and other supply resources.

The town of Ossining, which was originally named Sing Sing when it was first incorporated in 1813, has about 25,000 people. In 1901 the townspeople changed the name to Ossining to differentiate the town from Sing Sing Prison, built in 1826, which had become infamous as a very harsh institution. You can see Sing Sing Prison from the waterway—or at least the two water towers on the prison grounds. Sing Sing is still an active prison in the New York State prison system. Ossining, by the way, is a very long walk, or a short taxi ride, uphill from any of the dockage in Ossining. For that reason, the town is not really easily accessible to boaters. Also, the water becomes shallow once you get outside the channel here. You will often see local boaters moving through the area, but you need to exercise caution unless you know that you are following exactly the same path somebody else has used to go in to shore and that his boat required the same or more water depth as yours does.

The Shattemuc Yacht Club is the most north here, followed by the restaurant. Inquire at (914) 941-3311.

Then Westerly Marina is also on the east shore north of the large fuel storage tank farm. Its entrance is south of a partially sunken barge that protects the slips from river-traffic wakes. Then there are the sailboats on moorings to the south of the entrance.

Westerly Marina (914) 941-2203

Storm protection: √√
Scenic: * *
Marina-reported approach depths: 7 feet
Marina-reported dockside depths: 5 feet
Floating docks
Gas
Diesel
Rest rooms
Showers
Dockside water
Power connections: 30A/125V, 50A/125V
Mechanical repairs
Travelift/hoist
Ship's store
Restaurant: off site
VHF-monitored channel: 68

Patrons of the Hudson Riverboat Company restaurant (914-762-4564) should arrange for a slip at the Shattemuc Yacht Club (914-941-8777). The restaurant has outdoor dining, a lounge, a snack bar, and a raw bar. Lunch and dinner are served Tuesday through Sunday.

Shattemuc Yacht Club (914) 941-8777

Storm protection: ᴠᴠ
Scenic: * *
Marina-reported approach depths: 6 feet
Marina-reported dockside depths: 4 feet
Floating docks
Gas
Rest rooms
Showers
Dockside water
Power connections: 30A/125V
What's special: private club with adjacent restaurant and swimming pool
VHF-monitored channel: 16

Croton Point

As you leave the Tappan Zee and go north into Haverstraw Bay, Croton Point forces the channel to the west shore of the river.

In this area the river bottom ranges from soft muck to hard sand.

> **SKIPPER TIP:** The very end point of land on Croton Point to the south is called Teller's Point, and at high tide it is about 1,200 feet shorter than it is at low tide. So if you're coming into it at high tide, make sure you give it more than a quarter-mile clearance, because you are dealing with water that becomes exposed land as the tide goes out.

Just make sure that when you pick up the buoy off of Teller's Point that you don't go too close to shore on the wrong side of it. William Teller bought Teller's Point from the Indians for a barrel of rum and some blankets. He named it after himself.

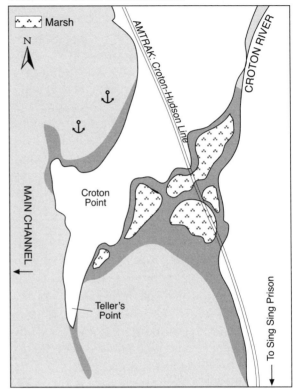

CROTON POINT ANCHORAGE

NOT TO BE USED FOR NAVIGATION

Croton Bay and River

The shallow, expansive bay is tucked behind Teller's Point in Croton Bay and is the terminus of the 100-mile-long Croton River. The railroad tracks effectively block the river from the Hudson for boaters.

Just north of Croton Point is a popular local anchorage. The only problem with this anchorage area is that it would be exposed if a northwest wind develops. At the north side of Croton Point (1½ nautical miles north of where you just were) is an informal anchorage near the shore. It is very exposed to wind and weather, however. Leave the main channel at red buoy #22 and head east, leaving 30-foot water depths to

8- to 10-foot levels. Stay at least a quarter-mile north of the land as you approach.

Croton Point Anchorage

Storm protection: √
Scenic: * * *
This anchorage area is just 8 feet deep, with a sandy to mud/clay bottom. You should swing with the wind if it is blowing, since the current does not seem to have a big effect in here. A great lunch stop but a mediocre overnight choice unless you absolutely know no bad weather has been forecast.

The Half Moon Bay Marina sits in front of the housing development associated with it. A bulkhead to protect the slips from river-traffic wakes somewhat hides the boat's superstructures, but sailboat masts are visible. Most off-site conveniences are a half-mile walk. The other facility for boaters in this area is the Croton Yacht Club, which is for members only.

Half Moon Bay Marina (914) 271-5400

Storm protection: √√√
Scenic: * * *
Marina-reported approach depths: 6 feet
Marina-reported dockside depths: 2-8 feet
Waste pump-out
Rest rooms
Showers
Dockside water
Power connections: 30A/125V, 50A/125V
Restaurant: off site
Grocery: off site
Convenience store: off site
What's special: few transients

A final suggestion if you're landing in the Ossining, Croton Point, and Croton-on-Hudson area. Take a taxicab ride to tour the Van Cortlandt Manor, originally built in 1683 as a hunting lodge and located in Croton-on-Hudson. It was expanded in the 1750s, burned in 1777, and was rebuilt in 1780. Thus, the house is pre-Revolutionary War, and it was lived in for seven generations. The last Van Cortlandt died in 1940, and the house has not been occupied since then by a family. A member of the Rockefeller family purchased it after it had deteriorated and facilitated its restoration, which is considered very authentic.

Malaria

Some of the land used during the 1880s was affected by the prevailing beliefs about what caused malaria ("bad air" in Italian). Until the mosquito was found to be the source of the disease's spread, decaying marshland was thought to put off some sort of toxic gas. Therefore, people didn't want to live anywhere near these areas because of the gas, and the lowlands were drained whenever possible. It also has been suggested that some railroad barons of the time popularized the notion that the lowlands were malaria-ridden to bring down land values so the railroads could buy them up. Of course, the railroads wanted these lands for their tracks so their trains could run at the same elevation as much as possible.

Ranges

Now is the first opportunity for you to use a special navigational skill if you are so interested. Notice the two broken parallel lines with a solid line in their center. The broken lines indicate the narrow channel, while the solid line leads to an extended dotted line that ends at two range markers, each at different heights. These also are lighted for night use.

SKIPPER TIP: Keeping the vertical stripes lined up one on top of the other while your vessel is in the solid-line portion (not the dotted line—you are too close to shore for this set of ranges when in the dotted area) will help you stay within the narrow channel indicated by the dashed lines. This particular channel has a bend in it; therefore, use the northern set of range markers (off Verplanck Point) to finish this section of the narrow channel. Now that you have accomplished this, you can navigate using range markers both on the Hudson River and on other passages you make.

Historic Dutch Jokes

The Dutch were great practical jokers. They liked to make jokes and play jokes on newly-wed couples. They would run their horses at full gallop through town, fire off guns, and shout at night to wake people up. Just for a joke, they liked to frighten the Indians. One guy sailed his sloop past Sandy Hook right up to the edge of Manhattan Island and dropped anchor about two in the morning. He waited until early dawn and then fired off three guns so that their sound, echoing against the fort walls, woke everybody up at once. They all jumped out of bed. He thought that was funny.

Another game was pulling the goose. You would ride your horse at full gallop underneath a goose that was hung upside down by a rope. The goose's head was greased so it wasn't easy to hold on to, and whoever could pull that goose down was the winner of that game. This was also done with rabbit and eel. The winner got to keep the animal as his reward.

Another popular but sick game in New Amsterdam and Fort Orange was called clubbing the cat. A cat was put into a cask, which was then hung between two stretched-out ropes; players would then stand back and throw clubs at the cask. The winner was the person who broke the cask to let the cat escape—much like a piñata in Mexico.

When the British took over, they didn't really want to put up with any of these antics and didn't see them as funny.

Haverstraw

You are approaching Haverstraw Marina, perhaps the largest marina in the east. It is successful, friendly, and very complete. They have saunas for transients! Haverstraw is a Dutch word that refers to a certain style of oat straw that was grown in the local lowland marshy areas. The town, which has a population under 10,000 people, is a taxi ride away, not a walk. North of the Haverstraw Marina is the Rockland Bergen Boat Club, a private club for members only. If you want to overnight at Haverstraw, facilities are limited to the Haverstraw Marina property because of the distance from town. However, the marina has a broad selection of businesses and amenities that will satisfy most boaters' needs on site.

The restaurant just outside the marina is leased out. If you are not staying at the marina, go back outside the marina, and just immediately south of the main Haverstraw Marina are the restaurant docks. However, here you have to watch water depth. It doesn't seem to be quite what it is reported as, because even in a boat that draws 3 feet, I was turning up some substantial silt immediately in front of and maneuvering around the docks. The marina restaurant, by the way, might have different docking arrangements each season as winter weather takes away and management improves. If you are an overnight guest of the marina and want to use the restaurant, make sure your slip assignment puts you within close walking distance, because the marina's size can create problems if you need to walk it end to end. Prime rib is a good choice for dinner, and a portabello mushroom, arugula, and radicchio sandwich makes a nice lunch.

Again, depending on your boat speed, you might not be ready to stop, except for lunch at Haverstraw, when you come through here, but do. It is an excellent property, has very good water depth inside, a well-stocked hard-parts and lubricants fuel dock, and bountiful ship's store. Sailors: This is one of the best support facilities for your craft on the Hudson.

Haverstraw, by the way, is in an area that is identified as a separate bay. This area is where the river is technically the widest—it's about 3 miles wide within the Haverstraw Bay. Also, because of the wind and river currents created by tidal changes, it is a fine area for a good sail. Long runs and required knowledge of the tides make it a good challenge. The historic Haverstraw Reach matches the length of the bay.

The town of Haverstraw is built on a delta or flats area. This area of sediment was deposited here by glacial streams from the Pleistocene era, when the water level of the Hudson River was probably 100 feet higher than it is today. You can see that the Haverstraw and northern shorelines are very irregular and have a couple of promontories in them: One is called Stony Point; the other is called Grassy Point. Man has put some connectors together here, so Grassy Point is not so isolated from the mainland anymore. Did Captain Kidd, a New York

HAVERSTRAW MARINA

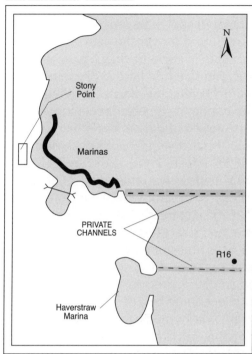

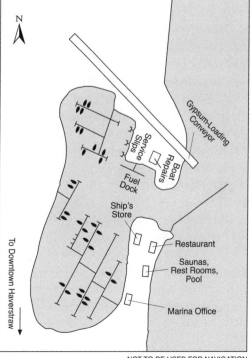

NOT TO BE USED FOR NAVIGATION

resident at times, really bury treasure here, as rumor has it? It cannot be proved or disproved. If anyone found it over the years since Kidd was executed in England, they have not talked about it. The riverbed here is predominantly clay, and Haverstraw had a thriving brick industry during the nineteenth century.

Haverstraw had only a few houses as late as 1795. The first street wasn't even designed until 1803. The area was described in 1794 as having fields of rye under cultivation and a very pretty riverbank with a large forest of chestnut and oak trees growing alongside it.

Commercially, the Haverstraw area was quarried for limestone by 1790. The quarrying was replaced by brick making, which started sometime before 1810 and was successfully operating by 1815. Even to this day, bricks are synonymous with Haverstraw. We can all appreciate that at one time 2,400 people were employed in the brick-making business here, which produced 300 million bricks a year. The brick-making clay and the vast amount of wood from the nearby forest needed to make bricks made it a natural activity. Later on, James Wood invented a process of adding in a little anthracite coal dust to create better bricks. The coal needed was available nearby via a side canal that entered the Hudson River at the city of Kingston. This side canal, the Delaware & Hudson Canal, went into Pennsylvania and its coalfields. This last inventive refinement and the canal cut to access the town made Haverstraw the brick-making capital of the lower valley.

Haverstraw was busy in the 1850s with its brick business, not only the brickyards but also the kilns, landings, and docks needed to deliver these goods to market. The hills of sand and clay at Grassy Point were completely strip-mined to support this brick-making industry. This commercial activity changed the landscape here, and when you see a brick building that is 200 years old in New York, the materials probably came from Haverstraw.

There were 42 brickyards operating in the 1880s, mostly concentrated in the Grassy Point area. However, by 1890 the essential ingredients of sand and clay from local deposits were almost depleted. The brick business died.

Here are approach instructions for Haverstraw Marina: The marina is on the west shore at red buoy #26, 11½ miles north of the Tappan Zee Bridge. Other landmarks: The marina is north of the power plant (and its two stacks) by about a mile and south of the large crane and the pier for the U.S. Gypsum Company and its feeder shaft. The fuel dock and its supply of lubes and hard parts is to the right—the north side—once you are inside.

Haverstraw Marina (914) 429-2001

Storm protection: √√
Scenic: * * *
Marina-reported approach depths: 25 feet
Marina-reported dockside depths: 8 feet
Floating docks
Gas
Diesel
Waste pump-out
Rest rooms
Showers
Laundry
Dockside water
Barbecue
Picnic tables
Power connections: 30A/125V, 50A/125V, 50A/125V
Travelift/hoist
Restaurant: yes, plus the Tiki Hut bar and an outside dining deck

Convenience store: on site
What's special: friendly, complete marina
    with swimming pool, saunas, and play-
    ground
VHF-monitored channels: 09, 16

Stony Point Bay, which is north of Grassy Point on your chart, has as its most memorable feature for the cruiser a very large ship's chancery, or store, at Willow Cove Marina (914-786-5270). The marina is just about where Stony Point Bay appears on your chart. Also in the bay are Penny Bridge Marina, Minisceongo Yacht Club, and then a half-mile farther north the previously mentioned Willow Cove Marina. These last two have had a privately maintained buoy system that, when lined up with the marina entrance through the bulkhead, leads you into the deeper areas. Caution: This area is shallow; deeper-draft vessels should contact the marinas here for approach instructions. By the way, as with some of the other areas, a visit to the town of Stony Point (population less than 15,000) does require a taxi ride.

Penny Bridge Marina (914) 786-5100

Storm protection: √√
Scenic: * *
Marina-reported approach depths: 3-4 feet
Marina-reported dockside depths: 4 feet
Floating docks
Rest rooms
Showers
Picnic tables
Power connections: 30A/125V
Mechanical repairs
Gas-engine repairs
Stern drive repairs
Outboard-motor repairs
Travelift/hoist

Ship's store
What's special: few transients
VHF-monitored channel: 16

Minisceongo Yacht Club (914) 786-8767

Storm protection: √√
Scenic: * *
Marina-reported approach depths: 5 feet
Marina-reported dockside depths: 5 feet
Gas
Waste pump-out
Rest rooms
Showers
Laundry
Dockside water
Barbecues
Picnic tables
Power connections: 30A/125V
Souvenir store
Restaurant: on site
What's special: private yacht club
VHF-monitored channel: 09

Willow Cove Marina (914) 786-5270; 786-8781

Storm protection: √√
Scenic: * *
Marina-reported approach depths: 5 feet
Marina-reported dockside depths: 4 feet
Floating docks
Waste pump-out
Rest rooms
Showers
Laundry
Dockside water
Barbecues
Picnic tables
Power connections: 30A/125V
Below-waterline repairs
Mechanical repairs
Gas-engine repairs

Diesel repairs
Stern-drive repairs
Outboard-motor repairs
Travelift/hoist
Ship's store
What's special: pool
VHF-monitored channel: 12, 16

Stony Point Bay Marina and Yacht Club
  (914) 786-3700

Storm protection: √√√
Scenic: *
Marina-reported approach depths: 5 feet
Marina-reported dockside depths: 5 feet
Waste pump-out
Rest rooms
Showers
Dockside water
Picnic tables
Power connections: 30A/125V
Mechanical repairs
Gas-engine repairs
Generator repairs
Travelift/hoist
Mast stepping
Convenience store: off site
What's special: few transients
VHF-monitored channel: 09, 68, 16

Henry Hudson and Haverstraw Bay

It was September 14, 1609, some 12 days after Henry Hudson had explored the mouth of the Hudson River. He had taken his vessel, the *Half Moon,* and had gone as far as Haverstraw Bay, which he called a lake in his writings. A day or two later Captain Hudson and the natives had a meal ashore consisting of freshly killed pigeons and a fat dog (the dog was skinned using shells from the riverbank). In return, the next day Hudson brought the chiefs on board the *Half Moon* and gave them some wine. One of the chiefs got so drunk he had to sleep it off on board. Worried about their companion, the natives came back the next morning and were so pleased to see that he was safe that they gave Henry Hudson presents of tobacco and shelled beads.

As you look at your chart, just south of Verplanck (east bank) you will note an area called George's Island, so naturally you expect to see an island. However, it's not an island anymore—it's been filled in and connected to the mainland. That area labeled George's Island, by the way, has a very large launch ramp for trailer boaters. Another piece of history here: Cornelius "Commodore" Vanderbilt wanted to put a railroad through here, but the local residents who were the surviving members of the Verplanck family resisted and blocked that idea. A considerable amount of time passed before the family agreed to sell a railroad right of way to the owner of some of the most famous yachts of the New York Yacht Club and the America's Cup, Mr. Vanderbilt.

On the east shore on the north end of Haverstraw Bay about 13 miles north of the Tappan Zee Bridge is the Cortland Yacht Club, which is a private club and just near the Viking Boatyard. Viking has a casual dining restaurant, and Cortland has a poolside snack bar. The approach to both requires you to pick up privately maintained markers. Many boaters start their approach south in the main channel off Grassy Point. Here they pick up the main channel's range markers on Verplanck Point. They follow those range markers closer to land than they are intended to be used for—almost to the forward range marker with its lights at 25 feet. Here boaters look to starboard to see and then pick up the private aids. Viking's entrance becomes visible as you

THE MIDDLE HUDSON RIVER 71

approach the aids, and Cortland requires a turn to the south.

Cortlandt Yacht Club (914) 737-9483

Storm protection: √√
Scenic: * *
Marina-reported approach depths: 3.5 feet
Marina-reported dockside depths: 3.5 feet
Floating docks
Rest rooms
Showers
Dockside water
Power connections: 30A/125V
Restaurant: on site
What's special: private yacht club with pool
VHF-monitored channel: 09, 16

On the east side of the river is:

Viking Boatyard (914) 739-5090

Storm protection: √√√
Scenic: * *
Marina-reported approach depths: 4-12 feet
Marina-reported dockside depths: 4 feet
Floating docks
Rest rooms
Showers
Dockside water
Mechanical repairs
Gas-engine repairs
Generator repairs
Travelift/hoist
Ship's store
Restaurant: on site
What's special: 60-ton travelift
VHF-monitored channel: 09

Stony Point

Stony Point had a spur road sometime between 1790 to 1810. After 1790 Dundenberg had a river landing that let the produce

from the farms, forest, and mine be brought to market. The lower Hudson Valley in the 1830s and earlier seemed to grow quite a bit of wheat on river bottomlands very close to the river. Of course, as the river changed paths because of the Ice Age, different bottomlands had been exposed. Wheat was a very popular crop from about 1780 to 1825 because Europe had a big demand for it, which the Hudson Valley wheat farmers were partially able to fill. Other crops grown in the area were rye, barley, corn, and flax.

Stony Point housed the laborers and the proprietors who worked for the brick industry and the quarries that were operating at Haverstraw from the 1870s to 1880s. The railroad arrived at Stony Point from New York City in 1875.

Stony Point was the site of a battle on July 16, 1779, in which the Americans, led by Gen. "Mad Anthony" Wayne, defeated the British and boosted the colonists' morale. A museum here supplements the historical battle site.

> **SKIPPER TIP:** Stony Point starts Sailmakers Reach, which runs north to Peekskill.

Stony Point lighthouse on the west shore (this is the third lighthouse, as we cruise northward, that was built because of the Erie Canal's opening) first began operating in 1825. Built on top of an old powder magazine, this is the oldest lighthouse on the Hudson River that still exists. After operating for a hundred years, the lighthouse was decommissioned and has been a part of the historical site that was created for the Stony Point battlefield. Stony Point's battlefield commission has controlled the lighthouse since 1946.

Liberty Ships

In its recent history, this area has stored the mothballed "liberty" ship fleet. A liberty ship was a tanker-freighter that was mass-produced, sometimes at the rate of one or two a week, for the British in the early days of World War II. Once the United States declared war on Germany, the liberty ships were produced in even higher numbers for the Americans. About 190 such liberty ships were anchored here from the end of World War II to 1971, when they were sold off for scrap.

These ships were all surplus after the war, but nobody was ready to do anything with them other than store them. Mothballed and stationary, this huge fleet of ships was lined up like ducks in several rows along the western shore of the Hudson just north of Stony Point. Nothing was done with the ships for the most part, although some were used for grain storage in the mid-1960s. If you're driving this area in a car, you can see on Route 9 West a marker consisting of two large liberty-ship anchors with a plaque commemorating the liberty fleet that was once mothballed there.

Take your eyes up and look west now. It's Dundenberg Mountain (1,086 feet), Bald Mountain (1,100 feet), and other peaks. What a vista!

River Channel Overview

You are now coming to a section where the river becomes somewhat winding and also narrows to less than a half-mile wide, and sometimes only one-third of a mile wide. There is still commercial traffic, as there is all the way up to Albany, so keep an eye out for these fellows. They need to use the channel and might maneuver in ways that could cause you concern.

Current can be a problem in this section. Most say the currents are less than 2 miles per hour, while reports of 4 miles per hour—particularly for a short time in mid-channel—are whispered about. Smaller boats that can only run at displacement hull speed might want to wait it out or progressively maneuver across the width of the river to find a slower flow during high-current periods.

Verplanck

Moving north of Grassy Point and onto the east shore is the village of Verplanck, which was named after the family who owned the property along the eastern shore of the Hudson during the early colonial and revolutionary periods. The Indians called it Meahagh. The granddaughter of Van Cortlandt, the original buyer in 1683, married Philip Verplanck, whose family gave this area its name. Because the family sided with the Americans, many improvements to their property were burned by the British in the American Revolution. But Gen. George Washington came back to defeat the British force there and took the land back for the Americans and the Verplancks.

Tomkins Cove

Your chart shows a rock quarry on the west shore of the Hudson at Tomkins Cove. This wedge of marble and schist is what remains of Hog Hill, a 200-foot-high limestone cliff that was pretty well flattened out by the quarrying activities that began in 1838 and continued until after the Civil War. The Tomkins Cove Lime Company employed 100 people to knock down the limestone to sell as manure for the fields of New Jersey and to pulverize for gravel. The Tomkins Cove operation used a million bushels of stone per year from about 1850 to

1860. You can best find the site today by looking for the five stacks on shore just north of it.

North and east of that is the Indian Point Nuclear Power Plant, which opened in 1963 and expanded to twice its output in the late 1970s.

Jones Point

On the western shore coming up is Dundenberg Mountain, which is Dutch for "Thunder Mountain." Rising some 1,086 feet above us, it is the first truly big rocky mountain on the trip. At the foot of Dundenberg is Jones Point, which is a better reference point for boaters. This area was also called Kidd's Point. After Captain Kidd, then a New York City resident, was killed by the British in England for piracy in 1701, his crew is believed to have sailed to this point, where they ran aground during a storm. Kidd's ship, *Quedah Merchant,* sank, and the crew took off inland.

> **SKIPPER TIP:** Sailors, take note: If you have a southeast wind, the wind gains strength the farther north you go. In a northeaster you would appropriately shorten up on sail here, since it becomes puffy enough that you can get knocked down. Hudson River sloops, at least, used to get knocked down by these gusts. The sloops would wait in the lee of Dundenberg Mountain if a west wind were blowing because it would become a bow-on wind once you rounded the point into the race ahead. This lee waiting point often got busy—as many as 50 sail craft could be there waiting for a wind shift or a favorable tidal change.

At the foot of Dundenberg Mountain was a ferry dock called Caldwell's Landing, nicknamed Gibraltar. A toll road was built in 1809 to tie into this landing and connect it to the interior lands. By 1814 a second toll road also tied it to Fort Montgomery and to the forest of the Dean iron mine. The highland iron industry, which came and went pretty quickly in this area, was peaking at this time.

Peekskill

The National Maritime Historical Society and its magazine, *Sea History,* are based in Peekskill. This group of about 15,000 members has an interest in keeping the legacy of sea, sail, and other marine activities alive. A recent issue of the magazine had articles on American flagged vessels, Christopher Columbus, Gloucester fishing schooners, the Falkland Islands, and ship models made of ivory.

Peekskill is separated from the main channel by Peekskill Bay, as marked on your chart. The bay is shallow and must be traversed using the marked channel that takes you directly into Peekskill. Channel depth varies from 3 to 4½ feet. The channel within the bay is U-shaped. You can see a small waterway off Peekskill Bay, Annsville Creek, which is also very shallow. Peekskill has a population of about 25,000 and is a taxicab ride from the marina facilities.

> **SKIPPER TIP:** Cook's Reach starts north from here to 1 mile north of the Bear Mountain Bridge. The next reach picks up from there and goes to just north of the northern side of West Point.

Peekskill, granted by the king in 1665, had its first trading post established in 1697 and was incorporated as a city in 1940. Like so many areas along the Hudson, Peekskill was the site of some Revolutionary War activity, and you can correctly say that "George Washington slept here." In fact, Peekskill was the site of the conference of American generals, during which they decided to fortify Pollepel's Island and Constitution Island to defend the Hudson.

At the very southern edge of Peekskill Bay is a fine marina, Charles Point Marine. North of Indian Point and south of Charles Point on your chart, the marina is inside Lents Cove 16 miles above the Tappan Zee Bridge. Although primarily for seasonal tenants, the marina always seems to have a few slips for transients. It is clean, attractive, and serves lunch, dinner, and Sunday brunch. Also, if you are able, have Sunday brunch here. However, beware that the water is shallow (4 feet) on approach and at the docks. The water at the dock specifically for the restaurant is shallower (3 feet) than at other docks. Also, any vessel drawing more than 3 feet will churn up considerable silt. Be cautious at lower tide levels. Charles Point Marine, a new boat dealer for Sea Ray brand boats, is very accommodating and willing to help all boaters. If you're thinking of stopping, ask for updated local conditions.

Charles Point Marine (914) 736-7370

Storm protection: ∿
Scenic: * *
Marina-reported approach depths: 4 feet
Marina-reported dockside depths: 4-6 feet
Floating docks
Gas
Waste pump-out

Rest rooms
Showers
Laundry
Dockside water
Power connections: 30A/125V, 50A/125V
Below-waterline repairs
Mechanical repairs
Gas-engine repairs
Ship's store
Restaurant: on site
What's special: new boat dealer
VHF-monitored channel: 09

North of Charles Point and south of Travis Point is the private yacht club, Peekskill Yacht Club.

Peekskill Yacht Club (914) 737-9515

Storm protection: ∿
Scenic: * *
Marina-reported approach depths: 5 feet
Marina-reported dockside depths: 3-4 feet
Floating docks
Gas
Rest rooms
Showers
Dockside water
Power connections: 30A/125V
Restaurant: on site
What's special: private yacht club

Iona Island

Iona Island, just south of Bear Mountain, is an area of flat and marshlike land. Only about 15 percent of it is high enough to use. A railroad track runs through it and the little bit of water remaining there. The water is so shallow in that particular area past the railroad tracks that it is inaccessible. You can, however, anchor in front of this railroad track just north of Iona Island. Even if you decide to row or swim ashore, do not do so. Yes, you can see a bunch of steel-door storage areas that were used to keep Navy artillery shells, but it is not safe. These huge swing-out doors cover up caves that were blasted out of bedrock.

In 1878, people aboard the *Dayline* cruise boat indicated that the view from Iona Island of Dundenberg and Bear mountains was akin to the unspoiled beauty of parts of the Canadian wilderness: no settlement, no industry, fully forested and foliated from base to summit.

Just before the Civil War, Iona Island was becoming a resort area and a playground for people who would come up on an excursion boat (such as the *Dayline,*), go up to West Point, and stop here on the way back. The island also was used by farmers to grow grapevines and seeds as cash crops. Spring comes earlier here, and the weather is more akin to that in New York City than in other upstate towns because of the influence of the Hudson River Valley and the Atlantic Ocean.

With the start of the Civil War, Iona Island was closed to the public because it was federal land that was needed as a supply depot for the navy.

One theory of how Iona Island was formed states that a remnant of Anthony's Nose was torn off from the cliff base by glaciers thousands of years ago. At the same time the presence of Iona Island helped straighten out the river path to the current course.

Bear Mountain and Anthony's Nose

Bear Mountain, on the west shore, is more than 1,305 feet tall. Named after its bear population, it also functions as a year-round resort and contains some ski trails, a lodge, restaurant, pool, museum, and major hiking trails. Just north of the Bear Mountain Bridge is a lit-

tle creek (Popolopen Creek) that comes out on the west shore of the Hudson. This was the site of the Fort Montgomery Furnace, which was an iron-smelting business operating between 1830 until just after the Civil War. Anthony's Nose and Bear Mountain formed the southern part of the narrow channel of the Hudson River. Below this the channel is wider to New York City and stays narrow from here up to Storm King Mountain. Bear Mountain used to be a lot taller than it is now. The mountain was leveled as part of a development project to provide a new home for a New York State prison. When the local citizens saw what was going to happen to the mountain, they organized a drive to save Bear Mountain. The state government listened and stopped the project. The mountaintop, which features an observation tower, is accessible by car. At the tower level you can find rest rooms but no vendors or food services.

On the eastern shore now we're going to go all the way up to the next turn in the Hudson River. The promontory jutting out is Anthony's Nose, which is named after the ancient Roman general Marc Anthony, Cleopatra's boyfriend. Supposedly this mountain formation reminded somebody early on of what Marc Anthony was thought to have looked like. Another justification for calling it Anthony's Nose is to honor St. Anthony, who started the whole idea of monastic life. By the way, Anthony's Nose has a 200-foot railroad tunnel running through it.

Bear Mountain Bridge

At Anthony's Nose is the Bear Mountain Bridge, which was built in 1924 and set a record for being the world's longest suspension bridge at the time. Vertical clearance is more than 180 feet. The bridge serves both

Routes 6 and 202, and—again—the toll is paid on one shore only: That is, if you're traveling east you pay a toll; if you're traveling west there is no toll. The Bear Mountain Bridge ties into Bear Mountain, whose peak is immediately south of the bridge.

The Hudson River: Man-made and Natural

Be careful not to be attracted by an abandoned marina on the east shore. Its many submerged pilings and dock sections make navigating unsafe.

SKIPPER TIP: Passing north of Anthony's Nose near the east shore, take note that the water can move swiftly. When the tide is going out, you have to be careful not to be taken off course and outside the channel.

There is good deep water here, and the only real navigational problem occurs because of the river channel's width narrowing, causing a strong tidal current. In fact, this area has been nicknamed "the Race."

The watercourse that runs through the town of Highland Falls, on the west shore, has a 100-foot drop. The Dutch called it Buttermilk Falls. This rush of water once powered mills for flour, grist, sawing, and cider making. Today the area is a support village for West Point military academy.

In Highland Falls the Cozzens Hotel sat forward near the river's edge as a promontory and resort property in 1878. As shown by a contemporary atlas, the town of Highland Falls was more inland directly behind it. The hotel had been relocated to Highland Falls just before 1850. It is now Ladycliff College.

In 1685 the Hudson highlands were bought as a single land area from the local Indians and given to an early colonist named Evans, a ship's captain. He kept the land intact, neither subdividing nor selling it off. Therefore, it was not populated until sometime after 1710, some 25 years later, when it had a different owner. The migration of Yankees by 1750 from other colonies and from Westchester and Long Island helped develop Highland Falls.

On the west shore about a mile south of West Point and less than a half-mile north of the falls, you will find Highlands Falls Marina.

Highland Falls Marina (914) 446-2402

Storm protection: √√
Scenic: * *
Marina-reported approach depths: 30 feet
Marina-reported dockside depths: 8-30 feet
Floating docks
Rest rooms
Dockside water
Power connections: 30A/125V
Woodworking repairs
Fiberglass repairs
Mechanical repairs
Ship's store
What's special: few transients and smaller craft (under 25 feet) only

The east shoreline near Garrison and Foundry Cove, which had a view of Buttermilk (Highland) Falls, is dotted with some upscale homes originally built for the wealthy entrepreneurs from New York City.

Garrison Yacht Club (914) 424-3440

Storm protection: √√
Scenic: * *
Marina-reported approach depths: 12 feet

Marina-reported dockside depths: 3 feet
Floating docks
Rest rooms
Dockside water
Barbecues
Picnic tables
Power connections: 30A/125V
What's special: private yacht club

Garrison Anchorage

You can anchor off the east shore just south of the Garrison Yacht Club and its moorings. You need to anticipate being in about 35 feet of water depth with a mud bottom. There is a swift current here during tide changes.

West Point

The factories of Dean, Sterling, and Queensborough iron works were busy in the very early days of the United States and continued through the Hudson River Valley's peak manufacturing eras. The links (described below) for the great river chain that crossed the Hudson just above West Point came from these factories. Some mining, mostly for the academy at West Point, also was done up on the other side of the river at Cold Spring. The Queensborough furnace ceased operations in 1812, and the rest of this industry has now mostly disappeared.

> **SKIPPER TIP:** There are eddies just below the pier on the west shore.

First occupied in 1720, Constitution Island was the site of a fort during the Revolutionary War, but it was unused afterward. In 1836 a New York City lawyer, Henry Warner, bought the island from the Philipse family, the

A view of West Point from the south.

second owner. His heirs deeded it to the government under President Theodore Roosevelt in 1908-09. However, the Audubon Society owns the marshes here. An early name for Constitution Island was Martelaers Rock. The island and the Warner family home, which dates to 1836, are sometimes accessible via a special two-hour afternoon tour from West Point. Inquire at (914) 446-8676.

During the post-Revolutionary War period, West Point was in part a tourist attraction. People would travel on a steamer to vacation there. The academy, formally established in 1802, had 32 cadets as early as 1794. Vacationers would tour the parade grounds and buildings and view demonstrations (such as cannon practice over the Hudson) there early on.

The Sterling Iron Works, 13 miles west of the river near Sloatsburg, is credited with having produced the iron chain links that were stretched from West Point (specifically Gees Point) to Constitution Island during the Revolutionary War. The links were 2 feet long, 2½ inches square, and weighed about 140 pounds each. A few are on display in the museum on the grounds of West Point. The links were made buoyant by being attached to tree stumps. Once attached, the floating chain was stretched across the Hudson River to block all boat traffic. This blockade chain was put in place in April 1778 to stop the British from winning land battles up north and then using the Hudson to split the rest of the colonies from New England by simply sailing the length of the Hudson. This chain fence, built by the Americans in response to the burning of Kingston by the British, and West Point were the targets Benedict Arnold tried to help the British capture in 1780. For being a turncoat to his country, Benedict Arnold's name has become synonymous with betrayal.

The Hudson River is only 1,400 feet wide here around the West Point area, which is its narrowest point. It also can exceed 200 feet in depth, which is about as deep as the Hudson River gets. Underneath that bottom, though, the riverbed itself consists of sand, clay, and boulders resting atop bedrock, which is another 700 feet thick. This valley could almost qualify as a fjord, something that's pretty hard to find in the United States.

> **SKIPPER TIP:** Sailors: The next reach runs from Constitution Island to 2¼ miles north of Storm King Mountain. Then another reach continues onto Diamond Reef.

West Point just before the Revolutionary War was described as having a fairly good selection of deciduous oak and hickory trees and a chestnut forest. It also had some scrub oak and pitch pine amongst the rock outcroppings.

From the river West Point is quite an impressive sight. West Point is America's oldest occupied military post, first run by Maj. Sylvanus Thayer. West Point, however, is not boater-friendly because it is at the top of a point and requires a major uphill walk or a cab ride from any of the marinas in the nearby area. However, if you're going to make the commitment to visit, make sure you stop by Thayer Hall, which holds quite a bit of information, including some nautical displays and the blockade chains. On the west shore everything is uphill, so it is quite a hike to get on top of the cliff—the village of Highland Falls included. Inquire at (914) 938-3590. The other marina opportunity is West Point Yacht Club, whose dock may be available for very short-term transients. The south dock of West Point itself also might be available. North of West Point on the western shore, the river continues to curve around to port.

West Point Yacht Club

Storm protection: √
Scenic: *
Marina-reported approach depths: 30 feet
Marina-reported dockside depths: 4-10 feet
Rest rooms
Barbecues
Picnic tables
What's special: you must have prior permission
VHF-monitored channel: 09, 16

West Point (south dock) (914) 938-2137; 938-3011

Storm protection: √
Scenic: *
Marina-reported approach depths: 30 feet
Marina-reported dockside depths: 4-10 feet
What's special: prior permission from the West Point academy harbormaster needed
VHF-monitored channel: 09, 16

World's End is an area so nicknamed because of the water depth, which here exceeds 200 feet. You can imagine a sailor from olden times, Henry Hudson perhaps, running soundings in this area with a lead line and getting readings typically in the 125-foot range. Then all of a sudden he gets a 200-foot-plus reading. On that basis he wonders if the world isn't coming to an end. A lead line, by the way, is a length of line with a lead weight affixed to its end. The lead is allowed to fall underwater to the bottom. Because the line is marked with various measurements, one can read water depths with it. Also, a proper lead line has a recess on its bottom where wax can be attached. The wax is supposed to hold a sample of the bottom material so one can see what type of bottom exists (sand, gravel, silt, etc.) for the anchor to dig into and hold. A pleasure-boater version is cataloged and available from Defender Industries. Inquire at (860) 701-3400.

One of the early tourist pastimes was watching artillery practice. The military would fire rounds and blast sections of rocks off the various promontory points. Furthermore, if you can believe it, tourists also enjoyed propagating graffiti. Masons, actual and aspiring, were fond of chiseling their names into the rock. Other graffiti artists resorted to painting on their names and dates. Although I have not seen the graffiti, I have been told that it remains visible.

Cold Spring

Just north of Constitution Island and the site of the great Revolutionary War chain blockade is the village of Cold Spring, a source for spring water for early sailors and today a bedroom community noted for its antique shops. It has a quaint downtown shopping area and a few fine restaurants. The dock at Cold Spring offers one of the best views of the area, with Storm King Mountain to the north and the West Point promontory and Constitution Island to the south. The railroad had reached Cold Spring in 1848 and Poughkeepsie the following year. In 1851 Lake Erie was finally connected to New York City by the railroad.

Cold Spring Boat Club

Storm protection: √√√
Scenic: * * *
Marina-reported approach depths: 5-10 feet
Marina-reported dockside depths: 3-6 feet
Floating docks

You'll occasionally see marshy areas along the Hudson. The marsh shown here comes into view when looking south toward Denning Point, near Beacon, New York.

Rest rooms
Dockside water
Restaurant: off site
Deli: off site
Grocery: off site
Convenience store: off site
What's special: private club for smaller
    boats (although I have seen a 40-foot
    sailboat end tie for an overnight here);
    phone number unavailable
VHF-monitored channel: 16

Cold Spring Anchorage

North of the Cold Spring Boat Club and south of the town's wharf. Approach straight in (east) toward the boat club from the main channel. The bottom is foul on either side.

Swim Stop

North of Little Stony Point on the river's eastern edge is an excellent swim stop. The channel is black and white here or, more accurately, white and blue. If you go outside the channel at 90 feet of water, you can almost instantly be in 3-foot-deep water.

Storm King Mountain

Storm King Mountain reaches 1,355 feet into the sky. It looked like a huge pile of butter to the Dutch, so they called it "Butter Hill." An early roadway runs along it about 200 feet above the water on which you are cruising.

Storm King Mountain is one of those areas that writers and artists alternately would characterize as wooded or denuded. Storm King had a forest including oak, beech, chestnut, and walnut trees. Twenty years later someone would come by and say "pretty barren area up around Storm King." Then he would come back another 40 years later and say "Gee, there are woods on Storm King." The woods have been cut down and then regrown several times over.

Just north of Storm King Mountain, which has an elevation of some 1,200 feet, was Cornwall Landing, and just north of Cornwall Landing is Round Top. At Round Top, about a mile in from the river, the Mountain House hotel once stood in 1880.

Cornwall on the Hudson

On the western shore, the next area up is Cornwall on the Hudson, which is a long walk up the hill. It does have some shops and some restaurants. The Cornwall Yacht Club services this area and is best known for its fuel dock. Just before you come to Plum Point there is a possible anchorage area, but it is not a designated anchorage. That is your second opportunity for an overnight stay besides the Cornwall Yacht Club. On the eastern shore you will see Breakneck Ridge, which is about 1,200 feet high, although it was higher in the past. This area has been quarried for its granite for a number of years. State Highway 9 D runs through a tunnel here, as does the Metro North railroad. You have deep water with the channel, although the channel is fairly tight and the river is fairly narrow. On the eastern shore you will find a couple of opportunities for swimming. An area labeled on your chart as Break Neck Point is locally called Sandy Beach. During the weekends you'll see small boats tied literally to a tree in this Sandy Beach anchorage area. Just north of this and slightly north of the Cornwall Yacht Club is Pollepel's Island. The castle on the island, now in ruins, can best be seen once you have passed it as you head north.

Butter, cows, sheep, and lambs were shipped from Cornwall Landing to New York City on steamers in the late 1800s. These same areas, as well as the northern part of New Jersey, supplied fruit such as apples, peaches, melons, and grapes; some vegetables, including potatoes; chickens; and various milled flours. (Cornwall Landing is now no longer is use.)

Cornwall was just starting to be settled at the time of the Revolutionary War, while the landing and other commercial activities started around 1800. Cornwall then began to develop a reputation as a center for business on the river. It had docks; it had raspberry and strawberry nurseries; it had a shipyard. The small creek just north of Cornwall facilitated these activities. Cornwall had a boarding-house that started to flourish right after the Civil War because a steamer from New York City started daily service to the town. Other steamers ran farther up river than Cornwall, but the sole daily steamer run had Cornwall as its northern terminus. Portable cottages were put up and taken down just to meet the high occupancy rates during the summer resort season in Cornwall.

Cornwall is on the Cornwall plain, which is about a 10-mile-wide area of granite that has been overrun by glaciers and has a good amount of sediment, which appears somewhat billowy. So much of this lower part of the Hudson is considered still within the greater Appalachian physiographic area. The Appalachian mountain range that we learned about in grade school basically starts in Canada and goes all the way down to Georgia, not too far inland from the Atlantic Ocean.

You are looking at a mountaintop of 1,403 feet at Crow's Nest. Perhaps a dozen summits in this area are taller than 1,400 feet, including South Beacon and North Beacon, each more than 1,500 feet tall.

The River Width

The river and the deep-water channel widen now. Depths can run 25 to more than 40 feet. The shallows also become more expansive outside the channel.

Ruffles Have Ridges

From here to an equal distance north of the bridge (about 8 miles), a very small chop is quite common on the Hudson. Remembering the potato-chip commercial "Ruffles have ridges," I think of this surface as ruffled water.

Cornwall Yacht Club (914) 534-8835

Storm protection: √
Scenic: * * *
Marina-reported approach depths: 15 feet
Marina-reported dockside depths: 6 feet
Floating docks
Gas
Rest rooms
Showers
Dockside water
Barbecues
Power connections: 30A/125V, 50A/125V
Restaurant: on site
What's special: private yacht club
VHF-monitored channel: 09

Pollepel's Island

On the starboard side is Pollepel's Island, where a family named Bannerman built a cas-tle. The island was purchased in 1900 by David Bannerman, who wanted a place to store his private stock of Civil War and Spanish-American War surplus. He built a house there for his family and an arsenal to contain the war surplus. Bannerman, who wanted it as a summer resort for his family, died in 1918 before it was completed. Pollepel's Island also was a site of fighting during the Revolutionary War.

The 7-acre Bannerman Island and surrounding waters are now shown on your charts as ruins and obstructions. Remember that although I think of it as Bannerman Island, in reality it has had several different names over time, including Cheese Island. Pollepel's Island stands off the main shore by about 1,000 feet. From 1967 to 1969 the island was operated as a state park. In 1969 all the buildings burned down, leaving just the castle's rock remnants. Landing is not permitted on the island, and going between the island and the shore is too shallow for most powerboats or sailboats.

Parts of the original "castle" on Pollepel's Island can be seen by boaters traveling the channel just north of Storm King Mountain.

A canoeist enjoys the beauty and solitude along the Hudson River.

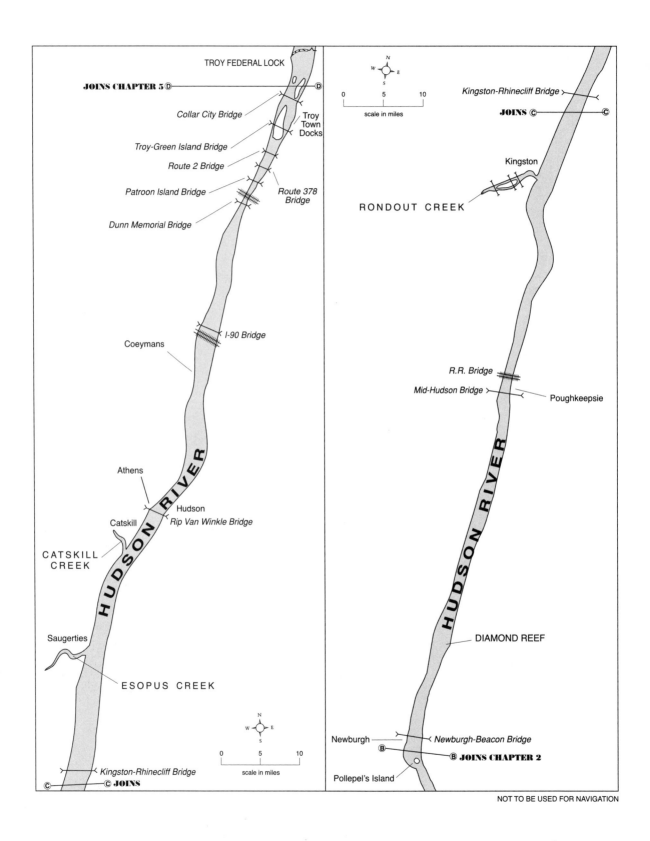

TROY FEDERAL LOCK

JOINS CHAPTER 5 ⒹⒹⒹ

Collar City Bridge

Troy
Town
Docks

Troy-Green Island Bridge

Route 2 Bridge

Patroon Island Bridge

*Route 378
Bridge*

Dunn Memorial Bridge

I-90 Bridge

Coeymans

Athens

Hudson

Rip Van Winkle Bridge

Catskill

CATSKILL
CREEK

HUDSON RIVER

Saugerties

ESOPUS CREEK

Kingston-Rhinecliff Bridge

ⒸⒸ JOINS

N
W E
S

0   5   10
scale in miles

N
W E
S

0   5   10
scale in miles

Kingston-Rhinecliff Bridge

JOINS ⒸⒸ

Kingston

RONDOUT CREEK

R.R. Bridge

Mid-Hudson Bridge

Poughkeepsie

HUDSON RIVER

DIAMOND REEF

Newburgh

Newburgh-Beacon Bridge

Ⓑ

Ⓑ JOINS CHAPTER 2

Pollepel's Island

NOT TO BE USED FOR NAVIGATION

CHAPTER 3

The Upper-Tidal Hudson River

SKIPPER TIP: Please use NOAA charts 12347 and 12348.

Your cruise up the Hudson continues on a waterway similar to what you have enjoyed this far. This continues until just past Kingston. North of Kingston you must take care to stay off the shallow-water areas.

The Towns of Newburgh and Beacon— and the Bridge

You'll find two towns here. First is the city of Beacon, which has a population of about 20,000. Newburgh is not much larger, with a population between 30,000 to 35,000.

Your only concern in this area would be to keep an eye out for old abandoned pilings or other submerged objects that pepper this shoreline. These were industrial towns long ago, though they're primarily residential now.

In October of 1709 the first group of German settlers set sail for New York. Nine weeks later they landed on what is now New York City's Governors Island. They stayed there until the spring of 1710, when they sailed to and settled in the area now called Newburgh.

By then this group had been reduced by

The glistening sun on a warm fall afternoon beckons boaters to relax on the Hudson River.

illness to 1,800 people from the original 2,400. In the spring of 1710 a second wave of German immigrants—as many as 2,800 passengers—arrived in New York harbor. These Germans also settled Elizabethtown, Georgetown, and Newtown, as well as Hunterstown, Queensbury, Annsburg, and Haysbury.

Newburgh

Newburgh was the center of operations for the Americans during the Revolutionary War. Gen. George Washington had his headquarters here for more than 16 months in a home owned by Jonathan Hasbrouzk. While he was encamped here near the end of the war, Washington formulated his orders to disband the Continental Army. Today the house and the grounds immediately surrounding it are a historical site. In early June, Martha Washington's birthday is celebrated. The site is open from the late spring to mid-October, the same season as many other riverfront attractions along the Hudson. Inquire at (914) 562-1195.

Road turnpikes were actively constructed in this area between 1800 and 1815. Newburgh at this time was competing with Kingston for river-traffic commerce also. Newburgh had a brick-manufacturing plant in the 1830s, but the two areas differed primarily in the amount of farmland, which increased going inland. Newburgh's surrounding countryside was a pretty fertile region. Boaters need to be aware that remains of a shipyard, ferry terminal, and steamer landing dot the shoreline here. Newburgh was finally incorporated in 1865.

The marina closest to Washington's headquarters is Gull Harbor Marina. If you just want to stop for lunch, go to Gully's restaurant, located on a barge just south of the marina. A temporary caution: The launch ramp here is

to be renovated, so be alert for short-term navigational hazards. From any of these locations, walk out to the riverfront street and continue a quarter-mile uphill. There you'll find the entrance to George Washington's Revolutionary War headquarters.

> **SKIPPER TIP:** Be advised that when arriving by boat in the Newburgh area your chart shows a generous water depth right up to the water's edge. But because of the 300-plus years of history here, you must watch out for uncharted snags. There are many abandoned bulkheads and piles all over this town's shoreline. It was used as a whaling port first, then as a steamboat landing, and then as a shipyard area.

Fishkill Creek and its inland village of Fishkill are on the eastern edge of the river. The creek, its inland village, and Beacon were all part of a land grant in 1682. Initial settlement seems to have been in 1714. The first house from the initial settlement is now a museum. A ferry service crossing the river was started in 1743. In the 1800s cotton milling, brick making, hat making, and wagon making were industries here. The state hospital noted inland on your chart is for the criminally insane. A hospital has been on this site since Revolutionary War days.

On the east shore of the Hudson you now come abreast of the city of Beacon, which gets its name from the twin-peaked Mount Beacon. The north peak is a little more than 1,500 feet high; the south peak is more than 1,600 feet tall. Both peaks are littered with commercial-radio antennas because these are the highest points all the way to the Atlantic coastline eastward and therefore can transmit line of sight (radio) transmissions quite a distance.

Some of the areas around Gull Harbor Marina are as shallow as 3 feet. Gull Harbor Marina's rest rooms are located in a metal-shed building that seems to be leased out, so these facilities are somewhat suspect. North of Gull Harbor Marina and Gully's restaurant are the Newburgh Yacht Club and another restaurant. The Newburgh Yacht Club is intertwined with a fairly new apartment-condominium complex. You would have to take a taxi to visit George Washington's headquarters from the yacht club.

Henry Hudson and Newburgh

In September 1609, Henry Hudson stopped his travels on the Hudson River with his vessel, the *Half Moon*. One of the natives had come aboard and was caught in the process of stealing some shirts and a pillow. The native was shot, and everybody on both sides scattered. The following day the *Half Moon* had to skedaddle because Indians in war canoes were firing arrows at the boat in revenge.

Gull Harbor Marina (914) 565-7110

Storm protection: √√
Scenic: *
Marina-reported approach depths: 10 feet
Marina-reported dockside depths: 3-10 feet
Rest rooms
Showers
Dockside water
Power connections: 30A/125V
Mechanical repairs
Travelift
Ship's store
Restaurant: off site (next door on a barge)
What's special: transients likely to need a
  reservation

Just south of the Newburgh-Beacon Bridge and on the west shore at red buoy #50 is a members-only yacht club.

Newburgh Yacht Club (914) 565-3920

Storm protection: √√
Scenic: * * *
Marina-reported approach depths: 7 feet
Marina-reported dockside depths: 4-7 feet
Gas
Diesel
Rest rooms
Showers
Dockside water
Barbecues
Picnic tables
Power connections: 30A/125V
Ship's store
What's special: private club with a swim-
  ming pool

Newburgh-Beacon Bridge

This almost 8,000-foot-long bridge has a center-section vertical clearance of 150 feet. It opened in 1963, with the second (southern) bridge opening in 1985; both serve as a connector for Interstate 84. Newburgh is the western terminus of the bridge, with Beacon as the eastern.

Three miles north of the Newburgh-Beacon Bridge on the eastern shore are first the Chelsea Yacht Club and then the Chelsea Carthage Landing Marina. On the western shore a mile farther north is North Anchorage Marina.

Chelsea Yacht Club (914) 831-9802

Storm protection: √√
Scenic: * *
Marina-reported approach depths: 3-50
  feet
Marina-reported dockside depths: 3-5 feet

Rest rooms
Showers
Power connections: 30A/125V (very limited)
What's special: private club

Chelsea Carthage Landing Marina (914) 831-5777

Storm protection: √√√
Scenic: * *
Marina-reported approach depths: 3-50 feet
Marina-reported dockside depths: 4-9 feet
Rest rooms
Showers
Dockside water
Picnic tables
Power connections: 30A/125V
Travelift/hoist
Ship's store
VHF-monitored channel: 68, 72

North Anchorage Marina (914) 562-5373

Storm protection: √
Scenic: *
Marina-reported approach depths: 10 feet
Marina-reported dockside depths: 3-5 feet
Rest rooms
Showers
Dockside water
Picnic tables
Power connections: 30A/125V
Mechanical repairs
Gas-engine repairs
Stern-drive repairs
Outboard-motor repairs

Danskammer Point

Farther north is Danskammer Point. A power plant is located there, which you can identify by its towers, tanks, and stacks. A commercial wharf also is there, but it's not open to private pleasure vessels. In 1890 the steamship *Cornell* ran into this point with such force that the overhanging rock ledge broke off. The site—now occupied by an electric company's power plant—is where Henry Hudson reported seeing Indian dancing in 1609. Some 55 years later, another Dutchman also witnessed Indian ceremonial dancers here. He named it "dance hall," or Danskammer in Dutch. Farther north, the next hospital noted on the chart services U.S. veterans. Chelsea Yacht Club, to the east, is sailboat-oriented.

River Channel

Most boaters favor the western side (left side heading north toward Albany) of the channel in this area of the Hudson River. If you look at your chart, you'll see good water depth that varies from the high 30-foot range to 40 feet deep, and these depths all run pretty close to the shoreline.

Shallow Diamond Reef

A little north between Cedar Cliff on the west shore and New Hamburg to the east, both marked on your chart, is the 5-foot water depth of Diamond Reef. It is marked by red buoy #56 almost mid-river, which is the middle of three red markers in a row. You'll find good striped-bass fishing here. Three miles north is another navigation marker for another relatively shallow spot—27 feet (recall all sizes and drafts of vessels use the Hudson River and that is shallow water for some tankers). Then 2 miles north is the last of the five buoys and shallow points. These last two are marked by combination red/green aids indicating that the channel goes by on either

DIAMOND REEF

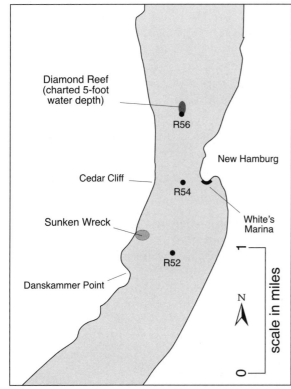

NOT TO BE USED FOR NAVIGATION

side and you may pass by on both sides of the buoy.

> **SKIPPER TIP:** Diamond Reef starts the next reach for boats under sail. It goes 10 to 11 miles north to Crum Elbow, which is just north of Poughkeepsie.

Back on the eastern shore 6 miles north of the bridge is another marina. Locate it by the moored boats just south of it.

White's Marina (914) 297-8520

Storm protection: √√

Scenic: * *
Marina-reported approach depths: 15 feet
Marina-reported dockside depths: 3-10 feet
Floating docks
Gas
Rest rooms
Showers
Dockside water
Picnic tables
Power connections: 30A/125V
Mechanical repairs
What's special: few transients
VHF-monitored channel: 09

New Hamburg Yacht Club (914) 297-9874

Storm protection: √√
Scenic: * *
Marina-reported approach depths: 15 feet
Marina-reported dockside depths: 3-4 feet
Gas
Diesel
What's special: private yacht club

West Shore Marine is obviously on the western shore and to the south of the Marlboro Yacht Club. Watch out for current as you first approach, but it diminishes closer into the docks.

West Shore Marina (914) 236-4486

Storm protection: √√
Scenic: * *
Marina-reported approach depths: 12 feet
Marina-reported dockside depths: 10 feet
Floating docks
Gas
Diesel
Rest rooms
Showers
Dockside water
Barbecues
Picnic tables

Power connections: 30A/125V, 50A/125V
Fiberglass repairs
Below-waterline repairs
Mechanical repairs
Gas-engine repairs
Stern-drive repairs
Generator repairs
Travelift/hoist
Ship's store
Restaurant: on site
What's special: new boat dealer
VHF-monitored channel: 09

Marlboro Yacht Club (914) 236-3932

Storm protection: √√
Scenic: * *
Marina-reported approach depths: 20 feet
Marina-reported dockside depths: 10 feet
What's special: private yacht club

Lone Star Industries operates the eastern shore's gravel crusher and quarry. They also run the quarry on the west bank. North of that is the old off-season landing for Hudson River steamboats.

SKIPPER TIP: Lange Rock (in English "Long Reach") is printed on your chart on the land area of the west bank of the river. The chart makers are trying to tell you this is the area of the "Long Reach" delineated in old-time sailing directions.

Inland on the west bank lie large orchard operations of strawberries, raspberries, currants, and grapes. Blue Point (west shore) is home to another winery. This area on both sides of the Hudson River is a mecca of small farms and locally grown produce, some of which is facilitated by the Cornell Cooperative

Extension (914-677-8223). A simple listing of just the summer crops is going to wear us both out, but here it goes: apples, blueberries, melons, cherries, grapes, peaches, pears, plums, prunes, raspberries, strawberries, beans, beets, broccoli, cabbage, carrots, cauliflower, celery, corn, cucumbers, lettuce, onions, peas, peppers, eggplant, potatoes, pumpkins, radishes, rhubarb, spinach, squash, and tomatoes.

On the east shore and below Poughkeepsie is a private club.

Pirate Yacht & Canoe Club (914) 486-9878

Storm protection: not rated
Scenic: not rated
What's special: private club

Now immediately north of the railroad bridge and on the western shore is a marina.

Mariner's Harbor Marina (914) 691-6171, 691-6011

Storm protection: √√
Scenic: *
Marina-reported approach depths: 35 feet
Marina-reported dockside depths: 5-15 feet
Gas
Diesel
Waste pump-out
Rest rooms
Restaurant: on site
What's special: mostly a restaurant tie-up for good food; few transients

Poughkeepsie, FDR, Hyde Park, and the Vanderbilt

Poughkeepsie was first settled in 1687 and incorporated in 1854. Railroads came to town in 1849. A major boost for the community came when it opened its first railroad bridge across the Hudson in 1888. That bridge (vertical clearance of 137 feet) is now abandoned. As the Industrial Revolution exploded in town, products such as shoes, shirts, thread, hardware such as horseshoes, and dairy equipment were made here. IBM is the major industry now. For more than fifty years the Intercollegiate Rowing Association races were held on the Hudson here, ending in 1950.

A municipal launching ramp is right next to the train station. Adjacent to the launch ramp are two floats where just-launched trailer boats and cruisers can tie up. This landing can accommodate one cruiser or three runabouts for a short-term tie-up. Please, no overnights. Be cautious about water depths if you avail yourself to this free tie-up. A snack bar is in the building at the head of the ramp. Rail is an effective way to get around in this part of the country, and you can take either a Metro North train into New York City or an AMTRAK train upstate to Albany, and even to Lake Champlain and Montréal. Nothing else is close by, however.

Mid-Hudson Bridge

The Mid-Hudson's vertical clearance is 167 feet. This bridge was first used on the last day of August 1930. Note: Some think this bridge is just one notch below the level of beauty exhibited by San Francisco's Golden Gate.

Two miles north of the bridge is the Hyde Park Marina. Two additional marinas are two and three miles north of it. Please read ahead for their descriptions and the shoreside descriptions through the Vanderbilt mansion to decide if and where you want to stop.

Hyde Park Marina (914) 473-8283

Storm protection: √√
Scenic: * *
Marina-reported approach depths: 40 feet

Marina-reported dockside depths: 3-12 feet
Floating docks
Gas
Diesel
Rest rooms
Showers
Dockside water
Picnic tables
Power connections: 30A/125V
Mechanical repairs
Restaurant: on site
What's special: Brass Anchor restaurant on site
VHF-monitored channel: 09, 16, 68

The CIA

In New York State, CIA stands for the Culinary Institute of America, an outstanding cooking school. It moved to its just-off-the-shore Hudson River location in 1972 after more than 25 years in Connecticut. A private school, it does have several dining rooms open to the public. Chefs, sous chefs, and waiters and waitresses are all students of the school. It features outstanding food, fun service, and a cook's heaven of a gift shop, and is open for lunch and dinner. The school is just a taxi ride away from all marinas in the area. Tables are sometimes booked months in advance. Call as soon as you can (914-452-9600). If you cannot get a reservation, call them back two days ahead, and then the day before, and the day of your visit, and you might get a table. I hear that cancellations are heavy at times because people book months in advance and then have to cancel just before their reservation comes up because of a change in their plans. Also, during the first few days of a new semester, because the students rotate through the school and assume new duties, you might experience occasional slow service, dropped meals, snafus, and other snags. Of course, CIA has another meaning down below in Washington, D.C.

This whole area had some 30 gristmills in operation in the 1830s. Orange County, just below here, was noted during the same period for its cheese products. By 1840 both Orange and Rockland counties were turning to drinkable milk as their main source of commerce because it could be shipped via steamer downriver to a growing New York City.

FDR Home

To the east, peeking out between the trees is Franklin Delano Roosevelt's home. An only child, he was born there in 1882. He and his wife Eleanor are buried in the rose garden. Roosevelt led a life in politics from 1911 until his death while president of the United States in 1945. Eleanor died in November 1962. Roosevelt served as a New York State senator, assistant secretary of the Navy, governor of New York, and then president from 1932 to 1945. He contracted infantile paralysis in 1921 in the midst of his political career. Expanded for the last time in 1916, from 15 rooms to 37 rooms, the core of the building dates back about a hundred years earlier. Open to the public. Inquire at (914) 229-9115.

Across the river from FDR's home in the 1930s lived a man called Father Divine, or Major Devine, an African-American radio evangelist and businessman who owned land there and south of Tarrytown in Westchester County. Father Divine was recognized by locals as the man who traveled around in a white stretch limousine, usually accompanied by several women.

Rogers Point Boating Association (914) 229-2236

Storm protection: √√
Scenic: * *
Marina-reported approach depths: 40 feet
Marina-reported dockside depths: 8 feet
Gas
Waste pump-out
Rest rooms
Showers
Barbecues
Picnic tables
Power connections: 30A/125V
Ship's store
What's special: private club

Hyde Park

Hyde Park, called Stoutenburgh for a short time, was first occupied by the Dutch about 1705. The town was established in 1821.

Five and a half miles north of the bridge and south of the Vanderbilt Mansion is a marina.

Andros River Road Marina (914) 229-2316

Storm protection: √
Scenic: * *
Marina-reported approach depths: 20 feet
Marina-reported dockside depths: 2-3 feet
Barbecues
Picnic tables
What's special: runabouts can tie up to a pier; cruisers must pick up a mooring due to very restrictive bridge clearance; best walking access to Vanderbilt Mansion

Vanderbilt Mansion

Also to the east, the Vanderbilt Mansion, now open to the public, was built in 1898 on acreage that was home to society leaders all the way back to an early New York governor in 1702. The Vanderbilts employed 17 staff

ANDROS RIVER ROAD MARINA

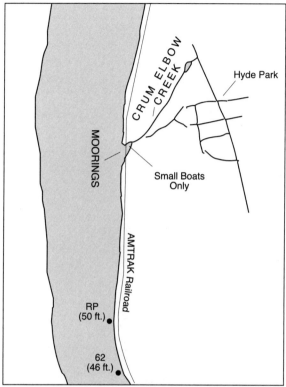

NOT TO BE USED FOR NAVIGATION

members when they owned the house. The estate lent its original name, Hyde Park, to the town. Both the mansion and the beautiful grounds overlooking the Hudson make the estate really worth seeing. Plan on stopping for several hours to take it all in. Inquire at (914) 229-9115.

East River Bank

In the process of laying out their route here along the east side of the river, the railroads had to fill in the land between the mainland and Bolles Island, making the island a part of the mainland. It is now a peninsula, not an island, but no one has changed the name.

Your chart will note other examples of this along the way north.

Poughkeepsie Yacht Club (914) 889-4742

Storm protection: √√√
Scenic: * * *
Marina-reported approach depths: 8 feet
Marina-reported dockside depths: 8 feet
Floating docks
Rest rooms
Showers
Laundry
Dockside water
Barbecues
Picnic tables
Power connections: 30A/125V
What's special: private yacht club
VHF-monitored channel: 09

Esopus Island

Esopus Island is a mid-channel Hudson River Island. Farther north on the Hudson, other islands will provide a diversion for the river waters as this one does. Take either side as a route around it, but if you go to the east, please slow down in respect for the yacht club there. The island is well marked. Do be cautious, however, on the north side of it, since it stays shallow and rocky well north of the visible land area of the island. About 1¾ miles is the next buoy (green buoy #63). It defines the western edge of the channel as well as warns boaters off the shallower water there behind it.

Norrie Point Marina (914) 889-4200

Storm protection: √√√
Scenic: * *
Marina-reported approach depths: 12 feet
Marina-reported dockside depths: 4-6 feet
Waste pump-out

Rest rooms
Showers
Dockside water
Barbecues
Picnic tables
Power connections: 30A/125V, 50A/125V, 50A/220V
VHF-monitored channel: 09

SKIPPER TIP: Do not go out of the channel while the river swings west. It is only 1 to 3 feet deep here and boulder-strewn on the bottom as well.

Lighthouse/Navigation Aid

The abandoned Esopus Meadows Lighthouse makes an outstanding green channel marker. Built in 1872, it is on a man-made rock island. It replaced one that was authorized and funded in 1837 but did not operate until 1839. That first one was damaged by winter ice in 1855 and again in 1867. This one also was attacked by river ice in 1929. Please watch your wakes when passing the lighthouse. An effort is ongoing to further restore the landmark. Note: Keep well off from the next two red buoys because they sit on the edge of the shallow water.

*Hidden Harbor Yacht Club (914) 338-0923

Storm protection: √√
Scenic: * * *
Marina-reported approach depths: 3 feet
Marina-reported dockside depths: 3 feet
What's special: private yacht club *
* This club is just south of the entrance to Rondout Creek.

SKIPPER TIP: Sailors Only—If you plan to continue your cruise through any locks, then you must unstep your mast. Marinas that have done this work are: Certified Marine Service, Hideaway Marina (smaller masts), and Rondout Yacht Basin, all in Rondout Creek. In Catskill they are: Jeff's Yacht Haven, Riverview Marine Services, and Hop-o-Nose Marina. In New Baltimore and Coeymans, you'll find Shady Harbor Marina and Coeymans Landing Marina (smaller masts). If you have anything big and fancy, you should call beforehand to assess a marina's abilities to meet your needs.

For powerboaters who do not understand the fuss over this, let me explain: You need a marina crane to lift up the mast after a wood-bracing system has been constructed on deck to hold the stick, and all the rigging on board for the mast and sails must be taken down. Much of the detail work is usually done by the skipper. Plus, since a mast is almost never aboard unstepped while one cruises, "little things" like being able to see to steer need to be thought through.

Kingston/Rondout Creek

Entrance to this cruise stop is easy and well marked. Two jetties, which can be underwater at high tide, extend out into 12- to 14-foot water depth reaching toward the deepwater channel. This is a man-improved channel within a 3½-mile-long natural creek. The north jetty is more prominent, since it is marked by a lighthouse that was built in 1915.

You turn left off the main Hudson River channel, and—once nearly parallel to the lighthouse—head for a spot in the creek's channel about 100 feet south of the lighthouse. As you close in on the entrance channel, the two sides of the channel will become clear. The entrance path curves slightly, but the curve is evident. Slightly favor the north side as you go in, as over the last 300 years a lot of things have gone down or been left to rot on the south side. This channel and its north-side bulkhead have just been totally updated. Boaters never had it so good.

Although they're no longer used as navigation aids, the variety of unique lighthouses along the length of the Hudson River are a special treat. This is the Rondout Lighthouse, which was built in 1913 to replace the previous lighthouse that marked the entrance to Rondout Creek and Kingston.

It is a 20-minute cruise to the rear, wooded area of the creek. The sights along the way are plentiful, and several marinas offer overnight stays. Don't miss this stop. I have stayed here for a short weekend and used taxis to expand my range of sightseeing choices—and still I needed another day to take it all in.

Please note: I am combining at least two historical towns into one stop, since all are served by one set of docking opportunities. Names for towns in this area include Ar-karkarton, Seepus, Esopus, Wictwyck, Kingston, Connelly, Rondout, Bolton, and Columbus Point.

Ship Museum

This creek is home to the worthwhile Hudson River Maritime Museum, which presents the story of boating history on the Hudson River, with a focus on the period from 1825 to 1925. Its exhibits include photographs, storyboards, and water and land-based vessels. The museum staff often runs a launch out to the lighthouse. A tie-up might be available. Inquire at (914) 338-0071.

Boat Show

A wonderful celebration of classic boats is held in the creek each year in mid-August. The weekend can bring in more than 1,000 feet of boats dockside, plus more on land. From runabouts to cruisers, built nearby and in Great Lakes cities, they come for the display of the history of boats. The show does put a burden on available dock space during this weekend. If you come by during the show, call ahead for a reservation at the marina of your choice.

Kingston History

Kingston was razed by the British. Only one

Classic boats are shown flying dress flags for an area festival.

house was left standing out of the 115 burned after the torching on October 13, 1777. The church, courthouse, schools, and markets also were burned. It only took three hours for the town to burn to the ground. The British also burned houses north of Kingston and two big houses at inland Clermont on the opposite shore as well.

In 1828 a canal that led to Pennsylvania was built at the end of Rondout Creek. Coal and blue stone were freighted in here via barge from 1828 to 1904, when the canal was closed. Almost all the sidewalks in New York State use this blue stone—most of which came through this canal.

The American Indians farmed in this area. Europeans came in 1614, and after some false starts a permanent settlement was established around 1652. From 1658 to 1661, a wood stockade was built around that settlement, enclosing 25 acres. The Dutch Reformed Church was organized about the same time. Kingston was the capital of New York State from 1777 to 1783. The state senate met in a home inside the stockade in 1777 for the first time. This building is open to the public; call (914) 338-2786. Fulton's steamboat (whose invention was financed nearby) in 1807 sparked development. Then the canal advanced the area's importance. Railroads

came in 1872. A train museum is here; call
(914) 331-3399. As for boats, Hudson River
sloops, cable ferries, ferries, towboats and
barges, tugs, steamboats, and cruise ships pro-
liferated. Because there is a lot to see and do,
everybody seems to stop here.

> **SKIPPER TIP:** There are three bridges in
> Rondout Creek. Bridge clearance is lim-
> ited to about 56 feet in Rondout Creek.

The tie-up opportunities inside the creek are
so numerous that I would be overwhelmed by
the selection. Let me say that I strongly prefer
Rondout Yacht Basin, probably because the
staff and Jim, the owner, have always been
what I like to see in people involved with
boating: upbeat, quick to offer help, straight-
shooting, can-do—and all of this with a smile.
Can the other stops do this? Sure. You pick
your favorite. Perhaps you should cruise all the
way in to the beginning of the abandoned
D&H Canal at the Anchorage Restaurant and
Marina and then make your choice.

First, inside the creek is the rescue squad
dock. A distance in from it is the Hudson River
Maritime Museum, then a 56-foot-vertical-
clearance bridge, and the Kingston Municipal
Dock; now to the north of the island, the Great
Hudson Sailing Center under an 86-foot-verti-
cal-clearance bridge and the Hideaway Marina.

South of the island in the channel way past
the same 86-foot-vertical-clearance bridge is
Rondout Yacht Basin. Then Jeff's Yacht Haven,
followed by Certified Marine Service, the
Kingston Power Boat Association (private),
Ulster Marina, a third bridge (railroad) of 144-
foot vertical clearance, Tidewater Marina, and
Lou's Boat Basin #2, the anchorage area, Lou's

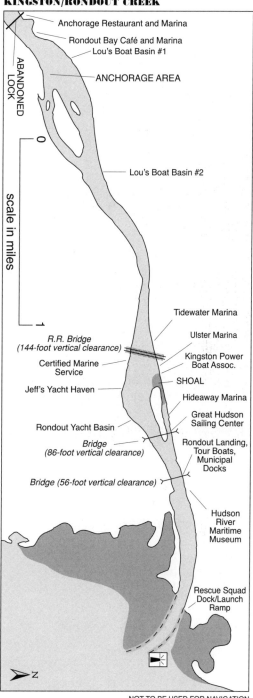

KINGSTON/RONDOUT CREEK

Anchorage Restaurant and Marina
Rondout Bay Café and Marina
Lou's Boat Basin #1
ANCHORAGE AREA
ABANDONED LOCK
Lou's Boat Basin #2
scale in miles
Tidewater Marina
Ulster Marina
R.R. Bridge
(144-foot vertical clearance)
Kingston Power
Boat Assoc.
Certified Marine
Service
SHOAL
Jeff's Yacht Haven
Hideaway Marina
Great Hudson
Sailing Center
Rondout Yacht Basin
Rondout Landing,
Bridge
Tour Boats,
(86-foot vertical clearance)
Municipal
Docks
Bridge (56-foot vertical clearance)
Hudson
River
Maritime
Museum
Rescue Squad
Dock/Launch
Ramp
N

NOT TO BE USED FOR NAVIGATION

Boat Basin #1, Rondout Bay Café and Marina, and the Anchorage Restaurant and Marina.

Hudson River Maritime Museum (914) 338-0071

Storm protection: √√
Scenic: *
Marina-reported approach depths: 12 feet
Marina-reported dockside depths: 8 feet
Wharf
Rest rooms
Dockside water
Power connections: 30A/125V, 50A/125V
Gift shop plus books
Restaurant: off site
Convenience store: off site
What's special: in the past, free dockage with membership

Kingston Municipal Dock

Storm protection: √√√
Scenic: *
Marina-reported approach depths: 12 feet
Marina-reported dockside depths: 5-8 feet
Restaurant: off site
Convenience store: off site
What's special: always improving

Great Hudson Sailing Center (914) 338-7313

Storm protection: √
Scenic: *
Marina-reported approach depths: 9 feet
Marina-reported dockside depths: 7 feet
What's special: a few slips

Hideaway Marina (914) 331-4565

Storm protection: √√
Scenic: * * *
Marina-reported approach depths: 6 feet

Marina-reported dockside depths: 6 feet
Floating docks
Pump-out
Rest rooms
Showers
Laundry
Dockside water
Picnic tables
Power connections: 30A/125V
Below-waterline repairs
Mechanical repairs
Travelift/hoist
Mast stepping
Ship's store
VHF-monitored channel: 16

Rondout Yacht Basin (914) 331-7061

Storm protection: √√
Scenic: *
Marina-reported approach depths: 12 feet
Marina-reported dockside depths: 10 feet
Floating docks
Gas
Diesel
Waste pump-out
Rest rooms
Showers
Laundry
Dockside water
Barbecues
Picnic tables
Power connections: 30A/125V, 50A/125V, 50A/220V
Below-waterline repairs
Mechanical repairs
Travelift/hoist: 35 ton
Mast stepping
Ship's store
Deli: on site
Convenience store: on site
What's special: pool, cable TV
VHF-monitored channel: 09, 16

Jeff's Yacht Haven (914) 331-9248

Storm protection: √√√
Scenic: *
Marina-reported approach depths: 8 feet
Marina-reported dockside depths: 8-10 feet
Floating docks
Rest rooms
Showers
Laundry
Dockside water
Picnic tables
Power connections: 30A/125V, 50A/125V,
    50A/220V
Ship's store
What's special: smaller marina
VHF-monitored channels: 09, 16

Certified Marine Service (914) 339-3060

Storm protection: √√√
Scenic: * *
Marina-reported approach depths: 8 feet
Marina-reported dockside depths: 8-10 feet
Floating docks
Gas
Diesel
Rest rooms
Showers
Dockside water
Power connections: 30A/125V
Below-waterline repairs
Mechanical repairs
Gas-engine repairs
Diesel repairs
Stern-drive repairs
Generator repairs
Travelift/hoist
Mast stepping
Ship's store
VHF-monitored channel: 09, 16

Ulster Marina (914) 339-3943

Storm protection: not rated

Scenic: not rated
Marina-reported approach depths: 12 feet
Marina-reported dockside depths: unknown
Floating docks
Rest rooms
Power connections: 30A/12V
Below-waterline repairs
Mechanical repairs
Gas-engine repairs
Stern-drive repairs
Outboard-motor repairs
Ship's store
What's special: crane for repairs

Tidewater Marina (914) 331-4923

Storm protection: not rated
Scenic: not rated
Marina-reported approach depths: 8 feet
Marina-reported dockside depths: 8 feet
Power connections: 30A/125V
What's special: for vessels 24 feet and
    smaller on a seasonal basis

Lou's Boat Basin #1 (914) 331-2706

Storm protection: not rated
Scenic: not rated
Marina-reported approach depths: 8 feet
Marina-reported dockside depths: 8 feet
Dockside water
Power connections: 30A/125V
What's special: seasonal slips only

> **Rondout Creek Anchorage** is on the
> south side of the creek outside of the
> channel buoys. It has little wind and a
> mud and rock bottom. Water depth varies.

Lou's Boat Basin #2 (914) 331-4670

Storm protection: not rated
Scenic: not rated
Marina-reported approach depths: 8 feet
Marina-reported dockside depths: 8 feet

Gas
Diesel
Rest rooms
Dockside water
Power connections: 30A/125V
What's special: seasonal slips only

Rondout Bay Café and Marina (914) 339-3917

Storm protection: √√√
Scenic: * * *
Marina-reported approach depths: 8-14 feet
Marina-reported dockside depths: 8 feet
Gas
Diesel
Waste pump-out
Rest rooms
Showers
Laundry
Dockside water
Power connections: 30A/125V
Mechanical repairs
Gas-engine repairs
Diesel repairs
Stern-drive repairs
Outboard-motor repairs
Generator repairs
Inflatable repairs
Travelift/hoist: 18 ton
Ship's store
Restaurant: on site

Anchorage Restaurant and Marina (914) 338-9899

Storm protection: √√√
Scenic: * * *
Marina-reported approach depths: 5 feet
Marina-reported dockside depths: 3-5 feet
Rest rooms
Showers
Dockside water
Picnic tables

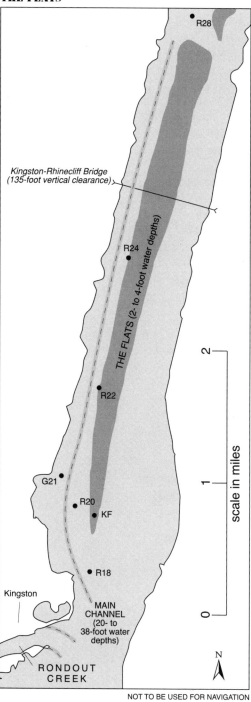

THE FLATS

Kingston-Rhinecliff Bridge (135-foot vertical clearance)

THE FLATS (2- to 4-foot water depths)

R28
R24
R22
G21
R20
KF
R18

Kingston

MAIN CHANNEL (20- to 38-foot water depths)

scale in miles

N

RONDOUT CREEK

NOT TO BE USED FOR NAVIGATION

Power connections: 30A/125V
Restaurant: on site

The Flats (Shallow Water)

Now that you are above Kingston, the Kingston Point Reach Channel leads you toward the western edge of the river and far enough over to be safely away from the Flats. For almost the next 4½ miles north the river has a shallow spot, a broad one, right in the middle of it—sometimes as shallow as 2 to 3 feet. I have seen keel sailboats and trawlers hard aground here—seemingly in wide-open water. The towing-service boats have the best franchise here, second only to the one in Beaufort, North Carolina. At high tide, most pleasure boats might make it, but why take the chance? The Flats continue north of the Rhinecliff Bridge.

The shallow water introduced by the Flats continues now, on up to Castleton-on-Hudson. White areas of the chart attempt to indicate 18 feet (3 fathoms) of water. While a glance at the chart makes navigation look nightmarish, the actual cruising is an easy and logical trip from buoy to buoy.

> **SKIPPER TIP:** Stay clear of local fishermen's nets—they can be extensive in length. Just look for the small floats and buoys.

Bridge

Opened in 1957, the Kingston-Rhinecliff Bridge (with vertical clearance of 135 feet) is just under 8,000 feet long.

Just shy of 2 miles north of the bridge on the east shore is Gore Vidal's former home, Edgewater. A two-story house in the federal style built in 1820, it sits right on the water, located in Barrytown and before Trap Cliff on your chart.

Montgomery Place

In that the channel runs along the west side of the width of the river, let me tell you what you are missing to the east. Roughly located parallel to where Hogs Back is printed on your chart on the east shore, about 150 feet above the water's edge, is Montgomery Place.

This mansion was built in 1805 on a 434-acre property. Remodeled twice (in 1840 and 1860), it finally was bought when in a state of great disrepair by Historic Hudson Valley Association in 1986. It was restored and opened to the public by 1988. Inquire at (914) 758-5416.

Now the sad story. A young married general named Richard Montgomery was going off to fight the British during the American Revolution. Leaving from Saratoga (farther north on the Champlain Canal system at Lock 5), he kissed his wife good-bye, promising to be brave. And brave he was, leading the charge against the city of Quebec late in 1775, where he was killed. His actions there were so gallant that, it is recorded, he was spoken of in favorable terms in the British Parliament. Janet Montgomery then had this house built and lived in it 50 years as a childless but always cheerful widow.

But there is more. General Montgomery's body was not returned right away, even after an act of the Continental Congress ordered a plaque created to honor him. Forty-three years later, in 1818, the governor of New York, De Witt Clinton (the Erie Canal proponent), had Montgomery's body recovered to lay it in state at the capitol in Albany. The body was then transported by steamer down the Hudson to be buried in New York City with full military honors. When the steamboat carrying the body passed by this house, the widow was notified and, by her request, she stood alone on the home's terrace. The steamer stopped. A band on board played the "Death March," and a military salute was fired off. She fainted.

Bigger Ruffles

This area seems to have, more often than not, waves as big as those found anywhere on the Hudson. In a blow and in a small craft, I would consider a lay day for the sake of the crew.

Even water as deep as 8 feet is shallow to commercial-vessel traffic today and all sailors before 1800. Sailors named each shallow area to both personalize them and soften their images. Some of these names are still used today, at least on NOAA charts. Hogs Back and Saddle Bags come ahead before Saugerties.

The Town of Saugerties and the Lighthouse

The town of Saugerties is accessed from the river via Esopus Creek. South of it is the old steamboat jetty now silted in. Stay clear! Next comes the creek, which is fed by an inland lake. The creek has good water depth into the marinas and a yacht club located here.

The lighthouse, now abandoned, stands guard on the north of the two points of land. A house as well as a lighthouse tower, it was built in 1835 and rebuilt in 1869.

Saugerties, an early mill town, had its first such business as early as 1663. Saugerties is Dutch for "sawmills." It is somewhat uphill from the creek.

Saugerties Marine (914) 246-7533

Storm protection: √√√
Scenic: *
Marina-reported approach depths: 12 feet
Marina-reported dockside depths: 8 feet

Built in 1835 and rebuilt in 1869, the Saugerties Lighthouse marks Esopus Creek and is the oldest on the Hudson River today. The entrance channel lies south and west of the lighthouse (on the left side of this photo).

Floating docks
Gas
Diesel
Rest rooms
Showers
Laundry
Dockside water
Picnic tables
Power connections: 30A/125V
Mechanical repairs
Ship's store
Restaurant: off site
What's special: few transients; a long (half-mile) uphill walk to town

Lynch's Marina (914) 246-8290

Storm protection: √√√
Scenic: *
Marina-reported approach depths: 12 feet
Marina-reported dockside depths: 10 feet
Floating docks
Gas
Rest rooms
Dockside water
Picnic tables
Power connections: 30A/125V

Clermont

It's interesting to talk about how some of the Americans dealt with the advancing British army during the Revolutionary War. At Clermont (inland and east from here) the Livingston family put their books into a fountain that had been drained and then they covered that with some old sails. On top of that they put manure to further disguise the whole thing. They also created false caves. They would take any steep ravine, quickly throw down some cut-down trees across it to make a false cave for storage of household effects, disguised with as much brush as possible.

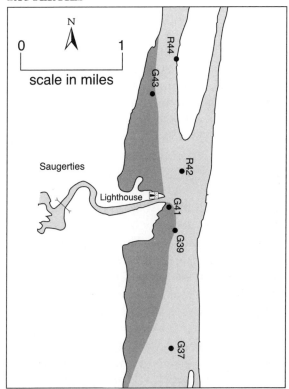

NOT TO BE USED FOR NAVIGATION

Steamboats

Inland (off your chart) on the east side is the estate and town of Clermont. It is roughly about equal to the rock-mounted red navigation light located on Green Flats. The estate is one of three in the area of the Livingston family. This one belonged to Robert Livingston Jr., one of the authors of the Declaration of Independence. Also, as the chancellor of New York State, he swore in George Washington as president of the United States in New York City in 1789. Later, he went to France with Thomas Jefferson to represent the new federal government. There he met Robert Fulton. Located here is a replacement home that has some of the original house (built in 1729-30) that was burned by the British in October 1777 when they razed Kingston. It was enlarged and remodeled three times through 1893 and was occupied by Livingston's descendants until just before the Vietnam War. The house is now open to the public. Inquire at (914) 537-4240.

Fire on the water! A steamboat has a fire to make steam. Cinders from the fire went up the smokestack and could catch sails or a boat's deck on fire. Fire on a waterborne vessel has been a big worry to boaters from early times. John Finch had the first steamboat around the Hudson Valley as early as 1796. He demonstrated it on a lake near New York City. Earlier Finch had operated a steam-powered packet ferry service on the Delaware River, but he discontinued it because it was unprofitable.

Fulton, however, had in Robert Livingston Jr. a potential father-in-law who was a New York powerhouse. An act of New York's legislature gave exclusive steamboat rights to the company with which Fulton and Chancellor Livingston were connected—even though 15 different steamboats built by eight different inventors had been constructed by this point. Fulton named his boat *Clermont*. Thus, the *Clermont,* the sixteenth boat and the one made by Robert Fulton in New York City, finally established in history the beginning of a steam-powered ferry packet service. By the way, the full name of the vessel was the *North River Steamboat of Clermont*. Remember, the Hudson was called the North River for awhile.

In the 1820s steamboats were beginning to be used extensively in this Hudson area and in North America. Recounted below are some events that shaped their early progress. First, a court case in 1824 broke a steamboat monopoly and allowed increased competition

in all steamboat activities. Then, in 1825 the Erie Canal opened, and by the 1840s Hudson River steamboating was peaking as a New York-to-Albany service function. By the 1860s, the steamboats were on a downward spiral, primarily because of some steamboat fires in which people died, constant newspaper reporting of price-fixing, and riverboat races that usually resulted in explosions. To put the final nail in the coffin, in 1851 the New York Central Railroad opened a Hudson River line, so now steamboats had direct competition along the same route. However, tourism and recreation in the upper Hudson River Valley quickly blossomed because the steamboats allowed large numbers of people to get there. New Yorkers could visit for a weekend if they wanted to—or for a Fourth of July picnic—and no longer had to limit themselves to the Harlem Park area of New York City. A requisite amount of industry had been built up to supply coal and lumber to the steamboats. Boat building, boiler fabrication, and related industries occurred in places such as Nyack—and these activities required a number of employees to support them all.

Just to give you an idea of the size of this whole industry, in 1825 some 13 steamboats were operating, and an estimated 100,000 cords of wood were cut to provide fuel for these boats. A cord of wood measures 128 square feet. It is estimated that almost the whole Hudson Valley forest was clear-cut about every 30 to 40 years. Contemporary artistic representations of the valley alternately depict specific areas as forested or deforested—depending on when an artist painted, sketched, or wrote the piece. These discrepancies confused some artists and historians for a while, until they realized that these clear-cutting activities were causing the dramatic changes in the landscape.

In 1840 steam packets started to burn anthracite coal instead of wood, except when they were racing. Wood was still used during races to get a better fire and a higher head of steam.

Steamboat races on the river were very popular, although after a number of explosions and fires many people thought the races were inappropriate. One such ill-fated race started in Albany in July 1852. After a series of landings and exchanging of leads, one boat caught fire and was deliberately beached to save the passengers. It hit the riverbank with such force that it plowed some 8 or 10 feet onto land right near the railroad tracks. The accident was over in 20 minutes, and about 80 people lost their lives in the crash. Because of this crash, in 1852 the state legislature passed a steamboat inspection act, which led to the discontinuance of steamboat racing on the Hudson.

A steamboat breakfast in 1829 was English beefsteak, French toast, and buckwheat pancakes. Fares for a steam packet from Albany to New York in the early 1800s started at seven dollars, dropped to two dollars by 1840, and got down to fifty cents. Passengers had to pay extra for food and a stateroom, however. Also, many of the Hudson River properties for the wealthy had their own steamboat landings or docks. Thus, the patrons of these estates could use both the regular steamship packets as well as their own private boats.

Capitalizing on the pyrophobia of potential passengers, businessmen from Jersey City, New Jersey, entered the competition by building a customized showboat. This boat was built on a barge and towed along behind river steamers. Because explosions and fires were common in the early days of steam travel, ladies and gentlemen could thus ride on the towed barge, far from potential fires. This mode was considered a more genteel (and safer) way of traveling up and down the Hudson River.

The Hudson River also had some showboats like those we associate with the Mississippi River, except these were totally oriented toward being entertainment palaces rather than full-service steamers. One such boat early on was 90 feet long, 22 feet wide at the waterline, 42 feet wide at the deck line (22 feet by 42 feet = Wow!), and powered by a 90-horsepower engine. The boat drew 7 feet. Seats were from twenty-five cents to three dollars. This vessel contained a stage that was 42 feet by 45 feet, with a 16-foot-tall scenery backdrop.

The excitement of the steamboat era, when people looked to the river for fun as well as commerce, matches modern-day pleasure boaters' high level of appreciation of the Hudson River. The steamers carried tremendous loads of people. They offered a real commuting path between the two centers of New York State at this time: Albany and New York City. A sense of grandeur, masterful woodworking, and ornate detailing combined with the newness of mechanical power to fascinate the public. The real lack of safety took a long time to undermine this. But as you cruise on the river, just picture a steamboat race, with smokestacks belching hot cinders, the river water frothing furiously on the paddlewheels, and the passengers gaily wagering and cheering their captain on to victory. It was an exciting time.

Marshland Grass

Standing fields of grass growing on marshland edges of the Hudson begin to appear now and continue to a point somewhat north of New Baltimore.

Confusing Navigation Aids

The main channel is to the west side of the river here. There is also, alas, an unmarked deep-water path on the east side. These are separated by a shallow flat or bar. On this flat is a rock-island-mounted navigation light at a height of 27 feet above the water. Since the light is visible at a greater distance than the channel buoys, some people aim for it, thinking it marks the channel. It does not, and it is located within the shallow water. Just pay attention, use the correct buoys, and you'll be fine.

Next up, North Germantown Reach is a longer narrow-channel reach to keep vessels in the deepest water section. The range markers are only to the south and are located on land at heights of 26 feet and 45 feet. Line these up, one on top of the other, to stay in the channel. Smaller boats in fair weather will not use them except to practice navigating, because the buoys are more than sufficient to keep you in the channel.

Silos

Jutting out from the shallow water and marshland to the west are six silos. Cement is loaded into barges from there. The place is marked on your chart as "silos (northern of six)."

Catskill

Catskill Creek is the most placid creek on the Hudson, making it a delightful place for a quiet visit. The creek is mostly deep water (favor the north side) and a truly serene place midweek that is a delight to your eye from after 5 P.M. until sunset. Then the shadows fill in where the rock- and tree-lined land edges meet the water until they become one, their separation lost in darkness. If you yearn to tie

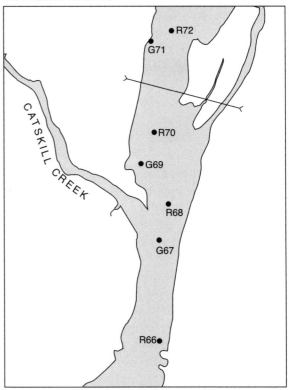

CATSKILL CREEK

NOT TO BE USED FOR NAVIGATION

up overnight in a heavily wooded park, tie up at Catskill to see another special side of a Hudson River cruise.

The Catskill Creek approach channel is easy. Its north side is a land promontory that—together with the south side, which is delineated by buoys—shows you the channel off the Hudson.

> **SKIPPER TIP:** Continue to favor the north shore to miss an unmarked rock just 3 feet below the surface just before you're east of the bend. It can be a surprise because it is surrounded by deep water.

The other promontory is Hop-O-Nose. An early fur trader, Claes Uylenspiegel, named it that after noticing that the landmass matched the shape of the nose of a local Indian, Mr. Hop.

Catskill competes with upriver Troy to lay claim as the home of the man who inspired our modern-day Uncle Sam icon. Although he was born and raised in Troy, "Uncle Sam" Wilson moved here after the War of 1812 ended. Catskill named a bridge that crosses the creek in town "Uncle Sam" to honor him and solidify its claim.

Incorporated in 1806, this area was on the path of very early 1800s roads, and stagecoach lines were established through here. The area also was an early ferry landing. By 1838 a steamboat route to New York City was instituted. At one time or another, Catskill Creek has boasted a resort and has been home to hide-tanning, metal-mining, metal-fabrication, and liquor-distillation industries. The town has a current population of 6,000 people.

Catskill Marina (518) 943-4170

Storm protection: √√√√
Scenic: * * * * *
Marina-reported approach depths: 30 feet
Marina-reported dockside depths: 10-15 feet
Floating docks
Gas
Diesel
Rest rooms
Showers
Laundry
Dockside water
Barbecues
Picnic tables
Power connections: 30A/125V, 50A/220V

Ship's store
Gift shop
Restaurant: off site
Grocery: off site
Convenience store: off site
What's special: a pool; the most transient-oriented marina in Catskill Creek

Hop-o-Nose Marina (518) 943-4640

Storm protection: √√√
Scenic: * * *
Marina-reported approach depths: 10 feet
Marina-reported dockside depths: 10 feet
Floating docks
Gas
Diesel
Rest rooms
Showers
Laundry
Dockside water
Picnic tables
Power connections: 30A/125V, 50A/125V, 50A/220V
Mast stepping
Restaurant: on site

Riverview Marine Services (914) 943-5311

Storm protection: √√
Scenic: *
Marina-reported approach depths: 12 feet
Marina-reported dockside depths: 8 feet
Floating docks
Gas
Diesel
Rest rooms
Showers
Laundry
Dockside water
Power connections: 30A/125V
Welding
Mechanical repairs
Gas-engine repairs

Diesel repairs
Stern-drive repairs
Generator repairs
Travelift/hoist
Mast stepping
Ship's store
What's special: new boat dealer
VHF-monitored channel: 68

Catskill Yacht Club (518) 943-6459

Storm protection: √√√
Scenic: *
Marina-reported approach depths: 7 feet
Marina-reported dockside depths: 6 feet
Floating docks

Gas
Power connections: 30A/125V
What's special: private yacht club

Rogers Island

Site of an Indian battle in 1625, Rogers Island is surrounded by marshland. You cannot circumnavigate it even in a dinghy. Not much is there to see, anyway. The land is very low-lying, and not much has been done with it since the time of the Indians.

Athens-Hudson Lighthouse

This two-story Mansard-roofed lighthouse rests on a massive stone base. Built in 1874, it

The mid-channel Athens-Hudson Lighthouse—north of buoy #78—was built in 1874.

is now abandoned, though it still marks the western edge of the main channel.

Rip Van Winkle Bridge

Opened in 1935, the bridge has a vertical clearance of 146 feet and is named after the Washington Irving character Rip Van Winkle, whose story is set in this area.

Athens

Although it made a strong early start toward development into a major city, Athens has been bypassed by the New York Thruway and the main river channel and is no longer on the beaten path. The original deed for the land in this area goes back to 1665, and the town's first family is said to have come from the Lake Champlain area and settled here before Henry Hudson sailed by in 1609. Historical records do show that a house here was occupied by this same family, the Van Loons, by 1709. The original name for Athens was Loonenburg,

named after the founders. Shipbuilding, whaling, steam-powered ferry service, and railroad operations were active in the early years.

Today Athens offers shopping and antiques for boaters. A waterfront bed and breakfast, the Stewart House, features fine dining (try the salmon), plus there are additional restaurants, a deli, a convenience mart, and antique stores near the Athens Town Dock.

Athens Town Dock has 6- to 7-foot water depths dockside and often a 10- to 17-foot-deep approach off the main river channel. No services and no overnight tie-ups are offered, but lunch and shopping stops are free. The wooden floats accommodate three to five vessels.

Hagar's Harbor Marina (518) 945-1858

Storm protection: √√√
Scenic: * *
Marina-reported approach depths: 10-17 feet

A tie-up at the Athens Town Dock gives boaters access to restaurants, convenience marts, and antiquing opportunities. On the afternoon we stopped by, the local fire department was exercising its equipment!

Marina-reported dockside depths: 10-16 feet
Floating docks
Gas
Rest rooms
Showers
Dockside water
Barbecues
Picnic tables
Power connections: 30A/125V
Restaurant: on site
Deli: on site
Convenience store: off site
VHF-monitored channel: 16, 68

Hudson

Founded by Quakers in 1784, Hudson has a population of about 10,000 and is the county seat for Columbia County. An early official port of entry and whaling hub, Hudson was the homeport for some two dozen vessels.

Hudson Power Boat Association (518) 828-9023

Storm protection: √
Scenic: * *
Marina-reported approach depths: 20 feet
Marina-reported dockside depths: 12 feet
Floating docks
Gas
Waste pump-out
Rest rooms
Showers
Dockside water
Barbecues
Picnic tables
Power connections: 30A/125V
What's special: private yacht club
VHF-monitored channels: 09, 16

Whaling

The whaling industry was in Hudson, first called Claverack Landing, by 1783 and contin-

ued to expand until 1797. Between then and the War of 1812, the British continuously increased ship and cargo rules on the young United States. These rule changes made whaling unprofitable. As a result, whaling dried up and the ships were effectively mothballed. Then it underwent a resurgence in 1830; one ship during this period had cargo valued at $80,000.

Newburgh and Poughkeepsie were part of the whaling revival, too. However, the whaling industry in New York ended for good in 1837. At that time a panic ensued, and whale prices dropped to a low level. Prices stayed low, and the whalers just couldn't make it a paying proposition anymore.

The town of Hudson's initial whaling fleet consisted of 25 sailboats. In 1790 Hudson became an official seaport—which meant that customs officers and government seals, which confirmed that taxes had been paid, were available at its wharves. Nevertheless, in 1797 Hudson lost by one vote to Albany for designation as the capital of New York State. This close shave conveys a sense of the town's importance at that time.

When whaling died out, freight shipping and passenger traffic replaced it as a source of business. Catskill, Peekskill, Hudson, Poughkeepsie, Newburgh, Kingston, and Marlboro freighted cargo such as ostrich feathers, elephant bones, tortoise shell, ebony, gold dust, and Spanish dollars to keep its fleet afloat.

As steamboats replaced the sailboats, the sailboats no longer carried passengers. From 1815 on, they became freighters carrying brick, cement, bluestone, hogs, and butter. Even as late as 1860, 200 sailboats were still engaged in commercial traffic on the river.

The captain of a trading vessel going up and down the Hudson River functioned as an

A tug pushes a river barge up the Hudson while a boater enjoys an afternoon dip.

agent for the whole town. The townspeople would give to the captain a shopping list of what they wanted, along with goods that they wanted to sell, and the captain would transport both the list and the goods downstream, negotiate the sale of the goods, and buy the merchandise. He would then return home, where he would give the person the requested goods and, if there was any, the change from the purchase.

Middle Ground Flats

North of the lighthouse begins the island known as Middle Ground Flats. The "middle" part of the name goes back to the early days of river traffic, when a channel passed on both sides of the land area. Middle Ground Flats can be circumnavigated if you have local knowledge or are cautious. So can Stockport

Middle Ground about 2½ miles north, as can Coxsackie Island (formerly Bud's Island) another 2 to 2½ miles farther north.

> **Middle Ground Flats Anchorage Area:** The bottom can be foul in spots all around this area. Anchor after securing local knowledge. You must ensure you cannot swing into the main channel, since very large commercial traffic might pass by during the night. Water depths vary. Many of these conditions apply to the Stockport Middle Ground and Coxsackie Island anchorages.

Do not attempt to go around Rattlesnake Island, however, since it is hard to find a clear path at its north end.

The Coxsackie Yacht Club is west off the

main river channel, west of Coxsackie Island, and on the western shore. It is north of the town of Coxsackie. There are some anchorages north of the club, but beware of a shallow, foul spot. Secure local knowledge before anchoring here.

Coxsackie Yacht Club (518) 731-9819

Storm protection: √
Scenic: *
Marina-reported approach depths: 12 feet
Marina-reported dockside depths: 12 feet
Floating docks
Gas
Rest rooms
Showers
Dockside water
Picnic tables
Power connections: 15A/125V
What's special: private yacht club

Navigation Hazards

Along and continuing just north of Rattlesnake Island, you are better off staying in the middle of the marked channel if you are cruising through. There is the rock base for red buoy #66 to the east and then the natural shallow spot just north of navigation marker #RI just past it.

Kinderhook

To the northeast, off the chart, is the village of Kinderhook. It is the birthplace of the eighth president of the United States, Martin Van Buren. His home for the last 50 years of his life, Lindenwald, is here. Inquire at (914) 758-9689.

Houghtaling Island Anchorage

To the east side of the main river and on the inside of Houghtaling Island is a lengthy side

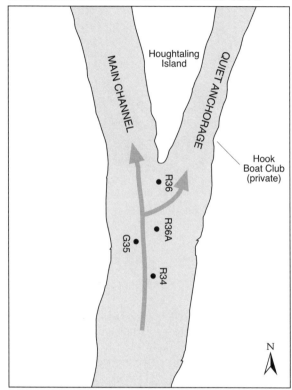

THE HOOK ANCHORAGE AND BOAT CLUB

NOT TO BE USED FOR NAVIGATION

channel. There are anchorages and a private boat club here.

Houghtaling Island Anchorage has a mud bottom with 3- to 11-foot water depths. Good protection from the wind is available. Locals who anchor here feel like they have left civilization and joined the "community" of the Hudson River of 200 years ago.

Hook Boat Club (518) 758-6030

Storm protection: √√√
Scenic: * *
Marina-reported approach depths: 17 feet

Marina-reported dockside depths: 3-8 feet
Rest rooms
Power connections: 15A/125V
What's special: private club
VHF-monitored channel: 16, 09

New Baltimore and Coeymans

Both on the west shore, you will see New Baltimore first, then Coeymans as you proceed north. New Baltimore has an early history of shipbuilding, first for Hudson River sloops, then schooners and, finally, Erie Canal barges. All of this, of course, has disappeared.

Coeymans, a Dutch name, is pronounced "quee-mans." A rock breakwater there is efficient in stopping wakes caused by passing river traffic at low tide. Be cautious, because the breakwater is mostly submerged at high tide and water depth is shallow inside it until very near the boat slips. While the depth is well marked by privately maintained navigational aids, most of us just do not believe that we must go that close to shore and to the floating docks to remain in six feet of water, but it's true. The safest course to be sure you have sufficient water depth is to stay just 15 feet off the boats in the slips. Hail the marina on 09, 13, or 16 VHF channels; they will talk you in

Shady Harbor Marina, on the western shore, offers a full-service restaurant for lunch, and dinner, along with a great view. One of the nicest facilities on the Hudson, it is well worth an overnight stop.

Just north of Shady Harbor, you'll find the marina at Coeymans Landing. The lengthy rock breakwater that parallels the shore makes this one of the "quietest" marinas because it minimizes the wakes from the river's traffic.

unless they are at the gas dock. Their radio is inside the ship's store. Like many marinas, this radio has a remote speaker broadcasting active channels, so marina staff (and everyone else) can hear you dockside but cannot respond. Be sure to positively project the seaman you really are so you will not be embarrassed later! This is a good idea to keep in mind at all times.

Which marina to choose? First, let me say that each has great showers, laundry, and rest-room facilities. Shady Harbor Marina in New Baltimore has a more upscale restaurant as well as boat sales—both of these amenities attract land-based patrons from the surrounding area, so this marina tends to be busier.

Coeymans Landing Marina, two miles north in Coeymans, not only offers the rock break-water that reduces wake action but also hosts a friendly burger-and-fries-style restaurant. Marina owners Hedy and Carl are always working and have a helpful, friendly attitude for anyone who stops by.

Shady Harbor Marina (518) 756-8001

Storm protection: √
Scenic: * *
Marina-reported approach depths: 10 feet
Marina-reported dockside depths: 10 feet
Floating docks
Gas
Diesel

Pump-out
Rest rooms
Showers
Laundry
Dockside water
Picnic tables
Power connections: 30A/125V, 50A/125V
Fiberglass repairs
Mechanical repairs
Gas-engine repairs
Stern-drive repairs
Generator repairs
Travelift/hoist: 20 tons
Ship's store
Gift shop
Souvenir shop
Restaurant: on site
What's special: boat dealer; plus swimming pool
VHF-monitored channel: 09

Coeymans Landing Marina (518) 756-6111

Storm protection: √√√
Scenic: * *
Marina-reported approach depths: 8 feet
Marina-reported dockside depths: 7-10 feet
Floating docks
Gas
Diesel
Waste pump-out
Rest rooms
Showers
Dockside water
Picnic tables
Power connections: 30A/125V, 50A/125V
Fiberglass repairs
Welding
Mechanical repairs
Gas-engine repairs
Diesel repairs
Stern-drive repairs
Outboard-motor repairs
Generator repairs

Travelift/hoist
Mast stepping
Ship's store
Restaurant: on site
VHF-monitored 09, 16, 13

The Ravena-Coeymans Yacht Club shares the rock breakwater with Coeymans Landing Marina. It is immediately north of the marina.

*Ravena-Coeymans Yacht Club (518) 756-9932

Storm protection: √√√
Scenic: * *
Marina-reported approach depths: 4 feet
Marina-reported dockside depths: 1-4 feet*

COEYMANS LANDING

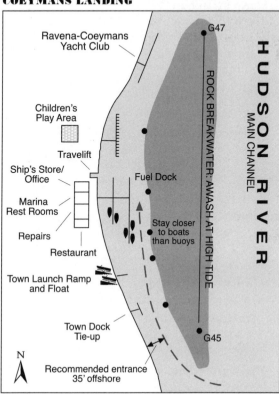

NOT TO BE USED FOR NAVIGATION

Floating docks
Rest rooms
Showers
Dockside water
Barbecues
Picnic tables
Power connections: 30A/125V
Restaurant: on site
What's special: private yacht club

* This yacht club owns its own dredge—but dredging is not a simple task. Ongoing dredging might improve dockside water depths.

Before the next bridge is a private yacht club.

Tri-City Yacht Club (518) 756-8313

Storm protection: √√
Scenic: * *
Marina-reported approach depths: 10 feet
Marina-reported dockside depths: 3-4 feet
Rest rooms
Showers
Barbecues
Picnic tables
Power connections: 30A/125V
What's special: private club

Bridges
Both the railroad bridges (built in 1928) and the Interstate 90 Cutoff Bridge (1959) have a minimum vertical clearance of 135 feet between them.

Castleton-on-Hudson
A bit farther up north and on the eastern shore is Castleton Boat Club, (518) 737-7077.

Castleton Boat Club (518) 732-7077

Storm protection: √√
Scenic: * *

Marina-reported approach depths: 9 feet
Marina-reported dockside depths: 6 feet
Floating docks
Gas
Diesel
Waste pump-out
Rest rooms
Showers
Dockside water
Barbecues
Picnic tables
Power connections: 30A/125V
Restaurant: on site
What's special: private yacht club
VHF-monitored channels: 09, 16, 68, 13

The Castleton-on-Hudson shore is dominated by the railroad tracks separating the river from the first street inland. The crossing points of this rail line have been reduced because of concern for possible accidents between cars and trains. A recent late-winter ice flood did some damage through here.

Albany Ho!
This is your first chance to see Albany's Empire State Plaza high-rise office buildings over the trees.

Port of Albany
Oil-tank farms begin the area of the Port of Albany. These commercial activities continue into downtown Albany. To the east is the turning basin for large ships.

Troy Town Dock, the last marina before the first lock, is now nine miles ahead.

Capital District Bridges
A series of bridges now marches between here and the Troy Federal Lock. Most local traffic is low enough to not require the opening of

The Albany Motor Boats' logo embossed on this step pad attests to an era—the 1920s and '30s—when these boats were manufactured in Albany, New York.

the few low bridges. Vertical clearances run from 25 feet to a fixed 60 feet without calling for a bridge opening. Dunn Memorial Bridge (state Highway 20), the first one, was the starting/finish line of the record-setting speed run on October 11, 1996 (described shortly). Here, on the west shore of the Dunn Bridge, is the location of Fort Orange, built in 1624. It is under the highway now.

Next up you might consider taking either side of the opening section toward the western

side of the second bridge, a swing bridge for railroads. Many local boats pass through the other sections of the railroad bridge, too. When closed, this bridge has a reported 25-foot vertical clearance. If it is open, the next lowest bridge is near Troy Town Docks. Its reported clearance is 29 feet.

Water Depth

The port area today tries to maintain a depth of 34 feet. This depth was achieved under the Eisenhower administration. Prior to that, sand and gravel bars controlled the accessibility this far north. In 1954-56, 32 feet was the controlling depth; the 1930s, 27 feet; and 1800-1900, 12 feet. Freighter traffic does not continue beyond the Port of Albany; therefore, water depths reduce from 32 to 14 feet as you head north.

Albany Yacht Club (518) 445-9587

Storm protection: √
Scenic: * *
Marina-reported approach depths: 20 feet
Marina-reported dockside depths: 10 feet
Floating docks
Gas
Diesel
Waste pump-out
Rest rooms
Showers
Dockside water
Picnic tables
Power connections: 30A/125V, 50A/125V
Restaurant: on site (weekends)
What's special: private yacht club; popular transient stop for visiting members of other clubs

Record Run

A local Chevrolet dealer, Jim DeNooyer Sr., 55, and his son, Jim Jr., 33, took three hours and seven minutes to run from the Dunn Memorial Bridge (Albany) down to the Statue of Liberty (New York City) and back again on October 11, 1996. They jumped into a 28-foot catamaran powerboat, went up river to get a running start, and crossed under the Dunn Memorial Bridge (the start/finish line) with the speed clocked on radar at 89 mph. I saw the radar readout myself. The Skater brand hull was powered by three Mercury outboard motors, each rated at 280 horsepower. These pushed the craft past the Castleton Boat Club at 105 mph, the only other time their speed was checked. The top speed of the rig was quoted as 125 to 130 mph, turning the engines at 7,800 rpm. They never opened it up, however. They consumed 150 gallons of aviation gasoline during the run.

The DeNooyers ran a round trip. The original one-way record run was set by Robert Fulton. He ran from New York City to Albany in 28 hours and 45 minutes in 1807.

The previous record run for this distance was set in 1984 by Betty Cook, a personal friend of mine, now deceased. She ran the same distance in four hours and 22 minutes in a twin-engine Mercruiser stern-drive-powered catamaran. She, unlike the DeNooyers, stopped to refuel. Betty was a grandmother at the time. Those who knew her miss her.

Albany Area Shoreline

The shoreline in the Capital District has a few grassy, wooded preserved recreational areas, but not many. Most of it is occupied by less-than-attractive commercial wharves that are seldom vibrant. There are good reasons for this. The river, connecting Albany (Fort Orange) and New York City (New Amster-

dam), historically moved more goods than people. Then the Erie Canal system opened. For a short time the canals were people movers to get the west populated. Within a decade or two, that role changed more to moving finished merchandise, raw materials, and agricultural products back and forth. However, passengers on the waterways at this time were not on a pleasure trip: They had the serious mission of finding a new life and home somewhere out west.

Then the railroad came along the shoreline. Trains require flat land and easy grades to work. Where better to find these than a river's shoreline? Trains carried both freight and passengers. They were noisy and belched smoke, and there was a wrong side to every set of tracks. Finally, the interstate highway came through. Rumor has it that the New York Thruway was to be routed on the east shore near Rensselaer and Troy, which local politicians in Albany saw as an instant guillotine (rightly so) to the growth of Albany. So they let the engineers run it over what was then the cheapest land in Albany—the riverfront—because industry and the trains were underutilizing it by then and everyone was moving to the suburbs. The politicians even let historic Fort Orange be buried underneath the highway.

Remember, too, that by then the river had been used without regard to consequences for 350 years. It smelled. Garbage floated in it. It was a sewer for every town and industry located near it. Federal and state Superfunds have since cleaned it up, making it an outstanding natural resource now that our society values nature and the environment. More improvements have to occur, and community and state leaders will make them happen.

Launch Ramp

Do not throttle up right away after the railroad bridge, since ahead on the west shore is a public launch ramp. Pass it slowly, because your wake will wash onto the floating pier and upset the positioning of any boat and trailer trying to launch or retrieve. Note: The water depth is shallow around the ramp and close to shore in and around the floating docks. Also, local rowing teams are in the water here early in the morning and for the last three hours of sunlight on almost a daily basis.

Tides and Current

The Hudson River is tidal all the way to the Troy Federal Lock. A tide range of 4 feet can be expected. Also, there can be other reasons why the water is "high." Springtime runoff can raise river levels. Industry, upstate lake levels, and city water needs also might have some effect on water depths and bridge clearance during the boating season. Recently, a reservoir was dramatically lowered in an attempt to move the saltwater/freshwater line further downstream in the middle of the summer cruising season. These events can create currents even where they usually are not. I have experienced a current of 3 mph at Troy Town Dock in mid-July.

Patroon Island Bridge

This 60-foot vertical clearance bridge carries a section of Interstate 90 across the Hudson. It effectively connects Boston, Albany, Utica, Syracuse, Rochester, and Buffalo to one another.

North of the bridge the channel moves over to the eastern half of the river.

The lift bridge in Troy, New York, raised for a tour boat.

At the Troy Town Docks, boaters "parallel park" alongside a float on the eastern shore of the river. This is a convenient place to stop, with several restaurants and other facilities nearby.

Troy-Menands Bridge

The Troy-Menands Bridge is a fixed bridge with a vertical clearance of 55 feet. It is state Highway 378 for cars.

Watervliet Arsenal

To the west is the arsenal where 16-inch gun barrels for battleships were made. On the battleship *New Jersey,* these guns can fire a shell 40 miles. That is, the ship can shell the huge sign at the Yonkers municipal pier while cruising in the Atlantic Ocean outside Ambrose light tower.

Established during the War of 1812, the arsenal has made weapons exclusively for the U.S. military (it can now do so for other countries as well). It is quarter-mile south of the red buoy off Poestenkill to the east.

Route 2 Bridge

North of the bridge, the channel west of Green Island is not usable.

Troy-Green Island Bridge

This bridge has a 29-foot vertical clearance.

Troy Town Docks (518) 272-5341

Storm protection: ⩗
Scenic: * *
Marina-reported approach depths: 20 feet
Marina-reported dockside depths: 20 feet
Floating docks
Gas
Diesel
Waste pump-out
Rest rooms
Showers
Laundry
Dockside water
Power connections: 30A/125V, 50A/125V, 50A/220V
Ship's store
Restaurant: on site
What's special: last marina before locks (so everyone stops here); some brand-new floating docks

Events within a taxi ride from Troy Town Docks or the Albany Yacht Club include:

May—
Albany Tulip Festival, (518) 434-6311
Canalfest, Waterford, (518) 237-7999

June—
Free concerts, Albany, (518) 434-6311
5K and 10K runs, Albany, (518) 273-0267
Riverfront Arts Festival, Troy, (518) 273-0552

July—
Fourth of July fireworks and celebration, Empire State Plaza, Albany, (518) 473-0559
Outdoor plays, Albany, (518) 434-2035

Specialty entertainment locations:
The Egg, Empire State Plaza, Albany, (518) 473-1845
Pepsi Arena, Albany, (518) 487-2000
Palace Theater, Albany, (518) 465-4663
Troy Savings Bank Music Hall, (518) 273-0038

Museums:
New York State Museum, Empire State Plaza, Albany, (518) 474-5877
Albany Institute of History and Art, (518) 465-4478

Historic Houses and Government Sights:
Schuyler Mansion (1761), Albany, (518) 434-0834
Cherry Hill (1787), Albany, (518) 434-4791
Ten Broeck Mansion (1798), Albany, (518) 436-9826
Governor's Mansion (1850), Albany, (518) 473-7521
State Capitol (1867), Albany, (518) 474-2418
Albany City Hall (1881), Albany, (518) 434-5100

Bed and Breakfast:
Mansion Hill Inn (also serving dinner), (518) 465-2038

Recommended Restaurants:
Nearby:
Troy Pub, Troy Town Dock, (518) 237-2337, (burgers, beer and snacks; excellent food)
Manory's, 99 Congress St., Troy, (518) 272-2422, (A long walk for breakfast, but reported to be Michelle Pfeiffer's favorite restaurant while she was in Troy filming the 1993 movie *The Age of Innocence*)
Cape House, 254 Broadway, Troy, (518) 274-0167, (seafood)

Farther but worth it:
Jack's Oyster House, 42 State St., Albany, (518) 465-8854, (You must try their cheesecake.)
Ogden's, Howard at Lodge St., Albany (518) 463-6605, (I recommend their salmon.)
Mansion Hill Inn, 115 Philip St., Albany, (518) 465-2038

Emergency Information:
Police and Fire: 911
Deaf Emergency TDD (New York State Police): (800) 342-4357 or 311
Poison Control Center: (800) 336-6997
U.S. Customs Emergency: (800) 522-5270 (24 hours)

Hospitals:
Albany Medical Center: (518) 262-3131
Albany Memorial Hospital: (518) 471-3111
St. Peter's Hospital: (518) 487-1324
Child's Hospital: (518) 487-7200
Stratton VA Medical Center: (518) 462-3311

Note: Troy Town Docks usually has information on what to do and where to eat. Also, the Troy Visitor's Center is a short walk from there. Local stuff: Two blocks north of the docks, the local Oldsmobile/Cadillac dealer has a framed 1917 newspaper advertisement showing its role as a distributor for Oldsmobile cars before it became a dealer.

Troy

Known as the Collar City, Troy took its nickname from the inventive work of Hannah Montague. She created the "detachable" collar for shirts in 1825 and gave birth to an industry. Arrow Shirt Co. made shirts until 1989 on River Street. It was the largest manufacturer of shirts in the world for many years.

Not a one-industry town, Troy over the years has had notable achievements in industry and transportation. Early on it was a market for farmers' produce. An early tavern owner lent his name to one area of town called Ashley's Ferry. Troy was the name in common usage by the time the village was formalized in 1798. This "come to market" aspect of early Troy fueled its growth. In 1802 a toll road to Schenectady (west of Albany) opened. Steamboat landings in 1808 or 1809 were established. Then the Erie and Champlain Canals opened. A small railroad was in place by 1842.

The valves for the Panama Canal locks were manufactured in Troy at Ludlow Valve Co., still an ongoing concern operated by fifth-generation family members. Plates for the ironclad *Monitor* were also made in Troy. Other industries over time were bricks, paper, stoves, bells, horseshoes, ammonium sulfate, steel, scientific instruments, and fire hydrants.

Fire in the Streets

Most of Troy burned to the ground in a catastrophic fire in May 1862. A wooden railroad bridge—the first ever to cross the Hudson—caught on fire one windy day. Those embers soon had Troy in flames. From morning to night in that one day more than 500 buildings burned and many lives were lost. Stories of people burning to death in the streets are told in some books.

Flood!

Notice the Dutch door at the entrance for the staff at the dockmaster's office at the Troy Town Docks. A recent midwinter rain on top of the frozen Hudson jammed ice into bridge supports, damming the river. Ice and water backed up until reaching the level of the split between the lower and upper parts of that Dutch door. Above the rest-rooms/laundry area a watermark shows the much-higher 1913 flood.

Collar City Bridge

This bridge is the third built to cross the river at this location. It was opened in the late 1970s after the second bridge collapsed in 1977. (Amazingly, no cars were on the bridge at the time.) The first bridge here was the first one across the Hudson. Opened to railroad traffic in late 1835, it was the one that caught fire and burned Troy in 1862.

Adams Island

North of the Troy Town Docks the channel goes west of Adams Island and east of Green Island. It is not well marked, but it does not seem to matter. I routinely go straight north along the eastern river edge and enjoy water depths in the high-teen to mid-20-foot range, but it is always safer inside the marked channel.

This area is not the end of the navigable portion of the Hudson River, but it is the end of the tidal Hudson, and the locks ahead pose challenges. Because of these conditions, and in deference to local boating customs, I end my navigation commentary for this area here.

History

The Hudson River was known to the earliest settlers, the Indians, as "the water that flows two ways," meaning it was tidal to people used to rivers (which flow one way) and lakes. Of course, these were the descendants of the people who came across the Bering Straight in the state of Alaska and crossed the entire continent to finally come to this area.

On the western shore of the Hudson River the Indian tribes called themselves Lenapes. Farther south, the Indian tribe was called Raritans, and farther up on that area they were called Hackensacks—and then came the Tappans and then the Haverstraws. These all joined the Lenape Bay Alliance. Midway up the river was another union of the Lenape Bay group called Wolf, and in alliance with the Wolves were the Catskills, or Wawarsings, and the Waranawankongs.

Manhattan Island was populated by the Manhattan tribe and the Wappingers. While up north, the strongest of all the Algonquin tribes were the Mohicans. They occupied the area that is now called Albany and continued up into the Lake George and Lake Champlain area. Hudson River Valley Indians were strong, muscular, and fairly tall. They also rubbed themselves with odorous greases of wild animals and typically walked around with just a pair of pants on—they were naked from the waist up during warm weather. They would wear hip-length leggings of tanned hide and some soft-soled moccasins.

An Indian would give himself a haircut by taking a hot stone and burning off his extra hair. That left a strip of stiff short hair running from his forehead to the back of his neck. Hanging from his crown was one long lock—the piece you would want to scalp if you were in a competing Indian tribe.

In cold weather the clothing became unisex. They would throw on a robe of some wild-animal skin (wolf, bear, or deer), something they could sew together with turkey feathers or wildcat gut. They would paint their faces and the exposed parts of their bodies using the clay from the riverbank, sometimes mixed in with berry juices. The men liked to wear necklaces, usually from shells or perhaps colored stones. A woman's necklace was an indicator of family wealth.

Indians made bows and arrows from hickory sticks, and with these weapons they hunted for deer, bear, and raccoon. They also fished for sturgeon, striped bass, slim herring, and shad. Oysters were prevalent in the river shallows, and the Indians ate the meat and used the shells in a variety of ways. These Indians used to travel up and down the river in dugout canoes made from tree trunks hollowed out by fire or scraping. Birch-bark canoes on the Hudson were very rare. These lighter canoes were used up in the north woods, where portages were required.

The Indians were living in a stream of water that flows two ways; they really didn't need to continually move their canoes over land between bodies of water. Therefore, a dugout canoe, although heavy, was more than satisfactory.

Indians cultivated maize (corn), pumpkins, and green beans. They farmed by following the changes in the sky. Because harvesting commenced by the autumn moon, planting was timed by the alternation of the constellations.

Marauding parties of Mohawk Indians threatened the Hudson River Indians. The Mohawk tribes usually stayed over in Mohawk and Genesee (the area around Rochester), but if for some reason an emergency came up, they would just come over to the Hudson

River Indians in full war dress and demand a tribute. The Algonquin tribes usually submitted meekly. About the only Indian tribe that would resist these people were the Mohicans.

History recounts that Henry Hudson, the first white man in this area, called these Indians a loving people. The Algonquins believed in supernatural beings. They had a goddess of the valley, Minewawa, and they thought that they had sinned whenever she hurled lightning down upon them or growled at them with thunder. She supposedly lived beyond the Catskill peaks among many other gods, and she also was believed to be the source for the new moon—she put it up and took it down. The Indians believed that when Minewawa took down the moon, she cut it up and cast the pieces into the sky, thus making the stars.

The Beginning of Dutch Settlement

By September 1609, Henry Hudson, in his 80-ton ship, the *Half Moon,* sailed north as far as where Albany is today, establishing the Netherlands' claim to the region. All was not "milk and honey," however. The *Half Moon* sent five men to explore the river even farther north. They had a good trip up, but on the way back two boats of Indians attacked them. John Coleman, the leader of the men, died in the boat from the arrow wound in his throat, and two of the other men were in agony because they were likewise struck by arrows. After spending all night rowing around the blackened river trying to find their way back, they finally found the *Half Moon* at 10 o'clock the following morning.

In 1614, the first trading-post fort, Fort Nassau, was established in the Port of Albany area. It was intended to support the skin and fur trade that was growing in the upper reaches of the river. A fortified log house, it served Dutch and other fur traders, mostly French-speaking white men who were hunting beaver, mink, otter, and wildcats for their skins. Each year this outpost was flooded in the spring and sometimes in the fall, too. It was destroyed by flood three years later in 1617. Unfortunately, no evidence has been found that verifies the fort's actual location. Fort Orange, built in 1624, provided a home for an initial settlement of 18 families, a government outpost, a small military presence, and the fur traders. This fort also was on the west shore, now located underneath the section of Interstate 787 that parallels the river and just north of the first auto bridge, Dunn Memorial, about 1½ miles north of what's believed to be Fort Nassau's location. The fort's primary purpose was trade, with perhaps an eye toward defending the colony from a takeover attempt by the Spanish. The fort was made of wood, consisting of flat planks laid lengthwise against some mostly upright logs to form the outside walls. The four corners had bastions where cannons were mounted. A moat was later established around it. Most of the buildings inside were brick, particularly the Dutch West India Company's New World headquarters, located in the middle of the fort's enclosure and built in the highest period style and decorated with the latest, most fashionable furniture and detailing. The lavishness must have demonstrated to everyone that the Dutch West India Company was the biggest power in the New World. The original fort was partially destroyed in a big flood in 1648. In rebuilding, again in wood, because the Spanish threat had never materialized, fur traders were allowed to build houses inside the fort if they would bear the expense of building a share of the outer wall. The fort was in disrepair when the English came and was finally abandoned in 1676. The ruins were still visible as late as 1790. By fall 1970, when remnants of the fort were studied, the pieces were found under about 6 feet of fill 200 yards from the Hudson River, whereas in 1624 the fort had been right up against the river's edge. Thus, the Hudson is 200 yards less wide than it was in 1624.

Meanwhile, the first eight settlers in Manhattan started by building small dwellings from sod—cellar homes that were more below than above ground. This settlement was called New Amsterdam. Soon they wrote to the West India Company to send them a preacher, supposedly to perform baptisms, but they hinted that they wanted marriages performed as well. Along with the preacher, a new governor was sent—Gov. Willem Verhulst, who replaced Captain May as leader of the colony. Three more ships also arrived. The *Horse, Cow,* and *Sheep* were named after their cargo. A fourth ship called *Mackerel* brought 45 additional colonists and a few fish. So now there were cattle grazing at the foot of Manhattan, in what is now known as Battery Park. Europeans had begun farming in the Hudson River Valley.

Later, in 1626, Peter Minuit, named director general of the colony, bought permission to occupy Manhattan from the native Algonquin tribe of the Wappinger Confederacy. This deal was the famous transaction in which he bought Manhattan for 60 florins' (or 24 dollars') worth of tools, trinkets, and glass beads.

Attempts to lure Dutch immigrants to the New World met with mixed success, so in 1629, the West India Company established a Charter of Freedoms and Exemptions, which became known as the patroon system. This feudal-type system authorized the distribution of huge riverfront estates to wealthy patrons or patroons from all over Europe who would each establish a colony of at least 50 people on their land within eight years. They could select a tract of land either 16 miles along one shoreline or eight miles along both shorelines of the Hudson River. The patroons also were granted tax incentives—they did not have to pay any duties for eight years, and the people who settled on their land didn't have to pay taxes for 10 years. This was the system under which Van Rensselaer acquired his holdings in 1629.

Within two months of signing up for the charter, Van Rensselaer decided to start buying land beyond this 8-mile limit. He bought as far as the entrance to the mouth of the Mohawk, which was 9 miles above his designated area, and he went as far as 11 miles below Albany. So he had about a 20-mile stretch on both sides of the river. The land wasn't all contiguous, however, and it was not clear exactly where his land's boundaries began and ended.

As an aside, Van Rensselaer never did come over to the New World to visit what he had named Rensselaerwyck. From afar, however, he attempted to control trade on the Hudson River by ordering a fort built at the southern end of his land and requiring traders to be under contract to him to use the river. They were then forced to sell only to him and to buy from him at outrageous prices.

When the Revolutionary War broke out, many farmers thought the war would be an opportunity for them to own their own land. They believed that if they helped free the land from the British, the feudal barons' hold on these large estates would be broken and the Tory properties would be divided among the tenant farmers. As it happened, however, the rich river families supported General Washington and, as a reward, the Van Rensselaers were allowed to keep their holdings. In fact, they advanced their position by absorbing the confiscated Tory lands themselves. Tenant farming at Rensselaerwyck continued well into the 1800s.

By the mid-seventeenth century, Fort Orange (Albany) and the land across the river at Rensselaerwyck (Rensselaer) were eventually inhabited by a diverse population that included Irish, Swedes, Germans, Danes, and English as well as the Dutch. In 1643 eighteen different languages were being spoken on Manhattan Island.

Between 1648 and 1651 the director of the Rensselaerwyck patroon ordered that a number of homes be built below the stockade of Fort Orange. Unfortunately, the homes would have been in the line of fire if there had been an Indian raid, the threat of which was the reason for the fort in the first place. Peter Stuyvesant, who was then governor of New Amsterdam, ordered this building activity stopped, but the director of the patroon wanted to maintain his property rights, so he refused and defiantly built a house within pistol shot of the fort.

Because nobody really wanted to deal with this argument during the winter, in the spring 1651 Stuyvesant dealt with the land grabber by going less than a mile north of Fort Orange and ordering the soldiers to march on the director's house to take down the patroon's flag. Then he simply drew some boundaries and claimed the land for the Dutch West India Company. He named this land Beverwyck, enclosed it in a stockade, and set up a court that was to take care of all of the criminal and civil cases for both Fort Orange and Beverwyck. This brought some law and order into what had been a freewheeling and loose fur-trading area.

The British Take Over

In 1664, five ships of the British Empire sailed through the Verrazano Narrows and took over the Dutch colony of New Netherlands, marking the beginning of the British colony of New York. The conquest was bloodless, and little changed in the region as a result. For the most part, the common men didn't care who ruled them because there was no change in their property rights or land usage. They did gain one advantage— some of the taxes they were paying to the original West India Company were removed, and the colony, with less taxation, began to prosper. A whole series of name changes ensued. New Amsterdam became New York. Rondout became Kingston. Beverwyck (the area north of Fort Orange) became Albany, and the River of Prince Mauritius became the North River. The English governors then decided to try to revoke the large land grants that had been the Dutch policy of settlement. They wanted unwinding because they thought the grants were slowing development.

Jumping ahead, in 1785 the first vessel to prove that the Hudson River craft also were seagoing vessels left Albany. The *Experiment* was the first American craft to make a direct voyage from the United States to China and the second such craft to reach Canton. She carried furs of squirrel, mink, foxes, muskrats, raccoons, bears, and fawns and also wildcat skins. The ship also carried some spirits, snuff, tar, turpentine, rosin, and varnish. The town of Albany was so overjoyed when Captain Dean came back from his China expedition that they named a street after him, which still exists today in Albany.

By the 1830s the Hudson Valley had become very busy. The Erie Canal opened in 1825. Its construction had started in 1818; the workers used the Hudson River to bring in supplies and machinery to the construction site. After 1825, the freight rate for cargo and passengers going west dropped 90 percent, creating a complete redistribution of how goods would be moved. In fact, it has been said that the Erie Canal thrust New York City and New York State into the leadership position that had previously been enjoyed by Philadelphia and Pennsylvania. In addition to the canal, by 1850 the railroads were active, and telegraph wires went up and down the Hudson. The Erie Canal opened up such vast new lands to agriculture that as a result, farmers abandoned parts of Long Island and New England. The wheat crop moved immediately to the western area of New York State—up to Lake Erie. The Genesee Valley initially offered twice the production yield of wheat per acre compared with the previous farmland, because the old lands had been worn out from extensive cultivation. Don't forget that during the 1800s to 1850s lands were often farmed until the soil was exhausted, and rather than trying to rejuvenate it, the land would be abandoned in favor of new virgin land that would be clear-cut for fresh farming.

The Erie Canal

On the morning of Wednesday, October 26, 1825, the Erie Canal opened with a bang! To celebrate the connection of a Lake Erie port to New York City, and from there to the world, a sound-off of weaponry boomed from Buffalo to New York City. A series of cannons was lined up in intervals stretching over 500 miles between these two cities. Starting in Buffalo, the first battery fired its guns. When the next battery east of it heard the sound echo through the mountains, it fired, and so the progression continued all the way to New York City. This series of signals—west to east—took 81 minutes to complete. Then the New York City battery started a return series of signals, which took 80 minutes to reach Buffalo.

The first packet through the Erie Canal was the *Seneca Chief*, which carried the dignitaries. The second vessel through was *Young Lion of the West*, which carried eagles, wolves, fawns, foxes, and raccoons to represent the variety of animals found out west.

The original canal construction was authorized April 15, 1817; started July 4, 1817; and was completed October 26, 1825, at a cost of $7,143,789. It had 83 locks. The first enlargement of the canal was authorized on May 11, 1835; construction started in August 1836; and was completed in September 1862 for the cost of $32,008,851. The Erie Canal went from 83 locks down to 71 locks. Today's Erie Canal has only 34 locks—and it costs a million dollars to fix just one town wharf!

CHAPTER 4

Locking Through for the First Time

The essential character of the canals is found in the locks. Boaters locking through for the first time have a true adventure in store. As the lock gates close, holding you hostage until the waters rise to the appropriate level, you realize nothing is between you and a giant wall of water except an ancient technology and the lock operator's authority. I still feel a sense of anticipation and excitement at each lock, and I enjoy the experience itself as well as the awareness that each locking through takes me closer to my destination.

Clearly, locking is a unique experience, very different from what most saltwater boaters have ever encountered. While not difficult, it does require some preparation and concentration, but the procedure—once mastered—is pretty much the same through all the locks on your trip through New York waterways. In this case, practice makes, if not perfect, at least a smoother, more efficient passage. For now, relax, pay attention, and prepare to enjoy!

Just What Is a Lock?

A lock is an artificial water basin used to connect portions of a waterway that stand at different levels. It consists of a long set of concrete walls with a pair of huge gates at each end. When a ship travels upstream, it enters the lock chamber through the gates at the lower water level while the gates at the upper end remain closed. Then the downstream gates are closed and water is pumped into the chamber. When the boat rises to a level equal with the upper waterway, the upper gates

open, allowing the vessel to pass through. For a boat passing downstream, the procedure is reversed, with the water being let out of the lock until the level inside the chamber is the same as on the downstream end. Then the lower gate opens. The average lock in the New York canal system is 338 feet long and 45 feet wide. It can accommodate as many as 30 boats, depending on their sizes, though usually only about four or five go through at a time; or one barge and tug measuring 300 feet by 43½ feet overall. By the way, if traffic on the waterway is heavy, there is a protocol for going through the lock: Military vessels advance first, with state and official boats next in priority, then commercial vessels carrying passengers, commercial tows, commercial fishing craft, and finally pleasure craft. You'll be glad to know that ships carrying munitions or explosives always go through alone.

All but two of the locks on your cruise through these waters are under the jurisdiction of the New York State Thruway Authority/Canal Corporation and are operated by personnel called lock operators. When locking through, it is important to remember that the lock operators are the masters of both the locks and the waterway in the area approaching the locks. They have full authority to direct and instruct anyone and everyone using the lock system. Do not challenge a lock operator. Make sure you understand the lock operator's instructions and follow them, not only for your safety and that of the other boats in the lock, but also because the lock operator might detain you or restrict your passage.

Making Your Boat Cruisable

Boaters can and do use just about any type of craft to go cruising, particularly in the generally protected waterways covered in this book. People cruise in everything from outboard-powered open skiffs to day sailers equipped with an auxiliary engine clamped to the stern and a tent for sleeping in beside the locks. However, I anticipate that most of my readers will be using a craft that the skipper and crew can sleep aboard and prepare some meals on. What I offer below is not a comprehensive course on how to turn any craft into an inland-waterway cruiser; rather, I present a few basic points that many skippers seem to consider only after they have started locking through and are forced to play catch-up in acquiring needed accessories. I hope these equipment suggestions save you some headaches and make your trip more enjoyable.

Locking-Through Equipment. Minimum equipment for locking through includes extra fenders, sometimes called bumpers by non-boaters, and at least two long dock lines, one for the bow and one for the stern, plus one boat hook. For a super-deluxe lockable boat, you need to add a second boat hook. This extra boat hook's presence inside the locks really makes things go more smoothly. For an ultra-equipped lockable boat, think of the crew. Lock lines, cables, and walls become slimy during the season; the cheapest cotton gloves can protect hands, and rags at each station to wipe one's hands after locking through are nice.

Minimum crew includes the skipper plus someone who can handle the bow. The skipper can usually take responsibility for the stern in boats up to 32 feet in length or 12,000 pounds in weight. Read the Welland Canal

chapter (16) for its crew requirements, which might overrule these specifications. For boats bigger than this, you might need a skipper, bow person, and a stern-line handler. A runabout can usually get by with just the skipper using one line or boat hook from the helm station.

Shore Power Connections. If your vessel has shore power connectors, they fit only one style of pier-side connection. Cruisers on these or any waters cannot be that inflexible. The most popular shore power connection is 30A/125V. If you want the widest selection of marina choices, you must be able to use these for your boat's electrical needs. Buy or make (if you know what you are doing; I don't) an adapter that uses this unique pier-side shape. Second, most free village-provided tie-ups and some marinas offer 15 A/125V (what I call an electrical extension-cord-style plug). Again, if possible have an adapter to fit this to your boat's system on board your vessel. It will be used on the trip, particularly on the Erie Canal section and in Canadian waters. When you use an undersized connection, be very careful not to turn on or use many electrical systems or run them for a long time. Turn off breakers to control the demand through these temporary connections to avoid starting a fire and ruining, or at least shortening the life of, on-board equipment. As they start up, electrical motors multiply many times their electrical load draw and then run on a much smaller draw. For example, if the refrigerator is cycling on, turn everything else off, then turn back on a few selected breakers once the refrigerator is running. Carry extra lengths of shore power cord; some tie-ups need them. I have run 125 feet of shore power cord to make a slip and its available electrical sources work for me.

Fenders. For fenders I use old dirty ones or inexpensive hay bales, which I don't mind getting messed up. Marinas near the beginning of lock passages usually sell straw- or hay-filled, vinyl-coated cloth sacks that you hang outside or in place of your boat's regular fenders. Set them to touch the lock walls first. They are cheap and are intended to last only through the locks and then be thrown away. Many locks have a slimy green growth on the walls that can permanently discolor your boat or good fenders, so be forewarned. In lieu of fenders, you can use old rags, boards, or errant children—whatever will keep your nice, shiny vessel from getting dirty and scraped up.

Dock Lines. The dock lines are used to keep the boat stable while it is inside the lock chamber. In most boats (but not all) two lines are used: one at the bow and one at the stern. Each line is secured to the boat on one end, while the other end is first passed around a weighted wire cable or similar system on the lock wall and then held by a crew member.

Because of the changing water level, you cannot make the boat fast to the cable. As water is bled in or let out to change the height within the lock, the crew at bow and stern pull in or let out the hand-held ends of these lines in order to keep the boat alongside the lock wall. *Don't make the mistake of attaching your lines to the lock wall—as the water level drops, you may find yourself dangling off the side of the lock!* Note: The structure of a few locks requires that you pass your line around fixed points on the lock walls. In these rare situations you must be ready with lines the length of about two-and-a-half times the lock lift (the height that the lock water level changes).

Multiple Boat Hooks. The crew member on the bow uses a boat hook to grab the cable or pole attached to the lock wall, enabling him to feed the bowline around it. I recommend a second boat hook for the skipper, so that once the boat's bowline is in place, she can leave the helm station, walk to the stern, use the hook to pull the cable close to the boat's stern cleat, and then run the stern line around the cable nearest it—all without wishing she had long monkey arms to reach for the cable. Yes, many cruisers only have one boat hook and pass it back and forth—but for only an additional twenty dollars you can buy yourself not only a second boat hook but much more comfort and control—and the opportunity to look like a skipper should!

SKIPPER TIP: Fender Boards: The Pros and Cons
Fender boards are another option for protecting your boat when locking through. They are simply boards of rough-cut lumber, hung by lines outboard (or outside) the boat's regular series of fenders. I recently used 1¼" x 8" x 14' boards on a 32-foot boat. A 42-foot boat might use a 2" x 12" x 20' board on each side, separated from the boat's gunnel by several fenders. The boards are usually rigged from the stern cleat forward or along the flattest length of the hull. A series of short (6-foot) boards, each supported by several fenders, also can be used.

Fender boards provide the greatest protection for your vessel from dirty lock walls, but they do have some distinct disadvantages:
- Fender boards can get fouled behind fixed lock cables.

- Their attachment lines wear quickly, so if you use boards, replace the lines daily—I had one end break inside a lock, and what followed was not a pretty sight!
- They are difficult to stow on board while you cruise open waters between lock systems.
- Fender boards can interfere with the open-water operation of your boat and often get hit by the spray and waves the boat creates, especially when it is on plane.

If you can deal with these limitations, then fender boards are invaluable equipment for keeping any lock slime off your boat.

SKIPPER TIP: On a busy weekend I take a contrary approach: I rig portside-only fenders and alert the lock operator via VHF radio of my need to use that side on approach. This way I make every lock, since no one usually wants the port side, and I am not likely to be rafted up against.

Mastering the Procedure

Before approaching the lock, sailboats must have masts unstepped, taken down, and secured. All boats should have their extra fenders out and rigged. These fenders form a pad between the boat's gunnel—or anything that projects beyond the gunnel—and the lock wall. In most cases, boats line up on the right, or starboard, side of the lock—the side that more frequently needs protection. Some skippers, however, believe in rigging fenders on both sides and regularly proceed with all fenders out while locking through. There are always exceptions to rules. Lock 17 on the Erie section is best used by a portside lock-through westbound. Portside fenders are typically used only when lock-through traffic is so great that the lock operator directs some boats to raft up on the port side of one or more vessels to get everyone through simultaneously.

If it is not a busy day, place your fenders on the normal or routine side for the lock. One side is typically favored based on the way the water flows in and out of the lock. Boats on the "wrong" side of the lock might have a little more bubbly experience, generated by the way the lock water either enters or leaves the grates at the bottom of the lock. In that situation, be prepared for a slightly rougher ride, with your boat moving around more, and some extra strain on your arms if you go willingly or by lock operators' directions to the other side of a lock. However, do not vex over this—it's not a big deal. When a certain side is really important, this guide and the lock operators will tell you what to do.

As you approach the lock, look for the green light as a signal that, first of all, the lock is ready, and second, the chief lock operator or assistant (and not just a bystander) is aware of your presence and is watching your progress. Do not proceed into the lock on anything but a steady green light. The lock might be open, but the absence of the go-ahead light indicates that the operator is either not on station or not ready to accept you yet. If you do not have a go-ahead, contact the lock operator by VHF radio, channel 13, and wait for a reply. After four minutes call again if there was no

Standing by in the lower pool while a lock "dumps" its water.

response—most locks are lightly staffed and the lock operator might need some time to reach a radio. Don't bother trying the Coast Guard on channel 16 because they do not tend the locks. You also can signal the lock operator with three short blasts on the horn or via a hailer. A good loud yell also works.

While waiting for the green light on the downstream side, it is a good idea to stay well below or away from the actual lock entrance. As it empties, the lock dumps the water out of the lock and into the channel downstream—right where you are waiting. This water will swirl around, creating quite a bit of turbulence (far more than experienced inside the lock), so keep plenty of space between you and other vessels, as well as you and the shoreline. Some skippers require everyone on deck to wear personal flotation devices (PFDs) while locking through; now is the time to get them on—the St. Lawrence Seaway requires them.

New York boating laws require PFDs on all children anytime they are over water, i.e., on piers as well as boats.

On the green-light signal, it's time to go. Take a deep breath, put your boat in gear at a dead-slow maneuvering speed, and ease forward with fenders rigged and in place. At this point someone should be on the bow, ready with the forward line. One end of the stern line should be secured and the other lying loosely coiled in the cockpit. A word of caution: Don't allow these rigged and ready lines to fall overboard where they might get fouled in your props. In most Canadian waters, do not rig your boat's lines; use those that the lock operators will hand down to you.

If you prefer, you might want to notify the lock operator that this is your first time locking, and perhaps he will keep an eye out for you or give you a little extra attention. It's really not necessary, however, because what needs to be done is fairly obvious, and you have plenty of time to proceed through each step. If other boats are locking through at the same time, try to line up with some ahead and some behind you, so that you can watch what they do. A bonus to this plan is that you won't find yourself right up against the lock gate, which can be somewhat intimidating with that wall of water leaking around its edges and straining to break loose behind it! Don't worry, it never does.

Now, proceed into the typical lock, taking your natural position along the chamber wall. You will notice posts, called bollards, along the top of the lock, or cables hanging from the side. They are spaced about every 12 to 15 feet apart along the length of the lock wall so that you can pick a set appropriate for the length of your boat—take two in a row if you

The view as we enter a lock on the high side of the river—the water level will be dropped to let us out at a lower elevation. Note the green "traffic light" in front of the low building, signaling that it's OK to enter.

are in the 17- to 20-foot range, skip the one in between if you are in the 30-foot range, and skip two in between if you are 40 to 45 feet long. The arrangement of the boats is simple: The first boat in goes to the front of the lock and the first set of cables, while the last boat takes the last set of cables. Position your boat's bow so the bow person can take the line and hand feed it around the bollard or around the cable on the lock wall. After this is done, for powerboats I usually kick the engine into reverse for just a second, with the helm hard over, to pull the stern of the boat in and stop forward travel, and then immediately put it in neutral. For full-keel sailboats I drive straight in as close to the wall as I dare, since these craft (and some others) cannot easily be backed and twisted to starboard readily. While the boat is responding to that maneuver, I walk to the stern, grab the cable there, and feed the stern line around it. Once your boat is secured, shut down the engine(s), including the generator set. Cutting the engine(s) is required in

Canadian waters and is practical. A lock at low water is a closed box without a lid—in consideration of others, do not stink it up.

Alternate arrangements in locks (they vary)

Two cruisers enter the lock behind us.

The water has been lowered about a foot within the lock, in contrast to the water level in the upper pool outside these gates.

Approximately 6 minutes later, the water has been lowered about 8 feet.

include 6-inch round pipes spaced 50 to 60 feet apart; a floating pier that goes up or down inside the lock with you; three-quarter-inch dock lines with 5-pound weights at their ends, so you pull down forcibly to hold your vessel in position; and ladder rungs to catch onto with a boat hook, changing rungs as the water moves up or down.

As soon as everybody is in, the lock gates behind you close, and after a few minutes you realize that the water level is changing. The crew at the bow and stern should be adjusting the lines continuously to hold the vessel steady as the water fills in or lets out. When the water reaches the same level as the waterway in front of you, usually in 8 to 12 minutes,

After another 10 minutes we've dropped more than 30 feet. You can still see the closed lock gates through which we entered, and the normal flow of water around those gates that "leaks" through in the process. At the base of the lock gates you can now see a sill that was approximately 12 feet below river level when we entered.

the forward lock gate opens and you can proceed without fear of a surge or tidal difference. The lock operator sometimes gives a signal to alert boaters to fire up their engines, cast off, and proceed forward slowly out of the lock. *Careful, do not swing the stern in or you will brush it against the lock wall as you depart.* No signal? Just leave, but only after the gates are fully opened, again making sure that your lines are properly taken in and stowed.

That's all there is to it. Once you have conquered your first lock you can consider yourself an "old salt." On the other hand, locks typically are not in salt water, so you're not really an "old salt," are you?

AT RIGHT: As the lower lock gates open, the water level inside the lock now matches that of the lower pool, into which we'll exit.

Enjoying lunch and a swim on the Erie Canal.

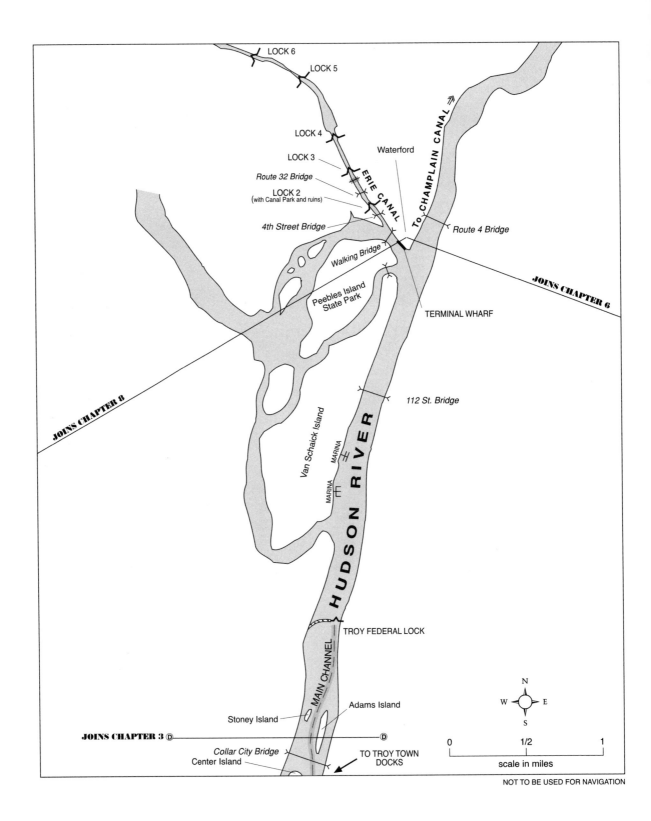

LOCK 6

LOCK 5

LOCK 4

LOCK 3

Waterford

Route 32 Bridge

ERIE CANAL

LOCK 2
(with Canal Park and ruins)

To CHAMPLAIN CANAL

4th Street Bridge

Route 4 Bridge

Walking Bridge

JOINS CHAPTER 6

Peebles Island
State Park

TERMINAL WHARF

JOINS CHAPTER 8

112 St. Bridge

Van Schaick Island

MARINA

MARINA

HUDSON RIVER

MAIN CHANNEL

TROY FEDERAL LOCK

N

W   E

S

JOINS CHAPTER 3 Ⓓ ─────────────── Ⓓ

Adams Island

Stoney Island

Collar City Bridge

Center Island

TO TROY TOWN
DOCKS

0   1/2   1

scale in miles

NOT TO BE USED FOR NAVIGATION

CHAPTER 5

Gateway to the Canals: Troy Federal Lock

SKIPPER TIP: Use NOAA chart 14786 for the Troy Federal Lock and the water course leading into the New York State canals beyond it.

Anyone who has cruised the open water knows the unique experience of the high seas. The unending expanse of the water and the mystery of the moon and stars set in the dark sky overhead command a sense of humility from even the most arrogant sailor. The canals have a different majesty. It comes from the doggedness of man rather than the omnipotence of God. It reveals itself in persistent trenches cut through rocky hill and grassy valley, and huge man-made steps, called locks, that permanently hold the sweat of men's brows. The canals are the stuff of legends. Even before the railroads, it was the canals that opened the interior of the United States to commerce and settlers. To travel these famous waterways is to follow in the wake of countless ships that represent almost two centuries of history and tradition.

Troy Federal Lock is the first in the upcoming chain of locks that takes boaters through either the Champlain Canal or the Erie Canal. Once through the Troy Lock, you can continue north on the Champlain Canal, past tiny Hudson River towns, through the glorious Adirondack and Green Mountain vistas, cruising the sixth-largest freshwater lake in North America until finally reaching Canada and the great St. Lawrence Seaway. Or you can head west along the Mohawk River via the Erie Canal,

through a panorama of central New York and the scenic Finger Lakes region, with either Lake Ontario or Lake Erie as your destination. Both routes together form a giant loop that either returns you to the Hudson or carries you on through the Great Lakes. Most travelers choose one course or the other to keep their cruise manageable in length and to avoid the very commercially trafficked Saint Lawrence Seaway.

If you select the Erie Canal route, then several days after you embark you will have three more choices to make. The most popular—my guess is by five to one—is to go west on the Erie Canal to the Oswego Canal cutoff and take it the 24 miles to Oswego on the southeast shores of Lake Ontario. From there you continue on two popular ways: the Thousand Islands (not to be missed) or the Welland Canal, which connects Lake Ontario and Lake Erie, with a stop along the way at Rochester.

Next, many boaters also choose to go past the Oswego Canal cutoff, continue on the Erie route to the fabulous Finger Lakes, and then cruise back to the Oswego cutoff. (This is outlined in chapter 12). This side trip adds two to four days onto your trip and a whole new set of lasting memories. Wine vineyards and a major founding site of post-World War II auto racing are just two of the experiences that reward a Finger Lakes cruiser.

Of course, Lake Erie also is a choice. It is easy to reach—just keep on the Erie Canal all the way west, past the Oswego and Finger Lakes cutoffs. (See chapter 14 for details on this route.) The cry "Go West Young Man!" was triggered—and a young nation expanded westward—by this route.

In selecting the Champlain Canal route, you will enjoy two days cruising on the canal, then the gorgeous, almost-120-miles-long, multifaceted Lake Champlain (where I could spend five days to a month), and an opportunity to cruise on to Montréal via additional rivers and canals in Canada. Either way, you will encounter memorable people and places and discover a new way of cruising that takes you through rocks and rapids, over dams and waterfalls, all by way of man's ingenuity.

Before leaving Troy Town Docks, purchase a lock permit, which is your pass to use the New York lock system. Permits also are available at most docks and marinas along the canal. The fees might change from one year to the next, but there are usually various designations according to the size of your boat and how many days you will be locking through. The permit is usually a numbered sheet of cardboard about the size of a license plate or a smaller decal for a season-long permit. Most people will be best satisfied with the seasonal permit. If you have bought a limited-time permit, at the first lock of each day the lock operator may or may not stamp it, but you should place the permit in sight on your windshield for going through subsequent locks. Decals are simply read and logged. Now you are on your way.

SKIPPER TIPS FOR LOCKING THROUGH:

- Be sure to read chapter 4, "Locking Through for the First Time," the night before entering Troy Federal Lock.
- Have your hay-bale fenders out, ready and rigged. Use these along with your other fenders to form a pad between your boat and the lock wall.
- Do not proceed into the lock on anything but a steady green light. This tells you that the lock is ready and that the lock operator is on station *and aware of your presence.*
- Stay well below or away from the actual lock entrance. Locks dump their water into the channel downstream, which is right where you are waiting.
- Be careful not to let your lines fall overboard and become fouled in your prop.
- Lock operators are the masters of the locks and the waterways approaching/exiting the locks. Make sure you understand their instructions and respect their authority while navigating the lock system.

SAILORS ONLY: All masts have to be unstepped (taken down) and secured before proceeding through any locks.

Heading north from Troy, about 1 mile above (north of) the Troy Town Docks, you arrive at Troy Federal Lock, likely your first locking opportunity on this cruise. Slightly bigger in size than the others, Troy Lock is one of only two in New York State that are federally operated. The other is in Buffalo, just past the far western end of the Erie Canal. In fact, the Army Corps of Engineers owns them both, and passage through them both is free. The rest of the locks are financed and maintained by the state of New York and require the permit available at area marinas. If this is your first time locking through, rest assured that the procedure is easy to do and pretty much the same through all the locks, whether they are state or federal, in New York State or Canada. With each repetition of locking through, you increase your proficiency and prepare yourself for a smoother and more efficient locking experience the next time.

As you approach the lock, make sure your extra fenders are rigged and remember that in most cases you need to protect the starboard side more than port. If you choose to forego the unique hay-bale fenders that are sold locally, specifically for locking through, be prepared. Unprotected fenders can get a grassy slime and dirt mixture on them that doesn't easily come off. By the end of your locking adventure you might wish you had just bought the hay-bale fenders in the first place.

If the lock is open, wait for the green light to go. If you don't see a green light, it might be because the lock operator hasn't yet seen you. You can let him know you are waiting by contacting him on VHF radio or signaling with your horn (three short blasts) or hailer. Then, when the light turns green, proceed at dead-slow speed into the lock, with lines rigged and bow crew member ready. There might be some floating debris, especially after a rainstorm. Remember too that any wake you create will follow you into the lock. If it is your first time and other boats are locking through with you, position yourself now so that boats are both in front of and behind you. Then you can get some pointers by watching what they do.

Commercial traffic, including tour boats, takes priority in the locks. This is the view looking south from the high-water side of the Troy Federal Lock.

Inside the lock chamber, pull up to the farthest forward and available 6-inch fixed pipe (spaced about 60 feet apart) on the lock wall. Run the bow and stern lines halfway around the pipe once, with a crewman holding the return loose end. Keep a watchful rein on those ends. If you are by yourself, perhaps just one line around the pole with both ends loose—one in each hand while pulling them toward you—might work for you. In this case, pad the extreme ends of your craft overly well with fenders to prepare for your craft's possible twists as the water rises. Once your boat is in place, kill the engine. When all the boats are in, the lock gate behind you closes.

Soon your boat starts to lift and you realize that the lock is filling up. The federal lock in Troy is a moderate 14-foot lift compared to some on the Erie Canal that are nearly three times that high (the highest on the Champlain system is 19½ feet). Still, you can feel the cold, wet walls towering above, as water drips down and the lock gate spews forth threatening reminders of the water trapped behind. Peering up at the lock operator and whatever spectators the site attracts, one tends to feel somewhat inconsequential—at least until the rising water puts one back on a par with the rest of the world. (Remember: You are the entertainment here, and a kind word to an onlooking child just might create a future boater.) As the level rises, the skipper and crewman in the bow gradually pull at the lines, keeping the boat parallel to the lock wall. Some skippers continuously push their boat off the wall to minimize wear and tear on the equipment.

After the lift of 14 feet, the forward lock gate opens quietly and without creating a ripple. Amazingly enough, the water inside is now level with the waterway in front of you. The lock operator might ask you, "Erie or Champlain?" He wants your answer so he can telephone ahead to alert the next lock operator that you are on the way so they can ready the next lock for you, if possible. At his signal, start your engine, pull in your lines, and go on your way. The first lock is behind you; you have gained a new boating skill, and your canal adventure has begun!

After successfully navigating Troy Lock, you now are ready to discover the New York State canals, just 3 miles (Erie) to 6 miles (Champlain) ahead. Two marinas are just ahead on the western shore: Van Schaick Island Marina is first, followed by Capital District Marina, 100 yards farther north. All food is off site for both these marinas. A restaurant-bakery with good, basic fresh food (except for the liver and onions) serves breakfast, lunch, and early dinner. It is a half-mile walk down a woodsy country road that is poorly lit at night. The restaurant is usually open Monday to Saturday from 6 A.M. to 9 P.M.; and Sundays from 6 A.M. to 3 P.M.

Van Schaick Island Marina is best approached from the south, where you should enjoy 10- to 13-foot water depths. Do not come straight in (abeam from the main channel), since it is shoal (around 3 feet deep). Depths are 8 to 10 feet deep near the shore. The marina property is large—8½ acres. Please note that this property is going through some changes and may or may not offer any services. Please call ahead to confirm what is available.

Van Schaick Island Marina (518) 237-2681

Storm protection: √√√
Scenic *
Marina-reported approach depths: 9-10 feet

Marina-reported dockside depths: 3-8 feet
Floating docks
Gas
Diesel-waste pump-out
Rest rooms
Showers
Laundry
Dockside water
Barbecues
Power connections: 30A/125V, 50A/125V,
    50A/220V
Ship's store
Restaurant: off site
Convenience store: off site
What's special: new boat dealer,
VHF-monitored channel: 9 and 13

One hundred yards farther north now is the other property, the Capital District Marina. To approach it, come in due west (water depths are 9 to 10 feet) or from an angle from the north (10 to 14 feet deep) off the main channel, not from the south. Capital District Marina is housed in an adapted two-car garage that has a rest room around back that is infrequently cleaned. Ask to use the other one that is off the inside ship's store/sales area. The marina is a single-finger dock of about 11 slips behind the bass- and deck-boat sales area and repair shop and represents owner Al Weber's initial commitment to seasonal and transient boaters. The end slip is about 40 feet long, but call ahead if your boat is more than 35 feet. A 70-footer can be accommodated by overhanging the bow and stern. The floating pier is well secured to the river bottom. In place are 30A and dual 30A power connections. A side comment: A member of the New York State governor's staff has docked here.

The business's hours of operation are Monday through Friday from 8:30 A.M. to 5 P.M. (but they often are still there at 8 P.M.); finding them open on Saturday or Sunday is a hit-or-miss proposition.

What's special? Inboard/outboard and outboard repairs. The owner, a former union negotiator, has a can-do attitude concerning other types of repairs and anything else you might need. He knows everybody and all other resources in the area. The marina also has a large inventory of Mercury O/B and Mercruiser I/O parts. Finally, a word about an outstanding mechanic, Frank, who is a top-notch Mercruiser I/O and Mercury O/B mechanic. He has been at it long enough to save you billable time by troubleshooting your problem, a feature that longtime boaters will appreciate. Capital District Marina usually has a journeyman apprentice mechanic as a backup for Frank. This business has both factory-replacement and unbranded parts available to save boaters additional money. Frank works on other brands, too: Chrysler, Johnson, Evinrude, Volvo, OMC, and inboards are routinely in the shop. Frank even finds the time to volunteer to drive the local ambulance. If you need repairs, you are in good hands with Frank.

The supplies/ship's store has a heavy selection of motor oil, lubes, waxes, props, and other supplies for trailer boats under 26 feet. Few snacks or soft drinks are offered.

Capital District Marina (518) 237-3442

Storm protection: √√√
Scenic: no rating
Marina-reported approach depths: 9-14 feet
Marina-reported dockside depths: 3-8 feet
Floating docks
Rest rooms
Dockside water
Power connections: 30A/125V, dual
    30A/125V

Fiberglass repairs
Welding
Below-waterline repairs
Mechanical repairs
Gas-engine repairs
Diesel repairs
Stern-drive repairs
Outboard repairs
Generator repairs
Travelift/hoist: off site
Ship's store
Restaurant: off site
Convenience store: off site
What's special: mechanic

Erie or Champlain

About 2.3 miles straight north from the lock, just on the other side of Pebbles Island, the waterway forks into two courses. A large 8-by-16-foot sign indicates this. Adjacent to this sign is a public launch ramp. A port, or westward, turn here will take you through the Mohawk River and Erie Canal, also called the

This large sign at the confluence of the Mohawk and Hudson Rivers in Waterford, New York, helps boaters easily find the way to either the Erie or Champlain Canals.

State Barge Canal, with either Lake Ontario or Lake Erie (or a Finger Lakes side trip) as your destination. About 100 yards in on the water course of the westbound Erie Canal—but before the first Erie Canal lock—is the Waterford village floating dock, the best place to tie up and access Waterford.

WATERFORD TERMINAL WALL

Inside the Erie Canal channel, the tie-up is at the first bridge, approximately 1,000 feet before the first Erie lock (Lock 2). Boaters will find full water depth right up to the floating dock. This place makes a good, free tie up if you have to wait for the lock or want a meal. There are no real boating amenities, but you will find 200 feet of floating pier (installed in early 1998) and a welcome center. The center plans to move into a permanent building in the future. It currently has canal literature, a lending library, a rest room, an information desk, and a telephone. The small community's main street is two-and-a-half blocks away. There you can dine on burgers, pizza, and Chinese food for breakfast, lunch, and early dinner. You'll also find a florist and an antique store.

This wall was a commercial wharf from approximately the 1920s to the 1970s. This stop will constantly be improving in the upcoming seasons. A drinking-water supply, electrical connections, and multiple shower rooms are in the works, set for completion in the next two years. I have always enjoyed bringing a towel and lying on the grass here to catch some rays—I still do.

On to the Champlain Canal

Now heading up toward the Champlain Canal, a quarter-mile north of the turnoff for the Erie Canal, the river passes under the fixed 126th Street Bridge (22 feet of clearance) that functions as the Route 4 automobile crossover from Troy to Waterford. Just south of the bridge, outside the channel on the east shore, is the Price Chopper supermarket dock with float. Watch the water depth around this dock (6 feet or less). As with all docks in the system, it is rumored each winter that if boaters do not use the dock, patronize the Price Chop-per supermarket, and let the manager know they did, the dock might not be open next season. The CEO of the chain is a boater, as other employees are, but business decisions are what run the docks.

If you're headed toward the Champlain Canal, just keep going north another 2¾ miles to reach Lock 1 of the system. Canals, villages, history, and quaint marinas are all there for you. The lake itself is nearby, too: a 3- to 10-day cruising ground of majestic scenery and special boating experiences.

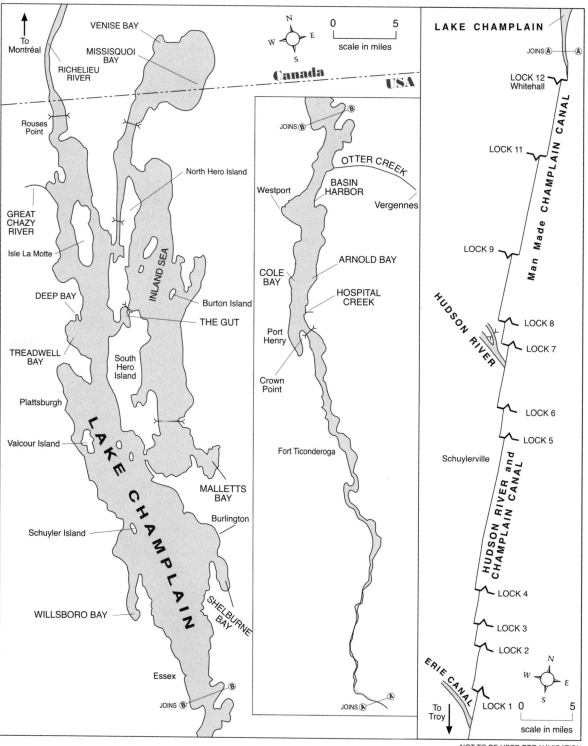

LAKE CHAMPLAIN

To Montréal

VENISE BAY

MISSISQUOI BAY

RICHELIEU RIVER

Canada

USA

N
W · E
S

0 · 5
scale in miles

Rouses Point

GREAT CHAZY RIVER

Isle La Motte

DEEP BAY

TREADWELL BAY

Plattsburgh

Valcour Island

Schuyler Island

WILLSBORO BAY

North Hero Island

INLAND SEA

Burton Island

THE GUT

South Hero Island

LAKE CHAMPLAIN

MALLETTS BAY

Burlington

SHELBURNE BAY

Essex

JOINS Ⓑ

JOINS Ⓑ

Westport

Cole Bay

Port Henry

Crown Point

BASIN HARBOR

OTTER CREEK

Vergennes

ARNOLD BAY

HOSPITAL CREEK

Fort Ticonderoga

JOINS Ⓐ

Ⓐ

LAKE CHAMPLAIN

JOINS Ⓐ — Ⓐ

LOCK 12 Whitehall

LOCK 11

Man Made CHAMPLAIN CANAL

LOCK 9

HUDSON RIVER

LOCK 8

LOCK 7

LOCK 6

LOCK 5

Schuylerville

HUDSON RIVER and CHAMPLAIN CANAL

LOCK 4

LOCK 3

LOCK 2

ERIE CANAL

LOCK 1

To Troy

N
W · E
S

0 · 5
scale in miles

NOT TO BE USED FOR NAVIGATION

CHAPTER 6

The Champlain Canal and Lake Champlain

The Champlain Route

Time or Distance from Troy Federal Lock
(All distances are +/- 3 statute miles)

Champlain Canal	Vergennes: 122 miles
Schuylerville (midpoint): 5 to 7 hours	Shelburne Bay: 130 miles (popular)
Whitehall (the northern end of canal 63 miles): 10 to 15 hours	Willsboro Bay: 133 miles
	Burlington: 134 miles (popular)
Lake Champlain	Valcour Island: 145 miles
Fort Ticonderoga: 85 miles	Deep Bay: 155 miles
Cole Bay Anchorage: 110 miles	Rouses Point: 170 miles (popular)
Westport: 112 miles	Canadian/U.S. border: 171 miles
Maritime Museum: 113 miles (very limited day slips and moorings)	Route to Montréal
	Sorel: 250 miles
Essex: 120 miles (very popular)	Montréal: 305 miles

SKIPPER TIP: Use NOAA chart 14786 for the Champlain Canal section and NOAA charts 14781, 14782, 14783, and 14784 for Lake Champlain.

Along the Champlain Canal route you'll be captivated by the varying and often majestic landscape as you cruise the waters first traveled by the American Indians in their canoes. On your canal and lake adventure you can almost hear the echoes of several hundred years of American history, including battles in the French and Indian War, the American Revolution, and the War of 1812. Today the shores along the Lake Champlain route are a summer playground for tourists looking for an escape from the city and a foliage festival for the legions of leaf-peepers who flock to this area in the fall.

Although the lower part of the Champlain route is not known for spectacular scenery, it has an appeal all its own. The landscape is dotted with small river towns whose glory days of paper and textile mills are long past. Some towns can provide needed provisions and rest stops, and many offer landmarks of historical significance. You'll also find that the canal itself is a source of constant fascination. From meandering river to rigidly defined trench, the approach changes dramatically from one lock to the next. Most of the locks are cut into the landscape so as not to disturb the natural flow

Twenty minutes after a summer sunrise, the majestic silhouettes along Lake Champlain's shores come into view.

of the river, and you can watch the rapids issuing forth through twists and turns. Several islands have formed where natural waterfalls were circumvented by the locks. These often are popular walking or picnic spots for local residents and small boaters. The locks themselves are never boring and each passage is a little different, requiring fairly constant attention. I find beauty in the opportunity to use newly acquired knowledge and skills with each locking experience.

The upper part of the system is a different story. Nestled between the Adirondacks to the west and the Green Mountains to the east, the Champlain gives cruisers plenty of opportunities to marvel at nature's artistry. You can imagine yourself in a canal boat, pulled by mules on a towpath here. Western civilization peeks through only occasionally. Finally, the canal opens to reveal the magnificence of Lake Champlain, where boaters can easily spend a week exploring its secluded bays, historic landmarks, and elegant resorts.

To get to Lock 1 of the Champlain Canal, you want to head straight north to continue on the main waterway, the Hudson River. The first lock is 3 miles (or 20 minutes) from the 6-by-16-foot sign that indicates a fork in the river.

Cruising

Why do it? Is the goal to be able to brag to your buddies back home how far you went in how short of a vacation time? Or is it to store away memories and have experiences that last? If you are a delivery skipper, then yes you do want to get the boat "there" and get back for the next job. If you're retired, then you already know it is not how long you live but *how* you live each day that is important. Do not rush a cruise.

I have gone out of my way to highlight the best attractions and amenities on these waters. This approach is sure to at least disappoint those good entrepreneurs in the marina industry who are not featured as heavily. But you bought this guide, from whose sale I get a royalty, so I'm serving you. My advice is that you reduce the distance you plan to cruise so you can enjoy it more. The perceptions, enjoyment, and insights gained by spending a day and two evenings at a location can be a hundred times greater than if you tie up at 7 P.M., eat dinner and cast off at 8:30 A.M. the next day for the next marina. Slow down and savor this!

Champlain Canal

The Champlain Canal opened in 1822—although some history books mark it as the spring of 1823—nearly three years before completion of the Erie Canal. The combination of river and man-made channel took five years to construct. The first boat through the newly constructed Champlain Canal was a southbound cargo-carrying workboat. Freight and trade were the reasons for the creation of the Champlain Canal, whose construction was authorized on April 15, 1817. (While the estimated cost of building the canal was $871,000, the total cost came to just under $1.8 million.) The addition of Canada's Chambly Canal in 1843 completed a thruway of water from the Atlantic Ocean at New York City to the St. Lawrence River—right through

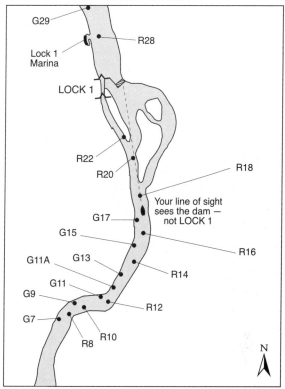

LOCK 1 — CHAMPLAIN CANAL

NOT TO BE USED FOR NAVIGATION

New York State. Before the Civil War era, which brought the railroads, water was the way one traveled. As late as 1803 there was not a road connecting upstate New York to New York City—just a horse path. The canal completion brought money, commerce, people, and towns, and developed the vast areas between New York City, Albany, and Montréal.

The Champlain Canal advertises a low overhead clearance of about 15 feet and a water depth of around 12 feet, still subject once in a while to high water, spot shoaling, and submerged hazards just like other waterways. There are 11 lock steps from Waterford to Lake Champlain, though the last is numbered 12.

That's because a change in the original plan eliminated Lock 10 and the rest were never renamed. The largest canal lift is 19½ feet at Lock 3, and the longest run is between Locks 4 and 5. The distance of that stretch is just over 14 miles—about a 90-minute ride at the 10-mph canal speed limit.

On to Lock 1

The water is deep (14 to 20-plus feet) between the channel markers in this stretch before the first lock. North of the 126th Street Bridge, the natural river outside the channel turns shallow, sometimes as little as 2 feet. Stay in the channel.

There is not an ocean tide above Troy Federal Lock, but the auxiliary uses of the river and the canal can always change water depths as much as 18 inches off standard. Spring runoff, recent heavy rains, freshwater needs of municipalities downriver, and the cooling and power needs of commercial plants can raise the water. Commercial plant operations, upriver reservoir replenishment, and high-clearance transit vessels can lower the water. The Champlain Canal personnel can selectively lower the water levels to accommodate boats; however, they usually do so only for commercial vessels. Call well ahead to arrange this, though. Inquire at (518) 747-4613. You might hear stories of 5 feet or more of flooding waters, but these extremes occur in the off-season before the system opens for boaters, although it has happened about once in the past 10 years in June because of continuous rain.

Just around the bend is the seasonal dockage of Riverbend Marina. It seldom has tie-ups available for transients, but the setting is bucolic.

Riverbend Marina (518) 695-6126

Storm protection: √√
Scenic: * *
Marina-reported approach depths: 12 feet
Marina-reported dockside depths: 6-10 feet
Floating docks
Waste pump-out
Rest rooms
Dockside water
Power connections: 30A/125V
What's special: few transients

Up ahead, the channel veers to the left fork just below Lock 1. There is selective 6- to 10-foot water depth outside the channel in the two eastern small coves before the overhead power cables there. A swim or lunch stop, perhaps? These water depths drop off to 1 to 2 feet farther up the bays.

As you approach, you will see the water wall of the falls that is east of the lock before the actual lock (which is more west) comes into view. That's the General Electric plant's pump house on the west bank.

Lock 1—14-foot lift. (518) 237-8566. VHF channel 13. Supervisor of the entire Champlain Canal (Locks 1 to 12): (518) 747-4613. Now roughly 5½ miles north of Troy Lock, you are at Champlain Lock 1. Lock 2 is 4 miles ahead. Lock 1 offers poles and weighted lines for boaters to use to control their craft while locking through. The Troy Federal Lock operator will have tried to telephone ahead to this lock's operator to tell them that you are on your way. If possible, all lock operators try to be ready for your arrival with lock gates open and waiting for your passage.

Note: If you ever are not going on to the next lock—whether because of a lunch, refuel, or an overnight stop—it is a courtesy to let the last lock operator know. He will alert the next lock operator. If you are ever sitting inside a lock waiting with an open back door (entrance gate), you'll know why this is necessary.

As you approach the lock, you should pleasantly alert the lock operator on your VHF channel 13: "Lock operator, Champlain Canal Lock 1, this is the motor (sail) vessel, Blue Sea, a 28-foot craft with blue (red, green, white) canvas" or some other distinguishing feature (black hull, blue cushions, fly bridge) that someone looking down from the lock on your vessel can use to tell your craft apart from the other boats nearby. Do not be too nautical. Many of the lock operators are not boaters and might not know a yawl from a ketch from a sloop. And keep it short. Finish with "requests a lock through northbound," because traffic on the Champlain is headed either north or south.

Wait four minutes and repeat if unanswered. The lock operator might not be able to respond sooner. Proceed on a green light only. Once inside the lock, the lock operator will come alongside to record your canal pass number. Please note that the method the lock uses to hold your vessel within the lock as the water level changes will vary from lock to lock.

This lock marks the northernmost point where Henry Hudson sailed his ship, the *Half Moon,* when exploring the Hudson River in 1609. It also marks the beginning of a waterway that takes you all the way up to and through Canada, coming out at the St. Lawrence Seaway some 55 miles seaward of Montréal. The route includes the navigable portion of the Hudson River north of Troy, the Champlain Canal and its locks, Lake Champlain, the Richelieu River, the Chambly Canal

Sail- and powerboaters share a lock in the Champlain Canal. The sailboat has its mast unstepped to clear bridges.

and its locks, more river, the Saint-Ours Lock, and finishes with the Canadian town of Sorel. Then the St. Lawrence River leads your cruiser into Montréal. The distance from Troy, New York, to Montréal is just about 305 miles. Now that you are experienced at locking through, you should have no problem here putting your new skills to use again.

The channel past Lock 1 is well marked, and I recommend that you stay in the channel, because the Hudson River has some shallow areas along here. Do not even cut the channel markers close. The channel typically runs about 12 feet deep, while the natural river is often only 2 to 4 feet deep outside the channel. Lock 1 Marina is on the river's western edge.

Lock 1 Marina approach instructions are easy because it is on the main channel and all angles of approach are about the same water depth. I suggest a northwestern course turning left when abeam the small white gazebo shoreside, since the entrance is 100 feet north of it. The river can have a southern current when the water is high. Therefore, aim high since the entrance is on the north end of the basin. Black poles in the water define the width of the basin's entrance channel. Water depth is 6 feet near shore and 3 to 5 feet inside the basin at dockside, while on the main channel the 60-foot outside float offers more water depth.

The marina has about 40 slips (with six to nine for transients), all floating docks, with some padding dockside. It offers 15A and 30A electrical connections, and only one slip can reasonably accommodate dual 30A shore power connections. The haul-out equipment is used primarily for winter-storage customers. This marina is home to mostly 28-foot boats, with too little water depth for fixed-keel sail

craft, although they may be accommodated on the side-tie float outside the basin on the main river. Locals pick Lock 1 Marina because of its enclosed basin that protects the southern half of the slips from river traffic. It is peaceful, with calm water, and the quirky improvements are a delight. The marina has one unisex rustic shower/rest room in the ground floor of the main office/upstairs residence. One washer, one dryer, a counter for folding clothes, and detergent are available.

The marina is open 9 A.M. to 5 P.M., but its owner, Kevin Lengyel, lives on site with his family. His bookkeeper/daughter also fills in when the owner—a commercial diver—has a job with his other company (Salvage). A miscellaneous selection of supplies and ship's store items can be found in the bookkeeper's office.

What's special about it? A breakfast/lunch snack bar is inside the hull and cockpit of a land-based 1953 wooden Chris Craft cruiser. The charcoal grills with tree-shaded picnic tables on a grassy peninsula festooned with decorative details make for a particularly restful self-cooked repast. Visit the grotto waterfall created by the previous owner, and walk next door to see a whimsical interpretation of a tugboat.

Probably because Lengyel is a commercial diver and an ex-farmer, a practical approach to vessel repairs is used here. The marina also can pull boats out using a yard trailer and tractor. Local marine mechanics can be called in from the immediate Capital District (population of 250,000) area.

Note: The on-site snack bar (inside the cabin cruiser) is leased out each season. It might not be open.

Finally, a small town, Waterford, is 4 miles

Along the western shore of the Champlain Canal (just above Lock 1), you'll find Lock 1 Marina. Check out its unique landscaping, complete with miniature boats, cannons, and treasure chests!

south. A large city, Albany, is within 10 miles. A nearby off-site restaurant might be open for banquets only.

Lock 1 Marina (518) 238-1321

Storm protection: √√√
Scenic: * * * *
Marina-reported approach depths: 6-12 feet
Marina-reported dockside depths: 3-5 feet
Rest rooms
Showers
Laundry
Dockside water
Barbecues
Picnic tables
Power connections: 15A/125V, 30A/125V

Yard trailer/tow vehicle
What's special: off-channel basin; bucolic, interesting grounds

Lock 2 is about 3 miles just ahead. The road you see to your port side or on the western shore is Routes 4 and 32 and more or less follows along this stretch of the canal. The right shore has a stand of trees that hides the cornfields farther east. By the way, the riverbed in this area is made up of a sand bottom with some mud, with rocks and boulders strewn about. During a recent winter when the water level was dropped to facilitate lock repairs, the riverbed was exposed. There were rocks ranging in size from 20-pounders to 1,000-pound boulders some four feet across.

The approach to Lock 2 has two factors that can affect your boat. First, to the west of the lock is a hydroelectricity plant. When operating, it tends to increase currents and push your craft toward the eastern shore. Second, the river dam to the east of the lock, when flowing with high water, will tend to push your craft westward. Both of these are easy to spot when they are running; just be on the lookout for them.

Lock 2—18½-foot lift. (518) 664-4961. Lock 3 is 15 minutes ahead after clearing Lock 2. Lock 2 was totally renovated in 1996. This type of lock is what the state of New York will build as it replaces worn locks. Lock 2 has the new system of 1-inch cables about 27 feet apart, secured top and bottom, where it is best to take a half-turn around a cable fore and aft with the bow and stern lines and to have the crew hold the loose ends, adjusting as the water level changes upwards. By the way, the lock operator has a perfectly detailed 1200cc motorcycle that is usually parked on warm, sunny days so the kickstand rests on the concrete pad at the northeast corner of the lock chamber. Pull in to the front spot inside the chamber for the best view of it. From Lock 2 it is another 2½ miles of winding channel to Lock 3, which sits just past the town of Mechanicville.

The next 2 miles take the channel from the western side of the river above Lock 2 to the east shore and then back to the west shore at Mechanicville. It moves east again at Lock 3. The channel, like all sections of the canal, is well marked. Do not leave it, because there are no good water depths for cruising outside it, even in the small shoreline notches. Local boats are required to fish outside the channel and have explored their own "deep-enough water" spots. Remember, however, that all aids to navigation must be removed and replaced each season due to winter ice. Do not approach them too closely just in case they are a little off station. Also, be cautious at the northern end of the island in this section because rocks are adjacent to the western edge of the channel.

Mechanicville

Mechanicville, with a population of 5,200, is the second-smallest city in New York State (it is incorporated as a city, not a town). It grew from the small industries that used the power of the Tenandaho Creek. This tributary to the Hudson fueled the country's first wooden-match factory along with shirt factories and paper mills. It has a public wall, or terminal, where you can tie up. The channel swings right in front of it. Charts of the canal waterways frequently label wharves "terminals" because these canals were created to accommodate commercial traffic, and the terminals were where loading and unloading of freight, as well as passengers, took place. Pleasure boats are always welcome to use these facilities unless otherwise posted, although they might be too rough to use and lack essential services that put the "pleasure" in pleasure boating. Mechanicville has remodeled its terminal to a limited degree to attract pleasure boaters. Water and electricity were available on my last stop here, and more amenities might be added. Immediately behind the dockage is the police station, and they keep a good eye out for the boaters in the summer.

> **SKIPPER TIP:** The Mechanicville Terminal Wharf is shallow at its south end. Stay at least 100 feet off the wall until you are north of the bottom (southern) third of the cement wall.

Mechanicville Terminal Wharf

This is a 300-foot-long cement wharf that has been improved for pleasure boaters. It has 15A electricity (like a household 3-pronged extension-cord plug). It also has some fresh water available. Water is shallow at the south end. It has 2- to 8-foot water depths.

Some of the downtown stores are very convenient, the large supermarkets less so. A breakfast and lunch deli is within blocks. Price Chopper, Grand Union, and a McDonald's are quite a bit farther to the north and west. When wharfside, look for fish at the south (shallow) end of the terminal where the creek feeds into the Hudson.

Lock 3—19½-foot lift. (518) 664-5171. Lock 4 is 12 minutes ahead. Lock 3 is just ahead on the eastern shore, about a half-mile north of town. It is the highest of the 11 locks in this Champlain section of your cruise. Howland Avenue Bridge, north of the terminal, shows a 24-foot clearance. After the bridge, head directly toward Lock 3 to stay in the channel. Be cautious as you approach the lock, because high water creates a current that first pushes you to port and then to starboard as you cruise up to it from the south. New York State Electric and Gas Co. is on the western shore.

After exiting the lock about six-tenths of a mile north of Lock 3, watch out for the overhead clearance at the railroad bridge. It might not be as much as what is shown on your chart (21 feet). It is good practice to always ask at the locks, if practical, for current local information about water levels, shallow water, and special hazards ahead. Be proactive in your questioning; be specific about your interests and concerns and your boat's special navigation needs.

Lock 4—16-foot lift. (518) 664-5261. It is not quite 2 miles from Lock 3 to Lock 4, where an additional length of channel was put in through the adjoining landscape around 1917. It is an hour and a half to Lock 5. From 1917 to 1919, much of the Champlain system was rebuilt and resized to accommodate larger-sized traffic. The Lock 4 channel allows the canal to bypass a series of dams and rapids on the Hudson River, leaving the natural waterway intact and creating a rather long entrance/exit from the lock. There is also a pleasant little park where local people and boaters picnic and watch other boats go through. Tie up north of the lock if you want to stop. It is always best to let the lock master know that you are tying up and how long you will be. The park was installed by the New York State Canal Corporation for everyone's enjoyment—just another nice touch that makes these cruising grounds so special. The bridge north of the lock has a 28-foot clearance.

Just north of the lock is the historic town of Stillwater, where three different forts were built in the 1800s. Stillwater also was the headquarters for Philip Schuyler, an American general in the Revolution. He led his command from a house that still stands there. Called the Dirk Swart home, it is currently a private residence, so please respect the owners' privacy. The name Stillwater comes from the Indians who populated this area for 3,000 years before Europeans came to the New World. The Algonquian-speaking Indian people came into New York State before 1000 A.D. The Indian nation

Near Stillwater the channel leaves the Hudson River for about a three-quarter-mile-long man-made cut. This sign clearly points the way for southbound travelers so they'll avoid the falls.

in this area was the Mohican. They occupied the area from Lake Champlain south to the Catskill Creek halfway down the Hudson River. Around the time of Columbus, the increasing presence of the Iroquois nations of Mohawks, Cuyugas, and others forced Deganawidah and Hiawatha (yes, that Hiawatha from Longfellow's poem "The Song of Hiawatha") to spread the word that some kind of a truce was needed among the Indians. This suggestion evolved into the League of the Five Nations. By 1609, when Henry Hudson discovered the Hudson, the Indians had a smooth working relationship among themselves in place for more than five generations. This con-

federacy of Indians worked so well as a method of governing that Benjamin Franklin wanted to model the American colonies' union after the Indians' agreement. Early in the settlement of the New World, a human-powered ferry ran across the Hudson at Stillwater, following the Indians' similar habit of using this area as the easiest river crossover within several miles. Because of the ferry and General Schuyler's headquarters, troop movements during the Revolutionary War were extensive. Stillwater is best accessed at Admiral's Marina immediately north of Lock 4.

On approach to Admiral's Marina, check water depth (usually 2 to 3 feet) both on your approach and at your slip. This marina is geared to smaller boats due to the water depth. The owners are Charles and Joann Dyer. Many boaters come by trailer and launch here. The marina has limited 15A shore power, night lighting, drinkable water, barbecues, and picnic tables. It also is a campground for travel trailers. The rest rooms are small and include showers that are cleaned and checked daily.

Admiral's Marina is open late, from 8 A.M. to 12 P.M., due to the bar it operates. Boaters can get supplies here more along the line of a corner convenience store with liquor than a ship's store. Repairs must be called in from outside.

A launderette is nearby (about a quarter-mile off site).

Admiral's Marina (518) 664-9039

Storm protection: √√
Scenic: *
Marina-reported approach depths: 2-3 feet
Marina-reported dockside depths: 2-3 feet
Gas
Rest rooms
Showers

Dockside water
Barbecues
Picnic tables
Power connections: limited 15A
Convenience store: on site
**What's special: great bar with a covered
    patio and a hot-dog-stand-style eating
    area**

SKIPPER TIP: Make sure that your average speed from one lock to the next does not exceed 10 mph or the lock operator may fine you or delay your passage.

The distance between Lock 4 and Lock 5 is the longest single level stretch on the Champlain Canal and a good opportunity to change your clothes, make a sandwich, or take a rest, letting a relief skipper take the helm.

Open Anchorage

Because this is not a "special anchorage area" delineated by the U.S. Army Corps of Engineers, you must show a white anchor light. Do not under any circumstances let your craft be in or swing into the channel. Commercial vessels can run later than you and must use the full channel width to maneuver. This "no obstruction to channel traffic 24 hours a day" is taken seriously throughout the system. Commercial traffic, although very light today, is a 150-year tradition. We pleasure boaters are the new kids on the block. We must respect each others' needs. New York State needs the revenue, too.

It is located between Locks 4 and 5 south and east of red marker #92 and has

---

10-foot-plus water depth. The adjunct high ground was used by soldiers during the Revolutionary War. The far western shore is a part of Saratoga National Historic Park.

The cruise of just over 14 miles to Lock 5 should take you a little less than an hour and a half at the canal's 10-mph speed limit. Let me explain about the speed limit and how it is enforced on the canals. The lock operators keep timed records of who is locking through, and they talk to one another by land telephone. This diligence often results in a lock ready or nearly ready for you when you arrive. For example, the operator at Lock 4 calls the operator at Lock 5 and lets him know what time you left, so that he can easily calculate what time you should arrive. If you get there too quickly, the lock operator will know that you are disobeying the 10-mph speed limit and speeding through the canal. If he catches you, a lock operator has the right to either fine you—which they almost never do unless you're a smart aleck—or delay your passage by refusing to open the lock to you. He can delay you up to 21 hours according to the laws under which the canal operates. The lock operator will usually make you wait a half-hour or so and then give you a good talking to. On the other hand, the speed limit is not strictly enforced between the locks unless you are bothering someone else by what you are doing. You might notice that local boats that do not use the locks—and therefore are not subject to scrutiny by the lock operators—often pull water-skiers or otherwise speed on the river. This is good news for people who think their boat is inefficient at 10 mph. They might decide to run at top efficiency and then slow down, or stop and wait, just out of sight of the next lock. Other boaters prefer to go slower than 10 mph when they are in front of a marina or a private dock, making up that lost speed by going faster when their boat's wake is not likely to cause any harm to other boats, docks, or the shoreline. Please understand, I am not necessarily recommending any course of action, except dead slow around fuel docks; I am just passing along my observations.

"Low bridge!" was a popular refrain on the canal. Bridges were built across the canal when it was first built by the canal contractors to let farmers access fields bisected by the canal. The bridges were built as low as possible due to price considerations, and canal boats were built as high as the bridges would allow clearance for to maximize profits, so people sitting on the top of canal boats had to duck in order to clear the bridges. It was the job of the helmsman or steersman to shout out, "Low bridge!"

Since canal boats carrying both freight and passengers traveled at 2½ mph, towed by horses walking on shore, passengers bored with canal travel would often step off at a lock, go for a walk to the next bridge, and jump back aboard the boat.

The queen ship of the canal system, the packet boat, would speed along day and night pulled by the best horses, which were changed often. Packets were capable of going as fast as 7 mph, exceeding the then 4-mph

A skipper solo-handling his single-screw, full-keel, 1913-vintage craft found himself sideways in this lock as the water was released. He traversed another 10 locks, however, without incident.

THE CHAMPLAIN CANAL AND LAKE CHAMPLAIN 159

speed limit, for which they were obligated to pay a fine of $10, which amounted to a 5 percent to 7 percent surcharge over their freight fees. It wouldn't be unusual for a packet captain to jump ashore at a toll office, throw down his $10, jump back aboard his boat, and keep on going.

Coveville Marina is a small marina coming up that is accessed via an improved channel in a natural waterway. I "chickened out" in starting up this channel the first time I tried it. However, the next year, after a visit by automobile and getting assurances from the marina staff, I successfully went up the shallow, very narrow channel. That time the vessel I skippered drew 3½ feet and had no problem, and the depth sounder indicated mostly 5-foot depths, some 4 foot deep areas, and a couple of areas 12 feet deep. Still, passage is very narrow. On a bright day with the sun overhead at midday, you can see the bottom just inches deep immediately outside the channel.

Coveville Marina is deep off the Hudson River (three-fourths of a mile, a 15-minute cruise) at the end of the side channel that is on the west shore at red channel marker #118. They usually have a billboard sign that alerts you to the channel entrance. The approach is shallow in places, starting at 5 feet, going to 4 feet well before the docks are in view. The docks have 4- to 8-foot-deep water, with water lilies everywhere, and are surrounded by a wooded water's edge that is very bucolic.

Dennis and Linda Nadeau own this small but well-protected 30-slip marina for mostly outboard-powered runabouts. It offers electricity, ice, bar (with limited food offerings), gas, and water. Rest rooms are inside the bar

labeled "inboards" and "outboards." Although there are no showers, a new bathhouse is in the planning stages.

The hours of operation for Coveville Marina are posted as 11:30 A.M. "til" because of the on-site bar. This bar/patio, which overlooks the marina, offers a whole pig roast the second weekend in August and live music some Fridays and Saturdays.

Coveville Marina (518) 695-6079

Storm protection: √√√
Scenic: * *
Marina-reported approach depths: 4-5 feet
Marina-reported dockside depths: 4-8 feet
Floating docks
Gas
Rest rooms
Power connections: 15A/125V
Restaurant: on-site bar has some food offerings
What's special: very narrow approach channel

Schuylerville and Saratoga Springs

A quarter-mile south of the Route 29 Bridge, and just over a mile below Lock 5, lies the diverted waterway that holds Schuylerville Yacht Basin. The turn on the chart book is easy to miss because it falls right at the edge of the page. Here the main channel makes a gradual turn to the right, while a slight turn to port takes you straight into the private channel for the Yacht Basin. At this point, depending on traffic and delays, you have been cruising for 5 to 7 hours since leaving the Troy Docks, and you might want to consider stopping here for an overnight stay or longer. The channel for the marina is protected from passing river traffic by an island and provides quiet, wake-free dockage.

SCHUYLERVILLE

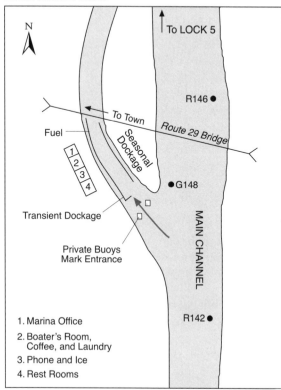

1. Marina Office
2. Boater's Room, Coffee, and Laundry
3. Phone and Ice
4. Rest Rooms

NOT TO BE USED FOR NAVIGATION

Schuylerville Yacht Basin is right in town, no more than two blocks from restaurants and other conveniences. Plug into their cable TV to pick up the Weather Channel. Remember, Albany is south and Glens Falls is just north, both of which are shown on the Weather Channel reports for this area. There is even an upstairs bowling alley in town if you are inclined to play a few strings before retiring to your berth for the evening. Submarine sandwiches, pizza, and fried seafood dinners can be delivered to the marina if you are tired. Saratoga Monument and Gen. Philip Schuyler's house are near. By the way, Indians burned General Schuyler's first house here in 1745,

the British Army burned the second one in 1777, and the replacement is what stands today. Schuylerville was originally named Old Saratoga when it was settled in 1690 and got its present name in 1831. The village has considered changing the name back to promote its historic past as a lure for tourism. However, in March 1997, voters in Schuylerville rejected the name change by a two-to-one margin.

This spot is the best stop for an extended look at the old, earlier version of the canal. Schuylerville also provides boaters with the closest access to Saratoga Springs, a summer playground for the rich and famous. During peak summer months, a number of reserved rental cars just sit there waiting for visitors needing transportation from their boats to Saratoga. Reserve yours by calling the marina well in advance.

Initially famous for its mineral baths, Saratoga became the resort of choice during the 1920s for everyone from movie stars to gangsters. Today it still boasts the northeast's premier thoroughbred racing at the Saratoga Racetrack, drawing followers from all over the world during its July-August season. In addition, this area features the Saratoga Performing Arts Center (SPAC), which presents the Metropolitan Opera in June, the New York City Ballet in July, the Philadelphia Orchestra in August, and a broad variety of rock, jazz, and pop artists throughout the summer. The city also is home to the Saratoga Raceway Harness Track, gourmet restaurants, chi-chi watering holes, antiques and collectibles stores, and unique boutique shops. Victorian mansions and tree-lined streets evoke an earlier era, while Skidmore College keeps the city thinking young.

From the beginning, the Saratoga Racetrack

offered the utmost in elegant surroundings, with covered viewing from the clubhouse, formal waiters serving champagne and shrimp, brightly colored red and white awnings, flowers in abundance, and flags and pennants flying daily. Construction began on the track in 1863 and was completed in 1864, under the shadow of the Civil War. Despite concerns about using horses for pleasure rather than as resources for the Union Army, the track opened for the August 1864 season, and racing at Saratoga has been an annual tradition ever since. The season currently runs from the last week of July through Labor Day. The track is open six days a week, Wednesday through Monday, with Tuesday dark. Attendance runs from 20,000 to 45,000 daily, with a handle of some $20 million a day. Routine clubhouse attire is suits and hats—definitely a no-jeans, no-shorts policy, and seats are usually sold out. Clubhouse boxes are nearly impossible to get because they stay in families for generations. However, I am told that if you approach a ticket agent, temporary sublets occasionally are available; if you score a coveted box, track etiquette calls for tipping the agent to express your gratitude. Others skip the clubhouse level, come in casual clothes, and still enjoy the racing and the atmosphere in the grandstand area, where neat and clean boaters' attire fits right in. Stakes and steeplechase racing are standard on the track schedule. Each year a canoe in the infield is painted in the stable colors of the most recent winner of the Travers, America's oldest stakes race. If you go to Saratoga—and I highly recommend it—do not miss "Breakfast at the Track," an opportunity during race season to enjoy a delicious meal while watching the horses go through their morning workout.

The nearby Saratoga Raceway Harness Track is open from mid-April through mid-November and provides an atmosphere of fun and excitement nightly. It is a half-mile track, whereas the thoroughbred track is 1⅛ miles. This track also opened under the threat of pre-war hysteria, in 1941, just six months before the bombing of Pearl Harbor.

Long before the Europeans inhabited New York, the Mohawk Indians used Saratoga's spa waters for their curative powers. At the north end of town is the High Rock Spring, which the natives introduced to the British in 1771. More than a half-dozen springs are in and around downtown Saratoga, including one at the racetrack that was named Big Red after the famous racehorse Man-O'-War. Bottled versions of the local drinking water are available in grocery stores and restaurants, and three bath facilities offer a full range of therapeutic and cosmetic services. You can get everything from a simple mineral bath for about $10 to a full day of luxurious pampering that will redefine cruising to any reluctant crew members. I suggest the truly decadent experience at the Crystal Spa, on Broadway, which offers mineral baths, massages, facials, aromatherapy, steams, body wraps, and saunas. Hair- and nail-salon services also are available.

The southern edge of town is flanked by a 2,200-acre wooded park that contains the Saratoga Performing Arts Center (SPAC), as well as a world-class golf course, various spas and pools, and the Gideon Putnam, a historic hotel that offers fine dining and a superb Sunday brunch. You also can visit the Racing Museum, where I discovered that the "old gray mare" of the children's nursery song, who "ain't what she used to be," raced at Saratoga during the Civil War era.

The "too hot to get" dinner reservation during the racing season in Saratoga is for Siro's (518-584-4030). Located across the road from the track but only open during the racing season, the place is very expensive and dressy. Console yourself with another dinner experience and feel good again with a stop at Ben and Jerry's Ice Cream (518-584-3740), which sells the original premium dessert made famous by its founders in Vermont. Ben and Jerry, by the way, were the inspiration for two of the dude-ranch guests in the Billy Crystal movie *City Slickers*.

For more information about Saratoga, check out the visitors center on Broadway, the main street of downtown. Also, do not miss the Victorian-era lobby of the Adelphi Hotel (1877) at 365 Broadway (518-587-4688). Then consider visiting the National Museum of Dance; the Canfield Casino, which now houses an historical museum; and the 2,800-acre Saratoga battlefield just south of town, where the Americans turned the Revolutionary War in their favor in two battles fought there in 1777.

Several boaters use their craft as a home away from home during the Saratoga racing season, staying for a day, a week, or the entire season that the track is open. Be forewarned, however, because your boat *will* be your hotel if you visit during high season. Every bed in the area is booked a year or more in advance.

Marina Information

It is an easy, well-marked approach to the Schuyler Yacht Basin, which is on its own side

Schuyler Yacht Basin is nestled in quiet water off the main channel below Lock 5. Transient boat docks are in the foreground; seasonal boaters use slips on the opposite shore.

channel west of and just south of the state Highway 29 Bridge and north of the overhead cable. Two buoys clearly delineate the width of the entrance channel and keep you well clear of any dangers. Cruisers here enjoy 10-foot water depth both on approach and for most of dockside (except right next to shore at some docks).

The marina's fuel dock is a safe place for boaters to get clean fuel. Both gas and diesel from newer dispensers are on site, with fuel replenished every three weeks, at most, in season. The pump-out is located here, and the rest rooms are very close, as is the office with boating supplies and T-shirts.

Schuyler Yacht Basin is a medium-sized marina that is the most oriented toward transients in this section of New York. Because this marina is so popular, call ahead to let them know you are coming. Grouped all together there, the transients enjoy a sense of camaraderie, while the seasonal tenants enjoy their own ambience across the protected waterway. Flowers, shade trees, grills, and picnic tables cover the spacious grounds. Both slips and side ties are offered on floating docks. Electrical connections of 30A, dual 30A, and 50A are available. Cable TV, dockside water, ice, and a boaters lounge also are offered. Many transient slips are at the marina (around 35 are set aside). Rental cars are either on site or will be called slip-side for travel into Saratoga 10 miles away. Judy and Phil Dean are always on site, have a "can-do" attitude, and want you to have a positive experience. They advertise that they can handle a 90-footer; if you are that big, call ahead to be personally talked in.

The marina has multiple shower rooms with benches in them for putting on your shoes and separate toilet rooms that are nicely detailed and constructed to minimize after-shower summer humidity. Judy Dean cleans them herself—sometimes several times a day. The laundry is complete (even soap) and in a large room that also functions as a comfortable boaters lounge complete with free book exchange. You will find yourself drawn into friendly conversation, picking up tips, and giving advice if you sip your morning coffee here in a bathrobe.

The hours of operation are officially during the daytime, but because the Deans live on site, they can reasonably accommodate a late arrival, but you must alert them. A supply/ship's store offers a practical selection of boaters' accouterments, and there is a small marine boutique in the marina office. They can arrange vessel repairs because they know everyone up and down the canal/river.

Schuylerville is two blocks to the west, where you can find breakfast, lunch, dinner, and groceries. However, before you buy groceries at Sully's, ask directions to the more than 150-foot-tall Saratoga Monument, which is dedicated to the local Revolutionary War battles and its American heroes. The town also has an antique, upstairs bowling alley, and you also can visit Gen. Philip Schuyler's 1777 summerhouse. An excellent dinner house is 2½ miles north and west, and it will sometimes send a car to pick up boaters from the marina. You also can have a second restaurant deliver pizza, fried seafood, or subs to the marina. The grounds of the Saratoga National Historical Park are within 10 miles. Saratoga (the community and racetrack) is also 10 miles away; do not fail to visit there. This stop is constantly improving; I personally look foward to seeing what is new each season.

Schuyler Yacht Basin (518) 695-3193

Storm protection: √√√
Scenic: * * * *
Marina-reported approach depths: 8-10 feet
Marina-reported dockside depths: 8-10 feet
Floating docks
Gas
Diesel
Waste pump-out
Rest rooms
Showers
Laundry
Dockside water
Barbecues
Picnic tables
Power connections: 30A/125V, dual 30A/125V, 50A/125V
Mechanical repairs
Ship's store
Gift shop
Restaurant: off site
Grocery: off site
What's special: a do-not-miss, transient-oriented marina with town two blocks away and fabulous Saratoga readily accessible
VHF-monitored channel: 9, 13, 16

After leaving Schuylerville, you are now headed for a cruise to the town of Whitehall, the birthplace of the U.S. Navy. The next lock, Lock 5, is about a mile north of the Route 29 Bridge, which has a vertical clearance of 28 feet. Several factors affect the level of the water in this section, and the whole Champlain Canal can vary as much as 1½ feet during the boating season or even daily. At least one energy plant periodically draws water from the river, thereby reducing the level. If needed, the lock operators can control the level to a certain degree. It takes about two hours and they prefer 48 hours notice, but if you call ahead, the operator will let some of the water down to accommodate your passage.

Lock 5—19-foot lift. (518) 695-3919. The next lock is 4 miles ahead. Ask the lock master if it is OK to tie up north of the lock; tell him you want to disembark to go see the old canal section west of the current canal you're on. You can see a lengthy piece of it here. Notice the size difference as well as the construction materials.

Once at Lock 5, I found that some of the ropes to hang onto were missing from the rings on top of the canal wall. They were deliberately removed because the lock had a leak in its sidewall, and a vessel resting there would get squirted with a wash as the lock water level lowered (I was headed south—therefore locking down). The New York State Canal Corporation would rather not shut down the system for repairs in season, but they go out of their way to protect boaters.

After proceeding through Lock 5, the Champlain Canal route leaves the Hudson River for nine-tenths of a mile. Here it goes around the natural falls, which are over on the eastern side of the waterway, and the shoreline starts to take on a more scenic appeal. You'll soon notice wooded areas and higher elevations as you enter the beginning of the Adirondack region to the west and the Green Mountains closer by to the east.

If you are like me, you probably think of the Green Mountains in conjunction with Ethan Allen and his Green Mountain Boys. Teachers use the heroics of this band of freedom fighters to capture the imaginations of their students when they teach about the American Revolution. I remember as a kid being mesmerized by stories about the Green Mountain Boys in the struggle for independence from the British.

From here to the north end of Lake Champlain is the region they called home.

Geologically speaking, the mountains in this area are part of an old mountain range. They have been worn down over millions of years from much higher peaks and shaped by the glaciers of the last ice age. The river you are riding on here also is in a channel that's millions of years old—a natural river, gouged deep by those same glaciers and relentlessly flowing toward the ocean.

At this point of the river, you are starting to see a little more elevation in the landscape. Here it is about a half-mile to the 200-foot-high hills on the right. This valley will narrow, then widen, and narrow yet again as you proceed north, and the hillsides close to the river will climb to 1,000 feet and higher.

The mountains are heavily wooded and in autumn create a magnificent panorama of color and texture. Boaters taking this trip in mid-October are treated to rich hues and sparkling patterns as sunlight and shadow play hide-and-seek over the rippling leaves, coming to rest on root-beer-colored water. Breathe deeply the crisp fall air and munch on a juicy red Macintosh apple as you experience these glorious moments in the year's cycle from a vantage available only to boaters. During times like these Mother Nature allows us to enjoy her fine handiwork in proper awe.

Lock 6—5-foot lift. (518) 695-3751. Seven and a quarter miles ahead at Lock 7, the canal route permanently leaves the natural river of the Hudson and becomes a mostly man-made channel using the available small creeks and lowlands and continuing all the way to Lake Champlain. This portion is sometimes called a ditch, as with the Panama Canal, but locals do not use that term and might find it insulting.

Upon exiting the lock, look west for some interesting architecture in the lovely older homes in Fort Miller.

Next up is the guard gate, a guillotine-style, raised steel gate that if needed protects the water level to allow for repairs downstream. Everyone passes under it at idle speed since the concrete sidewalls can ricochet boat wakes. This man-made structure seems to intrude upon an otherwise rural landscape full of farmlands.

Five miles ahead at Fort Edward is the Fort Edward Yacht Basin, which offers a free overnight tie-up for cruisers. Turn in toward Fort Edward immediately before Lock 7. Fort Edward Yacht Basin is a very enjoyable town-park wharf.

West River Marina (518) 747-8112

Storm protection: √√
Scenic: *
Marina-reported approach depths: 12 feet
Marina-reported dockside depths: 3-8 feet
Gas
Diesel
Rest rooms
Dockside water
Power connections: 30A/125V

Fort Edward

The canal channel to the far right takes you through the next lock on your trip north. Then you will notice that the natural Hudson River course to the left splits into two sections. The next channel immediately to the west or left of the lock is a narrow buoyed channel that leads into the town of Fort Edward. Here you can find a municipal wall to use as a tie-up and a diner/cafe within two blocks. This is nice small town, very clean and green in summer.

Free dockage is available at the Fort Edward Yacht Basin, which is really a town dock. To reach it you'll need to leave the main channel and take the cut just before Lock 7.

Overnight tie-ups are currently free. Just patronize the local businesses, because their combined efforts keep the terminal in good repair. Also, let them know you appreciate their hospitality. If you do stop at Fort Edward, be sure to watch for the two Model As that frequently seem to be driving around the town.

The next channel, just west of the one to Fort Edward, is the wider section of the natural Hudson. It is not buoyed and is only about 6 or 7 feet deep up until the bridge, which you can see about a half-mile ahead. This part also contains some underwater obstructions, so unless you are familiar with it, I don't recommend trying to navigate the wider of these two natural Hudson River channels.

The approach to Fort Edward Yacht Basin is a very specific route about a mile long off the main channel. It is the middle waterway of three. From the eastern shore, waterway #1 is the Lock 7 entrance, and on the opposite side of the lock (westward) is the channel that leads to waterway #2, the free tie-up called Fort Edward Yacht Basin. Waterway #3 (farthest west) is the main, natural river channel of the Hudson River. Do not go #3. (Pardon my little bathroom humor, but it does make you remember.) Now, hug the western side (non-lock side) of the Lock 7 approach, not the middle of the water space between the island of the Lock 7 approach. Water depth is 12 to 15 feet. Next, both red and green channel markers define the channel as it veers west and indicate that you should now run in the center of the waterway for best depth. Finally, favor the left side under the two bridges (19-foot and

26-foot overhead clearance). Water depth should not go below 7 feet (just inside of the bridges) in the whole approach. Tie up to the concrete wall to the north (your starboard). This route is not as hard to traverse as it reads.

Fort Edward Yacht Basin is a free, overnight tie-up created and maintained by the town's merchants; it is unstaffed and therefore has no telephone number. All they ask for is your business at their places of business. Be sure you let them know you came because of the free tie-up. It is on the water's edge of a nice park with trees, grass, and a gazebo. This tie-up provides boaters with water and a 15A electrical hookup. Take your trash with you. Town is on the other edge of the small park. Convenient stores, restaurants, a bank, a post office, and other shops are there. Look for the antique cars usually parked on the street near the insurance office. Farther east and several blocks away, in the Old Fort House Museum, is a pre-Revolutionary War display. This museum house was used by both sides during the American Revolution.

Fort Edward Yacht Basin

Storm protection: √√√
Scenic: * * *
Marina-reported approach depths: 7-15 feet
Marina-reported dockside depths: 5-8 feet
Dockside water
Picnic tables
Power connections: 15A/125V
Restaurant: off site
Grocery: off site
Convenience store: off site
What's special: free and nice

Past the town of Fort Edward, the natural Hudson River continues to meander, going first southwest and then north to its birthplace. Lake Tear of the Clouds, some 4,293 feet up the side of New York State's highest mountain, the 5,344-foot-tall Mount Marcy, is in the heart of the Adirondacks and the source of the Hudson River. Its discoverer, Verplanck Colvin, said of it: "A minute, unpretending tear of the clouds, as it were, a lonely pool, shivering in the breezes of the mountains, and sending its limpid surplus through Feldspar Brook and to the Opalescent River, the wellspring of the Hudson."

From Fort Edward the canal takes on a different character. The man-made trench is almost military-like in its regular sides and structured straightness.

Lock 7—10-foot lift. (518) 747-4614. Lock 8 is 15 minutes ahead after you clear Lock 7. Ask the lock operator about water levels. After passing through Lock 7, you come to the low-clearance Broadway Avenue Bridge, which shows a fixed vertical clearance of 15 feet on its western edge. This clearance is the lowest noted in the Champlain Canal section of this trip. If the water is high, clearance is less than 15 feet. The buoy channel markers are now replaced by railroad rails stuck into the canal bottom with a metal "flag" attached on top. They continue through the dug section. Civilization is not far away: On the eastern shore a golf course will soon appear. Lock 8, with an 11-foot lift, is just 2 miles ahead.

In the early 1800s, New York State was nearly all rural except for the areas downstate, in and around New York City, and the Capital District of Albany, Troy, and Schenectady. Nearby states such as Pennsylvania, Massachusetts, and Rhode Island were expanding toward more industrial economies. Pennsylvania produced iron and steel; Massachusetts and Rhode Island manufactured textiles and developed other industries. Meanwhile, the upper part of New York State remained primarily a one-industry, one-crop (grains) economy. The canals changed all that.

First came the construction of the canals themselves, which were mainly built through manual labor. Local people made up the greatest portion of the work force, but the high wages drew Irish, British, and German immigrants as well. It was brutal labor, accomplished over 14-hour days—when the ground wasn't frozen—and six-day workweeks. The trenches were dug with axes, shovels, and horse-drawn sand scrapers. Surveyors initially planned out the route, along with the location and lift of each lock. A swath had to be cut through the brush, and a man would bring a tree down by attaching a cable high up upon it and cranking through a reduction gear that cabled down to earth at a 60-degree angle from the tree. By turning the reduction gear, the tree was easily toppled, often with its roots, and then could be dragged away by a team of horses. Tree stumps not pulled out were cleared by using a pair of wheels 16 feet in diameter and fitted with a third 14-foot wheel in between them on a 30-foot-long axle. Rope was wound around the axle in such a way that a mechanical advantage was gained. After heavy chain was hooked around the stump, horses pulled on the other end of the rope and pulled the stump out. Seven men and a team of horses could grub 35 stumps a day using this method. Next, the ditch was dug through dirt, roots, and rock, all of which had to be removed. Finally, a stone edge was put in place to keep the sides firm and secure.

With the completion of the canals came the commercial and passenger vessels that forever opened New York State—and the country beyond—to industry and commerce, making the state a vital player in the nation's economy.

Lock 8—11-foot lift. (518) 747-5520. Lock 9 is 6 miles ahead. A good stand of evergreen trees flanks the approach to the lock. Once you go through Lock 8, you are at the highest level of the Champlain Canal. You have now been lifted a total of about 139 feet. At this level, the canal needs water fed to it to keep it full—and to keep your boat afloat! About 2.1 miles north of Lock 8 is the feeder canal that does just that. Actually, three streams or canals, including one that comes from Glens Falls, join together to supply the needed water. It has been shallow on the eastern edge of the channel between this feeder canal and the bridge a quarter mile north. This next bridge, state Highway 196, has a 21-foot clearance, but there is only 17-foot clearance at the New Swamp Road Bridge next up after that. Again, if this pool (the water between the two locks) is higher than normal, the bridge clearances will be lower.

Farther north of the lock is an abandoned Civil War-era warehouse built of wood. It was built right up against the canal's eastern shore. The individual loading doors are narrow and reflect the manual labor used during loading that was a part of the transportation of goods in our past.

This area's shoreline is one of dense foliage followed by various agricultural operations; then there is some scrub vegetation between the man-improved canal and the natural Wood Creek that's immediately east of it. Much of Wood Creek was used as a basis for the northern end of the Champlain Canal. The canal runs much more in a straight-line direction than Wood Creek, however. East Creek, Bond Creek, the Mettawee River, and Moses and Snook Kills also feed it or share their water-channel floor with man's energy to create the canal.

Canal traffic added new words to the evolving language of American English. For example, a "hoagie" was a boy who led the team of oxen or horses that towed the canal barge. Hoagie comes from a Scottish word that means "laborer." There were 5,000 hoagies on New York State canals by 1845. Hoagies worked two six-hour shifts a day—rain, sleet, or cold—and had to tend to their horse or oxen teams in the off-hours. (They also had a sandwich named after them!) Daydreaming was expensive: Towlines could quickly get tangled in either boats or bridges, and the result was that the team of oxen or horses would be dragged into the canal. Hoagies also had to have "eyes up" when passing. Remember, there was only one towpath that served both directions, no matter which side it was on. Therefore, passing boats had to agree that one of them would slack his lines and let that towline drop to the bottom of the canal so that the other tow could pass over it.

Canals also gave birth to the "towpath walker," also called a "pathmaster." His job was to walk a given section, usually 10 miles, of the towpath and berm carrying some manure and hay in a wheelbarrow. Using that mixture, he would stuff and stop a small leak, stamping it down to seal it. A manure/hay mix also was used by early boat captains to plug up boat leaks. A full bucket on a long handle was lowered over the side and dumped. The rushing inward water carried the mix to the leak and naturally plugged it. These repair techniques were backed up by speedy, slim repair boats pulled by fast horses and stationed frequently in different areas of the

canal, although more on the Erie section than the Champlain. Then, carrying a gang of workers, they would move along at the fast pace of 10 mph toward any bigger break.

Lock 9—16-foot lift. (518) 747-6012. It is 9 miles to Lock 11. The final three locks before Lake Champlain are all downhill steps. This simply means that instead of raising you to the water level ahead, as each one has done up until now, the locks lower you. (It is easier to lock through dropping down than going up a level.) The final lock brings your level to approximately 96 feet above water level at sea level, which is the average water level of Lake Champlain. There is a slightly different feel to these locks as the lock's walls drop around you, but the procedure is pretty much the same. Be careful to tend your lines steadily as the water goes down.

About 1½ miles north of the lock, hug the center to the western side of the canal channel to avoid obstructions. Otherwise, it's smooth cruising to Lock 11 for just under one hour. After the engineering drawings were completed for the canal route here, Lock 10 was eliminated and the locks were never renumbered. That's why there is no Lock 10.

Lake Champlain Water Levels

A word about Lake Champlain's water levels and the corresponding navigation charts. Chart depths are calculated from a low level of 93 feet. The average the lake has shown historically is 96 feet above sea level. Therefore, you will have on average 3 feet deeper water than what the chart shows at historical levels. Cruise through in May and the Champlain lake levels might be even higher than this. The soundings might be out of date, however. Some of them in the eastern United States go back to the 1920s. Also, the lake is higher in the spring than in the fall. While inside Lock 12 the operator will come alongside your craft to record your pass number. At that time, ask him about Lake Champlain's current water level. VHF radio Weather 2, out of Burlington, Vermont, quotes the lake water height level above sea level in its daily weather reports.

SKIPPER TIP: There are bridges ahead with 18- to 21-foot overhead clearances.

Fort Ann

On the western shore at the third bridge is the settlement of Fort Ann. Both Fort Ann (western shore) and Battle Hill (eastern side) have interesting military histories going back as far as February 1690, when English settlers at Schenectady were massacred (60 killed and 27 carried away) by French and Indian raiders. The attack caused tensions in the area and the subsequent fort-building frenzy, which included the one at Fort Ann, that continued until 1814, when the War of 1812 ended.

You will soon see your first majestic mountain looming in front of you from Lake Champlain—a foreshadowing of the majesty ahead. Immediate scenery includes dairy farms, cornfields, and the AMTRAK line.

Lock 11—12-foot drop. (518) 639-8964. It is roughly 6½ miles from Lock 11 to Lock 12. The one bridge (Ryder Road) between them has 18-foot clearance. Hug the center to western shore of the canal just as you approach Lock 11. It's shallow to the east. The lock is on the western side of the channel. The western shoreline is more defined on both approach and exit as compared with the low, almost marshy, eastern

shore. About a half-mile down the road from Lock 11, on the right shore, sits Great Meadow Correctional Facility on the outskirts of the town of Comstock. This maximum-security state prison is not visible from the water, but you can walk there if you desire to—or just go part way for a glimpse of the facility.

New York canals were first conceived by Cadwallader Colden in 1724 to ensure that New York would keep developing at a competitive pace with Montréal and Philadelphia. In 1792 the Northern Island Lock Navigation Company (a private enterprise) was formed to open a waterway between the Hudson River and Lake Champlain. Started in 1793 near Fort Edward, the canal failed and the company went bankrupt. It was 1822 when the first generation of the Champlain Canal was finally opened. The canal was financed as a public-works project, in a separate corporation, but its bonds were backed by the full faith and credit of the state of New York. The one you are riding in now is a newer version built over almost the same route. This one uses more of the Hudson River channel. It was constructed between 1917 and 1919.

About 2¾ miles north of Lock 11, you can see where the Delaware and Hudson Railroad line, now AMTRAK, just about touches the canal on its western shore.

SKIPPER TIP: It is mandatory that all southbound pleasure craft in Lock 12 lock through on the east wall, or raft up against a boat that is on the east wall, because of how water flows in and out of this lock chamber. If you forget, the lock operator will instruct you to do so to avoid lock turbulence.

Lock 12—15-foot lift (drop if heading north). (518) 499-1700. You can contact the supervisor for all of the Champlain Canal at (518) 747-4613. Lock 12 is located in the middle of the town of Whitehall, 63 statute miles from Federal Lock 1 in Troy. With this lock, you have now been lifted 139 feet and then lowered about 44 feet to the Lake Champlain level. The four bridges south of the lock have 16- to 18-foot clearances.

> **SKIPPER TIP:** Sailboaters, once clear of Lock 12, step your mast. It is more than 130 miles to limited clearance navigation again, and Lake Champlain is a beautiful sailing adventure.

Whitehall

Whitehall is the town's second name. Founded in 1759 and named Skenesborough, after Philip Skene, it was renamed after the Revolutionary War because, you see, Philip was a British army major. Also, the town was a part of the military history of the first two wars involving the young United States. During the Revolutionary War ships for the fledgling U.S. Navy were made here. In fact, Brig. Gen. Benedict Arnold was responsible for getting some American ships built right here using the local sawmill and recruiting labor from all over the colonies. Moreover, arms were stored in what is now Lock 12 Marina's main building from 1812 to 1814, the dates for the War of 1812. Shipbuilding continued but with a twist: The opening of the Champlain Canal in 1822 created a demand for canal boats and barges.

You have probably been running roughly 6 to 7 hours and might be thinking about finding

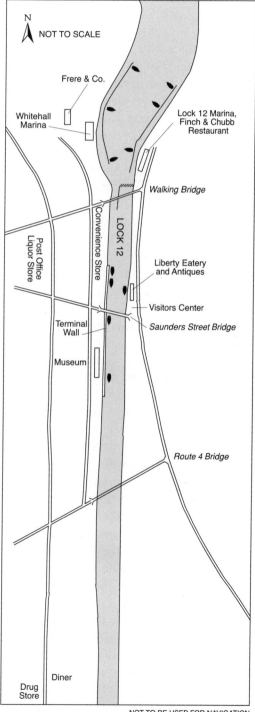

WHITEHALL

N NOT TO SCALE

Frere & Co.

Whitehall Marina

Lock 12 Marina, Finch & Chubb Restaurant

Walking Bridge

Post Office Liquor Store

Convenience Store

LOCK 12

Liberty Eatery and Antiques

Visitors Center

Terminal Wall

Saunders Street Bridge

Museum

Route 4 Bridge

Drug Store

Diner

NOT TO BE USED FOR NAVIGATION

a place to stop before venturing into the narrows of lower Lake Champlain. Everybody does—so much so that the canal people along with other agencies have targeted Lock 12 and Whitehall for major renovations. No specific plans are ready to be announced as this guide goes to press, but cruisers should expect good things to come in the next few years.

Straddling both sides of the lock, the town of Whitehall offers a nice full-service, family-run marina on the eastern shore with on-site gourmet dining. Located on the northern edge of town, the marina is about a 1,000-foot walk from the main street of Whitehall and all the usual town amenities. On the western shore is a marina well known for its repairs. Make your choice depending on your priorities.

On the western bank of the canal at Whitehall before Lock 12 is a cement wharf that serves as a public dock. It is quite exposed to channel traffic and wakes. Also on the western bank is the Skenesborough Museum, a treasure house of marine history and lore. After all, Whitehall is credited with being the birthplace of the U.S. Navy. The country's first fleet of either 12 or 15 vessels—history has lost the exact count—was constructed here in 1776. Benedict Arnold was its commander on Lake Champlain before he was renounced as a traitor for helping the British try to take West Point on the Hudson River later on in the Revolutionary War. The ships were engaged in a battle to stop the British from coming down from Montréal into New York in an attempt to control the Hudson Valley and thereby split New England from the rest of the colonies. Arnold's fleet did not win, but he was a hero. He forced the British to stop their southern campaign push for the winter due to the delay the battle caused. By the next spring, when the British

again began to push south (war was not fought back then in the wintertime), the colonials had had sufficient time to gather their forces to defeat the British at Saratoga.

Along with ship models and naval memorabilia, the museum also has on display the remains of the USS *Ticonderoga,* a boat built in Vergennes, Vermont, that was used during the War of 1812. South of the museum but also on the western side of the canal is a village park with rest rooms, picnic tables, and charcoal grills. Ask about the local farmers market that is held on the street in front of the park. North of the museum is Whitehall Marina and Frere & Co., a marine-hardware ship's store. Farther west from the terminal wall, still on the western side of the canal and across Main Street to Broadway (also called Route 4), are the following: a liquor store, a post office, the Village Diner (close by), the Silver Diner (farther away), and the train station. A train that runs between Montréal and New York City stops here daily.

On the eastern side of the canal waterway, starting from the south at the Route 4 Bridge, is a Stewart's convenience store and an ATM. Under new ownership, the Liberty Eatery and Antique Emporium is an overnight tie-up choice. Just walking around inside is an experience. Look everywhere and walk slowly to take in everything—it's fun! Take the time to meet the owners, Susan and Frank Coraldi. Now, staying on North William Street, go past the playground and up four to five blocks to antique stores and the chamber of commerce. Continue north past the Lock 12 walking bridge and you are at the Lock 12 Marina, with its gourmet restaurant, Finch & Chubb. Farther north is the golf course. Farther east up on the mountain is Skene Manor, named after the town's founder but built by a judge about 70 years after Skene died. Outdoor concerts are held in town every Friday in July and August from 7 to 9 P.M.

Whitehall Terminal Wall

Along on the western shore south of Lock 12 and north and south of Saunders Street Bridge is a long concrete wall for boaters to tie up overnight. Water depth runs 8 to 12 feet. Face south if you want the bow facing the water flow (a starboard-side tie-up). This is the water's edge of the park-like Skenesborough Museum property. There are picnic tables but nothing else on site. One would think that as the marinas in town served the public better, the town fathers would spend money on the terminal to keep it up to snuff. Perhaps, the exposure to boat wakes and increased canal traffic has made this a less desirable candidate for renovation. However, the possibility of future renovations here looks good.

Liberty Eatery and Antique Emporium (518) 499-0301

Storm protection: √√√
Scenic: * *
Marina-reported approach depths: 12 feet
Marina-reported dockside depths: 6-10 feet
Rest rooms
Showers
Dockside water
Power connections: 30A/125V
Gift shop
Restaurant: on site
What's special: the eclectic collection all over the restaurant
VHF-monitored channel: 16

Lock 12 Marina is north of Lock 12 by about 200 feet, on the eastern shore, with about 12-foot water depth all around.

In the main building are heated multiple toilets—men's and women's, plus separate, individual shower rooms that are well vented (you can use your hair dryer after your shower), with electrical outlets and mirrors that are cleaned and checked daily and then spot-checked. These facilities are simple but repainted yearly to impart a clean, fresh look and feeling. One washer/dryer with a folding counter is on site. Laundry soap is available.

The main building of the marina is a War of 1812 ammunition warehouse. Reservations are recommended for dinner and dockage in July and August and on popular holidays. As many as 20 slips are allocated for transients. This facility offers 30A/125V and dual 30A/125V electrical hookups. Nonpotable water is dockside, and drinkable water is at the fuel dock. They have a pool plus a hammock for transients and advertise that they can accommodate a 100-foot yacht. Phone ahead to work it out. Lock 12 Marina also is an inn if you want to get off the boat for a night.

Important note: Gourmet chefs Ray and Linda Faville own both the marina and its first-class restaurant. Try the salmon with mustard dill sauce or the filet mignon au poivre. Lunch and dinner are served. Let them know you are coming if it is going to be a later arrival than 7 P.M. dockside.

In the ship's store soft drinks, beer, snack food, charts, other books/magazines, boutique clothing, and convenience items are all in good supply.

Nearby activities include the town of Whitehall, birthplace of the U.S. Navy. A courtesy bus operated by the Whitehall Chamber of

Want to relax in a pool, a hammock, or over a gourmet meal? You'll find them all at the Lock 12 Marina. The Finch & Chubb restaurant on the second floor offers a commanding view of the waterway.

Commerce runs from 7:30 to 9:30 A.M.; 11:30 A.M. to 1:30 P.M.; and 4:30 to 6:30 P.M. daily from July 1 to Labor Day. It makes multiple stops, including Lock 12 Marina. No taxi service is in town.

Lock 12 Marina (518) 499-2049

Storm protection: √√√
Scenic: * * *
Marina-reported approach depths: 12 feet
Marina-reported dockside depths: 8-12 feet
Floating docks
Gas
Diesel

Waste pump-out
Rest rooms
Showers
Laundry
Dockside water
Barbecues
Picnic tables
Power connections: 30A/125V, dual 30A/125V
Ship's store
Gift shop
Restaurant: on site
Grocery: off site
Convenience store: on site
What's special: on-site gourmet dining
VHF-monitored channel: 09, 16

THE CHAMPLAIN CANAL AND LAKE CHAMPLAIN 175

Frere & Co. Marine Supply

This store is located on the western shore north of Lock 12 behind Whitehall Marina.

Boaters may use Whitehall Marina as a courtesy dock; just let the management of Whitehall Marina know where and why you are tied up.

Frere & Co. is an independent marine-supply house stocking 7,000 marine items. They have the usual items and often can make helpful suggestions. I have changed head (toilet) chemicals based on a dialogue with them. Free services include splicing on all line purchased, Nico pressing on wire rope, fabrication of lifelines, and occasionally minor machine work and fabrication. They stock some propellers and boat-trailer supplies.

A stop here is an excellent opportunity to replace dirty fenders and expand your vessel's horizons with a second anchor system or to add more anchor rode. Lake Champlain is more enjoyable if you have as a choice a good anchoring system with the ability to set out plenty of rode.

Whitehall Marina is on the west shore just north of Lock 12. Good water depth both on approach and dockside is here for cruisers.

Although this marina specializes in repairs and dry-stock/wet-slip seasonal tenants, it gladly works with transients. It has two showers and two toilets that were new in 1996 and are beautiful. No laundry is available, however. The walking bridge across the top of Lock 12 gives good access to all of town and gourmet dining across the waterway. There are limited 30A/110V electrical hookups. The on-site launch ramp is only limited by the trailer

available. Forty-five-foot yachts have used it for transportation to winter storage.

Nearby activities include the town of White-hall, plus Frere & Co., next door, the best marine-supply store between Burlington, Vermont, and Albany, New York, with discounted prices, good selection, and high volume.

Whitehall Marina (518) 499-1663

Storm protection: √√
Scenic: * * *
Marina-reported approach depths: 12 feet
Marina-reported dockside depths: 4-8 feet
Floating docks
Gas
Rest rooms
Showers
Dockside water
Picnic tables
Power connections: 30A/125V (limited)
Fiberglass repairs
Below-waterline repairs
Mechanical repairs
Gas-engine repairs
Stern-drive repairs
Outboard-motor repairs
Generator repairs
Yard trailer/tow vehicle
Ship's store: next door
Restaurant: off site
Grocery: off site
Convenience store: off site
VHF-monitored channel: 09

Lake Champlain

SKIPPER TIP: The lake is divided into four large NOAA charts numbered 14781, 14782, 14783, and 14784. This section covers the cruising grounds as detailed in these charts, starting with chart 14784. These charts are needed to transit Lake Champlain.

Just past Whitehall are the narrows of the southern part of Lake Champlain, the largest freshwater lake in the United States excluding the Great Lakes. Lake Champlain varies in width up to a maximum of 10 miles and is about 110 miles long. It contains 75 islands, and the deepest spot is 400 feet deep. The lake touches Canada to the north, Vermont on its eastern shore, and New York State on its western shore. It functions as the boundary between Vermont and New York, with the dividing line roughly following the line of deepest water near the middle of the lake. From top to bottom the western shore is New York territory, and all but the smallest piece above Lock 12 on the eastern side belongs to Vermont.

The lake edge on the Vermont side is much more meandering and the water shallower, with a progressive incline up the shore; whereas on the New York side the lake is typically quite deep near shore. This slow slope on the Vermont side causes about two-thirds of the lake's surface to be Vermont waters. You can touch a rock ledge from your craft and still be in 100 feet of water on the New York side, or travel inland on the Vermont side 6 miles up a creek to a former gunboat-building site used in the days of Ethan Allen and his Green Mountain Boys.

SKIPPER TIP: Red buoys are to your vessel's port.

SKIPPER TIP: The water level in Lake Champlain typically moves up and down 4 to 5 feet within each boating season, with the highest level in May and the lowest in October.

Lake charts figure from a water level of 93 feet above sea level. The observed range is actually from .6 foot below to 8.8 feet above this, with 96 feet being typical in July and August. VHF radio channel Weather 2, out of Burlington, Vermont, reports levels to the nearest tenth of an inch in its forecasts.

SKIPPER TIP: Be conscious of weather when transiting Lake Champlain. Prevailing winds, uneven in summer, are more consistent in spring and fall. The lake's width and size leave boaters exposed, particularly to the few storms coming from the west, although most (40 percent) come from the south. In midsummer these storms usually include thunder, lightning, rain, and a good amount of wind. There are less than half as many storms in September as compared with the months of June, July, and August.

SKIPPER TIP: Daytime high air temperatures average 78° in June, 82° in July, 80° in August, 70° in September, and below 60° by October.

SKIPPER TIP: Water temperatures for Lake Champlain run the gamut, with shore-edge temperatures being significantly warmer than those farther out, and temps dropping noticeably in deeper water. The lake seems to warm up late, with temperatures still around 60° in June, rising to 74° by August, and dropping back to 60° in mid-October.

SKIPPER TIP: Please keep the lake clean. Most of the communities along Lake Champlain use it as their drinking-water supply. Even though it is treated before use, the water should be respected. Vessels cannot be capable of dumping waste into the lake. Plumbing and wiring enabling this must be visibly disconnected and blocked, not just switched off, with the wastewater diverted to a holding tank.

SKIPPER TIP: Lake Champlain is a cruiser's lake. It offers an abundance of marina choices and an unending selection of anchorages. Most of these anchorages are not very specific as to where you should drop the hook, unlike in the waters farther south. Anchorages on the Lake Champlain portion of this guide will not be set off from the text unless there is a special circumstance.

SKIPPER TIP: NOAA charts 14784, 14783, 14782, and 14781 cover this first area. Note that the white area indicates at least 12 feet of water depth, while areas colored blue are less shallower depths—the first black line follows the 12-foot (2-fathom) line, while the inset line follows 1-fathom (6-foot) depth line.

The first 15 miles or so of Lake Champlain seem more like river than lake. In fact, at one point called the Narrows of Dresden, it is only about 125 feet wide. Boaters pass through several miles of marshland north of Whitehall and through valleys before the lake opens up at Stony Point.

You might notice one area called South Bay that is used by local boaters, but because of shallow water and low bridges—a reported 11-foot-vertical-clearance bridge with a reported 8-foot-vertical-clearance bridge beyond it—it is really only usable by runabouts that know where its hazards lie.

If you have been longing for breathtaking scenery and magnificent vistas on this cruise, you won't be disappointed now. Here are clear waters, evergreen and deciduous forest, a multitude of secluded anchorages, and, looming over all, the Adirondacks to the west and the Green Mountains to the east.

Sit back and enjoy the ride from Whitehall to Fort Ticonderoga as you travel through snaking passages and watch the mountains rise in the distance. Some 20 miles to your right, the Green Mountain summits rise more than 4,000 feet, while the Adirondacks to your left march in rows like soldiers. The first row stretches 1,200 to 1,600 feet; the second tier rises 2,200 to 4,600 feet; and the third, about 40 miles distant, reaches 4,000 to 5,300 feet high.

Lake cruising is soon upon you and, for the first time on this trip, you are facing open water. Unlike river and canal cruising, there are stretches where the shoreline is at a distance. Water depths run the gamut and are charted from 8 feet in the channel to one spot in the narrows of 400 feet. Remember that most depths shown on your charts are from a 1979 survey. In fact, using your depth sounder and a chart, you might be able to match them up to pinpoint your location in a fog. Be alert to the weather forecast—both the immediate weather and that of the following few days. Wind and waves are now important factors, and too much of either requires a prudent skipper to call for a layover day rather than foolishly risking vessel and crew. Since landmarks and aids to navigation are spaced out and not always in sight of one another, smart skippers chart a compass course and regularly check off their boat's progress as they follow it. Knowledge and planning are essential to avoid surprises on open water—and surprises are tough when you cannot touch bottom and walk away!

The channel in the narrows of Lake Champlain is often winding and slalomlike if you are in a craft cruising at 35 mph. Trees, marshes, rock walls, and a sprinkling of side channels delight your senses as you travel into the broader lake ahead at a hull speed of 6 mph. Except for the buoys and fixed markers, man has little presence here. Birds and a few

The narrow southern section of Lake Champlain can offer channel banks of sheer rock as well as weedy shallows.

animals outnumber us. The trees and the intermittent marsh reeds make green the primary color of the moment.

You might be sharing the waterway with canoes, a fleet of kayaks, and fishermen; you'll find adults and kids, men and women all enjoying a special time. This area is part of the Adirondack portion of New York, a large tourist and vacation area. Enjoy the view; be prepared for a surprise around the next bend. If you are cruising fast, slow down when you pass others. If you are going slowly, stop to let the other boat get past you quickly, and then turn into the boat's wash to get through its wake quickly and with a more pleasant motion.

I know of no good fishing spots in the narrows below Stony Point. Depending on how expensive it is to go "bump on the bottom" with your craft, you might want to try. Remember, lake level is usually at least 3 feet higher than the numbers on the chart but is based on data almost 20 years old. Ask a local fisherman. South and north of the Narrows of Dresden at Maple Bend and Red Rock Bay are the logical ones.

In 1993 the Coast Guard renumbered many of the aids to navigation on the lake. If your chart was printed before then, it will not show the current numbering *even* if it is the latest edition of that chart. The government does not reprint charts just because of buoy renumbering. You need a light list update, which is sometimes available from the local Coast Guard station or chart supplier.

Once north of Stony Point, the narrows end and the deepwater area widens—still nothing like the mid-lake but much more than just a narrow channel passage. Spot your aids to navigation on your chart and know where to expect them ahead. They are not that close together. Very few boaters will have to run a compass course here, but most will be more comfortable if they check off markers as they pass and know where to look for the next one.

Lake Champlain has been called several names. The Indians called it Sea of the Iroquois, The Lake Which is the Gate of the Country, and Reggio, to honor a Mohawk Indian chief. The Dutch called it Corlaer, after the Dutch governor of Fort Orange (Albany), Arendt Corlaer. Samuel de Champlain named the lake after himself in July 1609.

Champlain was 42 years old when he voyaged from Quebec, which he founded, down the Richelieu River, then called the Iroquois River, to its rapids, which were impassable to his ship. He then switched to Indian birchbark canoes and continued on to Lake Champlain. In July 1609 he went as far south as either Crown Point or Ticonderoga; on this fact historians cannot agree. After helping his Indian tribe allies (the Montaquois, the Ochatequois, and the Algonquins) in a successful battle against the Iroquois, where he used his musket to kill the Iroquois leaders and set the battle in their favor, he returned to Quebec never, it is said, to visit the lake again.

Champlain was an adventurer. Born in France the son of a naval captain, he joined the army in 1588 at the age of 21. He then moved to the navy, commanding his first ship at 22. He sailed to the Caribbean, Central America, and at least touched South America. He was at the Charles River in Boston and named Mount Desert Island in Maine. In 1600 he established the first French colony in America, picking the site of Quebec.

He was very much enthused with New France. He was a prolific writer, detailing his adventures and promoting settlement. The next known white man to visit the lake was Father Isaac Jogues, a Jesuit missionary, in 1642. He was tortured on Cole Island, losing a thumb, but escaped. In 1646 the Indians did finally murder him on a site along the Mohawk River.

Plunder Bay Marina is the first marina on the southern end of Lake Champlain. It is on the Vermont side of the lake opposite marker #78 at Orwell Bluff Light in the upper southern narrows of Lake Champlain. This smaller marina is limited in water depth depending on lake levels (at 95 feet lake level above sea level, a 5-foot draft vessel will have trouble on approach but not dockside). It has toilets, showers, and 30A/110V electrical hookups. Nearby activities are nil. I do not know of anything within a 10-minute walk.

Plunder Bay Marina (802) 948-2330

Storm protection: √√
Scenic: * * *
Marina-reported approach depths: shallow—check lake levels
Marina-reported dockside depths: 2-6 feet
Gas
Rest rooms
Showers
Picnic tables
Power connections: 30A/125V
Mechanical repairs
VHF-monitored channel: 09

Chipman Point Marina has for several seasons offered the lowest fuel prices on the lake. Gas there is usually priced 20 cents lower than market. The marina is on the Vermont shore between markers #76 and #78 in the narrows of lower Lake Champlain (three miles below Fort Ticonderoga). It is deep just off shore and

at the service dock and can be shallow at the slips near shore if the lake level is low.

The marina has about fifty slips on three finger floats right on the channel. No wake, please, if you do not stop. Historically, warehouses and then a small village grew here in the very early nineteenth century due to the deep water so close to shore at this point.

Chipman Point Marina on Lake Champlain operates from a historic warehouse on the eastern shore between buoys #76 and #78. It's known for good fuel prices.

Trade in molasses, rum, flour, nails, and iron was popular here. Now those warehouses house the marina. The water depth and outside long finger piers can easily accommodate larger vessels.

The buildings and grounds are very picturesque. Men and women both have a rest room with a shower. Mirrors and electrical outlets are provided. The marina offers marine supplies and groceries inside the historic warehouse. Some winter storage also is offered on site. As for repair capability, they mostly do mast stepping, light rigging, and painting. A mechanic can be called in. Restaurants and Orwell Village require a shuttle that is sometimes provided. Confirm its schedule prior to your visit.

Chipman Point Marina (802) 948-2288

Storm protection: √√
Scenic: * * *
Marina-reported approach depths: 15 feet plus
Marina-reported dockside depths: 3-10 feet
Gas: usually had at a bargain price
Waste pump-out
Rest rooms
Showers
Laundry
Picnic tables
Power connections: 30A/125V
Mechanical repairs
Travelift/hoist: 10 tons
Mast stepping
Ship's store
Convenience store: on site
What's special: possible shuttle to restaurant
VHF-monitored channel: 09, 16

Buoy 39 Marina also is a good fuel stop, but transient slips are only available if a seasonal

tenant is away on a voyage. Again, gas is offered, in general at about 20 cents per gallon under the competition. A pump out is available, and toilets and showers are on site. The facility is at buoy #73, which was renumbered from buoy #39, hence the name.

The marina has floating docks that wrap around a point of land for 18-foot to 40-foot vessels. Water, ice, and 30A/110V electrical hookups are all available. However, the marina has not had transient berths for the past two years. A ship's store with an especially large stock of lubricants is on site.

Buoy 39 Marina (802) 948-2411

Storm protection: √√
Scenic: *
Marina-reported approach depths: 20 feet
Marina-reported dockside depths: 3-8 feet
Gas
Waste pump-out
Rest rooms
Showers
Laundry
Dockside water
Picnic tables
Power connections: 30A/125V
Fiberglass repairs
Below-waterline repairs
Mechanical repairs
Travelift/hoist: 20 ton
Ship's store
VHF-monitored channel: 09

Fort Ticonderoga

Lake Champlain offers a wealth of material for amateur historians and Revolutionary War buffs. The site of strategic forts and significant naval confrontations, the lake still echoes the early colonists' struggle for freedom.

Perhaps the most famous historic landmark

Fort Ticonderoga is probably the most famous landmark on Lake Champlain. Built by the French in 1755, it was taken over by the British only a year later. Early in the American Revolution, the colonists seized it from the British in a surprise attack.

on Lake Champlain is Fort Ticonderoga. It sits about 22 miles north of Whitehall or 7 miles north of Stony Point, which is where the river widens before it narrows again at Chipman Point. The fort is just north of the entrance to the creek joining Lake Champlain to Lake George. By the way, this creek, called La Chute, is not navigable—it has dams—and really constitutes more of a land access between the lakes than a navigable water path. Even traveling by canoe at normal summer water levels requires several sections of portaging to reach Lake George via this route.

Fort Ticonderoga is reachable by boaters only via dinghy. You can stay south and west of the fort (by the river) at the base of Mount Defiance, anchor, and then walk around to the stairway. The fort is maintained by the Fort Ticonderoga Association and is open to the public for a small fee. Tours are given frequently. About a hundred years ago the fort was acquired by a private citizen, William Ferris Pell. He and his descendants restored it and then donated it for public access.

Fort Ticonderoga Anchorage

Anchor in 6 to 12 feet of water directly south of the fort. It is well protected in most wind directions. Even winds from the south (its open side) do not build much of a chop, just some wind to swing your boat. The bottom is mud and can be weedy. Do not use the tour-boat dock for your dinghy landing; it is better to beach it nearby. Do use the stairway path that passengers of the tour boat use to climb the hill to the fort.

First built in 1755 by the French, Fort Ticonderoga, then called Fort Carillon, offers a perfect view of the lake, making it an ideal defense position. A year after it was built, it was taken over by the British. Early in the Revolutionary War, the colonists captured the fort from the British in a surprise attack led by Benedict Arnold, who had joined with the forces of Ethan Allen and the Green Mountain Boys when Arnold's troops were delayed. This situation naturally led to a constant argument about who was in charge: Arnold, who held the higher rank, or Allen, whose troops they were leading and who had his own guerrilla approach to command.

The British, meanwhile, had not yet received word of the fighting in Boston and left only one night guardsman on duty at the fort. The colonists had the gates open and were inside (some versions of the story have the gates open before the boys got there) before the British forces knew what was happening. The fort was an important victory for the Americans because it had big-gun artillery not available to them in Boston, and Gen. George Washington needed firepower to shoot across Boston Harbor at the British—or at least at their ships in the harbor—from his stronghold position. The colonists, led by General Knox, a New England bookseller, stripped the fort of its guns and dragged them through the forest (no roads then) in the dead of winter, on 42 sleds pulled by oxen, all the way to where Washington was fighting in Massachusetts. Later in the war, the British took the fort back from the colonists and held it through several battles, eventually abandoning it for good.

If you visit on a clear, sunny day, you might want to go into the town of Fort Ticonderoga, hire a taxi, and ride up to the top of Mount Defiance, which is immediately south and west of the fort. At more than 900 feet, you will have an inspiring view of the entire area, as well as your boat down below you.

East Creek, on the Vermont side opposite Fort Ticonderoga, is too shallow and marshy for cruisers. It does have the oldest known evidence of Indians on the lake: a burial ground of the "Red Paint People," some 5,000 years old (3000 B.C.), has been explored by anthropologists and archaeologists.

As you proceed north, note the squiggly magenta (purple-pink) colored line on your chart. It is trying to warn you that there is a cable-operated ferry crossing the lake from the New York to the Vermont side and back. I note this because, if the ferry goes by, you want to make sure that the cable has plenty of opportunity to sink back down to the bottom before you pass either in front of or behind it, so that you don't get fouled. The cable drops down to the bottom of the lake about 400 feet in front of and behind the ferry itself. If you pass on the Vermont side of the ferry crossing (Larabees Point), note the stone wharf with the word Teachout's painted above it. A nice waterside landmark, it also is the home port of the tour boat Carillon that cruises this end of the lake. I have "tooted" the MV Carillon when passing but did not receive a return signal. A wave was welcomed, however.

Past the Teachout's wharf the natural deep water moves to the east. Be sure to pass east of buoy #68 to stay in comfortably deep water. I have seen a planing 38-foot fly-bridge powerboat go inside of it at a 95.8-foot lake level, but I would not trust it. Unlike the narrows, this section of the lake is not dredged; it is a path that has been worn down just slightly from what was created by glaciers in the last ice age.

This ferry runs just north of Fort Ticonderoga near buoy #69. Pass well behind it to avoid getting snagged on its underwater cable.

More spacious vistas on the eastern shore are here for you to enjoy as you pass Fivemile Point. Just 4 miles north, take caution: There are abandoned cement blocks between the western shoreline and the deepwater channel.

Crown Point Anchorage

The anchorage is located by heading north past the monument and its pier but before the bridge on the New York side of the lake. Rest rooms, barbecues, and picnic areas are at the park. It is not suggested as an overnight or unwatched anchorage, rather as a way to visit the monument park. It has 8 to 10 feet of water depth with a mud/sand/gravel bottom. It is exposed to wind.

Crown Point

Crown Point is the site of two more forts, the early French Fort St. Frederick, built in 1731, and a later British fort, Fort Amherst, built in 1759.

Fort St. Frederick was blown up by the French when they retreated from it in the face of advancing British troops in 1759. Much of each fort was carried away to build stone houses in this general area in the 1800s to 1900s. Therefore, unlike Fort Ticonderoga, these forts are only partial reconstructions, but they are interesting because you can see how they were originally structured and built. Located on the western, or New York, shore right at the Highway 903 Bridge, Fort St. Frederick Point also is more accessible to boaters, although you still must use a dinghy. Very big yachts won't make it in, but most should make it fine. While you are here, check out the early "American graffiti." Some 250 years ago people carved or chiseled their names and messages into the rocks around the forts. Finally, look across the bridge toward the Vermont side to Chimney Point, which was settled as early as 1690 and was originally a fur trappers' trading fort. Rumor has it that a wall of one of the homes there is from that original fort.

The natural deepwater area bends to the west just before the high bridge (91-foot clearance), making the span invisible to northbound boaters until they are quite close to it. It is a surprise to those coming around the bend. As a second surprise, the lake jumps to a mile and a half wide after the bridge. Sailors, set sail.

North past the bridge, Hospital Creek is so named because it was the site in 1776 where so many retreating American soldiers, who had taken over Montréal in 1775 but failed to take Quebec, were treated for the effects of a harsh winter and an epidemic of smallpox.

Champlain Bridge Marina is located on the Vermont shore in Hospital Creek (second cove north of the bridge). During times of higher lake levels, more than 5 feet of water is available, and it is not tricky. If the lake is at low levels, keel sailboats and inboards should use caution.

The marina is capable of handling up to 40-foot boats (water depth is the limiting factor).

This smaller-boat marina is full service, with 30A/110V shore power, water, ice, rest rooms, and showers all available. There is a supplies/ship's store on site. The marina is a new-boat dealer for three lines of boats and four outboard-motor brands.

Champlain Bridge Marina (802) 729-2469, (800) SAY-AHOY

Storm protection: √√√
Scenic: * *
Marina-reported approach depths: check current lake levels
Marina-reported dockside depths: check current lake levels
Gas
Waste pump-out
Rest rooms
Showers
Dockside water
Picnic tables
Power connections: 15A/125V
Mechanical repairs
Gas-engine repairs

Once beyond the Champlain Bridge—north of buoy #58—the beauty of Lake Champlain unfolds. This is the only bridge over the lake until you reach Rouses Point.

Stern-drive repairs
Outboard-motor repairs
Travelift/hoist: 8 tons
Ship's store
VHF-monitored channel: 09, 16

Port Henry is on the New York side just past the bridge. Through time it has been a major settlement on the lake, based on mining activities. It has marinas. Groceries and supplies here are up a hillside, and the walk is not that convenient. However, since you've been cruising about 39 miles since Whitehall, you might want to stop. On the plus side, Port Henry has swimming beaches with lifeguards, some fishing-guide services, and a vista that makes the climb worthwhile.

Bulwagga Bay

Tucked in behind Crown Point and south of Port Henry is a fishing cove for local boaters. Bulwagga Bay is shallow for a good distance from shore, a fact that keeps most cruising boaters away, as do the submerged pilings at the cove's entrance.

Velez Marina sells gas plus diesel fuels. The marina is behind sunken barges that act as a breakwater. It is a small marina in the town of Port Henry mostly for boats under 30 feet. Water depth is good on approach, but you need directions to avoid shallow water. The showers and toilets were unacceptable when I visited. Dockside electrical hookups are limited. The ship's store offers a limited selection that is mainly oriented toward lubricants. The town of Port Henry is probably best reached from the marina via a taxi ride.

Velez Marina (518) 546-7588

Storm protection: √√
Scenic: *

Marina-reported approach depths: 15-18 feet
Marina-reported dockside depths: 2-6 feet
Floating docks
Gas
Diesel
Rest rooms
Showers
Picnic tables
Power connections: 30A/125V (limited)
Yard trailer/tow vehicle

Van Slooten Harbor Marina is due west of the south side of the aid to navigation off Point Henry. Look for a white-roofed, red-sided building. The marina is populated by 20-foot to 35-foot boats and is a 35-slip facility. It is open from 8 A.M. to 5 P.M. (longer hours in July and August), and it has a small cafe on site. The supplies/ship's store has a nice selection on site as well. The marina offers winter storage and has a travelift on site. They can call in expert labor if need be. Waterside at the town of Port Henry: the Grand Union supermarket is about three-fourths of a mile away. The King's Inn, which has a golf course, is 2 miles away and might send a car to pick up boaters (inquire).

Van Slooten Harbor Marina (518) 546-7400

Storm protection: √√
Scenic: *
Marina-reported approach depths: 15-18 feet
Marina-reported dockside depths: 2-8 feet
Gas
Diesel
Waste pump-out
Rest rooms
Showers
Laundry
Dockside water

Picnic tables
Power connections: 30A/125V, dual
  30A/125V
Woodworking repairs
Fiberglass repairs
Below-waterline repairs
Mechanical repairs
Travelift/hoist: 15 ton
Ship's store
VHF-monitored channel: 09, 16

> **SKIPPER TIP:** You may now change charts over to 14783.

Cole Bay

Continuing up the New York side, you come to an island standing in Cole Bay, called, naturally enough, Cole Island. This is a nice place for boaters to drop anchor for lunch, a swim, or a little fishing. You can also tie a stern line to a tree on the island and drop a bow anchor toward the main shore, but please do not trespass by going ashore on the mainland.

Depending on the prevailing wind conditions, go north or south of Cole Island inside the 2-fathom line (12 feet of water depth). In the absence of wind, most boaters choose the south side either close by (150 feet) or about a quarter-mile off the island near the Stacy Brook outlet. Camp Dudley, the oldest of all YMCA camps, is located on the north side, along with a number of private residences. This is all private land, posted No Trespassing, and the residents in the area ask that they not be disturbed. The island is OK, however, for exploring.

A mile north of Cole Island is the south shore of Barber Point. Tucked in fairly close is an acceptable lunch/swim location. It can be shallow out at the point. For that reason do not

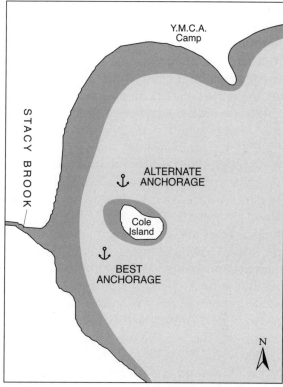

COLE BAY

NOT TO BE USED FOR NAVIGATION

approach this anchorage from the north. Use good judgment to find your spot.

Arnold Bay

On the eastern shore is Arnold Bay, named for the notorious Revolutionary War general. It is here that Benedict Arnold had to burn the flagship of his fleet, the *Congress,* and four other boats to escape the British in 1776. He left the water altogether and fled over land. History buffs can envision him and his first sailors of the U.S. Navy following the path that is now the road shown on the chart leading into the town of Vergennes and ending up at Crown Point.

Modern man needs his waste-treatment plant. That complex inside Arnold's Bay is visible and it is the best way to identify the bay coming from the west or southwest but not from most northern courses. The bay and the surrounding land gently slope, making for a shallow but usable anchorage area.

Next on the eastern shore is Button Bay, the open part of which is popular for water-skiing. As you proceed from the south and go north inside the bay (do not approach it any other way), you'll notice an island to the west. Be careful because it is shallow around the island, but it is well worth approaching by dinghy. The rocks on the island contain visible fossils. Fossils in the rocks here fascinate students and geologists, since they show that in ancient times the lake had a tropical salt-water climate. Fossils of coral, which only grows in consistently warm water, were the first tip-off. This and the mainland area immediately north is a state park, Button Bay. You can walk around and picnic. There are also some good trails on the mainland and a swimming beach. If you anchor here, please note that the bottom here is very weedy.

Westport

Opposite Button Bay, on the western shore, is the New York town of Westport. Westport has a good deepwater marina, food, fuel, and overnight dockage. If you want to anchor out here, contact the dockmaster at the service dock so that you can pay the fee for using their dinghy dock and also get advice on the best spot to anchor to avoid some of the heavy weed growth on the bottom here.

Westport Marina is at once modern, historic, clean, and fun. There is a floating-tire breakwater that causes a first-time visitor to come in from the northern end. This also is the best approach for the fuel/service dock. If you choose, you can exit to the south between the swimming beach and the tires. Water depth should not be a problem either way. The marina originally was a U.S. military aircraft base that also handled watercraft.

It has now developed a strong entertainment/dining presence on the New York shore of the lake. Starting in July and continuing through Labor Day, Friday and Saturday nights have live entertainment, and the on-site Galley restaurant provides food inside and out in a picnic-table atmosphere. Slips and side ties accommodate about 90 vessels. The marina has 30/110A and 50/220A electrical hookups, well water, ice, and a restaurant (breakfast/lunch/dinner) on site. The restaurant/bar is open from 8 A.M. to midnight in July and August. The marina's fuel and service dock hours are 9 A.M. to 5 P.M., but it can accommodate special situations (inquire). Rest rooms and three showers (recently renovated) are on site and are shared by the restaurant. The laundry has two washers, two dryers, and a clothes-folding area.

Westport Marina is the only factory-trained repair center for inflatables on the lake. It also leads the way in service and repair of marine A/C. Marina repair staff understand both processes very well and have most common parts for the brands they sell. They can troubleshoot, order, and install parts on those they do not. Plus they do work on outboards, stern drives, inboards, and sailboats (including mast stepping). They also offer winter storage of boats. The marina has a 25-ton travelift. On site is a store that is both a marine outlet and a gift shop—only bigger and broader than

WESTPORT MARINA

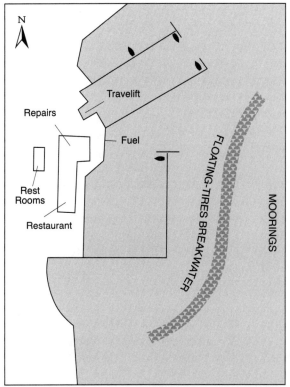

NOT TO BE USED FOR NAVIGATION

Waste pump-out
Rest rooms
Showers
Laundry
Dockside water
Picnic tables
Power connections: 30A/125V, 50A/220V
Woodworking repairs
Fiberglass repairs
Below-waterline repairs
Mechanical repairs
Gas-engine repairs
Diesel repairs
Stern-drive repairs
Outboard repairs
Generator repairs
Inflatable repairs
Travelift/hoist: 25 ton
Mast stepping: 60 feet
Ships store
Gift shop
Restaurant: on site
What's special: entertainment Friday and Saturday
VHF-monitored channel: 09, 16

most. This is a new boat dealer for inflatables and in-stock Johnson outboards as well as some hard parts (engine, pump, etc.) and sailboat-rigging supplies. Groceries, liquor, and additional restaurants are a 5- to 7-minute walk. A hardware store and other shops are 10 to 15 minutes away.

Westport Marina (518) 962-4356

Storm protection: √√
Scenic: * * *
Marina-reported approach depths: 25 feet
Marina-reported dockside depths: 3-13 feet
Gas
Diesel

Westport, originally named Bessboro by William Giuiland in the 1770s, is a very picturesque traditional summer-resort town with an excellent view of Lake Champlain. The town is oriented toward boaters and provides a map to let you know how to locate their shops, restaurants, and hotels. They have much to offer in terms of replenishing supplies, with a supermarket, liquor store, drugstore, and bank. There also are numerous antique stores, fine-art and craft shops, and a Laundromat. For a restaurant, I recommend that you call the Westport Hotel and Country Club. They will send a car to pick you up, and you might even be able to get in eighteen holes of golf on their course.

SKIPPER TIP: There are several good places on Lake Champlain to dock or anchor for the night, but it's a good idea to plan ahead. Most slips are reserved on a year-round or seasonal basis, and the few available for single nights on weekends go quickly. Sit down with your guide and charts and think about how far you want to go each day and where you want to stop, then call ahead to make reservations.

Partridge Harbor

Partridge Harbor is probably one of the best gunk holes on Lake Champlain, offering scenic vistas and secure protection during a storm. Naturally, because of this, you almost need to think in terms of staking out your claim in advance of popular days and weekends. On sunny summer weekends, people arrive early in order to claim their anchor spots. If you are hoping to stay the weekend, I suggest that you get there on Friday morning. Due to the harbor's popularity, proper courtesy calls for both a bow and stern hook in 6- to 30-foot water depths. Do not tie a stern line to a shore-based tree because this is private property and you would be trespassing. The confining nature and configuration of this harbor call for a little more sensitivity than most, so please be careful about noise, lights, and general usage of the area. It's worth it, however, because this harbor is a must-see in fair weather and is the best anchorage in the southern end of the lake during a storm.

Nearby Rock Harbor, Hunter Bay, and Basin Rock Harbor also have their fans. I certainly enjoy them. Beautiful solitude is at hand. All of these anchorages become weedy in their shallow areas in the second half of the summer. Basin Rock Harbor might require more anchor rode than most carry. Certainly make sure that the bitter end is well secured before you start paying out rode. All are a part of this 7-mile-long stretch of shoreline north from Westport to Whallon Bay that is the best series of lunchtime, afternoon, and overnight anchorages on the lake.

Glaciers formed and shaped the lake, its shoreline, and the surrounding countryside. It is said that there were multiple glacial periods, with some glaciers as thick as 10,000 feet. This glacier action created the deep bays, coves, and islands as they moved southward. Because the glacier period last occurred after an earlier tropical climate, and also after the inland-sea period, the land and waterscape we see today are a glacial legacy.

Basin Harbor and the Maritime Museum

Directly across from Partridge Harbor on the east shoreline is Basin Harbor. The harbor is the water access to the Basin Harbor Club, which is a gracious 700-acre resort, owned by the Beach family, that in various reincarnations has hosted summer visitors since 1886. A little more upscale than the self-contained summer-resort communities in the Catskills, Basin Harbor offers all-inclusive packages, usually for two weeks at a time, with a few special weekend programs. Its amenities include an expansive golf course, tennis courts, pool, and an on-site executive airport on a grass field. The club has a very small and restricted dock area, but if you can be accommodated, this is a fine place to catch a meal and admire the grounds, the main lodge, and 77 guest cottages—each with its own name and decor. While you are here, don't miss the opportunity to walk just a half-mile inland, but still on the resort grounds, to see the Lake Champlain Maritime Museum. This multi-building museum has quite a collection of local watercraft dating back several hundred years. There also is a class on constructing small wooden boats that is taught here throughout the summer. Finally, there is an accurate floating replica on display of one of the Revolutionary War gunboats, the *Philadelphia*. It was built by the museum staff and a corps of volunteers.

A must-see boat museum and a resort with the ambiance of the Basin Harbor property place this area on a par with the best that the Chesapeake Bay waters have to offer.

The Basin Harbor Club, updated continuously and run by the Beach family since 1886, is a week- or weekend-long full-service destination resort—and a complete one at that: private

One slip is reserved for transient guests of the Basin Harbor Resort, which is on the Vermont side of the lake north of buoy #53. Plan to catch a meal here at one of the restaurants if the slip is available.

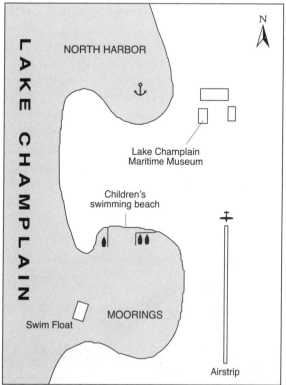

BASIN HARBOR

NOT TO BE USED FOR NAVIGATION

airstrip, boat harbor, dining rooms, 6,500-yard golf course, clay and all-weather tennis courts, pool, lake swimming, jogging trails, shuffleboard, croquet, outstanding flowered and treed 700-acre grounds, and the maritime museum. The marina is in a natural harbor with a few slips and moorings. A dockmaster in an outboard-powered inflatable is always on duty to assist you during core daylight hours. The resort is on the Vermont shore on the lower third of the middle of the lake. It is inside its own natural cove that has 8 to 10 feet of water at normal lake levels. This cove also is the swimming beach and has a swim-

ming float, plus a rental-boat and a children's boat area are in it sharing space with your vessel. If you stand off just outside the basin, the dockmaster will come out in an outboard-powered inflatable to offer you any needed services. One or two slips/moorings usually are available for museum visits tied in with a meal at the resort. Try the restaurant (of two) that is on the airfield and near the museum. The on-site store sells only beachgoers' supplies during limited hours. No overnight stays are available except by special arrangement coordinated in advance for resort guests. (Please note: Burlington is a very long taxi ride away.)

Don't miss the Lake Champlain Maritime Museum on the grounds of the Basin Harbor Resort.

Basin Harbor Club (802) 475-2311

Storm protection: √√√
Scenic: * * * *
Marina-reported approach depths: 8-10 feet
Marina-reported dockside depths: 4-8 feet
Floating docks
Gift shop
Souvenir store
Restaurant: two on site
What's special: a destination resort that reserves its marina facilities for its land-based guests (after that purpose has been fulfilled, those who want to have lunch at the club and visit the maritime museum are accommodated with all the graciousness of a special friend inviting you into their home, so tread lightly)

Lake Champlain Maritime Museum (at Basin Harbor Club Resort)

The Lake Champlain Maritime Museum is a must-see. Housed in its own buildings (one is an 1812 schoolhouse) and boat sheds on the expansive Basin Harbor Club Resort grounds, it appeals and satisfies several different enthusiasts. First, it has a full-size 54-foot replica of a Revolutionary War gunboat, the *Philadelphia* (it was built on site). You can climb all over the type of craft Benedict Arnold built and used in Whitehall, Valcour Island, Arnold's Cove, and Vergennes. It also occasionally sails the lake, bringing the history of this whole region right into your hands. Second, the collection of (often unrestored) vessels covering the last 150 years on the lake provides a sense of

Locals call it the "North Harbor"—although it's unnamed on your chart—and it's where most boaters anchor for a visit to Basin Harbor. In this corner of the harbor is a replica of Benedict Arnold's 1776 gunboat, the *Philadelphia*, which is part of the Lake Champlain Maritime Museum.

wooden boats and their historical construction and use. Displays of other artifacts with detailed storyboard explanations further illuminate olden times.

The bookstore offers both regional history titles as well as boating books. Some of these I have not seen anywhere else. Ongoing boat-building classes—from building a birch-bark canoe to a Maine coast dory—and the "build your own kayak and cruise it for a week" program are new twists on schooling that reach back to the days of Thoreau. Other classes aimed at children bring maritime history to life for them.

Special events—including battle reenactments, marches, costumes, and historical and modern-day boating presentations—are timed to happen at least once a month in the summer. Call for dates and events around the time you might be there. You might want to speed up or delay your trip to attend one of these events. For example, they host a small-craft boat show that primarily uses local builders and furthers interest in human-powered craft. Did I tell you about the tool-making classes using their on-site forge? The list of events goes on and on.

There is a second mooring/tie-up opportunity a third of a mile north of the resort and around the point that can be used to access the museum if you do not want to use the Basin Harbor Club's facilities. It has 7 to 9 feet of water depth fairly close to shore and has a weedy bottom.

The Palisades

If you are leaving from Basin Harbor, head about 340° magnetic to catch the New York shoreline nicknamed the Palisades. Follow them up to Snake Den Harbor, a good lunch-stop anchorage and one of the first opportunities to anchor and go ashore in a relatively undeveloped area. As your chart indicates, the water is deep right near shore. Because this is state land, you are welcome to tie a stern line to a tree on the shore and just use a bow anchor. Again, you need plenty of anchor line. Look for rockslides left over from the mining that took place here in the 1850s and 1860s. This general area also affords frequent opportunities to see bald eagles along the Palisade Cliffs. Plus, you might be able to maneuver close enough to the rock face to actually reach out and touch it! Grog Harbor, to the north, is so named because Major Rogers of "Rogers' Rangers" supposedly hid casks of wine, rum, and brandy there in 1756. This cargo was from a ship he had attacked the day before.

Vergennes and Otter Creek

Across the lake, at Fort Cassin Point, consider taking the entrance to Otter Creek, which leads to a 6-mile run up to the town of Vergennes. The creek shows water depths of at least 7 feet, mostly 11 feet at 95-foot lake-water level, in most instances in its center. Just watch out for downed trees both visible and hiding underwater. The creek is not wide—about 100 feet on average—and takes about an hour to make your way.

Just off Fort Cassin Point and well north of green buoy #51 is the entrance to Otter Creek. Do not go into Field's Bay. I stay 200 feet off Fort Cassin Point on the main lake. Then, at a dead-slow maneuvering speed, I proceed into Otter Creek. Entering Otter Creek, I stay 70 feet off the north shore and look for 10 feet of water depth (at 95-foot lake level), adjusting when I do not get it. The going is safer than you think. There are small craft tied up as well

This contingent of birds on a fallen tree helped me stay in deep water on one foray into Otter Creek.

as fishing activity, plus a few launch ramps, as you go in and throughout the passage. You can occasionally see through the trees to Porter Bay, too. This area is a good place to spot deer and other wildlife. If you walk the shoreline, you might find arrowheads, pottery, and other Indian artifacts. By the way, if you have a small-enough craft to portage around the Vergennes Falls, you can go another 100 to 200 miles farther up Otter Creek past these falls (including a few more portages). The creek offers quite different scenery from what you see out on the lake. You also will understand why the Indians called Otter Creek the "Crooked River."

Fort Cassin Point is not much to see now, but it was a battle site. While the Americans were building gunboats inland at Vergennes, Lieutenant Cassin was mounding up the land at the north shore of the entrance to Otter Creek to create a berm for cannon. On May 14, 1814, the British opened fire on this point and a several-hour exchange of fire ensued. Neither side won.

At the end of Otter Creek there are overhead power lines and the city of Vergennes and its waterfalls, which once were used to power mills and factories and still power a hydraulic plant. Vergennes, a very old town, was a source of shipbuilding for the American naval fleet during the War of 1812. On the one side of the public dock is the site of a shipyard where the sailing brig *Saratoga* was built for use in that war. While you are here, you can use the municipal or floating piers at no charge. The town posts a map to show you how to get around. Vergennes has restaurants, Nan's Bake Shop (a must-stop on the city's main street), a supermarket, liquor store, pharmacy, and hardware and clothing stores.

Although this is the view of the north side, the Vergennes Town Dock offers floats for tie-up on both sides of the river. Dockage is free, and it's a short (albeit uphill) trip to town for shops and good food.

Vergennes Town Dock (unstaffed; no phone)

Storm Protection √√√
Scenic ****
Wooden floating docks are available here for a dozen boats, with 15A/110V (extension-cord style) electrical hookups, set well back from the docks, for just four boats. I have used 125 feet of shore power cord and adapters to reach these plugs. This dock has 7- to 8-foot water depth at 95-foot lake level. The other dock has more. Town is 2 to 3 blocks away for the first nine boats and longer for three boats side-tied across the river.

Grounds are grassy and well treed.

This spot is a quiet, nice place to tie up. The town has a signboard of restaurant menus and a town map located near the electrical plugs.

You can tie-up for free (with free electricity if you arrive early) in this nice town within view of a historic waterfall. Check out a possible shuttle that goes around town and down to the Lake Champlain Maritime Museum.

Indians

Indians beat Samuel de Champlain in exploring Lake Champlain. They saw it as many things, including a "roadway." Canoe travel during Champlain's time was in increments of 5 miles per day. They used canoes, Champlain wrote in his journals, "made of birch bark strengthened inside with little hoops of white cedar, being about eight or nine paces long and one and a half paces wide in the middle." These carried three people or two paddlers and supplies. Portages over land between bodies of water were workable, but they had to be short. The natural proximity of the St. Lawrence River, Richelieu River, Lake Champlain, Otter Creek, La Chute, Lake George, Hudson River, and the Mohawk River opened up a huge territory to the Indians.

Kingsland Bay, Point Bay, and Converse Bay

Heading north, Kingsland Bay and two coves north of it are sheltered from most winds, including storms from the north. If you stay in the little cove that is the most westerly of the three, which appears as white, deeper water on your chart, you will have the best protection from weather in all directions. This cove is another place that is popular with local boaters, especially during a storm.

The large bay on the eastern shore of Lake Champlain, inside of Thompson's Point, is sometimes called Point Bay, but it is labeled on the charts as Town Farm Bay. There is a large marina here that is oriented toward seasonal tenants. It's not a good choice for an overnight stop since there are no restaurants on the premises or nearby, and a transient slip is available only if the seasonal tenant is away on a cruise. However, it does have a good ship's store.

To approach Point Bay Marina, I stay 300 feet off the southern shore of Thompson's Point starting at the flagpole to avoid the buoys marking two shallow spots in that bay. Water depth would only be a problem at low lake levels, but you must avoid a sunken barge near the fuel dock. It is a large 30-acre and 20-employee marina. Its ship's store is good and has charts, cruising guides, and other books in abundance, supported by a selection of soda pop and additional marine supplies. They also have a paperback-exchange section for cruisers. The marina does repairs, since it has both new and used boat sales on site as well as a large seasonal and winter storage business. Mercruiser, OMC, Volvo, Yanmar, Chrysler, and Ford/Lehman are all worked on. A travelift and a forklift move the boats in and out. They also do electronics, wood, metal, and fiberglass repairs.

Point Bay Marina (802) 425-2431

Storm protection: √√√
Scenic: * *
Marina-reported approach depths: 6-18 feet
Marina-reported dockside depths: 2-7 feet
Gas
Diesel
Waste pump-out
Rest rooms
Shower
Barbecues
Picnic tables
Power connections: 30A/125V, 50A/220V
Woodworking repairs
Fiberglass repairs
Welding
Below-waterline repairs
Mechanical repairs
Gas-engine repairs
Diesel repairs
Stern-drive repairs

Outboard-motor repairs
Generator repairs
Travelift/hoist: 25 ton
Mast stepping: 70 feet
Ship's store

Around the point and north are Converse Bay and its two islands. If you anchor at Converse Bay, stay north of Garden and Cedar Islands and as far east as is practical to get the best protection from all winds. Both islands, by the way, have submerged cables running back to the mainland on the south side. These are the two squiggly magenta lines on your chart. Don't anchor here because you could foul the cables and cut off their electricity. Again, because this is private property, any shore landing is considered trespassing.

Split Rock Point

Now the lake is ready to widen again. Split Rock Point, on the New York shore, denotes the beginning of the next segment of this magnificent lake. Wind and waves can change here more times than not. There is an aid to navigation—a red skeleton tower with a light at 93 feet—up on Split Rock Point.

An Indian custom was to toss trinkets overboard as they canoed past this point to pay respect to Indian Chief Reggio, who drowned here in rough water upon rounding the point. The lake was named after him for a while by his tribe, the Mohawks. Homage here to Chief Reggio is supposed to ensure safe passage and calm water. Today, make sure your trinkets stay on board: There is a federal law against throwing anything into the lake.

Essex

The town of Essex is one of my favorite spots in New York State. Listed in the National Reg-

ister of Historic Places, it is a very old town with a rock-solid maritime history. Ships were built here starting in the 1700s. The town's shipyards supplied ships for the Revolutionary War and the War of 1812; then they built canal boats to ferry people around the lake and pleasure boats when the need for them arose. The town of Essex is just a block inland from the marinas. Nicely maintained, it is a delightful shopping town with one or two outstanding restaurants. If you stay an extra day, you must have a long, leisurely meal at the Essex Inn. Built around 1810 and completely renovated in 1989, the inn has ten guestrooms—with no door locks on my last visit—and multiple dining areas. Dinner here is always

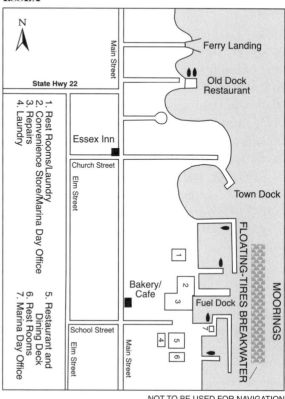

ESSEX

NOT TO BE USED FOR NAVIGATION

drawn out and entertaining, with mostly good gourmet food and a grand bed-and-breakfast/small-hotel atmosphere. For a one-night stay I must recommend the restaurant in a lovely cottage on the grounds of the Essex Shipyard. Its menu is short, but the large-portioned dishes are freshly prepared with flair. The place has a casual, country air, and you are not required to dress up for dinner after a long day on the lake. Both the restaurant and its patio overlook the lake, letting you soak up the ambiance of this special place.

I've heard some New Yorkers say that the New England-like character of both the architecture and the rocky edges of the shoreline detract from the "New Yorkness" of Essex, but I think the atmosphere is just terrific. I highly recommend a stop here.

There are two marinas at Essex, though originally it was all one property owned by two partners. As the result of some differences, they split the property into two marinas. The northernmost marina has been recently renovated, with all brand-new docks, electrical hookups, bathrooms, and a ship's store/convenience market right at dockside. Although the other marina first began as a shipyard, it does not suffer from heavy shipyard activities today. However, the marina is very active and in excellent condition, with a nice mixture of sail- and powerboats, both wooden and fiberglass. You'll find that this is the most atmospheric marina on the trip—more like a boat lover's museum without the title. Be sure to explore the boat sheds to see the antique wooden boats and enjoy the cafe/restaurant there that offers both lunch and dinner.

At Cabins by the Lake you can enjoy fully restored—but not updated—1920s-vintage accommodations. A cement pier is in front (watch the water depth!), so you can prearrange to tie up and spend the night on land if you prefer.

At the northern end of town, just north of the marinas, there is a landing for the ferry that commutes between New York and Vermont. Also nearby is a tie-up for smaller boats (3- to 8-foot water depths) that want to patronize the waterfront Old Dock Restaurant. Try the rack of lamb. Inquire at (518) 963-4232.

This general shoreline area doesn't really provide the kind of protection you would like to have for an anchorage, and you could have a rocky night if you anchor out on a hook or a mooring. Still, I encourage you to stop for the night, an afternoon, or for fuel in a marina at Essex. It is really something that you shouldn't miss.

Ships were built at Essex Shipyard from Revolutionary War times through World War II. Now it is a family-run marina for seasonal and transient boaters. It also repairs and restores boats. It is a very well maintained property and has a charm that is seen only at a select few marinas in the United States. Except for one floating dock, the fixed docks there pro- vide a sureness underfoot that only a pier built to withstand all four seasons can offer. It also offers 30A and dual 30A/110V and 50A/110V power connections; a drinkable water supply; night lighting; and picnic tables on site.

The on-site restaurant is separately man- aged and is open for both lunch and dinner. It has a must-see decor, with interior walls of varnished, knotty pine accented by white and deep-blue fabrics. Detailed with small flowers, the restaurant exudes a Green Mountain or Adirondack Mountain flavor both inside and on its dining deck. Up the marina's driveway and then right is a bakery/breakfast/sandwich shop that also has good food. Next door to the sandwich shop, a deli selling beer and wine may or may not be open.

You must explore the on-site boat-build- ing/repair shed, which approximates an unof- ficial boat show all summer long. A full marine railway for "inside a building" repairs, plus a launch ramp/yard cradle for outside haul-out, is available for below-waterline

The Old Dock Restaurant is a popular waterfront spot in Essex, New York—just south of the ferry that crosses the lake to Charlotte, Vermont. Docks are available in front of the restaurant's red- and-white frame building, which is easily visible from the water.

The Essex Shipyard offers pleasant dining facilities, including an outdoor deck with a commanding view of the lake. The Essex Marina next door, which has the fuel dock, is immediately off the right edge of this photo.

repairs. Large yachts occasionally come in for the annual wooden-boat show on a weekend in late July and end up spending the summer using the shipyard property and the town of Essex as a base from which to enjoy the lake.

The rest rooms and showers feature outstanding varnished-wood walls, doors, and stalls that have a warmth that is just right for boaters who prefer a special approach rather than today's cookie-cutter sterility. Vented doors and a vented cupola allow nature to disperse shower steam. The shower stalls are clean and are done in a smooth, Corian-style hard surface, with the ceilings repainted white

every year. The laundry, which has two washers and dryers, is in a separate building.

The Essex Shipyard, run by the Myers family, is on the western side of Lake Champlain about mid-lake in the downtown area of the small community of Essex. Enter it either north or south but not straight in, where there is a low-lying breakwater of floating tires. Good water depth is everywhere (12 to 15 feet). The Essex Shipyard is comprised of everything to the south of the fuel pier, which is part of the next-door property, Essex Marina. Nearby activities include Essex, a great historic town for exploring, browsing antiques, and dining out. There are several bed-and-breakfasts in town if you need one.

Essex Shipyard (518) 963-7700

Storm protection: √√√
Scenic: * * * *
Marina-reported approach depths: 12-15 feet
Marina-reported dockside depths: 5-10 feet
Gas: adjunct
Diesel: adjunct
Rest rooms
Showers
Laundry
Dockside water
Picnic tables
Power connections: 30 A/125V, dual 30A/125V and 50 A/220V
Woodworking repairs
Below-waterline repairs
Mechanical repairs
Marine railway
Yard trailer/tow vehicle
Ship's store: adjunct
Restaurant: on site
Deli: off site
Convenience store: adjunct
What's special: charm
VHF-monitored channel: 68

Essex Marina is at the downtown Essex waterfront. Come in from either the north or the south side to miss the low-riding tire breakwater. Essex Marina is on the north side of the central fairway; its fuel pier separates it from Essex Shipyard to the south.

The marina's fuel dock offers both gas and diesel and often super-hi-test (aviation gasoline), plus a wastewater pump-out. Boaters are cautioned to fender well: Some wave action can occur at the refueling station.

Essex Marina is an older medium-sized marina that was renovated during 1995 and 1996. It was completely reoutfitted with 30A and dual 30A/110V and 50A/110V electrical

hookups. If you need them, electrical adapters are for sale. In the past, this marina was a part of the Essex Shipyard and dates back to early boat-building activities at this site. Partnership problems led to an amicable division of the properties. This half had become rundown and was sold to Barry Hamilton, late of Philadelphia. He was the force behind the renovations, adding all-new electrical hookups, fuel dock, lighting, rest rooms, and a ship's store. It is first-class all the way—and clean. Its hours of operation in peak season are from 11:30 A.M. to 5:30 P.M. If no one is around, a buzzer is located at the entrance to the ship's store. Ring it again if no one shows up in five minutes. For a marina that doesn't do repairs, the on-site ship's store offers an oversized selection of boating supplies, plus an even larger selection of suntan oil, soft drinks, charts, camera film (the only place in town), and other items you might need.

Finally, the marina has two showers plus toilets in both the men's and the women's facilities, which still look very clean and new since the 1995 renovation. The bathrooms are housed in large rooms that are in their own building off a nice wooden patio deck with picnic tables. Experience the unique coin-operated showers (bring quarters). It is heated as needed. The laundry room—with two washers and dyers and a folding counter—was not open during my last visit because of poor local drainage and recent rains.

Essex Marina (518) 963-7222

Storm protection: √√√
Scenic: * * *
Marina-reported approach depths: 12-15 feet
Marina-reported dockside depths: 4-10 feet

Gas
Diesel
Waste pump-out
Rest rooms
Showers
Dockside water
Barbecues
Picnic tables
Power connections: 30A/125V and dual
    30A/125V and 50A/220V
Ship's store
Convenience store: on site
VHF-monitored channel: 09, 16, 68

Crossing the Lake: Yes/No

Leaving Essex, you'll find the lake is a little more than 2 miles wide. Going north, at the entrances to Willsboro Bay (New York) and Shelburne Bay (Vermont), the lake widens to about 8 miles. Depending on your destination, you might want to decide now which side you want to travel north on for the next few miles.

Going north on the New York side (western shore) for the 10 miles to the entrance of Willsboro Bay is simple. Stay at least two-thirds of a mile but not more than 1½ miles off the shoreline. You will pass outside three red buoys that mark shallow water to your port side, and you will go inside the Four Brothers, a series of offshore islands, keeping them to your starboard side. The first buoy, red #50, marks the shallow water from the outfall of the Bouquet River, a popular place for a swimming stop.

Proceeding across the lake and then north on the eastern shore, I suggest you take the longer, more offshore run of the choices available to you. It does get you to Shelburne Bay. After crossing over to the eastern shore from Essex to the north side of Sloop Island, turn north to about a 017° magnetic heading. That heading will take you outside Quaker Smith

Reef, which is 5½ miles ahead and at least three-quarters of a mile off the point of land, Quaker Smith Point. From there, head toward Saxton Reef, 1¼ miles north and east, clearing it on your starboard side. Then proceed toward Juniper Island 3⅓ miles north, passing inside it but outside the Juniper Ledge buoy three-quarters of a mile this side of Juniper Island. Shelburne Bay is now a right turn away. Quaker Smith Point along the way does offer anchorages on its north and south coves. Pick one based on wind direction. If you can cross the lake due east from Essex, you will pass Hill Bay, a public swimming beach. It has fire pits and picnic tables. Watch out for wind surfers as you cruise through here. There are those of us who would just as well sail up the center of the lake, too!

This lake was once much bigger, a great inland sea that extended over 20 to 50 times the area of the current lake. It was connected to the Atlantic Ocean, both north and south, and was salt water. The St. Lawrence River, Lake Champlain, and the Hudson River were one. Once the lake shrank to its current size, landmass disconnected it from the ocean and it slowly became what it is today, the sixth largest freshwater body in North America.

Shelburne Bay and the City of Burlington

SKIPPER TIP: Use chart 14783 to navigate Shelburne Bay and switch over to chart 14782 to go into Burlington.

For a quiet night's anchorage/dockage, go into Shelburne Bay, or, if you want a slip for the night and the nightlife of the big city, head for Burlington, Vermont.

SHELBURNE BAY

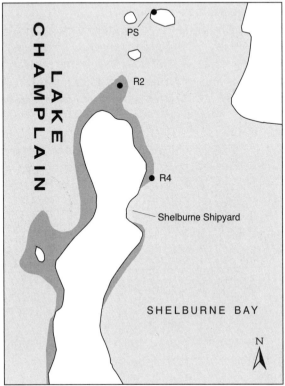

NOT TO BE USED FOR NAVIGATION

Shelburne Bay does not offer protection from winds coming from the north, but it is a good-sized bay with deep water and water access to the city of Burlington. The town of Shelburne has a shipyard that also functions as a marina with a ship's store. The origins of the Shelburne Shipyard, by the way, go back to 1826, and the ship's store is generally given the distinction of being the most complete on Lake Champlain's shores. This also is the best landing spot to get to the Shelburne Museum, although you need to arrange for a somewhat lengthy taxi ride from the shipyard to get there. The Shelburne Museum features American folk art and a tour of the Colchester Reef Lighthouse, which was built in 1871, decommissioned in 1933, and moved to the museum in 1952. Also on display is the *Ticonderoga* side-wheeler, an early steamboat that ran on Lake Champlain.

A closer place to visit, 2 to 3 miles down the country road that provides access for the shipyard to the mainland, is Shelburne Farms, a vast working dairy operation, and its upscale hotel Shelburne House (once the farm's manor). Here you can enjoy a wonderful Sunday brunch as well as other meals. The complex also has at its gatehouse a gift store with its mail-order products. Call ahead for any dining reservations.

You can also visit Shelburne Farms by anchoring south of Saxton Point. The ruins called out on your chart are an old rock crib that extends out from shore. Come inside it at about the 11 marked on your chart as a water depth. If this cove is busy with boats, I have been told that this means Shelburne House probably is holding an outdoor concert. The crowd of boats is listening to the music. Where else but on Lake Champlain!

Shelburne Shipyard is a good-sized marina with a wharf and floating finger piers. The shipyard has 20 employees in season. It is open 9 A.M. to 7 P.M. from June 15 to September 15, and 9 A.M. to 5 P.M. from April 30 to June 15 and September 15 to October 31. The ship's store has many books, charts, cruising guides, snack food, and soft drinks; marine supplies and hardware also are abundant. As far as repairs go, the shipyard stores more than 600 vessels every winter; has both a 50-ton and a 35-ton travelift on site; and does mast, rigging, fiberglass, wood, metal, electrical, mechanical, and stern-drive repair. All of these are routinely accomplished with a high standard of workmanship. Bottom- and much topside painting are done here, too.

One of the docks of the Shelburne Shipyard, an area institution for boaters. Not shown are the well-stocked ship's store and the tremendous facilities for repairs and storage.

Shelburne Shipyard (802) 985-3326

Storm protection: √√√
Scenic: * * *
Marina-reported approach depths: 30 feet plus
Marina-reported dockside depths: 3-10 feet
Gas
Diesel
Waste pump-out
Rest rooms
Showers
Laundry
Dockside water
Barbecues
Picnic tables
Power connections: 30A/125V, 50A/220V
Woodworking repairs
Fiberglass repairs
Welding
Below-waterline repairs
Mechanical repairs
Gas-engine repairs
Diesel repairs
Stern-drive repairs
Generator repairs
Travelift/hoist: 50 tons
Marine railway
Yard trailer/tow vehicle
Mast stepping
Ship's store
What's special: landmark repair yard
VHF-monitored channel: 09, 16

Years ago, the city of Burlington was a key port for the transportation of lumber. At one

SHELBURNE SHIPYARD

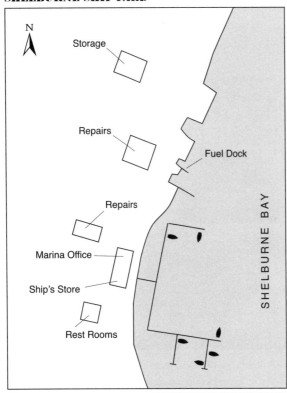

NOT TO BE USED FOR NAVIGATION

choice, which is the Burlington Community Boathouse. City-financed and operating under new management, this boathouse has several shortcomings. For example, only about half the slips have electrical power, and there are no shoreside showers for boaters to use. Plus, the docks need to be gated to keep visitors away from the boats. Although building some showers has been proposed, they will still be quite a walk away from the slips.

Having said that, Burlington's Community Boathouse is fine for an afternoon tie-up to access downtown Burlington, which is a great shopping city—largely because of strong community support for local business. The stores are constantly improving, and you can find outstanding bookstores and six or seven places to buy/sip coffee and other specialty items, as well as restaurants and all the services that you could possibly need. Burlington also is the home of the University of Vermont as well as other schools, and the synergy between the colleges and the local inhabitants provides a cheery, upbeat atmosphere that makes this a thoroughly enjoyable place to spend an afternoon.

For boaters, one of the potential problems with accessing downtown Burlington is that it is a hillside town: The six blocks or so to the shopping district are all uphill from the boathouse. Still, there is a free trolley every 20 minutes; use it and the negative becomes a positive. See, the city does like cruising boaters. It is interesting that the Burlington City Council establishes the harbor regulations, which are enforced by the harbormaster. This town is the only one I have come across where boaters write to the mayor for a copy of harbor regulations—although now these types of requests are being redirected to the

time it was ranked third in the United States for lumber tonnage transported. In the recent past, it was a port for barges carrying petroleum products. Today it is a bustling college town with a top-notch downtown shopping district. The city has two options in three marinas for cruising boaters wanting to tie up, or you can use the special anchorage area inside the harbor and marked on your chart. At the south end of town, there is the Ferry Dock Marina, sharing a small inner breakwater with Perkins Pier (for 22-foot and smaller boats only), which is within walking distance to town but still a ways from the center of downtown. It is farther south than the alternative

From the Burlington Boat House in Burlington, Vermont, you can take a trolley to the shopping-dining district and even take in a movie!

parks department. If the city leaders of Burlington ever committed the money to build a proper transient dockage and support system, this town would become a mecca for all boaters on Lake Champlain and probably a destination stop for anyone who considers cruising the eastern third of the United States. That's a multimillion-person pool of potential tourists. Attention business leaders: A proper marina and an orientation to transient boaters' needs are the keys to creating a whole new market for the community!

Burlington Community Boathouse rents powerboats and sailboats, accommodates a large dining yacht, and offers the residents of the city of Burlington waterfront access. In addition, it has transient slips; however, the gangways to the transient docks are not gated. There is an on-site cafe that offers free one-hour docking with a meal purchase. Also, the city's free shuttle bus stops here to take you the six blocks up the hill to the city's shopping area. The available power connections are 15A and 30A, but not all slips have connections. Call ahead for reservations and inquire about electrical hookups as you are assigned a slip number. An occasional wind-created chop can make it both hard to tie up and

DOWNTOWN BURLINGTON

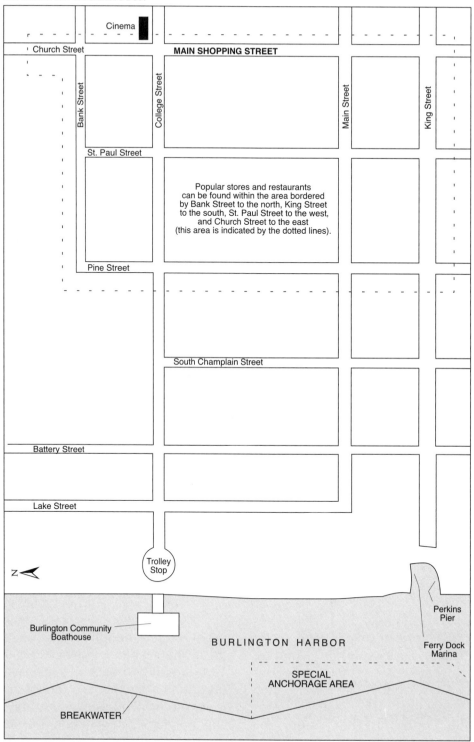

Cinema

MAIN SHOPPING STREET

Church Street

Bank Street

College Street

St. Paul Street

Main Street

King Street

Popular stores and restaurants
can be found within the area bordered
by Bank Street to the north, King Street
to the south, St. Paul Street to the west,
and Church Street to the east
(this area is indicated by the dotted lines).

Pine Street

South Champlain Street

Battery Street

Lake Street

Z

Trolley
Stop

Perkins
Pier

Burlington Community
Boathouse

BURLINGTON HARBOR

Ferry Dock
Marina

SPECIAL
ANCHORAGE AREA

BREAKWATER

NOT TO BE USED FOR NAVIGATION

somewhat uncomfortable overnight. Transient toilets and sinks are located in the main building. These rest rooms also are used by the many dining yacht customers, park visitors, and cafe patrons; they are cleaned frequently, however.

Burlington Community Boathouse (802) 865-3377

Storm protection: √√
Scenic: * *
Marina-reported approach depths: 15 feet
Marina-reported dockside depths: 4-12 feet
Floating docks
Rest rooms
Dockside water
Power connections: 15A/125V, 30A/125V (both limited)
VHF-monitored channel: 09, 16

Ferry Dock Marina shares an inner breakwater with Perkins Pier on the south side of Burlington. It is well protected. Enter from the southern end of the city's breakwater. Stay clear of both special anchorages buoyed off inside the Burlington Breakwater. Ferry Dock Marina is now to the northeast and is deep water all the way until inside the marina's inner breakwater, where depth can be shallow. Gas is available. A pump-out can be free with a large fuel purchase or overnight dockage plus top-off of fuel (inquire). Toilets and sinks are on site and are heated in cool weather. The marina shares its landing with the ferries that transit the lake. The potable water supply tastes excellent.

Ferry Dock Marina (802) 864-9804

Storm protection: √√√
Scenic: * *
Marina-reported approach depths: 15 feet

BURLINGTON COMMUNITY BOATHOUSE

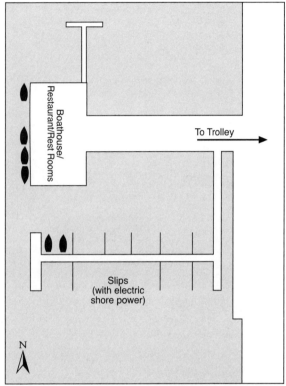

NOT TO BE USED FOR NAVIGATION

Marina-reported dockside depths: 3-10 feet
Gas
Waste pump-out
Rest rooms
Power connections: 15A/125V, 30A/125V, 50 A/125V
VHF-monitored channel: 09, 16

Perkins Pier shares an inner breakwater with Ferry Dock Marina on the south side of the city of Burlington. Transient boats are limited to 22 feet in length.

Perkins Pier (802) 865-3377

Storm protection: √√√
Scenic: * *

FERRY DOCK MARINA AND PERKINS PIER

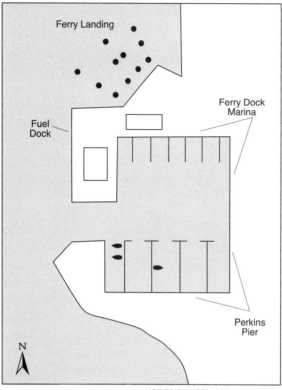

NOT TO BE USED FOR NAVIGATION

Marina-reported approach depths: 15 feet
Marina-reported dockside depths: 2-6 feet
Rest rooms
What's special: maximum boat size is 22 feet

Wreck Diving

One of the great fascinations of boating is the awareness that, while you are skimming along the surface of the water, beneath you exists another world with a life of its own—a world that occasionally claims victims from the realm above. Like any body of water that has been traveled for centuries, Lake Champlain has had its share of shipwrecks, and the state of Vermont now protects those wrecks as historic sites so that scuba divers may visit and explore them. Vermont is to be commended for this policy that recognizes the historic value of these wrecks. It is the only Northeastern state and, I believe, only one of four states in the United States to establish what are called "underwater historic preserves," which make shipwrecks accessible to divers.

Each underwater historic preserve is identified by one or more special-purpose yellow buoys. Divers' vessels tie up directly to the buoy for the duration of the dive to avoid using anchors, which might cause damage to a wreck site. Divers then follow the buoy's anchor chain down to the bottom. From there, a guide rope leads them across the lake bottom to the wreck. There are usually signs placed around the wreck to give information about the site. If you explore any of these underwater historic preserves, please do not penetrate the wreck. Instead, bring a light and use it to illuminate interior areas. Divers also are asked not to alter the site or remove any artifacts, and to report anyone who does. Pamphlets with details on how to participate in this innovative dive experience are available at local diver shops.

> **DIVER TIP:** To the best of my knowledge, neither Vermont nor upstate New York has a decompression chamber. However, the University of New Hampshire at Durham has one.

The most accessible wreck on Lake Champlain is the 88-foot canal sailboat *General Butler,* built in 1862 and sunk in 1876. After sailing the lake, the *General Butler*'s schooner-rigged mast would be unstepped and her centerboard raised in preparation for being towed down the Champlain Canal. Located just west of the southern edge of the Burlington Breakwater, marked by special buoys #A and #B, she now rests on her keel in 40 feet of water, with her bow pointing in an east-southeasterly direction. Her hull is intact.

The next most accessible shipwreck is the horse ferry. That is not the vessel's name but rather a title that indicates her propulsion power—literally that of two horses! This barge's "horsepower" came from two live horses that walked a moving sidewalk, or flywheel, forward. The flywheel was geared to two side paddles that in turn powered the barge. This power system did not work well enough to make horse propulsion very popular, but steam-powered side-wheelers such as the *Robert E. Lee* cruised the Mississippi and other rivers and this lake for years. The ferry now lies in 50 feet of water, marked by special buoy #E by Colchester Reef north of the city of Burlington, and even though it has mostly deteriorated, the wreck is a thrilling sight.

The third most accessible wreck site is an unnamed coal barge. She sank in 1884 and lies in 80 feet of water on a mud bottom south of Burlington and north of Shelburne Bay, just north of Proctor Shoal and marked by special buoys #C and #D. All of these sites are marked on chart 14782. There are more than two dozen diving sites on the lake. Please consult with a dive shop for local knowledge.

The water is significantly colder down deep in the lake where you find these wrecks, so make sure you are prepared. As with any diving, think carefully about safety issues and what equipment you will need. Local diving shops are your best resource for discovering this other—or under—side of Lake Champlain.

> **SKIPPER TIP:** Switch back to chart 14783 here.

Willsboro Bay

Across the lake from Burlington, about 8 miles away, is Willsboro Bay, a body of water that is as close to a visit to a Scandinavian waterway environment likely to be seen on the East Coast. Particularly on its western shore, you can literally hug the wall and have 50 feet or more of water under your bottom. I have touched the wall with my hand while my vessel was in 102 feet of water. Most of the western shore is unspoiled, except for a railroad track running about 100 feet up off the water; however, it does not disturb your view of the wooded shoreline. There are two marinas in Willsboro Bay, with the Indian Bay Marina being the smaller of the two. Take heed, Willsboro Bay is not a place to be anchored during a storm. The steep sides of the hills and mountains work against it being a safe-haven anchorage. There is no wind protection, and the water can turn angry.

Willsboro Bay Marina is a major 150-acre marina that is comprised of 70 percent sailboats and 30 percent powerboats. Half its tenants are Americans, the other half are Canadians. The bay itself offers protected sailing, plus it is within a day's sail of Mallet's Bay. It is a larger, full-service facility with four long finger piers that can satisfy a boater's needs year-round. The marina has 16 employees in season. Two buildings house two rest rooms each. Men and women each have three showers that are heated in winter and are sometimes cleaned twice a day. The ship's store has a large selection of marine supplies and

Although this bow rail is only 10 feet away from the rock wall, the depth gauge registers 102 feet of water below!

cruising guides rounded out with soft drinks, beer, snack food, and convenience items. The marina works on Merc, Volvo, Yanmar, Crusader, Force, Marinepower, Westerbeke, and OMC, doing mechanical repairs/rigging as well as wood, metal, and fiberglass repairs using a 15-ton crane, 25-ton travelift, and hydraulic yard trailers. Winter storage also is

offered. The fuel dock is at the north end of the marina on an extension of the travelift pier and sells both gas and diesel. It is open from 8 A.M. to 6 P.M. in July and August and shorter hours in the shoulder seasons.

Willsboro Bay Marina (518) 963-7276

Storm protection: √√√
Scenic: * * *
Marina-reported approach depths: 40 feet
Marina-reported dockside depths: 5-15 feet
Floating docks
Gas
Diesel
Waste pump-out
Rest rooms

WILLSBORO BAY MARINA

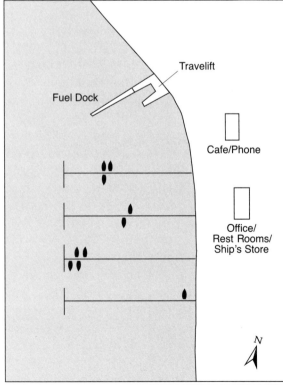

NOT TO BE USED FOR NAVIGATION

Willsboro Bay offers great sailing. The fine facility shown here is the Willsboro Bay Marina.

Showers
Dockside water
Barbecues
Picnic tables
Power connections: 30A/125V
Woodworking repairs
Fiberglass repairs
Welding
Below-waterline repairs
Mechanical repairs
Gas-engine repairs
Diesel repairs
Travelift/hoist: 25 ton
Mast stepping: 70 feet
Ship's store
Convenience store: on site
VHF-monitored radio: 09, 16

Indian Bay Marina (518) 963-7858

Storm protection: √√√
Scenic: *
Marina-reported approach depths: 40 feet
Marina-reported dockside depths: 3-8 feet

Floating docks
Waste pump-out
Rest rooms
Showers
Dockside water
Barbecues
Picnic tables
Power connections: 30A/125V
Mechanical repairs

Ferris Rock

Ferris Rock is marked on your chart. Located about 5 miles north (past Schuyler Island) and 1½ miles off the New York shore, it is infamous as a spot where vessels have foundered over the several centuries of travel on Lake Champlain. At lower water levels in the fall, the rock is exposed, but at normal water it is submerged, with just the marker visible to boatsmen. Be alert, because boaters continue to run aground here, even since the Coast Guard put up a lighted marker.

Port Kent

Ausable Chasm is inland from Port Kent and requires a taxi ride to reach. It's a natural wonder and a junior-sized Grand Canyon. Also, there are some artifacts from the lake on display there. Port Kent also is a landing for the ferry that runs to Burlington, Vermont. Look for the route as shown on your chart.

Mallet's Bay

Working your way north on the Vermont side, stay outside of the well-marked shoals, reefs, and islands that hug the shore here: Colchester Shoal; Colchester Reef, site of another buoyed underwater historic preserve; Hogback Reef; and Sunset Island. Then work your way inside of Jones Rock, Stave I Ledge, and Stave Island. Watch for the fire lookout tower on Stave Island proper.

> **SKIPPER TIP:** Stave Island has daily seaplane commuter traffic in season.

You now come across an opportunity to enter into Mallett's Bay, which is the very attractive cruising ground in the Burlington suburbs. It is perhaps the busiest area of the lake. Look at your chart and you will notice that the entrance through the railroad-track land berm is not straight in; you need to go slightly north of the entrance and come back down, staying in 6 or 7 feet of water and then going through a fairly narrow opening. Beware, sailboaters, because in a good wind this might be a bit difficult, but everybody does it. You then pass through the outer bay, 4½ miles by 4 miles in size, which is further sectioned off by an auto bridge and shallow water at its north

(or land) end, except for the entrance to Mallett's Bay.

Mallett's Bay is an outstanding area with a plethora of anchorages and also a few marinas. It is roughly 2 miles by 2 miles in dimension. Call ahead and reserve in high season, however, because this is premium space and, even though there is an abundance of slips, they are quite frequently full. In addition to the marinas on the south shore of Mallett's Bay, there are many good anchorages on the north shore, which is protected from everything but wind from the south. In only a couple of spots do you have to watch out for water depth; pay attention to your chart for these areas.

You will need land transportation if you want to access the city of Burlington from Mallett's Bay. It is about a 15-minute ride by car to Burlington from the closest marina.

Marble Island Resort and Marina is a 93-acre resort with a heavy marina influence. It has 60 slips, 50 moorings, and a 66-boat dry stack rack serviced by a 16,000-pound forklift. Both 30A and 50A/110V electrical hookups are dockside. Transient dockage fees include access to the hot tubs and two pools. Golf, tennis, basketball, and volleyball are on site; some of these activities must be paid for separately. Marble Island is at the entrance to Mallet's Bay. Just past it and inside is the resort. At low lake levels this resort is still mostly accessible. It has full rest rooms with showers. A washer/dryer is available. Marble Island is a beautiful waterfront resort used by boaters as an overnight or a weekend-long destination.

Marble Island Resort and Marina (802) 864-6800

Storm protection: √√
Scenic: * * *
Marina-reported approach depths: 30 feet

THE CHAMPLAIN CANAL AND LAKE CHAMPLAIN 215

Marina-reported dockside depths: 3-6 feet
Rest rooms
Showers
Laundry
Power connections: 30A/125V, 50A/125V
Gift shop
Restaurant: on site
What's special: resort property
VHF-monitored channel: 05

Mallett's Bay Marina is the larger full-service marina of Mallett's Bay. It is the marina destination on weekends for mid-lake sailors. Rest rooms, showers, and laundry are located in a nicer main building. The marina has a travelift for both repairs and winter storage and can step a 50-foot mast. However, groceries and restaurants are a 15-minute walk. Burlington's downtown is a 20-minute taxi ride away.

Mallet's Bay Marina (802) 862-4072

Storm protection: √√√
Scenic: * * *
Marina-reported approach depths: 20 feet
Marina-reported dockside depths: 3-8 feet
Gas
Waste pump-out
Rest rooms
Showers
Laundry
Dockside water
Barbecues
Picnic tables
Power connections: 30A/125V
Woodworking repairs
Fiberglass repairs
Below-waterline repairs
Mechanical repairs
Travelift/hoist: 15 ton
Mast stepping: 50 feet
Ship's store
VHF-monitored channel: 09,16

MALLETT'S BAY

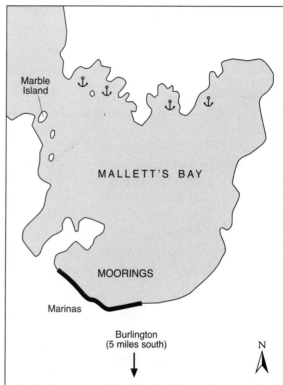

NOT TO BE USED FOR NAVIGATION

Champlain Marina (802) 658-4034

Storm protection: √√
Scenic: * *
Marina-reported approach depths: 15 feet
Marina-reported dockside depths: 3-6 feet
Rest rooms
Showers
Laundry
Picnic tables
Power connections: 30A/125V
Travelift/hoist: 25 tons
Mast stepping: 85 feet

The Moorings (802) 862-1407

Storm protection: √√
Scenic: * *

Marina-reported approach depths: 15 feet
Marina-reported dockside depths: 3-6 feet
Mechanical repairs
Travelift/hoist: 15 tons
Mast stepping: 50 feet

Valcour Island

Back out on the main lake and proceeding up the main channel to the west of Grand Isle, you notice Providence Island. It has a small natural harbor that is quite unprotected but is good for a lunch hook on its north side. Valcour Island, on the other hand, has several good anchorages and is accessible to boaters. If you only anchor out twice on your Lake Champlain cruise, you must spend one of

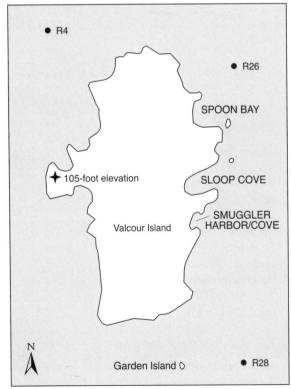

VALCOUR ISLAND

R4

R26

SPOON BAY

105-foot elevation

SLOOP COVE

SMUGGLER
HARBOR/COVE

Valcour Island

N

Garden Island   R28

NOT TO BE USED FOR NAVIGATION

those nights at Valcour Island. Approximately 95 percent of the island is owned by New York State, and the dense forest and trails on it make great hiking for boaters in the summer. You should not miss Smuggler Harbor on the island's eastern shore. It provides protection from wind coming from almost any direction and also is very scenic. If Smuggler Harbor is full, go immediately north to the next cove, Sloop Cove, and look for a spot, since this is the next choicest location and also is the second-prettiest strip of anchorage on the lake. The other choice anchorage area is in the southern part of the lake. Besides being very beautiful, Smuggler Harbor and Sloop Cove also are probably the best safe-haven anchorages in the northern part of Lake Champlain. Valcour Island, however, is not a good place to go charging around in your boat. All around the island are rock outcroppings, most of which are marked. Please give them a wide berth in order to stay off the rocks. On the mainland shore, west of Valcour Island on the southern end, are two marinas, Snug Harbor at Olde Valcour Marina and Snug Harbor Marina.

Snug Harbor at Olde Valcour Marina (518)
**   563-5140**

Storm protection: ₩
Scenic: * *
Marina-reported approach depths: 20 feet
Marina-reported dockside depths: 3-8 feet
Gas
Diesel
Waste pump-out
Rest rooms
Showers
Laundry
Picnic tables
Power connections: 30A/125V

Mechanical repairs
Mast stepping
Ship's store
VHF-monitored channel: 09

Snug Harbor Marina (518) 561-2134

Storm protection: √√
Scenic: * *
Marina-reported approach depths: 20 feet
Marina-reported dockside depths: 4-8 feet
Gas
Diesel
Waste pump-out
Rest rooms
Showers
Laundry
Dockside water
Picnic tables
Power connections: 30A/125V
Below-waterline repairs
Mechanical repairs
Mast stepping
Ship's store
What's special: new boat dealer
VHF-monitored channel: 09

The City of Plattsburgh

Cruising about 1½ miles north of Valcour Island, watch for the smaller Crab Island, the site of a U.S. field hospital during the War of 1812. You can get rather close to the obelisk monument that stands on the western shore of the island as a memorial to the soldiers who fought for Lake Champlain in that war. Both American and British soldiers are buried there. The island offers little protection for an overnight anchorage, but a lunch stop off the western shore can be pleasant if the wind conditions are right.

Cumberland Point and the city of Plattsburgh sit on Cumberland Bay, a strategic site

The monument at Crab Island, which commemorates all those soldiers who died fighting for Lake Champlain. The island housed a field hospital during the War of 1812, and both American and British soldiers are buried there.

where battles were fought both in 1776 during the Revolutionary War and in 1814 during the War of 1812. Plattsburgh is the location of an Air Force base as well as the Plattsburgh campus of the State University of New York. However, the Air Force base , which used the canal to transport jet fuel, has closed down, and with it much of the barge traffic on the Champlain Canal has ceased. If you do stop, walk the trail along the Saranac River. The city has a large marina, shown on your map as the Dock and Cole Co. Marina, which is now called the Plattsburgh Boat Basin. A low-lying breakwater there that protects the slips from wave action is marked by a light pole at each end. Just do not find yourself going between these poles when high lake levels obscure both poles and breakwater. The breakwater is due for a raise. If you like a lively atmosphere, do not miss the bar/restaurant here. Try the garlic chicken soup.

Plattsburgh Boat Basin (518) 561-2800

Storm protection: √√√
Scenic: *
Marina-reported approach depths: 12 feet
Marina-reported dockside depths: 3-10 feet
Gas
Diesel
Waste pump-out
Rest rooms
Showers
Dockside water
Picnic tables
Power connections: 30A/125V, 50A/220V
Fiberglass repairs
Below-waterline repairs
Mechanical repairs
Travelift/hoist: 35 ton
**Restaurant: on site (the most jumping joint I
    have seen on the lake at a marina)**
What's special: great bar and restaurant
VHF-monitored channel: 09

Cumberland Head Ferry

North of Plattsburgh, the western shore juts out in a large landmass called Cumberland Head. The deep water of the lake narrows from 4½ miles wide to 1⅓ miles wide. There also is a ferry route here and three submarine cables all shown with magenta-colored lines.

Lake Champlain Sovereignty

The French, the Dutch, and later the British all laid claim to Lake Champlain at one time or another. These multiple and conflicting claims haunted the area for years, often cul-minating in hand-to-hand combat to decide ownership. In July 1609 Samuel de Champlain, standing in the lake, claimed it for France. In September 1609 Henry Hudson claimed the lake for the Dutch while he was 50 miles south of it. The Americans and British fought over it in the War of 1812.

In 1690, the English and Dutch established an outpost at Chimney Point and a presence at Otter Creek. Otter Creek was not kept up and became French by 1709. Battles between the French and the English, both using Indians, continued from 1690 until 1713, when the Treaty of Utrecht divided the lake as French north of Split Rock and English below it. This treaty did not prevent the French from going south after a few years. By 1731 France's Fort Frederic was in place at Crown Point, which is well south of Split Rock.

Built in 1755, Fort Ticonderoga was upgraded in 1757, with stone walls replacing the original wooden walls. This massive building effort involved some 2,000 men. By 1759 the French, transferring forces from the lake forts northward to help defend Quebec, were too weak to defend their positions on the lake. The French abandoned Fort Ticonderoga and blew up their Fort Frederick (Crown Point) as they left. All French land claims were taken over by American colonists. In May 1775 Ethan Allen and the Green Mountain Boys with Benedict Arnold captured Fort Ticonderoga. (Benedict Arnold then fought the British fleet in October 1776 in the battle at Valcour Island.) War on Lake Champlain, however, ended for good when American Commodore McDonough, using boats built in Vergennes, won in the Plattsburgh engagement against the British fleet in September 1814.

> **SKIPPER TIP:** You may now change to chart 14781.

Young Island and Bixby Island

Young Island and Bixby Island are both nesting grounds for various bird species, some of which have declining populations. It is important not to disturb them while their young are hatching, and boaters should try to stay clear of these islands during the months of May, June, and July.

Deep Bay Inside Treadwell Bay

Treadwell Bay is a large bay on the New York side of the lake. It is the entrance to what many consider the most scenic anchorage on Lake Champlain: Deep Bay. Also, there is one large-sized and fairly new marina here, the Marina Champlain. Deep Bay is a secure anchorage in that it is protected from everything but a fairly rare wind from the south. Be cautious, however, if you head for Deep Bay. It is not difficult to access in broad daylight, but in less than ideal conditions the channel is easy to miss because it is marked by only one day buoy on the east (red) and another one to the west (green). Both are widely spaced apart, so they together do not form a visible entrance throat. If you don't stay in the correct area, you can run aground, so consider Deep Bay an anchorage best entered with good sunlight overhead. Good anchoring in 20 to 30 feet of water is available to you inside the bay, and good water depth (6 feet plus) is at the one small landing dock on the eastern shore at the head of the bay. A perfect gunk hole for all cruisers for either an extended stay or an overnight. With this reputation, the bay can

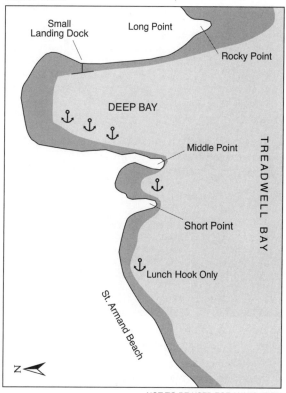

DEEP BAY

NOT TO BE USED FOR NAVIGATION

become crowded on peak weekends, so have alternatives.

If Deep Bay is crowded and you just want a lunch hook, go west to the next bay over, on the other side of Middle Point. Shallow-draft craft can go even more west—past Short Point but before the public beach at St. Armand Beach. I have anchored here in 4 feet of water (it is more shallow than the charts lead you to believe) 100 yards off the north shore. It is an excellent spot to scrub your boot-top stripe or to do other hull detailing while enjoying beautiful lake water yourself with the crew splashing all around.

At Deep Bay on the New York side of the lake, this float offers space only for brief tie-ups. Otherwise, everyone anchors out.

Marina Champlain is a large marina that was dug out of the low-lying land like an open-pit mine. Nine finger piers for 400-plus craft are available. Sailboats and larger powerboats are in the first couple of fingers (due to deeper water) in the fairways and slipside. Smaller boats are docked farther to the west. It has first-class docks, buildings, and a travelift. Due to the shallower water inward past the first few fingers, deep-draft vessels might need to call ahead for overnight dockage, but anyone who requires less than four feet should not be concerned about being turned away. Although this marina is a mile from Plattsburgh, New York, and 17 miles south of Canada, 99 percent of the seasonal tenant boats are Canadian-registered. There are multiple sinks, toilets, and showers for

both men and women—all generous-sized, well lit, and located inside the main building, which also has two washers and two dryers for boaters.

The fuel dock is on the first finger inside the basin and to the north of the entrance channel. There is a small office located on that float. Both gas and diesel are available, as is a pump-out. They sell enough fuel here to staff the fuel dock seven days a week. Note that you can measure your boat as you fuel, since that finger is marked off in feet on its face board. The facility is officially open from 8:30 A.M. to 7:30 P.M., but someone is often around until 11 P.M. during the peak season. The ship's store is just inside from the pool and also functions as a snack bar/deli/convenience store. There also are tennis courts. As an interesting

St. Armand Beach is two coves west of Deep Bay. Since it's a bathing beach, stay well clear from its shore and anchor just east of the beach.

aside, the mechanics' workroom is an underground cement bunker under the travelift. Look for it. The city of Plattsburgh is a mile away. The marina will call you a cab. Half a dozen restaurants are in a strip about halfway between town and the marina.

Approach instructions: The marina is on the western shore inside Treadwell Bay in a west by south direction off red marker #2. Sailboat masts are visible behind the earthen berm that separates the marina from Treadwell Bay, with the entrance on the south side. This entrance is marked with private buoys on both sides of the approach channel. Check water depth based on current lake levels and local knowledge, because there has been shoaling in this entranceway.

Marina Champlain (518) 563-1321

Storm protection: √√√
Scenic: * *
Marina-reported approach depths: 4-20 feet

Marina-reported dockside depths: 2-6 feet
Floating docks
Gas
Diesel
Waste pump-out
Rest rooms
Showers
Laundry
Dockside water
Picnic tables
Power connections: 30A/125V, 50A/220V
Below-waterline repairs
Mechanical repairs
Travelift/hoist: 50 ton
Mast stepping
Ship's store
Convenience store: on site
What's special: newer facility
VHF-monitored channel: 09, 16, 68

The Inland Sea Side Trip

A day- to weeklong side trip, the Inland Sea is the vast area of Lake Champlain that is off the main north-south passageway. This title

MARINA CHAMPLAIN

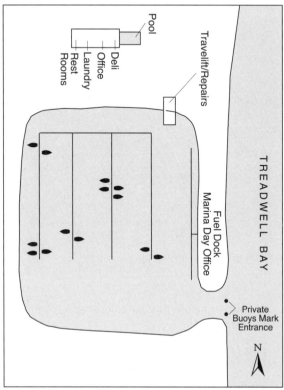

NOT TO BE USED FOR NAVIGATION

does not appear on your charts because it is a local designation. It is north of Burlington, Vermont, in the eastern half of the north lake. Actually, Mallet's Bay outer bay would be included as a part of the Inland Sea, because the low man-made causeway on its outer bay only separates it due to height and water limitations blocking cruisers from using it as an access point.

Cruisers who have the extra time will enjoy this area. Clear water, empty anchorages, and mostly undisturbed land vistas make for a restful time. Marinas in this area offer just enough support to seasonal and cruising boaters in their search for solitude.

Be prepared to backtrack if you take the Inland Sea adventure. Access from the main lake is limited. Your craft's height and depth requirements might cause you to enter and exit at the same point on and off the main north-south route.

Southern Access Point, Inland Sea, and the Gut

Between North Hero Island and Grand Isle (also called South Hero Island) is an entrance to the Inland Sea using the bay called the Gut. This is the most popular route in. Heading north, stay outside Young Island, Bixby Island, and their shoal water. Locate green buoy #3 delineating the Middle Reef and using it as your northern edge of the channel, turn right. Now you will see the low-lying landmass directly ahead. It is a railroad fill that has a non-bridged opening for boaters in it. Spot the next green marker #3, which should be visible to you as you see the opening between the land points. This heading takes you through and into the Gut. Once in, two red markers, #4 and #6, direct you to turn northward to stay in deeper water. Now turn right again. The bridge is now a straight run 1½ miles eastward. Beyond it is the Inland Sea.

Tudhope Marina is just past the bridge to the south. The marina describes itself as being at the bridge, Grand Isle, Vermont. Water depth can be a problem for the near-shore slips, especially at low lake levels. The marina has 80 slips on floating docks that go in April 15 and are hauled out October 15. Water, ice, and 30A electrical hookups are offered. The rest rooms are in a separate bathhouse next door to the main building. The supplies/ship's store carries marine supplies, some parts, and light groceries on site. They offer off-site labor

THE GUT

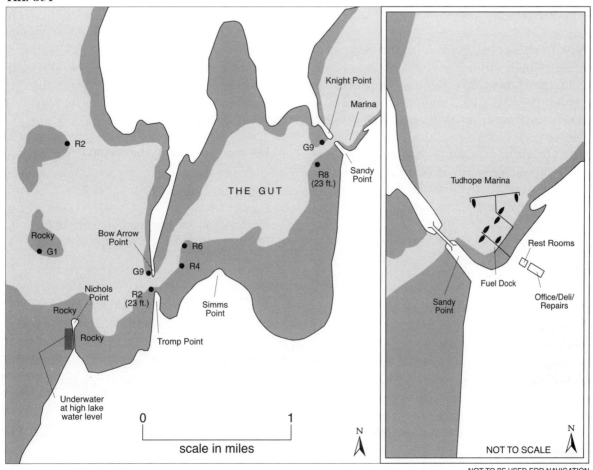

NOT TO BE USED FOR NAVIGATION

with their forklift to solve any problem you bring them. Bigger boats (15,000 pounds) are taken in and out of winter storage with a rented crane in the spring and fall.

Tudhope Marina (802) 372-5320

Storm protection: √√√
Scenic: * *
Marina-reported approach depths: 7 feet
Marina-reported dockside depths: 2-6 feet
Gas

Diesel
Waste pump-out
Rest rooms
Showers
Dockside water
Picnic tables
Power connections: 30A/125V
Woodworking repairs
Fiberglass repairs
Below-waterline repairs
Mechanical repairs
Mast stepping

Ship's store
VHF-monitored channel: 09

Northern Access Point—Inland Sea

Six miles north of the Gut is an entrance to the Inland Sea using Carry Bay. Here you hug the North Hero Island shoreline as you head north, especially as you approach Townes Reef (marked with a red buoy #2) only a quarter-mile offshore. Go inside it and the North Hero shoreline. North of Pelots Point the land becomes a narrow peninsula that you now go through to get into Carry Bay. You might want to take advantage of the marina at Carry Bay, marked on your chart about midway from east to west. Marina Internationale is a medium-sized marina with three finger docks that provide about 60 slips plus another 80 moorings. Transients are welcome to use both. However, on my last visit there were no flush toilets on site, and the place looked like it needed some sprucing up. Drinkable water is available only at the pump-out dock; nonpotable is at each slip. Pelots Bay provides pretty good anchorage with protection from most breezes, although it is probably one of the least scenic anchorages described in this guide's section on Lake Champlain.

Marina Internationale (802) 372-5953

Storm protection: √√
Scenic: not rated
Marina-reported approach depths: 12-14 feet
Marina-reported dockside depths: 3-7 feet
Picnic tables
Power connections: 15A/125V

Staying in deep water now takes you north between North Hero Island and Alburg Tongue land area. Three and a half miles north is a fixed bridge with 26 feet of clearance shown, but this is almost always less due to lake levels being above 93 feet. Listen to Weather 2 on your VHF for a current lake-level report. Past the bridge, the channel continues into the Inland Sea, and Dunham Bay Searay Marina is to your starboard.

Dunham Bay Searay Marina (802) 372-5131

Storm protection: √√√
Scenic: * *
Marina-reported approach depths: 30 feet
Marina-reported dockside depths: 3-8 feet
Floating docks
Waste pump-out

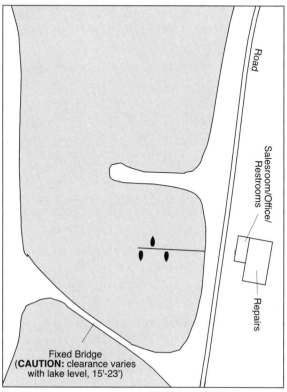

Fixed Bridge
(**CAUTION:** clearance varies with lake level, 15'-23')

NOT TO BE USED FOR NAVIGATION

Rest rooms
Dockside water
Barbecues
Picnic tables
Power connections: 30A/125V
Woodworking repairs
Fiberglass repairs
Below-waterline repairs
Mechanical repairs
Gas-engine repairs
Stern-drive repairs
Outboard-motor repairs
Generator repairs
Ship's store
What's special: a master Mercruiser
   mechanic runs the service department
VHF-monitored channel: 09, 16, 68

Fifteen miles north of Dunham Bay Searay Marina is an opportunity to go as far north on Lake Champlain as you can get. The area north of Rouses Point over on the main lake and north of the Canadian border is a remote cruising ground. Here Excellence Marine is at the northwestern end of the large Missisquoi Bay just south of Venise-en-Quebec inside the smaller bay, Venise Bay in Canada. Your charts show 3 feet of water near the docks, but the lake is almost always high enough above charted depths to allow for 6 feet of water even at dockside. The small, friendly marina of about 25 boats offers year-round care of its customers if they so choose. Boats range in size from runabouts to 35-foot cabin cruisers. A store, less than 10 minutes away, offers what the on-site ship's store does not have.

Excellence Marine (514) 244-6230

Storm protection: √√
Scenic: * * *
Marina-reported approach depths: 3-6 feet

Marina-reported dockside depths: 2-6 feet
Waste pump-out
Rest rooms
Showers
Picnic tables
Power connections: 15A/125V
Below-waterline repairs
Mechanical repairs
Ship's store: limited
Convenience store: off site
VHF-monitored channel: 16

Missisquoi Bay measures 3½ miles by 4 miles and is known for its wildlife. Excellent fishing also can be found here. There are two problems in accessing the bay. First are the bridges, of which there are two. The first is charted as the Canadian National Railway (now Central Vermont Railway), which has less than 11-foot reported clearance when closed (which would be further reduced by lake water levels). This bridge has to be hand-cranked to open for boaters. Twenty-four-hour notice is required—call (802) 527-7123. Then there is a second bridge for Highway 78. This is charted at a reported 18 feet but has since been rebuilt. Now it looks to be a 45- to 55-foot clearance. The U.S./Canadian border is about 3 miles north of the Highway 78 Bridge.

To clear Canadian Customs here, you are required to go directly to the Philipsburg Town Dock. This can be modified somewhat if you make prior arrangements at an extra fee. Inquire at (800) 461-9999. Because all the reporting possibilities from the bay for U.S. Customs are in shallow water (Campbell's Bay Campground at Donaldson Point) or across (I've been told) private property at the border crossing of Interstate 89, try to phone in to U.S. Customs. A local U.S. Customs station telephone number is (802) 868-2778. I suggest you call them ahead of time. Tell them your draft, your lack of a dinghy, and what you want to do; then, if they so bless, cross into Canada on Missisquoi Bay following their instructions. (Always remember this cardinal rule: Do not stretch the truth to customs officials. Please see appendix A for more information on clearing U.S. and Canadian Customs.)

Burton Island

It is a 9-mile side trip from the southern-access-point trip to reach Burton Island State Park. Burton Island is about 3 miles around and contains 250 acres of parkland. A part of the Vermont state park system, it has hiking trails, picnic areas, a swimming area, a concession where you can rent a rowboat or a canoe, a park store, a restaurant, and a visitor's center. If you need supplies, take the launch that runs during the summer from the island to Kill Kare. From there, take a taxi into the small town of St. Albans Bay. Kill Kare landing dock, which is marked on your chart as "Public Dock Ramp," operates the ferry in conjunction with Burton Park. There is a fee.

This is a place to go to relax, read a book, and feel as though you have finally escaped civilization. Or, as many people do, you also can go swimming, hiking, or camping on any of the island's many campsites.

From the Gut (southern access point to the Inland Sea), pick out Burton Island and head to its northeast side. You say you can't distinguish it from all the other wooded shorelines? I couldn't either. Try this: Find a starting point off Ladd Point, at about where your chart shows 31 feet of water depth, and steer 096° magnetic. That maneuver will cause you to hit the right island. As always, this heading is not

a course to steer—you must develop that. (Please see appendix D for more information.) As you near the island, you must adjust your course—this 096° will take you straight onto the land, but you can now find the island.

At Burton Island, stay well north of the island and keep an eye on your chart. On the northern side, as you approach the marina, the water shallows rapidly. You need to stay well off shore until you are far enough east that you can take a straight shot south into the marina landing area at a dead-slow maneuvering speed. Both slips and moorings are available here. There is not much water depth, however, so deep-keel sailboats might want to pass on this stop unless they can secure current local knowledge. At Burton Island, inquire about boater accessibility to Wood and Knight Islands.

Burton Island State Park (802) 524-6353

Storm protection: √√
Scenic: * * *
Marina-reported approach depths: 6 feet
Marina-reported dockside depths: 2-6 feet
Gas
Pump-out
Rest rooms
Showers
Barbecues
Picnic tables
Power connections: 15A/125V
Restaurant: on site (snack bar)
Convenience store: on site
VHF-monitored channel: 09

North Hero Island

If the hiking/camping/exploring aspects of a visit to Burton Island are not your cup of tea, there is a delightful alternative, one that offers a chance to immediately involve yourself in the daily goings-on of the middle-class society of summer-home dwellers on North Hero Island. This group is one most cruisers will identify with. North Hero Island is 12 miles end to end. It has three landing choices on it, two of which are described in this guide, where you can come ashore and look around. Two have been previously mentioned—Marina Internationale, and Tudhope Marina—and the last is listed here. Each offers a very different feel, and you will experience a unique segment of island life at each. To me, the most enjoyable is Hero's Welcome, the only one at which I had a sense of belonging within 10 minutes of landing at its moorings. It is 3 miles north of the southern entrance to the Inland Sea, and it also is accessible from the northern one. You can cruise (circumnavigate) North Hero Island using the two entrances/exits to the Inland Sea.

Hero's Welcome is part of the Inland Sea area of north Lake Champlain on North Hero Island inside City Bay. Head north, then west from red buoy #2. See your chart or call for instructions. Getting there is not hard if you draw less than 7 feet. Gas is available here on the 200-foot dock. The rest rooms are spotless, with one for handicapped people. Hero's Welcome is not a marina because it only offers 28 moorings with a floating finger for landing and refueling. For land access, a shuttle boat can chauffeur you in, you can use your own dinghy, or you can even drive the shuttle boat in yourself. The dock is put in in April and taken out in October.

There is a wonderful general store here that serves as a bakery, a deli, a gift shop, a bookstore, and a chart agent. The store's hours of operation are daylight; however, the bakery is open from 6:30 A.M. to 9 P.M. seven days a week. The store's other functions are open shorter hours, but you can talk them into open-

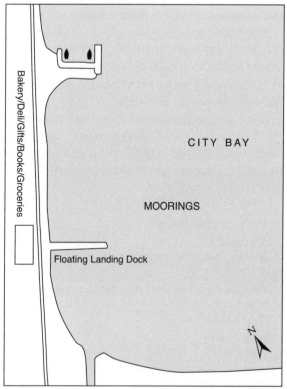

HERO'S WELCOME

Bakery/Deli/Gifts/Books/Groceries

CITY BAY

MOORINGS

Floating Landing Dock

NOT TO BE USED FOR NAVIGATION

ing up early or staying late if need be. They are open weekends only in April and September, and seven days a week in May, June, July, and August. Please note that everyone at the store shares the warm, helpful attitude of the ownership. You can fall in love just spending a half-hour here; spend an hour and the "thunderbolt" will hit you. This store is best described as having several functions. Besides being a real bakery, its general store has books (including cruising guides), charts, clothes, groceries, fresh fruit, beer, wine, soft drinks, ice, and camping and marine supplies. They also sell furniture: outdoor and patio furniture, directors' chairs, and other such summertime accouterments. The store has a fax service, a pay phone, and a U.S. Post Office.

For boat and engine repairs, walk to the adjacent separate business, Northland Boat Shop (802-372-5452), about 500 yards inland. They primarily work on stern drives and outboards. They are authorized to repair Mercruiser and Johnson products, but they also work on Volvo, OMC, and Yamaha. They haul boats up to 26 feet long themselves and use an outside service for larger boats.

Hero's Welcome (802) 372-4121

Storm protection: √
Scenic: * * *
Marina-reported approach depths: 4-12 feet
Marina-reported dockside depths: 3-8 feet
Gas
Rest rooms
Ship's store
Gift shop
Souvenir shop
Deli: on site
Grocery: on site
Convenience store: on site
VHF-monitored channel: 16

Heading all the way south on the Inland Sea, you come back closer to areas that are populated year-round. As I have outlined before, the outer bay of Mallet's Bay is separated from the Inland Sea by a man-made land berm with a bridge. No cruiser can safely pass through here due to the shallow water, but on the north side of this area—in addition to a motley crew of windsurfers, runabouts, fishermen, and some swimmers—you will find Sandbar State Park and the Apple Bay Marina. It is shown on your chart at the western terminus of the land bridge as Apple Island Campground and Marina. This facility really serves trailer boats that love this area. Cruisers might want to secure local knowledge if their vessel has a deep draft. It is tricky getting in here.

Apple Bay Marina (802) 372-5398

Storm protection: √
Scenic: *
Marina-reported approach depths: 3-8 feet
Marina-reported dockside depths: 3-10 feet
Gas
Rest rooms
Showers
Laundry

North on the Main Lake

On the side of Long Point opposite Deep Bay and on the main north/south route of Lake Champlain, there is a series of recesses in the west shoreline. A mile and a half north of the point is Mooney Bay Marina, which dominates Mooney Bay. Deep water is at hand on approach; inquire about slip-side depths after being assigned a slip, because some can be shallow. Two floating-tire breakwaters protect this very large marina (200 slips, 14 acres, 15 peak-season employees). Its hours of operation are from 9 A.M. to 8 P.M. during high season and from 9 A.M. to 5 P.M. during shoulder season. The supplies/ship's store offers a small selection of soft drinks, beer, snack food, boat supplies, and charts. A leased-out dinner house might be open. The marina handles new boat sales as well as winter storage, inside winter storage in massive clean buildings, and repairs: outboard, stern drive, inboard, generators, painting, and mast stepping.

Mooney Bay Marina (518) 563-2960
Storm protection: √√
Scenic: * *

Marina-reported approach depths: 30 feet
Marina-reported dockside depths: 4-10 feet
Gas
Diesel
Waste pump-out
Rest rooms
Showers
Laundry
Dockside water
Barbecues
Picnic tables
Power connections: 30A/125V
Below-waterline repairs
Mechanical repairs
Gas-engine repairs
Outboard-motor repairs
Travelift/hoist: 35 ton
Mast stepping: 60 feet
Ship's store
VHF-monitored channel: 09, 16

Mooney Bay Marina (North) at Monty Bay is next up off the western shore on the main channel inside Monty Bay. It is about 3 miles north of Mooney Bay Marina and under the same management.

Mooney Bay Marina (North) (518) 846-7900

Storm protection: √√
Scenic: *
Marina-reported approach depths: 7-13 feet
Marina-reported dockside depths: 2-5 feet
Gas
Diesel
Waste pump-out
Rest rooms
Showers
Laundry
Barbecues
Picnic tables
Power connections: 30A/125V

MOONEY BAY MARINA

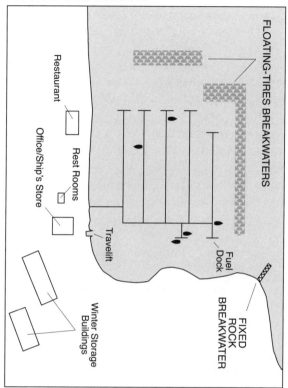

NOT TO BE USED FOR NAVIGATION

Ship's store
VHF-monitored channel: 09

This is followed by a very sailboat-oriented facility, Gilbert Brook Marina.

Gilbert Brook Marina (518) 846-7342

Storm protection: √√
Scenic: *
Marina-reported approach depths: 4-8 feet
Marina-reported dockside depths: 3-6 feet
Waste pump-out
Rest rooms
Showers
Laundry
Dockside water

Picnic tables
Power connections: 30A/125V
VHF-monitored channel: 68

At North Point (New York side) and The Head (Vermont side), the main lake continues north for its last almost dozen miles after a short westward set. The lake is shallow now for some distance from shore on both east and west sides. The wind is often calm in the mornings, with the best wind in the late afternoon. Summer Place Campground and Marina has gas for boaters and local knowledge of the sometimes-fouled shallow water.

Summer Place Campground and Marina
    (802) 928-3300

Storm protection: not rated
Scenic: * * *
Marina-reported approach depths: 3-8 feet
Marina-reported dockside depths: 2-6 feet
Gas
Waste pump-out
Rest rooms
Showers
Ship's store
Restaurant: on site
VHF-monitored channel: 09

The deepwater channel is still about a mile wide until you're at the north end of Isle La Motte and north of the Isle La Motte Light (45 feet high on a black skeleton tower on land). Here the deepwater channel necks down to a third of a mile wide. A jog to the east is required. Do not miss the jog, because the reef at Point au Fer has grounded many lake travelers. It is marked by a red buoy due north of the land that holds the Isle of La Motte Light. (Note: This buoy was not numbered once when I went through here.) That is how much

you need to jog east. Now line up the three green buoys #11, #9, and #7, starting with the most southern, #11, a mile north and east from the red buoy at Point au Fer Reef. Check these off as you pass each of them to be precise.

A side trip west below Point au Fer Reef locates the mouth of the Great Chazy River. A turn to the west gives you the opportunity for a change of scenery, since the landscape spreads out into flat stretches of farmland beyond the tree-lined river edge. The river is not very long, maybe a mile, nor as exciting as Otter Creek, but you might want to make the detour to visit the two marinas that are on the river right next to one another. Both provide more water in and around their service docks and slips than the 4- to 5-foot depth reported at the entrance to the Great Chazy River from the lake. The entrance to the river is your critical point of water depth.

Chazy Boat Basin (518) 298-2010

Storm protection: ⩗
Scenic: *
Marina-reported approach depths: 4 feet
Marina-reported dockside depths: 3-6 feet
Gas
Waste pump-out
Showers
Power connections: 30A/125V
VHF-monitored channel: 16

Chazy Yacht Club (518) 298-2797

Storm protection: ⩗⩗
Scenic: *
Marina-reported approach depths: 4 feet
Marina-reported dockside depths: 3-6 feet
Floating docks
Gas
Diesel
Waste pump-out
Rest rooms

Showers
Barbecues
Picnic tables
Power connections: 30A/125V
VHF-monitored channel: 68

Rouses Point

Located just a mile short of the Canadian border, Rouses Point offers three marinas from which to choose. The Marina at Lighthouse Point is probably the biggest, and it has a customs' station and the most amenities. Gaines Marina, under new ownership, is about half sailboats and half powerboats and, as a U.S. Customs point, has some transients. At the third, Barcombs Marina, be a little wary of the water depth. All three are in the same general area and about equal distance from essential land-side stores and services—namely, a supermarket, liquor store, and laundry.

Beyond the Rouses Point marinas is a high auto bridge. This bridge is a fixed auto bridge for Route 2. Clearance will vary between 45 and 55 feet, approximately, based on the lake's water levels. If your mast is up, check the vertical clearance signboard at the bridge before proceeding. Fort Montgomery is next to port, and the Canadian/U.S. border is a third of a mile past the fort.

The Marina at Lighthouse Point is a pleasant experience and is either your last U.S. marina for some time to come if heading north or your first coming down into Lake Champlain from the Richelieu River. The marina is competent in all overnight stay qualities. Its fine Italian restaurant located on the bulkhead of the marina property ranks as superior. It is a separate business but is accessible to all marina guests via the pool outside its windows. The building functions as a gateway between the town and the marina piers. A small bar with

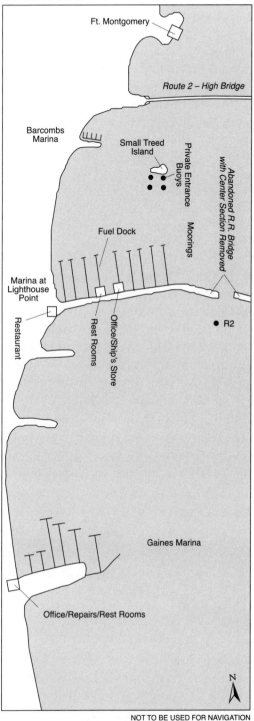

ROUSES POINT

Ft. Montgomery

Route 2 – High Bridge

Barcombs Marina

Small Treed Island

Private Entrance Buoys

Abandoned R.R. Bridge with Center Section Removed

Fuel Dock

Moorings

Marina at Lighthouse Point

Restaurant

Rest Rooms

Office/Ship's Store

R2

Gaines Marina

Office/Repairs/Rest Rooms

N

NOT TO BE USED FOR NAVIGATION

the Weather Channel tuned in offers a nice rest stop while you wait for a table.

That said, boaters also will enjoy a morning shower in one of six available in the overly large rest rooms at the marina. Four sinks and five toilets (stalls somewhat tight for long-legged men) also are in the clean room (painted yearly). Both the men's and the women's rest rooms and the laundry room share a newer building that is heated in cool weather. A large selection of soda, snack food, some gift items, books, and magazines expand the usual ship's store selections.

Also, barbecues and patio tables are located on several nice patio areas on each pier gangway. The main pier also is a piece of history; this property was the railroad bridge across the mouth of Lake Champlain in earlier times. Numerous photos dotting the marina buildings illuminate this historic time.

The approach to the marina is south of the high auto bridge (45- to 50-foot clearance, depending on lake levels) and on the north side of the abandoned railroad bridge that forms its spine. Do *not* go straight in; rather, go to the northern edge of the marina and follow a well-marked side channel into the maneuvering basin and the service dock, which is at the base of the two buildings about halfway in among the finger piers. Worry about water depth at low lake levels inside the entrance channel or confirm available water depth with the marina before approaching.

The Marina at Lighthouse Point (518) 297-6392

Storm protection: √√
Scenic: * *
Marina-reported approach depths: 5-10 feet
Marina-reported dockside depths: 7-12 feet
Floating docks
Gas
Diesel
Waste pump-out
Rest room
Showers
Laundry
Power connections: 30A, dual 30A/125V, and 50 A/125V
Dockside water
Barbecues

The Marina at Lighthouse Point uses this old railroad bridge as the backbone of its various finger piers. It also houses barbecue/patio decks, a ship's store, and other facilities.

Mechanical repairs
Travelift/hoist: 25 ton
Mast stepping
Ship's store: large
Restaurant: on site
VHF-monitored channel: 16, 68

Gaines Marina is a workmanlike, fully func-
tioning marina. Using their facilities and often-
times outside expert labor, they haul, repair,
and offer seasonal slips to 35- to 55-foot vessels. The clean but basic rest rooms (with
showers) match the overall theme, and all
facilities are housed in the former street-side
garage with painted block walls. In the front of
the same building, a few supplies are at hand
in the office/ship's store. Other amenities are
a short walk to Rouses Point's small downtown
shopping area. The new ownership seems to
be upholding the marina's reputation for handling all types of craft while enhancing the
marina's level of personal comfort.

**Gaines Marina [formerly Gaines Garage
   and Marina] (518) 297-7000**
Storm protection: √√

Marina-reported approach depths: 3-6 feet
Marina-reported dockside depths: 8-11 feet
Floating docks
Gas
Diesel
Waste pump-out
Rest rooms
Showers
Power connections: 30A/125V, 50A/220V
Dockside water
Below-waterline repairs
Mechanical repairs
Travelift/crane: 25 ton
Ship's store
Restaurant: off site
What's special: haul-out abilities
VHF-monitored channel: 16, 68, 72

Barcomb Marina suffers from lack of water
depth and has oriented its business to boats
less than 23 feet. Its focus is on seasonal tenants, but give them a call if you need service—
they are there to help. Call (518) 297-6112.

From here you can continue on to Montréal, if you choose, using the next chapter in
this book to guide you.

The "new" bridge north of Rouses Point and the stone fort beyond it are the last landmarks
northbound before entering Canada.

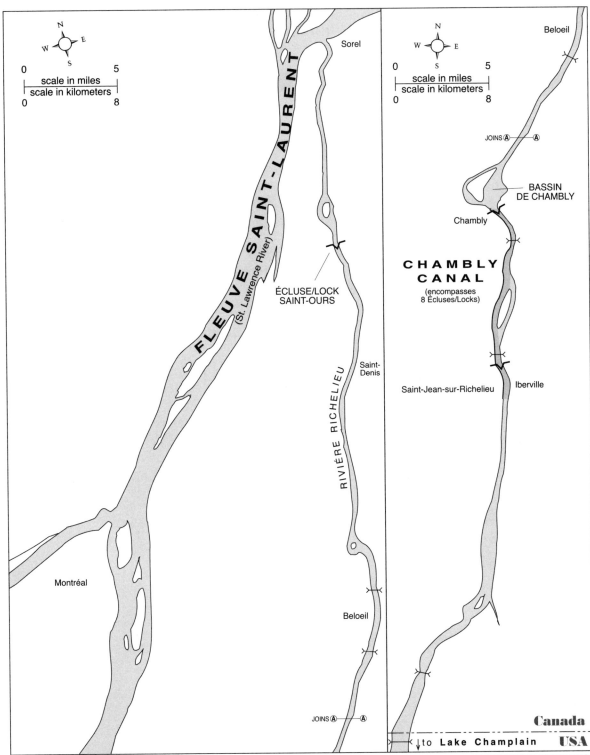

FLEUVE SAINT-LAURENT
(St. Lawrence River)

Sorel

N
W · E
S

0   5
scale in miles
scale in kilometers
0   8

ÉCLUSE/LOCK
SAINT-OURS

RIVIÉRE RICHELIEU

Saint-
Denis

Montréal

Beloeil

JOINS Ⓐ ━━ Ⓐ

Beloeil

N
W · E
S

0   5
scale in miles
scale in kilometers
0   8

JOINS Ⓐ ━━ Ⓐ

BASSIN
DE CHAMBLY

Chambly

CHAMBLY
CANAL
(encompasses
8 Écluses/Locks)

Saint-Jean-sur-Richelieu   Iberville

Canada

↓ to Lake Champlain   USA

NOT TO BE USED FOR NAVIGATION

CHAPTER 7

The Route North to Montréal from Lake Champlain

The Canadian Route

SKIPPER TIP: The charts for the route from Lake Champlain to the St. Lawrence River via the Richelieu River and the Chambly Canal are Canadian charts 1351 (the southern half) and 1350 (which covers the northern half). These chart numbers refer to eight separate chart sheets that are sold as two separate sets of four. This section covers those charts. Also be sure to read chapter 4, "Locking Through for the First Time," before approaching any locks.

The Canadian portion of this cruise takes you the roughly 80 statute miles of the route up the Richelieu River, into the Chambly Canal, and then back to the Richelieu to meet the St. Lawrence River at Sorel. Then the distance is less than 55 miles west and south to Montréal.

SKIPPER TIP: Do not discharge any waste here or on the St. Lawrence River. Your craft must route these products to a holding tank. Any wiring or plumbing that would circumvent this holding-tank system must be visibly disconnected and plugged, not just switched off.

Water Depths and Clearances

An important word about charted water depths and overhead clearances: Limitations of 6 feet of water depth and 25 feet of vertical overhead clearance are shown on the Canadian charts from here to Sorel. These same charts (in an addendum folder) then add as much as 4 feet on average onto any water depth noted on them for the month of June (but not every year) and 1¼ feet on average in August to adjust the charts for spring water runoff and other conditions. Thus, the water is always deeper and the clearance is always less than what is shown on the charts. These averages are based on data from the past 50 years. The most water ever required to be added to all printed chart depths was 6½ feet for the month of June during these same 50 years (the least was 1½ feet). In the same context, the depths have never in 50 years been less than the charted depths within the boating season, even as late as the end of August. These increases in water levels will likewise reduce overhead clearance an equal amount. Please ask for local knowledge of water levels when you travel through.

SKIPPER TIP: Red aids to navigation are to port on the waterway heading north.

Canal Locks

Minimum lock sizes for the first nine locks are 111 feet long and 22½ feet wide, with the biggest one a foot longer or wider. Lock lifts (southbound) or drops (headed north) range from just over 5 feet to 15½ feet. The Saint-Ours Lock, which stands alone, measures 311 feet by 45 feet. There are 10 locks, including Saint-Ours, the last of the locks in this section from the Canadian border to Montréal.

You need to stay in the channel on the Richelieu River, not only for the water depth but also to avoid weeds. These weeds grow thicker as the summer progresses, and they are more prevalent outside the channel than in. Skippers with engines running, please watch your gauges for any signs of overheating, which would indicate that you have ingested some weeds and have clogged the water intakes to either the generator or main engine(s). Also, be ready for false echoes on your depth sounder that prevent you from knowing your true depth. Anchoring will usually be in weeds with a mud bottom. Now a word about mosquitoes: All these weeds and marshland invite stagnant water, the breeding habitat for some pests. How can I phrase it, wordsmith that I purport to be? There are mosquitoes. There, it's out. They are not as bad as those elephant flies in Georgia in June, but they are here and you must confront reality. Be screened in before feeding time, which is usually late afternoon until mid-evening.

> **SKIPPER TIP:** The "high" season to cruise this river and canal way is the last three weeks in July, which usually offer the best balance of weeds, canal operating hours, water depths, and weather.

Also, be aware that charts are going to show water depths in meters and distances in nautical miles as opposed to inland U.S. charts, which show them in feet and statute miles. Be prepared to convert speed limits as well, which will be in kilometers rather than in miles per hour. For example, 16 kilometers as a speed limit equals about 10 miles per hour.

> **SKIPPER TIP:** Please see appendix B for metric conversion tables.

Temperatures

Montréal is about five degrees cooler than New York City during the cruising months. Daytime highs are in the mid- to high 70s in June, July, and August, and the mid-60s in May and September.

Note: Please now turn to Canadian chart 1351, sheet four of four.

Fort Montgomery

This fort was once surveyed as being on the Canadian side of the border, thereby making it useless. Because of this mistake, it has been known in its history as Fort Blunder. Construction was started in 1816 by the U.S. military, stopped after the survey, restarted after a second survey showed it to be inside the United States, but in the end it was never manned. Now it makes a good place to change charts and take a photo.

The river is a mile wide for the next 3 miles northward; the channel is buoyed (red to your vessel's port) and almost in the middle of the river. The white areas reflect water depth of at least 5 meters (16½ feet); light blue, at least 2 meters (6½ feet); and dark blue, less than that.

Depths are based on data collected some eighteen years ago.

At the lighted red buoy #E558, two-thirds of a nautical mile (say three-quarters of a statute mile) north of Fort Montgomery is the secondary channel to the U.S. and Canadian Customs wharf. Use the buoys to follow the secondary channel into Customs, a course of about 355° magnetic. (Please consult appendix D, "Compass Headings," to convert this to a course to steer.) Watch water depth. In spots it can be as little as .7 meter (2¼ feet), whereas in early May this same spot also can be 2.7 meters (8¾ feet) deep at the higher range of recorded river levels. Thus, you need local knowledge of water levels as you are transiting. Canadian Customs is at the end of the jetty. As an aside, if you do not go "bump on the bottom" getting in and out of here, you should have sufficient water all the way to Montréal (excepting that special situation, unknown shoal conditions).

Canadian Customs

> **SKIPPER TIP:** Check the appendix for more specific information about customs rules and regulations in Canada.

After crossing into Canada, you normally check into Canadian Customs at your first marina stop. Clearing Canadian Customs on the Lake Champlain route means stopping at the Customs Pier (often this is unmanned; if so, use the telephones provided), which is a mile north of the international border of the United States and Canada. By the way, any amount of liquor, opened or unopened, full or half-full,

is totaled, and then you are assessed a tax on that amount if it is over the "personal use" limit. You are "importing" that liquor whether you intend to sell it or not.

Some travelers—to protect themselves from problems later, especially if they have new cameras or other expensive items aboard—go through U.S. Customs before leaving U.S. waters to reveal those items that might be suspected as duty items on their return. I never have. The purported advantage is that there is no question of paying a duty on those same items when they pass through U.S. Customs later on their re-entry. I've passed in and out of both U.S. and Canadian Customs by car and by boat probably a dozen different times, and I have never had a problem on either side. I found customs officials to be very agreeable, except where liquor was concerned. If you cruise with a substantial liquor supply, you are going to be paying one heck of a duty on the same liquor every time you move across the Canadian/U.S. border. So perhaps you should just drink up—but not while you are under way. By the way, I have checked with other boaters, and they say they have never had the problem with liquor that I have had. I might be too honest in what I declare, or their customs officers either accepted their claim that their alcohol was for personal consumption or simply forgot to ask the question—something that has happened to me on occasion. (Again, please see appendix A for more complete information on clearing U.S. and Canadian Customs.)

> **SKIPPER TIP:** About 21 statute miles ahead, there is a bridge that will not open to boat traffic during lunch hours

(11:45 A.M. to 1:15 P.M.). This and the hours and days of operation of the Chambly Canal system dictate that you plan the timing of your arrival there to account for some waiting time. The locks can handle 3 to 12 vessels at a time, depending on size. If it is busy, you will have to wait your turn. Also, since this canal requires a 6-mph speed limit, whoever you lock through with will cruise with you for approximately the next four hours.

Now back on the main channel from the secondary (customs jetty) channel, the distance between lighted red buoy #E550 and the next buoy is a statute mile. Binoculars are helpful here. Lining up one on top of another, you can use the range markers on land two miles ahead at 13-meter (42½ feet) and 22-meter (72 feet) elevations, which cause you to steer an approximate 15.5° magnetic course. Or you can just steer without heeding the markers. When boating, remember to adjust this and all other courses outlined in books and charts by using your own good, basic chart work. (Please see appendix D for more information.)

Your first Canadian marina is the only one on the east bank. Marina Noyan is fully found, except that it does not offer repairs or refueling.

Marina Noyan (514) 294-1098

Storm protection: √√√
Scenic: *
Marina-reported approach depths: 6-7 feet
Marina-reported dockside depths: 4-6 feet
Waste pump-out

Rest rooms
Showers
Laundry
Dockside water
Picnic tables
Power connections: 15A/125V
Ship's store
Restaurant: on site
Convenience store: on site
VHF-monitored channel: 68

Next, keep between the buoys marking both sides of the channel to stay in deeper water and miss the shoal to the east. Coming up are a marina and two bridges, one for trains, the other for cars. Canadian charts show auto roads as medium gray lines, while railroad tracks are narrower black ones. At the marina on the western shore, a snack bar, gas and diesel refueling, and repairs can be found, but the rest-room conditions were unacceptable on my last visit. In general, the quality of the overnight stay for transients in the marina facilities in this section is more uneven than in other chapters in this guide; you'll usually find your stay clean and pleasant. For this reason, not all dockage opportunities in this area are fully described in this guide. You also probably will eat better around here than you'd expect in rural areas, if you choose wisely. Enjoy the food, and wear slippers in the shower. (If you have diet restrictions, bring along a French/English food dictionary.) The culture is different, with its own heritage and customs. Please do not be an ugly American; you are a guest in their country. Vive la différence. Several million people relish the Canadian culture. The opportunity to sample their experiences is one reason why many of us enjoy cruising so much.

Change Charts

North of the sister buoys #E522 and #E521 change charts to chart 1351, sheet three of four. Lighted red buoy #E518 is on both chart sheets.

Only 9 nautical miles of cruising (about 10 statute miles) have passed since leaving the Canadian Customs stop north of Rouses Point; now there is a secondary channel into Saint-Paul-de-Ile-aux-Noix and its multiple marinas. Many people find an excuse to stop here and just walk around on Canadian soil. The mari-

nas here are nice, and the multiple side canals give this area a tremendous waterfront presence. Use the secondary (marina) channel to access that waterfront. Turn left, using red #EA30 for your southern channel marker. Additional markers lead you the rest of the way. The red accordion line on the chart marks the path of an underwater power cable between the mainland and Fort Lennox. The dashed curved line also shown on your chart indicates a ferry-crossing path from the western shore to the island fort.

SOUTHERN CANADIAN MARINAS OF THE RIVIÉRE RICHELIEU

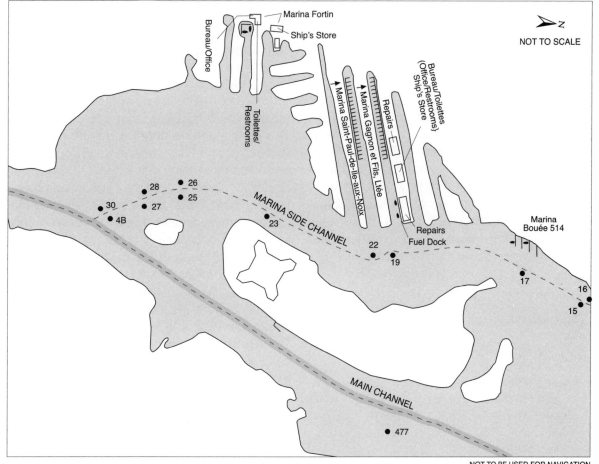

NOT TO BE USED FOR NAVIGATION

Marinas

Note: No marinas in this area have on-site restaurants. The nearest eatery is a 10 -minute walk, as is an IGA supermarket.

Marina Fortin, the second-largest marina on the Richelieu River, is a complete operation. It also is a new-boat dealer specializing in Sea Ray Brand boats. Clean rest rooms with showers and a laundry are on site. The marina hauls and repairs inboards as well as stern drives, is an authorized Mercruiser dealer, and offers an extensive parts inventory. The ship's store has a complete inventory. Transient boaters can find most of what they need here. The marina and its store are on the far inside end of three quiet canals. The fuel dock does not sell diesel nor can 50A shoreside power connections be accommodated.

Approach is easy. The marina usually sets out a private marker or two between buoys #EA26 and #EA23 to point out the best passage over potentially shallow water in the approach before the canal, which itself is deeper. Water depth on approach most years would be 7 feet in May and down to 3 feet in September. Depending on the finger float, add 1 to 2 feet at the marina itself. Inquire if you want current water-depth information and instructions, especially if one of the markers is missing.

Marina Fortin (514) 291-3333

Storm protection: √√√
Scenic: * *
Marina-reported approach depths: seasonal (call for current depths)
Marina-reported dockside depths: seasonal (call for current depths)
Floating docks
Gas
Waste pump-out

Rest rooms
Showers
Laundry
Power connections: 30A
Dockside water
Mechanical repairs
Ship's store
Restaurant: off site
Groceries: off site
What's special: Sea Ray dealer
VHF-monitored channel: 16, 68, 72

Marina Saint-Paul-de-Ile-aux-Noix is a smaller business serving mostly local boaters. It has some facilities, but no fuel or laundry. Inquire at (514) 291-3010.

If you stop, I recommend the Marina Gagnon et Fils, Ltée. (Gagnon and Sons Marina, Inc.), since they are the biggest around, they sell diesel fuel, and they have the nicest rest rooms—really nice rest rooms. Look for the cream yellow buildings with red metal roofs. This large marina is populated with 35- to 40-foot boats, and I have observed 55-foot yachts comfortably resting dockside. A new boat dealer for Carver, Wellcraft, Sonic, Celebrity, Hatteras, and Doral brand yachts, this marina features very clean, newly renovated rest rooms and showers. It does major repairs, hauling, and storage. The marina repairs CAT and Yanmar diesel repairs as well as Johnson, Mercruiser, Volvo, OMC, and Cruisader gas engines. Fiberglass, electronics, mechanical, and below-waterline repairs are available, too. Three on-site travelifts facilitate all repairs, and a crane performs mast stepping. While it is not in a league with Rybovich-Spencer (West Palm Beach, Florida), Atlantic Yacht Basin (Norfolk, Virginia), Hood/Little Harbor (Newport, Rhode Island) or the Hinkley Yard (Southwest Harbor, Maine)—Gagnon and Sons is the major repair

Marina Gagnon et Fils (Gagnon and Sons Marina) is exceptionally clean and pleasant, with a well-stocked ship's store and complete repair services.

yard in this neck of the woods. It is an excellent place to pick up needed charts and other boating equipment. Food is a 10-minute walk, both for groceries (IGA) and a restaurant. Finally, I like the fact that the owners run this business on site and readily try to satisfy any of your requests, even for small things.

On approach, depth can be as shallow as 6 feet (very rarely), so inquire if need be. Because it can be so weedy (especially later in the season) that a depth sounder will return depths false enough to frighten any prudent skipper, call ahead.

Marina Gagnon et Fils, Ltée. (514) 291-3336

Storm protection: √√√
Scenic: * * *

Marina-reported approach depths: 7 feet
Marina-reported dockside depths: 5 feet
Floating docks
Gas
Diesel
Waste pump-out
Rest rooms
Showers
Laundry
Power connections: 30A/125V
Dockside water
Fiberglass repairs
Mechanical repairs
Travel lifts: three plus a crane
Diesel repairs
Gas-engine repairs
Ship's store
Restaurant: off site
Groceries: off site

What's special: new boat dealer
VHF-monitored channel: 68

Marina Bouée 514, the smallest of this group of marinas, is farther north but still inside the secondary (marina) channel. My visit by car was a hit-or-miss kind of experience, but the marina was expanding and the staff might have been distracted from ongoing operations. The marina is deep down a side channel, so look for its sign. Inquire at (514) 246-2402.

The very historic Fort Lennox has been restored, has some grounds, and makes a nice tourist stop. While land-based visitors to this National Historic Park and Island access the fort from the mainland by ferry from its own peninsula in the group, boaters have two other options. Second choice: Take your dinghy across the secondary channel to access the western side of the fort. Beach or anchor near the ferry dock. Midweek, at less busy times, ask if you can tie up your dinghy to the far inside of this dock. Third option: If there is room, use the public dock on the eastern side of the fort's island, which is off the main north-south channel, and not the secondary channel containing the marinas. Do not dock on the broad face of this pier, since it is used by commercial traffic. Whether in your vessel or a dinghy, tie up or anchor out off the north end of the pier. Boat wakes can be a problem here, so pad your boat well with fenders. In all events, Fort Lennox is surrounded by a moat; the only access over it is on the fort's north face. The fort was built first in wood (1759), then replaced soon after by the current stone structures. In the summer of 1776, approximately 3,000 British troops were stationed here. Fort Lennox also figured in the War of 1812: Both it and Fort St. John were home to five British warships.

Note: Anchoring here either off the main channel, south of the underwater power cable, or west of both the island and of the secondary (marina) channel is not formally recognized. Therefore, take all precautions to ensure that you cannot swing at anchor into the channel, because the water, flowing north, will swing your stern north in the absence of wind.

Leaving the marina, the side channel continues north for 2 statute miles, enjoying water deeper than that of the southern approach, before rejoining the main channel between lighted red buoys #RGR and #E458.

Main Channel Route

If you do not access the secondary (marina) channel at red buoy #EA30, stay on the main channel, which goes east of Fort Lennox. Once past its island but just as you pass alongside lighted red buoy #E476, you can use the range to the south on the eastern shore, with lights at 16 feet and 30 feet. It makes a course of approximately 010° magnetic.

At lighted buoy #E458, both channels join into one. Continue north another 4 nautical miles using the northern range lights on the western shore even farther ahead at 20-foot and 62-foot elevations for a course of 019.5° magnetic. A nice lunch stop is Restaurant/Marina Saint-Tropez, located between buoys #E437 and #E434. Inquire at (514) 291-3300.

On the eastern shore is Marina Sabrevois. This complete facility includes a 40-seat restaurant, which in season is open for three meals plus snacks. Keep it simple here and try the steak. Watch water depth, although early in the season it should not be a problem for most boats. North of buoy #E437, look for the blue roof with the word Marina stenciled on it. Call (514) 347-0525.

Marina Sabrevois (514) 347-0525

Storm protection: √√√
Scenic: * *
Marina-reported approach depths: 4-7 feet
Marina-reported dockside depths: 6-8 feet
Gas
Waste pump-out
Rest rooms
Showers
Dockside water
Picnic tables
Power connections: 30A/125V
Ship's store
Restaurant: on site
Convenience store: on site
VHF-monitored channel: 68

Change Charts

Once you are parallel to either range marker, go to chart 1351, sheet 2 of 4. Using this chart sheet, continue another 5 nautical miles north to Saint-Jean-Sur-Richelieu, a good-sized town. The channel hugs the western shore here, but there are marinas on both shores. Marina Iberville Performance Marine tries to devote 20 percent of its slips to transients. Smaller boats can meet most needs on site except haul-out, diesel fuel, diesel-engine service, and pump-out. Inquire at (514) 358-4821.

Marina Iberville Performance Marine (514) 358-4821

Storm protection: √√
Scenic: *
Marina-reported approach depths: 3-6 feet
Marina-reported dockside depths: 4-10 feet
Gas
Rest rooms
Showers
Laundry
Dockside water
Power connections: 30A/125V

Fiberglass repairs
Mechanical repairs
Gas-engine repairs
Stern-drive repairs
Outboard-motor repairs
Generator repairs
Ship's store
VHF-monitored channel: 68

There is free dockage along the wall opposite lighted buoy #E401 at the very beginning of the canal. Most passing river traffic does not throw a large wake here, but the Le Nautique Saint-Jean Marina offers an alternative. A new-boat dealer for the seriously upscale quality Regal brand boats out of Orlando, Florida, this marina features good food (meals and snacks) and a bar, all in a fun boating atmosphere. A small but very complete ship's store is also on site. Long floating piers extend south to provide dockage. They are a Mercruiser sales and service facility also.

Le Nautique Saint-Jean Marina (514) 347-2341

Storm protection: √√√
Scenic: * *
Marina-reported approach depths: 15 feet
Marina-reported dockside depths: 5 feet
Floating docks
Gas
Diesel
Waste pump-out
Rest rooms
Showers
Power connections: 30A
Dockside water
Mechanical repairs
Ship's store
Restaurant
What's special: simple libations at their
   bar/restaurant
VHF-monitored channel: 68

Just after this marina and public wharf, the channel separates itself from the main river into its own canal. Not far beyond two bridges is your first lock, Lock 9, about 24 statute miles north of Rouses Point. Please note that the first bridge you pass is not open between 11:45 A.M. and 1:15 P.M. and has a 10-foot vertical clearance when closed at charted water levels.

The Chambly Canal

SKIPPER TIP: You need to pay a fee to use the canal. Permits can be purchased at the first lock on the Chambly Canal. They are available as a daily pass as well as in other designations. Let the lock tender know where you are going and how long you expect to take to get there. If you are not certain, he will advise you on which pass to buy. The Chambly Canal should take four hours to transit midweek and as many as six hours on busy weekends. By the way, if you decide to go down to Alexandria Bay and the Thousand Island region via the St. Lawrence River beyond Montréal, you will travel through locks much larger than those you've encountered so far, and you will share them with ocean and lake freighters, which can be somewhat intimidating. Also, because of the volume of commercial traffic on the St. Lawrence, which has priority, you might experience delays there. There are no locks, however, between Sorel and Montréal, so you can cruise from Lake Champlain to Montréal by going through just this first set of nine locks and then the Saint-Ours Lock, south of Sorel.

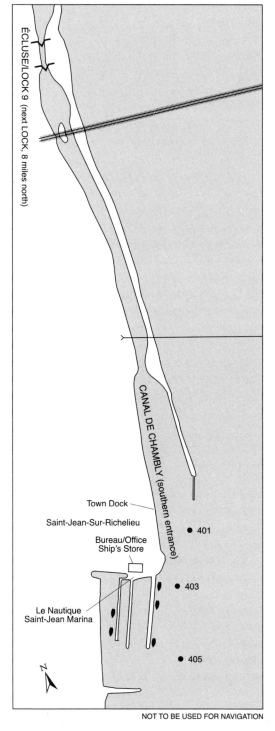

CHAMBLY CANAL

NOT TO BE USED FOR NAVIGATION

Please read chapter 4, "Locking Through for the First Time." The Canadian differences: a) the lock tenders have to hand-crank the lock gates and are in love with their jobs; b) they will hand you dock lines to hold your craft with (do not tie off); and c) the speed limit is 6 mph or no wake, whichever is slower.

The city of Saint-Jean-Sur-Richelieu marks the southern entrance to the Chambly Canal. This canal system is roughly 10 miles long and has a total lift (descent) of some 90 feet over nine different locks, with lifts ranging from 5 to 15 feet. Unlike the U.S. locks, these are hand-operated—that is, the lock tenders must manually crank the lock gates open and closed. Be prepared for happy, outgoing lock personnel. Seemingly always dressed in shorts, athletic, and ready to help, they really do present an image of enjoying their work. In fact, with the sun shining down in a blue sky with wisps of fairylike clouds contrasting with the grass and earth edges of the canal meeting the dark waters, you can almost believe you are in an animated Disney movie—and the lock tenders and you are the actors. Really, this canal is very pretty, as it meanders between the town and the river with a bike path shadowing its course. If not a Disney movie, this feels like boating in a park.

SKIPPER TIPS: The system's hours are longest from the third week of June to mid-August: 8:30 A.M. to 8 P.M. daily. During the last part of August the hours are 8:30 A.M. to 5 P.M. Early and late in the season, the canal is closed Tuesday, Wednesday, and Thursday, and it might have shorter hours. Inquire at (800) 463-6769; (514) 447-4805.

The Chambly Canal has a number of swing bridges (these open for the boaters and often use red and green lights like the locks) and overhead cables running across it. All have different clearances that vary a little depending on the seasonal water level. It's a good idea to ask how the water level inside the canal is running because it might be different from the river levels.

SKIPPER TIP: Chambly Canal telephone numbers.
First lock heading north: **Lock 9**—St. Jean: (514) 348-3392
Last lock heading north: **Lock 1**—Chambly: (514) 658-6525
Canal System office: (514) 658-0681; (514) 447-4805

A mile down the canal is the Highway 35 Bridge (28-foot vertical clearance). Within the canal, small buoys direct boat traffic away from shallow water and other hazards only where and when needed. These may narrow the channel width to about 25 percent to 50 percent of the waterway. After another mile there are two additional bridges. These both swing wide to allow vessels to pass. Houses now line both sides of the canal. You are their moving scenery show. I told you that you are in a movie.

Pleasure craft exiting a lock. Note the crisp bike path alongside and the perfectly manicured lawns—you'll feel like you're traveling through Disneyland.

There are another seven swing bridges plus additional fixed bridges and overhead cables ahead. Ahead in Chambly are eight locks. Just keep on cruising.

Between buoys #C32 and #C16, change your chart to sheet 1 of 4 of chart 1351. These aids appear on both sheets.

The village of Chambly, 37 statute miles from Rouses Point, was developed around Fort Chambly, originally built in 1665. The fort has been reconstructed and is open to the public. Lock 8 to Lock 1 all come now within the last nautical mile and a quarter of the canal. Lock 8 itself is behind a swing bridge for northbound cruisers. One swing bridge and then a fixed one (8.8-meter or 29-foot vertical clear-

ance) for Highway 112 are ahead, followed by Lock 7. All this happens in about 500 meters (1,640 feet). Another quarter-mile is the series of Locks 6, 5, and 4. All the while the canal banks reflect a back-to-nature path of trees, grass, and walking paths offering a bucolic break in a city. Look right to spot the old fort. Now another swing bridge blocks the last set of locks. Locks 3, 2, and 1 are a real set. The back door of one lock is the front door of the next. These locks complete the Chambly Canal. There is a long wharf for tying up after the last lock to the east. On the backside of it, further to the east, is Marina de Chambly.

The Bassin De Chambly is a lake about a mile and a third in diameter. It is 20 feet deep at its deepest spot, while most of it is about 8 feet deep. The buoyed channel keeps you in water depths of 7 to 14 feet. The town of Chambly and the fort are on the south shore, and the smaller town of Saint-Mathias is on the northeast side.

On the lake there are boater facilities. First, Marina de Chambly is a large, several-hundred-slip marina with 25 percent of its slips available to transients. Thus, this marina is most often considered by cruisers even if they just want to visit the fort and then continue on. Excellent water depth is pretty much everywhere except for the last finger pier east. It is a steep but not long stair climb up to the town level from the marina's water level. Another quarter mile east has you at the fort and its extensive park grounds.

Marina de Chambly (514) 651-1316

Storm protection: √√√
Scenic: * * *
Marina-reported approach depths: 8 feet
Marina-reported dockside depths: 6 feet
Floating docks
Gas
Waste pump-out
Rest rooms
Showers
Laundry
Power connections: 30A/125V
Dockside water
Barbecues
Some mechanical repairs
Snack bar
VHF-monitored channel 68

On the north side of the lake on the western shore between red buoy #E244 and the public dock of Saint-Mathias on the eastern shore is Marina Ile Goyer. Its 40-ton travelift is the largest on the Richelieu River, and boat repairs from fiberglass to engines are the marina's specialty. Watch water depths.

Marina Ile Goyer (514) 447-1968

Storm protection: √√
Scenic: *
Marina-reported approach depths: 6 feet
Marina-reported dockside depths: 6 feet
Floating docks
Gas
Waste pump-out
Rest rooms
Showers
Laundry
Power connections: 30A/125V
Mechanical repairs
Travelift
What's special: commitment to repairs
VHF-monitored channel: 16, 68

For boats under 6 meters (20 feet) there is Marina Léveillé (514-658-1423). It has moorings for this size boat (usually two to three are available for transients) and a restaurant. Also, Guy Aqua Sports is for shallow-draft vessels (depths might be 3 to 4 feet and no shoals). Inquire at (514) 658-6765. Next is Marina Saint-Mathias, a full-service marina with a restaurant.

Marina Saint-Mathias (514) 467-3868

Storm protection: √√
Scenic: * *
Marina-reported approach depths: 20 feet
Marina-reported dockside depths: 4 feet
Floating docks
Gas
Waste pump-out
Restrooms
Showers
Laundry

Power connections: 30A/125V
Dockside water
Mechanical repairs
Ship's store
Restaurant
VHF-monitored channel: 68

No matter where you might have jumped off on our run to Sorel, we pick up at the last set of buoys at the north end of Lake Chambly, buoys #E244 and #E243. The Richelieu River heads northeast now. Water depth increases, ranging from 5 meters (18 feet) to more than 8 meters (26 feet). After you pass the public dock of the town of Saint-Mathias, the western side channel joins the main river. Often this side channel's brown-colored water indicates where the shallow water is before it mixes in with the main river channel. It does get shallow very quickly along the channel's western edge.

Change Charts

Please go to chart 1350, sheet 4 of 4, once you are under the three sister overhead cables (92-foot vertical clearance). They are shown on both the previous (chart 1351, sheet 1 of 4) and new chart.

It is 2½ miles to the railroad bridge. Buoy #E234 warns you off the 3-foot-deep shoal just west of mid-river. The next buoy, about three-fourths of a mile ahead, is there to push you over toward the western shore. The railroad bridge (27-foot vertical clearance) in McMasterville/Beloeil swings open if need be.

> **SKIPPER TIP:** A strong current swirls around this and the next bridge. Skippers are advised to use caution. Downstream boats have the right-of-way.

Marina du Phare de Beloeil, the only operation in this area with rest rooms with showers, is located just south of the Route 116 auto bridge and is nestled between the road that runs along the top of the west shoreline and the river channel about 9 statute miles north of Chambly.

Marina du Phare de Beloeil (514) 464-5257

Storm protection: √√
Scenic: *
Marina-reported approach depths: 10 feet
Marina-reported dockside depths: 20 feet
Floating docks
Gas
Waste pump-out
Rest rooms
Showers
Laundry
Picnic tables
Power connections: 30A
Dockside water
Mechanical repairs
Restaurant
VHF-monitored channel: 68

Aids to navigation north of the bridge seem to disappear for awhile. If you stay on the center line of the river for the next 5 miles, you will be OK. Water depths here should easily be more than 4 meters (13 feet).

A special opportunity to sleep ashore as a break from sleeping on your boat is available at Hostellerie Les Trois Tilleuls. Primarily for bigger runabout-sized boats, its small area holds maybe a half-dozen vessels. Watch water depths. Inquire at (514) 856-7787.

At buoys #E208 and #E207, please change your chart to sheet 3 of 4.

The channel takes the western route around both Ile aux Cerfs and the Ile de Jeannotte.

This is well buoyed. At #E199, pick up the range markers astern on land with lights at 39-foot and 56-foot elevations. They keep you on a course of 034° magnetic.

Next up is Port de plaisance Saint-Charles-sur-Richelieu, which offers diesel as well as gas fuels. This marina, while owned and operated by some very nice folks, has marginal rest-room facilities (they really look like an afterthought) and is about 3 miles from a restaurant; there is no taxi or courtesy-car service to help you travel that distance.

Port de plaisance Saint-Charles-sur-Richelieu (514) 584-2017

Storm protection: √√
Scenic: *
Marina-reported approach depths: 3-4 feet
Marina-reported dockside depth: 3-4 feet
Gas
Diesel
Waste pump-out
Rest rooms
Showers
Dockside water
Picnic tables
Power connections: 15A/125V
Below-waterline repairs
Mechanical repairs
Gas-engine repairs
Diesel repairs
Ship's store
Snack bar
VHF-monitored channel: 68

A mile farther, Marina Auberge Handfield is the waterfront connection for a full-service motel. Perhaps the land-side accouterments are more complete than what is available at the marina. The motel even offers a sauna—that makes it for me. Boaters should not worry too much, however. What services that are in place are very satisfactory; just do not expect more than the listing.

Marina Auberge Handfield (514) 584-2226

Storm protection: √√
Scenic: * *
Marina-reported approach depths: 10 feet
Marina-reported dockside depths: 10 feet
Floating docks
Rest rooms
Showers
Laundry
Power connections: 30A
Dockside water
Restaurant: on site
What's special: motel with sauna
VHF-monitored channel: 16, 68

One of several small ferries that cross the river.

Cable Ferry

At buoy #E178 a cable-operated ferry crosses the Richelieu River. The auto and passenger ferry uses a cable to push-pull its barge across the river.

> **SKIPPER TIP:** Do not cross within 400 feet ahead of or behind a cable ferry, since the cable needs at least that distance to drop back down to the river bottom. It is safest to stand off and stay well clear of the ferry and its route while it is in operation.

Three nautical miles north of the ferry crossing, the buoys #E153, #E151, #E149, #E147, and #E145 guide you toward the western shore and around the mid-river shallow water. There are also ranges here to do this. Northbound, the first range (to be used from buoy #E153 to south of buoy #E149) is ahead with lights on the western shore at 12 meters (39 feet) and 19 meters (62 feet); it causes you to steer 025° magnetic. The second range (to be used starting at buoy #E145) is astern on the western shore at 13-meter (43-foot) and 17-meter (56-foot) light heights.

This range is effective until just south of buoys #E136 and #E135, a course of 069° magnetic. The third range is picked up here then. It is astern with lights at 9 meters (30 feet) and 16 meters (52 feet). It steers a direction of 041° magnetic.

It is best to go to chart 1350, sheet 2 of 4, at buoys #E132 and #E131, which are at Ile Larue (Larue Island).

Now there is another cable ferry crossing the river. This one is detailed in bright red trim.

Freshly painted, its colors seem Day-Glo.

On your chart, north of the ferry crossing and at buoys #E124 and #E123, a course heading of 156° true is plotted to allow you a path into the public dock at Saint-Denis.

North of buoy #E113, some 2 miles north of where you picked it up, stop using the range and steer, after a gentle turn more northward, targeting on buoy #E108.

Saint-Ours Lock

After the bend, the river channel and your vessel's path are set up for the approach to the Saint-Ours Lock (514-785-2212), which is my favorite lock. Never mind the island, the lockmaster's house, the grounds. They are all first-class, but so are others in this system and in other locations. What makes this my favorite lock is the tie-to float inside the lock. All vessels tie to it. Then, as a set, the boats and the float rise or fall (northbound) to the next level. Everyone always raves about this system, which I agree is a better one. Now, back to the lock approach.

Two miles south of the lock are the range lights on the western shore at 9 meters (30 feet) and 17 meters (56 feet). They are astern as you go between buoys #E100 and #E99. Line them up for a course of 008° magnetic. Replace this range and course at the next buoys, #E98 and #E97. Here pick up the range ahead on the eastern shore and east of the lock. Lights for it are at 5 meters (16 feet) and 8 meters (26 feet). It is a course of 016°. Notice also that buoys here (starting at #E100 and #E99) are in sets all the way into the lock.

The lock 30 miles north of the end of the Chambly Canal locks is anticlimactic after this approach. If anything, the lock is easier than others with the float inside it. The lock has a

A view of Saint-Ours Lock, looking north, as the lock gates open to the lower pool. Note the floating finger alongside the boats—you'd tie up to this instead of the wall.

lift of 1.52 meters (5 feet). It is 311 feet by 45 feet in size and offers 12 feet of water depth. This version was built in 1933 to replace the one built in 1849.

Exit the lock and head for the set of buoys #E86 and #E85, and then move north past #E81 and come alongside #E80. Now a new range is astern with its lights at 14 meters (46 feet) and 18 meters (59 feet). It produces a course of 017° magnetic. Leave this course at buoys #E72 and #E71. You are now about 12 statute miles from the St. Lawrence River.

Another cable-operated ferry is located between #E76 and #E72.

SKIPPER TIP: Do not cross within 400 feet ahead of or behind a cable ferry, since the cable needs at least that distance to drop back down to the river bottom. It is safest to stand off and stay well clear of the ferry and its route while it is operating.

The last marina on the river is about 4 miles north of the lock.

Marina Camping Par Bellerive (514) 785-2272

Storm protection: √√
Scenic: * *
Marina-reported approach depths: 6-8 feet
Marina-reported dockside depths: 5-6 feet
Floating docks
Gas
Waste pump-out
Rest rooms
Showers
Laundry
Barbecues
Picnic tables
Power connections: 30A/125V
Restaurant: on site
What's special: camping
VHF-monitored channel: 16, 68

The main river channel goes east around Ile Deschaillons.

Go to chart 1350, sheet 1 of 4, at either #E45 or #E42, since these both appear on the respective sheets.

Buoy #E35 keeps you to the west of a bar that can be as shallow as 3½ feet. At buoy #E23 you are pulled over to the eastern side of the river. The next 3 miles are not buoyed. Just stay in the middle and you'll be OK, barring an unusual situation. This buoys you into downtown Sorel (eastern shore) and Tracy (western shore). The last 2 miles of the Richelieu River become an industrial seaport.

The auto bridge of Route 30 is a wide fixed bridge with 19-meter (62-foot) vertical clearance. Here the chart directs you to the top of the sheet to an insert chart of a different scale that shows more detail.

The bridges in the Sorel section of the Richelieu River offer traffic an opportunity to pass to the right of center in each direction. This setup allows cars heading both ways to have their own bridge opening to use.

The marinas at Sorel are out beyond the Richelieu River and in the St. Lawrence River. Using the proper approach channels, they are about a nautical mile and a quarter to the east.

Sorel Marina Approach

Proceed a quarter-mile out the Richelieu River onto the St. Lawrence River on a heading within 010° to 035° magnetic. This positions you for a right turn (to the east) to a new 111.5° magnetic heading. This course takes you between the entrance-channel buoys and avoids the shallow water (2 to 3 feet deep) outside this channel. It is also the course steered by using the range marker lights at 7 meters (23 feet) on the dividing jetty to the marina's entrance and the east jetty's light at 8 meters (26 feet), about where the Canadian Coast Guard office is located.

Marina de Sorel (514) 742-9056

Storm protection: √√√
Scenic: * *
Marina-reported approach depths: 5 feet
Marina-reported dockside depths: 5 feet
Floating dock
Gas
Diesel
Waste pump-out
Rest rooms
Showers
Laundry
Dockside water
Power connections: 30A/125V, 50A/125V
Restaurant: on site
What's special: bar
VHF-monitored channel: 16, 68

Marina de Surel (Parc Nautique Fédéral)
   (514) 743-2454

Storm protection: ᐱ
Scenic: *
Marina-reported approach depths: 6 feet
Marina-reported dockside depths: 6 feet
Floating docks
Gas
Diesel
Rest rooms
Power connections: 30A/125V
VHF-monitored channel: 16, 68

St. Lawrence River

> **SKIPPER TIP:** Use Canadian charts 1338, 1339, and 1310 to cruise from Sorel to Montréal.

Please now open chart 1338.

Leaving Sorel for the trip upriver to Montréal via the great St. Lawrence River is a new kind of adventure. The positives: deep water, wide channels, and a world-class city at your feet just ahead to explore. Some negatives: wind conditions that create a chop; a high current starting at 1½ mph and increasing to at least 6 mph; big-ship traffic, usually more than one in view at most times; and aids to navigation that sometimes are better spotted by radar than from a pleasure craft's helm.

Your route boils down to this: Turn left at the north end of the Richelieu River; know what channel markers you are looking for and where they should be in proper order, ahead of time; and do not play chicken with freighters. If conditions are too windy and choppy, lay over in Sorel until it calms down, just like you do at home.

Water Depths

The white, light, and dark blue shadings of water depths on charts really do not offer a small-craft operator any navigational help. As an example, dark blue can be water from 1 to 17 feet deep. The chart is biased in favor of large freighters, not us. The Saint Lawrence, like all major rivers, is a watershed for vast land areas. Spring runoff and other factors pump up the water level above charted depths (or below them). The chart has a table displaying this. Also, the chart is based on survey data mostly not more than a decade old, which is good compared to charts for many areas.

Vessel Speed Abilities

Based on my experience, I would not transit the St. Lawrence in a marginally powered displacement pleasure craft. Charted currents seem minor. Let me make it plain: I have never been in a swifter current in 40 years of boating than those around parts of the Montréal waterways. I believe you need plenty of reserve power to enjoy this passage.

A 52-foot powerboat heading to the southwest on the Fleuve Saint-Laurent (St. Lawrence River) towards Montréal. Notice the spray blowing up onto the fly bridge—this river can be rough.

To Montréal

The St. Lawrence is 6 cables wide (about three-fourths of a statute mile) at the mouth of the Richelieu River. Go straight out at least a quarter-mile to be in more than 30-foot deep water. Head west-northwest for more than 2 miles upstream to pick up navigation markers that lead river traffic into the turn south. At this point there are a series of ranges that keep large vessels in the channel. On this river you'll need binoculars to effectively use these ranges. Vision must be able to cover 4 to 5 miles. That is beyond my visual ability without binoculars. Eight and a half miles from Sorel, an adjacent small-craft channel begins by going straight rather than taking the turn to the south of the main ship channel. The two channels parallel each other. Pick either one. I prefer the main channel because it is wider.

On chart 1339 the big-ship and the small-craft channels cross. After this, the small-craft channel only has a 6-foot minimum water depth and a vertical-clearance limitation of 32 feet (or less). Perhaps you'll want to change to the big-ship channel here by turning right.

This crossing of channels is a good place to switch to Canadian chart 1310. Warning: It is a confusing chart change. You must change over by matching up buoy numbers. The reasons: The chart's scale changes. The small-craft channel is not delineated the same between the two charts, and depths are marked in meters rather than feet.

The downtown Montréal marina shown in the insert labeled Quai Alexandra is the place to be. Use the marina as a base to explore one of North America's great cities.

PORT D'ESCALE du VIEUX de MONTRÉAL

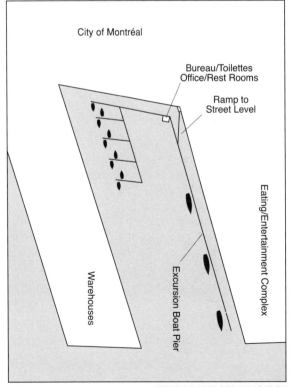

City of Montréal

Bureau/Toilettes
Office/Rest Rooms

Ramp to
Street Level

Eating/Entertainment Complex

Warehouses

Excursion Boat Pier

NOT TO BE USED FOR NAVIGATION

Port D'Escale du Vieux de Montréal (514) 283-5414

Storm protection: √√√
Scenic: * *
Marina-reported approach depths: 35 feet
Marina-reported dockside depths: 15-35 feet
Floating docks
Rest rooms
Showers
Laundry
Dockside water
Power connections: 30A/125V, 50 A/220V
Restaurant: off site
Convenience store: off site
What's special: This marina is in downtown Montréal.
VHF-monitored channel: 68

Alongside today's Lock 2 on the Erie Canal, you can explore locks built prior to 1862.

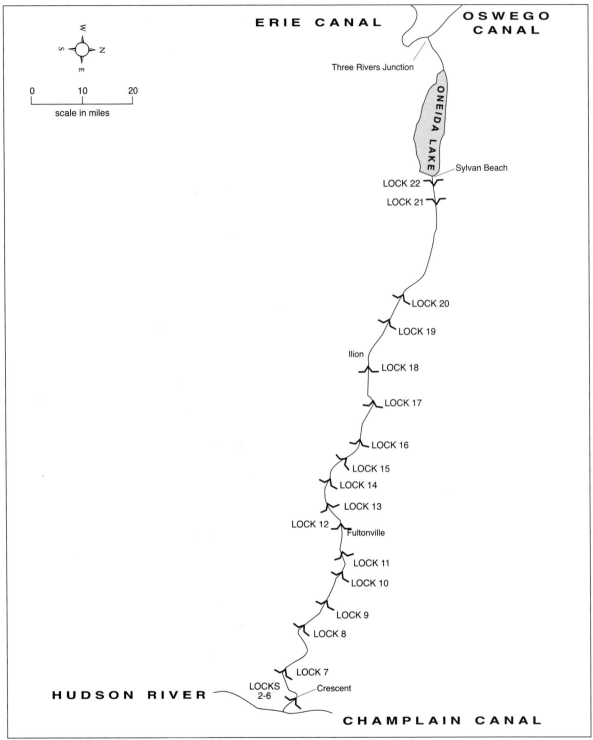

ERIE CANAL

OSWEGO CANAL

Three Rivers Junction

ONEIDA LAKE

Sylvan Beach

LOCK 22

LOCK 21

LOCK 20

LOCK 19

Ilion

LOCK 18

LOCK 17

LOCK 16

LOCK 15

LOCK 14

LOCK 13

LOCK 12

Fultonville

LOCK 11

LOCK 10

LOCK 9

LOCK 8

LOCK 7

LOCKS 2-6

Crescent

HUDSON RIVER

CHAMPLAIN CANAL

W N S E

0   10   20

scale in miles

NOT TO BE USED FOR NAVIGATION

CHAPTER 8

The Erie Canal (Area 1) West to Three Rivers Junction

Distances from Troy Federal Lock (all distances +/-3 miles)

Crescent Boat Club: 10 miles
Poplar Motor Hotel: 52 miles
Ilion Village Marina: 92 miles
Sylvan Beach: 133 miles
Three Rivers Junction: 160 miles
Oswego (Lake Ontario): 184 miles
Clayton (in the Thousand Islands): 245 miles

Alexandria Bay (in the Thousand Islands):
257 miles (do not miss this place)
Seneca Lake (Finger Lakes): 210 miles
Watkins Glen (on Seneca Lake): 246 miles
Buffalo: 352 miles
Welland Canal: 370 miles

SKIPPER TIP: Please use NOAA recreational chart 14786

Erie Canal (Area I): Hudson River to Three Rivers

The Erie Canal is the stuff of legend, folklore, and song, as well as the water route that opened up New York State, and the broader Atlantic coastal eastern United States, to the West more than 170 years ago. The canal was built with the sweat and labor of thousands of men, who made 50 cents a day for their back-breaking work. Finally completed at the cost of about $50 million, the canal was the engineering feat of its time. This man-made waterway revolutionized trade and transportation in the young country because it carried both freight and people east and west. Today, however, relatively few commercial vessels share the third generation of the canal with pleasure cruisers eager to explore this historic and often charming waterway.

The Erie Canal cuts a path across New York State that connects Albany to Buffalo. Along the way you'll see bucolic farmlands and apple orchards alternating with now-abandoned mills and factories—the remnants of the canal's once-glorious past. The canal and surrounding lands are rich in history, from battles in the French-Indian War to the tribulations of martyred Jesuits along the Mohawk River to the first Women's Rights Convention in Seneca Falls. Native sons and daughters of the region include William Burroughs, inventor of the adding machine; George Pullman, who invented the railroad car named for him; and nineteenth-century feminist Elizabeth Cady Stanton. Whatever your interests, you can't beat the Erie Canal for the diversity of its landscape and its history.

The canal gives you a variety of options for your trip, each with its own unique appeal. You can go all the way west to Buffalo and

Lake Erie, where you can share the lake with its large commercial traffic and have access to the other Great Lakes; turn off early and take the route to the stunning Finger Lakes, where you can relax on crystal-clear lake waters or visit nearby wineries; or you can go west at Three Rivers Junction and head north on the Oswego Canal to take advantage of Lake Ontario and the resorts that dot the Thousand Islands along the St. Lawrence River. Any way you choose to go, chances are you'll find special attractions and memorable moments along the way.

West from Waterford

The Waterford Terminal Wall, highlighted in the preceding chapter, is first up and comes before the entrance to the first Erie lock, which is called Lock 2 (there is no Lock 1).

At Lock 2 there is the remainder of the second-generation lock set that was built in 1842. The New York State Canal Corporation has posted several storyboards here on the canals and their history. The lock gates have been removed, but this place is still a more than worthwhile stop. Figure on an hour to tie up, have a look and a walk around, read the storyboards, and get moving again. Add that to the straight transit time mentioned previously. Please let the lock operator know in your initial contact with him that you want to stop here. You must tie up at the Waterford Terminal wall to properly see the earlier lock set. I suggest that you do to maximize your pleasure-cruise experience.

Passing under a second bridge, you are at the entrance of the first lock of the Erie Canal, which also is called the State Barge Canal—

You should easily see the bridges that precede Lock 2 as you enter the Erie Canal. This photo was taken from the main waterway, about 2,000 feet from the first lock entrance. Note that the directional signboard is also pictured in chapter 5.

Erie section, with either Lake Ontario, Lake Erie, or a Finger Lakes pleasure trip as your exit from the canals.

These two bridges that you pass under, both of which are in your line of sight, have 27-foot and 26-foot clearances, respectively. If you are planning to go to Oswego, be aware that the lowest bridge clearance from Troy Federal Lock is 20 feet. On the other hand, if you are heading to Buffalo, you'll need to get down to less than 15 feet as a minimal clearance. The canal's waters are said to be 12 feet deep. (These clearances and depths are according to the New York State Canal Corporation and can vary with high or low water levels and shoaling like any waterway. Always check with a lock operator for local conditions.)

Notice on your chart that you are not actually on the Mohawk River here. The Mohawk River/Erie Canal route is a mixture of the natural river channel and a canal cut through farmland and around natural waterfalls. The Mohawk, as your chart indicates, is not navigable in many sections because of falls and dams. You can see some of them from your boat, and they make this route quite interesting. Just a bit later on, the waterway and the Mohawk become one for a while and then separate again.

Don't be intimidated when you arrive at Lock 2, which is the first lock. The lift is more than 33 feet high, more than twice the height of the Troy Lock, and the chamber is a bit smaller. As you pull up to the wall, you might feel as though you are down in the bottom of the Grand Canyon. There is no cause for alarm, however. The procedure is the same here as in Troy, and Lock 2 gives you a good introduction to the rest of the Erie Canal, where locks lift as high as 40 feet.

Erie Canal First Locks

Locks 2 through 6 are taken as a set; you cannot stop once you start through from either direction. As a group they are sometimes referred to as the Waterford Lock Flight or a Flight of Locks. The total distance they encompass is less than two miles, yet their combined lift takes you up a little higher than 167 feet. Expect that this particular series will take about two hours to transit. If you are in sequence, go for it—skip lunch and put up with growling stomachs—and perhaps some growling crew members. If you are out of sequence, tie up to the wall, secure the boat, and read a good book or go for a walk.

LOCK 2 (First Lock of the Erie Canal system)

NOT TO BE USED FOR NAVIGATION

The Troy Federal lock operator may have asked you "Erie or Champlain Canal, Skipper?" You might have not understood, been too nervous to answer, or answered incorrectly. No matter; he was just trying to telephone ahead to the next lock operator that you are on your way. That lock operator wants to try to be ready for you when you arrive. His goal is to have the lock gate open just as you drive up. If you are not going on to the next lock, whether you're making a lunch or an overnight stop, it is a courtesy to let the lock operator know. He will alert the next lock operator. If you are ever waiting and waiting inside a lock with an open back door (entrance gate), you'll know why this is necessary.

As you approach the lock, you should pleasantly alert the lock operator on your VHF channel 13: "Lock operator, Erie Canal Lock 2, this is the motor (sail) vessel, *Much Fun,* a 30-foot craft with blue canvas . . ." Go on to describe your boat in enough detail that someone looking down at your vessel from the lock can tell you apart from other boats nearby. Do not be too nautical. Most of the lock operators are not boaters; many do not know a yawl from a ketch from a sloop. And keep it short. Finish with "requests a lock through westbound," because traffic on the Erie Canal is headed either east or west. Wait three minutes, maybe five, and repeat if this is unanswered. He may not be able to respond sooner. Proceed on a green light only. Note: The method that lock personnel use to hold your vessel within the lock as the water level changes should be different than that in the Troy Federal Lock. Every lock in this run will use one of three different locking techniques.

Alongside Lock 2 is a full set of prior-generation locks. The Erie Canal has gone through three generations since it originally opened in 1825, and the waterway you are riding on today is the third and most recent generation. That is why it is no longer always called the Erie Canal. The size of the locks, the depth of the water, and the width of the waterway were all generously increased, and the actual path was altered with each generation and each change. Most of this most recent incarnation was developed between 1910 and 1920, though the individual locks themselves continue to be rebuilt. The state usually chooses one or two locks a year to renovate in the off-season.

Heading westward toward the first lock of the Erie Canal, you can see traces of another era. While the staircase to today's Lock 2 is on the left, water rushes down the remains of an earlier generation of the locks, since their gates have been removed.

Lock 2—33.6-feet lift. (518) 237-0810. VHF channel 13. The supervisor for Lock 2 through Lock 9 is available at (518) 237-0613. Lock 3 is three-eighths of a mile ahead.

The Lock 3 operators know you are coming because Lock 2 will have likely telephoned them about you. Therefore, I suggest you wait seven minutes before hailing on VHF channel 13 to request a lock opening. The lock might be in the process of lowering (called dumping) its water to your level or waiting for eastbound traffic. Do call in after seven minutes, though, and ask for a rough time estimate if one is not offered. All boats can either stand off at idle or tie up below a lock to wait for the next lock opening. Lock operators know this and try to give time estimates so each skipper can decide which action to take. Bridge clearances are charted at 21 feet. Locks 3, 4, and 5 should

have similar ropes and cables. Take a look to port (southward) when exiting Lock 3; you'll see the repair yard for this section of the canal.

Lock 3—34.6-feet lift. (518) 237-0812. Lock 4 is again about 2,000 feet ahead.

> **SKIPPER TIP:** There often are eddies in the last 200 feet of the lower approach into Lock 4.

Lock 4—34.6-feet lift. (518) 237-0818. Lock 5 is roughly 1,000 feet ahead.

Lock 5—33.3-feet lift. (518) 237-0821. Lock 6 is again about 1,000 feet ahead after Lock 5.

Lock 6—33-feet lift. (518) 237-4014. Lock 7 is 8 miles ahead.

The view eastward from Lock 3 includes a railroad trestle and the New York State Route 4 bridge in Waterford.

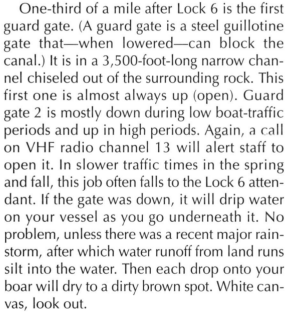

A raised guard gate on the western terminus of the "flight of five" near Crescent, New York.

The guard gate in its lowered position.

One-third of a mile after Lock 6 is the first guard gate. (A guard gate is a steel guillotine gate that—when lowered—can block the canal.) It is in a 3,500-foot-long narrow channel chiseled out of the surrounding rock. This first one is almost always up (open). Guard gate 2 is mostly down during low boat-traffic periods and up in high periods. Again, a call on VHF radio channel 13 will alert staff to open it. In slower traffic times in the spring and fall, this job often falls to the Lock 6 attendant. If the gate was down, it will drip water on your vessel as you go underneath it. No problem, unless there was a recent major rainstorm, after which water runoff from land runs silt into the water. Then each drop onto your boar will dry to a dirty brown spot. White canvas, look out.

Immediately past the set of Locks 2 through 6 and the two guard gates, the canal joins with the Mohawk River; there are some shallow areas. You need to stay in the channel, which is well marked with buoys, because this is one of the few areas of this particular cruising ground where the water outside the channel is a problem. Be careful, especially later on by the Crescent Boat Club, which is on the other side of the big bridge ahead. There, as you go out from their dock in a westerly direction, there are some rocks, even though the chart shows good water depth. You can avoid them by both entering and exiting the same way, from the east.

Trip Planning

Are you going to cruise nonstop 8 to 10 hours today from Troy Town Dock? Let's talk about planning your Erie Canal trip day by day. Some spots are more popular than others. This guide will point them out as a service to you. But don't let these stops "force" a schedule on your trip. That would be a shame. Cruising is a precious experience. It should be savored. Pace yourself as you see the trip unfold. Do not, however, rush through these waters. You will have only a memory of a seemingly endless narrow run of water. Bring home some lasting reflections of people, sights, and history by adding time to your schedule to make the extra stops or by spending a day shoreside exploring one, two, or three places. Cruising is not how far you can go; it is experiencing as you go, wherever you go.

Let's practice. The Poplars Motor Hotel, between Locks 12 and 13, has been a popular stop for boaters primarily because of its pool. However, the trip there from the Troy Town Dock takes between 8½ to 10½ hours. That estimate does not include the aforementioned stop at Lock 2 to see the historic first-generation Erie Canal display. Alternatives:

> a) Leave Troy Town Dock very early, say 7 A.M. Have lunch on board. That should get you into the Poplars Motor Hotel before dinner; or
> b) Leave Troy Town Dock late. Stop at Crescent Boat Club after about 4½ hours to 5½ hours running time, which includes a stop at Lock 2. Continue cruising a second day, breaking up the day by dropping anchor for lunch and a swim, and then proceed on to an early stop at the Poplars.

Speed Limits

Throughout this section of the Erie Canal, the speed limit is 10 mph (or less). However, as soon as you clear the guard gate and rock-walled channel throat, you see water-skiers and jet-skiers whizzing by far faster. Why? They are not being timed from lock to lock as you are. In order to have the next lock ready for you, the previous lock operator telephones ahead, tells the next lock's personnel that you are coming, and gives the time you left. The New York State Canal Corporation estimates

the run between Lock 6 and Lock 7 at 65 minutes. Each run between locks has a similar time estimate. If you show up sooner, the lock operator at Lock 7 assumes you have been speeding. He has the authority to fine you and/or delay your locking through for up to 21 hours. In reality, he will usually delay your request for a westbound lock-through with a lame excuse that prevents him from immediately opening the lock. He may suggest that the delay will be long enough that you tie up below the lock. Then, after a while, he will open the lock. Once you are at the top of the lock, he will give you a good talking to before letting you proceed.

However, if every boat, marina, and homeowner on the canal has been forced to ask you on VHF channel 13 to slow down or phoned the lock to complain about a mountainous wake or a dangerous situation you have created, then the lock operator will have the police waiting for you.

Most lock operators will give you some leeway because they really do not want to police you. Because they may get better fuel mileage at faster speeds, many boaters speed in open stretches, slow down for gas docks, and minimize their wakes around docked boats, still trying to stay close to the correct time. The lock operators want everyone to win.

Furthermore, if you leave a lock with three or four other boats, with rare exception the next lock operator will hold his lock open until you are all in—even that small displacement boat going 4 mph because of a dirty bottom, bent prop, and other ills. When one slow-going boat is so out of sync with the rest of the group, perhaps a quiet talk with the lock operator before you begin a longer stretch will convince him to help you pull ahead to separate from the slower boat. Do not compromise his authority by confessing to him that you'll speed. Just point out that based on the slower boat's past performance from lock to lock, you will be at the next lock 25 minutes before the slow vessel and would like a lock through without that slower boat. Finally, if you are stopping for any reason and not directly continuing on to the next lock, let the prior lock operator know, so the next lock operator is not worried about you.

Water Depths

Like all waterways, the canal's water levels can vary somewhat, on either a whole section of it or on a given pool (the water in the canal between two locks). However, it does not usually do so on this eastern run of the Erie Canal. Always ask the first lock operator you visit each day.

Spring runoff, downriver communities' water-supply needs (there are reservoirs that feed the canal system and/or other state needs), and farm and industrial usage can all affect the current water level. Stories of extremes of 5 feet over normal water levels are almost always before the canals open for a given boating season, although about once in every 10 years this can happen in June after heavy winter snows and a lot of spring rains. Please remember that bridge clearances are reduced by an amount equal to the increase in the water depth. If your bridge clearance is limited, you must take it upon yourself to be very diligent about water levels, especially in those pools that have the low bridges.

Cruising Again

Now, back onto your travels past guard gate 2.

> **SKIPPER TIP:** There is a launch ramp on the north shore (to your starboard) that creates lots of cross traffic in your path.

There is a popular stop located at green buoy #7 on the island to the south. People beach even large stern-drive-powered boats here and picnic. It stays deep quite near shore right at this little beach area but not west of it.

Red buoys are to starboard on the Erie Canal heading west. Stay to the right of the green buoys to enjoy deep water. The route of the original canal that was inland from here to starboard has been filled in and is no longer visible here.

The first bridge up after the Waterford Flight is the rather new Route 9 auto bridge (vertical clearance charted at 23 feet, but it may be less). On the north shore is the wharf for a local cruise boat. On the southern shore, you'll find Albany Marine Service (this side of the bridge—east) and Crescent Bridge Marina on the far side—west of the bridge. This is more a boat storage area without basic transient facilities. The phone number is (518) 786-3010. Albany Marine Service is a small, family-style marina set up to supply parts to many local boaters and be a home for about 60 year-round (winter and summer) vessels. Transients are welcome, but the regulars know the path in. There are no private markers to help you on approach, so watch water depth. Weeds also are prevalent close to shore.

Albany Marine Service (518) 783-5333

Storm protection: √√√
Scenic: **
Marina-reported approach depths: 3-12 feet

Marina-reported dockside depths: 3-4 feet
Fixed docks
Gas
Diesel
Waste pump-out
Rest rooms
Barbecues
Power connections: 30A/125V
Fiberglass repairs
Welding
Below-waterline repairs
Mechanical repairs
Gas-engine repairs
Diesel repairs
Stern-drive repairs
Generator repairs
Travelift/hoist
Parts store
Ship's store

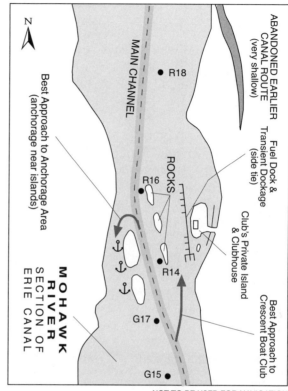

CRESCENT BOAT CLUB

NOT TO BE USED FOR NAVIGATION

About a mile west of the Route 9 Bridge is the departure point from the channel to head in for Crescent Boat Club docks. This club includes one of the friendliest groups of unassuming people you will run across in boating. They have a very nice facility on their own island, which is member-owned and -monitored. If you are westbound, heading toward Buffalo or Oswego, the approach to the marina is nice, wide, and deep. The boat club does request that you respect their policy of reciprocating only with other yacht-club members.

If you stop, perhaps they will extend the same courtesy to you that they did to me when I cruised through once. Among other courtesies, a member literally gave me the keys to his car and said, "Here, it is liable to rain, and it is too far to walk to a restaurant, so take my car—I don't need it right now—and enjoy." They are just a really nice group of people. Such experiences make fond memories and remind me of

why I got involved in boating in the first place. This private boat club goes all out to enjoy boating, and if you are of a similar ilk they will try to accommodate you overnight. Call ahead first, perhaps a day or so, when you know your plans. Tom, their consistently energetic but unpaid dockmaster, tries to be there (with several assistants if it is windy) to greet you on arrival. His extra efforts show how the club values you. For those who, like me, hate to go outside marked channels to cross unknown waters for any reason—a required feat to reach the Crescent Boat Club's docks—let me just say: 1) you can get on the rocks here; and 2) a $14 million, 126-foot megayacht easily overnighted here on its way to the Great Lakes, as have other large vessels before it.

The best approach is roughly from the east proceeding westward; leave the channel between buoys #15 and #17. Head somewhat northward for the end of Crescent's east- and west-oriented floats. There is usually a 50-foot houseboat or a 45-foot trawler on this end of the floats. You will be in 14-foot water depths early on in leaving the marked channel, dropping down to 10 feet near the end of this 2,000-foot run outside the channel. If you are in 7 feet or less water depth anywhere but within 30 feet of the dock, make an adjustment because you are off course.

The gas dock is centered on the outside float and in front of the clubhouse. The best exit, as it always is in unknown waters, is to go out the way you came in. Hint: Look behind you as you go in as a reference for when you leave.

Crescent Boat Club (518) 371-9864

Storm protection: √√
Scenic: * * * *
Marina-reported approach depths: 8-14 feet
Marina-reported dockside depths: 6-11 feet
Floating docks
Gas
Waste pump-out
Rest rooms
Showers
Picnic tables
Power connections: 30A/125V
What's special: private club
VHF-monitored channel: 13

Boat Clubs vs. Yacht Clubs

New York waterways have more boat clubs than yacht clubs. What is the difference? Most boat club members dress less formally at club events, have far more workdays for members, and have a "regular guy" membership compared to many yacht clubs. If you are a boat/yacht club member cruising well away from your own club, most clubs will reciprocate a one-night stay, but always call ahead. There are some private facilities for members only. I often will make a donation to the club's treasury of about 75 percent to 90 percent of the cruising area's going transient rates, i.e., 75 percent of the top rate I paid the previous night. If things are tough at home, donate less or match their extended courtesy in some other way.

More Marinas

Opposite buoys #14 and #16 and behind the island is a dead-end deep channel that is a favorite but not officially designated anchorage. Stay closer to the islands than the mainland for best water depths. Prior to the twin-arched bridges up next to the west, there are two marinas for craft under 30 feet in length. To the north, or your boat's starboard side, is Diamond Reef Marina, which is rather run-down. Call (518) 235-5748. The other on the south shore is a first-class rural facility. Blains Bay Marina offers good, clean year-round homes to more than 150 smaller boats. Almost all are seasonal (and winter storage) customers. There are no restaurants nearby, nor anything interesting to walk to, the same shortcomings common to the other locations in this area. Watch water depths at both marinas. At low water levels, ask for specific directions and advice.

Blains Bay Marina (518) 785-6785

Storm protection: √√√
Scenic: * * *

Marina-reported approach depths: 3-6 feet
Marina-reported dockside depths: 2-4 feet
Floating docks
Gas
Rest rooms
Showers
Picnic tables
Power connections: 30A/125V
Fiberglass repairs
Mechanical repairs
Gas-engine repairs
Stern-drive repairs
Travelift/hoist
Ship's store

Now you pass underneath a major fixed bridge called the Thaddeus Kosciuzcko Bridge. It has a vertical clearance of 30 feet and a horizontal opening of 200 feet for boaters. On an auto map, this bridge is part of Interstate 87, which is also called the Adirondack Northway, or "the Northway," as it is called locally. The Northway is an extension of the New York State Thruway and completes a continuous route from New York City straight into Montréal. This area is a strict no-wake zone. Notice that some of the homes to the port are nicer than to starboard. The lower ground to starboard can flood sometimes. Just past the bridge, heading west, be careful not to misread on which side to pass the mid-river island. Pass that island on the right side, so that it is to your port. The no-wake zone ends here.

Starting at buoy #24 (well past the Interstate 87 Bridge), keep an eye out, because to the north (starboard) of your boat, just a bit inland, is the old abandoned Erie Canal. It comes into view in a few different spots in this area and, since it still has water in it, is pretty easy to identify. The waterway originally was 40 feet wide and 4 feet deep, with a towpath on one

side and bucolic scenes surrounding it. Perhaps the best spot to see it is just as you come up to the old ferry landing at Vischer's Ferry.

Vischer's Ferry, which is now a small community, was once an operating ferry landing, and the structure for the north-side landing is still there. You can see a couple of old granite blocks, each roughly 2 by 1½ feet in diameter, that were used as a part of the ferry landing. Before there were highways or bridges, ferries were commonly used to transport both freight and people across the Mohawk River. You are now at the end of the waterway defined by Lock 6 and coming up on Lock 7. The channel hugs the riverbank to port.

Schenectady

Lock 7—27-foot lift. (518) 374-7912. After this lock it is 65 minutes to Lock 8, which is 11 miles west.

Once through the lock, on the south shore you come upon two of the city of Schenectady's four General Electric plants. Schenectady itself is just beyond the bend in the river. For many years Schenectady and General Electric were synonymous, but now General Electric has moved many of its facilities to other areas, both within New York State and elsewhere. The first facility you see, which looks like an old factory, is the Atomic Power Laboratory, which you can spot by the large tank that is a part of it. Next on the General Electric tour is the Research and Development Lab, which is best identified by a single stack visible from the canal.

On the south side of the waterway is a small waterfall. Depending on the time of year, it flows with varying intensity. About 15 feet high above the water, it is pretty. I have been within half a boat length of it and showed 10

Typical area for short-term tie-up offers a place for boaters to wait until the lock is available.

feet of water depth on the sounder. I have lunched and swum the afternoon away after anchoring in 12 feet of water well off the opposite (north) shore (because boat traffic goes past to the south side of the river's center line). However, you cannot anchor here overnight—you are too close to the dam. Let me point out the huge modern house constructed so as to look old on the top of the northshore cliff. It was built as a private 35-room residence for a local insurance executive. It has a $42,000 a month mortgage, according to a report by Schenectady TV station WRGB. Also take note that the shore rises as you proceed west, and you get a bit of a sense of going through a canyon.

Just as you make the shallow port turn around the curve on the Mohawk River, you see the Schenectady Yacht Club ahead on the north shore, which is actually in a town called Rexford. It is roughly a 2-mile walk from the Schenectady Yacht Club to downtown Schenectady and some of its historical sites. Unless you have a bicycle on board, Schenectady just does not seem to be boater-accessible. If you stop at Schenectady Yacht Club for any reason, look for the nearby remains of an aqueduct that was put in when the original Erie Canal was built.

Schenectady Yacht Club and the other marinas in the Schenectady area suffer from the same problem that Crescent Boat Club has: There are no dining opportunities close by. For most people, this dearth takes the area out of the realm of a reasonable overnight stop. Most people who stop overnight want to be able to get off their boat and have a meal shoreside.

Schenectady Yacht Club (518) 384-9971

Storm protection: √√
Scenic: *
Marina-reported approach depths: 10-13 feet
Marina-reported dockside depths: 3-8 feet
Floating docks
Gas
Diesel
Waste pump-out
Rest rooms
Showers
Dockside water
Power connections: 30A/125V
What's special: private club

Schenectady is one of the older towns in New York State. First established as a site for fur trading in the early 1600s, Schenectady became a Dutch settlement in 1661. In 1664 the English took over, and in February 1690, the settlement was nearly destroyed by a French and Indian raid. The town was originally built inside a stockade. The French incited the Indians to come down from Canada and burn the stockade, killing 60 people and carrying 27 away while burning most of the town. The survivors were left to fend for themselves.

If Schenectady were a little more boater-accessible, the historic improvements left over from that original stockade era would make a nice walking tour, as would the housing development that General Electric put in for its upper echelon executives and scientists from 1930 to 1950 (a very early version of a master planned development). In 1848, Schenectady became a center for locomotive-engine manufacturing. Then in 1861, the turret gears and assembly for the USS *Monitor* ironclad ship were made here. General Electric itself, incorporated in 1892, traces its roots back to 1886.

Schenectady is also the home of Union College, founded in 1795, which has a nice campus and lovely grounds. It was the location for the filming of the 1973 movie *The Way We Were,* starring Barbra Streisand and Robert Redford. Unfortunately, the two-mile walk into town from the Schenectady Yacht Club is somewhat uphill.

One more point of interest about Schenectady is that one of its main downtown streets is wider than most because it was once a section of the old Erie Canal. When the original canal was abandoned and it was decided to use the Mohawk River in the new section, the canal was filled in and became Erie Street, a section of Erie Boulevard.

Three-quarters of a mile past Schenectady Yacht Club is an abandoned bridge. The granite rock pilings are still in place, but the trestle part of the bridge has been taken away. About one-third of a mile past these pilings is a seaplane base. Usually there is at least one seaplane in residence, which is a neat sight. They often sit back from the waterway in a shed-type garage.

Mohawk Valley Marina (518) 399-2719

Storm protection: √√
Scenic: *
Floating docks
Rest rooms
Showers
Dockside water
Power connections: 15A/125V
Below-waterline repairs
Mechanical repairs
Gas-engine repairs
Diesel repairs
Stern-drive repairs
What's special: new boat dealer
VHF-monitored channel: 13

A mile and a half farther down from the seaplane base is a railroad bridge. Vertical clearance here is well over 20 feet. Be aware of the north shore because there is a barge tie-up area here. You want to make sure that they are not doing something with those barges that requires you to give way.

Wilson's Marine Service (518) 382-0077

Storm protection: √√
Scenic: *
Marina-reported approach depths: 7-13 feet
Marina-reported dockside depths: 3-6 feet
Floating docks
Wharf
Gas
Diesel
Rest rooms
Showers
Dockside water
Power connections: 30A/125V
Mechanical repairs
Gas-engine repairs
Diesel repairs
Yard trailer
Ship's store
VHF-monitored channel: 13

Another bridge follows, auto this time instead of railroad, with a vertical clearance of 21 feet. Next, you come to the third General Electric plant within the city of Schenectady. This is the main GE plant, and it is much larger than either of the other two. Much of the original Erie Canal route went over the land on which that facility now sits. Another fixed bridge comes up right after the GE plant.

The Route 5 auto bridge has 27-foot vertical clearance. On the north side of the river, and in some places the west side, across from Schenectady, is the town of Scotia. Scotia is home to a General Services Administration depot, or GSA. It also has a Naval Reserve training center and a Naval supply depot. I think it is interesting to find this located right here in the middle of upstate New York.

The fourth General Electric plant comes up on the south side. The river makes a right turn, after which you are in line to see, off in the distance, Lock 8.

Lock 8—14-foot lift. Call (518) 346-3382. Lock 9 is 30 minutes ahead. Lock 8 has a different type of dam structure than you have seen so far. This dam is movable, with an overhead trellis, not unlike a railroad-bridge support system. The fact that it is adjustable just makes the dam a little different, but it doesn't change the locking procedure. Lock 8 is the same as all the other locks you have been going through, except for the 14-foot lift or rise, which is somewhat less than what you have seen so far on the canal route. It is, however, the same lift as the Troy Federal Lock.

Almost midway between locks is Arrowhead Marina and RV Camp. Run by an elderly couple, it is a basic but fine stay-over. The atmosphere is a restful place, and water depth is good.

Arrowhead Marina and RV Camp (518) 382-8966

Storm protection: √√√
Scenic: * * *
Marina-reported approach depths: 12 feet
Marina-reported dockside depths: 12 feet
Floating docks
Gas
Waste pump-out
Rest rooms
Showers
Dockside water
Power connections: 30A/125V, 15A/125V

The run from Lock 8 to Lock 9 is a little more than five miles. A little more than halfway is the railroad bridge for the old Boston and Maine Railroad (24-foot vertical clearance). Just past that is the water tower that identifies Schenectady International, a chemical corporation. Up on the cliff on the west (or south) riverbank, you can see the main freight yard for the railroad.

This region along the Mohawk between Locks 8 and 9 was a campground and gathering area for the Indians, as well as a burial ground, centuries before European civilization came to the New World. Thus, the land around here is very rich in American Indian artifacts. As the countryside becomes more rural, it's easy to imagine a more primitive time, like that captured in the 1939 film *Drums Along the Mohawk*, the story of a group of upstate New York settlers during the Revolutionary War.

Coming back to the present, if you are getting hungry, you can stop and tie up just before or after Lock 9. Just across the bridge, on the south side of the river, there is a place you can walk to less than a mile away where you can buy pizza, soft-serve ice cream, or just a can of soda.

Lock 9—15-foot lift. (518) 887-2401. To reach the supervisor of Locks 2 to 9, call (518) 237-0613. Lock 10 is 35 to 40 minutes ahead. Again, this is a standard lock. The road that crosses above it is Route 103.

West of the lock just as you start to turn left here, you will see, on the right-hand side, multiple railroad tracks and an arched tunnel through which a small brook runs. The hillside here rises about 500 feet, and this brook is the natural runoff from the hills down into the river. Once you make the first turn, on your left

you can see relatively new homes and a new sea wall. You then have a fixed railroad bridge with 23-foot vertical clearance directly ahead. It is a pretty straight run after the railroad bridge. Again, be cautious passing the mid-river island. You want to pass this one on the left side, keeping it to your right. Just below the lock's dam is a reported hot spot for bass.

There is a long history of commercial traffic on the Mohawk River. Even before the Revolutionary War, as early as 1720 traders transported their wares along here on wooden cargo vessels called bateaux. These were flat-bottomed, double-ended boats, just under 28 feet long and about 5 feet wide.

Around 1797, the bateau was replaced by what is now called the Schenectady boat. This boat was roughly 60 feet long with an 8-foot beam and carried 12 times the cargo of the earlier boat. However, it was too big to be portaged around falls. The Schenectady boat originated during the Revolutionary War, when George Washington used similar vessels to move his troops and supplies. (This boat is the same design as the one pictured in the famous painting of Washington crossing the Delaware River.) The boat was in use until about 1825, when the Erie Canal opened up and started accommodating even larger vessels.

These pre-canal boats usually were pulled or dragged by tow ropes employing either human or animal power. In wider sections of the river, they were rowed or poled, though some occasionally sailed. In the sailboats, the sail-rigging system was designed to fold down to fit underneath any low bridges that crossed the river (built for farmers to access fields bisected by the canal). In fact, there were several bridges across the river that had been built before the use of these bigger freight-carrying boats, and they were set at whatever height was convenient to access the shore bank. So the second-generation boats were all built in such a way that they just barely cleared these bridges, and then only if the occupants ducked down. It was with these boats that the custom of shouting "Low bridge, everybody down" began, though it later became associated with the Erie Canal. By the time the canal came through in 1825, there were already bridges in place across the Mohawk, and their height set the precedent for the bridges that followed. That is one reason why, even today, you need to limit your clearance on this route, although it is a lot higher than it was then.

Lock 10—15-foot lift. (518) 882-5450. The supervisor for Locks 10 to 16 can be reached at (518) 853-3823. It is about 25 minutes to Lock 11.

Take a look at the lovely flower garden at Lock 10. It is well cared for and a bit nicer than those at most of the locks. The flower gardens are traditional at the locks and come from the early custom of having a whole family be responsible for running each lock. The job of lock operator used to be a year-round position. Each lock usually has had a chief lock operator and an assistant, known as a canal structure operator; some of the locks employ a third person to assist.

Everything You Always Wanted to Know About Lock Operators . . .
Chief lock operators also are often responsible in the off-season for reconditioning their machinery, including the generators and the mechanical devices that enable the locks to function. They

---

also paint all of the buildings and grounds. The lock operators I've talked to really have a sense that their lock is their domicile, and they show a pride of ownership. Lock operators in the New York State Barge Canal System are now employed by the New York State Thruway Authority. Before 1993, however, they came under the Transportation Department of New York State. Several of the chief lock operators still remember when there were few pleasure boats going through and the boat activity on the canals was all commercial.

For some of the lock operators, this experience with commercial traffic from a bygone era has created a mind-set that is not always receptive to pleasure boaters. It's unfortunate for us, but these few (less than 5 percent) lock operators in the state canal system seem to have the attitude that they are there to control the pleasure boaters. Many seem to think that pleasure boaters do not have adequate knowledge to make a lock-through. These few leave a sour taste in the mouth of out-of-state boaters. The Canadian lock operators, on the other hand, are employed by the Canadian Department of Parks and Recreation and generally think of themselves as being similar to forest rangers. They typically wear shorts and function as educators about the outdoors, locking through, and the canals.

Immediately after passing through Lock 10, you see Adirondack Power and Light on the south shore bank. Then, after a slight bend, there is a small cove that is not really marked well on your chart. This is probably the first instance in which the chart and what you see do not match up well. Next there is an eroding granite seawall that is part of an old carpet plant. After that, also on the north shore, there is an old launch ramp in disrepair, with a small float that may or may not have broken away by the time you pass by.

Mohawk Carpet was named for the river that it fronted, and the original building has since been torn down; its former site is a parking lot for tractor-trailer rigs. This was the company's original location, though the plant has long since moved to the South. Some of these types of buildings have been used for other purposes over the years, but most of them have fallen victim to fire and disuse and serve only as early industrial-era archeological sites.

Depending on the time of the day, this may be a good time to think about where you will stop for the night. I recommend the Poplars Motor Hotel in the town of Fultonville. Poplars is about 12 miles ahead between Locks 12 and 13. That's a little more than an hour of running time, plus some locking time, for a total of about 2¼ hours, although this will vary by the speed of the two lock-throughs. Poplars is probably the biggest boater-oriented complex on this eastern section of the Erie/Mohawk Canal, and it is definitely one of the better spots for an overnight stay, so you may want to plan your day to arrive there for dinner.

Amsterdam

You are now coming to the city of Amsterdam, hometown of movie star and author Kirk Douglas. Just as Troy was a factory town that used the available supply of water to power the earliest types of manufacturing plants, Amsterdam also made use of the river to power its industries. Just west of the bridge in

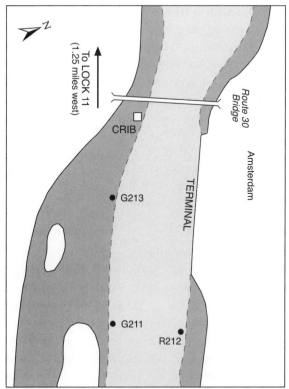

AMSTERDAM TERMINAL

To LOCK 11 (1.25 miles west)

CRIB

G213

TERMINAL

G211

R212

Route 30 Bridge

Amsterdam

NOT TO BE USED FOR NAVIGATION

the middle of downtown Amsterdam, you can see the remains of the old bridge that preceded the Route 30 Bridge (38-foot vertical clearance) that you just went under on the Mohawk River.

Amsterdam originally was settled by the Dutch, who also named it. However, a large proportion of the population traces its ancestry back to German and Italian immigrants who came to this area to work in the carpet mills.

Downtown Amsterdam is somewhat accessible to boaters who stop at the terminal, which is a commercial industrial wharf. Get permission if you are a pleasure boater. Call ahead to the lock operator if you want to use the Lock 11 entrance/exit approaches or if you want to take a break for lunch or a tour. In either event, you have to cross the railroad tracks just before the fixed bridge on the north shore and then work your way into town. A pedestrian walkway is in the works here. From here it is reasonable walking distance to Guy Park State Historical Site on the north shore of the Mohawk in Amsterdam. Here you find a museum housed in the Georgian mansion where Indian Agent Guy Johnson once lived. The museum focuses on the Erie Canal and its impact on westward expansion.

Cigars

If you enjoy the relaxation and comfort that a fine cigar provides, you must stop in Amsterdam. Three generations of Amsterdam's citizens operate a low-overhead store for good to superior cigars. Call them; if at all possible, they will come to your boat to bring you back to their location if you need to buy a box or two. They are fun, down-to-earth people to whom most boaters will instantly relate. It is interesting that each partner has a different background: one is the mayor of Amsterdam, one's a professional firefighter, and the other works in the school system. Inquire at (518) 843-4568.

Lock 11—12-foot lift. (518) 829-7331. Lock 12 is 30 minutes ahead.

About halfway to Lock 12 is Fort Johnson, built in 1749. It sits on the north shore, just past the first island but before the second island. On the south bank, across from the fort and town, you can see some of the original wall from the Erie Canal. This is the Schoharie Crossing State Historical Site. It is about 1½ miles from Lock 11 and 2¾ miles from Lock 12, too far in either case to be practical,

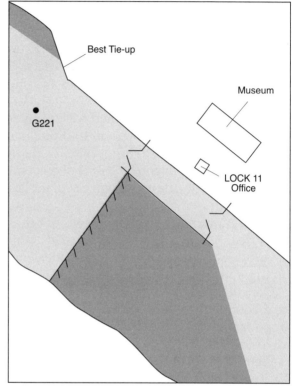

LOCK 11

Best Tie-up

Museum

G221

LOCK 11 Office

NOT TO BE USED FOR NAVIGATION

although the state suggests that you use Lock 12 to visit the substantial early-canal ruins at Fort Hunter, which also is on the south side of the river. Your only other plan might be just to jump off your boat and swim ashore until a boaters' landing is in place.

This section is pretty and has tall grass on each bank. There are three large mid-river islands on the waterway. In all three cases, stay in the channel by passing the islands to the left, keeping them on your starboard side.

Lock 12—11-foot lift. (518) 829-7331. Lock 13 is one hour ahead. Lock 12 is named Tribes Hill, the same name as the surrounding area. You have traveled 46 miles from Troy to this lock and lifted about 278 feet above sea level. This is the last lock before Poplars Motor Hotel.

After locking through, look to your port side for a wide-open waterway. This is the Schoharie Creek and the head of the Schoharie Valley, which stretches to the south. During earlier days, from 1817 to about 1850, this area was the breadbasket of the United States. Nebraska had not yet been settled, and this place raised the grain that fed the East Coast. Grain was just one of the products that was transported along the rivers and canals down to New Amsterdam, now New York City.

There is a launch ramp and a reasonable anchorage spot in the Schoharie Creek. Look for some plaques in this area that describe the story of the Schoharie Creek aqueduct that was built in the 1840s and carried the second generation of the Erie Canal over the creek. You can get a bit closer to the aqueduct by taking a short run upstream from the anchorage area. Go about a half-mile up the unmarked channel, but watch the depth here. Although it is marked on the chart to be generous, there might be some obstructions such as trees or other hidden obstacles down there. The Schoharie Creek does continue south another 75 miles to its source.

The first-generation canal was just a little farther (about a half-mile) south or upstream from here. One of the things that used to happen routinely on the original canal during flood times was that during the spring runoff, the water of the creek would sweep away the barges. They were block-and-tackled across the creek on the original canal. Their lines would break under the pressure of extreme high water, and a barge and its crew and cargo would find themselves riding down the rapids on the then-wild Mohawk River. The remains of the old canal aqueduct are visible there to boaters.

A little farther up the creek (beyond where boaters can reach) is Interstate 90, which is the east/west section of the New York State Thruway. There are two sections to the Thruway. Below Albany, the north/south section consists of Interstate 87. Above Albany, I-87 becomes the Northway and the New York State Thruway turns to the west as I-90. In the late 1980s, the Thruway bridge over the Schoharie Creek had a problem with the creek overflowing during storms. The bridge collapsed, and several people unknowingly drove their cars onto the bridge that was no longer there. Their cars crashed to the rocky ravine below, and they died. Remains of that original New York State Thruway bridge are still visible around the new bridge that replaced it.

Just past the bend in the Mohawk, there are some beige buildings on the south-shore hill marking the Shrine of Our Lady of Martyrs, formerly the Mohawk village of Ossernenon. In 1646, a French Jesuit priest, Father Isaac Jogues, and Brother Rene Goupil were brought here by the Indians after their capture. Goupil was killed by the Mohawks, and Father Jogues buried him here in a ravine. Near these buildings is a memorial to a Mohawk Indian maiden, Kateri Tekawitha, who has been honored as a "Blessed" by the Catholic Church. These sites are not boater-accessible because they are a little more than 2 miles to the west from the Schoharie Creek anchorage area. The highway between the hillside shrine and the Mohawk River Canal is I-90, or the Thruway. It parallels the canal in this section.

On the south shore you will come up on Fultonville, named after Robert Fulton.

POPLARS MOTOR HOTEL

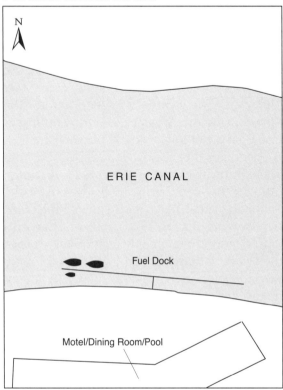

NOT TO BE USED FOR NAVIGATION

Although he did not actually invent the steam-powered vessel, his political connections allowed him to claim that credit, and the inaccuracy persists in many history books. This is the location of Poplars Motor Hotel, a popular inn, restaurant, and marina. The restaurant serves smorgasbord style at most meals, and I noticed a little German accent to the cooking. There is a substantial cold-salad bar.

Poplars also has motel rooms, a cocktail lounge, and a swimming pool. The pool is open to marina guests, and towels are available in the laundry room area, which is also the boaters' shower room. There is a substantial bank of washers and dryers here. In the morn-ing, however, these are primarily used by the housekeeping staff to take care of the motel's laundry needs, so do your wash at night.

As you tie up at Poplars Motor Hotel, be aware that the train tracks run along the far shore of the river, just to the north of the hotel. At the same time, the front of the hotel—the side with the street entrance—is across from a truck stop, so be prepared for a bit of noise in the marina all night long from those two sources of activity. The Mohawk has cut a river valley right across the state, creating a natural route from east to west that historically opened up the state to the rest of the U.S. As a result, all transportation, whether it is via water, rail, or highway, uses the valley to facilitate travel from one side of New York State to the other. All three modes of transportation seem to meet at Poplars.

Poplars Motor Hotel (518) 853-4511

Storm protection: √√
Scenic: * *
Marina-reported approach depths: 5-12 feet
Marina-reported dockside depths: 4-7 feet
Floating docks
Gas
Waste pump-out
Rest rooms
Showers
Laundry: big
Dockside water
Power connections: 15A only
Restaurant: on site
Grocery: off site
What's special: pool
VHF-monitored channel: 13

Across the river canal way from Poplars is the town of Fonda, which has the ConRail multiple railroad tracks running through it. One of the town of Fonda's claims to fame is that it provided the stage name for the movie star Henry Fonda, who was raised there. A half-hour west of the fixed bridge that runs through Fonda and Fultonville is the next lock, Lock 13.

Lock 13—8-foot lift. (518) 922-6173. It is roughly 50 minutes to Lock 14.

About 15 minutes (or 3 miles) west of the lock, the landscape rises into a hill about 700 feet high on the south side and two hills, about 800 feet and 600 feet high respectively, on the north. One can imagine that these would provide a good vantage point for anyone who wanted to maintain control of this portion of the valley. Remember the Tribes Hill lock name? These are the hills that Indian tribes used to control their areas. Please note that right after the bend in the river, the channel narrows and danger is indicated by the white buoy with the orange diamond on it.

SKIPPER TIP: As you travel through the narrow channel, tell your crew that the white buoy with the orange diamond on it represents danger. In this case, the buoy is used to indicate that the river is shallow immediately outside the channel. Have your crew take note of what these navigation aids look like so that they can watch for them in the future.

After you make the turn and are heading due west, the channel markers on the north set the channel to the southern half of the river. This creates an informal anchorage area, right at the base of Knauderack Creek. Informal

means that it is not marked as an anchorage area on the charts, so you must show an appropriate anchorage light if you stop here. You should be able to anchor outside the channel in that location and have decent water depth. It's unlikely you'll want to anchor here, however, because in the summertime the locks operate until late in the evening.

The town of Canajoharie is on the south shore at Lock 14. There is a terminal on the south shore just before the Route 10 Bridge (30-foot vertical clearance) crosses the river. You can tie up there to access this small town. Get permission. There is a grocery store with the standard necessities, including newspapers and ice. If you do not need provisions, take a hike to the south. It is worth the effort to follow the Canajoharie Creek into the pothole or gorge area, which is called Wintergreen Park. The name Canajoharie—an Indian word that best translates into English as the "pot that washes itself"—comes from the interesting formations here.

Canajoharie is the home of Beechnut chewing gum and baby food, whose plant is still located in town but is a substantial walk from the terminal. The Beechnut operation generated considerable wealth, and one result was that the Beechnut family established the Canajoharie Art Gallery, inside the town library, containing a significant collection of paintings.

Lock 14—8-foot lift. (518) 673-3314. Just west of Lock 14 you can tie up and enjoy an island park where you can go walking, biking, or picnicking. From here cruise to the Fort Plain Bridge (vertical clearance of 23 feet), right before Lock 15, which is about 20 minutes from Lock 14.

Lock 15—8-foot lift. (518) 993-4161. This

lock also has the last moveable dam on the western route from Albany. The bridge over it has 20-foot clearance. It is 40 minutes to Lock 16.

Located just past the lock, Abeel Island causes the river to fork. Take the right fork, which is marked by the channel.

SKIPPER TIP: If you have a dinghy or canoe, you can take a very nice side trip to the back side of Abeel Island. You would anchor to the east end of it, where there is more water depth, and canoe or row along the back side of the island. The area through here is pretty. You also can anchor, if it is a quick stop, just outside the channel at the west end of Abeel Island and row to the island from that direction.

A mile and a half before Lock 16 is the town of St. Johnsville, with a municipal marina located on the north shore, just before the bridge. It is indicated with a red aid to navigation and has its own basin. There is a launch ramp there, and the town is accessible. The origin of the St. Johnsville Municipal Marina was in commercial loading and unloading of barge freight. It has been improved for pleasure boaters. The bridge has 24-foot vertical clearance.

St. Johnsville Municipal Marina (518) 568-7406

Storm protection: √√√
Scenic: * *
Marina-reported approach depths: 10-13 feet

Marina-reported dockside depths: 5-13 feet
Gas
Diesel
Waste pump-out
Rest rooms
Showers
Dockside water
Restaurant: off site
Deli: off site
Grocery: off site
Convenience store: off site
What's special: diesel fuel

Lock 16—20-foot lift. (518) 568-2636. It is 50 minutes to Lock 17. Once past the lock, the waterway turns into the barge canal, leaving the natural channel of the Mohawk River for a man-made cut to follow through the landscape. Watch your speed in the canal cut. Now that you are in the Erie Canal, the channel markers mostly become posts, similar to those used for mailboxes.

Roughly a mile and a half past Lock 16, you pass beneath the River Road fixed bridge with plenty of vertical clearance (23 feet); a little later, the same road again crosses over the canal (29-foot clearance). However, some 2 miles farther west is one of the guard gates. This is the only time that I thought that the clearance shown on the charts did not match up with what I observed. The guard gate is marked at 24 feet, but it seemed substantially less than that, probably in the high teens. I don't know if the guard gate happened to be low at the particular time I went through, or if there was some other problem, such as a typographical error on the chart. If you are pushing clearance at 17 feet or 18 feet, I suggest that you slow down and approach this gate with caution.

Just past the guard gate, Nowadaga Creek turns off on the south side of the canal. There is a gravel area that comes in right at that point. Right after that, on the north shore, you see the Mohawk River again. Bridge vertical clearance is 23 feet. You are approaching a dam off the channel to the north. Just upstream of the dam, take note of a couple of cribs out in the waterway. The tour boats that carry passengers through this region tie up here, so it is a possible anchorage area. However, in addition to watching your depth, you have to make sure that you get a good hold so that you don't go over the dam, which is just to the north of you. At this point the cut channel becomes a part of the natural Mohawk River again.

Continuing west, there is a monument to Gen. Nicholas Herkimer on the south shore, up about 400 feet high. If you want to visit the monument, go forward to Lock 17, tie up (secure permission first), and then walk back. It's a good hike of about two miles and 400 feet uphill. A bridge with only 20-foot vertical clearance somewhat hides Lock 17, which is behind it.

Lock 17—40½-foot lift. (518) 823-0650. Lock 17 has the highest lift of its type in the world. I find it slightly intimidating, though there is nothing special about the locking process itself. The vertical-lift gate makes this a different style of lock. With this type, the lock gate lifts up over your boat, somewhat like a guillotine. You pass underneath it, and it drops down behind you.

> **SKIPPER TIP:** The lock operator usually recommends that small craft keep to the south wall of the lift (port side for westbound traffic).

Because the gates are particularly efficient, this lock can actually empty or fill in less than 10 minutes. It is 25 minutes to Lock 18, if you do not stop. You can contact the section supervisor for Locks 17 to 22 by phone at (518) 733-9530.

Vertical-lift gates are said to be common in Europe, but I have not cruised there so I can't verify that information firsthand. However, I do know that in the Erie/Mohawk/Barge Canal system, there is one major drawback to the vertical-lift gate. Now picture this: The gate sits in mossy water collecting a slimy growth before it lifts open to let boaters pass through. As you go under the gate, this wet mossy growth drips canvas-staining drops on boat covers, awnings, fly-bridge canvas, bow-deck covers, whatever. If it is not flushed off with water fairly quickly, ideally within a half-day, it becomes ingrained in your canvas. After passing Lock 17, I spent a considerable amount of time over three days because I let the drops sit there—washing my canvas (sunbrella fabric) *seven* times to scrub this stuff out of the fabric weave. So after you pass the lift lock, if you have access to clean water, I suggest you flush off all of your canvas to get rid of those little black dots—and the sooner, the better!

Little Falls

Two-thirds of a mile west of the lock and 1,000 feet before the next guard gate is a small wharf, Bentons Landing, that is sized and oriented to pleasure boaters and provides good access for the afternoon to the town of Little Falls. Since you've been cruising about four hours from Poplars Motor Hotel, it is probably a good time to stop for lunch anyway. A tie-up is also available at the Little Falls Terminal Wall 2,500 feet ahead, but it is a longer walk into town. Since my last visit, this has all been scheduled to be renovated. Little Falls is a good-size town with groceries, a coffee shop, restaurants, and newsstands. You can easily enjoy yourself strolling around for a half-hour or so. For lunch, check out the Canal Street Inn or the deli right in town, maybe three blocks in from the waterfront tie-up.

As you walk into town you can see again that the canal is a ditch dug along the south side of the Mohawk River, and both the canal and the river are to the south of town. Only Bentons Landing is on the same side of the canal as the town, but you have to walk over a bridge to cross the natural Mohawk River. This gives you the chance to see the ruins of some of the old aqueducts that were a part of the early version of the Erie Canal, including the remains of a more than 1,000-foot-long arched aqueduct made out of quarry stone that provided water for the Mohawk River and let some of the boats and cargo going through come into Little Falls. You can also see some of the dams, making it easier to understand the water-height changes. This very interesting little stopover helps reveal the early structure of the canal.

As I have pointed out, there is a Little Falls commercial terminal. However, it is on the south shore and about a mile walk into town because you have to cross the waterway. I prefer the small, wooden, boater-friendly wharf because it is closer to restaurants. A third of a mile past the wharf, the Mohawk River and the dug canal again become one.

Long before the Erie Canal came through, the first locks ever in the state of New York were put in around Little Falls. Prior to 1798, you could take a small 30-foot boat, typically something that carried about 3,000 pounds of cargo, and pull it and push it upriver from Albany to Little Falls. Then either the boat, the cargo, or both would be off-loaded and portaged around the Little Falls area. In 1798 a private canal company, Western Inland Lock Navigation Company, improved the system by building locks around Little Falls to allow ships to navigate the 39-foot drop. After the locks went in, the small bateau was replaced by a vessel that was double in size and could carry as much as 24,000 pounds of cargo. These boats, along with the company's improvements, were an important factor in the expansion of the country to what was then considered the West. For example, with the advent of these locks in 1798, shipment from Albany to Seneca Lake of a load that weighed a ton dropped in price from $100 to $32. Considering the value of the dollar back then, one realizes that the freight charges were often more than the cargo's original cost.

By walking across some of the bridges in Little Falls, you can imagine what a job it must have been to portage up and around the gorgelike terrain. The locks made a big difference to this part of the world, and people began to recognize their value, even 30 years before the first Erie Canal.

Lock 18—20-foot lift. (518) 823-2419. This lock is a little more than 3 miles west of Little Falls Terminal. The stretch between Locks 18 and 19 at a distance of 13 miles (75 minutes) is a long run in the Erie section this side of Oneida Lake. Other long stretches are Locks 20 to 21, at 18 miles (1 hour 50 minutes); Locks 24 to 25 at 31 miles; and Locks 33 to 34, between Rochester and Lockport, at about 63 miles.

SKIPPER TIP: Just before the lock, the Mohawk River veers off to the right and is not navigable. The man-made canal channel continues straight through.

About 2 miles west, past Lock 18, and less than a mile east of the first fixed bridge after the lock, there is a potential anchorage. I do not recommend that you anchor here, though, because there are multiple obstacles underneath the water that could entangle you or your anchor rode, and I am suspicious of the water depth.

Continuing west are two fixed bridges in a row. The first one is a local bridge for South Washington Street (22-foot vertical clearance) and the second is the State Thruway (or I-90, with a vertical clearance of 30 feet).

Now the New York State Thruway crosses both the man-made canal and the Mohawk River. Guard gate 5, next up, (vertical clearance 24 feet) precedes the Mohawk Street Bridge (vertical clearance 22 feet).

Just past this third bridge, the Mohawk and the canal become one again. Also, immediately on the north shore is a barge wharf with somewhat shallow water depth near shore. Watch out for the traffic here.

Just past the barge wharf, the natural river gives you a bit of shallow water close to shore on both the north and south sides. You are also coming into a more bucolic region, with lush vegetation and trees overhanging the river, just like those in the jungle ride at Disneyland—if you want your imagination to take a stretch to sharpen your mind. Watch out! There's an alligator to port!

Ilion and Frankfort

Just a mile or so ahead is the town of Ilion. The town calls their tie-up Ilion Village Marina. This is a nice long wharf that has just about all the basic services you need. One of the nice things about Ilion Marina is that Anthony's Restaurant will send a car down to the marina, pick you up, take you back to their Italian restaurant, and then bring you back—all on an on-call basis. When I went through, they picked me up in a Lincoln Town Car. This is typical of the individual (if somewhat homespun) service that the town, the merchants, and the marina all provide. The Ilion Marina, by the way, is also an RV park. You will have a chance to see about 20 RVs and the same number of boats on any given summer night. Clean, newer rest rooms; lots of water pressure wharfside; easy electrical hookups—it is all here plus more.

Another advantage of the Ilion Marina is that there is a cable hookup. For $1 you can rent their cable-system line, which will be run to your boat hookup. You get to watch cable TV maybe for the first time since starting this canal cruise, and if you timed your trip correctly, you don't have to miss an episode of *Home Improvement*!

The town of Ilion offers another chance to replenish supplies. In addition, you can tour the Remington Arms Museum. The Remington Company made guns and weaponry throughout U.S. history, and the museum is its hall of fame for firearms. It takes a while to get there, and you have to decide between a cab ride and a very long walk. Before you go, check on the museum's hours and decide whether this is of interest to you. I think people who do not particularly care about firearms might still enjoy taking the stretch and exploring what this museum has to offer.

Ilion Village Marina (315) 895-7449

Storm protection: √√√
Scenic: * *
Marina-reported approach depths: 10-13 feet

Marina-reported dockside depths: 8-10 feet
Wharf
Gas
Diesel
Waste pump-out
Rest rooms
Showers
Dockside water
Barbecues
Picnic tables
Power connections: 15A/125V
Restaurant: off site (car pickup can be arranged)
Grocery: off site
What's special: Remington museum

Vertical clearance for the Central Avenue Bridge is 22 feet. Just west is Ilion's sister town, Frankfort, a major rail-line distribution center and switching yard. There is a commercial terminal where the Mohawk River meets the Erie Canal again. The terminal is immediately past the Railroad Street Bridge, with a vertical clearance of 31 feet, which is the only bridge in Frankfort and the next one after Ilion's downtown bridge. Because of Ilion's amenities, most people prefer to stay there rather than Frankfort. On the far (west) side of town is the Moss Road Bridge, with 22 feet of vertical clearance.

Frankfort Harbour Marina

Storm protection: √√
Scenic: *
Marina-reported approach depths: 12 feet
Marina-reported dockside depths: 3-6 feet
Rest rooms
Power connections: 15A/125V
What's special: not really a marina—more an unstaffed terminal wall

The Erie Canal channel and the Mohawk River separate again, and the canal runs quite close to the ConRail Railroad on the north side of the waterway. A little farther down, just before Lock 19, ConRail crosses over the canal, leaving a vertical clearance of 22 feet.

Lock 19—21-foot lift. (315) 733-5041. This lock is almost hidden by the railroad bridge. It is about one hour to Lock 20. About 1½ miles after the lock, the canal is in need of some dredging around channel markers 538 and 540. It gets down to as little as 8 or 9 feet on most depth sounders. Typically, the lock is dredged when it reaches about this point, so we can assume it will soon be (or has been) brought back to its more generous depth of 12 to 13 feet.

Low Bridge

Immediately past the fixed Newport Road/Dyke Road Bridge (vertical clearance 20 feet), the Mohawk River again touches the canal. You can see that the canal is at a different level than the river, and the effect is a waterfall on the south side. Just a mile past that, the channel is narrowed by an additional 15 feet or so because some tree branches have fallen into the water.

Utica

You are now coming into the city of Utica. Utica Harbor and its system, which is primarily for the Niagara Mohawk power company and Utica's local fuel company, have a different water level from the canal, so there is a lock to lift you out of the Erie Canal and into the harbor. This harbor lock, which is not numbered, rises 6 or 7 feet. It is available to you only by appointment. Be careful while making a port turn here. Do not cut it too sharply, because there is some trash submerged in shallow water at the southeast corner where the channel of the Erie Canal merges into the Utica Harbor Lock.

Utica is a good-size city, and going into the Utica Harbor gives boaters an opportunity to access the city with a relatively short walk, not much more than a mile. The Utica Terminal is very industrialized, however. It has been suggested to me that boaters should not leave their craft unattended here, although I have had no personal experience that would support that concern.

The entire Utica section of the main canal route, at least 3 to 4 miles, is just chock full of fuel-oil and other commercial terminals, plus six bridges (at vertical clearances 20 feet, 22 feet, 23 feet, 20 feet, 22 feet, and 22 feet). Somewhat north and west of town, however, as you travel west on the Erie Canal, is Marcy Marina, about 2½ miles from the Utica Harbor Lock, or about a mile east of where the New York Thruway Bridge (vertical clearance 22 feet) crosses over the canal again. Marcy Marina is a rarity along the Erie Canal, in that it has its own basin off the canal. Take a taxi to Utica 3 miles back east and south of the canal.

Marcy Marina (315) 736-7617

Storm protection: √√√
Scenic: * *
Marina-reported approach depths: 10-13 feet
Marina-reported dockside depths: 3-5 feet
Waste pump-out
Rest rooms
Dockside water
Power connections: 15A/125V, 30A/125V
Mechanical repairs
Travelift/hoist

Lock 20 is just ahead, five-eighths of a mile past the New York Thruway Bridge.

Lock 20—16-foot lift. (518) 736-4617. Lock 20 completes the upward locking on this segment of the Erie Canal. This lock has a nice park area. It is 18 miles (1 hour, 50 minutes) to Lock 21. These miles are at a plateau level of the canal section between the Hudson River and Oneida Lake. You will go down 50.1 feet to meet the lake level in the next two locks. You, your crew, and your vessel have climbed 419.1 feet and traveled 108 miles from Troy Federal Lock.

In this area you might start to notice what appears to be a false edge to the shoreline. You can see some stagnant water behind the rock pilings along the side of the canal. To me, the water is an indicator of one of the earlier generations of the canal, before it was shored up or modified. You are now approaching the city of Rome. From Lock 20 to 21 there are 10 bridges at (going east to west) vertical clearances of 22 feet, 22 feet, 22 feet, 35 feet, 22 feet, 33 feet, 22 feet, 22 feet, 22 feet, and 24 feet, and one guard gate at 22-foot vertical clearance.

Rome

The first tie-up opportunity is Riverside Marina. A half-mile later but still east of downtown Rome is the Rome terminal, which is a wood wharf. Riverside Marina, located between markers 635 and 637, is approached via a long throat of water under the railroad tracks. Your chart, NOAA 14786, shows a dam here. The dam is really about three-eighths of a mile south, farther down in the throat. The marina is a new-boat dealer for outboards and stern-drive-powered runabouts and bass boats, but they fix everything, even if they have to somewhat disassemble it to get it under the low bridge at the entrance. The marina staff can't do everything, but they are used to assembling the resources needed to get your boat diagnosed, fixed, and back out cruising. Groceries, food, and movies are far away from the marina; expect to use a taxi.

Riverside Marina (315) 337-5720

Storm protection: √√√
Scenic: * *
Marina-reported approach depths: 3-4 feet
Marina-reported dockside depths: 2-4 feet
Floating docks
Wharf
Gas
Rest rooms
Dockside water
Power connections: 15A/125V, 30A/125V
Woodworking repairs
Fiberglass repairs
Welding
Below-waterline repairs
Mechanical repairs
Gas-engine repairs
Diesel repairs
Stern-drive repairs
Generator repairs
Travelift/hoist
Ship's store

The Rome terminal has been somewhat revamped so as to be usable by pleasure boaters. It has picnic tables and a small bridge that crosses the canal and connects the terminal to downtown Rome. At the time of my last visit, it did not have any basic transient boater facilities beyond a place to tie up.

While you are in Rome, you might want to visit Fort Stanwix. This fort was named after its original builder in 1758, but the name changed briefly to Fort Schuyler, after the Revolutionary War general. During the war, the fort was controlled first by the Americans and then by the British, but finally the Americans took it back again. The fort is not called out on your chart, but try this: On your chart, slowly run your finger up the blue-colored water of the Mohawk River 1½ inches north of where it meets the canal to just above where the railroad bridge crosses it. Fort Stanwix is just to the west of the river, below the next bridges crossing the Mohawk. Check to find out the hours it is open during the season you are there.

> **SKIPPER TIP:** Just past the immediate downtown Rome area, the canal widens for a private terminal and then narrows back down, and you are again cruising at the normal canal width.

As an aside, just past Rome is a section of the waterway that opened several years before the full Erie Canal was completed. Right at the very end of 1818, a short stretch of the original Erie Canal was opened here. Two years later, that short stretch had expanded and covered a little more than 90 miles, going from Utica, which is east of where you are now, to the Seneca River, which is to the west. Of course, the entire canal wasn't opened until 1826, and you are not cruising in that original canal.

Erie Canal Village

East of Rome and pretty far north of the canal route is Erie Canal Village. This is where the construction of the original Erie Canal began. The village has been reconstructed to replicate the era of the canal during its heyday, and it is probably the best tourist—and most touristy—attraction along the Erie Canal. The only problem is that there is no transportation specifically for the purpose of taking tourists from the current canal where your boat is on to the village, and you have to be aggressive to find a taxi to get you there. The touristy aspect of the village might detract from your enjoyment of it, anyway.

Just east of marker #657 is one place where the original canal path crosses at a diagonal to today's third-generation waterway, which you are on.

By Lock 21 you have had a good 18-mile plateau run since the last lock. In fact, if your plan is to go on to Lake Ontario via the Oswego Canal connection entrance, this is the longest plateau of your canal cruise. Now you are going through two downward locks in quick succession. Heading west, these are the first downward-descending locks you will have encountered, but don't be concerned. The procedure is exactly the same for going down as for going up, except it goes a minute faster and there is less water movement.

Lock 21—25-foot lift (or drop in this case). (315) 336-8229. It is 1¼ miles to Lock 22.

Lock 22—25.1-foot lift (another drop). (315) 336-4329. It is 29 miles to Lock 23, which is on the other side of Oneida Lake. Most boaters will wait until the next morning to begin crossing the lake to enjoy the resort town of Sylvan Beach.

These locks bring you down from the high plain of the Rome section of the Erie Canal and into the short run before the eastern shore of Oneida Lake.

Oneida Lake

The canal opening onto Oneida Lake is less than half an hour away, and right at this edge of the lake is the town of Sylvan Beach. Syl-

van Beach has merry-go-rounds, a beach (well over a mile long), lots of restaurants, amusement rides, a grocery store at the north end of town (a good walk back with your grocery bags), flea markets, drugstores, a canal-front park, newsstands, arcades, video-rental stores, an active bandstand—everything a vacationing boater might want.

Sylvan Beach is a summer resort town: first for beachgoers, then for the amusement-park lovers, fishing boaters in their runabouts and small boats, and canal cruisers. Oriented toward families that want a break from their daily lives, this destination serves them well.

There are marinas on both the north and south sides of the canal to access the town. In terms of facilities, both sides seem to be somewhat similar, but the marinas on the north side offer direct access to town, making them slightly more attractive. In reality, there is not a major time difference walking to town from either side.

SKIPPER TIP: The Oneida Lake chart 14786 in the NOAA chart book is a different scale from the previous and subsequent chart sheets. This makes you think it is smaller than it really is. Get out your dividers and walk it off.

Consider spending an extra day at Sylvan Beach to go fishing by boat, and give your crew a chance to walk around town and take advantage of the shore activities offered by a popular resort.

Oneida Lake is 370 feet above sea level, about 20 miles long and 4 miles wide. It is an excellent fishing lake and attracts many

Sylvan Beach's sands stretch along the edge of Oneida Lake for miles and are a main attraction for summer visitors.

boaters. There are markers all the way across the lake to signify the channel path you are supposed to follow, but they are spaced about a mile apart, so have someone looking out to the west for the next one ahead. They are easy to follow if you keep a sharp eye out. The lake is typically 20 to 40 feet deep in the channel. There really is not much of a problem if you get outside the channel on the eastern half of the lake, except for one spot that is well marked with additional buoys to help keep you on track.

Keep in mind that Oneida Lake is capable of having either a short, sharp, steep-sided chop or a mirrorlike calm. For this reason, you should check weather conditions—note the wind speed, which is what causes the chop— before deciding whether to spend the night at Sylvan Beach or to wait until you reach Brew-

erton on the far-western end, where the lake again joins the canal. Particularly if you are in a boat that's 25 feet or smaller, take into account your boat speed and figure out how long it will take you to cross the lake. Then, if you have a clear weather report, make your run and stay at the opposite shore. Otherwise, I think you are better off staying overnight at Sylvan Beach and starting out in early morning, when the lake is usually calm.

All the marina stops are after the Cove Road Bridge, vertical clearance 24 feet, and the Coast Guard Auxiliary facility.

Skinner's Harbor is both on the main channel (fuel dock) as well as inside most of the deepwater area of a lagoon on the north shore. It has about 100 slips, the largest in the Sylvan Beach area. Town is about six easy blocks away. Transient boaters can hardly ask for more. If you are coming in on a high-season weekend, you might find it full or at least requiring a creative force-fit for your craft in some regard. I used more shore power cord here than anywhere else to plug in my craft on one cruise through the Erie Canal, but the stopover is a delight.

Skinner's Harbor (315) 762-9986

Storage protection: √√√
Scenic: * * *
Marina-reported approach depths: 11 feet
Marina-reported dockside depths: 3-10 feet
Floating docks
Gas
Diesel
Waste pump-out
Rest rooms
Showers
Dockside water
Barbecues
Picnic tables
Power connections: 15A/125V, 30A/125V
Fiberglass repairs
Below-waterline repairs
Mechanical repairs
Stern-drive repairs
Outboard-motor repairs
Travelift/hoist
Ship's store
Restaurant: off site
Grocery: off site
Convenience store: on site

Holmes Marina (315) 762-9950

Storm protection: √√√
Scenic: * *
Marina-reported approach depths: 10 feet
Marina-reported dockside depths: 3-10 feet
Floating docks
Rest rooms
Dockside water

Barbecues
Picnic tables
Power connections: 15A/125V
Restaurant: off site

Lone Pine Marina (315) 762-5544

Storm protection: √√√
Scenic: * *
Marina-reported approach depths: 4-6 feet
Marina-reported dockside depths: 2-6 feet
Floating docks
Rest rooms
Picnic tables
Power connections: 15A/125V
Restaurant: off site

The **Sylvan Beach Terminal Wall** starts at the other (western) end of the lagoon that Skinner's Harbor also occupies. This shorter section is the better one for a tie-up because it is off the main canal channel. Depths are 6 to 8 feet here. This same wharf continues westward along the north shore even under and past the Sylvan Beach Bridge. Depths here can range to 12 feet. This is a very public lunch stop; it is not a recommended overnight tie-up. Many vacationers stroll by or relax here to watch you and the passing boats. You and your craft may be a close substitute for a circus sideshow for them. Also, the activities of the resort's downtown can be heard here. There are no facilities here, and some boaters might need to secure dock lines to anything nearby to hold their crafts to the terminal.

If you want to spend some time on Oneida Lake itself, follow the south shore, which is

Along the eastern shore of the lengthy Sylvan Beach Terminal Wall, free tie-up is available just before entering Oneida Lake.

more developed and offers more lakefront amenities. The lake does get shallow near its edge throughout its length on both the south and north shores, but there is a lot more to see and do on the south shore. Also, Verona Beach State Park is there.

As you proceed to the last western quarter of Oneida Lake, the length between the channel markers increases now to about 2 miles. It is impossible to see them from a non-fly bridge boat, so you need to watch your compass and keep on a reasonable, plotted course to get to Brewerton.

On the west side of Oneida Lake, you pass beneath the Interstate 81 Bridge (vertical clearance 24 feet), which is wider than the average highway bridge, and enter the Oneida River. I-81 is the major north-south thoroughfare in the region and the auto route to Canada and the Thousand Islands. Part of I-81 is the Thousand Island Bridge, which connects the United States with Canada across the St. Lawrence Seaway.

The town of Brewerton sits on the south shore just as the lake meets the river on the western shore of Oneida Lake. Brewerton offers marinas and other services for boaters, though it is more residential and far less of a resort town. From here west, you start to notice that the number of private homes increases. You see everything from fishing shacks to mobile homes, elegant vacation retreats to year-round residences, all built along the Oneida River, the canal, and the other rivers of the region.

The next bridge is state Highway 11, with a 24-foot vertical clearance.

Be alert through this area, especially when visibility is low. Some of the marinas on the south shore of the waterway use all sorts of innovations to prevent boat wakes from disturbing other boats, such as a sea wall constructed out of a couple of old wooden barges. These are not marked and not lit at night, so be careful as you enter these marinas. Better yet, call ahead on your VHF radio to the dockmaster to get his advice on navigating the approaches to his marina. Brewerton has a history dating back more than 300 years. French explorers first came through just after 1600, followed in the middle of the century by French missionaries. Continuous settlement began in 1789. Though the original Erie Canal did not go through Brewerton, the third generation was built to go through the town in 1917. Before that, a feeder canal carried freight and travelers from Brewerton to the Erie route. The feeder canal had trouble remaining economically feasible, however, and was eventually abandoned.

In Brewerton there is the Ess-kay Yard. It is not quite a half-mile west of the railroad bridge, the third bridge on this side of the lake, just about across the water from red buoy #150. A fully found repair, seasonal, and transient marina, it has slips both on this Oneida River section of the Erie Canal (6- to 9-foot depths) and in an enclosed basin (3- to 9-foot depths). The ship's store there goes well beyond the normal range of charts, nautical books, and cruising guides, and the balance of the marine-supplies selection is excellent, also. Be prepared to spend some time just exploring this special treat for the skipper and crew. The town's shopping district is complete, but getting there is a walk east and then south on Route 11. The larger strip mall of stores is even farther south, about the equivalent of eight to nine more blocks.

On the north side of the waterway is first the remains of Fort Brewerton; north of that is an auto speedway. The racing on Friday nights in the summer makes a good show.

Other marinas in the Brewerton area include Bradbury Boatel, Trade-a-Yacht Marina, and the Brewerton Boatyard.

Bradbury Boatel (315) 676-7060

Storm protection: √√√
Scenic: * * *
Marina-reported approach depths: 3-4 feet
Marina-reported dockside depths: 2-4 feet
Gas
Waste pump-out
Rest rooms
Showers
Dockside water
Picnic tables
Power connections: 30A/125V
Fiberglass repairs
Below-waterline repairs
Mechanical repairs
Ship's store
VHF-monitored channel: 16

Trade-a-Yacht Marina (315) 676-3531
Storm protection: √√√

Scenic: * * *
Marina-reported approach depths: 4 feet
Marina-reported dockside depths: 3-4 feet
Gas
Diesel
Waste pump-out
Rest rooms
Showers
Dockside water
Picnic tables
Power connections: 30A/125V
Fiberglass repairs
Below-waterline repairs
Mechanical repairs
Travelift/hoist
Ship's store
VHF-monitored channel 16

Brewerton Boatyard (315) 676-3762

Storm protection: √√
Scenic: * * *
Marina-reported approach depths: 10-12
    feet
Marina-reported dockside depths: 3-8 feet
Gas
Diesel
Waste pump-out
Rest rooms
Showers
Dockside water
Picnic tables
Power connections: 30A/125V
Fiberglass repairs
Below-waterline repairs
Mechanical repairs
Ship's store
Restaurant: off site
VHF-monitored channel: 16

Ess-kay Yard (315) 676-2711

Storm protection: √√√
Scenic: * * *

Marina-reported approach depths: 6-12 feet
Marina-reported dockside depths: 3-9 feet
Gas
Diesel
Waste pump-out
Rest rooms
Showers
Dockside water
Barbecues
Picnic tables
Power connections: 30A/125V, 50A/220V
Fiberglass
Below-waterline repairs
Mechanical repairs
Travelift/hoist: 14 ton
Ship's store
Bookstore
Restaurant: off site
What's special: hammock on site
VHF-monitored channel: 16

Take note that in this next 7- to 8-mile-long area, there are several branches off the main channel of the canal that private homeowners use for boat docking, but these are not marked nor maintained as official channels. Therefore, it is a "boater beware" situation. In some cases, your chart will show you the water depth; in other cases, you need local knowledge in order to use these side feeder channels. Most are the natural path of the Oneida River. When this generation of the canal was laid out, the engineers "straightened" the river by way of canal sections or "cuts," as shorter man-made sections are called. Because of the many private homes and private boat docks in this area, and depending on your sense of obligation to your fellow boater, you might want to drop below the 10-mph speed limit that is generally used for the canal and recognize that the no-wake rule is more appropriate here, regardless of what is posted.

About 2 miles past the Interstate 81 Bridge, the canal's path diverges from the river and again becomes a man-made canal ditch. When you come to the fork, take the left (or south) fork to stay in the Erie Canal. Sounds like something out of a Western film, doesn't it? It's easy to stay on course because a large sign posted where the Y starts to fork directs you to follow the Erie Canal. If you leave the canal by going straight from here, the Oneida River becomes shallow in spots and is navigable only for about another 2 miles before it ends in a dam. If you follow the canal route, however, you round the corner, go under the Caughdenoy Road Bridge (vertical clearance of 24 feet), and in 1 mile you are at Lock 23 and the guard gate (vertical clearance of 25 feet).

Lock 23—7-foot lift (or drop heading west). (315) 676-4171. The next lock depends on the path you choose ahead. Lock 24 (toward Lake Erie) is a 19-mile run, while Lock 1 of the Oswego Canal (Lake Ontario and the pathway to the Thousand Islands) is 9 miles ahead. Lock 23 has improved park-like grounds and rest rooms.

Pirates Cove Marina (315) 695-3901

Storm protection: √√√
Scenic: * *
Marina-reported approach depths: 6-12 feet
Marina-reported dockside depths: 3-5 feet
Gas
Diesel
Rest rooms
Picnic tables

Power connections: 30A/125V
Fiberglass repairs
Welding
Below-waterline repairs
Mechanical repairs
Ship's store
VHF-monitored channel: 16

It is roughly 5 miles from Lock 23 to Three Rivers, where the waterway forks again. Here you must choose either to continue on toward Buffalo with access to two of the gorgeous Finger Lakes or to take the route to Oswego, which is a port city on the edge of Lake Ontario. Three Rivers is the convergence of the Oneida, Seneca, and Oswego Rivers. Heading west, a hard starboard (right) turn takes you north on the Oswego River. The city of Oswego is 24 miles downstream. A large 8-by-16-foot billboard sign on the western bank indicates the direction to Oswego, while another on the northern bank points the way for people coming in from Buffalo. If you want to cruise toward Buffalo, skip Oswego and take the turn to port onto the Seneca River.

SKIPPER TIP: If the Thousand Islands and Lake Ontario is your destination, please change charts to the section inside the chart book called "Oswego Canal." Otherwise, please turn to Erie Canal (Area II). All routes use NOAA recreational chart 14786.

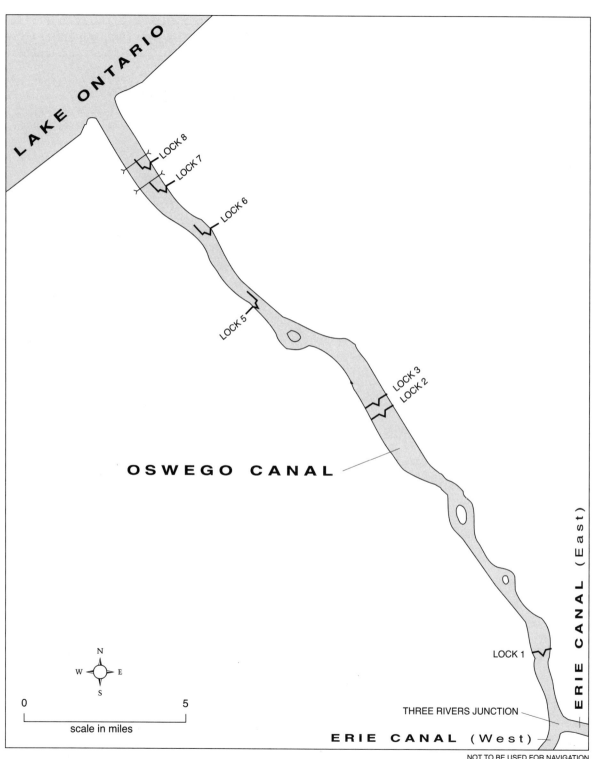

LAKE ONTARIO

LOCK 8

LOCK 7

LOCK 6

LOCK 5

LOCK 3
LOCK 2

OSWEGO CANAL

ERIE CANAL (East)

LOCK 1

THREE RIVERS JUNCTION

ERIE CANAL (West)

N
W   E
S

0   5
scale in miles

NOT TO BE USED FOR NAVIGATION

CHAPTER 9

The Oswego Canal to Lake Ontario

The Oswego Canal

> **SKIPPER TIP:** Use NOAA recreational chart 14786 for the Oswego Canal. Also be sure to read chapter 4, "Locking Through for the First Time," before approaching any locks.

The Oswego Canal is the canal watercourse that takes you the 24 miles from the Three Rivers Junction on the Erie Canal to the port town of Oswego on Lake Ontario. Oswego is a jumping-off point on Lake Ontario's southeast shore. The single most popular run from there is north to the Thousand Islands area of the St. Lawrence River, a multinational summer playground that integrates boating into daily life like no other place in the world. Otherwise, cruisers can head out west across the lower part of Lake Ontario and incorporate a visit to the city of Rochester on the way to the Welland Canal—principally a canal dedicated to commercial ships, not pleasure boaters—which provides access to Lake Erie. The longest cruise would be to the northeast corner of the lake to Toronto, a cosmopolitan showcase of some of the best of Canada. It's a shorter cruise to Trenton, Canada, on the northern lakeshore, which opens to the start of the Trent-Severn Canal path to Lake Huron's Georgian Bay. This selection of destinations can take a day or consume a summer.

The Oswego Canal has seven locks. Unfortunately, the canal engineers had planned and numbered eight locks and then decided to drop the fourth lock out of the system. I will expand upon the numbering as we go along. Vertical bridge clearances are 20 feet or more, and water depth in the channel strives for 14 feet, with 13 feet over the lock sills, inside the locks' entrances/exits.

> **SKIPPER TIP:** Your charts note that this is the point in the Three Rivers where the aids to navigation colors change sides as compared to coming from the west. They stay the same if you are westbound on the Erie Canal. In any event, as you go from here north on the Oswego River to the town of Oswego and Lake Ontario, all red markers and buoys will be on the eastern side of the channel (your starboard).

The trip from Three Rivers to the Lake Ontario breakwater is at best a 5-hour run, and it will likely take 6 hours of running, with some waiting and locking time combined. All the locks are "downhill," i.e., progressive drops in water levels to take your vessel down to the Lake Ontario water level. The drop over the seven locks is 118½ feet. The Oswego River flows north, a rare phenomenon in the United States. The St. John River near Jacksonville,

Florida, is the only other north-flowing river I know of in the eastern half of the United States.

Starting Out North

Three-quarters of a mile north from the Three Rivers Junction on the western shore is a Coast Guard Auxiliary base painted light gray with white trim. The building has a blue diagonal stripe with a red band on it. Another mile up a shopping center and a car dealership are just visible from the river. Go farther up another half-mile to Henley Park to tie up and walk back for a visit there.

Henley Park

Storm protection: √√
Scenic: * *
Marina-reported approach depths: 10-12 feet
Marina-reported dockside depths: 7-10 feet
Waste pump-out
Power connections: 15A/125V
Note: usually unstaffed (no phone number)

Stowell Island, aka Treasure Island, comes up now on your starboard side. This area was routinely traversed by French explorers as early as 1625. By 1650 Jesuit missionaries also had joined the explorers and came down from Canada to convert the American Indians to Catholicism. In 1656 about 50 people set up the first mission close to present-day Syracuse and the adjacent Onondaga Lake. However, they were unsuccessful in converting the Onondaga Indians. By 1658, having antagonized the tribe into a retaliatory attack, the missionaries fled. On the run from the Indians and still far from safe haven in Canada, the group, according to legend, left a cannon and gold on what we now call Stowell Island. Thus, it also has the name Treasure Island. No, the gold has never been found.

A bit more north of the island are the remains of the concrete supports for a now torn-down trolley bridge. The trolley ran between the cities of Syracuse and Oswego about 100 years ago. Buoys #13 and #17 keep you off these as well as lead you into Lock 1.

Phoenix

The town of Phoenix is 2 miles from the Three Rivers Junction. In 1916 Phoenix had a major fire in its downtown district. Almost all that you see and visit in Phoenix was constructed after that fire except for the bridge next to Lock 1, which survived.

Phoenix's first white man, settler Adam Paddock, built a log cabin in this general area in 1801. Known as the Three River Rifts, the natural rapids here have always forced a land portage around them of boat, freight, passengers, and crew. Everyone from the early American Indians to the French in the 1600s and early Americans in Paddock's time has had to circumvent the rapids here. At any rate, a trading post was conveniently located here for those having to get out of the water.

In 1829 a sawmill was constructed here to use the power created by a dam on the canal. From that first industry, commerce then broadened from just trading to a more diverse commercial base. Five boat yards, furniture factories, silk mills, a distillery, and paper manufacturers were all in place before the fire. That fire, which started in the machinery of a chair factory, changed the town. While most homes were rebuilt, few of the factories were. Times had changed; the railroad replaced the canal as the cheapest freight conveyance, and industries moved on to other towns. Today, Phoenix is a nice, small village of about 2,500 people.

Just before the lock there are two buildings

that at first glance look like a single structure. The taller building is the bridge house, built in 1917. It controlled a drawbridge that was torn down about 20 years ago. Like many lighthouses, it has only a single room on each of its three stories. The other building, constructed just before World War II, is called the "buoy house." The New York State Canal Corporation stores the Oswego Canal buoys here during the winter months.

On the far side of the river is Long Lake, one of eight hydropower plants on the river. Long Lake was built in 1991 and can produce 3,000 kilowatts of electricity, which in turn is sold through the Niagara Mohawk Corporation.

> **SKIPPER TIP:** Once at the lock, be careful about overhead clearance. The lock has a bascule bridge that does not open all the way. Therefore, you have restricted clearance on the port side of your vessel.

Lock 1—10.2-foot lift or drop, going northbound for the Thousand Islands. (315) 695-2281. VHF channel 13 or three long blasts. The section supervisor can be reached at (315) 428-4589. Lock 2 is 60 minutes ahead. Enjoy the landscape improvements here; they are the pride of the local people and serve as their welcome to you. Check with the lock operator for a lunch tie-up near the bridge if you need to get some grocery items, eat a meal (there are about a half-dozen inexpensive restaurants nearby), do some banking or laundry, post mail, or pick up a newspaper from the businesses nearby. Also, you might enjoy the Bridge House Museum, which features exhibits on canal, boating, and Phoenix his-

tory. Inquire at (315) 695-3543. Finally, the village has a Canal Days festival in June. Find out more by calling (315) 695-2484.

Hydropower

Hydropower is using the energy contained in moving water to produce electricity. Long Lake Energy Corporation owns the first hydropower plant, Niagara Mohawk owns six others, and the city of Oswego owns the final plant along the 24-mile Oswego River/Canal. Combined, these plants can meet the electricity needs of 40,000 people.

To make electricity, flowing water is diverted from the river into a pipe. This flow is controlled by floodgates to increase/decrease the amount of water. Boaters should stay clear of these gates on the high side of a hydroelectric plant because they suck water toward them when open. Also, they discharge water back into the main waterway on the low side, creating a "set" (or current) that also can move your craft around. A wise skipper will always try to spot these entrance and exit points to properly maintain control of his vessel.

From that intake pipe the flowing water hits a paddlewheel (today a bladed wheel called a turbine). This water pressure turns the blade, creating mechanical energy. This turbine is connected to a shaft whose turning powers the generator and produces energy. This electrical energy is conducted to transformers via transmission lines. The transformers convert the electricity to a voltage level a business, home, or boat can use. They make you wonder why boats do not drag a paddlewheel behind them rather than having a gas- or diesel-powered generator set on board.

It is interesting to note that neither the water nor the air used in this process is polluted during it. Hydropower is a source of clean energy. In fact, the whole process beats extra oxygen into the water, which is better for the river's fish population. No wonder the fishing is good here!

Back on the cruising track now. Buoys on the Oswego route were placed to keep you in the channel and to mark items such as rocks on the channel edges that can be hard on your boat and underwater gear. Stay particularly well inside the channel from buoys #29 and #31 early on.

History

The Oswego Canal opened up Lake Ontario to New York City via its route to Albany and on down the Hudson River. The Oswego Canal was competing for commerce with the Erie Canal-western section, which makes its way across western New York to Lake Erie. The Erie Canal eventually won the contest because of the complex engineering required to complete the half of the Oswego route closest to Lake Ontario. The engineering difficulties there were perceived as even greater than those involved in building the canal between Albany and Schenectady, the last section of the Erie to open.

The politics of opening up one versus the other lake also figured in the selection. The Erie route was seen as a way to increase commerce and travel to the West, whereas the Oswego route was perceived as a commercial boon for Canada. As it turned out, New York State built its canal to Lake Erie first—it opened in 1825. Simultaneously, the state built the Champlain Canal on its territorial portion of land toward a link with Canada and the St. Lawrence River, but Canada did not finish its portion (Lake Champlain north to the St. Lawrence River) of the New York City-Montréal connection until 1843. The original Oswego Canal route was

finished in 1829 after the difficult Erie section of Schenectady-Albany was completed in 1825, when engineering advances and practical canal-building experience made it more possible. All of these New York State canals were substantially replaced in a rebuilding program from 1915 to 1918.

You are in a natural river course here, improved by man, which results in a channel that is not the full width of the waterway at all points. So watch for shallow water outside the channel. There also are some side backwaters that are not marked for boaters; be cautious about water depth if you venture on your own. There can be currents depending on seasonal rains or water usage by dams and powerhouses. The bridges have clearance of 20 feet or more. Some might have to be opened to achieve this, but this is done for you.

Hinmansville Bridge is a doubled-arched bridge of just 20-foot vertical clearance. Although the two arches (80 feet and 95 feet) are not symmetrical, it is a pretty bridge. It was built when this generation of the canal was constructed. The Hinmansville Bridge marks the location of the hamlet of Hinmansville on the east shore. John Hinman first settled the area around the time the Oswego Canal opened. He wanted to start a town by using the canal traffic as a foundation. He did succeed in making it a popular stop for canal boats, which would exchange horses for a fresh team. The town did not have a readily available power source for factories to tap into, however, so only work tied to the canal traffic was available to employ the citizens. When the canal's commercial traffic waned, this area became a bedroom community.

Once past the bridge, look to your starboard past the strip of land. You should see what remains of the stone blocks of the Hinmansville locks from the original Oswego Canal system. Also, the towpath for that system runs now for about a mile north. The channel is not well marked here on its east side, but it does get shallow if you get too close—so watch your water depth as you sightsee.

Starting at buoy #46, the earlier-generation Oswego canal, which was mostly a separate channel from the river, is again somewhat visible to starboard. As before, please do not let your enthusiasm to see these remains take your attention off strictly staying inside the marked channel. It is shallow outside it. Also, parts of the old canal's foundation and locks can be underwater just out of sight here, particularly around buoy #58. In 150-plus years of canal presence, lots of hard objects can accumulate to create trouble underwater and out of sight. Just stay where everyone else in your size vessel goes to avoid trouble. For most of this section there is a land berm between this earlier route and where you are cruising now, but they do occasionally merge or touch one another. Then at buoys #54 and #56 the Ox Creek tributary comes in from your port side. I was told that Ox Creek many years ago was much shallower, more like a creek than a river, as it looks now. This raising of the water level was triggered by the needs of the canal system. But back when the water was lower, a small, wooden bridge crossed the creek. This bridge collapsed as a team of oxen crossed over it. People called it Ox Creek thereafter. Note: You must be alert for shallow water here even in the main channel. The creek flow can narrow down that navigable channel.

Bird Watching

Before you reach Big Island, around buoy #68, the eastern shore is home to a small state wildlife preserve. The Curtiss-Gale Preserve only covers 45 acres, as compared to the Montezuma Preserve of 6,500 acres near the Finger Lakes and the Erie Canal Locks 24 and 25. Here, however, is an undisturbed forest of black cherry, beech, and oak. This and the other natural vegetation make it an ideal bird sanctuary. The original donors, H. Salem Curtiss and Thomas and Ida Gale, conceived the idea for this place. These gifts as well as other land were assembled by the state to create and secure this area for future generations. It is not directly boater-accessible. You must go farther north about 2 miles to the Canalview Marina and then taxi or walk back to it if you want to explore. Look for songbirds and migratory waterfowl as you pass by. The next caution for navigation comes up just as you are coming up to Big Island, on the western shore. Here the channel makes an exaggerated loop to get around some shallow water that is just east of Big Island. To protect your boat bottom, follow the channel even if it seems exaggerated.

Next up on the east side were the spawning grounds of 10 million barrels of beer. That was a year's production for the former Miller Brewing Company, which is visible on your starboard side. This plant was constructed in 1974, but it has since closed. How much water did it take to brew the beer? I believe this plant used 1 billion gallons of water each year. You can do the math.

How about chocolate aromas to pique the appetite? The Nestle chocolate factory's chimney just might be in your view after you pass the Miller Brewery. Founded in 1900 and merged with Nestle in 1929, the "chocolate works," as old-timers call it, can sometimes be smelled more than seen from the canal.

Another large local employer here is Sealright Company, a paperboard-container manufacturer. It was first powered when it was a pulp and paper company directly by the river water, but no longer. Like so many others along the canal, this site has a history. Here the paper-container business replaced a paper manufacturer, which was preceded by a pottery factory that sat on the former grounds of a British fort named Bradstreet (I'll expand on the fort in just a bit), which, in turn, was built on Iroquois Indian burial grounds.

Ahead now is Fulton and Lock 2 in downtown Fulton. Nearby are two hydropower plants: Oswego Falls West on the far (west) side of the river, which can produce 1,460 kilowatts; and Oswego Falls East, right next to the west side of Lock 2, has the capacity to generate 4,500 kilowatts. Twenty-five hundred feet before Lock 2, navigation aids #79 and #81 a) keep you away from the rock-strewn river waters immediately west of them; and b) narrow the channel width to lead you into the extended lock entrance channel; and c) in poor lighting conditions make you aware of the large cement blocks on that side of the channel.

Lock 2—17.8 foot-lift. (315) 592-4155. Less than a half-mile farther is Lock 3. There are rocks outside the channel to the west in this passage between the locks. Before the canal was built, both the American Indians and the Europeans needed a portage around the falls. The area containing the rocks marks the site where a fort (Fort Bradstreet) was built. The portage usually ran through here, between the two locks, on the land on which the library sits.

Lock 3—27-foot lift. (315) 592-5349. This is the largest lift (or drop) on the Oswego Canal. Lock 5 is 40 minutes north; there is no Lock 4. Lock 3 is the second lock in the city of Fulton.

There is an opportunity to tie up between both locks and after Lock 3; check with the lock operator. The area between the locks is somewhat closer to stores and restaurants, however. The exit from Lock 3 is a man-made channel. This channel ends and you rejoin the river course after about 3,500 feet. This merger area is one place where current can affect your craft.

Canalview Marina (315) 598-4123
Storm protection: √√
Scenic: *
Marina-reported approach depths: 7-12 feet
Marina-reported dockside depths: 5-8 feet
Waste pump-out
Rest rooms
Dockside water
Power connections: 15A/125V, 30A/125V

Lock 3 has two hydropower plants. Near the lock is the Fulton plant, built in 1925 and updated about 15 years ago so that it now can produce 1,250 kilowatts. It is interesting that today's plant uses as part of its foundation the remains of an 1880-era waterwheel power plant that was located here. That first plant once powered factory machinery by way of a series of leather belts, pulleys, and shafts. On the far side of the river is a 10,000-kilowatt plant, built in 1909 and renovated about the same time as the Fulton plant. Niagara Mohawk operates both plants.

Just past Lock 3 you will see some boat docks just for smaller runabouts on the eastern shoreline, which is still within the town of Fulton. Fulton hosts a river festival in August. Inquire at (315) 598-4231.

Fulton, originally called Oswego Falls by Europeans, was renamed in 1826 after Robert Fulton, the man history books credit as the inventor of the steamboat. In 1759, Fort Brad-street, the one mentioned earlier as the current location of the paper-container business, was established by British forces as a part of a defense system for the French and Indian War. After the later Revolutionary War and the coming of the Industrial Revolution (and the canal), Fulton grew. Sawmills, gristmills, wool mills, and mills to manufacture silk items were all established. In fact, the biggest employer in town during World War I was a wool mill that made cloth for uniforms for the "doughboys" being sent to Europe, just as it had done for the Union soldiers during the Civil War. The mid-1800s was the peak of canal-boat building in town. Later, as the eastern United States matured from a frontier subsistence lifestyle to one in which a few luxuries were in demand, eels were "fished" at the falls, dried, smoked, and shipped to the East Coast cities as a delicacy.

The town always has been proud of the library since its construction in 1905. It was a gift of Andrew Carnegie, the steel magnate, on the condition that his original $15,000 be matched yearly by a contribution of $1,500 from the town.

SKIPPER TIP: Be alert to the channel markers as you make the next bend—they may cause you to twist and turn a bit.

Immediately on your forward starboard bow is Pathfinder Island. This famous piece of dirt is the setting for James Fenimore Cooper's novel *The Pathfinder*. Much of the novel takes place during a trip down the Oswego River in 1759. The book was published in 1840. James Fenimore Cooper was raised well east of here in Cooperstown, New York

(also known as the location of the Baseball Hall of Fame), which was named and settled by his father, Judge William Cooper, in 1786. You are heading due north here as you pass Pathfinder Island.

Fishing

Fishing in the Oswego Canal can be so rewarding that your one-day trip will turn into a week as you sample the offerings, test your skills, and enjoy fresh fish morning, noon, and night. Good fishing requires an adaptive attitude, as it does in most areas, to local conditions and seasons. Late September and into October is special: It is the time of the spawning run.

The river waters here have northern pike, walleye pike, yellow perch, white perch, largemouth bass, smallmouth bass, crappies, silver bass, blue gills, carp, bullheads, and channel catfish. In Oswego Harbor you can add to this list steelhead trout, lake trout, and smelt. As a general rule, the closer you get to Lake Ontario, the more numerous are the fish. Get a New York State license, ask for local specifics, and go for it.

Licenses, tackle, bait, and advice are available from private businesses in Phoenix (315-695-2573), Fulton (315-592-7355), and in several places in Oswego. Note: The county normally outsells all the other New York State counties in fishing licenses. Taxidermy is available in both Phoenix and Oswego. (Its existence must really be proof that trophy fish are in these waters.) Additional information and brochures can be obtained by calling (800) 248-4386.

As a general rule, I hate passing on fishing tips because they haven't made me a fisherman yet. Here they are anyway. Spring first brings steelhead close to the Oswego Harbor end of the river, and later white perch, bullhead, crappies, catfish, and carp. Summer begins bass season. Smallmouth bass are below the dams and locks, particularly in deeper water. Look for northern pike and largemouth bass in weedy, stagnant areas of the river, since this type of water can best be found in this river/canal. Try Ox Creek and the area around Battle Island. Walleye are best found where there are quick drop-offs in water depths. Fall, as I have said before, is the time for runs of brown and lake trout.

The low-lying land to the west creates a marsh area. Then Battle Island State Park and Battle Island run along the west river shore from before marker #102 to buoy #107A. Battle Island is so named because it was the site of a French and Indian War engagement in 1756. The British won this one. Most of the land for the state park was donated by F. A. Emerick in 1916. Later, his son, Stanley Emerick, gave additional land here to complete the park and its 18-hole golf course. Between #107A and #111 the brave ones among you cruisers may try to anchor in 7 to 9 feet of water outside the channel. I didn't.

Now the canal channel opens up in width. The shore fills in the pretty scenery with willow, beech, ash, and sugar-maple trees. The channel is almost the full river width, particularly on the western shore.

Just before you come to the next lock is Fletcher's Gas Station on the western shore. Fletcher's has the local reputation of generally having the lowest priced gas on the canal system. Once when I passed through, their posted price was 34 cents a gallon below the typical prices I was paying. Note that local boaters will go out of their way, maybe travel through a lock, to fill up at Fletcher's. Therefore, you need to be cautious that you do not get timed by the lock operator as you pass

through Lock 3 and then, because you are speeding along with these local boats that have no intention of going through the next lock, show up at the next lock (Lock 5) quite a bit early. As on most of the canal system, vessels are timed between locks so that the lock operator can be ready for you as soon as you arrive. A by-product of this helpfulness is it becomes painfully obvious to the next lock operator if you exceed the 10-mph canal speed limit. Those boaters who go through one lock but not the next do not seem to be held to the same standard.

When a lock operator catches you speeding, he has the choice to either fine you—which is almost never done—or delay your passage by refusing to open the lock to you. He can delay you up to 21 hours according to the laws under which the canal system operates. Don't worry: The lock operator usually will make you wait a half-hour or so, give you a good talking to, and then send you on your way.

Fletcher's Gas Station (315) 342-1094

Storm protection: n/a
Scenic: n/a
Marina-reported approach depths: 10 feet
Marina-reported dockside depths: 5-10 feet
Gas
Rest rooms
What's special: gas prices

Glaciers
So much of the landscape that you see around you has been influenced by the glaciers that came through here more than 15,000 years ago. This area and also the Finger Lakes south and west of the Oswego Canal were carved out as glaciers advanced and retreated. These mountains of ice dragged off

soil, dropped it in another place, pushed boulders around, and ground down mountaintops. The whole area was under water, at one time, as a massive inland sea. It was the glaciers that redefined that flat, shallow body of water into the land and multiple lakes we enjoy today.

The bridge just before the lock is called Minetto Bridge, after the town. It has a vertical clearance of 24 feet and a weird slant to it. This is the third bridge across the river here. The first one, made of wood, was built before the Civil War. The second one, which was located north of the lock, was constructed in 1872. Some of its remains are visible in the water once past the lock. The current bridge was built in 1915 and updated in 1993.

Lock 5—18-foot lift. (315) 343-5232. It is on the western shore. Lock 5 can have current both above and below it. Lock 6 is 4 miles (25 minutes) ahead. There is no Lock 4. A Lock 4 initially had been planned, with all the blueprints drawn and the locks titled, and then Lock 4 was eliminated from the plan very late in the game after canal construction had started. Therefore, you end up with a seven-lock system that has locks numbered 1 through 8 with no Lock 4. At Lock 5 is the Minetto Hydropower plant, capable of generating 8,100 kilowatts.

Just past the lock on port side is an old brick factory building, which is in the continual process of falling down. I point it out because its existence underscores the idea that in the earliest part of the Industrial Revolution any place with fairly rapid waters, a waterfall, or a change in water levels was always an attractive location for a factory.

Now your path really widens for most of the run to Lock 6. The channel stretches almost shore to shore after buoy #137. On the western

shore here, look out for a tunnel that was used by a local brewery, since closed, to store and ship its product via the Oswego Canal. Lock 6 is on the eastern shore, so most boaters really do not avail themselves of this wide channel; they just continue to cruise down the eastern shore. At Lock 6 on the western shore is another hydro plant, which produces 8,000 kilowatts.

Locks 6, 7, and 8 are all within a half-mile of each other. They are usually taken as a set, because once you are in the series the lock operators want you to continue through all three of them. The locks themselves, keeping pace somewhat with the downwardly cascading river, have a combined drop of 45.6 feet. Starting here, the natural river is an excellent photo opportunity; have your camera out for the runs between the locks.

Lock 6—20-foot lift or drop. (315) 343-9001. Lock 7 is 5 minutes ahead.

You are now in a section of canal that was one reason why the original westward (Erie) canal did not automatically go to Oswego. Although this was a travel route used by Indians, early settlers, and Revolutionary War troops, the engineering required to fashion a navigable canal here was too complicated to make this route an attractive choice to New York State.

Lock 7—14.2-foot lift or drop. (315) 343-6304. It is immediately short of Lock 8.

Lock 8—10.8-foot lift or drop. (315) 343-0280. This is the last lock in this canal. Lock 8 empties and fills differently here than the other locks. The lock operators crack open the lock gates to let the water in or out of the lock. This style of filling/emptying is called a siphon lock and lets you experience another method of locking through. The river channel becomes full width after buoy #4, about 1,000 feet north of Lock 8, but the variable current is less on the eastern shore. The Port of Oswego, which leads into Lake Ontario, is immediately ahead.

Oswego

Among other noteworthy things, Oswego is a college town, and rumor has it that anyone going to school here learns how to drink better than students at most other colleges (SUNY-Plattsburgh on Lake Champlain also has this reputation—everybody must want the title). Because of its proximity to the lake, Oswego has severe winters, with biting windchills and heavy snows. Perhaps the desire to ease the harshness of these winters is what helps foster the town's "party-on" image.

The Port of Oswego also has several different features that will entertain you if you spend a day or two waiting for a weather break to venture out onto Lake Ontario. Historic Fort Ontario is in downtown Oswego, probably within a 15- to 20-minute walk of the marina. There is an auto racetrack, where races are held every Saturday night in the summertime. The H. Lee White Marine Museum is on the western shore. Nautical history of the harbor, the canal, and the Great Lakes is the museum's focus, along with a gentle bias towards encouraging children to appreciate history. The museum features paintings, pictures, models, boats, and artifacts. Included are a display on the canal, a tug that participated in the World War II D-Day mission at Normandy, and the last steam-powered vessel to operate on the canal. Inquire at (315) 343-4503. Another history-related attraction, the Oswego County Historical Society is located in the Richardson-Bates House (315-343-1342). Movies and restaurants round out your entertainment choices. Boaters have two special events in Oswego in which to participate.

First, Waterfest is held in late June; then the better known Harborfest (quite a regional event) comes along in July. For more information, call (315) 343-7681.

SKIPPER TIP: Oswego has a taxicab company, Zeller Taxi, that will be helpful in getting you around the area. Inquire about rates and services by calling (315) 342-2000.

Oswego's auto racetrack (315-342-0646) is a paved, five-eighths-of-a-mile banked track open all summer long. It has hosted speedway racing since 1951. A cab ride gets you over there. After buying a pit pass, walk around to see the cars, drivers, personnel, and crew up close. Even the most experienced cruisers will enjoy a very different night out here at the racetrack. Oswego also has a boater-accessible movie theater, perhaps the first one you might ever come across. Again, it's a cab ride or walk (it is close) from the marina. The old converted movie theater has three or four screens and features a good selection of first-run movies.

The nearby town of Sterling, west of Oswego, is the site of the Renaissance Festival during the weekends in July and some weekends in August, depending on the year. Take a cab and do this festival. The taxi will take a full car (generally three people) for about $16 to $20 each way. The fest is a re-creation of English Renaissance times, when men were gentlemen who jousted and ladies were damsels in distress. The costumes are great, and the experience is fun. Eat a whole turkey leg torn off and served without utensils—you just gnaw at it. Or enjoy spinach pies, fish and chips, hot apple dumplings, apple cider, spiced wine, or trifles. Both adults and children delight in this wonderfully charming and entertaining fair. Allow a full afternoon or more to properly visit; when the festival opens at 10 A.M., there's usually a line of people who are coming back to enjoy it again.

I really cannot tell you how delightful it is to watch the comedy and entertainment of the Renaissance Festival. There is a sketch involving three to four people in a mud hole who get thoroughly dirty, and if you are in the first couple of rows in the audience, you too will get splattered—so be forewarned. Another attraction is the live jousting. Lots of handicrafts—including leather goods such as belts, shoes and purses, and wood products—are sold in booths. Get yourself a sword, a manzania-wood table, or a King Arthur wooden bed frame for the master bedroom at home. You can try out period costumes and hats, child-size wooden shields, and swords for mock fighting. Live demonstrations cover glassblowing, weaving, bookbinding, and printmaking. Thirty-five acres are set aside just to host this festival. If you go by taxi, the main advantage is they can drive you right up to the main admission ticket gate, bypassing the huge parking lot, and you will have an absolutely delightful afternoon. Call (315) 947-5783.

Fort Ontario (315-343-4711) has an active history. The fort you now see, reconstructed numerous times, is shown as it looked in 1868. The first fort was built by the British in 1755, although other sources say 1727. Take your pick. It was destroyed by the French and rebuilt by the British in 1759, and rebuilt yet again in 1782. The current version was fashioned between 1839 and 1844, then again in 1929, and then during World War II. An on-site museum details the fort's history and displays extensive military collections. The historical timeline there covers about 200 years. The fort was active from the French and Indian War through World War II.

Fort Ontario is the only one of three British forts rebuilt after they were all destroyed by the French Marquis de Montcalm. After burning the settlement, the shipyard there, and the fort, he took six ships, 120 cannons, and 1,600 prisoners with him. It was at Fort Ontario that the American Indian Ottawa chief, Pontiac, signed a peace treaty in 1766. James Fenimore Cooper served a tour of duty here from 1808 to 1809. Scholars think he gathered the background setting and details for his novel *The Pathfinder*, published in 1840, during his stay here.

Oswego is slated to receive a substantial amount of money for improvements from various government agencies now through 2002. Listed below are the current marinas for boaters as this guide goes to press.

Oswego Marina (315) 343-1967

Storm protection: √√√
Scenic: * *
Marina-reported approach depths: 18-20 feet
Marina-reported dockside depths: 5-9 feet
Gas
Diesel
Waste pump-out
Rest rooms
Showers
Laundry
Dockside water
Picnic tables
Power connections: 30A/125V
Below-waterline repairs
Mechanical repairs
25-ton hoist
Restaurant: on site

Deli: off site
Grocery: off site
Convenience store: off site
Note: everyone stays here, but watch out
   for angled steel under the finger piers (it
   can scar your hull sides)
VHF-monitored channel: 16

Wright's Landing (315) 343-8430

Storm protection: √√
Scenic: *
Marina-reported approach depths: 8-15 feet
Marina-reported dockside depths: 4-6 feet
Waste pump-out
Rest rooms
Showers
Dockside water
Power connections: 30A/125V
Restaurant: off site
Deli: off site
Grocery: off site
Convenience store: off site
What's special: close to maritime museum

West Side Terminal Wall

Storm protection: √
Scenic: n/a
Marina-reported approach depths: 18-20 feet
Marina-reported dockside depths: 4-6 feet
Wharf
Rest rooms
Restaurant: off site
Deli: off site
Grocery: off site
Note: mostly commercial fishing boats tie
   here; watch for current

East Side Terminal Wall

Storm protection: n/a
Scenic: n/a
Marina-reported approach depths: 18-20 feet

Marina-reported dockside depths: 6-12 feet
Wharf
Restaurant: off site
Deli: off site
Grocery: off site
Note: barely acceptable because of current,
   boat wakes, and traffic

Oswego History

Oswego was the first freshwater port established on the Great Lakes for the United States. Although the first Europeans—fur traders and missionaries—traded and proselytized, respectively, from sometime after 1600, a port was not formally established until 1725. Two of the three forts also built in the 1700s flanked the meeting of the river and Lake Ontario. Fort Oswego was to the west, while Fort Ontario was built on the eastern shore where it still stands today.

The Oswego River's rapids (or rifts, as they are termed locally) encouraged the development of mills along the river. The Oswego Canal, the last to open of the three major sections, provided every kind of freight with a connection to New York City and the Great Lakes. As a result, a boat-building industry soon sprang up. Canal boats for the river sections and schooners for the open lake were built in newly established local yards. The *Vandalia* was the first steamer to use the screw propeller, which was installed on her in Oswego. The mere shipment of goods via this canal was an industry. For example, salt from Syracuse was shipped to the Midwest and Canada, and grain was brought back through on the return trip. This trade pattern established the practice of storing goods in Oswego while awaiting future shipments or transfers from canal barges to Great Lake sailing freighters. Many grain elevators lined the western shore of the harbor. About 900,000 tons of freight traveled the Oswego Canal in 1870.

In 1848, Oswego further diversified its economy. Thomas Kingsford opened a starch factory using a process he developed to get starch from corn. Also, the 9,000 students of today's State University of New York at Oswego owe some of their heritage to a school founded here in 1861 and absorbed into the New York State system five years later.

The canal's importance, however, waned. By 1900, freight was just 3 percent (30,000 tons) of what it had been in 1870. I understand that the Welland Canal, in Canada west of here, was not wide enough at that time to accommodate modern vessels. This shortcoming cut off Lake Erie to and from Lake Ontario traffic. Furthermore, more convenient sources of salt were discovered, making its importation from Syracuse less vital. These factors, plus toll fees and how they were structured, all but dried up a major part of the Oswego commerce.

Today, three nuclear power plants nearby plus the hydropower plants make today's Oswego a center for generating electricity.

Although Oswego Harbor's depths are 22 feet or more today, they once were only 10 feet. In 1866, the depth was increased to 12 feet, with the current depths coming much later. A lighthouse has been here since before 1800. In 1836, it was moved to the breakwater. It was moved again in 1881 and then built in 1934 at its current location at the end of the western breakwater.

Lake Ontario

Lake Ontario is a major deepwater lake. It is the fourteenth largest lake in the world—about 195 miles long and 50 to 55 miles at the widest part. It is one of two Great Lakes that touch New York State (the other is Lake Erie). The lake's water level is usually 245 feet above sea level, but it can change, particularly from spring (when the lake is higher) to fall (when it's lower). Weather reports for boaters will include the lake levels if it is off by much. Oswego Harbor itself is protected by a breakwater.

This harbor is set up to handle commercial-freighter traffic as well as pleasure-boat traffic. Do not underestimate the commercial aspect of Oswego Harbor; it is the biggest U.S. port on Lake Ontario. It was a trading post even in Indian times, being in the strategic position as the terminus of an inland water route. Before the canal was built, the various waters had to be linked together by portages between them and around the rapids, but substantial trade was going through here even then.

Because of their high traffic and sudden storms, the Great Lakes have many occupants down in Davy Jones' Locker. Wreck diving is popular, and the shipwrecks are easy to access. One wreck is only 4½ miles west of Oswego Harbor, at a depth of 12 to 25 feet, with the boiler having only 3 feet of water depth over it. On a calm, sunlit day you can see it from the surface. A Great Laker, the *David W. Miller* was built in 1874 and foundered in 1919. She was 202 by 34 by 13 feet. In case of diving accidents, there is a decompression chamber at the Health Science Center of the State University of New York in Syracuse; local contact for it is Oswego Hospital (716) 349-5511.

Travel Routes

Boaters use two main routes on Lake Ontario. First, you can hug the south shore and travel to Rochester (just less than 60 miles from Oswego) and beyond to the Welland Canal (an additional 85 miles or so); or you can go just about due north and enter the St. Lawrence Seaway and quickly come upon Clayton (also about 60 miles) and Alexandria Bay (11 miles farther), both of which are in the Thousand Islands. Here New York and Canada share some interesting islands, actually numbering more than 1,750. They range from less than 50 square feet (the size of an average family's bathroom) to 20 square miles. In the seventeenth century, the French were the first Europeans to explore the Thousand Islands. They named them on their maps *Les Milles Iles,* or "the Thousand Islands." The name does add a little more drama than an exact count of the islands, doesn't it?

The Thousand Islands are an outstanding cruising ground. Island formations of all shapes and sizes combine with the rocks, trees, boats, and water in a beautiful, magnificent way. Going from Oswego to Clayton or Alexandria Bay is a 4-hour powerboat run or

10-plus hour sail. You want to pick your water on Lake Ontario if you're not a Class II (more than 26-foot) boat. Even larger vessels should watch out, because summer storms can quickly develop, and in a storm many eastern harbors do not offer the protection many would like. When the stormy lake does not want you, amuse yourself with Oswego and its amenities (the movie theater, the Renaissance Festival, the auto racetrack, museums, and Fort Ontario). The town has plenty to offer.

All locks monitor VHF 13. The Great Lakes Coast Guard uses VHF channel 16 for distress calls. Hail the lock operator on VHF 13 to request a lock-through, or use your ship's horn (three long blasts). Notify the last lock operator if you do not intend to proceed directly to the next lock. As usual, they try to telephone ahead so the next lock is ready for you. Fuel, fishing, lunch, bird watching, exploring, sightseeing, historic places, and overnight stops are all available on the Oswego Canal.

Lock Number	Location	Lock Phone Number	Police	Ambulance	Fire Department
1	Phoenix	(315) 695-2281	(315) 593-1223	(315) 695-3436	(315) 695-3436
2	Fulton	(315) 591-4155	(315) 593-1223	(315) 592-4145	(315) 592-9575
3	Fulton	(315) 592-5349	(315) 593-1223	(315) 592-4145	(315) 592-9575
5	Minetto	(315) 343-5232	(315) 593-1223	(315) 343-5522	(315) 343-5500
6	Oswego	(315) 343-9001	(315) 593-1223	(315) 343-1313	(315) 343-1313
7	Oswego	(315) 343-6304	(315) 595-1223	(315) 343-1313	(315) 343-1313
8	Oswego	(315) 343-0280	(315) 593-1223	(315) 343-1313	(315) 343-1313
Section Supervisor		(315) 428-4589			

Fishing is great in New York!

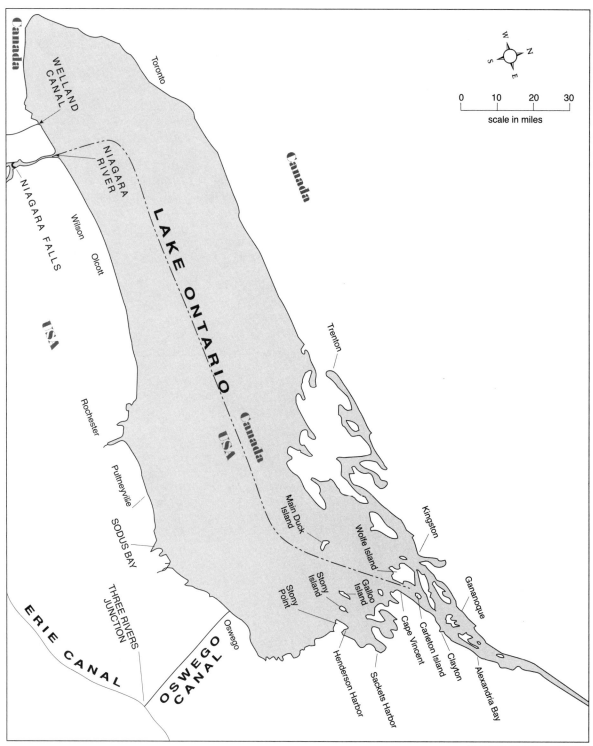

Canada

WELLAND
CANAL

Toronto

NIAGARA
RIVER

NIAGARA FALLS

Wilson

Olcott

USA

LAKE ONTARIO

Canada

USA

Canada

Rochester

Trenton

Pultneyville

SODUS BAY

Main Duck
Island

Kingston

Wolfe Island

Gananoque

THREE RIVERS
JUNCTION

Oswego

Stony
Island

Stony
Point

Galloo
Island

Carleton Island

Clayton

Alexandria Bay

ERIE CANAL

OSWEGO
CANAL

Henderson Harbor

Sackets Harbor

Cape Vincent

scale in miles

0   10   20   30

NOT TO BE USED FOR NAVIGATION

CHAPTER 10

The Southern and Eastern Lake Ontario

SKIPPER TIP: Please use these NOAA charts: 14803 for Lake Ontario and 14813 for the Oswego Harbor (regardless of which direction you cruise in), plus either A, B, or C.

A. If you want to go to the Welland Canal (west), you'll need the following additional NOAA charts: 14804, 14805, 14806, and 14810. For the Welland Canal itself, you'll need the Canadian chart 2042. And then you'll need some harbor charts to stop along the way: 14814 (Sodus Bay), 14815 (Rochester Harbor), and 14816 (Niagara River).

B. If you want to go to the Thousand Islands (north and east), you'll also need chart 14802.

C. If you intend to stop at Henderson Harbor, Cape Vincent, or Sackets Harbor, you'll also need 14811.

Lake Ontario

A large open-water adventure is ahead. Please consult local knowledge and current weather forecasts before embarking on this portion of your cruise. I have waited two days at Oswego for a window of calmer weather to make a trip to the Thousand Islands from Oswego. On the other hand, I've also had the opposite experience. On one cruise I put out towels and pillow rests so the crew could sunbathe as we crossed Lake Ontario northward from Rochester. The lake was a mirror that day, with just a few occasional wind ripples to keep the heat index down. It is recommended that besides having proper charts, you also should plan your cruise in advance. Know your compass headings, expected points of reference, and even some alternatives if something turns out different than you expected—good, general advice for any cruise.

You have two choices outlined in this section: A run to the Welland Canal across the southern shore of the lake, or a cruise north and then east into the heart of the Thousand Islands, the Northeast's most fabulous boaters' playground.

SKIPPER TIP: Water Depths

The water in Lake Ontario is normally 2 to 3 feet deeper than the levels shown on most charts, since they are based on a depth of 242.8 feet (74 meters) above sea level. The lake is typically at its highest level in early June. Check local sources or weather reports to know how much you need to add to charted depths so you can recalculate vertical clearances for bridges.

Seiche

On Lake Ontario you might experience a phenomenon called a seiche, in which the water is pushed up and deeper on one end of the lake from the other. This other end is then shallower than charted. This variance can last an afternoon or longer. It is caused by either barometric-pressure differences or strong winds literally blowing the water and piling it up at one end of the lake. Because this phenomenon can change water depths, check water levels using current local knowledge.

Lake Ontario:
Oswego to the Welland Canal

Once you cast off from any of the marinas in Oswego, you need to head out past the breakwater in a magnetic north direction. If you proceed all the way out toward the last breakwater, with the 30-foot-high flashing light at its west end, you can make a roughly 90° turn that will take you west to open water on Lake Ontario, with low- to mid-30-foot water depths. This distance of two-thirds of a mile offshore that can keep you in generally deep-enough water, but you'll be among (if not above) a variety of hazards, such as cooling intakes, industrial power-plant exhausts, sunken wrecks, and even some dumping areas. It's better to go out about 2½ miles offshore to clear all these obstacles, where the water is at least 70 feet deep.

> **SKIPPER TIP:** Window shapes in multi-storied buildings are generally visible to 3 miles offshore.

Port Oswego-Welland Canal Mileage
(All distances are +/- 3 miles)

Little Sodus Bay: 13 miles
Sodus Bay: 27 miles (popular stop)
Pultneyville: 38 miles
Rochester: 60 miles (very popular stop)
Olcott: 117 miles
Wilson: 123 miles
Niagara River: 136 miles
Welland Canal: 144 miles

It is about 13 miles to Little Sodus Bay—your first harbor to the west—depending upon how far offshore you cruise. The harbor has dual parallel breakwaters oriented in a north-south direction. The green light at 30 feet is on the eastern breakwater; the red light at a vertical height of 28 feet is on the western breakwater. This entrance channel is 7 to 16 feet deep, and most of Little Sodus Bay is 20 to 30 feet deep.

Keep away from most of the shoreline to stay in deep water. There are 300-foot-high hills on either side of the bay. The first marina is just inside the bay on the western shore. Most of the rest are about 1¾ miles down at the south end of the bay.

The Boathouse Marina (315) 947-6111

Storm protection: √√√
Scenic: * * *
Marina-reported approach depths: 12-16 feet
Marina-reported dockside depths: 4-8 feet
Gas

Diesel
Waste pump-out
Rest rooms
Showers
Dockside water
Barbecues
Picnic tables
Power connections: 30A/125V
Below-waterline repairs
Mechanical repairs
Gas-engine repairs
Stern-drive repairs
Outboard-motor repairs
Travelift/hoist: cruisers up to 45 feet long
What's special: closest to Lake Ontario

Fair Haven Yacht Club

Storm protection: √√√
Scenic: * * *
Marina-reported approach depths: 5-7 feet
Marina-reported dockside depths: 3-5 feet
**What's special: private yacht club; recipro-
    cal yacht club members are requested to
    contact the club (phone number unavail-
    able for publication here)**

Chinook Harbor Marina (315) 947-5599

Storm protection: √√√
Scenic: * *
Marina-reported approach depths: 4-6 feet
Marina-reported dockside depths: 2-4 feet
Gas
Rest rooms
Dockside water
Power connections: 15A/125V
Restaurant: on site
Grocery: off site
Convenience store: off site
What's special: near town
VHF-monitored channel: 16, 68

Bayside Marina (315) 947-5773

Storm protection: √√√
Scenic: * *
Marina-reported approach depths: 3-4 feet
Marina-reported dockside depths: 2-4 feet
Rest rooms
Showers
Dockside water
Power connections: 15A/125V
Travelift/hoist: 10 tons
Mast stepping: 50 feet
What's special: near town

Haven Marine (315) 947-5331

Storm protection: √√
Scenic: * * *
Marina-reported approach depths: 4-8 feet
Marina-reported dockside depths: 3-5 feet
Gas
Rest rooms
Showers
Dockside water
Barbecues
Picnic tables
Power connections: 30A/125V
**What's special: on-site bed and breakfast,
    plus it's near town**

It's an additional 7 miles or so to Port Bay, which also has marinas. However, the bay is marked by privately maintained aids to navigation, and water can be shoal at its entrance. You must have current local knowledge to enter Port Bay.

It's another 7 miles to Sodus Bay, which is a breakwater-protected bay with several marinas. Most of the town follows the bay's western shoreline, which is where the marinas are.

You must stay in the center third of the entrance channel for 10- to 15-foot water depths. Each of the breakwaters is marked by lights: green at 18 feet on the east, red at 51 feet on the western-breakwater end.

The bay is 2½ miles wide by 3½ miles long in a north-south orientation. Depths range from the low teens to the high 30-foot level.

All the marinas are either on the front face or backside of a .6 mile land arm that comes out from the western shoreline. Most pleasure boaters go around to the backside of this arm, making sure to stay in the 20-foot-plus deep water. Once around the arm, you will see the moored pleasure craft and the marinas. Watch water depths as you travel on this side, because it can shallow quickly.

Sill's Marina (315) 483-9102

Storm protection: √√√
Scenic: * *
Marina-reported approach depths: 6-20 feet
Marina-reported dockside depths: 5-7 feet
Gas
Diesel
Rest rooms
Power connections: 30A/125V, 50A/125V, 50A/220V
Woodworking repairs
Fiberglass repairs
Welding
Below-waterline repairs
Mechanical repairs
Gas-engine repairs
Diesel repairs
Stern-drive repairs
Outboard-motor repairs
Generator repairs
Travelift/hoist: 20 tons
Mast stepping: 100 feet
Ship's store
Restaurant: off site
Deli: off site
Grocery: off site

Convenience store: off site
What's special: near town

Krenzer Marine (315) 483-6986

Storm protection: √√√
Scenic: * *
Marina-reported approach depths: 7-9 feet
Marina-reported dockside depths: 2-5 feet
Gas
Waste pump-out
Rest rooms
Dockside water
Power connections: 30A/125V
Below-waterline repairs
Mechanical repairs
Gas-engine repairs
Stern-drive repairs
Outboard-motor repairs
Travelift/hoist: 25 tons
Ship's store
Restaurant: off site
Deli: off site
Grocery: off site
Convenience store: off site
What's special: near town

Sodus Bay Yacht Club (315) 483-9550

Storm protection: √√
Scenic: * * *
Marina-reported approach depths: 7-15 feet
Marina-reported dockside depths: 3-7 feet
Rest rooms
Showers
Dockside water
Barbecues
Picnic tables
Restaurant: off site
Deli: off site
Grocery: off site
Convenience store: off site
What's special: private club
VHF-monitored channel: 16

Anchor Marine Yacht Sales (315) 483-4052

Storm protection: √√√
Scenic: * *
Marina-reported approach depths: 19-25
 feet
Marina-reported dockside depths: 7-19 feet
Gas
Diesel
Waste pump-out
Rest rooms
Showers
Laundry
Dockside water
Barbecues
Picnic tables
Power connections: 30A/125V, 50A/125V,
 50A/220V
Fiberglass repairs
Below-waterline repairs
Mechanical repairs
Gas-engine repairs
Diesel repairs
Stern-drive repairs
Outboard-motor repairs
Generator repairs
Mast stepping
Ship's store
Restaurant: off site
Deli: off site
Grocery: off site
Convenience store: off site
What's special: some slips have very deep
 water dockside

Pultneyville is an additional 11 miles west.
You must have current local knowledge to enter Salmon Creek (Pultneyville). Private aids to navigation and/or ranges are put out to assist your getting in. It does shoal. There are two submerged jetties here also. Call before you enter.

Boaters suffer the hazards because of the fishing here. A number of record fish have come out of the river. Most every facility here serves fishermen in some capacity. Get a license and join right in.

Pultneyville Marina (315) 589-8922

Storm protection: √√
Scenic: * *
Marina-reported approach depths: 3-5 feet
Marina-reported dockside depths: 2-4 feet
Gas
Waste pump-out
Rest rooms
Showers
Dockside water
Barbecues
Picnic tables
Power connections: 15A/125V
Mechanical repairs
Travelift/hoist: for smaller cruisers (check
 with marina)
Ship's store
Restaurant: off site
Grocery: off site

Pultneyville Yacht Club (315) 589-9735

Storm protection: √√
Scenic: * *
Marina-reported approach depths: 3-5 feet
Marina-reported dockside depths: 2-4 feet
Waste pump-out
Rest rooms
Showers
Dockside water
Power connections: 15A/125V
Ship's store
Restaurant: off site
Grocery: off site
What's special: private yacht club

Rochester is another 22 miles farther west.

SKIPPER TIP: Most of the marinas in Rochester harbor are on the inside of a railroad bridge (vertical clearance: 10 feet closed). It is usually open, but if it is closed, signal one long blast followed by one short blast to request an opening. The bridge will answer the same if it will open, or five short blasts if it cannot or if it's going to close soon. You should return with five short blasts, indicating that you understand you must stand off to let the bridge close or stay closed.

Rochester Harbor is the Lake Ontario exit of the Genesee River. While there are dams that stop pleasure boaters, the river does continue on inland past the dam, crossing the Erie Canal on the other side of Rochester and then moving on to its mountain source. From 1840 to 1878 there was another canal that ran almost parallel to the north/south-oriented Genesee River, which connected Rochester to Portage (now Portageville).

A West Marine ship's store is a five-minute walk from most of the marinas, as is a selection of other shopping and eating venues. Downtown Rochester is a taxi ride away. Rochester is a good-sized city, so there's much to see and do. Don't miss the International Museum of Photography at George Eastman House (716-271-3361). Eastman's 49-room mansion is now a museum dedicated to photography and features thousands of cameras, prints, and movie stills.

Shumway Marina (716) 342-3030

Storm protection: √√√
Scenic: * *

Marina-reported approach depths: 4-16 feet
Marina-reported dockside depths: 4-6 feet
Gas
Diesel
Waste pump-out
Rest rooms
Showers
Laundry
Dockside water
Power connections: 30A/125V, 50A/125V, 50A/125V
Woodworking repairs
Fiberglass repairs
Welding
Below-waterline repairs
Mechanical repairs
Gas-engine repairs
Diesel repairs
Stern-drive repairs
Outboard-motor repairs
Generator repairs
Travelift/hoist
Mast stepping
Ship's store
Gift shop
Restaurant: on site
Grocery: off site
Convenience store: off site
What's special: a very complete marina
VHF-monitored channel: 09, 16

Voyager Boat Sales (716) 342-5150

Storm protection: √√√
Scenic: * *
Marina-reported approach depths: 4-16 feet
Marina-reported dockside depths: 3-6 feet
Rest rooms
Showers
Dockside water
Power connections: 30A/125V
Welding

Below-waterline repairs
Mechanical repairs
Gas-engine repairs
Stern-drive repairs
Travelift/hoist: 12 tons
Restaurant: off site
Grocery: off site
Convenience store: off site

Riverview Yacht Basin (716) 663-0088

Storm protection: √√√
Scenic: *
Marina-reported approach depths: 3-16
   feet
Marina-reported dockside depths: 2-5 feet
Gas
Diesel
Waste pump-out
Rest rooms
Dockside water
Power connections: 30A/125V
Fiberglass repairs
Below-waterline repairs
Mechanical repairs
Gas-engine repairs
Stern-drive repairs
Travelift/hoist: 14 tons
Ship's store
Restaurant: off site
Grocery: off site
Convenience store: off site
What's special: home to an excursion vessel

Pelican Marina (716) 663-5910

Storm protection: √
Scenic: *
Marina-reported approach depths: 10-16
   feet
Marina-reported dockside depths: 7-10 feet
Gas
Waste pump-out
Rest rooms

Barbecues
Picnic tables
Power connections: 15A/125V
Mechanical repairs
Ship's store
Gift shop
Convenience store: on site
What's special: very popular gas stop; on
   the main channel, so passing traffic can
   affect your craft; well-stocked ship's
   store/convenience store; very friendly
   marina staff

Rochester Yacht Club

Storm protection: √√√
Scenic: * * * *
Marina-reported approach depths: 4-19 feet
Marina-reported dockside depths: 4-6 feet
What's special: one of the premier clubs on
   the Great Lakes; extensive sailing program; host to many sailing competitions;
   outstanding staff; club does not accept
   credit cards, cash or checks (members
   are billed monthly), so have your club
   contact them well in advance on your
   behalf to facilitate payments (phone
   number unavailable for publication)

Genesee Yacht Club

Storm protection: √
Scenic: * *
Marina-reported approach depths: 5-16 feet
Marina-reported dockside depths: 4-7 feet
What's special: private yacht club (phone
   number unavailable for publication)

It is another 57 miles west to Olcott.

Hedley Boat Co. (716) 778-7771

Storm protection: √√
Scenic: *
Marina-reported approach depths: 4-7 feet

Marina-reported dockside depths: 2-4 feet
Gas
Waste pump-out
Rest rooms
Showers
Dockside water
Picnic tables
Power connections: 15A/125V
Ship's store
Restaurant: off site
Grocery: off site
What's special: in town
VHF-monitored channel: 16

McDonough Marine (716) 778-7048

Storm protection: √√
Scenic: *
Marina-reported approach depths: 4-7 feet
Marina-reported dockside depths: 2-4 feet
Gas
Rest rooms
Woodworking repairs
Fiberglass repairs
Mechanical repairs
Gas-engine repairs
Ship's store
Restaurant: on site
What's special: in town

Main St. Dock (716) 778-5462

Storm protection: √√
Scenic: *
Marina-reported approach depths: 4-7 feet
Marina-reported dockside depths: 2-4 feet
Power connections: 15A/125V
What's special: in town

Olcott Yacht Club (716) 778-5915

Storm protection: √√
Scenic: * *
Marina-reported approach depths: 8-9 feet

Marina-reported dockside depths: 3-7 feet
What's special: private club

Wilson Harbor is 6 miles west of Olcott.

Beccue Boat Basin (716) 751-6466

Storm protection: √√√
Scenic: * * *
Marina-reported approach depths: 4-5 feet
Marina-reported dockside depths: 3-5 feet
Gas
Diesel
Waste pump-out
Rest rooms
Showers
Dockside water
Barbecues
Picnic tables
Power connections: 30A/125V
Woodworking repairs
Fiberglass repairs
Welding
Below-waterline repairs
Mechanical repairs
Gas-engine repairs
Diesel repairs
Travelift/hoist: 30 tons
Ship's store
Restaurant: on site
What's special: very far inside the harbor
    across the east branch of Twelve-mile
    Creek from the state park

Tuscarora Yacht Club (716) 751-9975

Storm protection: √√
Scenic: * * *
Marina-reported approach depths: 3-5 feet
Marina-reported dockside depths: 2-4 feet
Power connections: 15A/125V, 30A/125V
What's special: on its own island; private
    club
VHF-monitored channel: 16, 68

Wilson Yacht Club (716) 751-6063

Storm protection: √√
Scenic: * * *
Marina-reported approach depths: 3-5 feet
Marina-reported dockside depths: 2-3 feet
What's special: on its own island; private
   club

From Wilson Harbor it is 12 miles to the
entrance to the Niagara River.
   On the Canadian side:

**Niagara-on-the-Lake Sailing Club (416)
   468-3966**

Storm protection: √√
Scenic: *
Marina-reported approach depths: 30 feet
Marina-reported dockside depths: 5-8 feet
Gas
Diesel
Waste pump-out
Rest rooms
Showers
Laundry
Dockside water
Power connections: 30A/125V
Woodworking repairs
Fiberglass repairs
Below-waterline repairs
Mechanical repairs
Travelift/hoist: 15 tons
Restaurant: on site
What's special: in a historic town with
   three forts, and a nice place to walk

On the U.S. side:

Williams Marine (716) 745-7000

Storm protection: √
Scenic: *
Marina-reported approach depths: 6-50 feet
Marina-reported dockside depths: 3-7 feet

Diesel
Waste pump-out
Rest rooms
Showers
Dockside water
Power connections: 30A/125V, 50A/220V
Woodworking repairs
Fiberglass repairs
Below-waterline repairs
Mechanical repairs
Gas-engine repairs
Diesel repairs
Ship's store
VHF-monitored channel: 16, 68

RCR Yachts (716) 745-3862

Travelift/hoist: 20 tons
What's special: repairs only

Youngstown Yacht Club (716) 745-7230

Storm protection: √√
Scenic: * *
Marina-reported approach depths: 6-50 feet
Marina-reported dockside depths: 3-7 feet
Waste pump-out
Rest rooms
Showers
Dockside water
Barbecues
Picnic tables
Power connections: 30A/125V
Restaurant: on site
What's special: private club
VHF-monitored channel: 68

SKIPPER TIP: Since all the Great Lakes
ultimately flow into Lake Ontario via the
Niagara Falls, the cumulative effect of the
sand and soil carried over centuries is the

Niagara Bar, where water depths can be less than 30 feet as far as 4 miles out from the shoreline. Be sure to pick up red marker buoy #2, which is roughly 4 miles off the entrance to the Niagara River, and stay to the outside (north) of it to clear the bar.

The Niagara River's centerline establishes the international border between Canada and the United States. Fort Niagara and Youngstown, New York, are on the U.S. side; on the west (Canadian) side of the river is Niagara-on-the-Lake and Fort Mississauga. You can clear customs at the Niagara River or wait until Port Weller and the Welland Canal, if you do not intend to land until then. If you're on your way to Canada, then refer to appendix A, "Clearing U.S. and Canadian Customs," and appendix B, "Metric Conversion Tables."

Niagara Falls

The American falls are 1,060 feet wide; the horseshoe falls, which are on the Canadian side, are 2,600 feet wide. The Canadian falls drop 158 feet, while the American falls have a drop of 168 feet. The falls were formed roughly 12,000 years ago as the last glacier moved back, exposed the Niagara escarpment, and allowed the waters of Lake Erie to flow north over that scarp into Lake Ontario. The falls have been eroding backwards (southward) toward Lake Erie since then. The Canadian side is eroding at a faster pace than the American side. It's been estimated that in 10,000 to 20,000 years (depending on the source), the falls will back up to the Buffalo area.

Today, the Canadian and American governments divert equal amounts of water from the falls through some hydropower plants to produce electrical power in a very clean manner. The hydroelectric plants have agreed not to

The Canadian falls on the Niagara River.

The American falls, looking south from Niagara Falls, Ontario, Canada.

turn off the falls because they are a scenic tourist attraction. Each side takes between 1.5 to 2 million kilowatts of electrical capacity from the river via diverted water. A description of the falls, by the way, came late in North American history. Although La Salle saw them in 1678, no one really wrote about them until one of his associates, Louis Hennepin, described them in his book *Nouvelle Découverte*, which was published in 1697.

Over the Falls

We all know that many tightrope walkers have traversed wires stretched over the Niagara Falls, and some people even have gone over the falls in barrels. But we seldom hear about boats going over the falls. On September 8, 1827, some promoters bought an unseaworthy ship named the *Michigan* and had her crew sail her as close to the falls as they could. Then, after the crew disembarked in a shore boat to safety, the *Michigan* went over the falls and disintegrated. It was one of the first promotional efforts by the local Canadian and American merchants to increase awareness of and promote tourism to the falls. Ten years later—in December 1837, during the Canadian rebellion then under way—some dissidents overtook the crew of the steam vessel *Caroline*, sailed her from her moorings, and caused her to go over the falls.

The Lake Ontario entrance to the Welland Canal is 8 miles west of the Niagara River. Use Canadian chart 2042 for the Welland Canal.

Lake Ontario: Oswego to the Thousand Islands and Cape Vincent

Leaving the Port of Oswego, you need to head up the open waters of Lake Ontario for just less than 50 miles to the beginning of the Thousand Islands and Cape Vincent. The initial part of this run is to the Galloo Island Light, just about due north. However, because of magnetic variation in the area, your compass course should be about 015° magnetic. This run is 28 miles from an imaginary point about three-quarters of a mile beyond the breakwaters of Port Oswego. On the open lake you'll find these imaginary lines or courses noted on most charts; you'll need to make adjustments to these headings for annual increase and decrease of the magnetic variation. In other words, you have to do your own chart work. But it does give you a sense of continuum as you change from chart sheet to chart sheet, or if you're moving through the pages of *Richardson's Lake Ontario Guide*.

This heading is intended to take you roughly 3½ miles off the western edge of Galloo Island and off its southwestern light that's set at 58 feet. It also takes you just west of Galloo Shoal, which has green buoy #3 and is about 2 miles east of the intended course line. The course allows you some leeway: Obviously, you could go almost 2 miles to the east and still not collide with the buoy, or you could go as much as 4 miles to the west where there's a red buoy. However, you do want to come close enough to the green buoy so you can see it. Avoid wandering west because that's the lane for southbound (down-bound) traffic crossing Lake Ontario. Commercial-freighter traffic uses these lanes, and you're being directed by this course along with the northbound freighter traffic toward the St. Lawrence Seaway/Thousand Islands area. If you wander to the west, that motion tends to take you bow-on into the path of southbound traffic coming from the St. Lawrence Seaway/Thousand Islands area. These aren't shipping lanes as you would see off the coast of California or in some other areas; rather, they're suggestions that give some sort of separation to this traffic.

West of red buoy #2 is Main Duck Island and its smaller sister, Yorkshire Island. Off Galloo Shoal (roughly 43° 53′ north, 76° 31′ west)—again this is an imaginary point some 3½ miles west of the Galloo Island shore (and 2 miles west of buoy #G3)—the course takes a jog to the right (eastward) and then continues for another 16 miles. The course swings about 20° to the east, a course setting somewhere around 034° magnetic. However, 10 miles after you make this course adjustment, you'll come upon vertically striped buoy #RW. Pass it on your port side—in other words, you want to be to the east of buoy #RW. Now make another easterly course adjustment, about 063° magnetic for the last 4½ miles to Cape Vincent.

Interim Side Cruise

Along the way to the Thousand Islands area, you may want to stop at either Henderson Harbor or Sackets Harbor. If so, the best place to turn for these harbors is about 5 miles north of the above-mentioned course change to 034° magnetic. As a reference point, water depth in this area on most charts is shown at 99 feet and then 87 feet—say 43° 56′ N/76° 29′ W. These two harbors—Sackets, which is about 19 miles to the east, and Henderson, which is about 20 miles to the east and then south—are alternatives if you're getting too rough a ride and want to change direction to get a better angle on the seas. Or you can continue on up to Cape Vincent. At this turning point, Cape Vincent is closer, about 10½ miles away, than either Sackets Harbor or Henderson Harbor. Please refer to the section "Direct Route: Oswego to Sackets Harbor/Henderson Harbor," which appears later in this chapter, for marina selections at both Sackets Harbor and Henderson Harbor.

Go another 15 miles east of Cape Vincent to reach Clayton in the protected water of the St. Lawrence River. Here, water conditions typically are more of a following sea created by the wind—that is, the waves are going in the same direction as your craft is heading—and therefore make for an easy ride. When you start your cruise up this last run, first you need to be to the right of green buoy #245. To your north or west (port side of your vessel) is Wolfe Island, one of the larger of the Thousand Islands, and to your starboard is the state of New York, but you are still short of Cape Vincent. Your position gives you Canada on one side and the United States on the other, with the internationally designated border running closer to the Wolfe Island side than the U.S. side, so you are cruising in U.S. waters.

Cape Vincent

Immediately east of green buoy #243 is the western entrance to Cape Vincent, along with its outer east/west-oriented breakwater.

> **SKIPPER TIP:** Horne's Ferry crosses the channel between green buoy #243 and the eastern edge of Cape Vincent's breakwater. The ferry runs between Cape Vincent and Wolfe Island, as it has since 1801.

The historic Horne's Ferry is respected for its important role in the development of this area. It provided the only access to Wolfe Island and the U.S. mainland. In fact, it was so critical that its workers were excused from military service early in America's history. The ferry dates back to 1801, when a man and his rowboat took people across this section of the St. Lawrence. English King George IV officially recognized the ferry in 1829 via a charter lease. The Horne family took it over after a daughter of the original operator married a Horne early in the twentieth century.

Cape Vincent's breakwater halts almost any major wave action. The town has had a history of lumber, coal, and pulp shipping and some shipbuilding. Its founder (then a holder of vast lands in upstate New York) planned for France's Napoleon Bonaparte to live here after his exile, but he never made it. Today, it's home to a U.S. Customs station, where commercial freighters pick up a Seaway pilot to transit the St. Lawrence Seaway. Although Cape Vincent is not in the heart of the Thousand Islands like Alexandria Bay, pleasure boaters and land-based tourists keep the friendly local merchants busy.

Cape Vincent Village Dock

Storm protection: √√
Scenic: *
Marina-reported approach depths: 3-10 feet
Marina-reported dockside depths: 3-5 feet
Picnic tables
What's special: public dock for up to 48-hour stays; can be rough-finished in places, and surge can be a problem; local boaters tend to fill it up early; unstaffed

Anchor Marine is toward the east end of the breakwater. It has dockage both outside and inside its own separate basin. It's very nice, with good access to town.

Anchor Marine (315) 654-2300

Storm protection: √√√
Scenic: * *
Marina-reported approach depths: 5-11 feet
Marina-reported dockside depths: 4-6 feet
Gas
Diesel
Waste pump-out
Rest rooms
Showers
Laundry
Dockside water
Barbecues
Picnic tables
Power connections: 30A/125V
Fiberglass repairs
Below-waterline repairs
Mechanical repairs
Gas-engine repairs
Diesel repairs
Stern-drive repairs
Outboard-motor repairs
Generator repairs
Travelift/hoist: 12 tons
Ship's store
Restaurant: off site
Grocery: off site
Convenience store: off site
What's special: in town
VHF-monitored channel: 16

Marker buoys now define the channel about every 1½ miles, although the red buoys are more frequent than the green. This marked channel keeps you in deep water, taking you to the side of Carleton Island that is west and north,

and then down the main channel towards Clayton, and beyond it to the resort town of Alexandria Bay, a boaters' paradise. (Please see chapter 9, "The Thousand Islands and St. Lawrence River" to continue cruising east.)

The Great Lakes Freighters

Throughout the era of commercial-ore freighting—from the local mines to the mills and from the cargoes of the great inland factories to the rest of the world—the ships that traveled the St. Lawrence River, Lake Ontario, and the other Great Lakes have had several different loading marks (levels) based on the season of the year during which the loaded boat traveled. Summer marks allow a boat (all Great Lakes craft are called boats here regardless of size) to be loaded down lower in the water, while winter marks require a vessel to be loaded more lightly in anticipation of winter storms. Of course, there are other seasonal variations, too. More boats have sunk on the Great Lakes in the month of September than any other time—although I haven't been able to document this, perhaps it's because the loading marks are out of sync with actual weather experienced at that time.

A wave of problems ensued when boats first converted from wood to metal and from sail to power. During this transition, a greater number of boats fell prey to accidents, fires, and wrecks as a result of increased speed, different handling characteristics, and the power systems/engineering of boats built with these new methods. During the last 20 years of the nineteenth century, some 6,000 vessels were wrecked on the Great Lakes—about 1,000 of them actually sank. By 1900, builders and crews had enough experience with these new technologies that the metal, engine-powered vessels became more reliable than the wooden sailboats.

Canoes

Much of the exploring, missionary work, and fur trading was done through the use of canoes. The native canoes could carry 12 to 14 men at one time. They were 35 to 40 feet long, bark-covered, and roughly 6 feet wide amidships, with a curved bow to slice through the water and deflect the rapids. Since bark skin was fragile, the men inside didn't touch it—instead, they sat or kneeled on a supporting suspended framework of thick tree saplings. This internal framework also made the canoe flexible, which helped its ability to go over rapids and handle the rough open waters of the Great Lakes. When the men disembarked, they did not bring the canoe up on shore—instead, the men got out while the canoe still floated freely on the water and carefully carried it up to land.

The men would spend all day in these canoes, singing songs to provide a cadence so they could paddle uniformly. The canoes hauled their tons of trade goods and supplies out to the Indian fur trappers. Once there, they would swap the kettles, knives, chisels, and axes for beaver pelts and return to Quebec with an equivalent tonnage of pelts. It was typical for these traders to paddle for 14 hours a day and then set up small camp sites on shore for meals and overnights.

Before the canals and the locks were built, all these major water trips required multiple portages either to go around rapids or to connect to the next river. Two men were expected to be able to carry the canoe. The others were expected to carry their weight in backpacks filled with either supplies going out or pelts coming back. Once the packs were loaded, the men often had a forced march or trotting pace for portages between 1 and 20 miles. Why the 14-hour paddling days? Why the forced-march portages? Simple. Canoes carried 21 to 22 days of rations. How far (and fast) they could go in that time gave them the best choice of beaver pelts. The quest for quality pelts forced them to make these unbelievable trips of strength and endurance.

Lake Ontario Wrecks

On November 12, 1832, a 6-man crew and 22 passengers coming from Oswego and bound for Sackets Harbor were on the side-wheel steamboat *Martha Ogden*. A wind shift kept her from using the sail the captain had spread out after a hull leak doused her steam boilers. Failing to control his ship first by steam and then by sail, the captain set two anchors. These dragged, and she finally foundered on the rocks. However, all aboard were saved.

On April 30, 1853, the steam vessel *Ocean Wave* caught fire 2 miles from the Duck Islands. She had left Kingston, Ontario, right after midnight, headed towards Oswego. Less than thirty minutes passed from the start of the fire to the sinking of the boat. The majority of the passengers were rescued by other vessels that had come after seeing the brightness of the fire against the lake skyline.

A couple of Lake Ontario firsts: In 1804, the first lighthouse on the Great Lakes was erected where the Niagara River enters Lake Ontario on the U.S. side. In 1840, the steamer *Vandalia,* which was built at Oswego, was the first commercial propeller ship, not only on the Great Lakes but anywhere in the world. It was the first steam vessel to have her engines aft as well, as opposed to amidships.

Lake Ontario: Early History

Lake Ontario, like all the Great Lakes, has had multiple glacier periods that have alternately covered and uncovered these vast land areas, formed the lakes, and then fed them with water when the ice retreated. Some historians believe that during the last glacier era glacier formations caused the ocean levels to drop 300 feet. This drop exposed land bridges that in previous times were under water. The bridges allowed animals and early man to start populating North America. The most famous of these land bridges was at the Bering Strait. Scholars think that about 9,000 years ago many people used a land bridge there to walk from Asia and settle in North America. These nomadic tribes simply followed the wild game south through Alaska and then eastward, eventually populating the Great Lakes and the northeast quadrant of the United States.

Geographically, cedar-dominated bogs were the first land types created upon the glaciers' last retreat. This cold and moist environment favored spruce, pine, and fir trees, all of which have the root system to dig into the topsoil. Beaver, musk ox, and other small animals filled the area. Throughout that 9000 B.C. to 1000 B.C. period, it is believed, people stayed nomadic and actually showed little change in their lifestyles. Archaeological remains, particularly of burial sites, show some awareness, but food gathering and finding shelter occupies most of the nomads' time. Because of the need for spearheads, copper came into some use and a few primitive agricultural tools were devised. Around 1000 B.C., one group of Native Americans seemed to take over, and they began farming pumpkins, squash, and other crops in good quantities. They became less nomadic and started settlements, usually just two, three, or four huts set up by a stream and built out of poles and tree saplings covered with bark or animal skins.

Spirituality evolved to include shamanistic customs: animal heads and skins and bags filled with sacred objects were used for soothsaying or medicinal purposes. These people made crude pottery, smoked tobacco in clay pipes, and clothed themselves in animal skin. For fashion statements they adorned their clothing with lace and beads. These people thrived from about 1000 B.C. to around 600 A.D.; then signs of this culture disappear.

Although other groups came in to populate the area after these people disappeared, the historical timeline has some unexplained gaps between the first group's demise to about the time of French and British settlement in North America. While some believe that these prehistoric people just described were the American Indians' ancestors, others think the American Indians were simply another wave of people to come across the land, perhaps from South America.

Native Americans are grouped by their language, and the language of the Indians around Lake Ontario was Iroquois. It has been suggested that when explorer Samuel de Champlain came through, there were about 43,000 Iroquois tribe members. The Iroquois tribes were Cayuga, Mohawk, Oneida, Onondaga, and Seneca. These Indians were farmers. They typically used a longhouse-style hut, inside of which six to twelve families lived. These houses, made up of bent saplings that were lashed together to form a tunnel-like structure, could be as long as 80 feet. The framework of the lashed saplings was then covered either by bark, skins, or some combination thereof. Something not often discussed is that many

Indians over their lifetimes would become blinded by smoke, since fires in the huts were not well vented. It was not unusual for Jesuit missionaries in their diaries to complain about smoke, noise, dogs, and dirt when they visited these Indian homes and settlements.

The "tribe" was a flexible concept to the Indians; groups could ally or disassociate over periods of time, generally based on disputes or the need to defend themselves from hostile outside groups. One of the strongest unions was the confederation of the Indians, or the Five Nations, which was formed around 1450 and affected the broad area around Lake Ontario, the Finger Lakes, and along the St. Lawrence River. Among this confederation of five tribes were the Mohawks, a warlike people who were considered the fiercest of the Iroquois. They were the ones who wore the crescent-shaped coxcomb style for their hair, used face paints, elaborately decorated their upper bodies for war, and fashioned small warrior shields from tree bark. The Onondagas tribe had their villages up higher on hills, seemingly almost geographically centered among the five tribes, and they tended to be the ruling group of the five nations. The biggest group, however, was the Seneca tribe.

However, it was the Mohawks who led the Five Nations into minor skirmishes to train for major conflicts, allowing the younger braves to gain combat experience and acquire war trophies while keeping the veteran warriors sharp, too. Always ready for war, the Mohawks required defeated enemies to join them and often had a large population of adopted tribe members in each of their camps. Finally, it must be noted that the torture techniques of the Mohawks (and therefore the Five Nations) were considered the most excruciating and the most violent of any of the American Indian tribes—not to suggest that all Indians engaged in torture.

Early European Settlers in the New World

In 1534 Jacques Cartier, hired by King Francis I of France to find a shortcut to China and all the wealth it contained, landed on Newfoundland with two small ships. He made it as far as the mouth of the St. Lawrence, where he met some Native Americans. History has it that he gave their chief an ax and two red hats. The chief in turn gave him beaver pelts and two young boys, whom he let be taken back to France. These young boys and the beaver fur made quite the hit back in Europe. The king commissioned Cartier for a second trip, this time with three vessels. He brought back the two Indian boys, and his kindness toward them helped him establish a trusting relationship with the American Indians. With the Indians' guidance, Cartier was able to locate the river entrance within the larger Gulf of St. Lawrence. In naming the river, he chose St. Lawrence, after the saint on whose feast day he discovered it.

On this second trip Cartier went as far as what is now Quebec, Canada. (By the way, the word Canada comes from the word *kanata*, which is Iroquois for "the village." Cartier, it is surmised today, simply misunderstood the Indians when he pointed—they were referring to the village, whereas he was asking for the name of the whole area.) Once on land, Cartier climbed to some hilltops to get a better view to the west and what he hoped would be China just ahead. From that vantage point he spied the rapids on the St. Lawrence River that would ultimately prevent his ships from going any farther west. Cartier named them the Lachine Rapids, French for "China rapids." During this trip Cartier was forced to stay over the winter because of ice on the river. While he was having a shipboard feast with the local Indian chief, Donnacona, Cartier spotted a break in the ice. Seemingly on the spur of the moment, he hoisted sail and left North America, having decided to take the chief back to his chief, King Francis I.

Although Cartier made a third trip to North America in 1541, he again failed to find China. The king of France, disappointed by the failure and distracted by a war he was waging with Spain, ordered no more immediate French expeditions to the New World.

In 1603 France had a new king, and he had a new explorer in his employ: Samuel de Champlain. In 1604 Champlain traveled to the St. Lawrence River, where he went as far as present-day Quebec and established a small village—four buildings—calling it Quebec after the Native American name *kebec,* which means "place where the waters narrow." In 1608, on Champlain's sixth voyage, he brought along Etienne Brule.

Brule, 17 years old at this time, became the first Frenchman to adopt the dress of the North American Indians. Brule also picked up their language and spent more time with the Indians than with the French while he was in the New World. He eventually gained the trust, admiration, and acceptance of the Indians, who considered him a good fighter and apparently a good womanizer. However, while he was currying favor with the Indians, he was losing favor with the French, particularly the very first few Jesuits who had come over to spread Catholicism.

Most of the French explored the areas with which the Indians were familiar. The French followed the Indians back to their settlements' hunting grounds and moved among their allied tribes. They were guided by the Indians and saw the rest of the New World through their lead. Because of this, Brule didn't go to the source of the St. Lawrence River, Lake Ontario. Instead, in 1610 he went up the Ottawa River and then portaged over a short section of land to Georgian Bay. By 1618, he had made the leap from Georgian Bay to Lake Huron, and from there up to Lake Superior. Again, he followed this course because of tribal patterns set out by the Indians, the friends and trading partners of the French.

During all of Brule's explorations, his relationship with Samuel de Champlain was held together by a thin thread. Brule eventually betrayed Champlain by helping the British capture Champlain. Four years later, in 1633, Champlain, freed from the British, wanted revenge on Brule. He asked the Hurons, whom he had befriended, to bring Brule to him for a court-martial. To further demonstrate their support for Champlain, the Hurons, upon capturing Brule, quartered him, broiled the quarters, and ate him—perhaps the first crème brûleé.

In 1634 another explorer, Jean Nicolet, built on Brule's work and—instead of going up to Lake Superior from Lake Huron—went west across the Mackinaw Straits to Lake Michigan and then on to Green Bay, Wisconsin. In 1669 Louis Joliet, again following Brule's route through the Ottawa River over land to Georgian Bay, went down Lake Huron, went past what is now Detroit, and discovered (via a portage around the Niagara Falls) Lake Erie and Lake Ontario for the French. Joliet only tried this trip down Lake Huron because he thought a new peace had been made with the Iroquois in that area. Joliet's discovery of the Ontario, Erie, and Huron Lake waterways made for a faster trip because they eliminated the need for multiple portages.

In 1672 New France got a new governor: Louis de Buade, Comte de Palluauet de Frontenac. He was a strong-willed man who wanted to solidify France's hold in the New World. One of his first moves was to build Fort Frontenac at what is now Kingston, Ontario. The presence of this fort neutralized England and the Five Nations tribes, who up until then had controlled Lake Ontario, and gave France free rein to traverse the lake. Frontenac also reestablished control over the fur trade and reactivated exploration with three goals in mind: finding a route to China; surveying the best sites for forts; and locating the best fur-trading markets. Frontenac asked Joliet to push forward on the exploration. In 1673 Joliet left the known waters and discovered for the French the Mississippi River, taking it down as far as Arkansas. Then Frontenac teamed up with another explorer, Rene Robert Cavelier, Sieur de La Salle, known in history as La Salle. Among other accomplishments, La Salle explored the Ohio River and went down the Monongahela and the Allegheny Rivers, envisioning them as routes for vast fleets of canoes, each burdened with heaps of beaver pelts, to Montréal and from there back to France. Finally, in 1682 La Salle took the Mississippi all the way down to the Gulf of Mexico, claiming the river and the land surrounding it for France. He named this land Louisiana, in honor of the king of France.

The Jesuit order was instrumental in these early exploration ventures. These tough, successful men gave up worldly security because they believed their duty was to spread the word of God. The Jesuit missionaries ought to be nicknamed the Catholic Marine Corps, because—like U.S. Marines—they went into the new areas first and reconnoitered for the explorers. Besides working to befriend the Indians and learn the new terrain, the Jesuit missionaries made maps, kept diaries, and translated the Bible into Indian languages. All these activities paved the way for the explorers who followed.

Ever since the first member of their order came to Canada in 1607, the Jesuits were busy exploring North America. The Jesuits sent their diaries back to Europe, where they were copied and printed in an annual volume called *Jesuit Relations*. Anyone hungry for new land could use this volume to learn about not only the customs and warlike tendencies of various tribes, but also what routes were best for forging into this new territory. The British, in their fight with the French for the same land, felt more threatened by the efforts of the Jesuits than by the French explorers. Whenever they could, the British would capture these missionaries and send them back to Europe to prevent further proselytizing and exploring in North America.

Another Jesuit priest, Brebeuf, survived 17 hours of horrible torture at the hands of the Iroquois. To show their admiration for Brebeuf, the Iroquois ate his heart so that his courage would enter them. By 1773 Canada had reduced the Jesuits' ranks down to just 11 missionaries. But by then the exploration of New France had been accomplished.

Beaver Pelts

Because beaver pelts made fine waterproof, stylish hats for European nobility, fur was a major reason the French went to the New World to trade with the American Indians. The hat material was made from the underfur of the beaver pelt, and it could be brushed to create a flat, felt-like material. The French wanted the fur, but they also wanted to establish a foothold in the New World. Therefore, the French kings who granted licenses for fur trading required these trading companies to establish settlements or bring people in to start a town. As the French advanced west, this system established many forts, towns, and trading posts, which helped New France expand more rapidly than the British colonies. Because the British gave their fur traders more leeway, their trade industry was scattered among a vastly larger number of independently acting entrepreneurs.

The British

Although the French had made strong progress in this North American territorial expansion, which was fueled by their fur traders and missionaries, the British began to catch up. They were concerned about the territory France had claimed, and the fact that the French territory running through the St. Lawrence, the Great Lakes, and down the Mississippi corralled the British and stopped them from expanding beyond their colonies. The British were looking for ways to overtake France when two Frenchmen became turncoats and provided the opportunity: Medard Chouart, Sieur de Groseilliers, and his brother-in-law, Pierre Esprit Radisson, were declared illegal fur traders by the French because they had violated French licensing laws. Legally or not, these two brothers operated a large fur-trading business; they had 60 canoes. When they were told their business was illegal, they

went over to the English side. There they laid out a plan to help the English beat the French at the beaver-pelt game.

Their plan was simple: To establish the Hudson's Bay Company farther north than the existing French pipeline. The route via the Bay Company wouldn't require the portages the French route had established by coming up the St. Lawrence, its rapids, and the nearby but unconnected rivers. Therefore, transportation would be faster and costs would cheaper, and the British could afford to pay trappers the highest prices. By outflanking the French traders with this new route in 1670, the British were able to pull ahead of France. The beaver-pelt business was profitable; profit margins could be 25 to 1. You'd pay a dollar and get $25 worth of pelts in exchange—a 2,500 percent mark-up! Naturally, after a couple of years the French narrowed their profit margin in order to pay trappers more money for the coveted furs. Once the fur prices were on equal ground, the English and the French found themselves at war. (I should note that hostilities were not isolated to the New World: France and England also were fighting for various reasons in the West Indies, India, Europe, and Africa.)

Although the fur trade was the war's primary cause, there were other ancillary issues in this war, some of which were just as important. Land ownership was a big factor in the war. The English felt hemmed in by France's exploration and its fort infrastructure down the St. Lawrence, around the Great Lakes, and down the Mississippi. The French had even come into Ohio and started to populate it as an offshoot to their fur business. The British needed more land if their thirteen colonies were ever going to expand. If the British won the war with France in North America (which they eventually did), the colonies would have room to grow.

However, once the British won control of North America from the French, they then had to win over the American Indians. In contrast to the French, the British were stuffy and unwilling to take the time to recognize the differences among tribes. This insensitivity created ill will between the British and the Indians. To act on the bad blood, Chief Pontiac developed a plan to attack all the British forts at once. This plot was discovered, however, so rather than a simultaneous attack on all posts, there were just some scattered attacks, and Pontiac was eventually forced to back down.

In the midst of this fighting, the thirteen colonies started the Revolutionary War and diverted Britain's attention from the Indian problem. However, the Indians didn't go away. Several years later Chief Little Turtle, of the Miami, Ohio area, came along and was so threatening to early American settlers that Gen. "Mad" Anthony Wayne was called out of retirement to deal with him. In 1794, General Wayne, using some 3,000 troops all at once in a battle and all lined up in row after row, wore out the natives, exhausted their supply of weapons, and finally crushed the Indian's powerful hold on these western territories.

Several years later Americans were still skirmishing somewhat with the Indians, but soon the United States faced another challenge: fighting Britain a second time, largely over British imprisonment of American seamen. This issue evolved into the War of 1812, during which Fort Niagara on Lake Ontario, located where the Niagara River empties into the lake, was captured by the British in 1813. On the opposite (Canadian) side, the Americans captured Fort George (Canada had sided with the British during the Revolutionary War and stayed with them in this conflict.) The Americans also burned Toronto, which at that time was called York, and the British burned Oswego. War activities on Lake Ontario pretty much ended with these battles.

John Jacob Astor

One of the richest and most successful men to come out of the fur trade was a German immigrant, John Jacob Astor. Once a young boy working in a New York City warehouse beating the dirt out of beaver pelts, he became one of the richest men in America. He began saving his money so he could buy a few pelts and resell them at a profit. Soon he was going directly to the Iroquois, the major suppliers, to buy pelts. He also established a return trade: he shipped furs to England and had musical instruments shipped back to sell in New York City. Astor, using many different techniques (some above and some below the belt), eliminated or bought out all the North American fur-trading competition except the Hudson's Bay Company. He eventually sold his total interest in the fur business in 1835, and the industry's prices collapsed soon afterwards.

Immigration

During the lull between the War of 1812 and the Civil War there was a surge of expansion westward into the United States. The fur trappers had been working the frontier for years, joined soon after by a wave of lumbermen who came to chop down the virgin forests. They were followed by the first big wave of settlers, mostly composed of immigrants fleeing economic and social problems back in Europe. Ireland's infamous potato blights and Germany's internal problems sent their citizens to the United States. Other Europeans came too. The new immigrants were brought west on the Erie Canal, which enabled families seeking a new life to make a trip that once was limited to only the most rugged explorers.

A series of potato-crop failures in Ireland in 1818 and during the 1830s and 1845 fueled Irish immigration to the United States. People from Scandinavian countries also arrived during this period. The first trickle has actually been traced to four young friends who—disappointed with their early work careers in their native Sweden—came as passengers on a freighter loaded with iron. They paid $26 each to cross the Atlantic Ocean. Based on advice from people they met along the way, they moved west from New York City, eventually making it all the way to Wisconsin. They were so pleased with what they saw there that they wrote back home, and from those letters more people came. By the 1850s approximately a half-dozen ships were bringing immigrants from Sweden into New York. The Civil War and the war industry that fed it caused the owners of mines to send delegates over to Sweden and bring back as many as 10,000 workers who would feed the war machine with their mining efforts. Twenty percent of the population of Scandinavian countries came to America from the late 1870s to the 1890s.

Citizens of Germany were disappointed with the failure of the Revolution of 1848, in which the people rebelled against state-mandated religion and heavy economic commitment to the military. The wave of German immigrants into the United States continued for about five years after 1848; its numbers included not only farm workers and the working class but also some of the failed leaders of the revolution and their educated followers. Additional waves of German immigrants came in the 1850s, 1870s, and 1880s.

This time period overall is associated with huge waves of immigration from Europe. Entire Swiss villages came over to the United States intact. The Dutch, who had founded all of early New York State, continued to come in and moved on west after the Erie Canal opened beyond New York State and into areas such as Michigan. As in Albany, New York, there are towns in Michigan that bear the Dutch names of Holland and Zeeland and still grow tulips today to honor their Dutch heritage.

Other immigrant groups included the Polish, the Welsh, and the Czech peoples. Many of them came into Pennsylvania, Ohio, and New York to work in the steel trades there and then moved farther west as the demand for steel grew. Russia's takeover of Finland in 1809 sent Finnish people to America. In the twenty years after 1850, some Danes came to America, many of whom worked in the dairy trades. Scots rounded out the ingredients in the "melting pot" that America was becoming.

Farmers

Early settlers often turned to farming to make a living. The land they farmed, after the timber people had moved through and cut down most of the trees, still had tree stumps. Since the stumps took several years to rot, new farmers just planted around these tree remains. The tree and underbrush roots in the soil also made the task of getting crops into the soil very difficult. The soil often wasn't fertile enough to provide a really good crop either—

it needed to be improved, usually with ash. Therefore, many of these first-generation immigrants resigned themselves to working on farms that might become viable property for their children—but not in their own lifetimes. The process of clearing and enriching the land—and therefore getting beyond a meager existence—would take at least a generation to accomplish.

Starting fires was one method that farmers used to clear their lands and improve the soil. The resultant product, ash, actually was a cash crop. After he plowed as much ash as he needed into his soil, the farmer would sell the remainder on the open market for the manufacture of soap, glass, and bleached cloth. And of course, beavers, ox, and minks were still around for farmers to trap and sell for additional income when winter set in.

Corn and wheat were the major crops, and some fruits (such as apples and pears) were popular. Farmers also raised hogs, both for private consumption and to bring to market. Curiously, ginseng cultivation was popular back then in the United States; the practice faded, but now ginseng is making a comeback as a Chinese herbal remedy. It was cultivated and developed in the Rochester area and other areas of western New York State.

To the west, lumber became a big industry. After clearing one forest, the nomadic lumbermen would advance farther west, and the settlers would come in behind them. In 1850, the Great Lakes area had seven vessels that specifically carried lumber; 45 years later there were 700 lumber freighters.

During all this intense harvesting and selling of lumber—where the market was still mostly on the East Coast—some of the logs would fall off the eastbound freighters or barges, become waterlogged, and sink to the bottom. Today people on Lake Ontario have made a cottage industry out of harvesting these underwater logs, which are highly sought after because the wood is of a grain no longer available in today's trees. So divers go down, identify the logs, and haul them up. These logs can be worth $10,000 to $20,000 each. The industry remains small but viable.

Industry

Early in the 1800s, it was possible literally to walk along and pick up iron ore right off the ground to use for smelting iron. Smelting required both ore and wood, which was to power the furnace. However, trees available for this purpose had become increasingly scarce in New York, Ohio, and Pennsylvania. Every 7 tons of iron produced consumed 1 acre of trees. The growing scarcity of raw materials pushed mining operations out toward Michigan, and factories became more concerned about the costs of bringing ore and wood to them. Cheap and effective freight methods became the key to the smelting industry because foundries were so bulky and expensive that businesses could not just pick up and leave when local supplies were exhausted.

Direct Route: Oswego to Sackets Harbor/Henderson Harbor

If you want, you can also hug the coastline after exiting the Oswego Harbor. Follow a very indirect course along the shoreline (about 1½ miles offshore). Go around the curve of Mexico Bay to the inside of Stony Island but east of Stony Point. This route is not popular because it is so much longer and is not

---

friendly to "cruiser"-sized boats. However, because this eastern end of Lake Ontario is a favorite camping area for many regional residents, a good support infrastructure for trailer-sized boats has been developed. Please note that most of these "marina" facilities are in campgrounds, and the presence of electrical outlets and showers does not mean that larger cruisers can fit. These resources were often put in for land-based campers, not boaters. Therefore, you cannot assume that a marina easily can accommodate your craft based on the marina amenities listed in this book.

As you cruise the coast eastward, Mexico Point, about 15 miles from Oswego, is your first stopping option. A good halfway reference point is the electrical power plant with its wide cooling tower. Mexico Point is off the lake within a breakwater-protected harbor/river entrance for the Little Salmon River. Lighted red marker #2 and lighted green marker #1 mark the entrance channel. The best approach is to go east of the entrance and then come in on a course that angles back west as well as south, because the breakwater on the western (red) side extends farther into the lake than the eastern (green) one.

**Dowey Dale Campground and Marina
(315) 963-7895**

Storm protection: √√
Scenic: * *
Marina-reported approach depths: 4-7 feet
Marina-reported dockside depths: 2-4 feet
Gas
Waste pump-out
Rest rooms

Showers
Power connections: 15A/125V
VHF-monitored channel: 68

**Salmon Co. Campground and Marina (315)
963-8049**

Storm protection: √√
Scenic: * *
Marina-reported approach depths: 4-6 feet
Marina-reported dockside depths: 2-4 feet
Gas
Waste pump-out
Rest rooms
Barbecues
Picnic tables
Power connection: 15A/125V
Woodworking repairs
Fiberglass repairs
Mechanical repairs
Gas-engine repairs
Stern-drive repairs
Outboard-motor repairs
Forklift
Ship's store
VHF-monitored channel: 68

Four miles farther east and turning north is the Salmon River entrance. It is best identified by its abandoned lighthouse, which has been decommissioned since 1850, when persistent shoaling problems at the entrance caused the U.S. government to abandon plans to maintain a viable commercial port here. It also is marked with aid-to-navigation lights: the red #2 is at 36 feet, and the green #3 is at 34 feet. It can be shoal, so please ask about conditions.

Lighthouse Marina (315) 298-6688

Storm protection: not rated
Scenic: * * *
**Marina-reported approach depths: contact
marina**

Marina-reported dockside depths: contact marina
Gas
Diesel
Waste pump-out
Rest rooms
Barbecues
Picnic tables
Power connections: 15A/125V (limited), 30A/125V (limited)
Woodworking repairs
Fiberglass repairs
Below-waterline repairs
Mechanical repairs
Gas-engine repairs
Diesel repairs
Stern-drive repairs
Outboard-motor repairs
Generator repairs
Travelift/hoist: for boats up to 34 feet long
Ship's store
VHF-monitored channel: all

Another 8 miles along the coast as you cruise northward is the entrance to North Pond, a 3-by-1-mile pond with a shallow entrance. I would call it a bay if I were naming it. There are numerous marinas inside, but the entrance is the problem. It can be shoal to 2 to 3 feet, the channel's location moves around, and the entrance is marked by private aids to navigation. Either have current local knowledge or trail a boat that you know draws more water than you do and follow its path exactly. Marinas are listed clockwise from the north.

Green Point Marina (315) 387-3513

Storm protection: √√√
Scenic: * *
Marina-reported approach depths: contact marina

Marina-reported dockside depths: contact marina
Gas
Rest rooms
Showers
Dockside water
Barbecues
Picnic tables
Power connections: limited 15A/125V
Fiberglass repairs
Mechanical repairs
Gas-engine repairs
Stern-drive repairs
Outboard-motor repairs
Ship's store
What's special: rents out cottages
VHF-monitored channel: 68

Reiter's Marina (315) 387-3881

Storm protection: √√√
Scenic: * *
Marina-reported approach depths: contact marina
Marina-reported dockside depths: contact marina
Gas-engine repairs
Ship's store
Restaurant: off site
Grocery: off site
Convenience store: off site

Seber's Shores Marina (315) 387-5502

Storm protection: √√√
Scenic: * * *
Marina-reported approach depths: contact marina
Marina-reported dockside depths: contact marina
Rest rooms
Showers
Picnic tables

Yard trailer/two vehicle
Ship's store
Restaurant: off site

Jones Marina (315) 387-3775

Storm protection: √√
Scenic: *
Marina-reported approach depths: contact
    marina
Marina-reported dockside depths: contact
    marina
Gas
Picnic tables
Power connections: 15A/125V
VHF-monitored channel: 68

Carnsie's Marina (315) 387-3554

Storm protection: √
Scenic: *
Marina-reported approach depths: contact
    marina
Marina-reported dockside depths: contact
    marina
Rest rooms
Power connections: 15A/125V
Restaurant: off site
Grocery: off site

North Sandy Pond Marina (315) 387-3522

Storm protection: √
Scenic: *
Marina-reported approach depths: contact
    marina
Marina-reported dockside depths: contact
    marina
Gas
Rest rooms
Showers
Picnic tables
Restaurant: on site
VHF-monitored channel: all

Eleven miles north of North Pond and 3½ miles south of the abandoned Stony Point Lighthouse, which was decommissioned in 1869, is the entrance to Stony Point Creek. On the north shore just off the lake and inside the creek is Stony Creek Marina.

Stony Creek Marina (315) 938-5580

Storm protection: √
Scenic: * * *
Marina-reported approach depths: 4-9 feet
Marina-reported dockside depths: 1-4 feet
Gas
Waste pump-out
Rest rooms
Showers
Dockside water
Power connections: 15A/125V
VHF-monitored channel: all

North of Stony Creek the land juts out far enough that following the coast line 1½ miles out will cause you to head northwest for a bit. This is Stony Point, which is marked by both the abandoned lighthouse and the current light 30 feet off the water level. Now deep water is close in toward land. You may elect to cruise about a half-mile offshore, but only for a short time. The channel waterway between Stony Point and Stony Island is about a distance of 2 miles wide, and its sister to the west, Galloo Island, is about an additional 3 miles offshore from Stony Island.

> **SKIPPER TIP:** North of Stony Point is a shoal area.

This dangerous shallow area is between you and the Lime Barrel Shoal buoy #1 (green). You must stay well off (at least 1 mile) the land area until you are parallel to this buoy to avoid the shoal. Once parallel (as far north as the buoy), turn so as to head into a point close to but just south of green buoy #1. You want to pass the buoy on your port side as you head east.

Henderson Harbor

Henderson Harbor is in the southern corner of Henderson Bay, which is large—about 2 miles wide by 6½ miles long in a northeast-to-southwest direction. Its most popular entrance is immediately south of Lime Barrel Shoal green light #1 and north of Six Town Point. Do not go too close to Six Town Point; it is rocky and has a shallower water depth. All of this is just about centered on the bay's western edge. Depths should be 12 to 15 feet. You can go north of here and enter in at least two other places, but why? Henderson Harbor is to the south, and the buoy is the best reference point from which to navigate. It is now 3½ miles south to Henderson Harbor.

Here are the marinas north-to-south in a clockwise direction.

RCR Yachts (315) 938-5494

Storm protection: √√√
Scenic: * *
Marina-reported approach depths: 7-11 feet
Marina-reported dockside depths: 2-5 feet
Gas
Diesel
Waste pump-out
Rest rooms
Showers
Dockside water
Power connections: 30A/125V
Woodworking repairs
Fiberglass repairs

Below-waterline repairs
Mechanical repairs
Gas-engine repairs
Travelift/hoist: 20 tons
Ship's store
Restaurant: off site
Marina office is in the main lodge
VHF-monitored channel: 09, 10

Captains Cove Motel Marina (315) 939-5718

Storm protection: √
Scenic: * *
Marina-reported approach depths: 7-9 feet
Marina-reported dockside depths: 2-4 feet
Rest rooms
Dockside water
Power connections: 15A/125V
What's special: also a motel

Cornell's Marina (315) 938-5523

Storm protection: √√√
Scenic: *
Marina-reported approach depths: 2-8 feet
Marina-reported dockside depths: 2-3 feet
Fiberglass repairs
Welding
Mechanical repairs
Gas-engine repairs
Diesel repairs
Stern-drive repairs
Outboard-motor repairs
Generator repairs
What's special: best known for repairs

Harbor Marina (315) 938-5311

Storm protection: √√√
Scenic: *
Marina-reported approach depths: 2-4 feet
Marina-reported dockside depths: 2-4 feet
Rest rooms

Showers
Dockside water
Power connections: 15A/125V
Mechanical repairs
Gas-engine repairs
Stern-drive repairs
Outboard-motor repairs
Generator repairs
Ship's store
What's special: factory-trained mechanics

Henderson Yacht Club (315) 938-9216

Storm protection: √√
Scenic: * * *
Marina-reported approach depths: 3-9 feet
Marina-reported dockside depths: 3-5 feet
Rest rooms
Showers
Barbecues
Picnic tables
Power connections: 15A/125V
What's special: private yacht club

Harbor's End (315) 938-5452

Storm protection: √√√
Scenic: *
Marina-reported approach depths: 3-5 feet
Marina-reported dockside depths: 2-3 feet
Gas
Rest rooms
Power connections: 30A/125V
Fiberglass repairs
Below-waterline repairs
Mechanical repairs
Gas-engine repairs
Generator repairs
Travelift/hoist: 15 tons

Lake Ontario Mariners (315) 938-5222

Storm protection: √√√
Scenic: * * *

Marina-reported approach depths: 3-5 feet
Marina-reported dockside depths: 3-4 feet
Gas
Waste pump-out
Rest rooms
Showers
Laundry
Dockside water
Barbecues
Picnic tables
Power connections: 30A/125V
Fiberglass repairs
Below-waterline repairs
Mechanical repairs
Gas-engine repairs
Generator repairs
Travelift/hoist: 20 tons
Ship's store
VHF-monitored channel: 19

Sackets Harbor

Just inside Black River Bay and on its south shore, Sackets Harbor has had a naval presence since the French first explored Lake Ontario. Today there is a nice town, settled in 1801, a museum, and three marinas. Commercial lumber freight was an alternative to military-related commerce in the town's early years. Activities during the War of 1812 seemed to cement Sackets Harbor's place in history books. The British troops holed up nearby—in Kingston, on Lake Ontario's Canadian north shore—and the Americans pumped men and materials into Sackets Harbor. A fleet was built and outfitted here for that war effort. Now it is a cruising ground for pleasure boaters. Note that it is an enforced no-wake zone once you pass the lighted red aid to navigation at a height of 25 feet, just outside the marina area. Also, some surge can occur at all the marinas in this area.

Navy Point Marina in Sackets Harbor, New York

Navy Point Marina (315) 646-3364

Storm protection: √√√
Scenic: * * *
Marina-reported approach depths: 7-11
 feet
Marina-reported dockside depths: 4-7 feet
Gas
Diesel
Waste pump-out
Rest rooms
Showers
Dockside water
Picnic tables
Power connections: 30A/125V
Woodworking repairs
Welding
Below-waterline repairs
Mechanical repairs
Gas-engine repairs
Diesel repairs
Generator repairs
Travelift/hoist: 20 tons
Ship's store
Restaurant: off site
Deli: off site
Grocery: off site
Convenience store: off site
What's special: town and museum
VHF-monitored channel: 09

Grunerts Marina (315) 654-2300

Storm protection: √
Scenic: *
Marina-reported approach depths: 2-4 feet

Marina-reported dockside depths: 2-3 feet
Gas
Rest rooms
Showers
Dockside water
Power connections: 15A/125V
Restaurant: off site
Deli: off site
Grocery: off site
Convenience store: off site
What's special: town and museum

Liberty Yachts (315) 646-2001

Storm protection: √
Scenic: *

Marina-reported approach depths: 2-6 feet
Marina-reported dockside depths: 2-4 feet
Rest rooms
Showers
Dockside water
Barbecues
Picnic tables
Power connections: 15A/125V
Travelift/hoist: 20 tons
Restaurant: off site
Deli: off site
Grocery: off site
Convenience store: off site
What's special: town and museum
VHF-monitored channel: all

I want my boat behind my home, too!

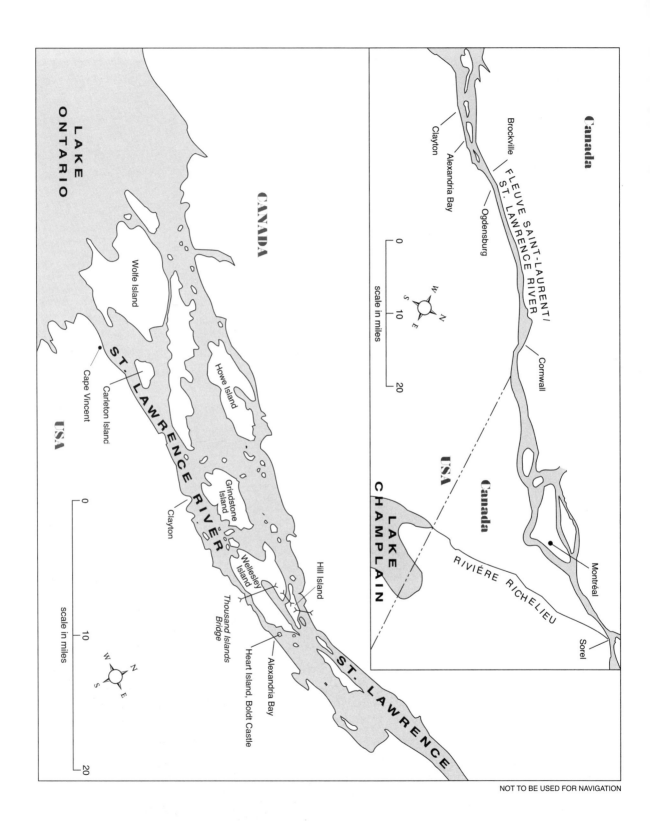

LAKE ONTARIO

CANADA

CANADA

USA

St. Lawrence River

Wolfe Island

Howe Island

Cape Vincent

Carleton Island

Grindstone Island

Clayton

Wellesley Island

Thousand Islands Bridge

Heart Island, Boldt Castle

Alexandria Bay

Hill Island

ST. LAWRENCE

0   10   20
scale in miles

N
W   E
S

FLEUVE SAINT-LAURENT / ST. LAWRENCE RIVER

Canada

Clayton

Alexandria Bay

Brockville

Ogdensburg

Cornwall

USA

Canada

Montréal

Sorel

RIVIÉRE RICHELIEU

LAKE CHAMPLAIN

0   10   20
scale in miles

N
W   E
S

NOT TO BE USED FOR NAVIGATION

CHAPTER 11

The Thousand Islands and the St. Lawrence River

SKIPPER TIP: You will need NOAA charts 14767, 14774, 14773, and 14772 for the trip from Clayton to Alexandria Bay.

Eleven miles apart on the New York side of the St. Lawrence, you'll find Clayton and Alexandria Bay—the jumping-off points for the Thousand Islands' summer residents and visitors.

Boats play a significant role in this island-hopping lifestyle and are far more important to the people of this area than other modes of transportation. Is my envy obvious? There aren't too many places in America where the automobile doesn't reign supreme!

Railroads initially brought people to these two towns from downstate, but once people arrived in the area, boats became the sole source of transportation. Over the last 100 years all supplies, trash, people, and pets have used boats to connect to shore. Children needed boats to get away from their parents. Dads needed them to join the family for the weekend after working on the mainland during the week. Staff needed them to bring back groceries to restock larders. And friends used them to visit other islanders.

Clayton hosts an annual classic boat show in early August on the grounds of its must-see antique-boat museum.

Stocking the Summer Islands

A family retreating to its island home for the summer did not travel lightly. Mom, dad, children, friends, close relatives, nannies, house and grounds staff, and operators and maintenance people for the boats—all would often be accommodated on a family's island homestead (not to mention pets and the occasional milking cow, too). Trunks and crates accompanied each entourage. Linens and china that had been removed from the previous summer's stay were brought back. If someone played music or had lessons assigned over the summer, a piano would be included in the family's freight. Paint, other maintenance supplies, and new annual plantings would either come with them or soon follow. Food was brought in out of necessity. All of this, of course, came to the island property by watercraft.

Different Boats for Different Folks

Various uses spurred the development of different types of boats over the years. Guides here have taken "city folk" freshwater fishing among the islands for well over 100 years. These guides, many of whom would build and repair their own craft over the winter months, developed rather efficient craft to take themselves and their clients to and from the best fishing locations. Thus, the Thousand Islands skiff was born, and each builder in the area had his favorite length, beam, depth, and shape for this design concept. Although still a workboat, any craft that does a job more efficiently than its counterparts can be admired by all boaters. So it goes for Thousand Islands skiffs.

When power came to boats, the Thousand Islands boaters embraced it. At first they put

engines powered by steam, gas, diesel, and naphtha into anything that floated. Then various combinations of engines and hull shapes started to gain popularity. The advent of boat racing was one of the spurs toward refining powerboats. The Thousand Islands were a hotbed for powerboat racing through the early 1950s. A series of slim-hipped runabouts named *P.D.Q.* ("Pretty Damn Quick") ran the river over the first quarter of the twentieth century. In their successive incarnations, the six runabouts in the *P.D.Q.* series almost mirror the early history and development of fast powerboats.

One local speedboat, *Pardon Me*, was built in Alexandria Bay. She is considered the world's largest runabout (48 feet) and is powered by a 1500-hp PT boat engine for really amazing performance. She is not just memorable for her performance, though—her planks are stained and brightly finished like a grand piano! Despite her size, she's really a day boat, since there are no overnight accommodations on board. You'll find *Pardon Me* on display in Clayton's Antique Boat Museum.

Canoes, launches, scows, yachts, tugs, fireboats, police boats, immigration boats, customs boats, dredges, skiffs, rowboats, houseboats, utilities, speedboats, Prohibition rumrunners, hydroplanes—all were built, used, and valued by the island residents. This museum is a boater's paradise that you and your crew can enjoy and admire.

While this chapter only describes the one main channel for the Thousand Islands, there are other marked channels and multiple cruising areas that are used by local boaters. Visitors who want to explore outside the main channel typically follow in the wake of local traffic. In the main channel, commercial freighters carry cargo between the Great Lakes and the world via the Atlantic Ocean, so there's plenty of water depth for your cruiser in that waterway. Elsewhere, who knows? The riverbed is primarily rock, as are the islands and the many shoals—and there are many of them. Going "bump on the bottom" here hurts. You must have up-to-date charts. Be sure to heed any recent "Local Notice to Mariners" on your charts. Be even safer and follow a larger boat when outside a known channel.

Leaving Cape Vincent, pick up green buoy #241 and then red buoy #240, and once again you're in the main channel headed east toward the town of Clayton. This channel takes you around the north side of Carleton Island. There is also a range ahead on Wolfe Island—at 35 and 70 feet—so when these are in alignment, your craft is in this reach.

Now use green buoy #237 and green buoy #235 to round Carleton Island. Pick up red buoy #234 2½ miles ahead, just off the Wolfe Island shore. As you get closer, look for green buoy #233 and adjust your heading now that you know the width of the channel.

Carleton Island

Used as a position from which to control the river, British forces built and maintained a fort here for more than 30 years before the War of 1812. At one time, 7,000 solders were assigned here. The last six Brits at the fort were "conquered" by a few Americans in an unauthorized raid led by a barkeep early in the war. Most of the fort has been disassembled and moved to another location near Kingston, Ontario.

You'll find Cedar Point 1½ miles past green buoy #233 and three-eighths of a mile past

Linda Island (quarter-mile long) that is marked by green buoy #231 at 33 feet high. There is a marina inside the point on its southeast shore. Stay in 25 feet of water depth until you are quite near the facility.

**Clark Bus and Marine/Cedar Point Marina
    (315) 654-2522**

Storm protection: √√
Scenic: * * *
Marina-reported approach depths: 7-10 feet
Marina-reported dockside depths: 3-6 feet
Gas
Waste pump-out
Rest rooms
Showers
Power connections: 15A/125V
Convenience store: on site
**What's special: home to flying tours over
    the islands**

Wolfe Island

Here Indians hunted bear, fox, and deer—however, the bear are no longer on this island, I'm told. Europeans felled the natural timber and quarried the limestone. Later, farming took over. The population surged to 3,600 during the American Civil War, but today the island has about one-third of that population.

Wolfe Island has a canal in the middle of it, as shown on your chart. It was closed in 1932 after 75 years of use. Locals have fun confusing visitors by giving directions based on above or below the old canal.

At the eastern end of the 16-mile-long Wolfe Island is the Wolfe Island Cut. This channel can take you over to other channels and a vast additional cruising area as a wonderful side trip. It is marked by red and green navigation aids at each of the ends of its three-quarter-mile duration. There is an additional buoy (unlit) in the middle of its eastern side. By the way, you can cruise all day in and out of U.S. and Canadian waters as long as you start and end in the same country and do not touch land during the trip.

Winter

Ice can and has closed the St. Lawrence River in winter. Then islanders have to resort to other means to connect with the mainland. Over the last thousand years walking, horses or other animals, snowmobiles, ski planes, sleighs and/or sleds have been the various means used. Farmers, ranchers, residents, military forces, deserters, escaped convicts, and smugglers all had a need to cross the frozen barrier.

Smugglers have always used the Thousand Islands area of the St. Lawrence River to do their unique type of work. During the Prohibition era—when selling liquor was illegal in the United States—it was perfectly legal in Canada. What a temptation! The speakeasies in U.S. cities would pay top dollar for something that was available only a mile or two away. The many islands here offered shelter and hiding places from the law—and only from the law. The islanders themselves did not consider liquor smuggling much different than fishing. Times were tough and the winters were cold. They had to put food on the table any way they could, and they did not always think that "the law" represented their best interests.

One smuggler reportedly would load a sleigh with illegal liquor and have his horse pull the load, on its own, across the ice to the other side. This animal, much like a homing pigeon, knew the "home barn" on either end of the short route. Other horses were renowned for their ability to avoid bad ice.

Bad or thin ice was an off-and-on problem. The river froze solid only during the coldest times. On the "shoulders" of these hard freezes, ice would have spots that would not support a horse or sleigh without cracking and letting them fall in.

A seemingly cruel but popular method of saving a horse was developed. An extra rope with a slipknot was tied around the horse's throat. If the horse fell through the ice, this rope was pulled tight with a yank, which stopped the passage of air, and the internalized air made the animal more buoyant. The horse was then pushed back down under the water—a wood beam would quickly be shoved under the animal as it popped back up to the surface. It could then be pulled out of a section of bad ice.

In recent times, automobiles have broken through the ice, too. Goods on a truck going to market have been swallowed up by cracks in the ice, driver and all. Teenagers, borrowing the family car for some special midnight fun run, have had a surprise dunking. Local communities have passed laws making some of this illegal today.

The next point is Bartlett Point. It somewhat hides the town of Clayton, which lies just east of it. The point is marked by green buoy #227, fixed at 23 feet. Immediately inside the bay, east of Bartlett Point, is the Clayton Yacht Club. The bay, which is on the western side of Clayton, is at least 6 feet deep about as far into it as the Clayton Municipal Dock. On a sunny day several runabouts circle this bay continuously. Many of these are classic wooden speedboats that are perfectly detailed, polished, and varnished to a furniture-grade finish. Be careful: the sun can bounce off the chrome and seem just like a flash from a camera! Smile for the camera and at the beautiful boating scene now before you.

Clayton

The town of Clayton occupies the entire point. Founded in 1822, it is both six blocks wide and long. The town was originally named Cornelia, only to be renamed Clayton in 1831 to honor John M. Clayton, a United States senator.

Boaters will find everything they need here: groceries, restaurants (you *must* try the Thousand Islands salad dressing—it was invented here), hardware stores, bars, pharmacy, library, marine stores, and launderette. All marinas are in town, too.

"High season" is August, when both the air and water temperatures are warmest. Clayton is full during the two weekends that month when the museum hosts its special events. However, any time children are on their summer vacations

CLAYTON

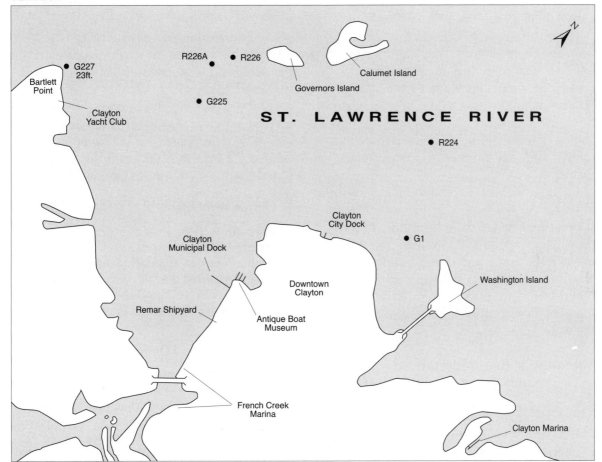

NOT TO BE USED FOR NAVIGATION

constitutes "the season." Try Alexandria Bay as a back-up place to stay and rent a car to visit Clayton for a day. The two towns are about a half-hour apart by car from dock to dock.

Early September also is very nice. I have visited here at different times throughout July, August, and late September. I almost always have had to put on a jacket during the September visit because any wind chilled the air quickly, even with strong, bright sunlight. But what a joy! Although the town seems comparatively empty by then, you still have access to all the amenities, and the water seems to be that much lovelier in the lower sun angles of early fall afternoons.

Do not hesitate to ride on the *Uncle Sam* tour boat before you go cruising outside the marked channels. It is an excellent way to scout out what you want to see and gives boaters who are new to the area a sense of boating "Thousand Islands style." It's a great source of regional lore and provides an opportunity to ask questions of very knowledgeable locals.

Clayton has built or repaired boats for most of its history. During World War II, 100-foot submarine chasers were built here as part of the town's war efforts. More than one shipyard in town has employed over a hundred people at a time. Small boats also were made in town. Hand-built in wood by a small workforce, many of these craft kept locals and tourists on the water.

The Antique Boat Museum

The Antique Boat Museum (750 Mary St.) is a must-see for any boat cruiser who comes within 100 miles! If you cannot come by boat, rent a car and make the trip. The museum in Clayton houses exhibits of regional boats, with an emphasis on those beautifully varnished mahogany speedboats. The museum bills itself as "the finest collection of historic freshwater boats and engines in North America," and I believe them! It houses 150 antique boats, 250 engines, and assorted nautical memorabilia. Admission is charged, but it's not the sole source of funding. A collection of this quality and selection has only been possible because the museum has a fairly long list of generous benefactors. The gift shop here can be an hour-long exploration by itself; you'll very rarely find a shop with as many books, objects, magazines, and posters on boating topics as this one. Antique boat rides are offered on an ongoing basis. The Classic Boat Show is held at the museum, usually on the first weekend in August—the absolute "peak" weekend. Every other year on the third weekend in August, when the second-heaviest volume of activity takes place, there are classic racing-boat demonstrations. The museum also operates a boat-building school. Call (315) 686-4104 for more information.

Clayton Yacht Club

Storm protection: √√
Scenic: * * *
Marina-reported approach depths: 3-7 feet
Marina-reported dockside depths: 2-4 feet
What's special: private club (phone number unavailable for publication)

Clayton Municipal Dock

Storm protection: not rated
Scenic: * *
Marina-reported approach depths: 6-10 feet
Marina-reported dockside depths: 4-6 feet
Wharf

What's special: on the west side of town and for short-term tie-ups only; usually filled up early in the day by local runabouts; electricity is available; overnight stays sometimes accommodated; next to museum and in town—useful while shopping, which is its intended purpose; no telephone

Clayton City Dock

Storm protection: not rated
Scenic: *
Marina-reported approach depths: 10-30 feet
Marina-reported dockside depths: 3-8 feet
What's special: short-term dockage for picking up supplies; good dinghy dock; no telephone

Antique Boat Museum (315) 686-4104

Storm protection: √√
Scenic: * * * *
Marina-reported approach depths: 2-6 feet
Marina-reported dockside depths: 3-5 feet
Gift shop
What's special: limited tie-ups for museum members only; memberships offered

Remar Shipyard (315) 686-4170, 686-3579

Storm protection: √√√
Scenic: * *
Marina-reported approach depths: 4-6 feet
Marina-reported dockside depths: 3-5 feet
Gas
Diesel
Waste pump-out
Rest rooms
Showers
Laundry
Power connections: 15A/125V
Woodworking repairs
Fiberglass repairs

Welding
Below-waterline repairs
Mechanical repairs
Travelift/hoist: 12 tons
Ship's store
Restaurant: off site
Grocery: off site
What's special: just inside and past the municipal dock in the west bay; a very popular fuel stop and a resource for live bait; houseboats and runabouts can be rented here

French Creek Marina (315) 686-3621

Storm protection: √√√
Scenic: * * *
Marina-reported approach depths: 3-5 feet
Marina-reported dockside depths: 2-3 feet
Gas
Diesel
Rest rooms
Showers
Laundry
Dockside water
Power connections: 30A/125V, 50A/125V
Woodworking repairs
Fiberglass repairs
Welding
Mechanical repairs
Gas-engine repairs
Diesel repairs
Stern-drive repairs
Outboard-motor repairs
Generator repairs
Ship's store
What's special: farther inside the cove than Remar Shipyard

Clayton Marina (315) 686-3378

Storm protection: √√√
Scenic: * * *
Marina-reported approach depths: 2-5 feet

Marina-reported dockside depths: 2-4 feet
Gas
Rest rooms
Showers
Dockside water
Power connection: 15A/125V
Mechanical repairs
Gas-engine repairs
Stern-drive repairs
Outboard-motor repairs
Ship's store
What's special: 1 mile east of town and past
   Washington Island

Overview: Clayton to Alexandria Bay

Alexandria Bay is 11 miles farther east on the St. Lawrence River. This route becomes very protected and offers a very scenic cruise along the way. The multitude of rock islands appears rugged but peaceful, with grass and trees clinging onto the sparse ground to keep from sliding into the dark water. The only bridge clearance ahead is the Thousand Islands Bridge (vertical clearance of 152 feet). Other than that, it is a well-marked channel with open cruising all the way.

A mile and a quarter east of Clayton are two sets of markers for the channel. First is the red fixed marker #222 at 28 feet; 1,000 feet farther east is the green buoy #221. Next you'll see green #217A and then red #218. Now pick out green #217 just over a mile ahead. From there, spot red #216A a half-mile away and red #216 a quarter-mile farther east.

The Thousand Islands Bridge, with 152-foot vertical clearance, is 2¾ miles ahead. This passage between Wellesley Island to your port and

A typical scene in the Thousand Islands: wooded, rugged isles with powerboats hopping between them.

the mainland to the south is called the American Narrows. Both land areas are on the U.S. side of the border. The channel narrows to a width of 500 feet here. Water depths range from 29 feet to almost 240 feet. There can be a 1- to 3-knot current (you are going with it as you head east) within this American Narrows section.

On the south shore at fixed green #199 at 28 feet (the Comfort Shoal Light), you'll find Keewaydin State Park and Marina. Stay closer to the light than Bella Vista Island on the west—say a ratio of one-third to two-thirds duration of the space between them. Look out for an unmarked shoal spot off the island that you need to avoid. You should be in at least 25-foot-deep water all the way.

> **SKIPPER TIP:** Boaters with pets need to have proof of rabies inoculation. Pets must be leashed as well if you bring them ashore in these state parks.

The marina is in its own small bay and has a floating tire breakwater to minimize boat wakes and wave action within it. Water depths are 6 to 9 feet except for a few slips closest to land that have 4-foot-deep water. The gas dock is to the south, where it can be shallow.

The marina is 2 miles west of the town of Alexandria Bay.

Keewaydin Marina is two miles from downtown Alexandria Bay. On the grounds of a former estate, it's a magnificent setting for a marina.

Keewaydin State Park and Marina (315)
482-3720; 482-3331

Storm protection: √√√
Scenic: * * * *
Marina-reported approach depths: 9-30
feet
Marina-reported dockside depths: 4-9 feet
Gas
Waste pump-out
Rest rooms
Showers
Dockside water

Barbecues
Picnic tables
Power connections: 15A/125V
What's special: swimming pool

Alexandria Bay

The riverfront resort town of Alexandria Bay holds special memories for anyone who's visited this town and the surrounding islands. It is a first-class summer resort, with specialty shopping, T-shirt shops, dining (local lore claims that Thousand Island dressing was invented *here*,

ALEXANDRIA BAY

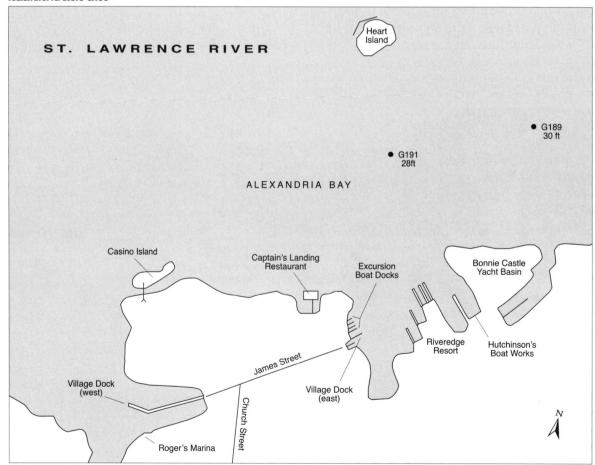

NOT TO BE USED FOR NAVIGATION

It must be a challenge getting into the front door of this cottage when the water levels are elevated in the spring! Behind it is the yacht house for Boldt Castle.

not in Clayton!), bars, nightclubs, and nighttime entertainment at four or five resort properties.

The main tourist street is James Street, which connects the town's two docks. Church Street leads you out of town to Highway 12, which connects to the International Bridge and Clayton to the west. Going the other way on Church Street, you'll find Fuller Street. Look for the Cornwall Store. Although it's not the original building, the site marks the beginning of the town. Azariah Walton, the founder of this business, cut down trees here and on the surrounding islands to sell as firewood to steamboats. That business then expanded into a supply store for the steamboat crew and passengers. Then local farmers and fishermen began to stop by for

supplies. Walton also became a customs agent. He had quite a business until the whole town (as well as the Thousand Islands area) went into the cellar after the stock market crashed in 1929.

Heading down along Fuller Street is the Church of the St. Lawrence. It has functioned as a fair-weather lighthouse of sorts since its steeple is quite a visible landmark for boaters on the river. If you go in, look at the yacht-like standard of the interior woodwork. It is so finely joined you'd think it could float. If you just walk by it, notice the pink-toned granite that makes up the foundation. This stone came from a local quarry. Now cross Fuller Street and climb all over Scenic View Park, which has great views of the river scene.

This is one of two Hutchinson's Marina locations in Alexandria Bay, offering dockage and full-service repairs.

Boldt Castle

George Boldt bought Hart Island in 1895 and changed its name to Heart. He even reconfigured the island's shoreline shape to look more like a heart. The seller was the estate of E. Kirk Hart (who passed away in 1893). Hart had named the island after himself because he disliked its former name, Hemlock Island. Boldt, the manager-owner of a premium hotel in Philadelphia and the Waldorf Astoria in New York City, committed much energy to making the islands popular with the superwealthy set over the next 10 years. His descendants still summer in the islands on one of his other properties.

You'll find this famous castle on the heart-shaped island directly across the waterway from the Riveredge Resort Hotel. Boldt Castle is a 120-room, four-story castle with a two-story basement whose construction was started by George Boldt as a gift for his wife, Louise. When she died in 1904, George Boldt telegrammed to stop all work immediately. Hundreds of craftsmen left their work where it was. Materials stayed crated, and the buildings were abandoned. Boldt had other island properties and continued to use them until his death in 1916 (when he died, he owned 60 boats in the Thousand Islands and had a boathouse with inside slips that could accommodate yachts 128 feet long), but he left Heart Island unfinished, exactly as it was the day his love died.

The castle deteriorated until 1977, when the Thousand Islands International Council took

A close-up of Mr. Boldt's yacht house, with a ceiling height and doors that once opened to accommodate a 128-foot yacht.

it over and restored it. It is accessible by way of your own private craft or by tour boat. Inquire at (800) 847-5263.

Regardless of where you stay, make it a point to find out what entertainment the resorts are offering and see at least two of these. Also, dine at least once in the Riveredge Hotel's elegant top-floor dining room either for Sunday brunch or dinner. Music, champagne, fine food, and the best view in town of Boldt's Castle are there for you and your crew to enjoy. You'll cherish the memory of your dining experience here.

First settled in 1818, Alexandria Bay only hit its current status of resort town to the Thousand Islands after 1880; until then, potash, barrel staves, and logs of native pine and oak were its industries. In 1823 Azariah Walton set up his steamboat station at the previously men-

tioned Cornwall Store. In 1830 an observer commented in his diary that there were about a dozen buildings in this area. By the 1870s community and business growth was exploding in several ways. A 65-passenger tour boat was put in service to take visitors around a few of the Thousand Islands for a five-cent fare, and a 300-room hotel was opened.

Moreover, in 1872 George Pullman (of railroad-car fame) had President Ulysses S. Grant vacation on his island. The press following the president liked what they saw and wrote glowing reports in all their newspapers. Pullman had bought the then-named Sweet Island in 1864. He was such a powerhouse businessman that the 1.6-acre island took on his name in local usage. The Methodist Church established a campground for its congregation in the Thousand Islands in 1874. In that same season Mr. Visger, the town boat operator, replaced his boat with one that could carry 300 passengers per trip.

The railroad in 1886 connected the islands with New York City. It was a 12-hour ride and required a transfer at Utica. However, the railroad opened up the area to the large number of wealthy residents and businessmen of the city. In 1888, a 500-passenger tour boat was put into service. During the 1890s the tour-boat operation had 20,000 passengers a year. The descendants of these boats that operate today are an excellent way for a boater to get an overview of the islands before cruising independently, because many of these toured areas lack aids to navigation. For example, there is Zavikon Island with a pretty wooden footbridge that connects it to a smaller island owned by the same family, both being their summer retreat. Each island flies a different flag—Zavikon a Canadian one and the connecting island an American flag—because for a long time the border was thought to run through the waterway crossed by the family's footbridge. Both islands are now thought to be Canadian, but the tradition of the separate flags continues.

In 1906 the ACA (American Canoe Association) bought a nearby island, Sugar Island, to encourage families to start canoeing and camping there during summers. These families were not superwealthy, but they did fall in love

The Captain's Landing restaurant in Alexandria Bay offers free dockage to diners.

A rare view: the Riveredge Hotel with empty docks. It must be off-season, since this popular spot is usually crowded with boats.

with the summer lifestyle. Many of the smaller islands were subsequently sold to families who wanted more amenities than a community campground offered.

Growth continued until the 1929 Wall Street crash and the Great Depression. The town and surrounding area went into a long period of decline until after World War II. Since then, in an uneven climb, it has again become a top destination for tourists.

Cruiser's note: The Thousand Islands cruising area continues east from Alexandria Bay for another 17 miles.

Riveredge Hotel (315) 482-9917

Storm protection: √√
Scenic: * * * *
Marina-reported approach depths: 5-10 feet
Marina-reported dockside depths: 4-8 feet

Wharf
Rest rooms
Showers
Laundry
Dockside water
Power connections: 30A/125V, 50A/125V
Gift shop
Souvenir store
Restaurant: on site (two)
Grocery: off site
Convenience store: off site
What's special: new upscale resort with gym, indoor and outdoor pools, hot tub, separate bathhouse for marina tenants, and on-site dockmaster; near town

Hutchinson's Boat Works (315) 482-9931

Storm protection: √√√
Scenic: * * *
Marina-reported approach depths: 4-7 feet

Marina-reported dockside depths: 2-6 feet
Gas
Diesel
Waste pump-out
Rest rooms
Showers
Laundry
Dockside water
Power connections: 30A/125V, 50A/125V,
    50A/220V
Woodworking repairs
Fiberglass repairs
Welding
Below-waterline repairs
Mechanical repairs
Gas-engine repairs
Diesel repairs
Stern-drive repairs
Generator repairs
Travelift/hoist: to 45-foot yachts
Ship's store
Gift shop
Restaurant: off site
Grocery: off site
Convenience store: off site
What's special: longtime premier repair
    facility; near town

Bonnie Castle Yacht Basin (315) 482-2526

Storm protection: √√√
Scenic: * * * *
Marina-reported approach depths: 3-20 feet
Marina-reported dockside depths: 3-6 feet
Gas
Waste pump-out
Rest rooms
Showers
Laundry
Dockside water
Power connections: 30A/125V
Mechanical repairs
Ship's store
Gift shop

The playhouse on Boldt Island—complete with a bowling alley—was home to the Boldts while they awaited completion of their castle. When Mrs. Boldt died prematurely, all work on the castle ceased, and the testimony of Mr. Boldt's affection for his wife was never completed.

Restaurant: on site
Grocery: off site
What's special: older, very large marina and
    resort complex

Alexandria Bay Village Dock (west)

Storm protection: not rated
Scenic: * * *
Marina-reported approach depths: 8-40 feet

Marina-reported dockside depths: 3-7 feet
What's special: a short-term tie-up while
   shopping—overnight tie-up may be
   arranged for a fee if marinas are full

Alexandria Bay Village Dock (east)

Storm protection: not rated
Scenic: * * *
Marina-reported approach depths: 8-11 feet
Marina-reported dockside depths: 4-6 feet
What's special: a short-term tie-up while
   shopping—may arrange overnight tie-up
   for a fee if marinas are full; dock is right
in the middle of the tour boat landing
and land activity, which can make coming here somewhat confusing and intense

Roger's Marina (315) 482-9461

Storm protection: √√√
Scenic: * *
Marina-reported approach depths: 3-5 feet
Marina-reported dockside depths: 2-4 feet
Gas
Diesel
Rest rooms
Showers

Boldt Castle's power house is quite impressive, since it single-handedly satisfied all the water
and electrical needs of Heart Island.

Dockside water
Woodworking repairs
Fiberglass repairs
Mechanical repairs
Ship's store
Restaurant: off site
Grocery: off site
What's special: limited transients

Captain's Landing Restaurant (315) 482-7777

Storm protection: not rated
Scenic: * * *
Marina-reported approach depths: 5-8 feet
Marina-reported dockside depths: 2-5 feet
Restaurant: on site
What's special: floating dockside dining and bar with excellent views of all the boating activity

East of Alexandria Bay is a good-sized channel except at green #181A and red #182 at 28 feet at Whiskey Island Shoal, where it narrows to one-eighth of a mile wide. An abandoned lighthouse, which was built in 1870 and is next to fixed red light #178 at 28 feet, is now someone's private summer home.

Want to go to church on Sunday? Red buoy #168 at 23 feet is southeast of Jorstadt Island, which is the home of an evangelical group that welcomes everyone to Sunday service. Water depths at the visitors' docks are 3 to 6 feet. The mansion housing their services was originally built for the founder of the Singer sewing-machine company (whose name was Jorstadt). If you stop, look for the secret passages and dungeon.

East of Jorstadt Island is Cedar Island, a boater-accessible state park. Go into the center between the two islands (they look like one island from your perspective) to access the dock. Be cautious: water is shallow here.

Cedar Island State Park Anchorage
Storm protection: ⩔
Scenic: * * * *
Marina-reported approach depths: 25-45 feet

A "laker" in the St. Lawrence Seaway channel passes in front of Boldt Castle.

Marina-reported dockside depths: 1-4 feet
What's special: state park of New York

> **SKIPPER TIP:** You will need Canadian charts 1436, 1435, 1414, 1413, 1412, 1411, 1410, 1409, and 1310. These numbers go from west to east (the direction you are traveling), and some of them will be in metrics—please refer to appendix B for metric-conversion scales.

This section is going to pick up traveling east from Superior Shoal to Montréal, Canada.

Cruising this part of the St. Lawrence River is not that popular for pleasure craft. It just does not have many facilities for pleasure boaters. The heavy big-ship traffic and variable currents also discourage cruisers. Therefore, while there is local small-boat traffic in many spots, you'll find very few cruisers here.

Furthermore, you can get quite a wind chop along the passageway and the marina facilities along it. These facilities are neither plentiful nor complete. Don't misunderstand: There is boating on the St. Lawrence River; it's just that fully found cruising marinas—the kind with on-site fuel and dockage, electricity, repair capacity for larger pleasure yachts—are few and far between. Onshore amenities such as restaurants, stores, and entertainment spots also are rare.

The St. Lawrence Seaway requires a minimum vessel size of 20 feet, and boaters are required to have the Seaway handbook (see chapter 16, "The Welland Canal," for information on how to get one), VHF radio with license, fenders, and other equipment. A knowledge of the French language is helpful, too.

By the way, the St. Lawrence Seaway, with its system of locks that finally allowed proper big-ship traffic passage through, was very late in coming. In 1951 Canada started working on the version of the canal in place today; the United States followed suit under President Eisenhower, funding the system's construction in 1954, and the St. Lawrence Seaway opened in 1957. In the 1800s there was a smaller canal system that just went around the rapids; before that, boats had been off-loaded and portaged around rapids. However, both of these methods were limited to smaller vessels. You might recall that Jacques Cartier's search in 1534 for a more direct route to China was halted by rapids. He named them the Lachine Rapids in recognition of his unsuccessful search for China.

Let's go forward from Cartier's time period another 150 years to 1689, when a Frenchmen named Dollier de Casson decided to build a canal to circumvent one set of the rapids. He began digging a canal intended to be 1½ feet deep—yes, 18 inches deep. However, by the time he had dug more than a mile of his canal, the local Iroquois murdered him and his workers. Years later, a second building attempt at the same location was not successful because of a lack of adequate financing. A small system of canals was finally established early in 1783 that allowed small boats to make it through and around the various rapids. With the Americans building the Erie Canal, Canada built another short canal around the Lachine Rapids in 1825. Because this canal was again undersized and barely adequate, the Erie Canal easily beat it out and became the preferred route for westward travel. In 1833 the Lachine and Beauharnois Canal started to rectify these logistical shortcomings.

Going forward to 1850: Between the canals, the locks, and the river, navigating from Montréal via the St. Lawrence to Lake Ontario was really simple, at least for vessels with rafts of 9 feet. In 1867 the Canadian government authorized an increase in the depth of this canal system to 14 feet, a step that took more than 20 years to complete.

Because the St. Lawrence is a border between the United States and Canada, the two countries have often collaborated on mutually beneficent engineering projects. However, the United States had an advantage: it had the Erie Canal, and it didn't need to transform the St. Lawrence system into an electrical powerhouse until later. On the other hand, Canada needed both electricity and a viable ship canal. The current and the rapids of the St. Lawrence were perfect conduits for electricity if a series of hydroelectric plants were integrated into a canal system by the countries, either separately or together. Once Canada announced in 1951 that it was forging ahead with plans to capture this untapped power source, the United States had no choice but to fall in step with them to make it a joint project by 1954. The allure of electricity was too great, and the series of canals, locks, and waterway that accommodated 14-foot draft vessels was then 60 years old. The renovations required massive manpower. In 1957, on the American side alone, 14,000 men were employed. On July 1, 1958, the new locks were finally opened with a bang. An existing dam that had been installed to let the old canal system stay open while the new system was under construction was detonated; the explosion flooded most of the old system. To commemorate this event, the U.S. Congress designated the Great Lakes as the fourth U.S. coastline.

St. Lawrence Seaway for Cruisers

It's important to know that pleasure craft cannot use sail power in the New York part of the St. Lawrence Seaway locks and canal. Furthermore, the 20-foot minimum length is augmented by a 1-ton minimum weight requirement. Along with a radio license, you'll need a VHF radio with channel 14, which is the Seaway's working channel. As we mentioned before, both fenders and dock lines are needed; in addition to that, life jackets must be worn in all locks and the approaches to and from them. Any of the Seaway locks—whether they're in the Welland Canal or in the section going from Iroquois Lock to Montréal—often will require pleasure boaters to raft up to each other. These raft-up lines are the responsibility of the boat that's rafting up to the boat against the lock wall; they must be able to free themselves from the raft-up if they need to. And speaking of up close and personal situations, a pleasure craft will sometimes be put in a lock with a vessel as big as 328 feet, a situation that can remind you of that old parental lesson: "It's fun to share."

The St. Lawrence Seaway's biggest vessel size is 730 feet long and has a cargo capacity of 28,000 tons. These ships lock through by themselves. The St. Lawrence Seaway section runs from Cape Vincent Harbor and continues to Montréal. The St. Lawrence River, which is 744 miles long from Lake Ontario to the Atlantic Ocean, is tidal below the city of Quebec and is about 90 miles wide at its mouth.

The first cargo vessel from the Great Lakes to go down the St. Lawrence and on to the Atlantic Ocean and Europe did so in 1844, a date actually preceding the completion of the Lachine and Beauharnois Canal. The sailing vessel *Pacific*, commanded by George Todd, left Toronto on Lake Ontario with a cargo of wheat, went down the St. Lawrence, and then crossed the Atlantic to Liverpool, England. By 1859 about 50 vessels a year were clearing the Great Lakes for overseas trips. Exports included flour, pork, hams, copper, lamp oil, nails, hides, and tobacco. Imports consisted of iron, paint, anchovies, tea, crockery, glass, salt, herring and—of course—immigrants. It was not until 1862, however, that a European vessel first came through the St. Lawrence to the Great Lakes.

Off Chippewa Point, look for green buoy #165 at 23 feet; it marks Superior Shoal. Find it and stay away from it, because it marks not only Superior Shoal but also a second shallow area just to its south.

At red buoy #162 and green buoy #163, you need to pick up and follow the course dictated by the range markers ahead at 32 feet and at 61 feet; the course is roughly 027° magnetic. (You must do you own chart work here to develop the proper course to steer; see appendix D.) Pick up fixed red buoy #160 at 28 feet and green buoy #159; before red buoy #152 steer to starboard and locate fixed green buoy #151 at 28 feet.

> **SKIPPER TIP:** The St. Lawrence River narrows ahead. Currents can run 4 knots in this narrow section.

The islands in the Brockville Narrows are the very last of the Thousand Islands. Just past them is the Canadian town of Brockville, which was founded after the American Revolution by British loyalists fleeing for their lives.

Originally named Elizabethtown, it was renamed to honor Major General Brock, who was a hero for the Canadian/British side during the War of 1812.

Stovin Island

Storm protection: not rated
Scenic: * * *
Marina-reported approach depths: 2-20 feet
Marina-reported dockside depths: 2-5 feet
What's special: an island access dock, with a small marked channel on the eastern end of the island to take you around the backside of Stovin Island; no phone

Excel Marina (613) 345-6372

Storm protection: √√√
Scenic: *
Marina-reported approach depths: 8-30 feet
Marina-reported dockside depths: 3-6 feet
Gas
Diesel
Waste pump-out
Rest rooms
Showers
Laundry
Dockside water
Power connections: 30A/125V
Below-waterline repairs
Mechanical repairs
Gas-engine repairs
Diesel repairs
Restaurant: off site
What's special: in town

Across the river is the New York State town of Morristown, which offers a chance to get off the river with Wright's Marina, a full-service facility on Louce Creek. The best approach is after passing the Three Sisters Islands. Now east of these islands, swing to something like a south-southwesterly course.

A fixed bridge keeps cruisers from going very far up Louce Creek. The marina is on the early eastern shore of the pleasure-boat docks that line this creek.

Wright's Marina (315) 375-8841

Storm protection: √√
Scenic: * *
Marina-reported approach depths: 9-13 feet
Marina-reported dockside depths: 3-8 feet
Gas
Waste pump-out
Rest rooms
Showers
Laundry
Dockside water
Power connections: 30A/125V
Mechanical repairs
Gas-engine repairs
Stern-drive repairs
Outboard-motor repairs
Generator repairs
Travelift/hoist: 5 tons
Ship's store
Restaurant: off site
Grocery: off site
**What's special: in town, but town is a slight
    walk upwards**

Channel markers now become less frequent because there are fewer shoal areas to warn you about. Stay well clear of green buoy #135: about a quarter-mile of the area around it is shallow.

It is another 10 miles to Ogdensburg and its sister town on the Canadian north shore, Prescott. Then another 10-mile cruise brings you to the first of the St. Lawrence Seaway locks, the Iroquois.

Ogdensburg, the older and larger of the two cities that lie across the river from each other, was built up around the Oswegatchie River from 1747 onward. It has a large collection of Frederic Remington's sculptures and paintings in the nearby museum, which is close to the marina and waterfront. Accessing the marinas requires pleasure boaters to rely on privately maintained navigation aids. The river has pushed its outfall far into the St. Lawrence River. Extending out farther from the western shore side are pilings, which are the remains of an old ferry pier. You must stay between the red and green buoys until you are near shore to avoid hazards like these.

Ogdensburg Alliance Marina (315) 393-1688

Storm protection: √
Scenic: *
Marina-reported approach depths: 7-15 feet
Marina-reported dockside depths: 3-10 feet
Gas
Rest rooms
Showers
Dockside water
Power connections: 15A/125V
Mechanical repairs
Ship's store
Restaurant: on site
Grocery: off site
What's special: courtesy car

The Lower Lakes Terminal, a major grain loading point for the Province of Ontario, is on the north shore east of Prescott.

Next up is the fixed bridge (vertical clearance of 129 feet reported) that connects the two countries at Chimney Point (New York) and Johnstown (Canada). At the bridge the channel narrows and a series of islands dot each side of it. Aids to navigation are spaced 2,000 to 5,000 feet apart.

SKIPPER TIP: There is a set of range markers on Gallop Island 2½ miles ahead at 28 feet and 48 feet—keep these lined up on top of one another and you will be in the channel.

Also along the Canadian shore is first the passageway, the North Channel, which continues east into the Old Gallop Canal. This combined route parallels the St. Lawrence River to the Iroquois Lock and was used to make the Great Lakes accessible to the Atlantic Ocean. Although local boaters still use sections of these waterways, don't use them yourself without local advice because of low overhead clearances and weed growth.

SKIPPER TIP: Be alert for currents increasing to 4 mph as you close in on the Iroquois Lock and Dam.

Because of a lack of hazards, aids to navigation start tapering off at red buoy #116 as you go east. Play it safe by picking up green buoy #115 at 28 feet—prudently staying slightly off the shore—and then aim your craft for the middle of Toussaint Island, where there are two red aids.

SKIPPER TIP: With binoculars you might be able to see a set of range markers behind you. Line up the towers with lights at 45 feet and 70 feet on top of each other and stay in the channel past Toussaint Island.

Small boats can "shoot" the dam at sluice gate #28; vertical overhead clearance is usually 8½ feet.

SKIPPER TIP: Sluice gates can close or partially close without notice.

Although shooting the dam sounds ominous, most of the time it is not. There just is not enough water level change between each side of the lock and dam to create a tense situation. The drop is usually about 1 foot. However, the lower pool next up is man-made Lake St. Lawrence, whose height is somewhat set by hydroelectric power needs and other factors. The more electric power needed, the more water has to flow past the turbines to spin the generators faster, and thus the water level drops.

Pleasure boaters must check in at the lock's small-craft dock before attempting to lock through.

SKIPPER TIP: Iroquois Lock is a half-foot to 6-foot drop. The higher number is for early in the season when water levels are higher, and the lower number reflects the typical later-season drop. The next lock is 21 miles ahead. Make contact with St. Lawrence Seaway personnel at the lock's small-craft dock.
- All vessels must carry the *St. Lawrence Seaway Pleasure Craft Guide.*
- Minimum vessel size: 20 feet and 1 ton.
- VHF radio channel: 14.
- Life jackets must be worn.

- Commercial traffic is a priority; pleasure craft can be delayed several hours.
- Be prepared for a "raft up" on busy days.
- Fenders and lines need to be rigged and ready.
- Current can be up to 4 mph both before and after locking through.
- A fee is charged to lock through.
- Montréal is roughly 100 miles past the lock.
- There are six more locks ahead.

The creation of Lake St. Lawrence did at least two things: it slowed a 25-mph current down to 2 to 4 mph, and it put a half-dozen towns under water. The town of Iroquois, downstream of the Iroquois Lock, was moved to today's location from its original, lower-elevation location somewhere underneath today's channel. Ranges are in place to help you stay in the channel past Ogden Island. The town of Morrisburg and Doran Shoal, which runs alongside the channel, are on the northeast side of Ogden Island.

Waddington, on the New York side of the lake, was settled in 1673. In the early American/Canadian times, the water level here was lower, and the passage for vessels was between Waddington and Ogden Island. The narrow passage, which forced a great volume of water through quickly, made this quite a run back then. The level of the speeding water also dropped quickly by about 6 to 10 feet, but only along the length of the island. Passing freighters had to go through here, and the power from the fast-moving water caused a robust commercial economy to develop in Waddington.

Two miles east of town is Cole's Creek Marina.

Cole's Creek Marina (315) 388-4237

Storm protection: √√√
Scenic: *
Marina-reported approach depths: 17-35 feet
Marina-reported dockside depths: 2-4 feet
Gas
Waste pump-out
Rest rooms
Power connections: 30A/125V
Fiberglass repairs
Mechanical repairs
Gas-engine repairs
Stern-drive repairs
Outboard-motor repairs
Ship's store
Restaurant: off site
VHF-monitored channel: 16

Five and a half miles east of here on the Canadian shore is the Morrisburg Crysler Park Marina, where you can clear Canadian Customs if you have been in U.S. waters until now.

Morrisburg Crysler Park Marina (613) 543-3254

Storm protection: √√√
Scenic: * * *
Marina-reported approach depths: 5-8 feet
Marina-reported dockside depths: 2-5 miles
Gas
Diesel
Waste pump-out
Rest rooms
Showers
Dockside water
Barbecues
Picnic tables
Power connections: 15A/125V, 30A/125V

Convenience store: on site (limited)
What's special: Canadian Customs office here
VHF-monitored channel: 68

If you stop at the marina, visit the Upper Canada Village, which is 1½ miles east. A recreation of life in the area during the 1860s, mills, factories, and farms are featured. If you do not stop at the marina, look towards the north shore at the fixed light red #68. The monument here honors the British-Canadian victory over the United States in 1813, during the War of 1812. On the New York side a preserve for wild waterfowl has been created by the installation of a series of dikes connecting the islands and the marshy areas.

At green #55 and red #56 you are in the approach for the next two locks and their canal. You can see the Alcoa aluminum plant on the New York shore at Massena. Slow down; the canal has a no-wake speed limit.

SKIPPER TIP: Eisenhower Lock is a 40-foot (+/- 2 feet) drop. The next lock, Snell, is 4 miles ahead.

Snell Lock is a 47-foot (+/- 2 feet) drop. The next lock is 45 miles ahead.

- After Snell Lock, currents and cross-channel currents can be as high as 7 mph.

The Cornwall Government Marina is on the north shore and behind Cornwall Island. Although you can use Polly's Cut on the west end of Cornwall Island to access the marina, it is tricky and has a high current. A better way is around Cornwall Island on its east end. Cruise 6 miles east to buoy #DCB, where the

side channel to the city of Cornwall meets the main channel. I hesitate to call this a side channel because it is so big. Well-marked and deep, it ends right at the marina's doorstep. Just cruise another 3¼ miles back west up the side channel.

Cornwall Government Marina (613) 932-8301

Storm protection: √√√
Scenic: *
Marina-reported approach depths: 30 feet
Marina-reported dockside depths: 3-5 feet
Gas
Diesel
Waste pump-out
Rest rooms
Showers
Laundry
Dockside water
Power connections: 30A/125V
Restaurant: off site
Grocery: off site
What's special: in town
VHF-monitored channel: 68

The International Bridge has a reported vertical clearance of 122 feet. Both sides of the waterway become Canadian about 3½ miles east of the bridge. This body of water is Lac St. Francois (Lake St. Francis), a natural lake that the St. Lawrence Seaway system raised when it opened in 1959. This rising water level covered some low-lying land areas, which often are too shallow for pleasure boaters to just cruise willy-nilly outside the channel. Yes, local boaters do run around in them, but let's hope they know the shallow-water locations. I say that because many boaters—having successfully cleared the bottom once without knowing the conditions that allowed them that luxury—often later (sometimes months later) find that those conditions have changed, and they get caught unawares by the shallow-water devil.

About mid-lake are the remains of the abandoned 15-mile-long Soulanges Canal. Now in the main waterway channel at the end of the lake, the Canal de Beauharnois is used by pleasure and commercial craft. The canal has the two locks plus three movable bridges. South of the main body of water, it bypasses all the rapids, thus reducing current speeds to a manageable level.

> **SKIPPER TIP:** Lock Beauharnois Upper is a 38-foot (+/- 2 feet) drop. The next lock is .8 mile.
> Lock Beauharnois Lower is a 39-foot (+/- 2 feet) drop. The next lock is 17 miles east.

After the locks, you are cruising on Lac Saint-Louis. Stay on the Seaway course for Montréal, just shy of 30 miles to the east. About half of this distance is in the moderately wide (225-foot) Canal de la Rive Sud, which bypasses the Lachine Rapids that stopped Cartier's very early westward exploration.

> **SKIPPER TIP:** Lock Côte-Ste-Catherine is a 34-foot (+/- 1 foot) drop. The next lock is 7¼ miles ahead.
> Note: Locking-through instructions are usually given only in French at these two locks.

> **SKIPPER TIP:** Lock St. Lambert is a 16-foot (+/- 3 feet) drop. This is the last lock on the St. Lawrence River.

Please refer to chapter 7 for information on Montréal.

Historic and current locks juxtaposed on the Erie Canal.

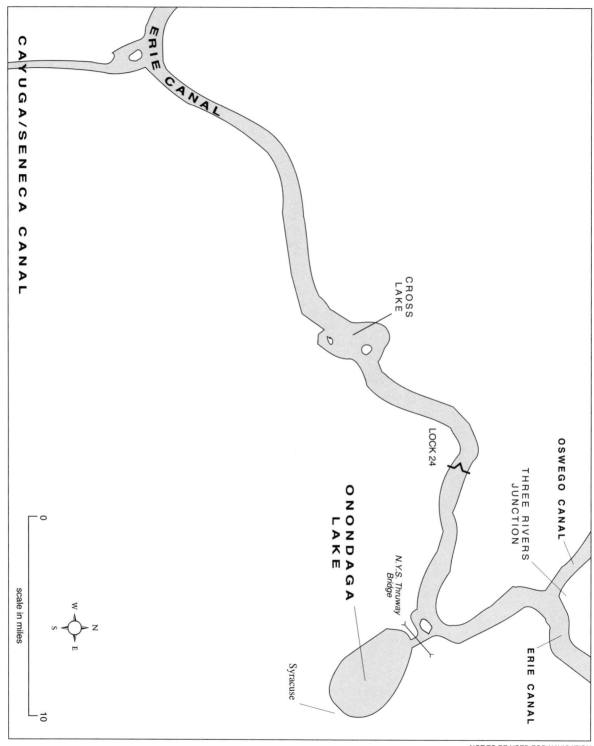

CAYUGA/SENECA CANAL

ERIE CANAL

CROSS
LAKE

LOCK 24

OSWEGO CANAL

THREE RIVERS
JUNCTION

ERIE CANAL

ONONDAGA
LAKE

N.Y.S. Thruway
Bridge

Syracuse

N
W — E
S

scale in miles

0

10

NOT TO BE USED FOR NAVIGATION

CHAPTER 12

The Erie Canal (Area II) West to the Cayuga/Seneca Canal to the Finger Lakes

SKIPPER TIP: Please use NOAA chart 14786.

This short section on the Erie Canal route takes you from the Three Rivers Junction—where you either break off for the Oswego Canal or here continue on the Erie Canal to the junction of the two Finger Lakes, the Cayuga and the Seneca.

Heading south from Three Rivers puts you immediately on the Seneca River. This Erie Canal section was the main waterway and therefore the primary travel route until the railroads came. The canal connected the then-populated eastern part of the United States with the virgin West. As people sought more space and land, they had to move West to fulfill their desires. The West also had a wealth of raw materials, such as forests that could be cut to supply the housing needs of a growing nation, along with farms and grazing lands. In designing the canal route to Lake Erie, the plan was to open up two other areas in the process, though for very different reasons.

The first was the salt at Syracuse. Syracuse, New York, was the salt capital of the United States when the first-generation canal opened. As you cruise through the third-generation Erie Canal today, you can travel the length of Onondaga Lake toward Syracuse. This route is and was an industrial-based connection, starting when Syracuse wanted to ship salt to the entire U.S. and Canadian markets. Even today railroad tracks hem the lake on three sides and diminish the beauty of this area as a cruising ground, giving it an industrial appearance. The side channel to take if you want to see this area is before the next lock, Lock 24.

The second area opened up by the canal allows access to the beautiful Finger Lakes. Two of these lakes—the Cayuga and the Seneca—are connected through a side canal. This vacation playground is a resort-oriented side excursion, and it always has been. A lovely, two- to four-day trip will let you experience what the Finger Lakes has to offer. The short channel way cuts off before Lock 25.

SKIPPER TIP: It is roughly 42 miles to the Cayuga/Seneca Canal. Only one lock is covered in this section.

River Cruising

The Seneca River meanders southward from the Three Rivers Junction. It is wide enough in spots to require navigation aids in select places to keep you in the channel. The marsh lowlands, prevalent as you go west, begin here. Now you'll pass Belgium and go under its Belgium Bridge.

Syracuse

A nice Erie Canal Museum is in downtown Syracuse, but it is about 3 to 4 miles inland from the lake. Pleasure boaters will need to take a taxi to get there because the marinas are in the Liverpool area north of downtown Syracuse. The museum is housed in an old weighlock building with a reconstructed Erie barge next to it.

Weighlocks were used early in the canal's history. At the beginning of every season, each barge on the canal system was weighed at the weighlock. There were seven of these buildings and scales spotted throughout the canal system. A barge loaded with cargo was weighed again as it passed through these seven spots. The difference reflected the cargo's weight and formed the basis for the freight charges.

The canal boats were weighed right outside of this museum building, since the earlier generation of the canal went down what is now a street in downtown Syracuse. That canal path skirted south of Oneida Lake by 12 to 20 miles and then turned west through what is now downtown Syracuse. On the current generation of the Erie Canal, you are cruising north of Onondaga Lake.

Syracuse really developed because of the salt that was mined from the salt springs along the sides of Onondaga Lake. Commercial production of salt began in 1789, but it was difficult to get it to buyers, since the market was on the East Coast and up in Canada. When the Erie Canal opened in 1825, followed by the opening of the Oswego Canal, both canals offered a cost-effective shipping route to buyers. Now salt could be shipped east along the Erie Canal to Albany, then down the Hudson River to New York City; or westward through the Erie Canal to Buffalo. Once in Buffalo, any port on Lake Erie was accessible. Similarly, the Oswego Canal opened up access to all of the cities along Lake Ontario. The salt industry peaked here in the 1860s—at

that point the Syracuse area had some 6,000 acres devoted to salt. Syracuse was capable of providing half of the nation's supply.

Salt comes from brine. Well houses pumped the brine from underground springs and up through wooden pipes to a settling pond. In the pond the water evaporated, leaving salt as a result.

Salt is still eaten by wild animals today—farmers often put out licks or salt blocks for them. Historically, salt was used as a preservative, although that role has now been replaced by refrigeration. The use of salt goes back to Roman times—in fact, the word "salary" comes from the Latin word for "salt." Soldiers were paid in salt. The expression "he wasn't worth his salt" also is tied to this: i.e., he wasn't worth what he was paid.

In early Syracuse, salt was used for barter in place of money. In 1817, for example, one bushel of salt was worth two pounds of pork. One hundred pounds of flour cost twelve bushels of salt. This system was a practical way to get around the fact that paper money was only manufactured locally in the eastern United States by often under-capitalized individual banks. Coins were the only federal money available. In fact, because of the Syracuse salt industry's growth—and the commerce created from it—the need for paper money here fostered a larger and better-financed banking system in the United States.

Money

Now for a short history on money in the United States, the Erie Canal and this region having been so instrumental in its development. Until 1862, the federal government issued only coins; it was individual or private banks that printed paper money. Banks were usually known only in their local areas, and any printed currency was only as good as the bank that had issued it. In 1862, the U.S. government issued the first paper dollar, which was called a "greenback" because of the green-tinted back side. Salmon Chase, Abraham Lincoln's secretary of the Treasury, designed that federal banking system.

After the Civil War, only select banks were authorized to issue federal paper currency. The others lost their right to do so. One authorized source was the Chase National Bank. It wasn't until the federal government reorganized currency in 1928 that the configuration of bills and coins we use today was created.

In 1799 Aaron Burr helped found the Manhattan Water Works Company. He and others controlled the company that had built the water-supply system for New York City. After that system was completed, the extra money not used in that business was dedicated to banking operations. Some of this money was used in 1817, when the Bank of the Manhattan Company purchased stock that financed the Erie Canal's construction.

After the canal opened in 1825, the bank continued to buy stock to improve and enlarge the canal. The canal stock dividends were paid out of the tolls assessed and collected at the canal's weighlocks. The profits that businesses generated by the Erie Canal were often deposited in financial institutions similar to and including the Manhattan Company. This wealth helped create a banking industry across New York State that grew by leaps and bounds. In addition to creating a reliable and respected system of banks, it also created sources of money available for other purposes—including loans—to further spur the growth of area businesses.

In 1829 Joshua Forman of Syracuse penned

the Safety Fund Act of New York, which began the true regulation of these banks at the state level, including an insurance fund to protect bank depositors. The New York banking industry, the most sophisticated at that time in America, was the model used by Secretary Chase to create a national banking system during Lincoln's administration. By the way, Secretary Chase lives on as a part of the name of Chase Manhattan Bank. He also is honored by the U.S. government, which put his picture on the $10,000 bill, the largest one in circulation.

An interesting anecdote: The Manhattan Water Company's founder, Aaron Burr, tried to involve Alexander Hamilton in his company. Hamilton supported the Manhattan Company's role in the New York City's waterworks, but he didn't like the idea of the company entering into banking services. Hamilton was a founder and director of the Bank of the United States and viewed the Bank of the Manhattan Company as a competitor. This financial conflict—along with Burr and Hamilton's political differences—led to the famous duel in 1804, during which Burr shot and mortally wounded Hamilton. The dueling pistols they used are a treasure in the historical collection of the Chase Manhattan Bank.

In 1820 the population of Syracuse was 250 people; in 1825 (the year the canal opened statewide), Syracuse had a population of 600. By 1830 Syracuse had grown to 11,000 people; by 1850, two years after Syracuse became a city, its population was 22,000. By 1865, Syracuse's population increased to 32,000. By 1920, when the canal no longer passed through downtown, the population was 171,000. Syracuse, like other small towns, blossomed because of the canal and the accessibility it gave to commercial interests.

Cruise to Syracuse

The Syracuse approach comes after the Route 370 Bridge, where the eastern leg of the U-shaped throat to the top of Onondaga Lake connects to your Erie Canal path and then goes on to Syracuse, which is at the bottom of the 4½-mile-long lake.

Halfway down the lake on the eastern shore is Onondaga Lake Marina Park in the town of Liverpool. There are aids to navigation to lead you in.

Onondaga Lake Marina Park (315) 453-6712

Storm protection: √
Scenic: *
Marina-reported approach depths: 5-7 feet
Marina-reported dockside depths: 3-5 feet
Waste pump-out
Rest rooms
Dockside water
Picnic tables
Power connections: 15A/125V
Restaurant: off site
Grocery: off site

The other docking opportunity using the same entrance channel is Onondaga Yacht Club, which is private and for members only. If you want to tie up there and you are an out-of-state yacht-club member, I strongly recommend that you have your club write a letter to them at least a month in advance of your planned visit. This club, founded in 1883, is seriously upscale. It is at the base of Tulip Street in Liverpool.

Onondaga Yacht Club

Storm protection: √
Scenic: * * *
Marina-reported approach depths: 5-7 feet
Marina-reported dockside depths: 3-5 feet

Floating docks
Waste pump-out
Rest rooms
Showers
Laundry
Dockside water
Barbecues
Picnic tables
Power connections: 30A/125V, 50A/125V
Restaurant: on site and off site
Note: phone number unavailable for publication

Continuing on the Erie Canal

If you do not go down to Onondaga Lake and Syracuse, you head straight, now southwest, passing the marshy Klein Island to your port.

There are three marinas in a row: First, Cold Springs Harbor, which is the smallest; next, J & S Marine is the largest; and the last, Sun Harbor, used to be known as Riverview Harbor.

Cold Springs Harbor (315) 622-2211

Storm protection: √√
Scenic: * *
Marina-reported approach depths: 4-6 feet
Marina-reported dockside depths: 3 feet
Gas
Diesel
Waste pump-out
Rest rooms
Dockside water
Power connections: 30A/125V
Woodworking repairs
Fiberglass repairs
Below-waterline repairs
Mechanical repairs
Travelift/hoist
Marine railway

J & S Marina (315) 622-1095

Storm protection: √√

Scenic: * *
Marina-reported approach depths: 4-6 feet
Marina-reported dockside depths: 3-4 feet
Gas
Diesel
Waste pump-out
Rest rooms
Dockside water
Power connections: 30A/125V
Woodworking repairs
Fiberglass repairs
Welding
Below-waterline repairs
Mechanical repairs
Gas-engine repairs
Diesel repairs
Stern-drive repairs
Outboard-motor repairs
Travelift/hoist

Sun Harbor (315) 622-3210

Storm protection: √√√
Scenic: * *
Marina-reported approach depths: 4-6 feet
Marina-reported dockside depths: 3-4 feet
Gas
Diesel
Waste pump-out
Rest rooms
Dockside water
Power connections: 30A/125V
Woodworking repairs
Welding
Below-waterline repairs
Mechanical repairs
Travelift/hoist

After two more bridges comes Lock 24.

How Locks Are Repaired

During the winter, the canal staff often uses temporary, corrugated steel dams to stop the water beyond the lock gate so that both sides of the gate can be worked on. Then the water level is lowered to reduce pressure on the temporary dam.

Work must be done in the winter because any breakdown during the operating season (about May 5 through November 15) will completely halt traffic. The canal is not like a highway, where a quick drop of some asphalt can quickly fix any problems. The canal system doesn't have that luxury. If the canal way cannot hold water, then no traffic goes through.

Winter Storage

In the off-season, a section of man-made canal ditch is drained of all of its water to prevent ice damage during the spring thaws. Most river sections, whether natural or artificial, have their water levels lowered about 3 feet or so during the winter for the same reason. The guard gates and canal locks are used to facilitate this job. Natural river sections that have not experienced much improvement maintain their natural water flow and levels.

Lock 24—11-foot lift. (315) 635-3101. You're going up again. It is 30 miles to Lock 25, about a 3-hour ride.

Check with the lock operator for a place to tie up if you want to get off your boat, or proceed three-fourths of a mile west to Cooper's Marina, a large facility.

Cooper's Marina (315) 635-7371

Storm protection: √√
Scenic: * *
Marina-reported approach depths: 5-10 feet
Marina-reported dockside depths: 3-6 feet
Floating docks
Gas
Diesel
Waste pump-out
Rest rooms

Laundry
Dockside water
Picnic tables
Power connections: 30A/125V
Woodworking repairs
Fiberglass repairs
Welding
Below-waterline repairs
Mechanical repairs
Gas-engine repairs
Stern-drive repairs
Travelift/hoist
Marine railway

Lock 24 is at Baldwinsville, a town named after its founder. The settlement was started in 1797 and then expanded when the good Dr. Jonas Baldwin—around the time that the Western Inland Lock and Navigation Company was doing its canal work—acquired this part of the land just before 1810. Dr. Baldwin built a dam (with a small canal and lock to get around the dam) that provided a source of water power, which turned Baldwinsville into a mill town. The second generation of the Erie Canal came through here, but not the first. Of course, by the third generation, hydropowered industry was in decline.

SKIPPER TIP: It is 11 miles to Cross Lake, which is about 1 mile by 4 miles in diameter. Your path will take you through the 1-mile dimension of Cross Lake. From there it's about another 16 miles to the Cayuga and Seneca Lakes cutoff. After that cutoff, you'll travel another 1½ miles or so on to Lock 25 (if you do not take the offshoot canal to the two Finger Lakes).

West of Baldwinsville you must stay in the marked channel, since it is shallow outside it.

Remember, you are cruising in the improved Seneca River, not a man-made canal section. The Route 690 Bridge is seven-eighths of a mile west of Cooper's Marina.

When you come up to the southernmost island, it is important that you bear *west*, not south. You can see that the state made a cut through a section of land for the Erie Canal to go straight, whereas the actual river makes a southern loop, which is uncharted and shallow.

The same thing occurs between buoys #398 and #409—about three-fourths of a mile later, take the clearly marked south fork around Big Island and head across Cross Lake, going on the north side of the mid-lake island named Little Island.

SKIPPER TIP: If you are using the NOAA chart 14786, look for your north directional arrow when you come to Cross Lake. Most editions of the chart book have that lake reoriented on the expanded-scale page for more detail. Therefore, you might be confused as to the location of Big Island and Little Island and what end you came in at. To avoid that confusion, NOAA provides a subsequent page with a standard chart that does not show the full lake. However, the chart does correctly show the way your logical mind would perceive it, and the proper location of Big Island on the east. Most of the lake that you are not going to access is north of where you are coming across, because Little Island is in the southern quarter of the middle of the lake. Therefore, when you come up to Cross Lake, look not only at the chart that you are following but also ahead two pages to the detailed chart for Cross Lake and the explanation page that shows both the inlet and outlet of the lake following the Erie Canal. What an explanation for a mile of waterway!

At the northwest corner of Cross Lake is Cross Lake Marina, which is designed primarily to accommodate small local runabouts.

Cross Lake Marina (315) 626-6718

Storm protection: √
Scenic: * *
Marina-reported approach depths: 3-6 feet
Marina-reported dockside depths: 2-3 feet
Rest rooms
Mechanical repairs
Gas-engine repairs
Stern-drive repairs
Outboard-motor repairs

On the other (west) side of Cross Lake, less than a mile away back on the Erie Canal path, are Quimby's Marina and the Cross Lake Boat Club, one on either side of the River Road Bridge.

Quimby's Marina (315) 635-7371

Storm protection: √√
Scenic: n/a
Marina-reported approach depths: 8-13 feet
Marina-reported dockside depths: 3-10 feet
Gas

Cross Lake Boat Club (315) 689-6171

Storm protection: √√
Scenic: *
Marina-reported approach depths: 8-12 feet
Marina-reported dockside depths: 3-8 feet

Rest rooms
Barbecues
Picnic tables
What's special: private club

Two more bridges and you come up to Hickory Island. Here you need to make a gentle port turn and take the south (or left) channel, which is the buoyed channel. Just past that and two more bridges, the Erie Canal separates its channel from the Seneca River. The Erie Canal route joins another river a little later ahead. This section of the canal is pretty much made up of marshland. There is a Howland Island Game Refuge on the north side of the Erie Canal cut, just past those 400- or 450-foot-high hills, along with the 6,500-acre Montezuma Marsh.

The various generations of the canal facilitated the draining of those marshlands, an act that destroyed the natural wildlife habitat. Living in the wildlife refuge today are quite a few birds, including eagles and ducks, which migrate there during the fall. Anyone on your crew who is not at the helm might enjoy taking the ship's binoculars and doing some bird-watching. You can see Canadian geese, more than 100,000 ducks, and a variety of animals (including deer, rabbit, and fox). Other birds, such as the great blue- and the black-crowned night herons, also use these areas.

To Enter the Cayuga and Seneca Canal

Hang a turn to port after the navigation aid #541 and before the red marker #2 on the island. This turn starts you down that canal to the two Finger Lakes, the Cayuga and the Seneca. Or go straight ahead, passing between the #542 and #543 markers to continue on the Erie Canal to Buffalo. If you are continuing straight ahead, please skip over the next chapter.

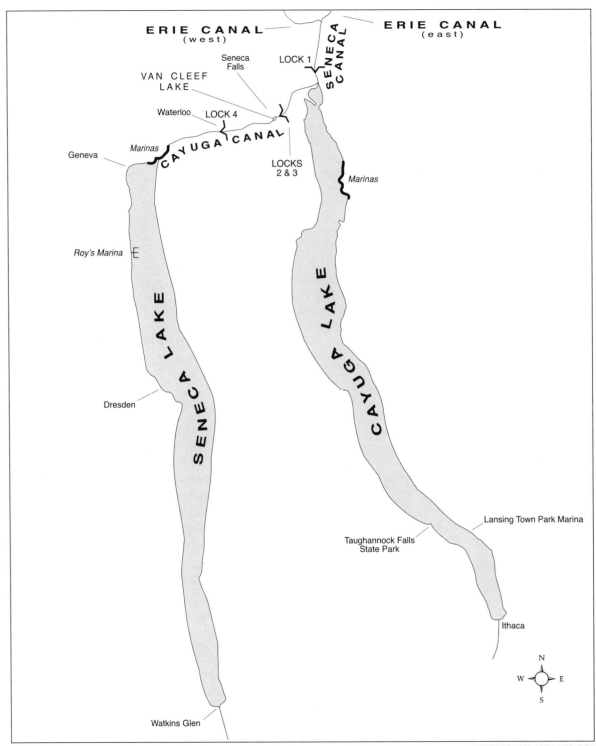

ERIE CANAL
(west)

ERIE CANAL
(east)

Seneca
Falls

LOCK 1

SENECA CANAL

VAN CLEEF
LAKE

Waterloo   LOCK 4

Geneva

Marinas   CAYUGA CANAL

LOCKS
2 & 3

Marinas

Roy's Marina

SENECA LAKE

CAYUGA LAKE

Dresden

Lansing Town Park Marina

Taughannock Falls
State Park

Ithaca

Watkins Glen

N
W   E
S

NOT TO BE USED FOR NAVIGATION

CHAPTER 13

The Finger Lakes

> **SKIPPER TIP:** Use NOAA chart 14786 (a book of chart sheets) for the Finger Lakes. A more detailed chart of both lakes is available on NOAA chart 14791, which is sold separately. Please note that NOAA puts these C/S Canal chart sheets inside the front of the 14786 book of charts. (Does that mean that after cruising here they liked this area best?)

Next up is the Cayuga-Seneca Canal (shortened to C/S in the NOAA book of charts). It's the path to the two largest and most pristine Finger Lakes. This canal has four locks. After the first lock, there's a **Y**-shaped juncture. The next three locks allow Erie Canal cruisers to access Seneca Lake. If you're planning to travel on Cayuga Lake, you'll only need to pass through Lock 1.

I have yet to meet a cruiser who didn't enjoy these two lakes! Some, in fact, just go this far on the Erie Canal, explore the Finger Lakes for two to four days, backtrack to the Oswego Canal, travel its 24 miles to Lake Ontario, and then continue on to the Thousand Islands. Using that route, they avoid about 140 miles of canal across western New York to Lake Erie.

Cruisers seem to prefer the Oswego Canal/Lake Ontario/Thousand Islands route because they don't want to miss the opportunity to cruise around 1,500 islands. If you're going on to Lake Erie from the Thousand Islands, you can get there via the Welland Canal, which connects Lake Ontario to Lake Erie. I'd guess that there are at least five cruisers heading for Lake Ontario for every one traveling the entire Erie Canal to Buffalo.

> **SKIPPER TIP:** The canal section leading to Seneca Lake has a vertical clearance of 15 feet, while Cayuga Lake is limited by the 16-foot height restriction (at normal water levels) of the Guard Gate south of Lock 1.

Shortly after heading south on the C/S Canal off the Erie Canal (red markers are to starboard), your vessel passes the Clyde River to the west and goes under the New York State Thruway (Interstate 90) and one additional bridge (Route 20) in this 4-mile run to Lock 1 of the Cayuga-Seneca Canal.

Lovers of wooden boats should be aware that there are at least two builders/restorers on these lakes: Beacon Bay Marine (315-252-2849), and Ford's Antique Boats and Motor (315-889-5539).

Lock 1—7½-foot lift. (315) 253-7523. The supervisor for this section is available at (315) 946-6192. It is 4 miles (25 minutes) to the pair of locks (Lock 2 and Lock 3) on the way to Seneca Lake; or go straight for 2 miles to the open waters of Cayuga Lake. There is a guard gate just behind Lock 1—vertical clearance at best is 16 feet here. You are 208 miles from the Troy Lock here.

Since the Erie Canal is lower than the two lakes ahead of you, the locks bring your craft up to their levels. Cayuga Lake is officially 381½ feet above sea level, and Seneca Lake is at 445 feet.

If you look at the Finger Lakes on a space satellite photo, you can easily see how the individual lakes look like spread-out fingers. Most people say there are 11 lakes that comprise the Finger Lakes region, but the five largest lakes are often referred to as the "Fingers of God." The lakes are oriented in a north-south direction, and the C/S Canal connects the Erie Canal to two of these lakes.

Canal Routing to Seneca Lake

Turn right 1,700 feet past the guard gate. This section is within the Montezuma National Wildlife Refuge. The marshlands generally continue for the first third of the 3½-mile run to the next set of locks after the turn.

Locks 2 and 3—24½-foot lift for each. (315) 568-5797. These locks are back-to-back. Also note that a bridge crosses over them and that the locks are followed by a guard gate to the west. Next up is Lock 4, 3½ miles west.

As soon as you get through these locks and the guard gate that follows, you are on Van Cleef Lake, which is about a half-mile long and perhaps an eighth of a mile wide. The depth of the lake is in the mid-20-foot range.

When you exit Lock 2 on the Finger Lakes (foreground), you'll automatically enter Lock 3 as you head westbound (off the right edge of the photo). Here the falls are parallel to the Lock 2 entrance, just opposite the lock's cement wall.

A view of Van Cleef Lake from Lock 3, looking west.

Stay away from the shores, since they are shallow as you get close.

You are now in the town of Seneca Falls, which was named for the 49-foot falls bypassed by Locks 2 and 3. Seneca Falls is probably best remembered in history for its association with the women's rights movement. In 1848 the first Women's Rights Convention was held here and produced its Declaration of Sentiments, which influenced the women's movement for many years after with its insistence on women's suffrage rights. Elizabeth Cady Stanton, a leading suffragette of the time, was its organizer. Downtown you'll find the National Women's Hall of Fame.

Seneca Falls provides a wharf for pleasure boaters west of both Van Cleef Lake and the first of three bridges on the north shore. This wharf's location makes the city very accessible to boaters. By the time you read this, the wharf will have been renovated to the tune of $1 million dollars. Listed below is what has been in place for boaters and what I have used. Under construction are: floating docks, a pump-out, improved electrical and water connections, plus some great landscaping and other landside construction.

The historic home of Elizabeth Cady Stanton is just outside of town—back where Lock 3 is, on the south side of the waterway. Food and groceries are available in Seneca Falls, as well as a chance to do laundry. Speaking of laundry, it was here in 1849 that Amelia Bloomer introduced her balloon-pants design for women, now known as "bloomers." Ms. Bloomer also was the first woman to own and publish a newspaper in America.

Seneca Falls Terminal Wharf is an improved tie-up for pleasure boaters. The 11-foot water depths are just off the wall. It is located west of the first bridge (Highway 414)—vertical clearance 15 feet. It ends before the next bridge west. Water, 15A electrical hookups, some shade trees, and a Welcome to Boaters sign are located here on the north shore.

Lock 4—14-foot lift. (315) 539-3242. The guard gate is west of the lock. Seneca Lake is another 5 miles west. Check with the lock operator for tie-ups. There are marinas both west of the lock and the town, as close as about 1½ miles.

Lock 4 is in the middle of Waterloo. Waterloo has a good-sized supermarket just north of and close to the lock; I prefer that market to others in the area. Waterloo is the official birthplace of the Memorial Day holiday. After a dispute with another town ensued over the holiday's origins, Congress ratified Waterloo's status through a special act. It was in Waterloo on May 5, 1886, that a community-wide observance of Memorial Day first took place to honor those who died in the Civil War. Throughout the town flags were draped in mourning or were flown at half-mast. The ladies of the town placed flower wreaths and bouquets on each veteran's grave. Businesses closed, and everyone marched to military music down to the village cemeteries. Thus was the tradition of Memorial Day born. The state of New York was the first to proclaim the day—originally called Decoration Day—a public holiday.

Past Lock 4 to starboard is an island park. West of town there are the six opportunities to tie up before and at the entrance to Seneca Lake itself. At one time a canal routed traffic just north of Seneca Lake to let barge traffic avoid the open water of Seneca Lake but still

reach Geneva. This detour is no longer in use and fairly well deteriorated, but the entrance to this old canal is visible just before you reach the last public marina and Seneca Lake. On chart 14786, page C/S-2, the old canal is shown as an inch-long blue finger of water. A last caution: Watch water depths as you enter the end of the canal and the beginning of the lake—they can be less than 5 feet. Securing up-to-the-minute local knowledge is your best bet here.

Hidden Harbor Marina (315) 539-8034

Storm protection: √√√
Scenic: * *
Marina-reported approach depths: 10 feet
Marina-reported dockside depths: 8-10 feet
Rest rooms
Dockside water
Power connections: 15A/125V, 30A/125V
Travelift/hoist

A & B Marine (315) 781-1755

Storm protection: √√√
Scenic: * *
Marina-reported approach depths: 10 feet
Marina-reported dockside depths: 2-3 feet
Waste pump-out
Rest rooms
Dockside water
Power connections: 15A/125V, 30A/125V

Inland Harbor Marina (315) 789-7255

Storm protection: √√√
Scenic: * * *
Marina-reported approach depths: 10 feet
Marina-reported dockside depths: 4-6 feet
Gas
Diesel
Waste pump-out

Rest rooms
Dockside water
Picnic tables
Power connections: 15A/125V, 30A/125V
Below-waterline repairs
Mechanical repairs
Gas-engine repairs
Diesel repairs
Stern-drive repairs
Outboard-motor repairs
Generator repairs
Travelift/hoist
What's special: most complete marina here

Barretts Marina (315) 789-4564

Storm protection: √√
Scenic: * *
Marina-reported approach depths: 10 feet
Marina-reported dockside depths: 3-4 feet
Gas
Diesel
Waste pump-out
Rest rooms
Dockside water
Picnic tables
Power connections: 15A/125V, 30A/125V
Below-waterline repairs
Mechanical repairs
Gas-engine repairs
Diesel repairs
Stern-drive repairs
Outboard-motor repairs
Generator repairs
Travelift/hoist

Waterloo/New York State Harbor (315) 539-8848

Storm protection: √√
Scenic: * *
Marina-reported approach depths: 5-10 feet
Marina-reported dockside depths: 3-5 feet
Rest rooms

Dockside water
Picnic tables
Power connections: 15A/125V, 30A/125V

Seneca Yacht Club (315) 789-4564

Storm protection: √√
Scenic: * *
Marina-reported approach depths: 5-6 feet
Marina-reported dockside depths: 3-5 feet
What's special: private club

Seneca Lake

A long north-south lake carved out by glaciers, Seneca Lake is about 33 miles long, between 1 to 4 miles wide, and is the largest of the Finger Lakes. Near here around 1450, Hiawatha and his companions gathered together the various Iroquois nations—the Seneca, Cayuga, Onondaga, Oneida, and Mohawk tribes—to form the Five Tribes confederation. By banding together, these tribes avoided warring among themselves or with other tribes. By 1675 this coalition not only had control of upstate New York, but it reached west to the Mississippi River. In 1722 another tribe—the Tuscarera, who came from North Carolina—joined the coalition, making it a six-tribe nation.

Seneca Lake also is a deepwater lake, with depths ranging from less than 100 feet at the north end of the lake to more than 600 feet at mid-lake. Throughout the lake you'll find areas where the water depths increase dramatically only a short distance from the shore, further enhancing the fabulous fishing and unique cruising grounds. This cruising trip really is nice.

Because of the water depths, the lake is usually cold. Along with the coldness, the lake's clarity has given it a good reputation for fishing. Brown and other kinds of trout, bass, perch, and walleyes all inhabit the lake and are ready for your line. Just make sure you get a license first. Scuba diving also is popular here because of the water's clarity, but you'll need a wet suit. Watch for the striped divers flag, which indicates that a diver is in the water. As a common courtesy, please stay away.

Since 1942 the United States Navy has maintained a presence on Seneca Lake, one of the few inland lakes where it conducts secret testing. Other government and scientific agencies also conduct training and/or testing here because the lake is so deep.

Rough Water

Like any lake in the hot, muggy days of summer, storms can pop up with little warning. Both lakes discussed in this chapter are three-to-four hour transits for displacement-type craft, meaning that some boaters sometimes might need every minute they can get to find protection from a summer storm. Wind and waves can build quickly. Keep an eye out for weather. Always keep your VHF radio on Weather 1 (Syracuse) or Weather 2 (Rochester) for reports. By the way, New York State is in the early stages of building marinas to offer more shelter on these stormy occasions.

Seiche and Other Water-Depth Influences

Whether you call it a wind tide, a barometric pressure differentiation, or uncharted shallow water—any cruising skipper on these lakes must be prepared for seiche conditions. In a seiche, water temporarily shifts so that one side of the lake is abnormally shallow, with correspondingly deeper water on the opposite side of the lake. Experts differ as to why this shift occurs, or whether it might be caused by one or more of the above-mentioned con-

ditions. The duration can be very short-term—for as little as an afternoon—or can last for several days. Skippers must adjust their approaches to marinas under seiche conditions or be prepared for it before they arrive at or depart from a marina. Even without a seiche, boaters might find that the lake's water levels fluctuate during the boating season. Please inquire from local authorities about current lake levels.

Geneva, on the opposite (west) shore of the north end of the lake, is not very accessible to boaters; it's a taxi ride around the top of the lake if you stop at the facilities near the lock, which are all on the eastern shore. Geneva is large and has some lovely areas. Dr. William R. Brooks, who discovered 27 different comets, called it home. At one time, Fay and Bowen, a very high-quality line of boats, was built here. After you have explored the more boater-accessible areas to your satisfaction, you might want to stop back at Geneva.

Don't miss the opportunity to cruise to the south end of the lake and travel the extension canal that takes you below Watkins Glen to the marina at Montour Falls. Watkins Glen was a destination resort with hotels during the Civil War. For the people of the Northeast it has always been a beautiful, pastoral, natural wonder—and a popular vacation spot for 200 years. Watkins Glen has the most visited state park in New York. Watkins Glen also has 19 waterfalls, most of which are in the park. The major attraction among these is the Minnehaha Falls. Visitors should check for special events, foremost of which is a waterfront festival usually held in mid-June.

Today, Watkins Glen is best known as one of the oldest sports-car-racing locations in the United States and is the home of the Watkins

The She-Qua-Ga ("Tumbling Waters") are one of the many falls you'll see near Watkins Glen, a town famous for its annual auto races.

Glen Auto Race. The racing activity began here in 1948 and continues today with a three-season schedule of races. A typical race schedule consists of one race in May, June, and July, followed by two in August and one in September. The early August race has the highest attendance. The track lap record is now more than 150 mph!

Jaguar 120s and MG-TDs brought back to the United States by GIs from Europe raced through the streets of Watkins Glen in the 1950s. Briggs Cunningham and Phil Hill (among others) drove, owned, or managed these cars that later inspired America's Corvette. Races such as these created the desire in the American public for cars that could professionally turn and brake on the roads as well as reach top speeds. A museum and a special area inside the town library commemorate the area's car-racing history. The current track was built in 1956 and is 2.45 miles in length. Boaters wanting to visit the track will have to take a taxi there—the track is 5 miles southwest of town.

If you are going to spend extra time on the lake, you'll want to visit a few of the wineries, since this is the wine country of the eastern United States. However, they'll also require a taxi to reach.

Because of water depth, anchoring is usually not a reasonable choice on the lake. If you do attempt to anchor out, make sure that your anchor rode's bitter end is well secured before dropping your anchor. Since most cruisers do not carry sufficient anchor rode to anchor in the water depths of the lake, marinas are the logical choice. You will find that most marinas are around the town of Watkins Glen, the south end of the lake, or on the C/S Canal before the lake's northern end. If you can, plan ahead and make reservations, especially in high season. Descriptions of marinas and an anchorage on the lake follow, going from north to south.

Located on the west shore are:

Roy's Marina (315) 789-3094

Storm protection: √√
Scenic: not rated
Marina-reported approach depths: 8-12 feet
Marina-reported dockside depths: 2-5 feet
Gas

Rest rooms
Power connections: 15A/125V, 30A/125V
Woodworking repairs
Fiberglass repairs
Welding
Below-waterline repairs
Mechanical repairs
Gas-engine repairs
Diesel repairs
Stern-drive repairs
Outboard-motor repairs
Generator repairs
Travelift/hoist

Sampson State Park

Storm protection: √√
Scenic: *
Marina-reported approach depths: 3-12 feet
Marina-reported dockside depths: 3-5 feet
Waste pump-out
Rest rooms
Dockside water
Picnic tables
Power connections: 15A/125V, 30A/125V
Note: unstaffed, so no phone number available

Dredden Anchorage is an unofficial spot where you can anchor in 6- to 18-foot water depths and be somewhat protected from prevailing winds. At one time, a short, steep canal connected Keuka Lake (west of here) to Seneca Lake, allowing access from Keuka to the C/S and Erie Canals. Since the Keuka Lake Canal was not profitable, it was replaced—first by a railway, and then in this century by a hiking path. Keuka Lake is the home of Pen Yan Boats, an old-line boat builder in central New York.

Showboat Motel (607) 243-7434

Storm protection: √
Scenic: * *

Marina-reported approach depths: 3-6 feet
Marina-reported dockside depths: 3 feet
What's special: docks for motel guests

At the south end of the lake there are another half-dozen marinas—but only one, Glen Harbor Marina, sells fuel. First is the only marina on the main lake, Village Marina, which is protected by a breakwater and offers a calm overnight stay. Approach from the east, staying close to the breakwater once inside for best water depth. The other marinas are down the channel.

Village Marina (607) 546-8505

Storm protection: √√
Scenic: * *
Marina-reported approach depths: 6-15 feet
Marina-reported dockside depths: 3-8 feet
Floating docks
Waste pump-out
Rest rooms
Dockside water
Picnic tables
Power connections: 15A/125V, 30A/125V

Glen Harbor Marina (607) 535-2751

Storm protection: √√√
Scenic: *
Marina-reported approach depths: 8-11 feet
Marina-reported dockside depths: 3-6 feet
Gas
Diesel
Waste pump-out
Dockside water
Power connections: 30A/125V
Below-waterline repairs
Mechanical repairs
Gas-engine repairs
Diesel repairs
Travelift/hoist

Lembeck's Marina (607) 535-2503

Storm protection: √√√
Scenic: *
Marina-reported approach depths: 8-11 feet
Marina-reported dockside depths: 3-6 feet
Rest rooms
Dockside water
Power connections: 30A/125V

Seneca Lake Boat Launch

Storm protection: √√√
Scenic: *
Marina-reported approach depths: 8-11 feet
Marina-reported dockside depths: 3-5 feet
What's special: a few tie-ups for trailer
    boats; unstaffed, so no phone number

Watkins Glen Yacht Club (607) 535-9955

Storm protection: √√√
Scenic: * *
Marina-reported approach depths: 7-10 feet
Marina-reported dockside depths: 3-5 feet
Rest rooms
Dockside water
Picnic tables
Power connections: 30A/125V
What's special: a private club

Ervay's Marina (607) 535-2671

Storm protection: √√√
Scenic: *
Marina-reported approach depths: 8-11 feet
Marina-reported dockside depths: 4-5 feet
Waste pump-out
Rest rooms
Dockside water
Picnic tables
Power connections: 30A/125V
Woodworking repairs
Fiberglass repairs

Below-waterline repairs
Mechanical repairs

Montour Marina Park

Storm protection: √√
Scenic: * *
Marina-reported approach depths: 6-8 feet
Marina-reported dockside depths: 2-4 feet
Rest rooms
Dockside water
Barbecues
Picnic tables
Power connections: 30A/125V
What's special: closest to falls; unstaffed, so
    no phone number

Cayuga Lake

After Lock 1 on the Cayuga and Seneca Canal, the right fork of the **Y** takes you over to Seneca Lake. Cayuga Lake is due south. Just head down the east (or left) fork—it's a straight shot.

Approximately 2,500 feet straight south of Lock 1 is Lockview Marina, along the eastern shore. Marshland is still the primary decor in this bay preceding Cayuga Lake, which seems additionally detached because a railroad bridge (19-foot vertical clearance) runs through some of the surrounding marsh at the north end. The lake here is shallow both north and south of the railroad bridge at its north end, so follow the aids to navigation until at least buoy #47. Better yet, go farther down to buoys #50 and #51, the last of the channel markers; you'll generally find that deep water here and solid shoreline replace the marsh and the flats.

Displacement cruisers on the lake should have marina reservations because of the lake's length. The marinas in Ithaca are about 34 miles from the railroad bridge. The lake is open enough to build a good-sized chop, and the shore offers few (if any) protected anchorage locations.

Cayuga Lake is a fairly long lake (about 37 miles long in a north-south direction) and averages about 2 miles wide. The lake is known for its great fishing and great surrounding wine country. Ithaca is located at the very southern end of the lake. This region of New York is one of the Northeast's vacationlands.

Beacon Bay Marina (315) 252-2849

Storm protection: √√
Scenic: * *
Marina-reported approach depths: 4-7 feet
Marina-reported dockside depths: 3-5 feet
Gas
Rest rooms
Picnic tables
Mechanical repairs
Travelift/hoist

Well west of buoy #48 is Cayuga Lake State Park, which is more for land-based visitors than boaters, but it does have a few slips and rest rooms.

Cayuga Lake State Park (315) 568-5163

Storm protection: √
Scenic: * * *
Marina-reported approach depths: 5-6 feet
Marina-reported dockside depths: 2-4 feet
Rest rooms
Picnic tables
What's special: limited slips for runabouts

Back on the eastern shore, there are three marinas as you head south. Castellis Marina offers fuel and is more complete than the others.

Willis Marina (315) 889-5208

Storm protection: √√
Scenic: *
Marina-reported approach depths: 4-7 feet
Marina-reported dockside depths: 2-5 feet
Rest rooms
Dockside water
Power connections: 15A/125V, 30A/125V

Hibiscus Harbor is best approached about a half-mile south of buoys #50 and 51, the southernmost navigation aids on the upper lake. Head east towards the promontory at first, then aim for the middle of the houses on shore. The marina's entrance is between them. There have been one or two privately maintained markers (black sticks) to further guide you into the marina's basin. Water depths have been more than 4 feet deep all the way in, but a prudent skipper should check with the marina on VHF radio channel 16 for up-to-date advice. It is a friendly, nicely landscaped, and pleasant stopover.

Hibiscus Harbor (315) 889-5086

Storm protection: √√
Scenic: *
Marina-reported approach depths: 4-8 feet
Marina-reported dockside depths: 3-6 feet
Gas
Waste pump-out
Rest rooms
Dockside water
Power connections: 15A/125V, 30A/125V
Ship's store
VHF-monitored channel: 16

Castellis Marina (315) 889-5532

Storm protection: √√
Scenic: *

Marina-reported approach depths: 5-7 feet
Marina-reported dockside depths: 4-5 feet
Gas
Diesel
Waste pump-out
Rest rooms
Dockside water
Picnic tables
Power connections: 15A/125V, 30A/125V
Woodworking repairs
Fiberglass repairs
Below-waterline repairs
Mechanical repairs
Gas-engine repairs
Diesel repairs
Stern-drive repairs
Outboard-motor repairs

Dean's Cove State Marine Park, on the western shore about a third of the way down the lake, is included here because it offers the only access to the multitude of the wineries in that section of Cayuga Lake. Plans are in the early stages to make this into a full-service marina.

Dean's Cove State Marina

Storm protection: √
Scenic: * * *
Marina-reported approach depths: 4-7.5 feet
Marina-reported dockside depths: 2-8 feet
Note: unstaffed, so no phone number

Long Point State Park

Storm protection: not rated
Scenic: not rated
Marina-reported approach depths: 5-100 feet
Marina-reported dockside depths: 3-6 feet
Rest rooms
What's special: tie-ups for trailer boats with
   a fair-weather anchorage for cruisers;

come in south of the floating dock as far as necessary for a water depth that's acceptable for you; dinghies can tie up to the float as long as they do not interfere with other activities; unstaffed, so no phone number

Taughannock Falls State Park is a very nice day stop for runabouts. It offers access to the falls, a 215-foot straight drop—higher than the Niagara Falls and the highest east of the Rockies. The falls are a powerful statement of nature and within a little walk from the marina. The grassy grounds and awesome falls make this place a must-see destination.

Boating access is restricted to runabouts because of its Japanese-style, half-round footbridge over the entrance channel to the dockage. Boaters shut out by the footbridge often are frustrated and wonder why the bridge is even there. Of course, the contingent of bass-boat and runabout owners now have a place they can point out to their crew (read: significant other) as accessible only to a boat constructed so low and open, thereby reinforcing their good purchase decisions! Seriously, clearance under the bridge is 5 feet at best and very narrow.

Taughannock Falls State Park

Storm protection: √√√
Scenic: * * * *
Marina-reported approach depths: 3-6 feet
Marina-reported dockside depths: 2-3 feet
Waste pump-out
Rest rooms
Barbecues
Picnic tables
Note: no phone number

Back on the eastern shore of the lake, a marina there has its own basin that protects from the chop on the main lake. Lansing Town Park Marina has 6- to 8-foot approach depths and as much as a 6-foot water depth at a few slips, but there are no supplies nearby. The marina's entrance is narrow, so approach by coming in directly on Myers Point Light. The swimming beach to the north of the entrance channel also is shoal. In contrast to the northern edge, the southern land edge of the entrance channel is recessed. Three pilings, somewhat aligned, define the southern limit of the entrance channel. All of this must be cautiously approached at a dead-slow maneuvering speed. Stay in the center of the channel for best depths, but remember that each year some silting does occur that can change everything. Pick a slip with enough water depth; the slips have less water depth as they extend north, and it's best to avoid the basin area with the busy launch ramp. If no one is around (there often isn't), then check in with a lifeguard.

Lansing Town Park Marina

Storm protection: √√√
Scenic: * *
Marina-reported approach depths: 6-10 feet
Marina-reported dockside depths: 4-6 feet
Rest rooms
What's special: tie-ups are few but well protected; swimming beach next door; no phone number

Finger Lakes Marine Service

Storm protection: √√
Scenic: *
Marina-reported approach depths: 5-10 feet
Marina-reported dockside depths: 3-5 feet
Gas
Rest rooms

Dockside water
Power connections: 15A/125V, 30A/125V
Below-waterline repairs
Mechanical repairs

Ithaca is a college town and home of the internationally known Cornell University. Cornell has a boathouse on an extension canal that is off of the south end of the lake; this canal takes you into downtown Ithaca. Also on this extension canal is the Allan H. Treman State Marine Park. Although very large, it is the only facility that does not put downtown Ithaca and the golf course within a half-mile walk—its location on the opposite side of the extension canal makes city access inconvenient. If the fishing and the views afforded by Cayuga Lake captivate you—and if you plan to spend some time in Ithaca—check out the winery tours in this area. That way you can enjoy the beautiful surrounding country as well as sample these well-known products.

At the southern end of Cayuga Lake are three marinas, plus the Cornell University Collyer Boathouse. Ithaca Boating Center, a moderate-sized marina, sells gas and is closest to town. Johnson Boat Yard and Marina is not much farther from town and is just a block from the golf course. Between these two is the Cornell University Collyer Boathouse, which is private. Finally, the major marina is the Allan H. Treman State Marine Park. Although larger (more than 300 slips), newer, and very clean, this marina doesn't sell fuel. All off-site amenities and the city of Ithaca are a mile away from this last marina.

The approach to the extension canal where the marinas are located is easy. Align lights #146 and #148 and pass them well to your starboard, but keep #147 to your port. It is shoal to the inside of all lights here; you must stay in the middle of the wide channel. Consistently correct your course if the wind or chop push you toward one side. The breakwater itself is outside of the channel, marked by light #148. You should have at least 8 feet of water depth all the way.

Allan H. Treman State Marine Park (607) 387-7041

Storm protection: √√√
Scenic: *
Marina-reported approach depths: 8 feet
Marina-reported dockside depths: 4-6 feet
Waste pump-out
Rest rooms
Showers
Dockside water
Barbecues
Picnic tables
Power connections: 30A/125V

Johnson Boat Yard and Marina (607) 272-5191

Storm protection: √√√
Scenic: *
Marina-reported approach depths: 5-11 feet
Marina-reported dockside depths: 3-4 feet
Gas
Diesel
Waste pump-out
Rest rooms
Dockside water
Power connections: 30A/125V
Woodworking repairs
Fiberglass repairs
Welding
Below-waterline repairs

Mechanical repairs
Gas-engine repairs
Diesel repairs
Stern-drive repairs
Outboard-motor repairs
Generator repairs
Restaurant: off site
Deli: off site
Convenience store: off site

Cornell University Collyer Boat House

Storm protection: √√
Scenic: * *
Marina-reported approach depths: 7-8 feet
Marina-reported dockside depths: 3-7 feet
Gas
Rest rooms
Restaurant: off site
Grocery: off site
Convenience store: off site
Note: private club; phone number withheld

Ithaca Boating Center (607) 272-1581

Storm protection: √√
Scenic: *
Marina-reported approach depths: 9 feet
Marina-reported dockside depths: 7-9 feet
Gas
Waste pump-out
Rest rooms
Showers
Dockside water
Power connections: 30A/125V
Restaurant: off site
Deli: off site
Grocery: off site
Convenience store: off site

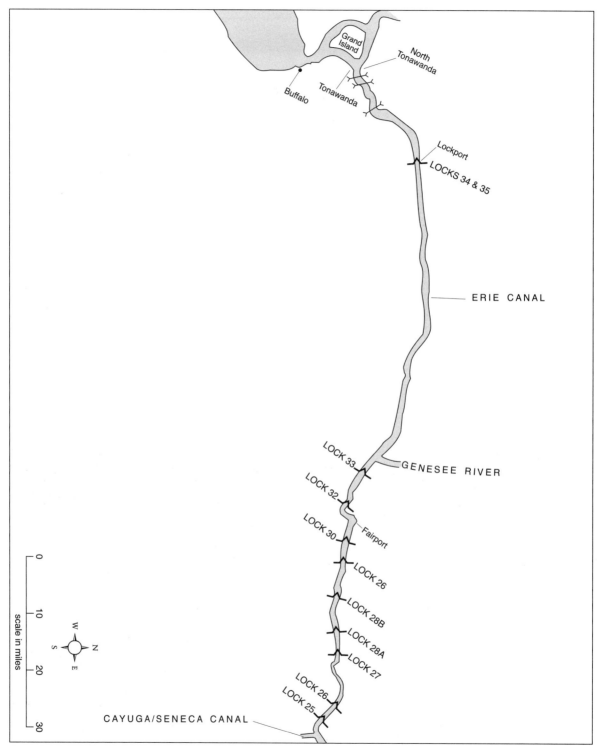

Grand
Island

North
Tonawanda

Tonawanda

Buffalo

Lockport

LOCKS 34 & 35

ERIE CANAL

LOCK 33

GENESEE RIVER

LOCK 32

LOCK 30

Fairport

LOCK 26

LOCK 28B

LOCK 28A

LOCK 27

LOCK 26

LOCK 25

CAYUGA/SENECA CANAL

0

10

20

30

scale in miles

N
W   E
S

NOT TO BE USED FOR NAVIGATION

CHAPTER 14

The Erie Canal (Area III) West to Buffalo and Lake Erie

SKIPPER TIP: Please use NOAA chart 14786 for this section. Also be sure to read chapter 4, "Locking Through for the First Time," before approaching any locks.

Now your cruise continues uninterrupted to the western gateway of the Erie Canal. After a quick run on the Niagara River and through the single-lock Black Rock Canal, your craft makes a comfortable approach to Buffalo. Beyond Buffalo are the open waters of Lake Erie and, if you choose, the Welland Canal.

This area of the Montezuma Marsh, at the north end of Cayuga Lake, is where so vast a number of the early canal workers contracted malaria from working in knee-deep water. The canal was almost stopped in mid-construction because the men got sick quicker than replacements could be hired, trained, and put to work.

The rare view of an empty lock—awaiting repairs—reveals the floor of the lock we otherwise never see.

The next lock, Lock 25, is a mile west of the Cayuga and Seneca Canal channel route.

Lock 25—6-foot lift. (315) 365-3241. The supervisor's telephone number is (315) 946-6192. Lock 26 is 6 miles (or 40 minutes) ahead. Just past the lock is Highway 89 overpass, also known as May's Point Bridge, which has a vertical clearance of 25 feet.

On the north edge of the canal channel is the Oak Orchard Marina and Campground.

Oak Orchard Marina and Campground
   (315) 365-3000

Storm protection: √√
Scenic: *
Marina-reported approach depths: 10-12 feet
Marina-reported dockside depths: 3-5 feet
Waste pump-out
Rest rooms
Showers
Dockside water
Mechanical repairs

Then past the marina, on the left, between markers #565 and #566 is a piece of the Clyde River that the Erie Canal used as a starting point for the canal extension that was cut through this area. As you cruise west, sections of the canal cut in and out of the Clyde River's path. In almost all cases, these little side channels off the marked channel are not navigable.

Lock 26—6-foot lift. (315) 923-9720. It is 2 miles east and south of the town of Clyde. Lock 27 is 1¼ hours farther down the road.

The town of Clyde was settled by the Scots. No one has to tell you—just read the street signs with such names as Galen, Sodus, and others reflective of Scottish origins. Besides being a mill town, Clyde also had several glass works. Clyde now has a weekend festival celebrating the canal in early July.

There was no formal tie-up in town the last time I was here. At that time some people even tried tying up underneath the Highway 414 Bridge or used the tie-ups of the boat-launch ramp just before it. If money keeps being invested in canal improvements, expect more amenities for boaters to be added in the future.

Clyde Boat Launch Ramp

Storm protection: not rated
Scenic: not rated
Marina-reported approach depths: 10 feet
Marina-reported dockside depths: 10 feet
Note: a few small-boat tie-ups; no phone number

The Clyde River continues to follow a similar course to the man-made Erie Canal channel, generally on the south side of it for the next couple of miles. After a couple of meandering bends, watch out for the low bridge between markers #652 and #658. This bridge offers only about a 17-foot clearance. A railroad bridge with about an 18-foot clearance follows. After two more bridges, you are then into Lock 27, which also is downtown Lyons.

Lock 27—12-foot lift. (315) 946-4062. Lock 28A is 1 mile ahead, while Lock 28B is 4 additional miles. In the springtime the Canandaigua Lake outlet can affect the water in the area east of the lock. This water can set your craft toward the lock's northern approach wall. Canandaigua Lake is one of the Finger Lakes, but it unfortunately is not accessible from the Erie Canal.

The town of Lyons was settled in 1789, just after the Revolutionary War. It was named by an early influential citizen, Mr. Williamson, after the town of Lyons in France, which he thought this area resembled. There is a limited ability to tie up along one of the walls here, so check with the lock operator. Restaurants, groceries, launderette, and newspapers are nearby in downtown Lyons. However, another one-third of a mile ahead to the west is a marina that offers a more legitimate tie-up. Although I recommend it, you should call ahead to make sure they can accommodate you; during the last few years they have been booked solid to seasonal tenants.

> **SKIPPER TIP:** Although many of the tie-up opportunities west of here are located every few miles and many are nice, the completeness of their amenities is at best spotty. Perhaps the navigator of your craft should flip through the marina listings ahead to make some timing and distance calculations, especially those in smaller runabouts who exclusively rely on shore-side services to cruise.

Lyons Canal Park

A standard wharf on both sides of the canal that offers a tie-up but no services. Watch out! Current here can be relentless.

Millers Marina (315) 946-9363

Storm protection: √√
Scenic: * *
Marina-reported approach depths: 10-12 feet
Marina-reported dockside depths: 3-10 feet
Gas
Diesel
Waste pump-out
Rest rooms
Dockside water
Picnic tables
Power connections: 15A/125V

Lock 28A—19½-foot lift. (315) 946-4410. Lock 28B is 25 minutes away.

Locks 28A and B were originally planned as one lock, combining the two lifts. Initial engineering drawings for this section of the canal specified a single lock, Lock 28. After that drawing was approved, planners decided to split that Lock 28 into two locks and relabel them Lock 28A and 28B. A dry dock for the use of the state's canal repair craft is located at Lock 28A's northern shore, west of the lock.

Lock 28A is the end of the chart sheets contained in the NOAA chart 14786. The canal continues on to Tonawanda and the Niagara River. The open waters of Lake Erie are about 130 miles from here. The New York State Canal Corporation, through other government authorities, tries to maintain 12 feet of water all the way, subject to local shoaling. Stay in the center third of the channel to be on the safe side.

Look for any change in the grass- and timberline in the marshland from now to the next lock. Any pattern change indicates where the first-generation canal path crossed this current canal cut.

Lock 28B—19½-foot lift. (315) 331-3296. This lock is in Newark. Lock 29 is an hour away.

Two more bridges bring you to Newark Canal Park.

Newark Canal Park

Storm protection: √
Scenic: *
Marina-reported approach depths: 8-12 feet
Marina-reported dockside depths: 4-6 feet
Wharf
Rest rooms
Restaurant: off site
Grocery: off site
Note: no phone number

After three more bridges (or 2 more miles), you enter the wide waters and its Widewaters Canal Park.

Widewaters is just that. The river joins the canal path, and these combine to make the waters wider. The waterway is about one-eighth of a mile wide here for about the length of a mile. Follow the buoys to stay to the north side of the river and in the channel. Two-thirds of the way through this mile run is a peninsula that projects part of the way for the Port Gibson Road Bridge. You'll pass four more bridges on the way to Lock 29.

Widewaters Canal Park

Storm protection: √
Scenic: *
Marina-reported approach depths: 10-12 feet
Marina-reported dockside depths: 4-6 feet
Rest rooms
Note: no phone number

Palmyra was originally settled by the American Indians, the Cayugas and Senecas. These tribes then migrated to Canada right after the Revolutionary War, opening the way for the first European settlers here, who in turn were then replaced by a population push instigated by some of the early major land companies. Finally, with the advent of the Erie Canal in 1825, little towns and cities really popped up along here, as did small industries tied in with the canal that offered the locals employment. However, orchards occupy much of this area today; various fruits and nursery stock (specifically roses) are cultivated here.

Late in the season, canal cruisers might want to try to time their transit so that they can enjoy this area's canal celebration, which is held in mid-September

Palmyra is very close to Smith Farm, which is just outside of town. Not far from the farm, John Smith, its owner, had a religious vision. On the Hill of Camorah about 2 miles south from here, he uncovered the Golden Plates, from which he transcribed the Book of Mormon. This religious book was first printed in town in 1830, and Smith went on to found the Mormon Church. You can visit all three: the printing building, the hill, and the farm. Arrange for a taxi in town. If you do go to town, pass by the intersection of the aptly named Church Street and the east/west-oriented state Highway 31: You'll find a church standing on each corner.

Lock 29—16-foot lift. (315) 597-4691. Lock 30 is 3 miles (or 18 minutes) ahead.

This canal has oversized grounds surrounding it. The lock was self-powered by a hydroelectric plant at one time in its past, and that power plant and its associated infrastructure are still here on the grounds. Also here is most of an aqueduct, in partial ruins, that carried an early version of the Erie Canal. It's fascinating to see and climb on. With all this to explore, plan to tie up for an hour or so. Take a nice stretch and enjoy a walk around. The area also does double duty as a park, so a picnic lunch may be just the right thing.

Palmyra-Macedon Aqueduct Park

Storm protection: √
Scenic: * * * *
Marina-reported approach depths: 8-12 feet
Marina-reported dockside depths: 3-5 feet
Rest rooms
Note: no phone number

SKIPPER TIP: Pass both of the upcoming islands to the south so they are starboard, which is where the channel is.

Three bridges are between Locks 29 and 30. There's also a road on the south shore that parallels the canal on the east side of Macedon.

Lock 30—16-foot-plus lift. (315) 986-5631. Lock 32 is 8 miles (or 45 minutes). There is no Lock 31.

Lock 30 is in Macedon, which was first settled by Webb Harwood in 1789. The village was incorporated in 1823, and the town was incorporated in 1856. If you cross Highway 350, which is the bridge east of the lock, on the south side of the canal just across the street you'll see a Mobil Oil building, and if you cross into their parking lot you'll see an almost-covered walkway. Right there is a stretch of the second-generation Erie Canal, including a set of locks, both east- and westbound. It's quite an interesting sight, and that covered walkway, although private property, is open all the time. The walkway has windows in it so you can safely look down on the lock without having to get near the edge of it.

A junior version of Widewaters comes up next, again about 1 mile long. The canal is fairly wide again and has a bridge near its western end. Continuing west, you will see a multitude of cabins sitting on the water's edge on a flood plain. Stay in the canal channel, though, because it's a mud flat for about two-thirds of the way over to those waterfront homes. Some of this shallow water is the path of the first Erie Canal. Remember, that version was only 4 feet deep, even when it was new in 1825.

If you look south (or left) just after you pass the Waynesport Bridge, near the wide waters end, which is 3 miles west of Lock 30, you might see a houseboat that seemingly sits on land. It's actually sitting on the bottom of what was the old man-made canal in its 1862 version. It's really not floating, but it got there floating on its own bottom on the old canal sections during high early spring waters. The boat is somewhat of a mystery for anyone coming through the current canal sections.

Six bridges are before Fairport, including the one at Main Street, a lift bridge. Telephone (716) 223-9412 to call for an opening. The second lift bridge is 27 miles ahead in Spencerport.

> **SKIPPER TIP:** The lift bridge at Main Street in Fairport is the first of a series of bridges (currently 15) spaced over the next 75 miles. These bridges must "open" just like a bridge on coastal waters often does to let cruising boats pass through. These, however, are manned by roving attendants—one person for several bridges. At busier times they open on a schedule, which—if timely—frees you from having to phone for an opening at each bridge. However, this guide does provide each bridge's contact telephone number. If you do stop or fall out of step, please let the bridge tender know. He has better things to do than open a bridge for a boat that is not coming. Like the locks, the bridge boys use phones to talk to each other and be prepared for every boat.

Although the number and operation of the bridges that need to open as you go west gets smaller each year, the number still seems high when you're cruising through.

Fairport

Overnight docking at Fairport is popular because of its power connections and its

396   CRUISING GUIDE TO NEW YORK WATERWAYS AND LAKE CHAMPLAIN

improved terminal wall, which is fitted with a 4-by-12-inch wooden facing for the length of the wharf that is a little softer on your boat than cement would be. Water and electricity are set up on the south wall. Rates in the past were 16 feet at $2.50 per night, 30 feet and smaller to 16 feet at $5 per night, and anything over 30 feet at $7 per night; when I visited, these prices were cut in half for those not using the power and water. Look for improvements here each year as money is available; the town really enjoys the interaction with canal travelers.

There is a small historical museum on Perrin Street. Also, don't forget to pick up from the Fairport Merchant's Association a flyer that lists all the downtown businesses. The association also is involved with sponsoring a canal festival in early June. One of the prominent citizens of Fairport, Henry DeLand, founded DeLand, Florida. He figured out how to make a big business out of baking soda. The DeLand Chemical Company building is visible from the canal.

Fairport/Packet's Landing Canal Park

Storm protection: √√
Scenic: * *
Marina-reported approach depths: 10-12 feet
Marina-reported dockside depths: 8-10 feet
Wharf
Dockside water
Power connections: 15A/125V
Restaurant: off site
Deli: off site
Grocery: off site
What's special: museum nearby; no phone number

There are nine bridges plus two guard gates after Fairport and before Lock 32. The guard gates protect local residents from the canal, which has been built up (as it had been in earlier versions) at a higher elevation than the local communities. The canal embankment has been pierced in the past, notably four times in the past 170 years, draining the canal and flooding the countryside. The guard gates in conjunction with the locks can minimize the damage if floods happen again in the future.

Great Embankment Park

Storm protection: √√
Scenic: *
Marina-reported approach depths: 10-12 feet
Marina-reported dockside depths: 8-10 feet
Wharf
Note: no phone number

Pittsford is the name given both to Lock 32 and a suburb of the greater Rochester area. Please be on alert—there are numerous bridge and road improvements under construction in the greater Rochester area. Keep your head up for navigational limitations that you must be prepared for. The lock itself is 1½ miles west of the town. The Genesee River, which is the river running north-south through Rochester, is 4 miles to the west, and the village of Fairport is back 8 miles to the east. Just before Lock 32 is the Clover Street Bridge, which hides the lock entrance from westbound traffic.

Pittsford Terminal Wall

Storm protection: √√
Scenic: *
Marina-reported approach depths: 10-12 feet
Marina-reported dockside depths: 8-10 feet
Note: no phone number

Pittsford Park

Storm protection: √√
Scenic: *

Marina-reported approach depths: 10-12 feet
Marina-reported dockside depths: 8-10 feet
Note: no phone number

Lock 32—25.1-foot lift. (716) 586-1837. The supervisor for this section can be telephoned at (716) 589-5689. Lock 33 is a mile away.

Lock 32 State Canal Park (716) 586-1837

Storm protection: √√
Scenic: *
Marina-reported approach depths: 10-12 feet
Marina-reported dockside depths: 8-10 feet
Waste pump-out
Rest rooms
Dockside water

There is a bridge just before Lock 33.
Lock 33—25.1-foot lift. (716) 244-2150. This lift height is the same as Lock 32.

Get ready! This is the long run. Starting at Lock 33, you've got another 63 miles before you come to the next lock-through. There, Lock 34 and 35 are one set. Then the canal ends at its western gateway in the Tonawandas. Let me warn you: there are more than 85 bridges and guard gates between here and the next locks. Some bridges are fixed, while others are capable of lifting up and out of your path. I will provide telephone numbers and other information on those bridges you'll need to contact about letting you through.

The Erie Canal runs through Rochester now, and that's really where you are, on the south side of the eastern outskirts of Rochester. You'll continue to swing south of Rochester for the next 10 to 15 miles as you head west. Most bridges here tend to be more modern, often because they carry the newer roads that were built as Rochester grew. The canal ditch itself

is wider through here compared to what you'll see farther west after leaving Rochester and progressing toward Buffalo. Lock 33 technically is in the town of Henrietta, which also is a suburb of Rochester.

I suggest you favor the north side of the upcoming guard gate. Last time I was there, the canal depth between the bridge and the east guard gate on the south wall was probably about 3 feet more shallow than on the north side. I caution you that similar depth impairment is always possible along either side of the canal. Always try to stay to the center of the channel.

The east guard gate and its corresponding west gate are there to protect the canal system from the Genesee River crossing ahead. The man-improved Genesee can affect the canal because it still drains a large watershed. At certain times, mostly early in the springtime, you can encounter a northern current as you cross the Genesee cruising west. Be prepared to compensate for it. You often can go on the Genesee River and head north toward the city of Rochester. The Court Street Dam (24-hour information line: 716-325-4882) ends your river adventure about 2½ miles downstream.

Just before the dam is Corn Hill Landing, which is a possible overnight tie-up.

Corn Hill Landing

Storm protection: √√√
Scenic: * *
Marina-reported approach depths: 6-10 feet
Marina-reported dockside depths: 3-8 feet
Note: no phone number

A daytime tie-up to access the Genesee Valley Park is, naturally enough, Genesee Valley Park Landing.

Genesee Valley Park Landing

Storm protection: √√
Scenic: * * *
Marina-reported approach depths: 8-12 feet
Marina-reported dockside depths: 3-7 feet
Rest rooms
**Note: sometimes has a current; no phone
   number**

Six miles past the Genesee River is Captain Jeff's Marina, which has gas and electricity. Pilot House, which has rest rooms, is another 3½ miles. Adams Basin Terminal Wall, which also has rest rooms, is 2½ miles farther. It is another 4½ miles to Brockport, which has electricity.

Captain Jeff's Marina (716) 426-5400

Storm protection: √√
Scenic: *
Marina-reported approach depths: 10-12 feet
Marina-reported dockside depths: 6-10 feet
Gas
Picnic tables
Mechanical repairs

Spencerport has the second of the lift bridges, and that's again at the main downtown street. Telephone (716) 352-5451 for an opening. There are cement-faced terminal-wall tie-ups both east and west of the lift bridge in Spencerport. Look for improvements in the future. Canal Days is a great local celebration held during the peak summer days of mid-July. The next lift bridge is 3 miles.

Pilot House/Spencerport

Storm protection: √√
Scenic: *
Marina-reported approach depths: 8-10 feet
Marina-reported dockside depths: 5-8 feet

Rest rooms
Note: no phone number

Well west of town is the next tie-up opportunity.

Adams Basin Terminal Wall

Storm protection: √√
Scenic: *
Marina-reported approach depths: 8-12 feet
Marina-reported dockside depths: 5-8 feet
Rest rooms
Note: no phone number

The Washington Street lift bridge is next. Telephone (716) 352-3548 for an opening. You'll then come to a pair of lift bridges in Brockport, which is 5 miles away.

Highway 260 is the reason for that formal-looking bridge across the canal now. From here all the way into Brockport there will be a road that just parallels the top of the south berm of the canal; it leads you right into Brockport and onto State Street. Brockport is about 2 miles west of the Highway 260 Bridge.

Park Avenue is the first of the pair of lift bridges in Brockport. Telephone (716) 637-4530 to have them both opened. About 5 more miles past them in Holly is the next lift bridge.

Brockport's hospital is on the west side of town about four blocks off the canal and west of the main street. The canal section through Brockport, as you can see, has a cement wall (or berm) on one side and rock gravel on the other side. At this point, appreciate that on the north side the land is probably 15 to 20 feet below the bottom-grade floor of the canal. The first (or the most easterly) of the two lift bridges in Brockport has bollards to allow you to tie-up to the terminal wall for access to Brockport, which has a division of the State University of

New York (SUNY). Go more to the west for electrical hookups. The park has a few picnic tables up there, and you can take a walk around Brockport, which is pretty, nice, and clean.

Brockport Port/Terminal Wall

Storm protection: √√
Scenic: * * *
Marina-reported approach depths: 8-12 feet
Marina-reported dockside depths: 5-8 feet
Wharf
Waste pump-out
Rest rooms
Dockside water
Picnic tables
Power connections: 15A/125V
Restaurant: off site
Grocery: off site
Note: no phone number

West of Brockport is a guard gate, followed by a second gate not too much farther beyond. West of the guard gates are several landings, which for the most part are not intended for overnight tie-ups. You'd be better off continuing on to Albion.

Just before you come into Holly, you'll see another cement-walled berm, which is there because the surrounding land is again well below the canal. The concrete helps strengthen the berm wall, making for better protection of Holly and its residents.

The lift bridge is for East Avenue. Telephone (716) 638-6456 for an opening. The next lift bridge is 3 miles ahead.

The Holly guard gate is well west of town.

The Halberton Road (Route 24) lift bridge can be telephoned at (716) 638-8183 for an opening. It is 6 miles to the two lift bridges in Albion.

The Highway 387 Bridge that crosses the canal is fairly modern and has beige-painted steel and galvanized hand railings. As it goes about replacing older bridges along the canal, New York State is implementing this type of structure.

The village of Albion, the seat for Orleans County, lies ahead after seven more bridges. Albion's two lift bridges are about one-third of a mile apart. Telephone (716) 589-6255 for an opening. After that the next lift bridge is 3 miles down the canal.

The Albion guard gate is next.

Albion Docks/Terminal Wall

Storm protection: √√
Scenic: * *
Marina-reported approach depths: 8-12 feet
Marina-reported dockside depths: 5-7 feet
Wharf
Note: no phone number

Eagle Harbor Road lift bridge is available by telephone at (716) 589-6700 to request an opening if needed. Three miles ahead, the next lift bridge is for Knowlesville Road. Telephone (716) 798-2050 to secure an opening if needed. The next lift bridge, on the far side of the town of Medina 5 miles away, has been remodeled, so an opening is not required. By the way, Medina has a canal festival over a weekend in the first half of July. The next bridge is 10 miles west at Middleport.

Knowlesville Terminal Wall

Storm protection: √√
Scenic: *
Marina-reported approach depths: 8-12 feet
Marina-reported dockside depths: 5-8 feet
Gas
Note: no phone number

Medina Terminal Wall and Park

Storm protection: ⩔
Scenic: *
Marina-reported approach depths: 8-13 feet
Marina-reported dockside depths: 5-8 feet
Power connections: 15A/125V, 30A/125V
Note: no phone number

Erie Basin Park

Storm protection: ⩔
Scenic: *
Marina-reported approach depths: 10-12 feet
Marina-reported dockside depths: 5-8 feet
Power connections: 15A/125V, 30A/125V
Note: no phone number

On the east side of Middleport is its guard gate.

Middleport Park

Storm protection: ⩔
Scenic: *
Marina-reported approach depths: 8-12 feet
Marina-reported dockside depths: 5-8 feet
Wharf
Power connections: 15A/125V, 30A/125V
Note: no phone number

Right in the downtown section of Middleport is a steel-decked drawbridge, over which passes the town's main street. The lift bridge is available by telephone at (716) 735-7250. The next lift bridge is 5 miles from here. Middleport is a little jewel of a town except perhaps for its downtown business district (for which renovations are planned); in particular, its homes and the surrounding small farms are very nicely maintained.

Niauga Orleans Golf Club is on the south canal side there; the next thing you'll see is the Wruck Road Bridge at the end of the golf course. The next bridge, with galvanized handrails and cream-colored steel high beams, is at Griswall Road.

Boaters Restaurant

Next up is a restaurant with its own docking basin. What will they think of next? The Basket Factory is a food lover's mecca for the surrounding 20 miles. Eat here and you will agree. The boat basin holds about a dozen slips, some with side walkways. A wonderful outside deck connects boaters to the restaurant. All in all, it's a delightful experience. Inquire at (716) 735-9001.

Just east of Gasport, the canal has a single-lane public-launch ramp and a couple of small slips for the use of the local trailer-boat community. The next guard gate is one-third of a mile west of here.

Gasport Landing

Storm protection: ⩔
Scenic: * *
Marina-reported approach depths: 10-12 feet
Marina-reported dockside depths: 5-8 feet
Wharf
Note: no phone number

About a half-mile past the guard gate is Gasport Road lift bridge, which is essentially in the center of town. The local ambulance service is located about 150 feet before this bridge. Call (716) 772-7700 for an opening. The next pair of lift bridges is 6 miles ahead.

The farms in this area usually are small. The most popular crops are corn and fruit (apples and grapes), although all kinds of foods are grown in this area. Much of the land here is low-lying and very fertile.

Most of the bridges crossing the canal around here have only one lane, so cars have to wait to the side of the bridge while opposing traffic passes. The majority of the bridges are the steel-platform type. One of these bridges, the Canal Road Bridge, is one lane wide and was built in 1910 (as were many of the bridges in this section of the canal). This one has tan-colored paint.

If ever as a kid you went to camp, your counselor or other older campers might have jokingly sent you on a "go fetch me" mission for a left-handed smoke shifter—all in good fun. Along this same line, as I was seeking local knowledge about the canal in Lockport (coming up), I was told that such a thing as "canal-effect snows" exist. Local lore has it that snow occurs only right over the canal—and not on the land immediately adjacent to it—because of the high moisture content of the canals. Believe it or not! However, I'd like you to know that—just as I didn't go running to fetch a left-handed smoke shifter when I was an 11-year-old camper—I didn't buy the jovial townspeople's bunk about "canal-effect snows," either.

Just beyond Old Niagara Road Bridge is the municipal marina, which has a boat-launching ramp as well as a place to tie up. If you need a meal, walk across the street about 200 feet to the Wide Waters Drive-In. In addition to offering ice cream during the season, they also sell burgers, hot dogs, steak and chicken sandwiches, fries, and onion rings. By the way, they call soda pop "pop," and they have two antique outboard motors in their inside dining room.

The fixed steel-deck bridge is for Old Niagara Road, only one lane wide. Look to the north shore outside the canal here: the land is just about the same height as the canal, and the berm holds back the waters.

Nelson C. Goehle Marine Park (716) 439-6624

Storm protection: √√√
Scenic: * * *
Marina-reported approach depths: 8-12 feet
Marina-reported dockside depths: 3-7 feet
Floating docks
Gas
Diesel
Waste pump-out
Rest rooms
Dockside water
Barbecues
Picnic tables
Power connections: 15A/125V, 30A/125V

The Adams Street Bridge is a drawbridge with a building for bridge attendants right there. The last of the lift bridges is now up ahead. Telephone (716) 434-7368 for an opening if needed. It is another 3 miles from the Adams Street Bridge to the combination Locks 34 and 35.

This green steel-deck bridge, closed to auto traffic, is the last bridge before Locks 34 and 35, which are about a quarter- to a half-mile away.

Most of Locks 34 and 35 were under construction between 1915 and 1920. You can still see an old lock flight there left over from the first-generation canal. A museum with a collection of historical photographs also is on hand.

The street bridge is hiding or partially obscuring Lock 34 and Lock 35.

Lock 34 and Lock 35 is at Lockport. The total lift of 34 and 35 is 49.1 feet. Lock 33 is some 63-plus miles back east.

Immediately past the lock, less than 1,000 feet and in sight while you are in the lock, is an extended bridge that covers the canal for some 400 feet because two different roads are essentially making an **X** pattern over the canal at this point.

Always favor the center of the channel here because it tapers slightly, maybe 1 to 1½ feet of extra depth in the immediate center of the channel, which you lose as you come out to the sides of the canal cut. The entire bottom is pretty much composed of the shale rock you see on the sidewalls lining the canal.

The bridge south of the city of Lockport is for Highway 93 (Pine Street); other bridges follow. Next up on the north or west shore is the town electrical plant. Notice that the canal really seems to be chiseled out of bedrock; the water's surface is about 30 to 40 feet below the land and the sheer rock wall.

The overhead power lines carry electricity from Lockport's electrical distribution area. This area as a whole is clean and nice, with a freshly manicured, well-maintained look about it.

About 4½ miles south and west of the locks and right after the bridge bearing the Lockport and Robinson Roads is the next guard gate.

The bottom of the canal here is pretty much mud clay with a little bit of sand mixed in (though the sand is not visible). The canal is about 20 to 30 feet below the surrounding land. After the guard gate, the artificially straight-running canal starts to show more of its creek origins as opposed to its man-made cuts.

Two miles past the guard gate, the canal merges with the Tonawanda Creek, which the state has improved so that it now becomes the canal way. This arrangement will carry your cruiser the rest of the way to the Western Gateway—the terminus of the Erie Canal and the Niagara River.

Hide Away Harbor Marina (716) 625-9666

Storm protection: √√

Shown here is the typical channel marker along the western section of the Erie Canal. The top section, including the diamond shape, will be painted either red or green.

Scenic: * *
Marina-reported approach depths: 6-10 feet
Marina-reported dockside depths: 3-6 feet
Rest rooms
Dockside water
Picnic tables
Power connections: 15A/125V
Mechanical repairs

Ellicott Creek joins the canal from the south within blocks of the Niagara River, 115 miles past where NOAA chart 14762 ends and just short of 20 miles west of the last lock.

You have an eight-lane public launch ramp

on the north shore, which is followed up by the particularly high Route 62 Bridge. You are still on the Tonawanda Creek section of the Erie Canal.

Just after you pass the six-lane public boat launch, you'll be looking at the East Robertson Street Bridge, which is a fairly modern fixed bridge. Next up after the Robertson Bridge, just a quarter-mile downstream, is Three Mile Island. Bear to the right or make a starboard turn to stay in the channel and go around Three Mile Island, which is quite pretty, heavily treed, and grassy.

Hi Skipper Marina is a fairly service-oriented marina with probably less than 20 slips on the north shore near the end of the canal.

On the Niagara River right outside the canal exit (or entrance, depending on your direction) is a broad waterway probably about a third of a mile wide on average and with a bit of a current. Even in late spring it can have some ice still on it, although it most likely won't be solidly frozen over. Ice here is different than ocean ice. The ice chunks here are not icebergs but certainly junior versions of them, with chunks projecting above water 18 inches and going as long as a 4-foot block.

Wardell's Boatyard (716-692-9428) is a full-service marina with limited transient dockage that is in poor condition. The yard is just past the last bridge on the north shore.

Past Wardell's on the north shore are a couple of small channels that host essentially run-down vacation homes with boat docks and a little water lagoon behind each of them. These structures are all built within 18 inches of the water level.

Also, if you head south, Buffalo is about 12 miles away. The island of Grand Island is across the waterway of the Niagara River; on the near side is the city of Tonawanda.

The Tonawandas

Both Tonawanda and North Tonawanda owe most of their existence to the creation of the Erie Canal. Europeans were here before the canal, but their presence was minor. Grand Island was heavily forested with white oak, long since clear-cut. The falls were several miles north. Early travelers faced a massive portage in getting around them. The Niagara River had a current that human-powered craft such as canoes could not handle well. Lake Erie was several miles south and accessed more easily from the southern half of present-day Buffalo.

First the French, then the British, and then the Americans all traded for fur in this general area for about 200 years before the canal's construction. However, they did not build sustainable communities on this foundation of trade until the canal came along.

Before the Erie Canal could change this area, there were decisions to be made, three of which turned into battles. First, was there to be a canal? Secondly, should it go to Lake Erie or Lake Ontario? And third, where should the canal join Lake Erie—at Lake Erie (Buffalo) or at the Niagara River (Black Rock and the Tonawandas)?

The canal was built in sections, with workers concentrating on one section at a time. After the first section started, work on the subsequent sections progressed simultaneously east and west. Some sections took longer than others. The section that ran through here was constructed fairly late in the building of the canal. Private contractors provided the workers and tools used. Like any army, these worker crews needed supplies, housing, and the proper tools, and boomtowns sprang up all over the canal path to support the undertaking. When construction was finished, the canal became an instant success, so much so that canal barges backed up, waiting at the locks but especially at Albany and the Tonawandas terminuses. Goods also had to be loaded and unloaded from barges to Great Lakes sailing freighters. All this commercial activity forced the creation of a whole shipping and industrial infrastructure here.

Tonawanda Stopover

North Tonawanda (population 35,000) has a unique attraction for you if you overnight here. Merry-go-rounds (or carousels) have been a part of America's leisure activities for a long time. We all have fond childhood memories of playing on these marvelous rides. The Allan Herschell Co. manufactured many of these carousels in North Tonawanda. The factory has been converted into a museum that offers carousel rides to visitors. Inquire at (716) 693-1883.

Nearby in Tonawanda and housed in an 1870 railroad station, the Historical Society of the Tonawandas (716-694-7406) covers both towns' histories. The Ben Long home (circa 1829) also is open to the public. Call (716) 694-7406.

Two festivals also occur in spring and summer: the Festival of Gold (716-285-2400) in mid-April, and the Canal Fest (716-692-5120) in mid-July.

If you're a fan of merry-go-rounds, don't miss the old Allan Herschell Co., now a museum devoted to these amusement rides in Tonawanda, New York.

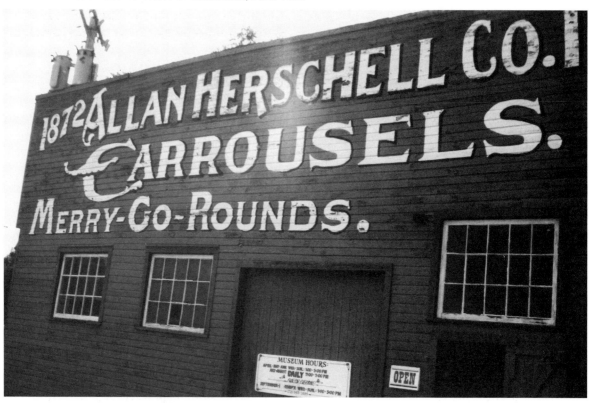

Ongoing Improvements

You are cruising in the western gateway of the canal system, which is undergoing a $3.3 million revitalization program at least through 2002. Plans include an amphitheater, bike and hiking trails, replacement canal walls, landscaping, and 400 feet of floating dock. Be alert for both navigational hazards and new things to enjoy each year.

Marinas in or near North Tonawanda on the Niagara River and on the Erie Canal include the following:

Niagara River Yacht Club (716) 693-2882

Storm protection: √√√
Scenic: * *
Marina-reported approach depths: 3 feet
Marina-reported dockside depths: 3 feet
Rest rooms
Power connections: 30A/125V
What's special: private club (members only)

East Pier Marina (716) 693-6604

Storm protection: √√
Scenic: *
Marina-reported approach depths: 14 feet
Marina-reported dockside depths: 10 feet
Rest rooms
Showers
Picnic tables
Power connections: 30A/125V, 50A/125V
Woodworking repairs
Fiberglass repairs
Welding
Below-waterline repairs
Mechanical repairs
Travelift/hoist
Ship's store
VHF-monitored channel: 16

Bow and Stern Marine (716) 692-2316

Storm protection: √√
Scenic: *
Marina-reported approach depths: 16 feet
Marina-reported dockside depths: 14 feet
Rest rooms
Power connections: 30A/125V
Mast stepping
Below-waterline repairs
Mechanical repairs
Travelift/hoist
Ship's store

Smith Boys (716) 695-3472

Storm protection: √√
Scenic: *
Marina-reported approach depths: 12 feet
Marina-reported dockside depths: 12 feet
Gas
Diesel
Waste pump-out
Rest rooms
Showers
Power connections: 30A/125V, 50A/125V
Mast stepping
Woodworking repairs
Fiberglass repairs
Welding
Below-waterline repairs
Mechanical repairs
Gas-engine repairs
Diesel repairs
Travelift/hoist
Ship's store
What's special: very well known

Placid Harbor Marina (716) 693-6226

Storm protection: √√
Scenic: *
Marina-reported approach depths: 6 feet

Marina-reported dockside depths: 6 feet
Gas
Rest rooms
Showers
Dockside water
Picnic tables
Power connections: 30A/125V, 50A/125V
Mast stepping
Mechanical repairs
Travelift/hoist
Ship's store

Wardell Boat Yard (716) 692-9428

Storm protection: √√√
Scenic: *
Marina-reported approach depths: 8 feet
Marina-reported dockside depths: 3-7 feet
Gas
Diesel
Rest rooms
Barbecues
Picnic tables
Power connections: 30A/125V, 50A/125V,
   50A/220V
Mast stepping
Below-waterline repairs
Mechanical repairs
Travelift/hoist
What's special: old but convenient

Hi Skipper Marine (716) 694-4311

Storm protection: √√√
Scenic: *
Marina-reported approach depths: 13 feet
Marina-reported dockside depths: 2-5 feet
Rest rooms
Dockside water
Power connections: 15A/125V
Mechanical repairs
Gas-engine repairs
Stern-drive repairs

Outboard-motor repairs
Ship's store
What's special: more for outboards than
   cruisers

Freight Rates

Erie Canal freight rates varied by cargo. The state of New York had the power to favor certain industries by lowering or raising cargo rates to sweeping effect. The foremost example of this effect on trade is salt, which for many years enjoyed an advantageous freight rate. However, the freight rate eventually was pushed up, making salt from Syracuse too costly to compete with product from other markets. This increase in freight rates for salt is often blamed for the decline in commercial traffic on the Oswego Canal.

Leaving the Erie Canal

As you come to the western end of the Erie Canal and go past the quick series of bridges, the waterway ends and enters the Niagara River. Directly ahead is Grand Island. Turn left, toward the southwest, favoring slightly the eastern side of the waterways' centerline. This area has water depth of mostly 14 feet, going to the lower 20s a bit down the line. There is a spot of 10 feet of water, but you should miss it by staying to the east (port) side of the center of the river here.

You are heading "upriver" on the Niagara River away from the Niagara Falls, with Tonawanda to port and Grand Island to starboard here toward Lake Erie. Buffalo is a little more than a dozen miles ahead, with about the next two-thirds of that distance on the Niagara River, followed by the last third along the inside of the Black Rock Canal, which parallels the river on its east (near) shore. Past Buffalo, you can continue your cruise, but on the open waters of Lake Erie to Port Colborne, which is on the north shore of Lake Erie and the southern end of the Welland Canal.

Grand Island

Home to 17,600 residents, Grand Island is a large island (5 by 7 miles) known for the wealth of its outdoor recreational choices. Interstate 190 runs over it, connecting the New York State Thruway (Interstate 90) and the Canadian QEW (Queen Elizabeth Way). Two golf courses called Beaver Island State Park and River Oaks are here. Families may enjoy the Fantasy Island amusement park. Two state parks, Beaver Island on the south end and Buckhorn Island at the north end, with amenities including a beach, round out some of the recreational choices on the island.

Grand Island splits the Niagara River into east and west branches. You are cruising on the east branch here about "amidships" on Grand Island's north-south length heading away from Niagara Falls and toward Buffalo. Powerboats can circumnavigate the island if they have enough speed and power to overcome the currents created as the water rushes toward the falls. However, I don't recommend testing the currents—it's unnecessarily risky. Besides, the channel ends far before you can see this high side of the falls. Rather, if you want to see some of the natural beauty of Grand Island, go south via the east branch side, enjoying it as you pass, then continue on, passing south of green buoy #1, to stay safely in these unmarked waters. Then go back up the deep west branch—fairly deep, but there are submerged wrecks and a few shallow spots—as far as you like. The channel is not marked with navigation aids but is generally

7 to 12 feet deep. There is a small-craft marina on that west branch, Big Six Mile Creek Marina. Inquire at (716) 773-3270. I suggest you get some local knowledge before starting out. The scenery along the west branch is very pretty and bucolic.

> **SKIPPER TIP:** That string of plus signs printed on your chart is the U.S./Canadian border, not a channel.

Listed here in order are the Grand Island marinas on the east branch of the Niagara River from north to south (Erie Canal Exit down towards Buffalo).

River Oaks Marina (716) 774-0050

Storm protection: √√
Scenic: * *
Marina-reported approach depths: 7 feet
Marina-reported dockside depths: 7 feet
Rest rooms
Showers
Laundry
Picnic tables

Holiday Inn-Grand Island (716) 773-1111

Storm protection: √√
Scenic: * * *
Marina-reported approach depths: 10-12 feet
Marina-reported dockside depths: 5-6 feet
Rest rooms
Showers
Restaurant: on site

Island Marine (716) 773-2839

Storm protection: not rated
Scenic: not rated

Marina-reported approach depths: 12 feet
Marina-reported dockside depths: 2-22 feet
Gas
Mechanical repairs
Travelift/hoist

Anchor Marine (716) 773-7063

Storm protection: √√
Scenic: * *
Marina-reported approach depths: 10 feet
Marina-reported dockside depths: 6 feet
Gas
Rest rooms
Showers
Dockside water
Picnic tables
Power connection: 30A/125V
Below-waterline repairs
Mechanical repairs
Mast stepping
Travelift/hoist
Ship's store
Restaurant: off site

Beaver Island State Park (716) 773-3271

Storm protection: √√√
Scenic: * * *
Marina-reported approach depths: 3-4 feet
Marina-reported dockside depths: 3-6 feet
Waste pump-out
Rest rooms
Showers
Power connections: 30A/125V

Cruising again, you'll see a high double bridge that is the Interstate 190 path over the Niagara River (99-foot vertical clearance). The river slowly curves to the east as you approach the bottom of Grand Island and the merger of its two branches. Here both Motor (or Pirates)

Island and Strawberry Island are mid-river with the channel passing east of them and almost hugging the east bank of the Niagara River. Do not go outside the channel here—it's shoal. South of green buoy #1 is the first real opportunity to leave the channel to go back up the west branch of the Niagara River, thus avoiding most of the shallow and hazardous water.

Continuing in the channel towards Buffalo and the Black Rock Canal past buoy #1, you'll see that the channel again swings east. This curve hides the beginning of the lock, but its outside, extended west entrance wall is seen early enough to herd you into the canal.

Black Rock and Canal

The canal and its one lock, normally with a lift of 5.2 feet, is here to provide a current-free passage for vessels to Buffalo and onto Lake Erie. Contact lock personnel either by phone at (716) 876-5454 or with two long and two short horn blasts. The Niagara River can have a 10-mph current in this section in addition to eddies. Local powerboats may abandon the comfort of the canal and brave the current, low-clearance bridge, and other hazards of the open Niagara River, but I don't recommend it. Hug the east side of the river and channel, use the lock, and you'll have no problems.

Past the lock is the International Bridge (17-foot vertical clearance), which swings open for boaters after one long blast of your ship's horn—if there are no trains on it. Since train traffic tends to move slowly across the bridge, you might have to wait awhile for the trains to pass. Up ahead, the Ferry Street Bridge is fixed at 100-foot vertical clearance. The city of Buffalo lies ahead.

These approaching pleasure boaters are about to lock through.

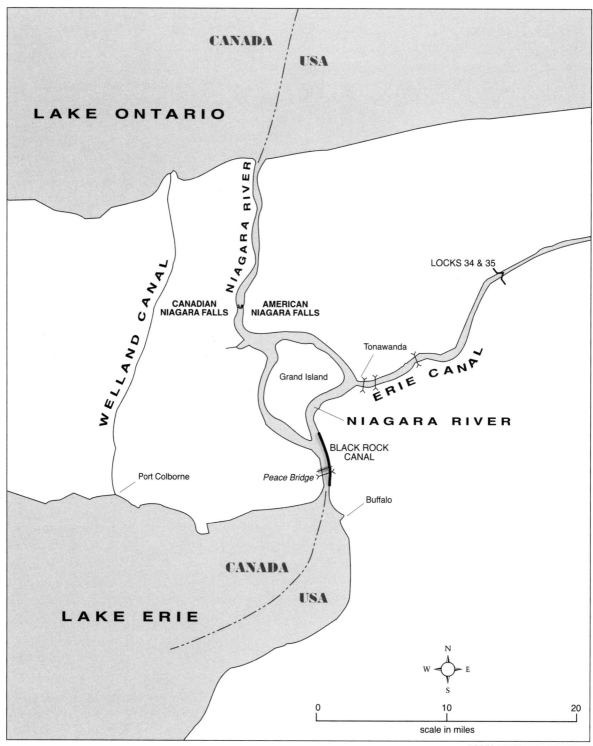

CANADA

USA

LAKE ONTARIO

NIAGARA RIVER

WELLAND CANAL

LOCKS 34 & 35

CANADIAN
NIAGARA FALLS

AMERICAN
NIAGARA FALLS

Tonawanda

ERIE CANAL

Grand Island

NIAGARA RIVER

BLACK ROCK
CANAL

Port Colborne

Peace Bridge

Buffalo

CANADA

USA

LAKE ERIE

N
W E
S

0   10   20

scale in miles

NOT TO BE USED FOR NAVIGATION

CHAPTER 15

The Eastern Lake Erie

Lake Erie

> **SKIPPER TIP:** Please use the following charts for this section: NOAA 14832, 14823, and 14822; and Canadian chart 2042.

Grand Island stretches along the horizon in this view of the Niagara River. The larger pieces of ice in this photo (shot in April) are at least five feet long.

This chapter follows the logical extension of the western terminus of the Erie Canal, the Niagara River to Black Rock Canal to Buffalo.

From Buffalo the chapter details a cruise across the north shore of Lake Erie to Port Colborne, Canada, the southern start of the Welland

Canal, a trip of about 18 miles. The Welland Canal is your connection from Lake Erie to Lake Ontario, since boaters cannot go over the falls on the Niagara River.

Lake Erie Access

At the south end of the Black Rock Canal you effectively have three choices. On a chart they are labeled North Entrance Channel, the Outer Harbor Northern Channel, and the Buffalo River Entrance Channel. Access to Lake Erie is via the North Entrance Channel. Slowly start a turn toward about a 220° magnetic heading using buoys #3 and then #1 as an apex. Pass south of the north breakwater ahead with its North Entrance light #7 at a 20-foot height, then go on past the West Breakwater with its Buffalo Harbor light at 71 feet.

Continue past buoys #1 and #2 for the 25- to 30-foot-deep open water of Lake Erie.

Buffalo Access

Another choice is the Buffalo River Entrance Channel. Leaving the southern terminus of the Black Rock Canal, you can swing right past buoys #3 and #1, then look due south to buoy #BR, passing to its north side, but then swinging 90° to the left around it and into the Buffalo River Entrance Channel. This industrial area has one pleasure-craft marina, RCR Yachts.

The final choice, the Outer Harbor Northern Channel, is simply the first name (of four) for the large area enclosed by a very long seawall that establishes the Outer Harbor of Buffalo. The next area inside this outer harbor is a designated anchorage area, which is the

From the observation deck of the Buffalo City Hall, you can view Lake Erie to the northwest. The rock wall that parallels the shoreline actually is the southern end of the single-lock Black Rock Canal.

As you face west from the observation tower, you can see the north breakwater (center of photo) with an abandoned lighthouse just visible in the distance.

A west-southwest view from the observation tower reveals the wall of the western breakwater (near top of photo). At the left edge of the view, you can see the Outer Harbor and its rock wall.

414 CRUISING GUIDE TO NEW YORK WATERWAYS AND LAKE CHAMPLAIN

most central of the three directional choices facing you at the south end of the Black Rock Canal. It requires a gentle starboard using buoys #3 and #1 as a pinpoint. However, just past the North Breakwater and its light #7 (North Entrance light), head south for a quarter-mile, then turn slightly east to 156° magnetic. Ahead is the anchorage area.

The Outer Harbor Northern Channel, more than 3 miles long, is necessary because wind and storms generally come across the lake from the west straight at Buffalo's shore. Since the lake is shallow, a wind-generated chop can quite readily develop. If winds are stronger and of long duration, the water in the lake can shift to the extent that the Buffalo end of the lake is several feet deeper and the opposite, western shore of Lake Erie is correspondingly several feet shallower. Discussed earlier, this phenomenon is known as a seiche. It's from a German word meaning "running water" that describes an effect on Lake Geneva in Switzerland similar to this one on Lake Erie. A seiche here can last from a few minutes to several hours and is caused either by wind or an imbalance in barometric pressure.

Lake Erie Weather and Temperature

Summer weather conditions can cause storms to form quickly, as they can on all the Great Lakes, but Lake Erie seems to take longer than the other Great Lakes in calming down enough to allow comfortable pleasure cruising. On a positive note, Lake Erie is the warmest of the Great Lakes, with water temperatures of 70° to 75° in August.

Attractions

On the Buffalo River is the Naval and Servicemen's Park, a multiship and -airplane dis-

play to honor all the branches of the U. S. military. Boaters can board the submarine USS *Croaker*, the destroyer USS *The Sullivans*, and the guided-missile cruiser USS *Little Rock*. Also on site are scale models of ships and aircraft, plus a jet fighter. There is an admission charge. Inquire at (716) 847-1773.

The Buffalo Harbor lighthouse is no longer in use, but it still stands near the Coast Guard base of operations between the Buffalo River and the outer harbor. It was built in 1833, rebuilt with a French lens installed in 1851, and restored in 1985.

QRS Music Rolls, the only manufacturer of player piano rolls in the United States, is located near the water in Buffalo. It offers guided tours (limited availability). Inquire at (716) 885-4600.

Farther inland are several more things to do. The Buffalo and Erie County Historical Society, located at 25 Nottingham Terrace in the only remaining building from the 1901 Pan-American Exposition, features commercial and industrial highlights from that exposition. Inquire at (716) 873-9644. Nearby is the very impressive Albright-Knox Art Gallery. Call (716) 882-8700 for more information.

Wilcox Mansion, an 1839 Greek Revival house, is the site of President Teddy Roosevelt's first inauguration. Because President McKinley was assassinated in Buffalo (the reason for President Roosevelt's inauguration here) in 1901, material about the assassination also is on display. Inquire at (716) 884-0095.

Buffalo's City Hall at Niagara Square downtown has an observation level at the twenty-eighth floor. You can see everything from this height—don't miss this! Call (716) 851-4200.

The Theater District is along and near Main St., just north of City Hall. Unfortunately, some live theaters stay dark during June, July, and August.

Taxi companies can be reached at (716) 896-4600 or (716) 852-4000.

Mid River Marina (716) 875-7447

Storm protection: √√√
Scenic: *
Marina-reported approach depths: 15-20 feet
Marina-reported dockside depths: 4-6 feet
Gas
Waste pump-out
Rest rooms
Showers
Dockside water
Picnic tables
Power connections: 30A/125V
Fiberglass repairs
Mechanical repairs
Gas-engine repairs
Travelift/hoist
Ship's store
Restaurant: off site

Harbour Place Marine (716) 876-5944

Storm protection: √√
Scenic: *
Marina-reported approach depths: 15-20 feet
Marina-reported dockside depths: 5-7 feet
Gas
Diesel
Rest rooms
Showers
Dockside water
Power connections: 30A/125V, 50A/125V
Woodworking repairs
Fiberglass repairs
Welding
Below-waterline repairs
Mechanical repairs
Gas-engine repairs

Diesel repairs
Generator repairs
Travelift/hoist
Mast stepping
Ship's store
Restaurant: on site
Grocery: off site
What's special: haul out to 35 tons
VHF-monitored channel: 16

Rich Marine Sales (716) 873-4060

Storm protection: √√
Scenic: *
Marina-reported approach depths: 20 feet
Marina-reported dockside depths: 10-15 feet
Gas
Rest rooms
Dockside water
Power connections: 30A/125V
Woodworking repairs
Fiberglass repairs
Welding
Below-waterline repairs
Mechanical repairs
Gas-engine repairs
Stern-drive repairs
Outboard-motor repairs
Travelift/hoist
Mast stepping
Ship's store

Buffalo Yacht Club (716) 883-5900

Storm protection: √√
Scenic: * * *
Marina-reported approach depths: contact
  marina
Marina-reported dockside depths: 3-5 feet
Waste pump-out
Rest rooms
Showers
Power connections: 30A/125V
Restaurant: on site

Grocery: off site
Convenience store: off site
What's special: private club; best access to
   city
VHF-monitored channel: 16

Erie Basin Marina (716) 842-4141

Storm protection: √√
Scenic: * *
Marina-reported approach depths: 14-17 feet
Marina-reported dockside depths: 5-14 feet
Gas
Diesel
Waste pump-out
Rest rooms
Showers
Dockside water
Barbecues
Picnic tables
Power connections: 30A/125V
Mechanical repairs
Ship's store
Gift shop
Restaurant: on site
Grocery: off site
What's special: second-best access to city
VHF-monitored channel: 16

Small Boat Harbor (716) 852-1921

Storm protection: √√
Scenic: * *
Marina-reported approach depths: 5-9 feet
Marina-reported dockside depths: 4-8 feet
Gas
Waste pump-out
Rest rooms
Showers
Dockside water
Picnic tables
Power connections: 30A/125V
Ship's store
Restaurant: on site

Great Lakes History

To understand Lake Erie, you need to know something about the history of the Great Lakes. They were created by the last retreat of the Wisconsin glacier about 15,000 years ago. Some of the land sank, creating stone bowls which are now the lake beds. Then erosion created different types of shorelines—some rocky, some sandy—but all are magnificent. The Great Lakes finally settled into their current configurations about 3,000 years ago.

Lake Superior has a height of 600 feet above sea level. Going from Lake Michigan and Lake Huron to Lake Erie, the height drops to 570 feet. Lake Ontario is only at 245 feet above sea level. The water volume of these first four Great Lakes flows through the Niagara River escarpment and over the Niagara Falls with all the pressure that water can bring. Talk about hard rock—that water has been flowing there for thousands of years.

All the Great Lakes are deep, except for Lake Erie, which is on average only about 58 feet deep, and much of it is only 20 feet in depth. Lake Erie has been described as a river because of its size and depth in comparison to the other Great Lakes. The deepest depth of each lake is as follows: Superior, 1,333 feet; Michigan, 923 feet; Huron, 750 feet; Ontario, 802 feet; and Erie, at only 210 feet.

The Great Lakes contain enough water to flood all of Canada, the second-largest nation on earth, under 12 feet of water. Lake Superior's surface area of 31,820 square miles makes it the second-largest lake in the world (the Caspian Sea is the largest), while Lake Erie ranks twelfth at 9,930. Lake Ontario is fourteenth in the world at 7,600 square miles.

Buffalo History

Today Buffalo proper has about 330,000 residents and is a part of a greater metropolitan area of 1.2 million people. It was a small trading area that very slowly grew into two communities: Black Rock and Buffalo. Much bad blood developed when the two towns competed with each other to become the western terminus of the Erie Canal, which was still being determined even as other sections of the canal were under construction. Each town won the designation only to alternately offend the canal builders and lose the distinction. After several years Black Rock officially won the right to the terminus. However, Buffalo won as well: in the intervening years it had grown larger, and after losing the decision it wrangled the right to have an extension canal built over to it. Black Rock was officially annexed into Buffalo by 1853.

Black Rock had two positives: a natural harbor and the Porter brothers. These two brothers, Peter and Augustus, along with their partner Benjamin Barton, owned Porter, Barton and Co. This firm controlled local shipping and, more importantly, the portage business then necessary to get around the Niagara Falls (this was prior to the Welland Canal and 20 years before the Erie Canal was authorized). They had money from that successful business and powerful political contacts, because since 1809 they had supplied the forts along the Great Lakes military frontier with salt, beef, flour, and whiskey.

However, Black Rock also suffered from a serious drawback: Vessels had to be pulled by oxen up the Niagara River to Lake Erie. Large vessels required a team of 14 oxen because the current was too strong against them and the prevailing western winds could not be overcome by sail power alone, which was all that was available.

In its favor, Buffalo had Buffalo Creek, which was deep enough, but a sandbar blocked the entrance to it. As a result, freight vessels had to anchor out, off-load into lighters (small boats), which then brought the cargo into the creek to be off-loaded onto land. The canal commissioners and De Witt Clinton, the father of the canal himself, preferred Buffalo. The locals got excited—they really wanted the canal designation.

After all, the first European settlers in Buffalo had been thrown off the land when the Holland Land Co. bought the whole area in 1800 and announced that they would be building a vigorous new town to be called New Amsterdam there. The town was built (or rebuilt) but still called Buffalo. Then in the War of 1812, the British burned down that development. It was rebuilt, and again the British burned it down. The people rebuilt again. The townspeople had endured much tragedy in less than 15 years. They needed the canal and the prosperity associated with it.

Here's a recounting of the battle steps:

1818—The Porter Bros. and eastern investors built and operated a steamboat on Lake Erie named *Walk-in-the-Water*. It ran from Black Rock to Detroit, but it still had to be pulled by oxen through the Niagara River current to Lake Erie.
1819—Buffalo asked for state aid. The state drew up plans for a 1,000-foot pier for Buffalo.

Black Rock countered with a proposed dam, an embankment, and a pier.

1820—Nine hundred feet of Stone Pier were constructed at Buffalo.

1821—Using the spring runoff channeled through a directed path, the Buffalo Creek's entrance sandbar was washed away to create a channel that was 5 feet deep and 90 feet wide. That winter, representatives from Buffalo went to Albany to ask for a law that would require the canal to end in their town. Meanwhile, there were accusations of bribery when two top engineers came out in favor of the Black Rock route. Finally, the steamboat *Walk-in-the-Water* met a storm and was wrecked, only to be rebuilt later.

1822—In February four engineers came out in favor of Buffalo. In March a new sandbar developed at the Buffalo Creek entrance, reducing the depth at the river entrance from 5 feet to 3 feet in less than a year. The *Walk-in-the-Water* replacement vessel was contracted to be built in Black Rock. Buffalo officials, upon hearing the news, offered the builder a 25 percent discount on lumber and promised an open waterway for a spring launch, agreeing to pay $150 a day if the waterway was not open May 1. The replacement vessel *Superior* successfully exited (after much channel work) on May 1 and called Buffalo her home port. In the meantime, Buffalo tentatively was to be the Erie Canal terminus. However, five schooners ran aground in the Buffalo harbor that year, and Black Rock was told that it would get the canal if an experimental pier worked to improve their harbor.

1823—Black Rock's experiment was deemed to work, and the state contracted with the Porter Bros. for a harbor at Black Rock. However, it was to be one of three harbors in a 12-mile stretch—Black Rock plus the Niagara River itself and Buffalo, with Buffalo the smallest. Assurances were given to the citizens of Buffalo that the small harbor still would have a good amount of trade.

1824—Buffalo was dissatisfied with its partial win. The city, charging the Canal Commission with corruption, incited the Canadians to threaten to blow up the piers and dams that were planned for the Niagara River. A big deal was made of that past winter's damages to the harbor in Black Rock. The Porter Bros. organized the Union Line Steamboat Company, holding 48 percent of the shares for themselves and spreading out support throughout the Great Lakes for Black Rock by getting other shippers involved in this company, which was dedicated to a Black Rock canal terminus. Meanwhile, population in 1825 grew in both towns: 1,031 people lived in Black Rock, 2,412 in Buffalo.

1825—At the other end of the canal, the businessmen in Albany, believing the continuing feud might impact their business, wanted it settled. In April, a bill passed the state legislature and was signed into law by the governor. Black Rock was named the permanent terminus, but an extension canal was authorized to be built when needed to reach down to Buffalo. The canal opened.

1826—Ice damage closed the Black Rock harbor, and freight was pushed over to Buffalo for handling.

1828—The Black Rock and the Buffalo harbors here were taken over by the state of New York from the local governments, since they affected the canal, and the canal was so successful that it drove the state's economy.

1829—Boats carried 3,640 bushels of wheat through Buffalo.

1837—Boats transported 500,000 bushels of wheat through Buffalo, a 137-fold increase.

1840—More than 8 million bushels of wheat came through Buffalo, 2,200 times the amount shipped in 1829.

1852—The Buffalo Harbor underwent another big expansion that increased the level of trade it could handle.

1853—Black Rock merged with the city of Buffalo.

Buffalo to the Welland Canal (Port Colborne)

Large freighters usually use the North Entrance to/from the Buffalo outer harbor and the Buffalo River starting with the Buffalo Harbor bell buoy. Some pleasure craft cut out of the marked North Entrance channel earlier than freighters, i.e., once past the Buffalo Harbor Light on the West Breakwater or once past the outside channel buoys #1 and #2. The bell buoy is about another 2 nautical miles farther out from these buoys on about a 215° to 220° magnetic course. To stay clear of the southward-projecting Point Abino later on, you need to go south anyway, so the bell buoy is not that farther out of the way. Follow this course. A second benefit of this path is that it keeps you well clear of Waverly Shoal, more so than the alternative courses.

The 25-meter (83-foot) white tower of Point Abino is less than 8 nautical miles from the bell buoy. Do not aim straight for it because the water is shallow nearby. Aim (or navigate) to an imaginary point about 1 mile south of it, a rough heading of 265° to 270° magnetic. My suggested setting is not accurate enough, but it does give you an idea of where to look and makes you do your own chart work. You should never blindly follow what some book tells you—not even this one!

> **SKIPPER TIP:** There is fishing on Lake Erie, commercial as well as sport. Commerical fishermen often use nets, especially on the section starting west of Port Abino to the Welland Canal entrance as far as is covered in this chapter.

Abino Bay, just east of Point Abino, has a satellite marina of the Buffalo Yacht Club. The shoreline is pretty from Buffalo to the point close in to shore. However, watch out for obstructions and shallow water depth. Locally savvy boaters zip in and out along here on the weekends.

Buffalo Yacht Club (416) 894-6111

Storm protection: √
Scenic: * * *
Marina-reported approach depths: 3-5 feet
Marina-reported dockside depths: 2-4 feet
Waste pump-out
Rest rooms
Showers

Power connections: 30A/125V
What's special: private club
VHF-monitored channel: 16

You'll need to adjust your course as you pass Point Abino to complete your run to the Welland Canal, which is about another 9 nautical miles west. Shoot to pass #EA2, a little more than 6 nautical miles ahead, to its south side to avoid the disposal and the anchorage areas. Freighter traffic will most likely be heading closer to a north-south course to the Welland Canal than your west-northwesterly course. The approach suggested here puts all of that large traffic in front of you, making it very visible and therefore easy to cope with. Because the Welland Canal is highly commercial, you might want to follow my advice.

From #EA2, the entrance buoys to the Port Colborne/Welland Canal breakwater is 1½ nautical miles.

> **SKIPPER TIP:** The West Breakwater projects farther south by at least an additional third of a mile as compared with the east jetty. Heading in from #EA2 in low visibility conditions, you must take precautions to avoid running into this breakwater extension.

Lake Erie Shipwrecks

The year 1850 was probably the worst for maritime disasters on Lake Erie. Because accurate passenger lists were not kept for steerage passengers, a total loss of life in that year has been estimated at more than 450 people. The first vessel to have a problem was the *Troy*. Its boiler blew up and burned the boat, forcing everybody over the side—a great many to their deaths. The *Anthony Wayne* also suffered a boiler explosion. The steam vessel *Commerce* sank after colliding with another boat, which limped to shore. Next, the *G. P. Griffith*'s cargo caught fire, causing the skipper to drive the boat at full speed toward shore since they were only 2 miles out. However, the helmsman managed to put the boat on a shoal area, thereby stopping any further progress of the boat toward land. Still, by this point the fire was raging, and many people died. Later in the year the steamboat *American*'s boiler exploded, killing some of the people on board. On the macabre side, these burned bodies often don't surface for weeks because the burnt skin lets out the decomposing gases that ordinarily would provide buoyancy.

Steerage passengers on a Great Lakes' boat were called by the quaint term "deck passengers." Passages on Lake Erie were typically in the 15- to 20-hour range, so deck space was more popular than cabins. For example, most of the boats in the heyday of the Great Lakes steamer carried a little less than half of their passengers in cabins and a slightly higher number on deck. As the vessels got larger, the ratio sometimes was 30 percent in the cabin to 70 percent on the deck. A final note on shipwrecks: in 1845 a total of 77 vessels were wrecked on all five of the Great Lakes.

Lake Erie's Battle

During the battle of Lake Erie in the War of 1812, the British had 63 guns, and the Americans had 54. However, the Americans were in smaller ships and had nine boats versus six for the British. The Americans won the battle. This was the only battle on Lake Erie, but it caused fear and fortification along all the Great Lakes.

A New York State Canal tug.

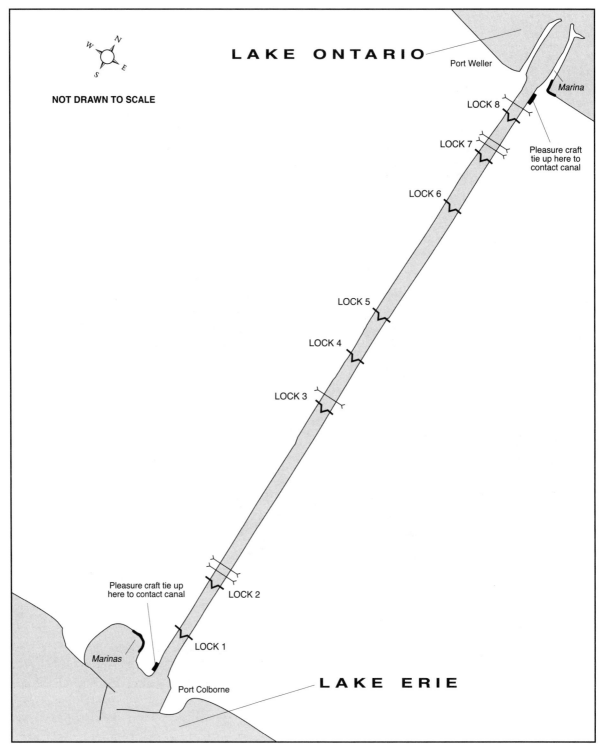

NOT DRAWN TO SCALE

LAKE ONTARIO

Port Weller

Marina

LOCK 8

LOCK 7

Pleasure craft
tie up here to
contact canal

LOCK 6

LOCK 5

LOCK 4

LOCK 3

Pleasure craft tie up
here to contact canal

LOCK 2

Marinas

LOCK 1

Port Colborne

LAKE ERIE

NOT TO BE USED FOR NAVIGATION

CHAPTER 16

The Welland Canal

> **SKIPPER TIP:** Please use Canadian chart 2042 for navigation for this section.

The Welland Canal is the current generation of the canal that completed the access between Lake Ontario and Lake Erie—and therefore the Great Lakes—for freighters and pleasure boats. The canal eliminated the portage required of freight and passengers to get around Niagara Falls. This canal, suited for big-ship traffic, is busy with large freighters. Pleasure boaters should anticipate that the canal system will take a full day, if not more, to transit. Canal authorities will advise you of this when you check in at either end using the telephones provided.

The Welland Canal drops vessels by 326 feet going northbound from Lake Erie to Lake Ontario. The first Welland Canal opened on November 30, 1829, when two brigantines—each with 7½ foot drafts—managed to go from Lake Ontario to Lake Erie. That original canal took 40 locks. Today's Welland Canal, which was rebuilt by the Canadian government over an extended period (1914 to 1932), maintains a depth of 8 meters (27 feet).

Marlon Marine (416) 834-6331

Storm protection: √√√
Scenic: *
Marina-reported approach depths: 20 feet
Marina-reported dockside depths: 7-10 feet
Gas
Diesel
Waste pump-out
Rest rooms
Showers
Laundry
Dockside water
Power connections: 30A/125V, 50A/220V
Mechanical repairs
Ship's store
VHF-monitored channel: 68

Sugarloaf Harbour Marina

Storm protection: √√√
Scenic: *
Marina-reported approach depths: 20 feet
Marina-reported dockside depths: 7-10 feet
Gas: adjunct
Diesel: adjunct
Rest rooms
Showers
Laundry
Dockside water
Power connections: 30A/125V, 50A/220V
Mechanical repairs
Ship's store
VHF-monitored channel: 68

Once you enter the canal, you come under the St. Lawrence Seaway Authority traffic control. Based on freighter and pleasure-boat traffic going both ways, you will be assigned a routing. The canal traffic control will keep an eye on you and the rest of the traffic around you to make sure everyone gets through in a safe and timely manner. However, because of the priority given to commercial freighters, you might have to wait before you can start your transit.

The Seaway Authority requires that you keep on board a Seaway handbook (entitled the *St. Lawrence Seaway Pleasure Craft Guide*). You can get one beforehand from the Seaway Authority by writing to the St. Lawrence Seaway Development Corporation, Box 520 Massena, NY 13662; or pick one up as you check in at the canal. The canal authorities also require you to have a VHF radio, which is their source of communication. As in most canals, you'll need to tie up and fend off, so an appropriate number of boat hooks and fenders (or bumpers) are needed to protect your craft while going through the canal. The canal is entirely within Canadian waters, so you'll also have to clear Canadian Customs at this point.

Starting at the south side of the canal, you come into the breakwater that protects a small bay. Stay within the marked channel inside the breakwater—it is shallow outside of it.

SKIPPER TIP: There's also an extension to the breakwater on the west side of the opening that projects farther into Lake Erie. Under limited visibility, be careful not to drive outside the opening and hit the breakwater.

There are some speed limits within the canal and its approaches, the lowest of which is 6 knots (7 mph) as you enter the breakwater. From there the speed limits are either 6 or 8 knots.

All the depths are in meters, since you're in Canada, you're using a Canadian chart, and the Canadians use the metric system. (Whatever happened to that plan to convert the United States to the metric system? I know that I am more comfortable with inches and feet, because I grew up with it, but the metric system is so logical.)

About 12 bridges and 8 locks dot the canal. There's a marina inside the breakwater but before the actual entrance to the canal. You need to land at the wharf (or quay, a word from Old French that means "wharf"), and use the phone there to contact the Vessel Traffic Control, giving them the necessary information so they can direct you through.

As you head north, the first lock is Lock 8, about 1.7 nautical miles from the breakwater entrance. Another requirement in the Welland Canal is to have a third crew member; a retired canal worker often will be available for hire if you're just traveling as a couple. The rules and procedures are laid out in the Seaway handbook that you're required to read.

SKIPPER TIP: At the ferry crossing at Port Robertson, near nautical mile 12.5, pleasure boaters are asked to slow down and limit their wakes. The ferry docks are used for boarding and disembarking passengers, so you don't want your wake to go over those docks.

Welland Canal Mileage

There are bridges before Lock 8 at 1 mile and then at 1.1 miles. Lock 8 is .6 miles ahead.

Next up is bridge 11, which is 11.4 miles past Lock 8; bridge 10, an additional 1.2 miles past bridge 11. The guard gate cut is then .9 miles; then Lock 7, which is 8 miles. Locks 4, 5 and 6—which are taken as a set—are .7 miles; and Lock 3 is about 1.3 miles from that measuring point. Bridge 4 is .6 miles; Lock 2 is 1.7 miles from bridge 4; and Lock 1 is 1.5 miles from Lock 2; and then the Port Weller Breakwater is 1.7 nautical miles from Lock 1. Then the exit channel, 1.7 miles long from Lock 1, leads into the Port Weller Harbor on Lake Ontario. There is an extended breakwater at this end. At the Lake Ontario end of St. Catharines there is a marina, however, that's outside the breakwater and requires you to make a hard right to go around the tip of the breakwater and come back.

St. Catharines Marina (416) 935-5522

Storm protection: √√
Scenic: * *
Marina reported approach depths: 10 feet
Marina reported dockside depths: 7-9 feet
Gas
Diesel
Waste pump-out
Rest rooms
Showers
Dockside water
Power connections: 30A/125V
Mechanical repairs
Ship's store
Restaurant: on site
VHF monitored channel: 68

Correct Sides of the Locks

Each of the locks in the Welland Canal has a favorite side that you are expected to hold against. At Lock 8, it's port; Lock 7, it's starboard; Lock 6, it's port; Lock 5, port; Lock 4, port; Lock 3, starboard; Lock 2, port; Lock 1, port—that's going down toward Lake Ontario. You'll want to have fenders and bumpers along to protect those sides, and if you are anticipating that you would be with other small boats that will raft with you, then you'll need to provide fenders and bumpers for both sides.

Additional Warnings and a Bon Voyage to You

A three-crew-member rule is imposed for upbound-directed vessels in the canal—that means traffic going to Lake Erie from Lake Ontario. The St. Lawrence Seaway handbook warns pleasure boaters that transit time on the Welland Canal might exceed 12 hours and that the crew is expected to be prepared to man their stations aboard their pleasure craft continuously for that time.

The Welland Canal is the only waterway in this guide that does not touch upon New York waters or shorelines. The chapter covering the Welland Canal marks the end of this cruising guide to New York and adjacent waterways. Although some readers—perhaps those looking for information only on the select areas they intend to cruise—will not read this guide from cover to cover, it is here that I end my narrative, and it is here that I wish you, "Good boating!"

Serene sailing on New York's waterways.

Clearing U.S. and Canadian Customs

In general, Canadian Customs is as easy as any I have cleared. Although each office is slightly different, whether it is at the top of Lake Champlain, at Lake Ontario, or at Lake Erie—all work well and quickly for the organized cruiser. Most boaters call customs from the first Canadian marina they reach. However, if there is a reporting station open, you must use it. These stations are plainly identified on your charts, as are international borders (indicated by a string of plus signs on a chart).

Upon landing in Canada, ask how to clear customs at that location. Customs officials expect that clearing customs is foremost in the minds of every skipper, so do not go touring, exploring, or meandering before doing so. If asked, you want to be able to say that you just got in and you made a beeline for customs. Only the skipper is technically allowed to disembark from the craft to clear customs; crew, pets, possessions, baggage, and merchandise are supposed to stay quarantined aboard your vessel until clearance is given.

After clearing customs, Canada will issue your pleasure craft a clearance number. You must remember this number, because at the very least, U.S. Customs will require it when you re-enter the United States. Furthermore, someone might ask for it on a dockage registration form as you visit different Canadian ports. Write it down and keep a copy of it with the ship's papers; give a second copy to whoever usually handles the ship's business when you come into a new port.

What documents are required? Check with Canadian Customs at:
Revenue Canada
Connaught Building
Mackenzie Avenue
Ottawa, Ontario, Canada
K1A 0L5

There also is a regional Customs office in Montréal at:
400 Youville Square
Montréal, Québec, Canada H2Y 2C2
(514) 283-9900

The Canadian Embassy in the United States is located at:
501 Pennsylvania Avenue N.W.
Washington, D.C. 20001
(202) 682-1755

In Montréal, there's a United States Consulate at:
1155 Saint Alexandre Street
PO Box 65, Station Desjardins
Montréal, Québec, Canada H5B 1G1
(514) 398-9695

In general, officials at Canadian borders ask for proof of ship's registration, ownership, and insurance as well as information on the vessel's size, name, and home port. Skipper, crew, and passengers ideally will have a passport or, failing that, a certified copy of their birth certificates, voter-registration cards, and so forth. Immigration officials are looking to keep out criminals (including anyone with a drunken-driving conviction) and anyone who does not already have a specific job lined up in Canada. Customs officials also want proof that people on board are crew or guests and not paying passengers; a skipper who fails to prove this can be considered operating a business and thus in violation of a myriad laws and regulations concerning Canadian commerce and taxation. During a phone conversation with customs officials, routine questions cover place of birth, citizenship, last port visited and date of departure, purpose and length of visit, and a rundown of any items to be declared.

Customs typically wants to itemize liquor, cigars, cigarettes, film, cameras, and portable radios. They are worried either that you'll sell these items in Canada or are bringing in amounts in excess of what is allowed. You may bring in up to 200 cigarettes, 50 cigars, 14 ounces (200 grams) of loose tobacco, 40 ounces (1.14 liters) of liquor or wine, or 24 containers of beer at 12 ounces (355 milliliters) each. In either case (sale or excess), a duty or refundable bond, as is appropriate, is required. Every once in a while, claiming that items are your "ship's store" is a sufficient answer to a request for full itemization for items other than liquor and tobacco. I have heard that on at least two occasions a "personal use" response has ended further inquiry into exact liquor supplies. Again, I am not advocating any specific behavior; I'm just reporting dockside scuttlebutt that I have overheard in my research.

Fresh food, meat, eggs, and other food items in small quantities, again listed as "ship's stores," might not create a problem; however, bringing a case of oranges or other kinds of fruits that can carry flies or pests from one country to another is discouraged. In fact, Canada has many regulations to prevent plant

pests from entering the country. Your vessel's initial quarantine is such a preventative measure. Likewise, you're probably better off not bringing over items such as live plants, bulbs, seeds, or other material that may propagate pests. Try to keep all fresh food at a minimum when you're crossing the border and replenish as you go.

In addition, if you are carrying prescription drugs, make sure they are clearly identified and in the original packaging with a label that specifies both what the drug is and that it is a doctor's prescription. It is also a good idea to bring a copy of your prescription and your doctor's phone number; a note from the prescribing doctor also can be helpful. If you are diabetic and bringing syringes with you, carry some evidence of your need for them (again, a doctor's note). As for marijuana, Canada does not recognize its medical use. Getting traveler's health insurance before visiting Canada in case you become ill or injured on your trip there also is a good plan. Often for a nominal fee, your health-insurance provider can extend coverage while you are in Canada.

Ship's pets—cats, dogs, or other animals—can be a problem in clearing Canadian Customs. While they are recognized as a part of life, they also can be classified as livestock. If you intend to clear Canadian Customs with pets aboard your vessel, I highly recommend that you get specific advice from Revenue Canada to ease the process. Under no circumstance do you want a pet to be quarantined while the rest of the crew cruises on without the animal. Customs sometimes requires a statement from a recent veterinarian visit stating that your pet has had all its shots (including one for rabies) and is in good health. Again, I would recommend that you call

Canadian officials for more specific advice.

Firearms in general are a problem in clearing Canadian Customs. Automatic weapons, handguns, and other kinds of firearms are illegal in Canada. Legal weapons can only be brought in for a specific hunting trip. Canadian law must be respected in this regard. Again, if you normally cruise with firearms aboard your vessel, you must get specific information from Canadian Customs.

Canada is home to many items of historical, cultural, or scientific significance, and there are restrictions in place to prevent these from leaving the country. If you want to take objects that are more than 50 years old out of Canada—fossils, archeological artifacts, fine and decorative art, technological objects, or books and archival material, for example— first contact the following agency to find out whether you need an export permit:

> Canadian Cultural Property Export
>   Review Board
> 15 Eddy Street
> Hull, Québec, Canada K1A OM5
> (819) 997-7761; Fax: (819) 997-7757

SKIPPER TIP: While in Canada, American boaters should make sure that receipts for marina charges or other purchases detail individual Canadian sales taxes collected—one of which is called the GST or "goods and services tax"—so that upon return to the United States they can apply for reimbursement of this tax, which by the end of a Canadian trip can amount to a pretty piece of change. This tax rebate applies to certain goods taken out of Canada and on short-term accommodations, which means fewer than 30 days at any one location (but there is no limit on the separate types of accommodation for which you may apply for a rebate). Therefore, be sure to keep your receipts while traveling in Canada.

For more information about how to apply for the GST rebate, pick up a copy of *Tax Refund Application for Visitors* at any Canadian Customs office.

United States Customs

Pleasure craft coming back into United States ports from Canada must immediately report to U.S. Customs. Again, the skipper alone should leave the vessel at the first opportunity and report to customs either in person or by phone. A customs official may or may not clear a boat over the phone. You might be directed to an appropriate facility so an inspection can be made of your pleasure craft, but this has never happened to me. As with Canadian Customs, all persons, pets, goods, baggage, and possessions should stay aboard the craft until customs is cleared.

There currently is a $25 user fee per year for pleasure craft to go in and out of U.S. Customs on an unlimited basis. If you want to clear on a Sunday or during holiday hours, there is a surcharge above this fee. The fee provides a numbered decal that is proof of payment. U.S. Customs, unlike Canadian Customs, suggests that—before leaving your last Canadian port— you make an advance phone call to U.S. Customs, if practical. Indicate where you're coming from and where and when you intend to arrive in a U.S. port. Provide the names, birth dates, addresses, and other details for everyone on board, as well as information on the ship—its ownership, registration, insurance, size, and name. This call theoretically will facilitate your clearing customs once you actually arrive at the port; if they're expecting you, the process can move faster. Documents required to enter the United States are the same as those for Canada; officials want to know who owns the boat, where the boat comes from, whether it is insured, and how and where it is registered. People on board need to prove they are U.S. citizens, and if they aren't U.S. citizens, they must provide immigration papers and/or follow up with immigration officials. A passport is preferred, certified birth certificate is accepted usually, and other documents often will suffice.

For more information on U.S. Customs, contact:

U.S. Customs Publications
1301 Constitution Avenue, NW
Washington, D.C. 20229
(202) 927-5580

Ask for Publication #512—*Know Before You Go.*

> **SKIPPER TIP:** If you have stayed outside the United States for more than 48 hours, then you get a merchandise allowance before you have to start paying duty on your Canadian purchases.

If you're traveling with pets, it's important that you check on the current rules and procedures when you're entering the United States. Guns have specific regulations, not only for U.S. Customs (a federal agency) but also for that state that you're coming into; i.e., New York State might require handgun permits that another state does not.

All in all, customs is nothing to worry about, but it does require organization and some pre-trip fact-finding and contact. After going through either country's customs agency, you'll find you've added one more experience to your book of cruising knowledge.

Metric Conversion Tables

Feet to Meters (rounded)		
Feet		**Meters**
3	=	.9
4	=	1.2
5	=	1.5
6	=	1.8
6.5	=	2.0
7	=	2.1
8	=	2.4
9	=	2.7
10	=	3.0
15	=	4.6
20	=	6.1
26	=	8.0
33	=	10
49	=	15
66	=	20
100	=	30.5

Air Temperature	
Celsius	**Fahrenheit**
-10	14
-5	23
0	32
5	41
10	50
15	59
20	68
25	77
30	86
35	95

Statute miles		Kilometer		Nautical miles
1	=	1.6	=	.868
5	=	8	=	4.4
6.3	=	10	=	5.5
10	=	16	=	8.7
20	=	32	=	17
30	=	48	=	26
50	=	80	=	43.5
100	=	160	=	87

Conversion Formulas

Statute mile to kilometer: multiply by 8, divide by 5

Kilometer to statute mile: multiply by 5, divide by 8.

Statute miles to nautical: multiply by 33, divide by 38.

Nautical miles to statute: multiply by 38, divide by 33.

Other nautical measurement terms:

6 feet = 1 fathom
100 fathoms = 1 cable
10 cables = 1 nautical mile (rounded)
6,080 feet = 1 nautical mile
3.281 feet = 1 meter
3 nautical miles = 1 league

Now you know that Jules Verne's *20,000 Leagues Under the Sea*, either the book or Disney film, means 60,000 nautical miles or 69,091 statute miles or 110,545 kilometers under the sea—what a piece of trivia for captains.

Here are some helpful, practical examples of the metric system from the Canadian Tourism Commission:

- A liter of milk is equal to slightly less than a quart of milk (1 liter = .88 quarts).

- A 340-milliliter soft-drink can holds approximately 12 fluid ounces (1 fluid ounce = 29.56 milliliters).

- A kilogram of ground beef equals slightly more than two pounds (1 kilogram = 2.2 pounds).

- On a pleasant summer morning of 72° F, it is also 22° C (F° = C° x 9/5 + 32).

Where to Get Charts, Information and Nautical Books

You can buy charts from the governments of the areas you want to cruise in or from chart agents. Governments offer a chart order form. Agents charge the same price and usually offer suggestions, choices, information, and limited (or a lot of) trip-planning ideas. Avoid those agents that do not do research, ask you pertinent questions, or make helpful suggestions about charts or harbors you intend to visit for your trip, etc. The governments cannot do this—that is why they authorize agents. "You pays your money and you takes your choice."

The following is a short list of chart agents.

N.Y. Nautical Instrument
    and Service Corporation
140 W. Broadway
New York, NY 10013
(212) 962-4522

The Book House
Stuyvesant Plaza
Albany, NY 12203
(518) 489-4761

The Armchair Sailor
543 Thames St.
Newport, RI 02840
(800) 29CHART (292-4278)
Fax (401) 847-1219
Web site: http://www.seabooks.com/

Landfall Navigation
354 W. Putnam Ave.
Greenwich, CT 06830
(800) 941-2219
(203) 661-3176
Fax (203) 661-9613

Dover Flag & Map
323 Main St.
Racine, WI 53403
(414) 632-3133
Fax (414) 632-3188

Safe Navigation Inc.
820 Long Beach Blvd.
Long Beach, CA 90813
(310) 590-8744

Complete Cruising Solutions
2051 Grand St.
Alameda, CA 94501
(510) 769-1547
Fax (510) 769-1573

The Nautical Mind
Radisson Plaza Hotel
249 Queen's Quay West
Toronto, Ont., Canada M5J 2N5
(416) 203-1163
Fax: (416) 203-0729
Web site: www.nauticalmind.com
E-mail: books@nauticalmind.com

Canadian government chart contacts:

Hydrographic Chart Distribution Office
Fisheries and Oceans Canada
1675 Russell Road
P.O. Box 8080
Ottawa, Ontario, Canada
K1G 3H6
(613) 998-4931
Fax (613) 998-1217

Information about Canada's nautical charts, sailing directions, small-craft guides, tide and current tables, and other nautical publications is also available on the World Wide Web at http://www.chshq.dfo.ca.

United States government chart contacts:

NOAA Nautical Charts
NOAA Distribution Division, N/ACC3
National Ocean Service
Riverdale, MD 20737-1199
(800) 638-8972
Fax (301) 436-6829

Notices to Mariners (Canadian) and *Local Notice to Mariners* (U.S.) describe amendments to charts and publications required because of changed conditions. Ask to be put on these marine lists up to 18 months before you go. Let them know in your request the chart areas in which you intend to travel.

Copies of these *Notices to Mariners* are available free of charge by writing directly to:

Director General, Aids and Waterways
Canadian Coast Guard, Transport Canada
Ottawa, Ontario, Canada, KIA ON7

United States Coast Guard:
District 1
Department of Transportation
408 Atlantic Ave.
Boston, MA. 02110-3350
(617) 223-8600

District 9
Commander (OAN), 9th Coast Guard District
1240 E. 9th St.
Cleveland, Ohio 44199-2060
(216) 902-6063

U.S. Coast Guard Web site: http://www.navcen.uscg.mil/nacen.htm

• Please note that government charts are not copyrighted. Many private businesses reproduce government charts in a different format: on waterproof paper, as with chart sheets from International Sailing Supply, or in a book that covers a specific area (such as Lake Ontario, for example). Richardson's is well known for chart guides to the individual Great Lakes, as is BBA-Chart Kit for the Atlantic Seaboard. Ask your chart agent for the advantages and disadvantages of privately printed chart guides, but be very cautious if the scale has been reduced: You need the original, full scale to read the detail, unless you are going to just cruise up the middle of the channels with no stops or breakdowns.

Compass Headings

		TRUE HEADING
+/-	**Variation**	(from your chart's compass rose in that area)
=	**Magnetic Heading**	(heading accounting for the earth's magnetic properties)
+/-	**Deviation**	(from your compass card when it was swung)
=	**Compass Heading**	
+/-	**Set & Drift**	(adjustment for current speed and direction)
+/-	**Leeway**	(effect of wind direction and speed)
=	**Course to Steer**	(finally, heading to keep your compass on)

Approaching a lock from the upper pool.

Community/Tourist Information Resources

New York City, the Hudson River, and the Capital District

- Albany Convention & Visitors Bureau, 52 S. Pearl St., Albany, NY 12207; (518) 434-1217
- Albany Visitors Center, 25 Quackenbush Square, Albany, NY 12297; (518) 434-5132
- Columbia County Chamber of Commerce, 401 State St., Hudson, NY 12534; (518) 828-3375 or (800) 724-1846
- Dutchess County Tourism, 3 Neptune Rd., Poughkeepsie, NY 12601; (800) 445-3131 or (914) 463-4000
- Gateway Tours, (518) 274-5267
- Greene County Promotion Department, P.O. Box 527, Catskill, NY 12412; (800) 335-CATS or (518) 943-3223
- Historic Hudson Valley, 150 White Plains Rd., Tarrytown, NY 10591; (914) 631-8200
- New York Convention and Visitors Bureau, Two Columbus Circle and 59th St., New York, NY 10019; (212) 397-8222 or 800/NYC-VISIT
- New York State Parks, 915 Broadway, New York, NY 10010; (212) 387-0271
- Orange County Tourism, 255-275 Main St., Goshen, NY 10924; (914) 294-5151, Ext. 1647 or (800) 762-8687
- Palisades Interstate Park Commission, Bear Mountain State Park, Bear Mountain, NY 10911; (914) 786-2701
- Putnam County Tourist Information, 110 Old Route 6, Carmel, NY 10512; (914) 225-0381
- Rensselaer County Tourism, 31 2nd St., Troy, NY 12180; (518) 274-7020
- Rockland County Office of Tourism, 11 N. Hempstead Rd., New City, NY 10956; (914) 638-5800
- Ulster County Public Information Office, 244 Fair St., P.O. Box 1800, Kingston, NY 12401; (914) 331-9300, Ext. 503 or (800) 342-5826
- Westchester County Visitors Bureau, 235 Mamaroneck Ave., White Plains, NY 10601; (914) 948-0047 or (800) 833-9282

The Champlain Canal and Lake Champlain

- Essex County Information Center, RR 1 Box 220, Crown Point, NY 12928; (518) 597-4646
- Franklin County Tourism, 63 W. Main St., Malone, NY 12953; (518) 483-6788
- The Lake Champlain Regional Chamber of Commerce, 60 Main St., Burlington, VT 05401; (802) 863-3489
- Plattsburgh/Clinton County Chamber of Commerce, Box 310, Plattsburgh, NY 12901; (518) 563-1000
- Saratoga County Chamber of Commerce, 494 Broadway, Saratoga Springs, NY 12866; (518) 584-3255
- Vermont Travel Division, 134 State St., Montpelier, VT 05602; (802) 828-3239
- Washington County Tourism, 383 Broadway, Fort Edward, NY 12828; (518) 746-2290
- Whitehall Chamber of Commerce (Washington Co.), 259 Broadway, Whitehall, NY 12887; (518) 499-2292

Canada

- Ministry of Culture, Tourism and Recreation, BCE Place, 181 Bay St, Suite 350, P.O. Box 851, Toronto, ON, Canada M5J 2T3; (800) 668-2746 or (416) 314-0944
- Québec's Historic Canals, Montréal District, 1899 Perigny Blvd., Chambly, Québec, Canada J3L 4C3; (514) 658-0681
- Tourism Québec, PO Box 979, Montréal, PQ, Canada H3C 2W3; (800) 363-7777 or (514) 873-2015; Home Page: http://www.gouv.qc.ca

Erie Canal and Lake Erie

- Amsterdam Chamber of Commerce, P.O. Box 309, 366 W. Main St., Amsterdam, NY 12010; (518) 842-8200
- Auburn/Cayuga County Chamber of Commerce, 36 S. St., Auburn, NY 13021; (315) 252-7291
- Bureau of Fisheries, Room 518, 50 Wolf Rd., Albany, NY 12233; (607) 753-1551; **Note:** a source of fishing information; anglers also may request copies of popular fishing brochures from any Department of Environmental Conservation Regional Fisheries office.
- Fulton County Chamber of Commerce, 18 Cayadutta St., Gloversville, NY 12078; (800) 676-3858 or (518) 725-0641
- Genesee Chamber of Commerce, 220 E. Main St. Plaza, Batavia, NY 14020; (800) 622-2868
- Grand Island Chamber of Commerce, 1763 Baseline Rd., Grand Island, NY 14072; (716) 773-3651
- Greater Buffalo Convention & Visitors Bureau, 107 Delaware Ave., Buffalo, NY 14202; (716) 852-0511
- Greater Fulton Chamber of Commerce, 189 S. 1st St., Fulton, NY 13069; (315) 598-4231
- Greater Oswego Chamber of Commerce, 156 W. 2nd St., Oswego, NY 13126; (315) 343-7681
- Greater Rochester Visitors Association, 126 Andrews St., Rochester, NY 14604; (716) 546-3070
- Herkimer County Chamber of Commerce, Box 129, Mohawk, NY 13407; (315) 866-7820
- Leatherstocking Country, 327 N. Main St, P.O. Box 447, Herkimer, NY 13350; (315) 866-1500 or (800) 233-8778
- Lockport Chamber of Commerce, 151 W. Genesee St., Lockport, NY 14094; (716) 433-3828
- Madison County Tourism, P.O. Box 1029, Morrisville, NY 13408; (315) 684-3911 or (800) 684-7320
- Ministry of Culture, Tourism and Recreation, BCE Place, 181 Bay St., Suite 350, P.O. Box 851, Toronto, ON, Canada M5J 2T3; (800) 668-2746
- Montgomery County Chamber of Commerce, 366 W. Main St., Amsterdam, NY 12010; (518) 842-8200 or (800) 743-7337
- New York State Canal Corporation, P.O. Box 189, Albany, NY 12201-0189; (800) 4CANAL4
- Niagara County Tourism, 139 Niagara St., Lockport, NY 14094; (716) 439-7300 or (800) 338-7890
- Niagara Falls Convention and Visitors Bureau, 310 Fourth St., Suite 101, Niagara Falls, NY 14303; (716) 285-2400 or (800) 421-5223
- Oneida County Visitors Bureau, P.O. Box 551, Utica, NY 13503; (315) 724-7221 or (800) 426-3132

- Orleans County Tourism Office, Route 31 West, Albion, NY 14411; (716) 589-7004 or (800) 724-0314
- Oswego County Department of Promotion and Tourism, 46 E. Bridge St., Oswego, NY 13126; (315) 349-8322 or (800) 248-4386; **Note:** Oswego County offers a toll-free tourism fun line, and a free fishing kit is available by request.
- Phoenix Chamber of Commerce, 811 State St., Phoenix, NY 13135; (315) 695-3599
- Rome Chamber of Commerce, 139 Liberty Plaza, Rome, NY 13440; (315) 337-1700
- Seaway Trail, Inc., 109 Barracks Drive, Madison Barracks, Sackets Harbor, NY 13685; (315) 646-1000
- Schenectady County Chamber of Commerce, 306 State St., Schenectady, NY 12305; (518) 372-5656 or (800) 962-8007
- Syracuse Visitors Bureau, 572 S. Salina St., Syracuse, NY 13202; (315) 470-1800 or (800) 234-4SYR
- Wayne County Tourism Office, 9 Pearl St., P.O. Box 131, Lyons, NY 14489; (315) 946-5470 or (800) 527-6510

The Thousand Islands/St. Lawrence River
- Alexandria Bay Chamber of Commerce, Box 365, Alexandria Bay, NY 13607; (800) 541-2110 or (315) 482-9531
- Cape Vincent Chamber of Commerce, P.O. Box 482, Cape Vincent, NY 13618; (315) 654-2481
- Chaumont Three Mile Bay Chamber of Commerce, P.O. Box 24, Three Mile Bay, NY 13693; (315) 649-5452
- Clayton Chamber of Commerce, 510 Riverside Dr., Clayton, NY 13624; (800) 252-9806 or (315) 686-3771

- Massena Chamber of Commerce, Box 387, Massena, NY 13662; (315) 769-3525
- Ogdensburg Bridge and Port Authority, Ogdensburg, NY 13625; (315) 393-4080
- Ogdensburg Chamber of Commerce, P.O. Box 681, Ogdensburg, NY 13669; (315) 393-3620
- St. Lawrence County Chamber of Commerce, Drawer A, Canton, NY 13617; (315) 386-4000
- South Jefferson County Chamber of Commerce, P.O. Box 73, Adams, NY 13605; (315) 232-4215
- Thousand Islands International Council, I-81, foot of 1000 Islands Bridge 13607; (800) 8-ISLAND
- Thousand Islands State Park and Recreation Region, Keewaydin State Park, Alexandria Bay, NY 13607; (315) 482-2593

Lake Ontario
- Sackets Harbor Chamber of Commerce, P.O. Box 540, Sackets Harbor, NY 13685; (315) 646-1700
- Watertown Chamber of Commerce, 230 Franklin St., Watertown, NY 13601; (315) 788-2520

The Finger Lakes
- Finger Lakes Association, 309 Lake St., Penn Yan, NY 14527; (315) 536-7488 or (800) 548-4386
- Finger Lakes Trail Chamber of Commerce, 34 Tompkins St., Cortland, NY 13045; (607) 753-8463
- Geneva Chamber of Commerce, P.O. Box 587, Geneva, NY 14456; (315) 789-1776
- Ithaca/Tompkins County Visitors Bureau, 904 E. Shore Dr., Ithaca, NY 14850; (800) 284-8422 or (607) 272-1313

- Ontario Chamber of Commerce, Ontario, NY 14519; (315) 524-5886
- Ontario County Tourism Bureau, 248 S. Main St., Canadaigua, NY 14424; (716) 394-3915 or (800) 654-9798
- Penn Yan Chamber of Commerce (Yates County), 2375 Route 14 A, Penn Yan, NY 14527; (315) 536-3111
- Schuyler County Chamber of Commerce, 1000 N. Franklin St., Watkins Glen, NY 14891; (607) 535-4300
- Seneca Falls Chamber of Commerce, P.O. Box 294, Seneca Falls, NY 13148; (315) 568-2906
- Yates County Tourism, 1 Keuka Business Park, Penn Yan, NY 14527; (315) 531-3000

Marina Etiquette

A short discourse now on the appropriate way to welcome yourself into a neighborhood that exists inside a given marina, which usually has a mixture of seasonal slip-holders and overnight transient boaters. A few words of suggestion—and a little sensitivity on everyone's part—will help this marriage of diverse interests be a satisfactory experience for all.

As you approach the marina, you must be sensitive to the size of your wake and to the fact that your wake continues to travel for a good distance. Most boat owners usually cut their throttles to a fast idle, even when they're still throwing a wake. When they arrive at the marina, their wake arrives behind them a minute later. This practice is not good. You're much better off if, when you come off plane or down from a cruising-run speed, you throttle back well away from the marina and cruise for perhaps 10 minutes to let the engines' and other systems' heat buildup dissipate, then shift into neutral, to confirm that your throttles are all the way down, then come back into forward gear at dead slow, doing your final approach to the marina at this speed (except during conditions of high wind and swift current).

If you need to refuel, by all means do that first. Almost all marinas are set up for you to take care of fueling before a transient slip assignment. Likewise, the marina staff expects you to do the same for pump-out, repair, and dining arrangements. In fact, if the fuel dock is not busy, many boaters first go in there even if they do not need fuel.

Most marinas monitor either channel 9, 13, 16, or 68 on your VHF radio. You can contact them while you're still several miles out and discuss with them your intentions and your needs. Occasionally, a marina feature that you need is not working or is being rebuilt, thereby affecting your final marina selection. Likewise, your vessel might have needs that are best met by specific dockage arrangements. For example, your shoreside power connections may favor one side of your vessel over the other. You might need to refill your water tank; that fill connection might be at the bow or the stern, making it more appropriate for you to tie up bow-in or stern-in. Many vessels carry an anchor or have a bow sprit that would project over a marina's dock if the boat is bow-in. You need to advise the marina as to what your intentions are so these problems can be worked out, either by giving you a deeper slip than you normally would be assigned or by your working with them to solve your needs and their dockage limitations to everyone's satisfaction. If you need repairs, often larger-sized marinas will have a different area of slips designated to take care of those needs. Similarly, if you want to barbecue, then you'd want to be close to a barbecue; the same with laundry, showers, play area, or a dog run. Perhaps you want a fairly quick meal and you're expecting rain: then you'd want to be close to the restaurant facilities. Along the same lines, if you have children with you who want to use a pool, it would be nice if the pool were in view of your vessel so that you can have some contact with them (although you certainly can't watch the children from the vessel). In all these cases, shopping around with various marinas via your radio can help you to choose the marina with amenities best for your needs.

Water-depth concerns often cause a skipper to select a certain marina. In tidal areas you need to be concerned that you're not going to touch the bottom at any time during your stay and that the entrance/exit channel depth is adequate when you intend to drop lines and depart. Also, ask about silt buildup, weed growth, and the bottom's composition, because all these factors can affect your vessel and your cruising experience. All these concerns can easily be covered and dealt with through an effective dialogue between yourself and marina staff.

If it's windy or the current is strong, it is appropriate to ask for assistance in getting your boat safely tied up with minimum stress to you and damage to the other vessels surrounding your assigned slip. I have had as many as three attendants help me to quickly secure a boat when conditions were bad. Yes, I do a fair share of single-handed cruising, but during this incident I had aboard a very competent crew member on a 30-foot twin-screw cruiser. The vessel was safely tied up with a minimum of stress because of the marina's staff assistance. And minimum stress is everyone's goal, isn't it? You cannot "showboat" if you crash.

Dockside attendants, if they go out of their way to help you secure your lines, adjust your fenders, plug in your shore power, and let you know where the ice machine is, may be appropriately rewarded by a tip, usually in the range of $1 to $5, depending on the extent of their courtesies. You do not have to tip, and many people don't, but it is a nice gesture to reward someone who has gone beyond the call of duty for your comfort and convenience.

When you tie up lines, it is important that you secure them in such a way that does not jeopardize a sister vessel's security or accessibility, if at all possible. The boat's skipper, being responsible for the vessel, also should always check other people's work. If you announce this beforehand and do it consistently, your boat will be better secured and no one will be insulted. Also, most marinas are going to ask you not to run cords or lines across walkways, since they might cause other people to trip over them. Basic courtesy also applies to shore power. Do not unplug someone else in order to plug yourself in, and once one end of a shore power cord is connected, it is important that you be extra cautious to keep it out of the water. You could shock the entire finger of the dock system with an electricity surge.

Some boaters like to keep their water supply connected, while others, thinking dockside water pressure too uneven, fill only their water tank and let it and the on-board pump system deliver fresh water to the rest of the boat. A helpful hint: Always run the water for two to three minutes to clean the line and then taste it before you use a local water supply. Although perhaps good water, it might have an unfamiliar odor or taste. In that case, just fill it up at the next stop.

Once you have your boat secured, everyone around you would appreciate you shutting down both your boat engines and your generator to minimize noise and any exhaust smell or smoke. Likewise, when you fire up in the morning, go easy, because nobody appreciates someone who immediately lets loose with a set of sport-boat engines, blasting to 3000 rpms. Be sensitive to your neighbor about the noise. Radios, guitars, halyards that are clanking in the wind—all should be adjusted with the idea that a noise that is music to you is an irritation to a neighbor with a sensitive ear. Most marinas and cruisers after 10 P.M. respectfully ask that all marina tenants quiet down and let those who need to get to bed early, ensuring them a glorious predawn departure.

Those who depart in early morning should in turn respect the fact that some of your neighbors may have been up late into the night in deep philosophical discussions about the meaning of various esoteric topics—or they just might have been partying too hard and too long. In either situation, please minimize the amount of time you run your engines slip-side or near seawalls and other structures that echo engine noise and other sounds. Also, be aware of the fact that basic, common dockside commands should be given in as low a voice as possible (or by using hand signals), and in no event should someone on the bow of the boat try to talk to someone on the stern of the boat. Because most people sleep with portholes and hatches ajar, any sound can carry across the water and seemingly right through these hatches and other openings, thereby disrupting someone else's sleep.

If you're going to clean fish, many marinas have a separate area for that task, and each marina has a different policy on what you do with the various parts: fish heads, tails, and bones. Clean up after you use a common area or piece of marina equipment. Barbecues, picnic tables, and walkways are all better left cleaner than when you arrived. Finally, just to be friendly, you might offer your neighbor a taste of your catch or barbecue, or at least a soft drink or a glass of whatever you're having. Remember that everyone at the marina is there to have an enjoyable time, so please do your part to have a good time while allowing everyone else to have their fun, too.

There's another adventure around the bend!

Boatbuilders of New York State

I was very surprised to discover in some of my poking around in the history of New York State boating and yachting that the Steinway piano company built powerboats in New York City. The company produced boats, which were powered by gasoline engines based on a European design, from 1891 to 1897.

Penn Yan Boats, which are still in production after more than seventy-five years, are made in the town that gave the company its name, Penn Yan. Penn Yan stands for "Penn-sylvania Yankee," and the town is located on the north shore of Keuka Lake, which is west of the middle of Seneca Lake in the Finger Lakes region. The two lakes were connected by a short canal from 1833 to 1877. Penn Yan pioneered its tunnel drive in the 1970s, which is still an option on a few inboard models, I believe. The tunnel drive allowed for a recessed propeller to decrease the draft of a boat. Penn Yan has built for inboards, out-boards, I/Os, and rowboats.

Other boatbuilders of New York have included: Consolidated, from Morris Heights and City Island (this yard's location and name are still in use today as a repair facility, which is under new management and is very helpful in all things marine); Nevins, also on City Island; and Purdy Boats Works, which was located on Long Island. Wheeler, which some say was the Rybovich of the north during the mid-1950s, was in Huntington, New York, later, I believe, moving down to New Jersey near Tom's River.

There also were some custom boatbuilders in the state. Hutchinson Boat Works, which is still a boat dealer and master service center in the Thousand Islands, built probably the most notable mahogany runabout, the 49-foot *Pardon Me,* which is on display in the Clayton Antique Boat Museum. Just imagine a 20-foot runabout water-ski boat, all mahogany, all brightly varnished. Now just enlarge that image to 250 percent, and that's *Pardon Me.* I understand that the driver or helmsman did not control the shifts; it was the job of the engine room personnel to shift the transmis-sion, which made the boat less than usable around docks. The skipper had to call out "for-ward," "neutral," and "reverse" when appro-priate. Of course, the engine that powered it is out of the PT boats from World War II, which also powered so many hydroplanes in the unlimited class. How about a $1,000 fuel bill for an afternoon of water-skiing? Another cus-tom boatbuilder/shipyard was Jakobeson Ship-yard in Oyster Bay, Long Island, which built an aluminum powerboat for Lawrence Rocke-feller to a Sparkman & Stephens design after World War II.

More production builders have included Richardson, which made Richardson's Cruis-ers in North Tonawanda at the western end of the Erie Canal. They popularized, along with Chris Craft, the idea of a production cruising boat, and in the early 1930s would sell any-where from 20 to 50 cabin cruisers (in the 28-foot range, which they called cruiserettes) during the January New York Boat Show. Then the owners of the cruiserettes would come to the factory in North Tonawanda the following May for delivery. After supplying a lead boat, fuel barges, and other amenities, the boat-builder would teach the new boat owners (who were often novice boaters) how to drive and use the boats. The lessons would take place on the Erie Canal. They would cruise east to Albany and then go down the Hudson River to the Battery area off Manhattan; by then, of course, the owners would have become very accomplished seaman. From there those proud skippers would take their individual boats home. This custom went on for a number of years and was an absolutely fascinating way to market boats.

Next was a company called Distin, a wooden-boatbuilder located in Saranac Lake. Also, the Thompson Boat Company was in Cortland before it moved to Wisconsin, which is where they were while I was growing up. There was even a company in Buffalo, Marine Mart, which sold kits for buyers to use in assembling their own boats. Sterling Engine Company, whose engines provided many yachts, was based in Buffalo.

Today there are still some boatbuilders in New York. One that I'm aware of is Hacker-craft, on Silver Bay on Lake George, making brightly finished, varnished wooden run-abouts. Singer Billy Joel also has had an interest in and has had a series of 36-foot boats built in New York at Coecles Harbor Marina and Boatyard.

The New York Boat Show, the oldest boat show in the United States, was the premier boat show when I was a kid, and it's still one of the higher-attended boat shows, now in the modern and bigger Jacob Javits Center in midtown Manhattan. This boat show dates back to 1905 and—except for during the world wars, when it wasn't held—has always been something to look forward to in the winter. I can remember my Uncle Tom driving in what turned into a severe snowstorm when I was in the fifth grade to fulfill a promise to take my friends and me to the show. What a gift. Thank you, dear uncle.

BIBLIOGRAPHY

Sources Consulted for This Cruising Guide:

Adams, Arthur G. *The Hudson River Guidebook*. New York: Fordham University Press, 1996.

Amende, Coral. *Hollywood Confidential*. New York: Penguin Books Ltd., 1997.

American Heritage New Illustrated History of the United States, 12 vols. New York: Dell Publishing Co., 1963.

Barry, Bob. *Daily Celebrity Almanac*. Walworth, Wisc: B&B Publishing, Inc., 1994.

Beach, Allen Penfield. *Lake Champlain as Centuries Pass*. Basin Harbor, Vt.: Basin Harbor Club and the Lake Champlain Maritime Museum, 1994.

Bell, David Owen. *Dockmanship*. Centreville, Md: Cornell Maritime Books, 1992.

Bellico, Russell P. *Sails and Steam in the Mountains: A Maritime and Military History of Lake George and Lake Champlain*. Fleischmanns, N.Y.: Purple Mountain Press, 1992.

Boyle, Robert H. *The Hudson River: A Natural and Unnatural History*. New York W.W. Norton & Company, 1979.

Braynard, Frank O. *Famous American Ships*. New York: Hastings House, 1978.

Browning, Judith H. *New York City: Yesterday and Today*. Stamford, Conn.: Corsair Publications, Inc., 1990.

Carmer, Carl. *The Hudson*. New York: Fordham University Press, 1989.

Chapman Piloting: Seamanship and Small Boat Handling. New York: Hearst Marine Books, 1994.

Chart No. 1, United States of America, Nautical Chart Symbols Abbreviations and Terms. 9th ed. Washington, D.C.: The Service, 1990.

Clements, John. *New York Facts: A Comprehensive Look at New York Today, County by County*. Dallas: Clements Research, Inc., 1986.

Cruising Guide to Lake Champlain. Burlington, Vt: Lake Champlain Publishing Company, 1993.

Ehling, William P. *Canoeing Central New York*. Woodstock, Vt.: Backcountry Publications, Inc., 1982.

Ellis, William Donohue. *Land of the Inland Seas*. Palo Alto, Calif.: American West Publishing Company, 1974.

Erie Canal Museum. Syracuse, N.Y.: The Erie Canal Museum, 1989.

Foster, Queene Hooper. *Chapman's Nautical Guide's Boating Etiquette*. New York: Hearst Marine Books, 1990.

Gerber, Morris. *Old Albany, Volume I*. Albany, N.Y.: Morris Gerber, 1972.

Glunt, Ruth R. *Lighthouses and Legends of the Hudson*. Monroe, New York: Library Research Associates, Inc., 1990.

Hacker, Richard Carleton. *The Ultimate Cigar Book*. Beverly Hills: Autumngold Publishing, 1996.

Hill, Ralph Nading. *Lake Champlain: Key to Liberty*. Woodstock, Vt.: The Countryman Press, Inc., 1995.

Hines, Doug. *The Captain's Coastal Directions*. Mt. Rainier, Md.: Doug Hines and Associates, Inc., 1992.

The Hudson Scenes Remembered. Poughkeepsie, N.Y.: The Antique Print Association, 1975.

Kemp, Peter, ed. *The Oxford Companion to Ships and the Sea.* Oxford: Oxford University Press, 1994.

Larousse's English-French, French-English Dictionary. New York: Simon and Schuster, 1971.

Leapman, Michael. *The Companion Guide to New York.* New York: Harper Collins Publishers, 1991.

Atlantic Coast. Vol. 1 of *Light List.* Washington, D.C.: U.S. Department of Transportation, 1996.

Lindquist, William C. *The Richardson Story.* North Tonawanda, NY: Richardson Boat Owners Association, 1984.

Lowry, Thomas P., M.D. *The Story the Soldiers Wouldn't Tell: Sex in the Civil War.* Mechanicsburg, Pa.: Stackpole Books, 1994.

The Luxury Yachts. Alexandria, Va: Time-Life Books, 1981.

Marian, Thomas W., and W. J. Rumsey. *A Cruising Guide to the Northeast's Inland Waterways.* Camden, Maine: International Marine, 1995.

Marinas. Toronto: Parks Canada and Ontario Ministry of Culture, Tourism & Recreation, 1993. [This booklet lists the services of 400 marinas.]

Martell, Alan R., and Alton Long. *The Wines and Wineries of the Hudson River Valley.* Woodstock, Vt: The Countryman Press, 1993.

Martin, Nick and Marsha Porter. *Video Movie Guide 1995.* New York: Ballantine Books, 1994.

McEwen, W. A., and A. H. Lewis. *Encyclopedia of Nautical Knowledge.* Centreville, Md: Cornell Maritime Press, 1992.

Merritt, Jim. "In New York and Connecticut: Shad Slump Make No Sense." *Field and Stream,* March 1997, 86.

Moore, C. Philip. *Yachts in a Hurry: An Illustrated History of the Great Commuter Yachts.* New York: W.W. Norton & Company, 1990.

Mulligan, Tim. *The Hudson River Valley.* New York: Random House, 1991.

The Nautical Seaway Trail: Chartbook and Waterfront Guide to New York State's Great Lakes-St. Lawrence River. Hammond, N.Y.: Blue Heron Enterprises, 1991.

New York: A Collection from Harper's Magazine. New York: Gallery Books, 1991.

New York State Canal Guide (Western Erie). Skaneateles, N.Y.: Mid-Lakes Navigation Co., Ltd., 1991.

Nutting, Wallace. *New York Beautiful.* New York: Bonanza Books, 1927.

O'Brien, Raymond J. *American Sublime: Landscape and Scenery of the Lower Hudson Valley.* New York: Columbia University Press, 1981.

O'Neill, Amanda. Biblical Times. New York: Crescent Books, 1992.

Powers, Judith, ed. *Northern 1997 Waterway Guide.* Atlanta: Intertec Publishing Company, 1997.

Ratigan, William. *Great Lakes Ship Wrecks and Survivals.* New York: Galahad Books, 1977.

Reed's Nautical Almanac: North American East Coast 1994. Boston: Thomas Reed Publications Inc., 1994.

Rinker, Harry L. *"The Old Raging Erie . . . There Have Been Several Changes": A Postcard History of the Erie and Other New York State Canals (1895 to 1915).* Berkeley

Heights, N.J.: Canal Captain's Press,1984.

St. Lawrence Seaway Pleasure Craft Guide. Massena, N.Y.: St. Lawrence Seaway Development, 1991.

Shank, William H. *Towpaths to Tugboats: A History of American Canal Engineering.* York, Pa: The American Canal and Transportation Center, 1982.

Smith, Susan Weston. *The First Summer People: The Thousand Islands, 1650-1910.* Toronto: Stoddart Publishing Co. Ltd., 1993.

The Smithsonian Guide to Historic America: The Mid-Atlantic States. New York: Stewart, Tabori & Chang, 1989.

Suisman, Charles A., Carol Molesworth. *Manhattan User's Guide.* New York: Hyperion, 1996.

Tantillo, L. F. *Visions of New York State: The Historical Paintings of L. F. Tantillo.* Wappingers Falls, N.Y.: The Shawangunk Press, 1996.

Thompson, Shawn. *A River Rat's Guide to the Thousand Islands.* Erin, Ontario: The Boston Mills Press, 1996.

Thompson, Shawn. *River's Edge: Reprobates, Rum-runners and Other Folk of the Thousand Islands.* Burnstown, Ontario: General Store Publishing House Inc., 1991.

Trent-Severn Waterway Boating and Road Guide. Peterborough, Ontario: Ontario Travel Guides, 1994.

Wagman, John. *On this Day in America.* New York: Gallery Books, 1990.

Young, Claiborne S. *Cruising Guide to Eastern Florida,* 3rd edition. Gretna, Louisiana: Pelican, 1996.

Young, Claiborne S. *Cruising Guide to Coastal South Carolina and Georgia.* Winston-Salem, N.C.: John F. Blair, 1992.

Young, Claiborne S. *Cruising Guide to Coastal North Carolina.* Winston-Salem, N.C.: John F. Blair, 1994.

Young, Claiborne S. *Cruising Guide to the Northern Gulf: Florida, Alabama, Mississippi, Louisiana.* Gretna, Louisiana: Pelican, 1991.

U.S. Coast Guard Auxiliary. *Boating Skills and Seamanship.* Washington, D.C.: Coast Guard Auxiliary National Board, Inc., 1988.

United States Coastal Pilot: Great Lakes and St. Lawrence River. Washington, D.C.: U.S. Department of Commerce, 1994.

Verplanck, William E., and Moses W. Collyer. *The Sloops of the Hudson.* Fleischmanns, N.Y.: Purple Mountain Press, Ltd., 1994.

Recommended Boating Periodicals:

Boating. New York: Hatchette Filipacchi Magazines. [A monthly magazine. Send subscription inquiries to P.O. Box 51055, Boulder, CO 80323-1055.]

Boating on the Hudson. Yonkers: Beacon Publishing Corporation. [A free monthly publication billed as "Your Where & When, Why, What and How Hudson River Information Source." For information, write 27 Beacon Street, Yonkers, NY 10701; telephone (914) 423-3329 or fax (914) 332-9103.]

Boating World. Atlanta: Boating World Magazine. [A monthly magazine. For information, telephone (770) 955-5656 or fax (770) 952-0669.]

Coastal Cruising. Beaufort, N.C.: Nautilus Publishing, Inc. [A magazine published six times a year. For subscription information, telephone (919) 728-2233 or fax (919) 728-6050.]

Cruising World. Newport, R.I.: The New York Times Company. [A monthly magazine. For information, telephone (800) 727-8473.]

Focs'le News. (A publication of the Hudson

River Maritime Museum). [For information write Hudson River Maritime Museum, 1 Rondout Landing, Kingston, NY 12401.]

Gazette: The Journal of the Antique Boat Museum. [For information, write the Antique Boat Museum, 750 Mary St., Clayton, NY 13624 or telephone (315) 686-4104.]

Great Lakes Cruiser. Royal Oak, Mich.: Great Lakes Cruiser, Ltd. [Published four times a year. For information, write P.O. Box 1722, Royal Oak, MI 48068-1722.]

Guides des Marinas. [An annual guide to marinas in Quebec. For more information, telephone (514) 273-9773.]

Heartland Boating. Martin, Tenn. [For information, telephone (800) 366-6893 or fax (901) 587-6893; Web page: http://www.gsn.com/heartland_boating.htm]

Hudson Valley. Poughkeepsie, N.Y.: Suburban Publishing Inc. [A monthly magazine that covers culture, history, current affairs, dining, fashion, and personalities of the Hudson River region. For subscription information, telephone (800) BUY-HVMAG.]

Lakeland Boating. Evanston, Ill: O'Meara-Brown Publications, Inc. [For subscription information, call (800) 827-0289.]

Maine Boats & Harbors. Camden, Maine: Maine Boats & Harbors Publications, Inc. [A monthly magazine. For information, telephone (800) 710-9368.]

Motorboating and Sailing. New York: The Hearst Corporation. [A monthly magazine. For information, telephone (800) 888-9123 or fax (515) 246-1020.]

Ocean Navigator. Portland, Maine: Navigator Publishing Corp. [Published seven times a year. For information, telephone (207) 772-2466, or send e-mail to OFFcirc@aol.com.

Offshore. Needham, Mass.: Offshore Communications, Inc. [A monthly magazine on northeast boating. For subscription information, telephone (617) 449-6204 or send e-mail to oshore@aol.com.]

Power & Motoryacht. New York: K-III Magazines. [A monthly magazine. For information, telephone (800) 284-8036.]

Rudder. [The official magazine of the Antique and Classic Boat Society. Published four times a year. For more information, telephone (315) 686-2628 or fax (315) 686-2775.]

Sail. Boston: K-III Magazine Corporation. [A monthly magazine. For more information, telephone (800) 745-7245.]

Sea. Irvine, CA. [A monthly magazine. For more information, call (714) 660-6150 or fax (714) 660-6172.]

Seaport: New York's History Magazine. New York: South Street Seaport Museum. [Published four times a year, this magazine is available with an annual $35 membership to the museum. Contact the Membership Department, South Street Seaport Museum, 207 Front St., New York, NY 10038.]

Soundings. Essex, Conn. [A monthly boating magazine. For more information, call (860) 767-3200 or fax (860) 767-1048; or send e-mail to: riptides@ix.netcom.com]

Trailer Boats. Mt. Morris, Ill: Poole Publications, Inc. [A monthly magazine. For subscription information, call (800) 877-5251 or send e-mail to tbmciro@aol.com]

WoodenBoat. Brooklin, Maine: WoodenBoat Publications, Inc. [A bimonthly magazine. For information, telephone (800) 877-5284.]

Yachting. Greenwich, Conn.: Times Mirror Magazines. [A monthly magazine. For subscription inquiries, telephone (800) 999-0869.]

INDEX

To help first-time visitors, the following codes in this index identify the *major* applicable waterway for the marinas, anchorages, bridges, reaches, and tie-ups listed in this guide. (Bold-faced codes in the index identify listings specific to the major waterways themselves.)